THE OTHER BATTLE

THE OTHER BATTLE

LUFTWAFFE NIGHT ACES VERSUS BOMBER COMMAND

PETER HINCHLIFFE

An Airlife
CLASSIC

Copyright © 1996 by Peter Hinchliffe

First Published in the UK in 1996
by Airlife Publishing Ltd

This edition published 2001

British Library Cataloguing in Publication Data
A catalogue record for this book
is available from the British Library

ISBN 1 84037 303 2

Typeset by Phoenix Typesetting, Ilkley, West Yorkshire
Printed in England by Biddles Ltd., Guildford and King's Lynn

Airlife Publishing Ltd

101 Longden Road, Shrewsbury SY3 9EB
E-mail: airlife@airlifebooks.com
Website: www.airlifebooks.com

Acknowledgements

Sources for a work such as this are of necessity many and varied. Firstly, there are the books read as background, some few of which I have drawn attention to under the heading 'Selected Bibliography'. Of those, I should like to make special mention of three. There is, of course, the indispensable Official History – *The Strategic Air Offensive Against Germany 1939–1945*, by Sir Charles Webster and Noble Frankland. Equally indispensable (I am tempted to say 'even more indispensable', but that would be a solecism) to the writing of this book was *The Bomber Command War Diaries* by Martin Middlebrook and his meticulous researcher, Chris Everitt. On the German side, Gebhard Aders' *The History of the German Night-Fighter Force* was fundamental.

I carried out research at the Public Record Office at Kew and at the National Archives and Records Administration in Washington DC, and I visited a number of Town Archives in Germany, among them those at Düsseldorf, Cologne and Hamburg. I owe my thanks to the members of staff of all these offices.

The vast majority of my information, however, came directly from participants in the battle, both British and German, either in the course of personal interview or by means of correspondence, and from others who have an interest in the air war over Germany. I list below those to whom my thanks are abundantly due, not only for the information that they gave me, but also for helping me to understand my subject: I fear that, human fallibility being what it is, I will have missed some out, and for that I apologise. I have decided not to include ranks, decorations and so on, nor to list British and Germans separately. I am sure that all of them who took part in the battle would agree, after all, that they were just ordinary men doing a job which, at the time, seemed necessary: Gebhard Aders, Herbert Altner, Hans Angersbach, Günther Bahr, Heinz Bärwolf, Martin Becker, Terry Bolter, Heinz Bönsch, Hermann Brandt, Franz Brinkhaus, Oliver Brooks, Willi Brünig, Karl Buschmann, John Chaloner, John Cox, Horst Diener, Wolfgang Dierich, Manfred Dieterle, Wolfgang Falck, Frank Faulkner, Otto Fries, Hermann Greiner, Ernst Güse, Walter Heidenreich, Friedhelm Henning, Hajo Herrmann, Werner Hoffmann, Jack Hyde, Hans-Joachim Jabs, Lothar Jarsch, Karl-Ludwig Johanssen, Wilhelm Johnen, Erich Jung, Ivan Kayes, Charles Kern, Walter Knickmeier, Fritz Krause, Josef Krinner, Erich Kubetz, Herbert Kümmritz, Otto Kutzner, Kurt Lamm, Gunter Lauser, Michael Moores LeBlanc, Hector Macdonald, Kurt Matzak, Ludwig Meister, Hermann Möckel, Johannes Mohn, Emil Nonnenmacher, Peter Oberheid, Peter Osborne, Fritz Ostheimer, Horace Pearce, Jean-Louis Roba, Lothar Sachs, Otto Schindler, Harry Shinkfield, Herbert Scholl, Daniel Schulz, Wilhelm Seuss, Peter Spoden, Alfred Staffa,

Gerd Stamp, Rudolf Szardenings, Thomas Terry, Herbert Thomas, Gerhard Wagner, Günther Wolf, Paul Zorner.

And finally my wife, Irene, whom I met when I arrived on my operational squadron in 1944 and married a year later to the day, for her help in checking the manuscript and her unfailing support throughout. Sadly, Irene died before *The Other Battle* appeared.

Foreword

by Marshal of the Royal Air Force Sir Michael Beetham GCB CBE DFC AFC
President of the Bomber Command Association,
formerly Chief of the Air Staff.

The Strategic Bombing Offensive of World War Two, *The Other Battle* as it is called by the author, was unique in that such a form of warfare had never been seriously attempted before and, in that form and on that scale, is unlikely ever to be repeated. The Offensive has been the subject of some controversy over the years since the war – not during the war – mainly because of its impact on the German civilian population. It is important, therefore, to understand why it was waged.

Firstly, and fundamentally, was the fervent wish to find some way of waging war without incurring the horrendous casualties of the trench warfare in World War One, and the coming of the aeroplane offered this opportunity. Secondly, once Germany had occupied most of Western Europe including the Channel ports in 1940 and we were back on our heels, there was no serious alternative strategy. For, if we were to survive, we could not just remain on the defensive. We had to strike back at Germany, and the British people, themselves under sustained and indiscriminate attack from the air, had to be given some hope of eventual victory. Thirdly, Bomber Command until late 1944 simply did not have the capability to find and attack precision targets in Germany at night, in poor weather and against formidable defences and could only, therefore, attack area targets such as industrial cities. There were certainly no scruples at the time on the part of the British Government or the British people with regard to the bombing of industrial cities, for the simple reason that the civilian population were all working hard in support of the Nazi war machine.

The bombing campaign was waged continuously throughout the more than five years of the war. It was a bloody and bitter battle in which more than half the Allied bomber aircrew who took part lost their lives. To them the German fighter force posed the main threat, and they too suffered heavy casualties.

This book tells the story of the battle as it was fought by both sides. Carefully researched, it describes the build-up of aircraft and equipment, notably radar equipment, the swings of the pendulum as one and then the other gained the initiative through new equipment or tactics, and the human element, the stresses and strains and the bravery of those who took part. In the end, by exerting relentless pressure, the bombers won this 'Other Battle' and thereby made a decisive contribution to final victory. I hope you enjoy reading this objective and realistic portrayal of the battle as much as I did.

Michael Beetham
Fakenham, Norfolk,
July 1994

Foreword

by Oberst a.D. Wolfgang Falck

I consider it a great honour to have been asked to write a foreword to the book that Peter Hinchliffe has written. It is a characteristic of this work, in which the author is at pains to give an objective account of the murderous battle between the RAF and the German night fighters *sine ira et studio*, that he has succeeded in exemplary fashion. It is surely no easy task to write objectively about a matter in which the youthful élite of two nations were killing each other.

The German night fighter force was a typical product of wartime. It is true that during the First World War some individual pilots experimented with night fighting on their own initiative and that night-fighting trials were carried out before World War Two, but there were no solid results. At that period it was difficult to imagine air warfare by night. Night attacks on targets in Germany and the occupied territories by RAF aircraft individually or in small numbers made it inevitable that we had to consider what to do in order not to have to accept the destruction by night without putting up a struggle.

In 1940, after the occupation of Denmark and Norway, I was stationed with my *Zerstörergruppe* at Aalborg in Denmark. Every night the bombers flew overhead on their way to their targets, and sometimes our airfields suffered low-level bombing and machine-gun attacks, so that we fighter pilots had to jump into our splinter-trenches instead of taking off and fighting. Morale-sapping experiences such as this led us to give thought to the technical, tactical and organisational ways in which we might defend ourselves. I wrote a report at that time with a number of appropriate suggestions, but it didn't go any further because we were posted to the Western Front on the border with France.

During this period there was an increase in RAF nuisance attacks, and the principal target was the Ruhr area. At the end of the campaign against France someone remembered my paper, and I was ordered by Göring to form *Nachtjagdgeschwader 1* and carry out night interception to defend the Ruhr industrial area. At that moment the German night fighter force was born.

It was not an easy job. The crews had no night-flying experience, the aircraft did not meet the requirements for successful operation by night, communication with the anti-aircraft organisation was cumbersome, the signals organisation was extremely underdeveloped and there was widespread ignorance of radar. But war stimulates inventiveness and compels men to take such action as is necessary. And so in the course of time these problems were to a large extent solved; new units were formed and the *Nachtjagd* became the newest and the most modern arm of the *Luftwaffe*.

At the beginning the RAF were greatly superior to the *Luftwaffe*, and in particular to the *Nachtjagd*, when it came to waging a war in the air by night. Under

9

pressure of circumstances, however, the development and production of the necessary equipment for our aircraft, and especially the development of ground and airborne radars, were afforded the highest priority in research and in industry. Thus it proved possible to make up lost ground in a relatively short time and to form a successful night-fighter force.

In practical terms the RAF was our only opponent. Our overriding priority was the defence of the territory of the *Reich*, which automatically also meant the German-occupied forward areas to the north and west. From time to time individual units in Italy, Sicily and even North Africa carried out night-fighter operations, and here too the RAF was the enemy. On the Eastern Front, in contrast, a sort of makeshift night fighting was developed, and it was only in exceptional cases that a night-fighter *Staffel* equipped with the necessary radar and radio control systems mounted on railway trains was brought into play, and then success rates were extremely high.

In accordance with the well-known saying, 'attack is the best form of defence', we decided that we should take steps to attack the bombers in their own country as they were taking off, to disrupt their night-flying operations and training and to lie in wait for aircraft returning to their bases. In this way an intruder organisation, which we called the *Fernnachtjagd*, or 'long-range night-fighter force', came into being. As we now know, these operations were extremely successful for us and unpleasant for the RAF. We shot down a large number of aircraft and the air traffic was effectively disrupted. But the German leaders did not believe these successes, so that from one day to the next intruder operations were forbidden. Today it is clear that from the German viewpoint this was a major error.

But in fact the night-fighter crews were not only fighting against the RAF. The night-fighter man is essentially a lone agent, and therein lies the main problem: unlike day fighters, who fly in formation and can usually see one another, he has to be completely self-sufficient when flying in the darkness. Frequently the first thing a man had to conquer was his inner self, and then how successful he was depended upon his own basic ability and his willingness to fly and to fight, plus, of course, his fair share of good fortune. The next problem was the weather, with fog, icing, and bad visibility. Then came failure of radio equipment, airborne radar and so on. There were times when hazards such as these caused us greater losses, often on take-off and especially when coming in to land, than we suffered operationally from enemy action. It must also be added that in the *Nachtjagd* we never had an aircraft specifically designed for the task of night fighting. We came from *Zerstörer* units, that is from day fighters. Thus, from the very beginning, the Bf 110 became the standard aircraft for night-time interception. Then, as experience was gained and continual improvements and modifications were made, it became the *Nachtjäger*. Then we operated with the modified and rebuilt Ju 88 and Do 17, and later with the Do 217. These types were also used for intruder work, being capable as they were of the necessary range and endurance. It was not until 1942 that we heard that a new, high-performance machine was being developed by Heinkel for reconnaissance operations. After a number of inspection visits and negotiations, first of all with Heinkel and then with the Ministry of Aviation, we succeeded in convincing our superiors that with relatively small modifications this aircraft could become the night-fighter of the future. In this way the He 219 became the first true *Nachtjäger*, and it proved itself in outstanding fashion.

In my view there was no other branch of the armed forces in which the high-frequency war played as great a role as it did in the *Nachtjagd*. I am not only thinking of radar equipment, which was put out of action by the dropping of aluminium strips, or of the monitoring by both sides of radio frequencies which were then tuned in to by the enemy and used to broadcast false information or instructions to mislead the crews; I am thinking more of the use of a wide variety of airborne radars. For example, the RAF introduced an IFF (Identification Friend or Foe) set. After our Signals Intelligence people had discovered the frequency of the equipment, we were able to use it to home in on our targets. The same thing happened with the fighter-warning device in the bombers. Once the frequency had been discovered we were able to use it to intercept our target. The high-frequency war was a decisive factor in the battle in the night skies, giving important advantage – or causing losses – first to one side and then to the other.

In the battle against the RAF the night-fighters' number one enemies were of course the Pathfinders. If they could be effectively countered, the success of a mass attack would be brought into question. But when Mosquitos were used for this purpose their high speed meant that we were seldom able to do anything about them. It is all the more gratifying, therefore, that today, about fifty years after these events, there is not only comradely contact, but also true friendship man to man and family to family, with reciprocal visits, between the Pathfinder Organisation and members of the former *Nachtjagd*.

In this matter, as with everything, Man is at the heart of the problem. Young men fought fiercely against each other. But in this night-time battle it was never the individual man that was the target, it was the aeroplane that was trying to drop its load of bombs on the night-fighters' homeland, particularly when the crew of the fighter could see the burning cities, perhaps where relatives lived; and on the other side were the members of the bomber crew who were fighting for their country, carrying out their orders and committing themselves selflessly in exactly the same way. The full realisation that these aircraft contained human beings like you and like me only came when crew members were taken prisoner and were fortunate enough to find themselves in the custody of an operational flying unit. Then it was as if everything that had happened was forgotten, and both sides came together as fellow human beings.

In my opinion there is nothing negative in human life that does not have, somewhere or other, a positive side. That also applies to this frightful and senseless war. Today, under the protective shield of NATO, our two nations are bound together in a common system of defence, our air forces work together in the closest of associations, and our two peoples, including veterans such as we who went through the war, have long since reached out to each other the hand of understanding across the graves of our dead. And from this mutual understanding, reconciliation and forgiveness have arisen many cases of genuine human friendship, as is shown by the participation of former warriors from both sides in reciprocal reunions, and by the many personal and family friendships that transcend borders and oceans.

Let us hope that with the publication of this book Peter Hinchliffe will have played a part in ensuring that the generations that follow us will learn from what happened in the past and will look to the future with goodwill and in the knowledge that international problems, no matter what they might be, can no longer be solved by means of force. It is up to all of us to make our individual contribution to the creation of a peaceful future.

Wolfgang Falck
St Ulrich a.P., Austria
February 1994

Contents

Introduction

The Battle of Britain was short and, in terms of the impact it had on the Second World War, clearly defined and conclusive. Fighter Command of the Royal Air Force won and the *Luftwaffe* lost, although it was a very close call. The immediate threat of invasion was lifted. The battle had lasted approximately four months and had cost the lives of approaching 600 RAF pilots. The other battle – the one waged between Bomber Command and the *Luftwaffe*, mainly in the night skies over Germany – lasted the full five-and-a-half years of the war in the West, and tens of thousands of British, Commonwealth and Empire and Allied aircrew men died.

The extent to which the outcome of that battle contributed to final victory has long been a subject of debate, increasingly so as years pass, memories fade and attitudes change. There are few today who would assert that the only good German is a dead one, but that was a saying in common currency during the war, as it had been, if perhaps not to quite the same extent, in the twenty-one years of uneasy peace from the end of hostilities between Britain and Germany in 1918 until their resumption in 1939. Nor was the other battle as compact and *sui generis* as the one that was fought in the skies over Britain from July to October 1940: whatever its impact, it was just one part of the strategic battle that was waged against the Third Reich on land and sea as well as in the air, one massive contribution to final victory.

For it was massive, over 1,300,000 tons of bombs having been dropped in the course of almost 400,000 sorties at the cost of well over 10,000 bombers and more than 70,000 aircrew casualties, 55,500 of them fatal. Statistics, however, are often cold and remote from real experience. A better perspective is given by the thought that the figure of 55,500 bomber aircrew who lost their lives during the war represents almost exactly fifty per cent of those who flew operationally. Another figure that has great relevance to the consideration of the Bomber Command effort, controversial as it remains, is that from the day of the Normandy landings to the end of the war just less than a year later the number of British soldiers killed in action was approximately 40,000: in 1916 more than half that number had been killed on the first day of the Battle of the Somme. The terrible slaughter of the trench warfare between 1914 and 1918 had left a nation determined that bloodshed on such a scale should never again be inflicted on the youth of the nation, and the concept of the bomber as a strategic weapon had had that resolve at its very roots.

When the Allied forces landed in France in 1944 they were venturing into a Continental Europe that had been softened up by the relentless bombing carried out by the British and American air forces, and as they advanced they were supported equally relentlessly, directly and indirectly, by the bombers. The contribution of the bombers cannot, it is true, be measured in as simple terms as can the contribution of Fighter Command in 1940, and many will argue that had the bombing effort been applied in a different manner its effect would have been even greater. That might be so, and it might not, because it is the easiest thing in the world to say what should have been done after everything is over and there is time to look back, to study, to consider all the angles and to reflect, but it is not so easy to say in advance and under all sorts of pressures what will be the most effective way of using one's resources. There is no such thing as retrospective predictability. But what, it is worth pondering, would have been the course and the outcome of the war without the Bomber Command effort, or even if some other strategy – for example, that of the precision bombing of selected targets as opposed to area bombing – had been attempted and had failed? There would quite doubtless be many who would say, 'We should have area-bombed their cities: we simply didn't have the equipment or the skills necessary for precision bombing.'

On one point concerning the bomber offensive there is virtual unanimity: those who took part in it as crew members were brave men. Theirs was a different sort of bravery from that of the fighter crews who defended Britain against the German bombers in 1940, a dogged courage that gave them to accept that each operation they took part in would involve flying for hours on end through a heavily defended air space, during which any moment might see their machine hit unseen by a German night fighter or anti-aircraft fire and burst into flames or simply explode, and that the chances of escape if they were hit were much against them. They coined phrases and made a joke of them – 'Press on regardless!' was one. Yet that is just what they did, and in reality it was no joke. Press on regardless of the knowledge that this night might be your last: you have already done twenty ops, and since you have been on the Squadron no one has finished a tour of thirty. Press on regardless of the fact that last night five aircraft from your Squadron didn't come back, and that on what should have been an easy target, Mailly-le-Camp in France, forty-two Lancasters in all out of a force of 346 were lost, which means that in all probability nearly 300 men like yourself died a violent death. Press on regardless of what happened just a few weeks ago, when your rear gunner, Chalky, took a German cannon shell in his face and you had to pull his body, still warm and blood-soaked, from the turret, while the skipper was throwing the aircraft about crazily to avoid the further attentions of a German fighter, possibly the one that had killed Chalky, possibly another one. And reflect, if you dare, that the forty-two Lancs missing represent more than twelve per cent of those involved in the attack, and you still have ten operations to do, so that if similar losses were to prevail from now on the odds against your survival would be twelve to ten. And remember the night five weeks ago when you went to Nuremberg and the German fighters had a field day and shot down almost a hundred bombers, each of which carried seven men. But press on regardless.

The Nuremberg raid on the night of 30/31 March 1944 saw the German night fighter force at its most successful, the German machines finding the bomber stream early and freelancing in it to devastating effect. It was the night that Hauptmann Martin Becker – 'Tino' to distinguish him from the other ace,

Ludwig Becker, by that time dead – and his crew shot down seven British bombers, so beating their previous best score of six in a night, achieved only a week previously: just a year later Tino Becker's crew would destroy nine bombers in a night, the highest individual score achieved in such a short period by any German night fighter crew.

Almost 800 four-engined bombers of Bomber Command took part in the tragic raid on Nuremberg, yet the raid was a failure, not only in terms of casualties suffered but also in terms of damage caused to the target it had set out to attack. The story of the questionable route planning, the inadequate weather forecasting and the navigational errors that resulted has been told many times. It remains the sort of operation that critics of Bomber Command seize on to support their own *post facto* rationalisation and theories when arguing that the Bomber Command effort was wasted. Yet eight months previously, in July 1943, Bomber Command had demonstrated its frightening potential by causing immense damage to the northern German port of Hamburg in a short series of raids that virtually destroyed the city and killed more civilians than had been killed in Britain during the whole of 1940 and 1941, when the German attacks had been at their most intensive. And of that attack Albert Speer, the German Minister of Armaments and Munitions, later wrote:

> 'Hamburg had suffered the fate Göring and Hitler had conceived for London in 1940 . . . Hamburg had put the fear of God in me. At the meeting of Central Planning on 29 July I pointed out: "If the air raids continue at the present scale, within three months we shall be relieved of a number of questions we are at present discussing . . ." Three days later I informed Hitler that armaments production was collapsing and threw in the further warning that a series of attacks of this sort, extended to six more major cities, would bring Germany's armaments production to a total halt . . . The next day I informed Milch's colleagues of similar fears: "We are approaching the point of total collapse . . . in our supply industry." '

If the Nuremberg raid marked the high point of the successes enjoyed by the German night fighters, the Hamburg raids had represented one of that force's low points. Built up to a considerable degree of efficiency since the beginning of the RAF bombing offensive, the *Nachtjagd*, to use the German name by which it was generally known and which I shall use frequently in this book, was rendered ineffectual when a form of blanket radar-jamming, 'Window', was first used by the RAF during the initial attack on the city of Hamburg during the night of 24/25 July 1943. The setback to the *Luftwaffe*, however, was only temporary, and four short weeks later the *Nachtjagd* destroyed forty out of a force of 596 bombers attacking the German ballistic weapons research establishment at Peenemünde on the Baltic coast, despite having been misled at first by a feint attack on Berlin, to which city the bulk of the night-fighter force were directed instead of to the real target some seventy-five miles to the north. In the brief period since the Hamburg catastrophe the *Luftwaffe* had adopted new night-fighting techniques that were eventually to make it a far more formidable and flexible arm than it had been before Hamburg.

Hamburg saw Bomber Command at its most formidable, Nuremberg saw the

Nachtjagd at its most effective. Two mighty forces were ranged against each other, matching skill against skill, technology against technology, bravery against bravery. For the German night-fighter crews, too, were very brave men, every bit as dedicated in the pursuit of their duty as were the bomber crews of the RAF. They saw the Pathfinders' markers going down over their cities, and they saw their cities burning, erupting, seething beneath them. They knew that their folk were dying down there, often in indescribable agony. They had been through air raids themselves, and many of them had lost members of their family. They knew that every bomber that they shot down was one less that could drop its explosives and its incendiaries on to their country and their people, and such knowledge lent strength to their resolve. But they knew, too, that Death awaited them every time their wheels lifted from the ground on an operational take-off. Losses among German night-fighter aircrew were very high, particularly among the novices. Apart from the defensive armament of the bombers that they attacked, the crews faced the hazards of operating in bad weather and, increasingly as the war went on, the terrible retribution meted out by the marauding Beaufighter and Mosquito intruders of the Royal Air Force that would appear, apparently from nowhere, and rake their aircraft with a lethal mixture of armour-piercing, explosive and incendiary cannon shells. For a *Luftwaffe* crewman there was no set number of operations after which he was rested, as there was for his opposite number in the RAF. He flew until he either died, was wounded, was badly injured in a crash-landing or, very rarely, was posted to less hazardous duties.

At the end of 1943 the German night-fighter force comprised approximately 800 aircraft, the great majority of which were twin-engined, while Bomber Command, at that time engaged in what has come to be known as the Battle of Berlin, was able to mount attacks by between five and nine hundred four-engined aircraft night after night, each carrying between three and five tons of bombs. Yet both these mighty forces had grown from virtually nothing over the four years that had elapsed since the outbreak of war in September 1939, at which time the Royal Air Force had no practical night-bombing capability and the *Luftwaffe* no specialised night-fighters. It was as if each side had entered the war without considering the possibility that bombs would be dropped at night, despite the fact that that very trend had been developing in the latter half of the First World War a mere quarter of a century previously. The first German night fighters in the Second World War emerged in response to penetrations of German airspace by British bombers, and once they had achieved their first successes the development of an integrated air defence system was quick to follow. As the increasing danger from night-fighters became apparent, Bomber Command began to change its tactics and its techniques. Electronics began to play their part, each side vying with the other for technical superiority and the operational advantage that went with it, and each new development on one side was countered by a response from the other. On both sides gallant men fought and died, and this is a book not only about the tactics of the night bombers and fighters, the machines and the electronic marvels they carried, but also about the men of both sides who manned the aeroplanes, operated the electronic equipment, and fought and died in the other battle.

Dedicated to those who died.

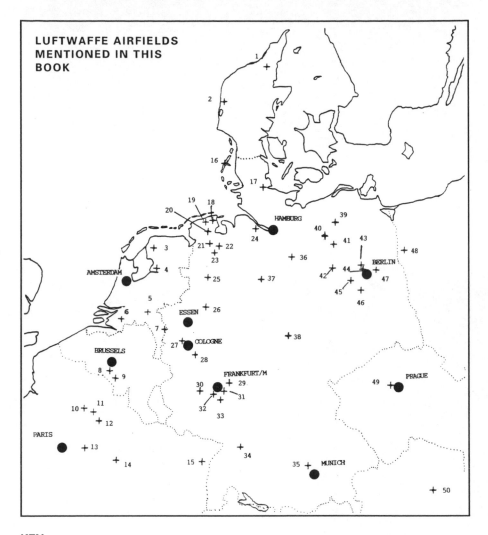

KEY

Denmark:
1. Aalborg
2. Grove

Holland:
3. Leeuwarden
4. Deelen
5. Eindhoven
6. Gilze-Rijen
7. Venlo

Belgium:
8. St. Trond
9. Florennes

France:
10. Tergnier
11. Athies/Laon
12. Juvincourt
13. Coulommiers
14. St Dizier
15. Hagenau

Germany (North):
16. Westerland
17. Schleswig
18. Jever
19. Wittmundhafen
20. Marx
21. Zwischenahn
22. Oldenburg
23. Vechta
24. Stade
25. Rheine

The Ruhr Area:
26. Münster/Handorf
27. Köln/Butzweilerhof
28. Bonn/Hangelar

Germany (South):
29. Langendiebach
30. Mainz/Finthen
31. Zellhausen
32. Rhein/Main

33. Darmstadt
34. Echterdingen
35. Schleissheim

Germany (Central):
36. Lüneburg
37. Wunstorf
38. Erfurt/Bindersleben

Germany (East):
39. Rechlin
40. Parchim
41. Neuruppin
42. Stendal
43. Döberitz
44. Staaken
45. Brandenburg/Briest
46. Jüterbog
47. Werneuchen
48. Königsberg
49. Prague/Ruzyn
50. Wien/Schwechat

CHAPTER ONE

Back to War

1939 – 1940

It was a unique battle, a bloody battle, a battle in which no quarter was asked and precious little given, and it lasted from the first night of the Second World War until almost the last. In the final analysis it was a close-run thing. Two great aerial forces, Bomber Command of the Royal Air Force and the German night-fighter force, the *Nachtjagd*, fought against each other in a confrontation of increasing complexity and ferocity. It was a battle in which tens of thousands of fighting men from both sides perished. Even higher was the cost in human life among the German civilian population. Yet when the war started the RAF was incapable of either navigating or bombing effectively either by day or night, while the *Luftwaffe* had no night-fighting capability whatsoever. The reasons behind this state of affairs were many, varied and complex, and it would be out of place to rehearse them here. Nevertheless, seen in the context of military history and given the experience of the First World War, when attacks on civilian targets had begun with the Germans launching their bomb-carrying airships and later their multi-engined aeroplanes against the British mainland, this was an odd situation. The two sides, the British and the German, had clearly reached different con-clusions as to the way in which a future war would be fought. There had, it is true, been half-hearted and inconclusive experiments by the Germans in the interception of bombers by night by means of standard day fighters, mainly the Bf 109, but the desultory nature of such experiments suggests that the German High Command did not seriously envisage that their homeland was likely to be subjected to bombing from the air during the hours of darkness. They began the war with neither night fighters nor a night-fighting policy.

The British, on the other hand, did have a force nominally dedicated to bomb-ing, and there had been some, if not very realistic, thought given to the problems of bombing by night. The RAF had been reorganised into functional Commands in 1936, with Bomber Command, Fighter Command, Coastal Command and Transport Command as the operational components. When the Germans invaded Poland on 1 September 1939 Bomber Command comprised thirty-three operational squadrons in five Groups of which one, No. 1 Group, was immedi-ately detached from the Command and moved to France, where it formed the bulk of the Advanced Air Striking Force. No. 1 Group was equipped with the Fairey Battle light bomber, a single-engined monoplane that carried a crew of three and which, underpowered and underarmed, was totally inadequate for the task of close-support bombing – indeed for bombing of any sort – and was to be withdrawn from front-line service in 1940 after the disastrous campaign in France, by which time it had taken many young pilots, observers and gunners to their death. Of the twenty-three squadrons that remained, six were equipped

23

with Bristol Blenheim medium bombers, while six had Vickers-Armstrong Wellingtons, five had Armstrong Whitworth Whitleys, and six had Handley Page Hampdens, all of which were classified as heavy bombers.

Of the twin-engined bombers on the RAF's inventory, the Blenheim was the fastest and most manoeuvrable, but even so, with a maximum speed of about 250 mph and light armament, it was no match for the fast Bf 109, which would be its principal opponent during daylight. It carried only a light load of bombs and its range was limited. The crew accommodation was such that even in ideal conditions accurate navigation was difficult. The observer – there was not as yet a specialist aircrew category of navigator – sat in cramped conditions alongside the pilot, which made even map reading an awkward business. The Hampden could carry more bombs a longer distance, but was much slower and, like the Blenheim, had only comparatively light defensive armament. It too provided only a cramped work location for the observer. The Whitley and the Wellington were true long-range heavy bombers with a proper navigator's 'office' and carried a respectable bomb-load, but were quite unsuited, as was to be discovered in action, to operation by day. They were slow, cumbersome in manoeuvre and vulnerable. The machine-guns with which all the RAF bombers were expected to defend themselves were of .303 inch calibre, inferior in both range and hitting power to the guns that were carried by German fighters. The Bf 109E, for example, carried two 20 mm (.79 inch) cannon and two machine-guns, all forward-firing, while the Bf 110 heavy fighter also had two 20 mm cannon and four machine-guns in the nose and one machine-gun looking aft. The guns of the RAF bombers at the beginning of the war were manned by so-called 'tradesmen gunners', basically ground crew airmen for whom air gunnery was a secondary job and whose practical training in defending the bombers with their guns was no more than superficial. Possibly worst of all, the petrol tanks of the British machines were not self-sealing, and even a short burst of incendiary or explosive ammunition accurately aimed would ignite the bomber's fuel and more often than not cause the aircraft to explode or rapidly become a mass of flame.

If the RAF was ill-prepared for a bombing war in terms of aeroplanes, it was even worse prepared in terms of navigational and bomb-aiming capability, particularly by night, so much so that one cannot but be surprised at the confidence in the efficacy of the bomber implicit in all the pre-war debate on how it might be used. Except in conditions of clearest daylight and minimal enemy opposition the crews would only rarely be able to find their way to their targets, and even if they did so they could not hope to hit them with any degree of accuracy. Some pilots and observers were better qualified, or gifted, when it came to air navigation, but they were facing what at that time was virtually an insoluble problem. Most cross-country flying that they had done in the course of their training had been over the British countryside where, if they got lost, as they frequently did, they could always call up for radio bearings and so determine, very approximately, their position, and when their flight was nearing its end they could call up on R/T for a course to steer to base. Even so, it was something of a hit-or-miss method of finding one's way about, but as long as they did get back to base the exercise was considered to have been completed, and no one really worried whether they had kept closely to their planned route or not. Indeed, so little confidence existed in air navigation, particularly by night, that commanders of squadrons rarely sent their aircraft aloft in the hours of darkness unless weather conditions were approaching the ideal. An analysis of flying hours for 1937, for example, shows that Bomber Command flew seventeen times as many hours by day as by night, while in 1939 the ratio was still as high as ten to one.

Navigation, then, was metaphorically a matter of hit or miss. Bomb aiming was literally more miss than hit. If, despite the odds stacked against them, a bomber crew should manage to find their target, there still remained the problem of dropping the bombs on it accurately, even in ideal conditions of visibility, conditions that very seldom prevailed. It was the observer's task to direct the pilot during the run-up to the target and to press the bomb-release button at the correct moment. To do this he would lie prone in the nose of the aircraft and aim at the target using a bomb-sight, attempting to align a cross on the sight by eye with the target on the ground. But visual bomb-aiming was subject to gross errors. In pre-war exercises all bomb-dropping training had been carried out in very favourable conditions and mostly by daylight on special target ranges and, of course, without any enemy action to deter the pilots from flying an accurate straight and level course or to give the observer 'itchy fingers' and make him release his bombs a second or two before the aiming point reached the aiming cross on his sight: and when an aircraft is covering the ground at, say, 200 knots, a second's error in releasing the bombs means a 170-yard error on the ground. Results in general had been less than satisfactory. Some squadrons, it is true, did attain a high degree of accuracy in bombing competitions, but the conditions were so artificial that the results could not be considered even remotely relevant to any operational situation that might face the Command in time of war.

In 1941 His Majesty's Stationery Office would publish a booklet entitled *Bomber Command*, the Air Ministry account of the bomber offensive from September 1939 to July 1941. In the preamble it claimed that at the beginning of the war the bomber force 'though in numbers far from equal to that of the enemy, was compact, ready and resolute'. That the crews were resolute is indisputable, as they were to prove in the hazardous and sometimes suicidal missions they were to be sent out on when the shooting war began; whether the force was compact depends on how one defines that adjective, but to claim that Bomber Command was operationally ready was quite wrong.

On Sunday the third of September 1939 Neville Chamberlain, the Prime Minister, broadcast to the nation that Britain was once again at war with Germany. Almost immediately air-raid sirens sounded in London and elsewhere, but the forecast onslaught from the air did not come, and those people who had gone to their shelters emerged when the all-clear sounded shortly afterwards. London was to be spared a major attack for the best part of a year. At midday a Bristol Blenheim aircraft of No. 139 Squadron lifted off from its base at Wyton, Huntingdonshire, to make the first operational sortie by Bomber Command in World War Two. The pilot's brief was a search for German shipping, and he photographed a number of vessels in the area to the north of Wilhelmshaven. There were other similar flights by Hampdens and Wellingtons in the course of the day, but of the twenty-seven machines that set out on maritime reconnaissance missions none sighted enemy warships.

It fell to the Whitleys of Nos. 51 and 58 Squadrons of No. 4 Group based at Linton-on-Ouse in Yorkshire to make the first night raids against Germany, ten machines setting out for Hamburg, Bremen and the Ruhr area that same night. Each Whitley was capable of carrying over three tons of bombs, but on these flights they dropped nothing more dangerous than propaganda leaflets, to a total number of over five million.

For the first month of hostilities the majority of the operational aircraft of the *Luftwaffe* were deployed against Poland, where the Germans, unable to reduce Warsaw by direct assault, unleashed an all-out bombing attack on the city on 24 September. There were voices in Britain, including that of the Director of Plans at the Air Ministry, Air Commodore J. C. Slessor, that argued that the RAF should take advantage of the Germans' preoccupation with the East to implement two strategic bombing plans that had been drawn up before the outbreak of hostilities, the 'Ruhr Plan' and the 'Oil Plan'. Both these plans embodied the conviction that telling, perhaps mortal, blows could be struck by Bomber Command against the power stations and factories in the sprawling industrial complex centred on Essen and against oil-producing and storage installations respectively. Other views prevailed, both professional and political, and no action was taken, although discussion of the two plans and the wisdom or otherwise of implementing them were to continue long after the Polish campaign was over. Not only was the Commander-in-Chief of Bomber Command, Air Chief Marshal Sir Edgar Ludlow Hewitt, doubtful whether his force was either powerful enough or capable of bombing with sufficient accuracy to inflict the sort of blows necessary to achieve the results required, but also, perhaps of even more influence in the decision, there was a considerable difference of opinion between Britain and France on the matter of bombing Germany. The French were adamant that Allied bombing should be exclusively tactical, directed against German troop movements and communications in the front-line area and its vicinity. Just as in the First World War, they feared reprisals against their cities, which were geographically easier for the *Luftwaffe* to attack than those in England.

The Germans would argue that their bombing of Warsaw was tactical in nature, necessary action taken to reduce a defended location that stood in the way of their Army's advance. In Britain it was seen as the indiscriminate bombing of a civilian target and therefore an element of justification for any future bombing action that might be taken against targets within Germany itself. For the time being, however, the RAF directed its bombing attacks against targets of a strictly 'legitimate' nature. Naval targets were the obvious choice, because attacks against them involved neither deep penetration of Germany itself nor great risk that inaccurately aimed bombs would hit non-military targets.

Before the year was out it had become clear that attacks by day against Germany were liable to such high losses for so little return that they were not a valid proposition. As early as the day after the declaration of war on Germany seven Blenheims and Wellingtons out of a raiding force of thirty were shot down while attempting to attack German capital ships and other naval vessels at Wilhelmshaven and Brunsbüttel. The majority of the damage was done by German flak, but it seems possible that two of the Wellingtons on the Brunsbüttel target fell to fighters. An early indication of the difficulty of aerial navigation was given when one of the Wellingtons mistakenly dropped bombs on the coastal town of Esbjerg in neutral Denmark, a navigational error of over a hundred miles and a gross map-reading mistake on the part of the crew, Brunsbüttel being at the mouth of the Kiel Canal and therefore quite easily identifiable from the air. The first two civilians to be killed in the course of Bomber Command attacks were not Germans, but Danes.

Bomber Command carried out a series of anti-shipping sweeps by day over the North Sea during this early period, but these were largely unproductive. Casualties were minimal. Whenever there were specific targets, however, losses tended to be heavy. Blenheims of No. 2 Group flew reconnaissance sorties over Germany during October and November and suffered a loss-rate of twenty per cent, mostly as a result of encounters with German fighters. On 29 September five Hampdens out of a force of sixteen sent out against maritime targets in the area of Heligoland did not come back. All five, the entire force dispatched from No. 144 Squadron, were shot down by German fighters. On 14 December German fighters shot down five out of twelve Wellingtons attacking a convoy of ships north of Wilhelmshaven. Just four days later, on 18 December, German day fighters destroyed twelve Wellingtons, exactly half of the twenty-four that had set out to bomb shipping, again in the sea area off Wilhelmshaven. Bomber Command had relearned the hard way the lesson that both the Germans and the combined Franco/British bombing force had learned in the First World War: daylight bombing was prohibitively expensive in terms of casualties. Henceforth Bomber Command would operate mainly by night.

While the costly experience of bombing by day had been running its course, the Whitleys of No. 4 Group had been doggedly, if with much frustration for the crews, pursuing their leaflet raids. In comparison to the daylight operations their losses were slight, only four machines of 113 dispatched before the turn of the year failing to return. The comparative losses played a very large part in the decision to switch Bomber Command's main effort to night-time. The nature of leaflet raids was such, however, that there was no possible method of assessing the relative accuracy of raids by day and by night. Bombs dropped on a major German city would surely attract reports in the neutral press, for example, whereas leaflets scattered over a wide area of the same city would scarcely merit a paragraph. Paradoxically, there was in all probability another factor that contributed to the low casualty figures – the inaccuracy of the British crews' navigation. During this phase of the war there was virtually no enemy night fighter activity, so that the main defensive hazard was flak. But the flak was concentrated around cities and towns, and unless the Whitleys flew into fairly close proximity of those towns they would not come under concentrated fire. Thus, for example, a bomber that set out for the Ruhr area and, due to faulty navigation, released its leaflets over the plains to the north would encounter only slight opposition, whereas had it found its intended and well-defended target things might have gone much worse for it. There is no evidence that any of the four Whitleys missing during this period fell to the guns of German fighters.

This was a period of experience gathering for the night bomber crews, and the experience they gained was not reassuring. Aircraft frequently got lost, the weather was a much greater hazard than the German defences, and the results were unquantifiable. In February 1940 the leaflet raids were resumed on an increased scale, Wellingtons and Hampdens joining the Whitleys in their endeavours. There were occasional reports by crews of sightings of German night fighters, usually Bf 109s, but still no evidence of any successes on their part. Up to April only six out of the 228 leaflet-dropping aircraft, which by now were operating as far afield as Poland, were lost.

It was well for the RAF bombers that there was no significant German night fighter effort at this time. The British aircraft were ill-equipped, and the gunners ill-trained, to defend themselves. The Whitley IV relied for its defensive fire on four .303 machine-guns, two in a turret beneath the fuselage, one in a nose turret and one in a rear turret. Larry Donnelly was a wireless operator/air gunner (WOP/AG) with No. 10 Squadron, stationed at Dishforth. His rank was Leading Aircraftman – it was to be some time before aircrew enjoyed a minimum rank of Sergeant. Telling how he tested his guns on his first leaflet raid he writes:

'I scrambled into the turret with difficulty, my bulky flying kit making it a tight squeeze. Lowering the turret by touch alone I loaded the two .303 Brownings. Depressing the guns to point to the sea I cocked them, switched on the reflector gun-sight and slipped off the safety catch. I looked through the sight and pressed the triggers. The two guns blazed away and I watched fascinated as the tracers and the incendiaries curved away in a fiery stream, for this was the first time I had fired the guns at night . . . At that time we had no information on the German night-fighter capability, so we did not know what to expect. Meanwhile Freddy in the rear turret tested his single VGO machine-gun. I didn't envy him. At least the mid-under turret and guns were hydraulically operated, but the tail turret and gun in Whitleys up to and including the Mk IVs had to be manually operated . . .

'The turret was covered with a transparent Perspex cupola which was fixed to the gun mounting and rotated with it. There was a gun aperture through which the elements – wind, rain, snow, you name it – entered when the turret was turned abeam. Getting from the turret to the fuselage when wearing full flying kit was almost an impossibility, so that the Tail-End Charlie was incarcerated in his turret for the duration of the flight. As most of the flights over Germany were to last from seven to ten hours the unfortunate tail gunners were left to suffer temporary paralysis of their nether regions to add to the other physical discomforts.'[1]

For navigation the crews relied on map reading, which, as already explained, was of little value, on DR Navigation supported by radio fixes and, theoretically at least, on astro-navigation. The radio equipment carried by the bomber was basic, and the bearings it produced were intrinsically susceptible to error. Hector Macdonald was a wireless operator who flew on Hampdens, an aircraft in which the crew accommodation was, to be charitable, much less than well designed. He writes:

'In those early days we were using the pre-war transmitter and receiver R1082/1083. They were efficient but in the cold conditions of a Hampden

---

[1] *The Whitley Boys* by G. L. Donnelly, published 1991 by Air Research Publications.

the coils for the various frequencies used to freeze up, and as they had to be changed manually this could be a problem. A signal would be transmitted on take-off, but then silence and a listening-out watch for messages from base. The next transmission would be to signify whether we had bombed the primary target or the alternative. Loop bearings always seemed to turn out satisfactory, but more so when we later had the then up-to-date Marconi set R1154/1155. In the Hampden the second pilot was the navigator, and he eventually became a first pilot. In flight, if the first pilot was killed or wounded there was not much hope for the rest of the crew. Whilst pilots *could* change places in flight, this was a hazardous occupation. A friend of mine, a W/Op, was killed along with the rest of the crew when the pilots attempted such a change-over . . .

'In the Hampden the W/Op had two Vickers gas-operated guns to use in addition to his radio duties. The second W/Op was in the lower position, and he had little else to do apart from operating the flare chutes if required and being custodian of the pigeons.'

The bombers were inadequately heated and the oxygen supply was neither sufficient nor readily enough accessible for operating at the heights the machines flew at, often over 20,000 feet. When it failed, as it not infrequently did, conditions became well-nigh intolerable. Of a leaflet raid to the Düsseldorf and Frankfurt areas in October 1939 the Air Ministry booklet *Bomber Command* (1941) reports:

'. . . such was the condition of the navigator and wireless operator at this stage, that every few minutes they were compelled to lie down and rest on the floor of the fuselage. The cockpit heating system was useless. Everyone was frozen, and had no means of alleviating their distress. The navigator and Commanding Officer were butting their heads on the floor and navigation table in an endeavour to experience some other form of pain as a relief from the awful feeling of frostbite and lack of oxygen . . . [The aircraft descended to 8,000 feet] and ice could be heard coming off the blades of the airscrews and striking the sides of the nose. Continuous movement of the controls was necessary to prevent them from freezing up.'

There was no comparable *Luftwaffe* activity over England at this time. Presumably the Germans did not calculate that propaganda leaflets were likely to diminish the British will to fight. Both sides remained reluctant to take the first step that might lead to all-out bombing. In the early hours of darkness on the night of 16 March 1940 a small force of German aircraft attacked a fully legitimate target, the British naval base at Scapa Flow in the Orkneys. Some of the raiders' bombs fell on land at the small settlement of Bridge of Waithe on the island of Hoy, where they hit cottages, killing one civilian and injuring seven. The Germans also hit a warship, HMS *Norfolk*, causing thirteen casualties among the crew, six of them fatal. The British Government ordered a reprisal raid, and a force of fifty Bomber Command machines, thirty Whitleys and twenty Hampdens, was sent three nights later to attack the German seaplane base at Hörnum on the southern tip of the island of Sylt, a target in the vicinity of which there were not thought to be any civilian residences. As was the practice at that period, each captain was responsible for planning his own route to and from the target, his bombing time and his direction and height of attack. The moon would be up for six hours that night, and the Whitleys were given a four-hour period during which to bomb while the Hampdens, which followed, were allowed a period of two hours. On their return a total of forty-one of the crews claimed to have bombed accurately, and an Air Ministry communiqué stated that 'the crews reported many hits'. Subsequent photographic reconnaissance, however, failed to reveal other than superficial damage.

Hörnum was a target that might have been tailor-made for a visual bombing attack. The long, narrow island of Sylt off the coast of Schleswig-Holstein runs north and south and is approximately twenty-five kilometres in length. The southern half forms a narrow finger ten kilometres long and only about a kilometre wide, and it should have been unmistakable from the air in the conditions of moonlight that prevailed on the night of the attack. Indeed, all the bomb aimers who claimed to have bombed the target reported that it had been easily recognisable. The RAF crews had demonstrated once more the difficulties inherent in aerial navigation and bomb dropping, and they had also manifested the propensity to exaggerate the accuracy of their bomb aiming that was sadly a persistent characteristic of bomber crews. Ominously too there was, in the comparison between the German raid on Scapa Flow and the RAF attack on Hörnum, an early indication, later to be alarmingly confirmed by the *Luftwaffe* attacks on Coventry and other cities, that in the matter of bomb aiming the Germans were more advanced than the British. They had at least hit a warship at Scapa Flow, whereas the much greater Bomber Command force had apparently caused only minimal damage to the German seaplane base.

There was one encouraging feature about the Hörnum raid: only one bomber, a Whitley, was lost. This compared most favourably with the losses that had resulted from the daylight raids in the same general area, tending to confirm that, as the leaflet raids seemed to indicate, losses by night were likely to be more tolerable than those by day.

On 9 April 1940 the Norwegian campaign began when German forces invaded Norway and Denmark at dawn. Bomber Command switched its role to one of tactical support for the Allied expeditionary force that went ashore at Narvik. The bombers were soon to suffer a serious reverse. On 12 April a force of eighty-three Wellingtons, Hampdens and Blenheims attacked shipping at Stavanger by daylight and came up against heavy flak and fighter opposition, losing nine bombers. The *Luftwaffe* lost five fighters, but the message that daylight raids were likely to be very costly had been underlined. From then on Bomber Command's attacks on Norwegian targets, mostly airfields, were mainly by night, as were their mine-laying sorties to the waters off Denmark and Norway. On 1 May the Allied expeditionary force began its evacuation from Norway, leaving the country in the hands of the Germans.

Irritated, if not as yet unduly alarmed, by Bomber Command's leaflet-dropping ventures into their territory, the Germans had begun to consider how their flak defences might be supported by fighters. Quite soon after the outbreak of war two fighter *Staffeln* were formed and designated as night-fighting units, 10./(N)JG 26 at Bonn-Hangelar to cover the Cologne area and 10./(N)JG 53 at

Heilbronn, further south near Stuttgart. Both units were equipped with the Bf 109.

The *Staffel* was the basic operational unit of the *Luftwaffe*. It is sometimes referred to in English language works as a squadron, but in fact was rather smaller than the RAF squadron, usually comprising nine aircraft, although there were exceptions. The next higher element was the *Gruppe*, made up of three *Staffeln* – sometimes anglicised as 'wings' – above which was the *Geschwader*, made up of three *Gruppen*. *Gruppen* and *Geschwader* had headquarters or staff aircraft attached to them: a headquarters flight was a *Stabsschwarm*. The designations of the flying units were compiled with Germanic logic. The basic element was the type of *Geschwader*: in the examples above 'JG' is short for '*Jagdgeschwader*', so that JG 53 means the Fighter *Geschwader* No. 53. *Gruppen* were given a Roman numeral, I, II or III, followed by a full stop, the German way of showing an ordinal number (III., for example, would mean 'third'). Individual *Staffeln* had an Arabic number followed by a full stop, so that 10./JG 53 would be the 10th *Staffel* of *Jagdgeschwader* 53.

To indicate their night-fighting role, 10./JG 26 and 10./JG 53 (clearly the figure ten indicates that this was a supplementary *Staffel*, additional to the usual *Gruppe* establishment of nine, or alternatively that a fourth *Gruppe* had been formed) were given the extra letter 'N' (for *Nacht* = Night). They did not, however, fly during the hours of darkness but at dawn and evening twilight, patrolling in the hope of coming across an RAF bomber. Not surprisingly, that hope remained unfulfilled.

The self-willed and pragmatic Commander-in-Chief of the *Luftwaffe*, the then Generalfeldmarschall Hermann Göring (it was not until July 1940 that Adolf Hitler appointed him to the unique rank of Reichsmarschall) remained unconvinced that there was a need for night fighters, and he informed the Inspector of Fighters to that effect, adding that there should be no expansion of the existing token force. Nevertheless a night-fighter *Gruppe* was formed at the turn of the year 1939/40 as part of JG 2, which had its headquarters at Jever, just to the west of Wilhelmshaven. Some of the fighters were positioned at Jever itself, some on the East Friesian island of Langeoog, to defend against attacks against naval targets in the Heligoland Bight area. The unit, IV./(N) JG 2, was equipped with the Bf 109D-1 single-seater, a version of the Bf 109 that was in the process of being phased out in favour of the Bf 109E because of the unreliability of its Daimler-Benz DB 600A engine. To aid vision and to obviate searchlight glare, the pilots flew their machines with the cabin canopies removed.

Successes were slow in coming. Oberfeldwebel Schmale claimed the destruction of an RAF bomber near Wismar on the Baltic coast in the small hours of 21 April 1940, but no Bomber Command machines are recorded as having been operating in that area that night, nor were any of those that did fly, most of which went to Norway, reported missing. Two further claims, both by Oberfeldwebel Hermann Förster, are, however, confirmed, the first for a kill on 25 April and the second for one on 14 May. His first of the two was one of a force of twenty-eight Hampdens mine-laying off the coast of Schleswig-Holstein. Probably an aircraft from No. 49 Squadron flown by Pilot Officer A. H. Benson, it seems likely to have been the first of the thousands of Bomber Command machines destined to fall to the guns of German night-fighters between then and the night of

14/15 April 1945, when a Lancaster attacking Potsdam had the unhappy distinction of being the last of the many. Förster's success on 14 May was possibly also a mine-laying Hampden. Both his victims came down near the island of Sylt.

At the same time as the single-engined Bf 109s of JG 2 were having their first tastes of success, the twin-engined heavy fighters, the Bf 110 *Zerstörer*, were also seeing what they could do to combat the night-time visitors from Bomber Command. Their experiments were to represent the first tentative steps along the road that was subsequently to lead to the formidable *Nachtjagd*, which would wreak such terrible retribution on the RAF bombers attempting to destroy German cities. The officer on whose initiative these first steps were taken was the then Hauptmann – he was later to attain the rank of Oberst – Wolfgang Falck, commanding I./ZG 1, stationed at Aalborg in Denmark, destined to become one of the legendary figures of the *Luftwaffe* of the Third Reich.

Born in August 1910, Falck had been one of the *Reichswehr* officer-cadets selected in 1932 to be sent to Lipetsk in the Soviet Union for training as a fighter pilot. He writes:

'In those days the War Ministry selected thirty officer-cadets for flying training each year from the approximately 250 who had already been accepted by the Regiments – before they joined their Regiment, that is. Training was "black", because Germany was not allowed to have an air force. The Regiments were not very pleased when they informed the Ministry which cadets they wanted only to be told, "You're not getting him yet, he's being detached for special duties first." When the Regiments came to work out their mobilisation plan they were a cadet – later an officer – short of establishment. After a year's flying training twenty went to their Regiment to get their normal training, while the other ten went to Russia for six months. Only then did we join our Regiment – it was quite a comedown to go from being a fighter pilot to being a recruit in an army 100,000 strong!'

On his return from Russia Falck reverted to infantry service, but with the emergence of the German Air Force from clandestinity he became a flying instructor at the *Luftwaffe* Fighter School at Schleissheim, just outside the Bavarian capital of Munich. Subsequently he was posted as a *Staffelkapitän* to JG 2, the Richthofen *Geschwader*, which was equipped with the Bf 109. Shortly before the outbreak of war, however, the *Gruppe* to which Falck belonged, III./JG 2, was detached from the *Geschwader* to form I./ZG 76 and to convert on to the new heavy fighter, the Bf 110 *Zerstörer*. In the attack on Poland on 1 September 1939 Leutnant Falck led his *Staffel* into action. The Polish campaign over, I./ZG 76 was sent to the Western Front, first in the Stuttgart area and then on the Lower Rhine. From there, on 17 December 1939, it moved north to Jever, and Falck saw further action when his *Gruppe* took part in the devastating action against the RAF Wellingtons the following day and shot down nine of the total of twelve destroyed, Falck himself claiming one. The remainder fell to Bf 109s. This success had resulted in part from reports of the approach of the RAF force received from two *Freya* radars, a Navy one on Heligoland and a *Luftwaffe* one at an experimental early-warning station on the island of Wangerooge commanded by Leutnant Hermann Diehl. It was radar that was ultimately to provide the solution to the problem of interception by night, and Falck was to play a leading role in its introduction.

In February 1940 Falck, who by that time had been promoted to Hauptmann, was given the command of a *Gruppe*, I./ZG 1: as *Gruppenkommandeur* he had under him three *Staffeln*, and among his pilots were men who would later make their name as night fighter aces, prominent among them Werner Streib, then an Oberleutnant, who ended the war as an Oberst with sixty-six victories to his credit, sixty-five of them at night. The term 'Father of the Night Fighters' (*Vater der Nachtjagd*) has been applied to both Wolfgang Falck and Werner Streib.

With the opening of the Norwegian campaign in April 1940 I./ZG 1 was deployed to Aalborg, near to the northern tip of the Jutland peninsula, where the airfield was a frequent target for night attacks by the RAF. At his own initiative and in discussion with his subordinates, Streib in particular, Falck began to think how something might be done about the unwelcome visitors from Bomber Command. Recalling the experience of 18 December 1939, he arranged for the operators at a nearby coastal radar station commanded by Leutnant Werner Bode to inform his Operations Room at Aalborg by telephone when they detected incoming British bombers. The radar used, the *Freya*, had a maximum range of 100 kilometres against a target at 10,000 feet, which was a typical altitude for the approaching bombers to fly at: the higher the bomber was flying, the earlier it would be picked up by the radar; the lower it was, the closer it would be before it was detected. With a bomber at 10,000 feet Falck would have perhaps fifteen minutes' warning of its arrival in the vicinity of Aalborg.

Falck encouraged his pilots to fly by night, and in consultation with Leutnant Bode and the officers in charge of the local *Flak* and searchlight contingents – not always an easy matter, because as a Hauptmann he was outranked by the majors and lieutenant-colonels commanding those units – he worked out a system of defence, trying it out first of all with three crews in addition to his own. He compiled a large-scale map of the area divided into a grid of rectangles (*Planquadrate*), each allocated two individual letters. When an aircraft was detected approaching from the west the radar officer would telephone to Falck's Operations Room the letters of the *Planquadrat* in which it had been picked up, upon which the Bf 110s would take off. No success having been achieved in this way, the next step was for his aircraft to take off and patrol at height in pre-arranged holding areas (*Warteräume*) while remaining in R/T contact with the radar station. When the radar officer reported approaching bombers and the *Planquadrat* in which they had been picked up, the *Zerstörer* would head in that direction. Still they had no success, but they were gaining confidence in their ability to fly by night, and they had made a simple, but significant, discovery. Other aircraft could be picked out at night more readily if they were silhouetted against the northern sky, particularly if seen from slightly below. Tactically, therefore, it would be advantageous to approach a bomber from the south and from a lower altitude. This would also, it was realised, have the advantage that the fighter, dark against the dark ground below, would be difficult for the bomber's gunners to see.

During the night of 30 April/1 May 1940 fifty RAF Whitleys, Wellingtons and Hampdens attacked airfields in Norway, including Falck's base, Aalborg.

Hauptmann Falck, Oberleutnant Streib, Oberleutnant Radusch and Feldwebel Thier took off and pursued the bombers as they headed westwards for England shortly before dawn on 1 May. Falck, Streib and Radusch made contact, opened fire and came under fire themselves, but their targets dived into low cloud, so that no claims could be made. Radusch's Bf 110 returned to Aalborg with a number of bullet holes. Three RAF bombers did not come back that night, but whether any of them were lost as a result of the encounter is not known. Be that as it may, the incident had given encouragement to Falck and his night-fighting pioneers, and he sent a detailed paper on his ideas, experiments and experiences to the *Reichsluftfahrtministerium*, the Reich Aviation Ministry, where it aroused considerable interest, so much so that almost immediately afterwards Generaloberst Erhard Milch, State Secretary for Aviation and, as Inspector General of the *Luftwaffe*, Göring's deputy, who was in temporary command of *Luftflotte 5* (Norway), went to Aalborg to discuss Falck's ideas with him personally. 'Never again did I hear of an operational report from the front line resulting in so quick and positive a reaction among the high-ups, who always know better than the men at the sharp end!' says Falck.

Immediately after this meeting high-level interest in night fighting fell into abeyance with the German invasion of Belgium and Holland on 10 May, but although Falck's endeavours had brought no tangible success they had provided the first, tentative lines on what was to become a blueprint for night-fighter operations in the Third Reich. Falck had perceived the value of early-warning radar and the necessity for a line of communication from the radar to the operational flying unit. He had conceived the idea of converting the readings received from the radar station into geographical positions so that the fighters could be brought into the proximity of the bomber, and he and his pilots had begun to formulate tactics suited to night fighting. Most importantly, he and his theories and practical endeavours had attracted official attention at a time when, as strategic developments were to show, the necessity for a powerful night-fighter force would soon become very apparent.

The essential element in Falck's concept was of course radar, although that word was not yet in general use. The British called it radiolocation, the Germans *Funkmesstechnik*, or radio measurement technology, and it was a very much more accurate method of detecting the approach of hostile aircraft than such methods as radio bearings, sound locators and message interception, which had first been used in the First World War. These older techniques in fact still played a very important part throughout World War Two in the defence of the Third Reich against Allied bombers, increasingly so as the British, and later the American, offensives developed, but it was radar in its many forms that provided the element of precision without which airborne interception could never have achieved the degree of efficiency that came to characterise it. Radar was also, incidentally, to revolutionise the crafts of aerial navigation and bomb dropping. To a great measure it was responsible for the way in which both bomber offensive and night-fighting evolved. For both sides it was an operational blessing, but at the same time it was a major constraint in their pursuit of ascendancy.

The basis of radar is the measurement of the time that it takes for transmitted radio energy to return to the point of transmission after having been reflected from a solid object: in the case of air defence radar the solid object will be an aircraft. Radio energy travels at a constant speed of approximately 186,000 miles a second. Once the 'there-and-back' time is measured, the simple formula '*Distance = Time × Speed ÷ 2*' will show how far away the aircraft is. It will readily be understood that mechanical devices such as stop-watches would be much too slow-working to register the infinitesimal intervals of time involved, but a solution to the difficulty had been found in the construction of the so-called cathode-ray tube, or CRT, which will certainly be familiar to the majority of readers. In its simplest form it appears to an operator as a circular screen, glowing green or amber, on which impulses from returned echoes are displayed along a horizontal or vertical line of light, known as a time-base. The distance along the time-base is directly proportionate to the time elapsed, and hence to the distance of the target away from the transmitter and receiver, so that the time-base can be marked with a scale against which that distance may be measured.

In order accurately to fix the position of an aircraft in space, two other factors in addition to the range are necessary: its direction, or bearing, and its altitude. There are two broad methods of measuring bearing by radar, but the simpler and more readily understandable one is to point the radar's receiving aerial directly at the target. The assessment of altitude is rather more complex.

The Germans were in the forefront of radio location, even though at the time they had no avowed air force. In about 1930 a certain Dr Rudolph Kühnold, a civil servant in the research department of the German Navy, was investigating the possibility of using radio waves to detect shipping and aircraft. A company, GEMA, was founded to develop his ideas and in March 1934 Germany's first practical radar was functioning in a building overlooking the harbour at Kiel. Once the potential of radar had been perceived and a workable device produced, things moved ahead with some rapidity. By 1936 GEMA had manufactured the prototypes of two radars that were to be of considerable significance in the war, *Seetakt* and *Freya*. *Seetakt* was a ship-borne gunnery radar, while *Freya*, the radar that would eventually alert Wolfgang Falck to the approach of British bombers, was a mobile early-warning radar for use against either ships or aircraft, and it was ordered in quantity by both the *Kriegsmarine* and the *Luftwaffe*. *Freya* had a range of twenty kilometres against a target flying at fifty metres, increasing to a range of 120 kilometres against a target at 8,000 metres, and it could be mechanically rotated through 360°. It worked on a frequency of 125 MHz, which meant that its wavelength was 2.40 metres. As the optimum length of a radio aerial is half the wavelength, this comparatively high frequency meant that, compared to the British early-warning radar CH, described later, *Freya* needed only a small aerial, which suited it well to a mobile role. *Freya* did not have a built-in height-finding function, although, as may be seen from the passage above about Wolfgang Falck's early efforts in the field of night-fighting, an estimate of a bomber's altitude could be made from the range at which it was first detected. The *Freya* was designated FuMG 80. A word might be in place here on the Germans' method of numbering their equipment, because we shall meet with such designations throughout this book.

The Germans are, it might be said, compulsive abbreviators, and they used their equivalent of acronyms widely long before they became fashionable in Britain. *Flak* and *Stuka* are examples: the Germans use not only the initials of words – of which several frequently go together to make a longer word – but sometimes also the first vowels, so that the two examples given are short for *Fliegerabwehrkanonen* and *Sturzkampfflugzeug* respectively. Most radio and radar equipments had designations beginning with *Fu* (short for Funk), although some of the earlier radars, like the *Freya*, had FuM (*Funkmess*). The 'G' stands for *Gerät* (equipment), so that a FuG would be a radio (or radar) equipment, a FuMG a radar equipment.

On the tenth day of May in the year 1940 the Germans invaded neutral Holland and Belgium to secure their northern flank. It was a copybook attack, awe-inspiring in its efficiency and striking power, with the German Army and Air Force, including parachute troops, working in close co-operation. Three days later the tanks of Generalleutnant Guderian, General der *Panzertruppen* and Commander of the *XIX. Armeekorps*, crossed the River Meuse into France at Sedan, thrusting for the Channel coast; by 20 May they were to reach Abbeville and three days later Boulogne and Calais, where Hitler would order them to halt. The majority of the British Expeditionary Force would escape from Dunkirk in an evacuation operation beginning on 26 May and ending on 4 June. In the meantime Holland and Belgium would fall, and France would sue for peace by the middle of the month. The *Blitzkrieg* lasted less than six weeks, and Hitler's generals could then pause for breath before beginning their assault on Britain.

The part that the *Luftwaffe* played in the campaign was pre-eminently a tactical one, with *Stukas* and other ground-attack aircraft in close support of the advancing troops on the ground and the heavier machines bombing pinpoint targets such as airfields. During the advance through Holland, however, heavy bombers of the *Luftwaffe* carried out an attack which, like those on Guernica during the Spanish Civil War and Warsaw in September 1939, was, and in some quarters still is, quoted in justification of the eventual British decision to move over to a campaign of unrestricted strategic bombing. Rotterdam marked another step along the road to the inevitable.

The city was encircled, but the Dutch were fighting tenaciously but hopelessly. On 13 May, under the cover of a white flag, the Germans sent two co-opted Dutch civilians to ask the Dutch Town Commander to capitulate and so prevent more damage to the already battered city and avoid further loss of life. The Dutch refused to treat with civilians, so two German officers were sent. In this way, and other similar ways, time was wasted and the German deadline of 1500 hrs approached. One hundred German He 111 bombers were ordered off from their bases at Delmenhorst, Hoya and Quakenbrück so as to be over Rotterdam at that time, but contingency plans were made for the bombing to be cancelled by means of red signals fired by the German troops on the ground should there be the prospect of a Dutch surrender. As negotiations were still continuing, the Germans sent out a recall signal to their bombers, but it was not received, possibly because the He 111s were at low level and their trailing aerials wound in. The bombers were split up into two forces, and the commander of one of the forces saw red signals that were fired from the ground, and so aborted the mission. The other force, however, bombed with devastating effect. Fifty-three He 111s dropped almost a hundred tons of high-explosive bombs, and a vast conflagration resulted. At 1700 hrs Rotterdam surrendered.

The toll was heavy: 20,000 buildings were destroyed and 78,000 people rendered homeless. Nearly one thousand died. Another act of frightfulness was added to the reputation of the Germans, but it was an act which, objectivity dictates, can now be seen to have been exaggerated in the way it was then presented to public opinion in Britain and elsewhere outside Germany. The fatality figure was propagated as up to 30,000 and the impression given that Rotterdam was an open city callously destroyed by wanton and indiscriminate attack. Both assertions were clearly wrong. The bombing of Rotterdam was not a strategic attack but a clinical close-support operation in the context of a military advance. That is not to condone it: the siege of Rotterdam took place in the course of the unprovoked invasion of a neutral country undertaken as part of Hitler's determination to dominate Europe.

Following the German invasion of the Low Countries on 10 May and until the attack on Rotterdam, Bomber Command had been striking at airfields and communications targets – bridges, railway, roads and so on – to delay the German advance. The first bombs on a German town were dropped during the night of 11/12 May when road and rail junctions near Mönchengladbach, just over the Dutch/German border, were bombed by thirty-seven Hampdens and Whitleys, of which three failed to return. Support bombing was also carried out between 12 and 14 May in the area of Aachen, where Germany, Belgium and Holland adjoin. But following the German attack on Rotterdam on the thirteenth the British War Cabinet under Prime Minister Chamberlain met and authorised Bomber Command to extend its activities to targets to the east of the River Rhine. What followed that night of the 15/16 May was not a retaliatory raid, as the attack on Hörnum on 19/20 March had been, but the *de facto* declaration of war by strategic bombing.

The announcement on 16 May that the previous night a large force of RAF bombers had attacked various oil and communications targets in the Ruhr area of Germany was overwhelmingly welcomed by the British public. After weeks of unremitting bad news, here was a bright spot. At last we were giving the Hun a taste of his own medicine. Now the Boche would learn what it was like to be bombed – see how he liked it! The decision was also welcomed by Bomber Command leaders and crews, who had been fretting under the political restrictions placed on their force and who were in general confident that they could bring Germany to her knees. Ninety-nine bombers – Wellingtons, Hampdens and Whitleys – were dispatched, and the Air Ministry communiqué reporting the raid was encouraging: 'Each crew was given specific military objectives and instructions that bombs were not to be dropped indiscriminately. A few aircraft failed to locate their objectives, and did not drop their bombs, but the majority found and bombed their targets with great effect causing widespread damage and many explosions.' Among the targets against which the RAF crews were sent were names that were to feature in countless Flying Log Books before the end of the war – Dortmund, Kastrop-Rauxel, Sterkrade, and Dormagen/Cologne for example – but despite the optimistic claims of the crews little damage was in fact caused, and some of that little damage was in places not on the crews' target lists. One Wellington was lost. Fifty-three German bombers operating by day had devastated the centre of Rotterdam, while almost one hundred RAF bombers operating by night had scattered bombs, largely ineffectually, over hundreds of square miles of Germany. It was a further strong reminder that bombing by night was an enterprise unlikely to bring success; it is hard after so many years to decide whether the euphoric Air Ministry claims were made knowing that they were false or in the unfounded belief that they were correct. Whatever the case, the strategic air offensive against Germany had begun. The gloves were off.

Further attacks followed. On 17/18 May, for example, seventy-two bombers went to Hamburg, Bremen and Cologne, this time with more success. German casualties were beginning to mount, at least forty-seven being killed and 127 injured in Hamburg and Bremen. Hans Brunswig, at that time a senior officer of the Hamburg Fire Brigade, describes the attack on his city in these terms:

> 'In the meanwhile, all hell is let loose outside: over the roofs of Harburg streak tracer trajectories from the 2 cm *flak*. Dull detonations can be heard, and the 8.8 cm *Flak* battery at the access road to the *autobahn* at Harburg is firing salvos, other heavy batteries near and far joining in. In the sky there is the cracking and the flashing of detonating *flak* shells – and on the ground, too, of impacting high-explosive bombs and dazzling-white incendiaries. Numerous parachute flares turn night into day.
>
> In rather hazy weather they had dropped about eighty high-explosive bombs and 400 incendiaries on targets lit by parachute flares, mainly in the Harburg industrial area, and in doing so had caused, in addition to considerable high-explosive damage, six major fires spreading over a considerable area, one medium-sized fire and twenty-nine minor fires. In addition thirty-four people (twenty-four men, nine women and one child) had been killed by explosive bombs and seventy-two individuals had suffered injuries of varying degree.'[1]

The war was beginning to come home to the German people, literally. The strategic offensive against Germany had begun, but for the moment the Air Staff had other preoccupations, additional tasks for Bomber Command. The German tanks were driving on across northern France and Belgium, sweeping aside resistance, while the *Luftwaffe* was taking a fearful toll of the French and British aircraft attempting to stop their advance. On the day of Rotterdam's agony, seventy British Battles and Blenheims, plus forty French machines, were shot down attempting to bomb bridges over the River Meuse. No. 82 Squadron, flying from Watton in Norfolk, sent twelve of its Blenheims to Gembloux, south-east of Brussels, on the seventeenth of the month to bomb German troops breaking through, and one came back. The other eleven were annihilated by *Luftwaffe* fighters. Bomber Command's heavy and medium bombers, the Whitleys, Wellingtons and Hampdens, joined in by night, attacking troop concentrations and communications targets in the front-line area, but they also went for oil and railway targets inside Germany itself. Losses were tolerable, and there were few reports of encounters with night fighters. On the night of 27/28 May 120 Hampdens, Whitleys and Wellingtons attacked oil targets at Bremen and Hamburg and rail targets at Neuss, Dortmund, Duisburg and elsewhere without

---

[1] Translated from *Feuersturm über Hamburg* by Hans Brunswig, published by Motorbuch Verlag, Stuttgart.

loss. The British bombers were still attacking individually, and German records show that in Hamburg the air-raid alarm was given at 0115 hrs on the eighteenth, the all-clear two hours and thirty-five minutes later. The raid on Hamburg caused little damage to Germany's second city, but one of the Whitleys from No. 10 Squadron attacking the Ruhr earned the distinction of shooting down the first German night fighter in the Second World War. Piloted by Squadron Leader Pat Hanafin, it had taken off from Dishforth in Yorkshire and was attacked on the way back from its target. The rear gunner, Aircraftman Stan Oldridge, shot the attacker down near Utrecht. It is likely that the German machine was one of Major Blumensaat's Bf 109Ds from IV./(N)JG 2.

The same pattern of Bomber Command operations continued until the Battle of France ended on 22 June. By day the Blenheims struck at objectives in the front-line area in an unavailing attempt to hinder the German advance, while by night the Hampdens, Whitleys and Wellingtons divided their efforts between tactical targets in France, Belgium and Germany and strategic targets in Germany. By day ninety-two aircraft were lost in the course of 1,601 sorties, by night only fifty-three from 3,484 sorties, comparative percentage losses of 5.75 and 1.5 respectively. Once again it was virtually impossible to compare the respective accuracy of the bombing. Still the Germans had only a token night-fighter force, and even that had not experienced success. Yet for the German nation and its leadership these were heady days, and now only Britain stood in the way of ultimate victory. But the euphoria engendered by success was tempered with unease, and that unease was caused by the British bombers that flew almost unimpeded, it seemed, over Germany almost every night. Bomber Command even ranged as far as Genoa, Turin and Milan after Italy's declaration of war on Britain on 10 June. In the pause between the successful conclusion of the French Campaign and the opening of the Battle of Britain, and despite the fact that the maximum effort possible would be needed for that undertaking, serious thought was at last devoted to the matter of night-fighting and some aircraft were made available, if only in small numbers at first.

Hauptmann Falck, who had carried out his do-it-yourself night-fighting experiments at Aalborg, led his *Zerstörer Gruppe* in the Battle of France, and when that campaign came to an end the unit was positioned on an airfield near Le Havre in anticipation of the assault on the British mainland. The *Gruppe* had had losses and he was awaiting new machines and crews for the attack on England, when out of the blue there came a telephone call that was not only to change the direction of Falck's career but also to mark the birth of the German night-fighter force that fought heroically, but in the end unavailingly, against Bomber Command in World War Two. The date was 22 June 1940, the very day on which the French signed the article of surrender at Compiègne, and the caller was General Kesselring.

Kesselring told Falck that it had been decided to set up a *Geschwader* dedicated to night fighting and that he, Falck, had been selected to do the preliminary work. He was to transfer that very day to Düsseldorf together with two *Staffeln* of his *Gruppe*, which had in the meanwhile been separated from ZG 1 and attached to ZG 26 as IV./ZG 26. For Falck and his men this was a very unpopular order. Keyed up for the forthcoming battle, they found themselves unexpectedly and unceremoniously plucked from front-line action, with its prospects of glorious participation in final victory over the main enemy, and consigned to the anticlimactic, possibly dangerous and, they thought, certainly unrewarding task of searching for elusive bombers in the vast, impenetrable blackness of the night sky over Germany. This was a time when there were decorations to be won and every operational pilot of the *Luftwaffe* wanted his share, and the *Nachtjagd* did not seem to offer that prospect. Falck protested to Kesselring, but to no avail. In fact the decision to transfer him and his pilots to night-fighting certainly extended their life expectancy, temporarily at least, because the Bf 110 *Zerstörer* were to suffer heavy losses in combat against the RAF Spitfires and Hurricanes during the Battle of Britain.

Only four days after his peremptory transfer to Düsseldorf Wolfgang Falck was summoned to a conference at Wassenaar, just north of The Hague on the coast of conquered Holland. A mere Hauptmann, the direct equivalent of a Flight Lieutenant in the Royal Air Force, Falck found himself among impressive company. Hermann Göring was pre-eminent, and with him was his close confidant, protégé and First World War flying comrade Bruno Loerzer, at that time the General commanding *Fliegerkorps II*. Generaloberst Albert Kesselring, commanding *Luftflotte 2*, was there, as was Generalleutnant Ernst Udet, also a wartime comrade of Göring and at that time *Generalluftzeugmeister*, Director General of Equipment (Air). Of this meeting Falck writes:

'Also among those present were General Kastner, Head of Personnel of the *Luftwaffe*; General Schmidt, Commander of *Luftgau VI*, Münster; and General Christiansen, officer in command of the *Wehrmacht* in the Netherlands. The discussions took place in a country house in Wassenaar that had, I believe, previously belonged to the Jewish arms dealer Wolff. In an ante-room was Oberleutnant Teske, signals officer of JG 1, Jever, who had been involved together with me in the successful daylight action against the RAF Wellingtons on 18 December 1939. I was called in. Göring delivered a long monologue on the way in which the war was developing. We would win, of course, but the occasional night attacks by isolated RAF aircraft were annoying. I had had thoughts on that subject, and he had decided to set up a new arm, the *Nachtjagd*. He was hereby appointing me to be *Kommodore* of the first *Geschwader* to be set up, NJG 1. I was to take my *Gruppe,* and to form a second *Gruppe* he was giving me Major Blumensaat's fighter *Gruppe*. I was to inform Blumensaat that he was relieved of his command and that he was to hand over to his senior Staffelkapitän, who was Steinhoff, and that his *Gruppe* would now come under me as II./NJG 1. Then he outlined a command structure that must, in terms of military history, be almost unique. Operationally I was to be subordinate to *Luftflotte 2* in Brussels, administratively to *Luftgau IV*, and in technical matters to the Inspector of Fighters. He added that I wasn't to get a swollen head because I was now a *Geschwaderkommodore* – other young officers would be following my example. (They were Lützow, Mölders and Galland.) Until then only officers from the First World War had occupied such a position. In addition I should give the personnel department the name of someone in whom I had confidence and would like to be *Kommandeur* of the *II. Gruppe*, and I should also ask by name for specialist officers for such things as Flak, Signals and so on. As signals officer I asked for Oberleutnant Teske. Göring laughed, said I couldn't have him, called him in and appointed him his personal adviser in all matters concerned with radar. As a second choice I asked for Leutnant Bode from the *Freya* station at Aalborg. The Blumensaat *Gruppe* had until that time been subordinate to the Flak Searchlight Regiment No. 1 – an absolute stupidity – so I asked Göring to put the searchlights under my command. He refused this with a laugh, but he recognised the strength of my argument and decided that the searchlight regiment and I should work in co-operation. He instructed me to inform Oberstleutnant Fichter to that effect. Just try to imagine what it was like in the conditions that prevailed at that time – I, a little captain, come into the office of the all-powerful and very self-important Regimental Commander to tell him, on behalf of the Field Marshal, that I am now a *Geschwaderkommodore*, the fighter *Gruppe* is now subordinate to me and that from now on the Regiment has to co-operate with me. It was a wonder that Oberstleutnant Fichter didn't have a heart attack!'

Wolfgang Falck handed over his own *Gruppe*, in its new I./NJG 1 identity, to his Aalborg comrade Werner Streib. He nominated Hauptmann von Bothmer to replace Blumensaat. Von Bothmer thus became *Kommandeur* of II./NJG 1 flying the Bf 109. Falck had himself gone to Düsseldorf as a *Gruppenkommandeur* with three *Staffeln*. Now he was a *Geschwaderkommodore*, a prestigious post usually occupied by an Oberst or Oberstleutnant. Never before had such a responsibility been entrusted to anyone with the lowly rank of Hauptmann. One has to allow for the fact that in general junior officers in the *Luftwaffe* tended to fill more responsible posts than did their counterparts in the RAF, but even so it was almost as if a Flight Lieutenant had been put in charge of an RAF Wing comprising several squadrons.

In selecting Falck for the new responsibility, Göring had behaved in a way that characterised his command of the *Luftwaffe* throughout the war. Göring was the master of the quick, fearless decision: 'Let there be a *Nachtjagd,* and there was a *Nachtjagd.*' Unhappily for the Third Reich, Göring was not God, and very many of his impulsive diktats had disastrous consequences. This time, however, his choice of Wolfgang Falck might well be described as inspired.

CHAPTER TWO

Feeling the Way

1940 – 1941

Now the threat to Britain was clear to all, particularly so to the new Prime Minister, Winston Churchill: 'What General Weygand called the Battle of France is over. I expect that the Battle of Britain is about to begin. The whole fury and might of the enemy must very soon be turned on us. Hitler knows that he will have to break us in this island or lose the war.'

There was no clear vision in the higher echelons of the RAF as to the way in which the force of heavy bombers, the only immediate means that Britain had of carrying the war to the Germans, might be used to try to alleviate the threat. On 19 June 1940 the Air Staff held a conference and decided that the best way to use Bomber Command would be to direct it against targets which would have 'the most immediate effect on reducing the scale of air attack' against Britain. A directive issued the following day required Air Marshal Portal, who had taken over as Commander-in-Chief of Bomber Command in April, to strike at targets associated with the German aircraft industry, including 'equipment depots'. Further targets specified were communications, principally railways and inland waterways, and attention was to be paid to the shaft lock and the aqueduct at Minden. 'Once the destruction of these targets has been achieved,' the directive continued, 'it should not be necessary to direct further attacks against the canal system at the present time.' There was no suggestion as to how the necessary bomb-aiming or navigational accuracy might be achieved. Oil plants and stocks in western Germany and in German-occupied territory were also to be attacked, and sea mining was to continue.

There were two more 'strategic' targets in the same directive that do not immediately strike one as having great relevance to reducing the scale of air attack on Britain – crops and coniferous forests. A low harvest was expected, said the directive, and hence it seemed probable that a very serious shortage of food might be felt in Europe that winter. Crops should therefore be attacked with incendiary pellets. Coniferous forests, of which there were extensive areas in Germany, were believed to be extremely vulnerable to incendiarism: some of them were in the vicinity of important military objectives and aerodromes, and a forest fire might have 'valuable results in dislocating German military and industrial activities, apart from the moral effect'.

Reading papers such as this after more than half a century it is hard to believe that they were written as Britain was facing invasion and shattering defeat, her army thoroughly, ignominiously, almost contemptuously thrust back across France. High-ranking officers responsible for directing the efforts of the nation's air force were solemnly directing their flyers to strike at targets that they should have known they could not hit and to scatter pellets and other incendiary devices

– the forests were to have been ignited by means of sandwiches of celluloid and phosphorus code-named 'Razzle' – to dislocate enemy industry and to affect the morale of the German population. At least it made a change from dropping propaganda leaflets.

Tentatively at first, and then with increasing might, the Germans began the aerial assault on Britain that was to be the preliminary to the invasion, *Seelöwe*. Bomber Command continued its night attacks against Germany and its sea-mining operations, and a more realistic target than crops and forests began to emerge. The Germans were concentrating barges in the Channel ports of Holland, Belgium and France to convey their invasion forces when the time was ripe, bringing them forward through the extensive inland waterway system in north Germany and the Low Countries. The first RAF attack was made in daylight on 3 July against barges at Rotterdam, and a series of similar raids was carried out intermittently by day and night, reaching a peak in September and effectively ceasing in October as the threat of invasion receded with the failure of the *Luftwaffe* to attain the air supremacy that was the prerequisite to the launching of Operation *Seelöwe*. But still the Bomber Command heavies went out night after night, ranging wide throughout Germany in the search for their allocated targets. At the same time, but mostly by day, the Command used its Blenheims to hit at tactical targets in France, Belgium, Holland and Germany, targets that included *Luftwaffe* airfields. Predictably the Blenheims of No. 2 Group suffered losses much higher than those experienced by the night bombers.

The Battle of Britain intensified and the Germans tacitly conceded defeat in September when they switched from attacks by day to bombing by night. The contribution made by Bomber Command to the Germans' abandonment of their plan to invade has never been fully assessed; to make such an assessment now would be an impossible undertaking. There is however one comparison that can be made without prejudice. While Fighter Command lost rather less than 600 pilots in the Battle of Britain, Bomber Command lost, at a conservative estimate, 1,000 aircrew members during the same period.

Still German night fighters did not pose a major threat to the Whitleys, Wellingtons and Hampdens that were invading the air space of the Third Reich on an increasing scale during the hours of darkness. Up to 100 bombers might set out for diverse targets on a typical night, and the night of 25/26 July saw 166 aim for targets in the Ruhr and airfields in Holland. Just a month later Berlin was the target for about half of a total force of 103 machines that operated that night, while others headed for Cologne, Bremen and Hamm.

The decision that Bomber Command should attack the capital city of Germany for the first time on 25/26 August was taken by the War Cabinet after London, Birmingham, Bristol and Liverpool had been hit by *Luftwaffe* bombers during the previous night. As a retaliation in kind the raid was a failure, with no significant damage being caused by the very few bombs that found the city or the very many that were scattered in the surrounding countryside. In London German bombs had fallen on Bethnal Green, East Ham, Stepney and Finsbury. It seemed that the Germans were extending their bombing to civilians, although in fact the crews had been briefed to bomb specific war-related targets, just as at the same time the RAF crews were being solemnly instructed to bomb 'legitimate' targets within the Fatherland. London, by virtue of distance and geography, was a much easier target for the *Luftwaffe* than Berlin was for the RAF, and it is not a matter of any surprise that the bombing concentration achieved by the *Kampfgeschwader* should have been greatly superior to that of Bomber Command. Yet the RAF seems honestly to have believed that its performance was better than that of the enemy. In considering a suggestion by Winston Churchill that the RAF might adopt a less selective bombing policy, the Vice-Chief of the Air Staff, Sir Richard Peirse, who opposed the idea, wrote: '. . . the reason for the effectiveness of our night bombing is that it is planned, and relentless until the particular target is knocked out or dislocated, whereas German night bombing is sporadic and mainly harassing.'

When Berlin was bombed Hauptmann Falck's NJG 1 was just three months old, but it had already had its first successes. During the night of 8/9 July Bomber Command had dispatched sixty-four bombers to ports in north Germany and airfields in Holland, as well as others to lay mines in sea areas. One Whitley had failed to return. It was probably the one claimed by Oberfeldwebel Förster off Heligoland. In the early hours of 20 July Oberleutnant Streib destroyed another RAF machine. The following night Streib made the second of the sixty-five kills he would achieve before the end of the war, shooting down a Whitley from No. 78 Squadron, Dishforth, which was piloted by Sergeant V. C. Monkhouse and which crashed in flames near Münster in Westphalia. There were further kills by NJG 1 during the remainder of the month, and they called the technique that they were by now using *helle Nachtjagd*, a system that had first been practised in inconclusive air exercises in 1936. A word of explanation is necessary. There have been various attempts to translate the term into English – 'bright night-fighting', 'illuminated night-fighting' and so on – but really it is better to understand what the term means and then stick to the German rather than use the literal translation. It simply means night-fighting with the aid of searchlights, and the Germans abbreviated it to *Henaja*.

When he arrived at Düsseldorf towards the end of June to devise a method of intercepting and destroying British bombers by night, Falck had a *Gruppe* of standard Bf 110 *Zerstörer*, I./NJG 1. A second *Gruppe* was immediately allocated to him, the Bf 109 formation IV./(N)JG 2, which thus became II./NJG 1. Each Bf 110C carried a pilot (*Flugzeugführer*) and a radio operator/air gunner (*Funker*). The Bf 110 was a heavy machine that lacked the manoeuvrability of its smaller, single-seated brother, the Bf 109, but it was a very stable gun platform. It seemed sensible to paint the Messerschmitts black for night-time combat, and that was done. A start was made with fitting dampers to eliminate the tell-tale emission of flames from the engine exhausts, even though such dampers caused a significant reduction in the speed of the machines. Night-flying practice was necessary for those pilots who were not already qualified.

Until it had been decided to make a serious attempt to create a specialised night-fighter force, all attempts at night fighting had been under the authority of Oberstleutnant Fichter, the officer commanding Searchlight Regiment No. 1. (*Flak-Scheinwerferregiment 1*). As explained earlier, this subordination was now removed and Falck's *Geschwader* given operational parity. Despite a certain degree of awkwardness at first, because Fichter outranked Falck by two grades, and despite the further complication caused by the fact that Falck was subordinate to *Luftflotte 2*, whereas searchlights came under the control of the Air

Districts, the *Luftgaue*, Falck did get co-operation, and the *helle Nachtjagd* was soon functioning.

Previously the freelance Bf 109s of IV.(N)/JG 2 had followed the searchlights; that is, they had patrolled in the vicinity of the defended areas in the hope of picking up a bomber in an individual beam or in a cone of lights. But the searchlights and the anti-aircraft guns were concentrated around locations expected to be likely targets for the RAF, principally towns and cities, which meant that to pursue a bomber in the searchlights was to risk coming under 'friendly' fire. There were no means in those days for a fighter to identify himself to the guns apart from firing a signal cartridge of a predetermined colour in the hope that the flak would hold off, a hope that was much more often than not in vain because the gunners had far more confidence in their own abilities than in those of the fighters, and once they had a target were very reluctant to cease shooting.

The RAF raids were widespread and Falck's resources were limited. It was clearly impossible for the moment to set up any sort of defensive barrier right across the broad front through which the RAF might be expected to arrive, stretching as it did from Schleswig-Holstein in the north to Normandy in the south. Looking at his battlefield Falck decided to install his first defences in a position from which they would give optimum coverage to Berlin in the east, the Ruhr industrial complex to the south and the coastal and shipping towns to the north. As his first tactical focal point he chose the city of Münster in the Westphalian plain, and he moved I./NJG 1 to Gütersloh, about forty kilometres to the east, although the *Geschwaderstab* remained at Düsseldorf. Ahead of Münster, to the north-west, Falck arranged for a belt of searchlights to be erected, searchlights which were withdrawn from the point defence of cities to form his so-called *helle Gürtel*, or illuminated belt.

Until the *Freya* early-warning radars could be integrated into the reporting system Falck had to rely on sound detectors to warn him of the approach of hostile bombers: the fighters were intentionally set back from Münster so that their engine noise would not be confused with that of their targets. When enemy attacks were expected the fighters, alerted by means of the code word *Fasan*, would take off and patrol behind the barrier of searchlights at an altitude slightly above that at which the RAF bombers were expected to come in, waiting for the sight of a bomber in the searchlight beams. Should he see one the night-fighter pilot would lose height and endeavour to manoeuvre into a position from which he could make his approach from astern and below (*von hinten unten*), pulling up to fire and then breaking away to one side, hoping to avoid the return fire from the bomber's rear turret. The *Flak* were strictly forbidden to fire within the searchlight belt. In general this was an unrewarding pastime, crews circling hours on end in the darkness in the vain hope of firing their cannon at a fat Wellington, a Whitley or a Hampden. In terms of kills, however, the Bf 110s did fare rather better than their single-seater fellows, the Bf 109s of II./NJG 1 under Hauptmann von Bothmer, which flew freelance over north Germany and Holland looking for trade, but without success. By the end of July 1940 I./NJG 1 had shot down six bombers by the *helle Nachtjagd* method, and returning RAF bomber crews were beginning to report increasingly frequent sightings of night-fighters.

Before July was out the seriousness with which the German leadership now regarded the bombing threat was underlined by the creation of a Night Fighter

Division. Chosen by Hermann Göring to lead the *Nachtjagddivision* was the forty-four-year-old Oberst Josef Kammhuber. Kammhuber had served in the infantry during the First World War and had remained in the depleted *Reichswehr* afterwards. In 1933 he had transferred to the *Luftwaffe* and trained as a fighter pilot. At the outbreak of war in 1939 he was serving as Chief of Staff to General Helmuth Felmy of *Luftflotte 2*, a post he was relieved of after one of his aircraft made an emergency landing at Mechelen-sur-Meuse in Belgium and the plans for the German offensive in the West, which an un-authorised passenger was carrying, were compromised to the Belgians. Hitler dismissed Felmy out of hand, but Kammhuber was granted a new appointment. After a short period as Chief of Staff of *Fliegerkorps V* he assumed command of KG 51, the *Edelweiss Geschwader*, surviving and being taken prisoner when his Ju 88 was shot down near Paris on 3 June but being freed just two weeks later when France capitulated. On 1 July Kammhuber became *Kommodore* of another bomber *Geschwader*, KG 1, but within three weeks he was transferred to command the newly formed *Nachtjagddivision*.

Kammhuber, although he lacked personal charisma, had a reputation as a brilliant organiser and a dynamic leader, and under his command the night-fighter force began to expand amoeba-like. A third *Gruppe* was added to the two that already existed, formed from a *Staffel* of Ju 88C-2 *Zerstörer* from KG 30, the *Adlergeschwader*. Other aircraft, Do 17s, were added to the *Gruppe*, which was confusingly named II./NJG 1, while von Bothmer's Bf 109 *Gruppe*, which already had that designation, became III./NJG 1. Hauptmann Graf Stillfried became *Kommandeur* of the new II./NJG 1.

It was becoming clear that there was no place in the new night-fighter organisation for the Bf 109, and gradually the pilots of III./NJG 1 converted to the Bf 110, only one *Staffel* of single-seaters remaining until October, when that was itself disbanded.

As soon as he took over the *NJ-Division*, Kammhuber set up his Divisional Headquarters in a magnificent castle at Zeist in Holland, just to the east of Utrecht, a forward position from which to direct the coming battle against the RAF. Kammhuber did not consider that defence was just a matter of waiting for the enemy to come and then trying to stop him: he believed in going out to meet him, in bearding the lion in its den, and he conceived an intruder role for the Ju 88s and Do 17Zs of II./NJG 1. They became the *Fernnachtjäger*, and Kammhuber used them to form the nucleus of his second *Geschwader*, designating them I./NJG 2 (the first *Gruppe* of *Nachtjagdgeschwader 2*) and moving them first to Schiphol, Amsterdam, and then to the airfield at Gilze-Rijen, between Breda and Tilburg, well situated as a base from which to mount offensive missions against England.

The Ju 88C-2s and the Do 17Zs of the *Fernnachtjagdgruppe* (*Fern-Nachtjagd*, usually written as one word, means long-range night fighting: the British used the term 'intruders operations') carried formidable forward-firing armament. As a *Zerstörer* the Ju 88C-2 was already fitted with three 7.9 mm machine-guns and one 20 mm cannon in an offset gondola beneath its nose. The Do 17Z-6 was a converted medium bomber, its original glazed nose exchanged for the nose of a Ju 88C-2 in which were mounted the same three machine-guns and one cannon as the Junkers machine carried. In another version, the Do 17Z-10, a completely new, purpose-built nose with the same weaponry was fitted, and that was the form in which it carried out the majority of its intruder raids against RAF bomber bases. All the Dornier long-range intruders were nicknamed *Kauz,* or 'screech owl'. *Kauz* also means a strange person, an oddball, but it is not known whether that meaning played any part in the choice of the name for the aeroplane.

It is always interesting to try to guess how code names originated and to come up with plausible answers. Strictly a code name, which by definition is intended to conceal the nature of the device to which it is applied, should be an entirely random word having no connection with that device. Frequently the temptation to be clever and choose a related word is too strong, and a potentially insecure code name emerges. A device known as *Spanner* was fitted to some of the night fighters. In German a *Spanner* can be several things, among them a trouser-press or a coat-hanger, but it can also mean a peeping Tom, which fits remarkably well with what the *Spanneranlage* (*Spanner-Anlage* means 'Spanner installation') was – an experimental device for seeing in the dark, a precursor of radar. *Spanner* was an infra-red night-vision piece of equipment. Modern infra-red detectors are usually passive devices; that is, they pick up heat transmitted from the target, for example from the engines of an aircraft. In the thirties, however, when it seemed that infra-red heat sensors might be an answer to the problem of detecting aircraft in the dark, the devices were infinitely less sensitive. *Spanner* Mark I was an active device; that is, it comprised an infra-red searchlight mounted in the nose of the aircraft to illuminate the target and a receiver to pick up the reflected energy. It was not very successful, the night-fighter pilots finding that if they got close enough to a bomber to see it on their *Spanner* they could usually see it with the naked eye.

The intruder *Gruppe* I./NJG 2 operated from Gilze-Rijen until October 1941. Although the standard establishment of a *Gruppe* was thirty aircraft, I./NJG 2's actual strength never exceeded twenty-one Ju 88s and Do 17s, and at times was much below that. In January 1941, for example, there were only seven aircraft on strength.

Hauptmann Karl Hülshoff took over as *Gruppenkommandeur* from Graf Stillfried, and from autumn 1940 onwards he was well served by the Radio Monitoring Service of *Luftflotte 3*, who were doing what British Admiralty intelligence officers had been doing in the First World War – listening in on the radio traffic between the enemy bombers and their ground control units, so that they were able to determine even before take-off how many bombers were on their way to the Continent and where they were setting out from. As soon as information began to reach him from the intercept service, the *Funkhorchdienst*, which might be an hour or more before the first bomber got airborne, Hülshoff would order off his first wave of fighters to head for the departure airfields in the hope of catching his prey over their bases. Soon afterwards a second wave would follow to try to intercept bombers on their way out over the North Sea. Finally he would try to mingle his fighters with the stream of bombers as they left for home, in the hope of being able to shoot them down as they approached their bases, landing lights on.

Although the intruder force was primarily intended to combat Bomber Command, its efforts were in fact spread much more widely, with frequent strikes against targets of opportunity. Any airfield from which night-flying was being conducted, which meant that it was illuminated, was fair game for attacks with 50 kg fragmentation bombs or strafing by cannon and machine-gun, while any aircraft intercepted in the air were attacked. Not only bombers but also, for example, training aircraft such as Oxfords and Tiger Moths caught in the air were ruthlessly dealt with, and many a fledgling pilot met his end in a ball of fire in the course of what had begun as a routine night-flying practice. I./NJG 2 made many claims for British aircraft destroyed: as very often happened with both German and British pilots, the claims outnumbered the true successes. Nevertheless the intruders were not without their effect, destroying as they did almost one hundred RAF aircraft between 24 October 1940, when their first kill was recorded, and their last success just under twelve months later, on 12 October 1941. They also caused damage to many more RAF machines, plus many casualties on the ground as well as among aircrew, and they in addition inflicted considerable material damage on buildings and airfield installations, not to speak of the wide disruption they caused to night-flying operations in England. Their successes were not earned cheaply. Twenty-six aircraft were lost over England or the North Sea, some to the formidable RAF Beaufighters that were operating in increasing numbers during 1941, and twice as many went down over Holland from various causes, both operational and non-operational.

In terms of the ratio of its successes and losses and of the nuisance and deterrent value of its operations over the British mainland, I./NJG 2 undeniably enjoyed a credit balance. With justification its flyers looked upon themselves as an élite force successfully carrying the war to the enemy. They found it hard to understand why, in October 1941, when Bomber Command's attacks against the Fatherland were continuing unabated, the unit was peremptorily detached from the air battle in the West and ordered to Sicily for operations in the Mediterranean theatre. Apparently Adolf Hitler himself had decided that the achievements of the *Fernnachtjagd* were not cost-effective, a surprising conclusion to reach when one considers the small size of the unit. There was no proof, the reasoning went, that the many aircraft that the crews said they had shot down over England had in fact been destroyed. In addition, the German population wanted solid evidence of bombers destroyed over their own country: stories of Wellingtons and Whitleys burning in the British countryside would affect the morale of the German man-in-the-street very little. What would give the necessary boost was bombers falling in flames from the sky over Berlin, Hamburg and Cologne. There would therefore be no more night-time intruder operations. Like Göring, Hitler was prone to arbitrary decisions, and one wonders whether the dissolution of Kammhuber's night-striking force was the correct one, as far as advantage to the Germans was concerned.

But that was in the future. While the intruder *Gruppe* was beginning to strike at the bombers on their home ground, Kammhuber was energetically pursuing his concept of a night-fighter defence, listening attentively to those, including Falck, who were at the sharp end, the pilots themselves. Clearly, *helle Nachtjagd* was not a satisfactory long-term solution. Once the RAF had realised that a barrier of searchlights had been set up in Westphalia, which they did very rapidly, they simply, and very understandably, flew around it. Kammhuber extended his belt of searchlights to north and south until they stretched from Schleswig-

Holstein southwards to Liège, a barrier of 486 lights thirty kilometres in depth extending a distance of about 900 kilometres. This was backed up with a shorter barrier to the west-north-west of Berlin between Gardelegen and Güstrow. In order to build up these barriers Kammhuber had to lobby energetically for an increased allocation of lights, and searchlight batteries had to be withdrawn from the defence of cities.

It would take the best part of a year before the job was completed, and in the meanwhile attention was focusing on a more effective means of directing the fighters towards the bombers, a combination of radar, an early-warning and control organisation on the ground and communications both within that organisation and between it and the fighters in the air, the searchlights and the flak batteries. To design, implement and test any form of air defence system while under an attack that might change its nature unexpectedly is neither an easy nor a quick task, and there were many experiments and failures on the way. Although it might with fairness be said that the Germans were ahead of the British in the technical aspects of radar, they lagged well behind in its practical application in the field of air defence. As early as 1935 a team of British scientists under Robert Watson-Watt had been working at Bawdsey, on the coast of Suffolk, on an air defence system based on radiolocation. The primitive radar that they used operated on the very long wavelength of about twelve metres, which meant that the aerials, in keeping with the 'half-wavelength rule', had to be six metres, or about twenty feet, in length. For best results a number of transmitter and receiver aerials, or dipoles, had to be used simultaneously, and they were mounted on very tall transmitter and receiver towers, necessary to see round the curvature of the earth, or, in the vernacular, over the radar horizon. The towers, constructed of steel girders, were between two and four hundred feet in height, and similar ones were eventually placed at several strategically located sites on the east and south coasts of Britain. The system was called 'CH', for 'Chain Home'.

Because the Germans were using the much shorter wavelength of 2.40 metres, which worked best with dipoles of about four feet in length as against the twenty feet required by CH, the German functional equivalent, *Freya*, could be equipped with a much smaller aerial array. With *Freya* this was a so-called 'bedstead' array, a rectangular construction about twenty feet square. In addition to permitting the equipment to be used in a mobile role, as against the permanent siting of CH, and because the radar had a narrower beam width, this meant that the *Freya* aerial could be rotated mechanically until it was pointing in the direction of its target, when the strongest signal reception would indicate its bearing. A precise assessment of maximum signal strength was, however, difficult to make, and a more sophisticated system was desirable. The measurement of distance was a simple enough matter, obtained, as explained above, by reading off the distance of the receiver 'blip' along the time-base on the cathode-ray tube. When it came to determining the bearing of a target, the Germans and the British developed rather different solutions. In brief, the British made an electronic comparison of the signal strength of echoes received from a target at two separate aerial arrays. Because the Germans were using a lighter, much more easily manipulated aerial, their solution was neater. It was called *AN-Peilung*. *Peilung* means direction-finding.

49

AN-Peilung was simply this: if, by means of an electronic switch, you transmit alternately from two sections of your aerial, one section looking left and the other looking right, in very rapid sequence – in the *Freya* the Germans did it seventy-five times per second – and arrange it that the receiver blips are alternately displayed on the left- and right-hand sides of a vertical time-base on the CRT in synchronism, you will apparently see a line cutting through the time-base instead of projecting from it to one side alone. As that part of your aerial looking more directly at the target will produce a stronger signal, and hence a longer blip, the impression your eye receives will be that of a line longer on one side of the time-base than on the other. If you turn your aerial in the horizontal plane so that the line is of the same length on both sides of the time-base, you know that you are looking directly at the target, and hence you can measure its bearing accurately. In conjunction with the range that you read along the time-base, you will be able to plot the position of the target. When *AN-Peilung* was introduced it brought a great increase in accuracy. The letters 'AN' refer to the signal on the time-base on the operator's radar screen. If the left-hand blip is short and the right-hand one long (·–), that is the equivalent of the Morse letter 'A', while the other way around (–·) equates to 'N'.

In one area, on the other hand, the British were greatly in advance of the Germans, and it is quite certain that without their superiority in that field Fighter Command would not have won the Battle of Britain. When the CH system was conceived it was as part of an integrated Air Defence System, with all readings from the radar stations, the Observer Corps, radio intercept stations and so on being fed, via a Group Filter Room where the plots from different radar stations were reconciled and 'tidied up', into a central Operations Room at Fighter Command Headquarters at Bentley Priory, to Sector Operations Rooms and, in the case of hostile flights, to Fighter Command Operations Room, where members of the Women's Auxiliary Air Force showed them on large, flat plotting tables, the General Situation Maps or GSMs. At these locations, then, there was an almost up-to-date representation of the air situation, and from the Fighter Command Operations Room fighters could be scrambled to meet incoming raids and then controlled towards the enemy either individually or in formations. When Kammhuber became the commander of the German night-fighter force he had no such organisation to help him in his allotted task, and so he had to design and develop one. *Helle Nachtjagd* was a first step, but quite obviously it could only be an interim solution: even at its best it was no more than a trawl net with a very wide mesh, and it did not greatly increase the number of British bombers shot down.

By means of their *Funkhorchdienst*, the Germans were able to listen in to the pre-flight and airborne R/T chatter of the RAF crews, so they could deduce when bombers were on their way; with *Freya* they could scramble their fighters and alert the searchlights and *Flak*. By moving many of the searchlights forward to create their *helle Gürtel*, they had to some extent deprived the *Flak* of their eyes, so to speak, in order that the night fighters might have a chance of catching a glimpse of the bombers before they reached their target.

Leutnant Hermann Diehl, the signals officer who in 1939 and 1940 had conducted the experiments against RAF raiders using the *Freya* on Wangerooge, had suggested that the *Freya* might be used as a close-control radar, that is, a radar by means of which a specific fighter might, using instructions sent from the ground station by radio, be directed against a specific bomber. His suggestion was that the radar, using the *AN* display described above, should be pointed at the bomber and the fighter alternately. From the screen it should then be possible to estimate the relative position of the two aircraft. By giving the pilot of the fighter headings to steer that would take him into the general vicinity of the target the controller, as he would later come to be called, could bring the two machines close enough together for them both to be illuminated by the radar beam simultaneously without the necessity for it to be moved to and fro, which meant that on the CRT the operator would see the blips for both aircraft at the same time. By directing the fighter pilot on to the heading that the bomber was flying he could tell him how far away from his target he was and, as the fighter was faster than the bomber, bring him in closer and closer, until visual contact was achieved.

The concept was good, the execution difficult. Diehl had tried it out by day, and in practice interceptions had brought fighters into the vicinity of targets. A great problem was that the *Freya* had no height-measuring capability, and in addition the controller needed a natural ability – as the subsequent experience of thousands of fighter controllers would show – to estimate relative position and movement in space. Falck had taken Diehl to Düsseldorf with him when he was charged with the first official experiments in night fighting, and he and Diehl explained the idea to Kammhuber in August 1940.

At first Kammhuber was not greatly enthused, but he was wise enough to authorise operational experiments, and he allowed Diehl to set up a *Freya* near the Dutch village of Nunspeet, between Utrecht and Zwolle in an area regularly crossed by incoming RAF bombers on their way to Germany. Live experiments began in early September 1940, and four weeks later, on 2 October, the first success was achieved when Diehl controlled Leutnant Ludwig Becker of 4./NJG 1 in a Do 17Z-10 into visual contact with a Wellington. Becker destroyed the twin-engined bomber: he had achieved the first radar-controlled 'kill' by night. He was destined to score a further forty-three before being killed himself in action in February 1943.

Encouraged by this first success in radar-controlled interception, Kammhuber proceeded to integrate the system into his air defence plan. A new term was added to the vocabulary of night-fighting – *dunkle Nachtjagd*, literally 'dark night-fighting', but better translated as 'radar-controlled night interception'. As with *helle Nachtjagd* (*Henaja*) it is simpler to use the German expression or its abbreviation, *Dunaja*.

Kammhuber began to set up an advanced defence barrier ahead of his belt of searchlights comprising a series of adjacent *Dunkelnachtjagdräume* (radar night-interception areas) along the Dutch and north German coastline, each equipped with a *Freya* from which a fighter controller using the AN system could direct a fighter against bombers. Yet another word was coined: a fighter-control officer was a *Jägerleitoffizier*, but this was abbreviated to *JLO*, and because 'J' and 'I' sound alike in German, this became a word in its own right, pronounced 'E-low'. Now, in addition to the night-fighters orbiting their beacons behind the searchlight belt, the RAF crews had to contend with fighters patrolling in front of the *helle Gürtel*, fighters that would appear unexpectedly. Whereas previously when they saw searchlights ahead or when they were suddenly caught in a beam they were alerted to the possible arrival of night-fighters, now a new menace faced them, the enemy unseen and unheralded.

This was, of course, a comparatively slow process. There was delay in the delivery of the radars: night-fighting was a new and untried craft, and there was reluctance on the part of the crews, many of whom were unwilling conscripts to the new force, to accept what seemed to be the black magic of radar; the initial phase was one of trial and error, of literally groping in the dark. There were problems integrating the old-fashioned, but still operative, sound detectors with the revolutionary new electronic device, radar. Techniques and concepts developed as experience grew, constantly being conditioned by the advent of new technology and the adaptation of existing equipment. In September 1940 a *Freya* radar was directly coupled to a searchlight by means of a so-called *Parasitanlage*, or 'parasite equipment'. The experiment was an immediate success, and the idea of radar-controlled searchlights was shown to be a practical proposition. Further lights were fitted with the *Parasitanlage*, and the first bomber illuminated in this way was shot down over Holland on 1 October 1940. Meanwhile a more accurate radar, the *Würzburg* (FuMG 62), was being introduced.

The *Würzburg* was a radar specifically designed for controlling anti-aircraft guns. Unlike the *Freya*, which used a rectangular 'bedstead' aerial, the *Würzburg* had a dish-shaped reflector with the aerial dipole itself at the centre; the reflector served the same purpose as that of a pocket torch, sending out a narrow beam of energy, and the same aerial was used, by means of a switching device, for both transmitting and receiving the signal pulses. The dish was about ten feet in diameter and, like the aerial of the *Freya*, could be turned in azimuth so as to point towards its target. It had a great advantage over the *Freya,* however, in that it could also be pivoted up and down to point directly at an aircraft, thus permitting the measurement of the target's altitude with some accuracy. Its wavelength was 5.3 metres and it had a range of twenty-five kilometres. In October 1940 the use of the *Würzburg* was being extended from guns to searchlights, and the danger to the bombers was increasing. Now that radar control of the searchlights was being introduced increasingly there was less chance of the lights' crews confusing fighter and bomber, and some fighters could be moved up to circle holding beacons, either visual or radio, within the searchlight belt itself so that they could be ordered forward into the *Dunkelnachtjagdräum* as soon as the forward listening posts reported the approach of bombers. From this advanced position they could either be vectored on to an unseen target by the *AN* system or could make visually for one illuminated by the radar-controlled searchlights. By the end of 1940 the *Nachtjagd* could claim the destruction of forty-two RAF bombers as against the thirty claimed by the *Flak*, a small number when compared to what was to come – in 1943 and early 1944 that figure would be a fairly representative one for a night's losses – but of ominous significance in comparison with what had gone before. These claims against night bombers represented less than a third of the total losses that Bomber Command suffered during the same period in diverse operations by day and night against widely scattered targets in Europe, so seen through British eyes the *Nachtjagd* had not even yet assumed the proportions of a major threat.

*   *   *

While the *Luftwaffe* was feeling its way towards a night-fighter force to combat the gradually increasing threat represented by the nocturnal raiders, the Whitleys, Wellingtons and Hampdens of the RAF, there were other happenings and factors that contributed to the remorseless escalation of the bombing war. Göring tacitly conceded defeat in the Battle of Britain and sent his bombers to attack London, first by day and then by night: his pilots were given specific war-related targets to attack, and there is little doubt that, in general terms and within the limitations of operational conditions, they tried to hit those targets.

But who decides what is a war-related target? From the German side it was argued that London itself came into that category, for it was from Whitehall and Westminster that the war effort was directed, and from the City that the commercial life of the country, essential to the conduct of the war, was conducted, while the London Docks were the arrival point of great quantities of war materiel. Inevitably civilian areas were hit and non-combatants killed in great numbers, and just as inevitably what was part of a military action to the men in the air was seen by those on the ground as the indiscriminate butchery of women and children. The hated enemy was at last showing himself in his true colours. Guernica, Warsaw, Rotterdam – now it was London's turn! Bombing of London and other British cities became a nightly event during the autumn and winter of 1940. On 7 September London suffered a devastating raid in which about 450 people were killed: it was to be the first of fifty-seven consecutive nights of air attack on the capital. Bomber Command machines ranged wide over Germany by night and also devoted their attentions to Italy. With the diminution of the invasion threat there was less call for attacks on the Channel ports, and so there were more bombers and bombs to spare for the German homeland. The nights were growing longer, so targets further afield could be contemplated. Total war was taking on a new meaning, and the self-delusory claims by both sides that their bombing was hitting only military targets were becoming progressively less tenable. During the night of 14/15 November 1940 the *Luftwaffe* attacked Coventry.

To the British public, Coventry represented a new level of German bestiality. To the Germans it was a brilliant success in the technique of night bombing, and they coined a new word, *koventrieren*, to 'coventrate' or to wipe out as the city of Coventry had been wiped out. Which version of the attack on Coventry is nearer the truth? One author, in a book on Bomber Command, refers to a very heavy attack that was 'quite obviously deliberately aimed at the civilian population'. This is a view so widely held, in Britain at least, that to challenge it is to incur the risk of provoking a reaction both vehement and indignant. Loss of life and damage to private property in Coventry were heavy, but were not a deliberate objective of the attack. That the Coventry raid was indeed well planned and executed was tacitly conceded by Bomber Command when, in an offensive which would relegate Coventry to one of the lesser happenings of World War Two, in magnitude if not in significance, they later adopted three of the techniques used by the Germans. Those three techniques were planned streaming, the use of radio navigation and bombing aids, and the employment of a pathfinding force.

An airfield-approach system known as *Lorenz* was in wide use in civil aviation. It operated on 30 MHz in the VHF band, and it required no special equipment in the aircraft other than a sensitive conventional radio receiver. Two directional beams side by side from one transmitter, one carrying the Morse letter 'E', a dot, and the other the letter 'T', a dash, overlapped with each other, and where they overlapped the Morse signals interlocked to produce a continuous note, an equisignal. Normally, when the system was used for airfield approach, that equisignal would be along the landing-approach path and needed to be audible over only a comparatively short range. If the pilot heard dots, he turned his aircraft to the right, if he heard dashes he turned it to the left, aiming to find and follow the equisignal.

In the Germans' navigational system, which they named *Knickebein* and which required a very much longer range, the overlapping dots and dashes were aimed at the bomber's target from a very powerful transmitter feeding a vast aerial array that had the effect of concentrating the equisignal into a very narrow beam, so that all the pilot had to do was to fly along it in the sure knowledge that he would pass over the target area. The equisignal of a second *Lorenz* beam was sent out from another similar, suitably situated transmitter so that it crossed the first one just ahead of the target. When the pilot reached the crossing point of the two aural beams he released the bombs. *Knickebein* was, however, discovered by British Scientific Intelligence fairly early in the war, and it proved easy to jam it and so to mislead the bombers. This was not a catastrophe for the *Luftwaffe*, because they already had a more sophisticated equipment, the *X-Gerät*, or 'X Equipment', which operated on a similar principle but on a higher frequency and which required a special receiver. More accurate than *Knickebein*, the *X-Gerät* used four beams, one along which the bomber approached the target and three that intersected with the first beam at separate points on the run-in to the target. The first crossing beam was simply a warning to the pilot to ensure that he was flying accurately along the equisignal approach to the target. When the observer heard the steady note of the second crossing beam he knew he was twenty kilometres from the estimated release point, and he pressed the button on the timing device of an automatic bomb-release mechanism, which began to compute the precise moment of release. At the third and final equisignal the observer again pressed the button, and the device dropped the bombs automatically in accordance with its computations.

The *X-Gerät* was more difficult to use than *Knickebein*, and it required special training. The attack on Coventry was accordingly led by a specialist unit with such training, *Kampfgeschwader 100*, which used a beam sent out from a transmitter near Cherbourg for its approach to the target and three beams from transmitters near Calais to provide the crossing equisignals. The He 111s of KG 100, flying from Vannes, which was between St Nazaire and Lorient so that a course for the Midlands would take them almost overhead the transmitter near Cherbourg, carried full loads of incendiaries and began marking the targets in Coventry with considerable accuracy at just after ten o'clock in the evening. KG 100 having performed their pathfinding function, other bomber *Geschwader*, the equivalent of what would later be called the Main Force by the RAF, aimed their bombs at their allocated targets: the Standard Motor Company works, the Coventry Radiator and Press Company factory, the Alvis aircraft engine works, the Daimler works and so on. It was a most successful raid by contemporary standards, with considerable damage being done to factories and production being much affected. But just as the Germans on the receiving end of RAF raids were experiencing, bombs cannot differentiate between what is moral and what is immoral, and 400 civilians met their death. The significance of the *Luftwaffe* raid on Coventry is not only that it was another clear step along the road to no-punches-pulled bombing, but also that it set a pattern, in terms of pathfinding at least, that the RAF would subsequently emulate to an extent that was, from the German viewpoint, disproportionately catastrophic.

There were other heavy German raids on British cities during the autumn of 1940: in addition to London, which remained the prime target of the *Luftwaffe*, Birmingham, Southampton, Bristol, Merseyside, Sheffield and other targets were attacked. Southampton in particular suffered severely in two night raids at the beginning of December, and on 13 December 1940 the War Cabinet authorised a raid on a German city in which specific targets were not allocated to crews but the centre of the city was the chosen aiming point. On the night of 16/17 December Bomber Command attacked Mannheim, using a similar pathfinding technique to that employed by KG 100 in their raid on Coventry the previous month, sending in a first wave of eight Wellingtons flown by experienced crews and carrying only incendiary bombs. The aim was 'to concentrate the maximum amount of damage in the centre of the town', according to a memo from the Commander-in-Chief, Sir Richard Peirse, to the Groups participating.

Bomber Command did not have the equivalent of the *X-Gerät* to guide the markers and the follow-up crews to their objective, but a look at the map might suggest that Mannheim should not have been a difficult target to find in the conditions of moonlight that prevailed on the night of the attack. The city lies on the east bank of the broad River Rhine, which runs almost due south-north, separating Mannheim from Ludwigshafen on the west bank. To the south of the twin cities the Rhine develops a series of very characteristic curves that should facilitate map reading. Coventry, by comparison, has no such clear identifying feature. Yet whereas the *Luftwaffe* raid on Coventry was a notable success, that by the RAF on Mannheim was a failure. One hundred and thirty-four bombers took part, less than a third of the number of German machines that bombed Coventry, but the eight Wellingtons that attempted to ignite fires to mark the target area achieved no concentration in their bombing, so that the following 126 crews scattered their bombs over a very wide area in and around both Mannheim and Ludwigshafen, the greater part of them falling in residential areas and killing thirty-four people, nearly all civilians. There was no significant damage to industrial property. Yet returning crews overwhelmingly reported that the attack in general, including their individual efforts, had been highly concentrated, and it was not realised that their claims were unsound until a Spitfire of the Photographic Reconnaissance Unit photographed the city of Mannheim the following week and the resultant pictures showed that damage was very widely dispersed. But just as raids such as that on Coventry were adding to the reputation for brutality of the *Luftwaffe*, that on Mannheim contributed to the growing view of Bomber Command crews as *Terrorflieger*.

The end of 1940, then, saw a force of RAF bombers still groping towards some sort of efficiency, but failing. It saw a young enemy night-fighter force rapidly growing and achieving its first tastes of success. It was beginning to dawn on the high command of the RAF that to ask the crews of Bomber Command to hit precision targets was to ask the impossible and, possibly reluctantly, possibly with unspoken relief, it was gradually coming to be accepted that with the forces and navigational facilities at Bomber Command's disposal the optimal way of using the bomber force lay in area bombing. Since May Bomber Command had flown over 17,000 sorties by night – not all of which were, of course, against Germany – and had lost about 340 aircraft, a loss rate of almost exactly two per cent from all causes. Of those lost, less than fifty had fallen to the *Nachtjagd*. That meant that for the aircrew the chances of being shot down or going missing as a result of other causes, including for example weather, faulty navigation or fuel shortage, or from a combination of such factors, on any one raid averaged out at two in a hundred, and of being shot down by a night-fighter only three in a thousand. Both sets of odds would shorten dramatically in the course of the next three years.

Above left: Bf 110 night fighter with SN-2 aerials. The large aerial array was dubbed *Hirschgeweih*, or "Stag's Antlers", by the crews. *(Buschmann)*

Above right: A Dornier Do 217 night fighter. *(Szardenings)*

Below: The date of this photograph is not known, but the belly-landed Bf 110 is apparently one of the earlier conversions to night fighting. The all-black paintwork and lack of the night fighter's coat-of-arms suggest that it is one of Falck's original machines, as does the *Spanner* equipment mounted forward of the cockpit. The letters show that it belongs to II./NJG 1. *(Henning)*

Above left: 1941: *Hauptmann* Greiner and his *Funker*. Greiner, awarded the Oak Leaves to the Knight's Cross of the Iron Cross, shot down fifty bombers. *(Greiner)*

Above right: Hajo Herrmann introduces *Reichsmarschall* Hermann Göring to his Wild Boar pilots. Westphalia, Autumn 1943. *(Herrmann)*

Below: Leeuwarden 1942. Left to right: *Oberleutnant* Prinz zur Lippe-Weißenfeld, Unknown, *Hauptmann* Lent, *Oberleutnant* Ludwig Becker. *(Greiner)*

CHAPTER THREE

Moving Forward

1941

Operationally 1941 was not a good year for Bomber Command, but it was a year of gradual expansion and re-equipment, a year of endeavour and experience, and the year in which, at last, lessons were learned and solid foundations for the implementation of the theory of strategic bombing established. In Germany, 1941 saw the *Nachtjagd* grow from its tentative beginnings into a major threat to the RAF bombing offensive.

The Commander-in-Chief of Bomber Command during 1941 and very early 1942 was Air Chief Marshal Sir Richard Peirse, the third officer to have held the post since the outbreak of war. Air Chief Marshal Sir Edgar Ludlow-Hewitt had been replaced in April 1940 by Air Marshal Sir Charles Portal, who led the Command for only seven months before handing over to Peirse on his appointment to Chief of the Air Staff in October 1940. Peirse inherited from Ludlow-Hewitt and Portal a force ill-equipped in terms of aeroplanes, weapons and navigational aids: when he handed it over to his own successor in January 1942 it was a force well placed to develop its potential. By then Bomber Command would have passed through an awkward, difficult adolescence and would be on the threshold of adulthood. But even so it would still be a long haul before maturity was attained.

On 15 January 1941 the Vice-Chief of Air Staff sent a new directive to Sir Richard Peirse in which he optimistically stated, 'On the assumption that our present scale of air attack on the enemy's oil plants is maintained, their oil position may be causing them grave anxiety by the spring of 1941.' The sole primary aim of Bomber Command, he went on, should now be the destruction of Germany's synthetic oil plants. Weather and visibility might sometimes make this impracticable, in which case the offensive 'should be directed towards harassing the enemy's main industrial towns and communications and may include periodically heavy concentrations against the former to maintain fear of attack'. It would be advantageous if cities connected with the oil industry were included in those selected. Without stating it explicitly the directive authorised an extension of the policy of area bombing.

It fell to the city of Hanover to be the first to be 'harassed' in accordance with this directive: 222 Wellingtons, Hampdens, Blenheims and Whitleys went there on the night of 10/11 February. Four bombers were lost over Germany, while Kammhuber's intruders, I./NJG 2, shot down three more over England as they were returning from the operation, one Wellington, one Hampden and one Blenheim. During the same night forty-three bombers attacked oil-storage tanks at Rotterdam in a fairly routine raid that had the distinction of being the first operation in which a four-engined RAF bomber, a Short Stirling, participated.

The specification on which the Stirling was based had been issued in 1936, and it was, in appearance at least, an impressive aircraft. Powered by four Bristol Hercules XI fourteen-cylinder sleeve-valve radial engines, it was 87ft 3in in length, with a wing span of 99 ft 1 in, and on the ground it stood 22ft 9in in height. For its length, its wing span was disproportionately short, being limited by the size of the hangars available when the aircraft was designed. On the ground it had a very distinctive nose-up appearance, supported as it was by a large and very solidly built undercarriage: indeed, so unusual was this item that the aircraft rapidly earned for itself the reputation of being an 'ingenious device for getting an undercarriage airborne'.

In terms of range and bomb-load carried, the Stirling was an improvement on the most efficient bomber hitherto, the Wellington, being able to carry a maximum load of bombs of 14,000 lb. As ever, the further the range the greater the necessary load of fuel, so that for a target eight hundred miles away from its base, and with an allowance for emergencies, a typical bomb-load would be 5,000 lb. The Wellington II, in comparison, had a maximum load of 4,500 lb, but it could carry only 1,500 lb to a similar target. The Stirling was only slightly faster than the Wellington. It carried eight ·303 Browning machine-guns in three turrets, one each in the nose and the tail and one atop the fuselage, the tail turret having four guns and the others two each.

As a bombing aircraft the Stirling suffered from two major disadvantages. Firstly, its inadequate wing area, a function of the restricted wing span meant that it was very slow climbing to its limited maximum altitude of 15,000 feet, and once it was there it was very sluggish on the controls. Secondly, although its maximum bomb-load of almost seven tons was very impressive, the dimensions and construction of its bomb bays limited the size of the largest bomb that it could carry to 2,000 lb at a time when bombs twice that weight were entering service.

Just a fortnight after the Stirling made its début there was another newcomer to the ranks of Bomber Command, the Avro Manchester, and only another two weeks later came the third new bomber, the Handley Page Halifax. Although the Manchester had only two engines, its performance did not fall far short of that of the Stirling, and it could climb higher and faster. It was not, however, a successful machine, suffering from frequent failure in its Rolls-Royce Vulture engines. After a total of 209 had been produced and eight squadrons of No. 5 Group converted on to the type from Hampdens it was withdrawn from service; not, however, before it had been turned into a four-engined bomber with Rolls-Royce Merlin engines, in which form it became the Lancaster, by any standards the best four-engined night bomber, and possibly the best bomber overall, of World War Two.

The third of the new aircraft, the Halifax, was the best of the newcomers, but even so it fell well short of the Lancaster when the latter eventually came on the scene. Powered by four Merlins, it first came into service with No. 35 Squadron at RAF Boscombe Down on 13 November 1940, and the squadron sent six to attack Le Havre on the night of 10/11 March 1941 together with eight Blenheims. It had a service ceiling of 18,000 feet at its top all-up weight, and it could climb to 15,000 feet in twenty-three minutes. Its maximum bomb-load was 13,000 lb, and with 8,500 lb of bombs it had a range – a there-and-back distance, that is – of 1,660 miles.

Although these new aircraft represented, for the Germans, an ominous augury for the future, their introduction into Bomber Command was of necessity slow. Production lines had to be set up, squadrons re-equipped, fresh crews trained and old ones retrained, airfields modified to accept the larger, heavier machines, and so on. Above all it was necessary to prove the new bombers in operational conditions. An indication of the very gradual nature of the transition to a force equipped with more modern aircraft can be gained by comparing two Bomber Command efforts of approximately the same numerical strength, one at the beginning of the year and one at the end. On 9/10 January 1941 the force that raided oil targets in Gelsenkirchen in the Ruhr comprised sixty Wellingtons, thirty-six Blenheims, twenty Hampdens and nineteen Whitleys, a total of 135 aircraft. On 27/28 December 1941, 132 bombers went to Düsseldorf, of which sixty-six were Wellingtons, thirty Hampdens, twenty-nine Whitleys and seven Manchesters. In the course of the year Blenheims, which could hardly be categorised as anything other than light bombers, had been withdrawn from main-line night operations against Germany. Apart from that and the inclusion of a small number of twin-engined Manchesters, the force was still mainly composed of Wellingtons, Whitleys and Hampdens. Blenheims were still flying operationally, but in an intruder role, mostly against *Luftwaffe* airfields. They would soon be replaced in that function by Beaufighters, and later by Mosquitos.

Tentative and slow though the introduction of the new-generation machines was, their impact was beginning to be felt. In the first few months of their operational being they were confined mainly to coastal targets, particularly, for example, to Brest, where German capital ships, among them the *Scharnhorst* and *Gneisenau*, were docked. Gradually they began to turn their attentions to the Fatherland, Berlin included, until in August thirty of them, nine Stirlings, nine Manchesters and twelve Halifaxes, were part of a seventy-aircraft force – the remaining forty were Wellingtons – that bombed the capital city of the Third Reich. Bombing success remained elusive: so far the navigators were still forced to rely on the methods and equipment that the Command had gone to war with. A war-related aiming point was given to the bomb aimers, the *Reichsluftfahrtministerium* headquarters in the centre of the city, but the bombs of the thirty-two aircraft that reached Berlin were widely scattered. It was a costly raid, too, nine bombers failing to return, a loss rate of almost thirteen per cent. During the same night a force of sixty-five Wellingtons and Hampdens visited Hanover. Four Wellingtons were lost, one of which was carrying out operational tests of a revolutionary radio device that was destined to represent a breakthrough in the craft of air navigation. It was called 'Gee'.

Gee was not a pure radar device: radar depends on radio energy being transmitted and an echo received, so that a range or position can be measured. Gee depended on a number of signals from separate ground stations being received in the aircraft and the time intervals between their reception being measured. Just as with the radar equipment we have already considered – CH, *Freya* and *Würzburg* – the device that made Gee possible was the cathode-ray tube. Gee was developed in 1940 by the Telecommunications Research Establishment (TRE), although the idea had in fact been conceived before the war. The mathematical principle on which Gee operated was that of the hyperbola.

A hyperbola is a line of constant distance-difference, and basically the Gee receiver in an aircraft could measure the difference between the distance the air-craft was from each of pairs of transmitters on the ground. The readings obtained could be plotted on a special chart that was overprinted with coloured hyperbo-las, each applying to one pair of stations. In ideal conditions a good operator could fix his position very rapidly, within a fraction of a minute. There were, of course, snags. Firstly, the range of the device was limited by the radar horizon so that if one were 240 miles from the transmitters, for example, one could not receive signals below an altitude of about 20,000 feet. Secondly, the further one was from those transmitters, the further apart were the hyperbolas and the more oblique the angle at which they crossed, so that it was increasingly difficult to obtain an accurate fix. Finally, Gee was very susceptible to enemy jamming.

Also in its experimental stages during 1941 was 'Oboe', which was not des-tined to come into general operational use until well after Gee. We might, however, have a preview of the device here, because it sprang to a large extent from the German *Knickebein* and *X-Gerät* already discussed in the account of the attack on Coventry.

Air Ministry Intelligence had become aware of the existence of *Knickebein* during the first months of the war, and a special unit to counter it had been formed in June 1940: it was called No. 80 Wing and was commanded by Wing Commander E. B. Addison. Addison it was who coined the term 'radio counter-measures', which was to become very widely used in its abbreviated form, RCM.

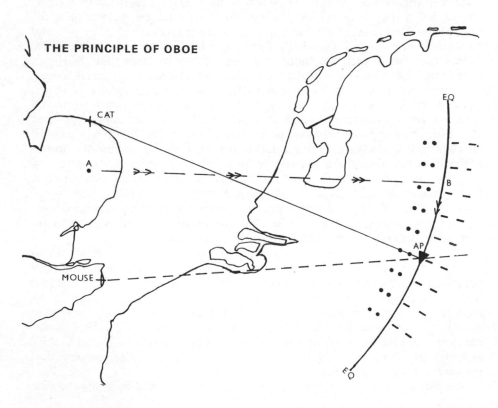

THE PRINCIPLE OF OBOE

No. 80 Wing worked very closely with the newly-formed Telecommunications Research Establishment, which developed Gee in 1940. Part of No. 80 Wing was the Wireless Investigation and Development Unit at RAF Boscombe Down, which in December 1940 became No. 109 Squadron. Equipped with Ansons and Wellingtons, it was charged with developing blind-bombing devices similar to those employed by the Germans. One of the operations that 109 Squadron carried out involved its Wellingtons flying along the German *X-Gerät* beam emanating from the Cherbourg peninsula and dropping bombs when they reached the cone of silence above the transmitter, which, however, they failed to hit. On the research and development side, fortunately, TRE and No. 109 Squadron had much greater success.

Oboe differed from *Knickebein* and *X-Gerät* in that it used radar, which was, of course, a much more accurate method of measurement than radio. Secondly, Oboe did not provide a bearing line along which the bomber had to fly to reach its target, but instead measured the aircraft's range from a ground station. One ground station, codenamed 'CAT', transmitted a rapid series of pulses: when each pulse reached the aircraft's receiver it triggered a device known as a 'transponder', which in its turn sent out a pulse which was, of course, much stronger than a simple radar echo would have been. Before take-off the precise distance of the aiming point from the ground station had been calculated, and the bomber approached the target along a curved line that was in fact the arc of

The *Oboe* aircraft, usually a Mosquito, was controlled by two ground stations, typically CAT, situated at Trimingham in Norfolk, and MOUSE, at Walmer in Kent. The aircraft set out from its base (A) and flew a course to enable it to intersect with a line (EQ) that was an arc of a circle with its centre at CAT and its radius the distance from CAT to its aiming point (AP), which was precisley calculated to take into account the aircraft's altitude and speed and the wind velocity. High-frequency signals from CAT activated a transponder in the aircraft, which sent back signals by means of which the ground operator could position the aircraft to within a matter of yards. To the west of EQ the crewmen in the aircraft heard a series of Morse dots, to the east a series of dashes. These signals interlocked on line EQ to form an equisignal. On reaching EQ at point B the pilot executed a starboard turn on to a heading to enable him to follow EQ southward. If dashes came through more strongly in his earphones, he would turn slightly to starboard, if dots predominated he would turn to port. In this way he followed EQ towards the aiming point. Meanwhile his progress was also being monitored by the operators in MOUSE, who transmitted specific Morse signals as the aircraft approached the aiming point to let the navigator know how far he had to go, culminating in a series of dots followed by a dash. When this dash ended the navigator released the bombs.

The Germans called *Oboe* «*das Bumerangverfahren*», the «Boomerang System», after the curved course on which the Mosquito approached its target. Flying at up to 30,000 feet and at high speed, the Mosquitos were virtually invulnerable to German fighter attack.

a circle with that distance as its radius and the CAT station as its centre. In effect the CAT station controlled the bomber along this curve, indicating to the pilot by a series of dots and dashes whether he needed to alter course to port or to starboard to stay on the precise, pre-calculated line: just as with the *Lorenz* blind-flying system on which the Germans had based their *Knickebein* bombing procedure, the pilot heard dots if his aircraft was displaced to one side, dashes if it was on the other side, and an equisignal when he was precisely on the curve. A second station, MOUSE, which was located about a hundred miles south of CAT in order to provide a good 'cut', measured the bearing of the release point and signalled to the aircraft the exact moment at which to drop its bombs. This it did by transmitting a letter 'B' in Morse eight minutes before the bomber reached the target, a 'C' five minutes from the target and a 'D' three minutes away. These were heard by the navigator in the Oboe-equipped aircraft, whose task it was to release the bombs or, more usually, the markers. Just before the moment at which the missiles were to be dropped the navigator heard five dots in succession followed by a dash lasting two-and-a-half seconds, at the end of which he pressed the bomb release.

As ever, there were disadvantages to the system. The first was one of range, which was again determined by the curvature of the earth and the altitude at which the aircraft was flying. One of Bomber Command's main target areas, however, the Ruhr industrial complex, was ultimately within manageable reach, and as visual bombing there was almost an impossibility by reason of the heavy industrial haze that was always present, Oboe represented a major means of overcoming that limitation. Secondly, one pair of ground stations could only control one aircraft at a time, in contrast to the universal availability of Gee. And similarly to Gee, Oboe, and particularly the earlier versions, could be jammed by the enemy.

Although conceived during 1941, Oboe took a considerable time before it became operationally available, early sets proving very unreliable in use. Experimental attacks on the *Scharnhorst* and *Gneisenau* in dock at Brest were carried out in December 1941, and the results, although far from satisfactory in themselves, were good enough to indicate that the system had potential justifying serious development work. It would be another year, however, before the system could be brought into general operational use, by which time the problem of achieving adequate range had been solved by the introduction of the high-flying Mosquito bomber. Because of the necessary one-to-one ratio between control stations and aircraft, Oboe would be used primarily as an aid to blind-marking of targets, but that lay in the future. Nevertheless, 1941 had seen, in the early work on Gee and Oboe, the beginnings of a solution to the closely related problems of navigation and bomb aiming that were still besetting Bomber Command.

While Bomber Command was moving slowly but surely along the road to greater efficiency, the *Luftwaffe* was devoting urgent attention to the extension and improvement of its *Nachtjagd* to combat the persistent visits by the RAF, visits that took place almost every night and which, although causing more inconvenience than significant damage to either the German war machine or German morale, were clearly not going to diminish. The appearance on the scene of the four-engined bombers, the *Viermots* as the Germans dubbed them, and the increasing tendency for the bombers to indulge in the bombing of city centres rather than to aim, no matter how inaccurately, at military targets, were portents that could not be ignored. Further, Bomber Command was by now obviously committed to night attack on an increasing scale, and even the requirement for front-line military aircraft in the east that resulted from the German invasion of the Soviet Union on 22 June 1941 did not greatly affect the priority that was by now being given to the production of night-fighters and the extension of the defensive system.

During 1941 new night-fighter units were set up, largely from Bf 110 *Zerstörer* formations. The original reluctance of aircrew to venture into the unknown and seemingly unrewarding field of night-fighting was gradually being overcome as successes mounted and new heroes of the *Luftwaffe* began to emerge, men such as Werner Streib, Ludwig Becker and Günter Radusch, new idols to the public and, to their brother pilots in the *Luftwaffe*, colleagues worthy of emulation.

In January 1941 the establishment of the *Nachtjagd* was sixteen *Staffeln* in three *Geschwader*, NJG 1, NJG 2 and NJG 3, including the *Fernnachtjagd*, I./NJG 2. This should strictly have meant a total of something like 144 aircraft, but both in terms of machines and crews units were seldom up to establishment. On average, for example, each *Staffel* had at that period less than four operational pilots. Things would improve during the course of the year, and meanwhile an intensive programme of construction and improvement of airfields suitable for night fighters was undertaken.

What was eventually the largest and most important *Luftwaffe* night fighter base was Venlo, situated astride the Dutch/German border about thirty-five kilometres to the west of the Ruhr and in the triangle formed by the German villages of Kaldenkirchen and Herongen and the small Dutch town of Venlo, and so ideally located for the defence of the concentration of industry centred on Essen – 'Happy Valley', as it came to be known to the crews of Bomber Command. The construction of the airfield at Venlo is worth describing in some detail to give an idea of the priority that, after years of disregard, was now suddenly being given to the *Nachtjagd*.

The area in which the airfield was built was flat, sparsely populated heath, a region frequented by nature-lovers and walkers. Within it there were two small flying fields, one on each side of the border, but they had neither permanent buildings nor facilities; it would be more correct to describe them as occasional landing grounds. In about August 1940, shortly after Kammhuber's appointment as commander of the *Nachtjagddivision*, surveying work was begun on the site, and on 1 October the construction work itself was started by a vast labour force: some reports say that 15,000 workers from Germany and Holland were employed on the project. Despite Dutch hatred of the invader, the Germans had no difficulty in recruiting Dutchmen to work on the site: there was a high level of unemployment in the area, and the money to be earned in round-the-clock shift work was good. Logistical problems were enormous, and their solution brought with it an atmosphere akin to that of the Klondike in the days of exploration for gold: there were neither good roads nor railway lines that could be used to bring the vast quantities of materials needed into the eleven square-kilometre area that the airfield would eventually occupy, nor were there any mains services.

Materials were conveyed by rail to the stations at Venlo and Kaldenkirchen, which changed almost overnight from sleepy wayside halts to frantically busy goods yards, and the materials were then transported to where they were needed on big lorries along hastily-constructed roads. The thousands of workers were brought in daily for their shifts by bus, largely from local premises – schools, monasteries and private villas – commandeered as hostels.

Three concrete runways were constructed in the west of the area, on Dutch territory, two of them 1,450 metres and the other 1,200 metres in length. Full night-flying facilities, including more than 2,000 airfield lights, were installed. Domestic and administration buildings were mostly built in wooded areas and widely dispersed as protection against attack from the air. Considerable attention was paid to making the airfield blend into the surrounding countryside, one of the measures taken being the camouflage-painting of the runways. There were heated hangars in which maintenance work on the aeroplanes could be carried out, and a sophisticated airfield control tower would come later. The network of roads within the area of the base measured in all approximately forty-eight kilometres.

By March 1941, only six months after the start of construction work, the airfield, although not completed to the last detail, was ready for occupation, and on the nineteenth of the month the Bf 110s of the first night-fighter *Gruppe* moved in, I./NJG 1, one of the most successful of the many *Nachtjagdgruppen* that fought against Bomber Command between 1940 and 1945.

While Venlo was being constructed other airfields in Holland, Belgium and north-west Germany were being enlarged and modified to accommodate the growing number of night-fighter units. Work also continued on extending the control system that was necessary to enable the night-fighters to function. By the end of 1941 there were six contiguous close-control zones (*Dunkel-nachtjagdgebiete*) along the Dutch and north German coastline, each with at least two *Freya* radars looking west, stretching from the Schelde estuary in the south to the island of Sylt in the north. They had as their identifying code words the names of animals or fish – *Hamster*, *Hering*, *Tiger*, *Löwe* (Lion), *Languste* (Lobster) and *Wolf*. These were the zones (*Gebiete*) in which the aim was to intercept incoming bombers by means of *AN* radar control. Parallel to and on average about 140 kilometres behind this line of early-warning radars was the searchlight belt, made up of *helle Nachtjagdräume*. (There is a small problem of linguistics here: both *Gebiet* and *Raum* can be translated as 'area', but a *Gebiet* tends to be larger than a *Raum*. For our purposes then, we might call a *Gebiet* a 'zone' and a *Raum* an 'area'.) Additionally, there were separate night-fighter zones around some of the larger cities – Hamburg, Bremen, the *Ruhrgebiet*, Cologne, Frankfurt am Main and Berlin. These latter zones were known as 'combined night-fighter zones' (*Kombinierte Nachtjagdgebiete*), and in them, in principle, radar, searchlights, flak and *Nachtjagd* worked in co-ordination. In practice *kombinierte Nachtjagd*, abbreviated *Konaja*, did not function very effectively: it proved impossible to design and put into operation a system that would ensure that the *Flak* did not fire on fighters attempting to press home their attack on bombers or would restrict the flak's fire to an agreed height, so that it was in effect almost as dangerous for a Messerschmitt to venture over one of these defended areas as it was for a Wellington or a Halifax.

The formidable searchlight belt that the RAF bombers had now to penetrate stretched from Schleswig-Holstein, east of the island of Sylt, in the north to the area east of Brussels in the south. It comprised six so-called *Scheinwerfer-Grossräume* (larger searchlight areas), each of which was made up of three smaller *Räume* measuring about thirty kilometres from north to south and twenty kilometres deep. The combined result was a formidable barrier: each *Grossräum* was occupied by three *Scheinwerfer-Abteilungen*, or searchlight sections, one in each *Raum*. In each of these smaller areas the establishment of the searchlight section was nine 150 mm lights, the centre one of which was the master searchlight, the one that would first pick up its target and on to which the others would focus to form a 'cone'. Each light was controlled by a *Würzburg C* radar.

During the period under consideration an improved version of the *Würzburg* was coming into use, the *Würzburg-Riese*, or Würzburg Giant, which, as its name implies, was larger than the original equipment. For practical purposes the range of the *Riese* was up to sixty kilometres, as compared with the twenty-five kilometre range of its predecessor, and it could be rotated through 360° and had a built-in height-finding capability. Würzburg Giants were being placed ahead of the *helle Gürtel* to provide radar-controlled interception zones in addition to those covered by *Freya* radars on the coast. At the same time 200 mm lights, also controlled by *Würzburg-Riesen*, were being located ahead and behind the original *helle Gürtel* to provide it with more depth.

A new form of intercept control technique was developing. When controlling either anti-aircraft guns or searchlights each *Würzburg* or Würzburg Giant made use of a plotting table (*Auswertetisch*), a simple map of the area covered by the radar on which the position of targets could be plotted from data passed through by the radar operators. This plotting system was extended to the close control of fighters, with the position of both bomber and fighter being told through to the same table from two separate radars, the *rote Riese* (Red Giant) and the *blaue Riese* (Blue Giant) respectively. At first the positions were plotted by hand in appropriately coloured chinagraph pencils, but an ingenious improvement was designed in which, by means of mechanical linkages, the positions of fighter and bomber could be shown on a ground-glass surface by green and red points of light projected from below. This improved version of the plotting table was named the *Seeburg-Tisch*, and on it the controller had a continuing picture of the relative position of the night-fighter he was controlling and the bomber he was trying to destroy. The fighter pilot still had to hope to pick up his target with his naked eyes. This was the first stage of what later came to be known as the *Himmelbettverfahren*, or *Himmelbett* procedure.

Although the Würzburg Giant was extending the capability of both *Henaja* and *Dunaja*, any form of fighter control using searchlights was of course very much affected by the cloud and general visibility conditions prevailing, and the skies over Europe are seldom completely clear, particularly in autumn and winter. And longer nights meant deeper penetrations by the RAF. The *Nachtjagd* was making progress, but it was becoming increasingly clear that until some non-visual system was available to take the fighters closer to the bombers further significant improvement in results could not be expected. There was an obvious requirement for a device in the fighter by means of which the pilot could manoeuvre his aircraft into a firing position. Some of them still carried *Spanner*, and a second version, *Spanner II*, had been introduced, a passive equipment that in theory used the heat from engine exhausts to detect its target; but if anything *Spanner II* was even less satisfactory than *Spanner I*. The solution could only be found in radar. In terms of bombers destroyed, *Dunaja* lagged well behind *Henaja* during 1941. By the end of September 1941 only about fifty RAF bombers had been shot down in radar-assisted interceptions as against about 325 in co-operation with the searchlights.

With the increasing size and complexity of the problem of air defence by night, the need for a more centralised system of overall control was becoming apparent. In England this problem had been faced and solved before the outbreak of hostilities, and the RAF's success in the Battle of Britain would have been impossible without the reporting and ground-controlled interception (GCI) system based on the coastal CH radars. In Germany there was no such system. Tactical co-ordination between searchlights and fighters within the *helle Gürtel* was exercised by the commander of the local searchlight regiment, who usually operated from the fighter airfield associated with his area, where he co-operated with officers of the night-fighter *Gruppe* within the Operations Room (*Gruppengefechtsstand*), while the fighter controllers themselves worked at the radar sites. This was clearly unsatisfactory, and Kammhuber set up a *Divisionsgefechtsstand*, literally a Division Battle Headquarters, at Zeist near Arnhem, into which all reports of enemy and friendly operations were sent by telephone and where the tactical air situation was displayed on a vast vertical map. At about this time the term 'Kammhuber Line' was coined by the RAF crews to describe the system of night fighters and searchlights they had to penetrate to reach their objectives.

Both in England and in Germany radar, under the stimulus of wartime necessity, was making rapid advances. The Germans needed some means of 'seeing' at night that would be an improvement on the *Spanner* infra-red device and that very unreliable night vision instrument, the human eye. In Britain, work on an airborne interception (AI) radar had begun before the war, and the first night fighter aircraft, Blenheims, had been equipped experimentally with AI in autumn 1939. The radar the Blenheims carried, AI Mark III, operated on the comparatively long wavelength of one-and-a-half metres and used external aerials mounted on the nose and wings. At first the experiments were not very promising: this was a new field of endeavour for both designers and crews. Nevertheless the potential of AI was recognised, and the number of Blenheims dedicated to air defence by night was increased. Success was slow in coming, and it was not until July 1940 that the first German bomber, a Do 17, was shot down by an AI-equipped night fighter that had detected its target and made its final approach to it by means of its radar, and the second success did not come until November, the same pilot, Flying Officer Ashfield, achieving both 'kills'. Enemy night fighters were still groping for their targets without any on-board aid except, in very rare cases, for the quite inadequate *Spanner*.

It was recognised at quite an early stage in Britain that better results in the field of radar in general, and of air-intercept radar in particular, could be achieved by increasing frequency and so decreasing wavelength, and by March 1941 a practical centimetric AI had been constructed and tested, and an operational device, AI Mark VII, introduced into service in December the same year. At the heart of the British equipment was a remarkable invention, the magnetron, which we will discuss further when we look at the airborne navigation equipment H2S. Suffice it here to say that the magnetron made it possible to produce high-power electromagnetic energy at a very short wavelength, in the order of 10 cm. That in turn meant that aerials necessary for transmission and reception could be correspondingly small and therefore easily manipulated to focus and 'aim' the beam sent out from the fighter. A great advantage was that the aerials could be housed in a specially designed plastic housing, so that they had virtually no adverse effect on the flying characteristics of the machine.

The Germans lagged well behind the British in the field of centimetric radar, and because they had not foreseen the need for a night-fighter defence of the *Reich* they had neglected to make any provision for an airborne interception radar of any sort.

In late 1940, well after the first British AI successes had been achieved, Kammhuber, realising the deficiency, had sent an urgent request to the German radio industry for the development of such a device. Despite objections from the Commander-in-Chief of the *Luftwaffe*, Hermann Göring, who had little understanding of or patience with the whole idea of night-fighting, including radar – 'A fighter isn't a movie show!' – Kammhuber's request was supported by the Aviation Ministry and in particular by the far-seeing General Wolfgang Martini, Head of *Luftwaffe* Signals and Communications. Among the firms so canvassed was Telefunken, and they responded to Kammhuber's request by suggesting that a radio altimeter, *Lichtenstein A*, might be adapted for the purpose. Feasibility tests were conducted, and the idea proved to be a good one.

There was, however, a problem. The device operated on a wavelength of about 60 cm, six times that of the British equipment, so an external aerial array was necessary. The ideal length of an aerial compatible to the wavelength of the equipment was in the order of 30 cm, or one foot, and a number of aerials and reflectors would be required to transmit and receive the electromagnetic energy necessary to 'see' an enemy bomber and to focus that energy into a beam ahead of the fighter. The aerial array that was designed comprised four sets of eight vertical dipole aerials and reflectors mounted in a square arrangement on the nose of the aircraft. Development was delayed at first by a *Luftwaffe* High Command veto on the use of outside aerials on the grounds that they would hinder the performance of the aircraft. Eventually, however, it was accepted that external aerials were indispensable, and German night-fighters began to appear with arrays on the nose. There was justification for the High Command fear that performance would suffer, pilots finding that their maximum speed was cut by about 40 kph and that they could not climb quite as high or quite as quickly as they had been able to do without the aerials. It was realised in scientific circles in Germany that a change to short-wavelength radar could solve the problems associated with the use of aerials inside the fuselage of the fighters, just as it had already done in England, but in 1942 Hitler himself vetoed new development of work on centimetric radar, thus robbing the *Luftwaffe* of what might have been a considerable advantage in the war against the bombers.

First operational tests of the *Lichtenstein* air-interception radar were carried out by 4./NJG 1, a *Staffel* of II./NJG 1, at Leeuwarden in north-west Holland, where a group of technicians from Telefunken had the responsibility of persuading the pilots of the value of the equipment and of teaching them how to use it. It was not an easy task. The technicians met with much resistance from the pilots and radio operators to what, in their eyes, smacked of black magic, in addition to having an adverse effect on the performance of their aircraft. Among those who at first treated the new concept with suspicion, but who was later to become a complete convert and outstanding exponent of the craft of night-fighting, was Helmut Lent: he shot down 102 British bombers by night before he himself was killed in action in October 1944.

It is not hard to understand the original reluctance on the part of pilots and wireless operators to commit themselves to what was, at the time, a revolutionary concept. Until the advent of airborne radar the tasks of the *Funker* had been confined to using the radio equipment for communications and for obtaining navigational assistance in the form of bearings and homing instructions, plus, as the occasion demanded it, the use of the rearward-firing armament. Now he was confronted by small, circular, flickering green or amber displays, of which he had to make sense and the readings from which he had to interpret in the form of instructions to his pilot. It was a responsibility that did not sit easily on the shoulders of many of the older wireless operators. Nor was it easy for many of the traditionally educated *Zerstörer* pilots, accustomed to being in absolute control of their machine and deciding tactics almost by reflex action, to believe in the seeming magic of radar to the extent that they could trust their radio operator to direct them to the attack position.

The display unit that the radio operator had to read comprised three small cathode-ray tubes set horizontally, each about ten centimetres in diameter. The one on the left showed a trace around the tube a short distance in from its periphery, and at irregular intervals on the trace were peaks, or blips, pointing outward. Each of these blips represented the echo from an aircraft, and the distance of an individual target could be determined by comparing the blip against a kilometre scale drawn on the face of the tube. The other two screens had linear displays, the first one horizontal and the second one vertical, on which echo signals produced by the *AN* system explained above were shown as straight lines cutting the time-base. From the first screen the operator could see what other aircraft were ahead of him and within the beam of his *Lichtenstein* up to a theoretical maximum range of about eight kilometres. He could switch in shorter-range displays on the other two tubes, and from the centre one he could tell whether the target was to the left or the right of the fighter's nose, from the right-hand screen whether it was above or below. He could, of course, also read the precise range of the target from the second two screens. Using this information he could give the pilot instructions that would bring him into a position from which he could attack the bomber.

The original device tested by NJG I, *Lichtenstein BC* (FuG 202), did not, at first glance, have a startling performance. Properly handled it proved capable of picking up a target aircraft at a range of between two and three kilometres and tracking it to within about 200 metres. That, however, was an enormous improvement on what had gone before, and a step of major significance to the air battle. Now there was, in more ways than one, light in the darkness. If a German night-fighter could be controlled from the ground to within two miles

A *LICHTENSTEIN BC* DISPLAY

Lichtenstein BC (FuG 202) was the first airborne interception radar used by the German night-fighter force. It searched forward of the aircraft in a 70° cone. Theoretically the range of the device was the equivalent of the fighter's altitude, but in practice it was much less. The radar-operator's display unit comprised three small-diameter, circular cathode-ray tubes, fluorescent green in colour, on which the time-base and signals were shown in lighter green. The left-hand CRT was the long-range search display and had a circular time-base. Other aircraft within range were shown as peaks towards the periphery of the screen. The centre screen was a short-range display showing whether the target aircraft was above or below the fighter, while the right-hand CRT showed whether it was to port or starboard. From these three flickering tubes the *Funker* would attempt to direct the fighter towards its target, aiming to be directly astern of and slightly below the bomber, the ideal position from which to carry out an attack.

This display shows a target at a range of 1.7 kilometres above and to the right of the fighter. In practice the screen was even less clear than the sketch above. *Lichtenstein BC* was eventually replaced by a radar operating on a longer wavelength, *Lichenstein SN–2*, the display unit of which had only two CRTs.

or so of a British bomber, that bomber's chances of survival would be poor indeed.

As related above, on 2 October 1940 Leutnant Ludwig Becker of 4./NJG 1 had been the first *Luftwaffe* night-fighter pilot to destroy a British bomber in the *Dunaja* environment. By now promoted to Oberleutnant, Becker assumed responsibility for the early operational tests of *Lichtenstein*, and unlike the majority of his fellow pilots he was enthusiastic about the possibilities opened up by the new 'eyes' that Telefunken had provided for him. By this time, in common with the other members of his *Staffel*, he had exchanged his Do 17Z-10 for the more powerful Do 215B-5, a special night-fighter version of the Do 215 reconnaissance-bomber, and in the early hours of 9 August 1941 he gained his, and the *Nachtjagd*'s, first AI victory, one of the forty-four Wellingtons sent by Bomber Command to attack Hamburg. This first success by the redoubtable Becker was quickly followed by others on 15 August, 23 August, 11 September and 2 October 1941. *Lichtenstein* was deemed to have proved itself, hitherto conservative-minded aircrew became progressively more enthusiastic, and orders for series production were placed with Telefunken. Under the code word *Adler* – the same pseudonym that had earlier been allocated to the planned knockout blow by the *Luftwaffe* against Britain in 1940 – a project was launched to equip, as a first step, the Messerschmitt Bf 110E/U1 night-fighters of I./NJG 1 at Venlo with *Lichtenstein BC*.

It was still to be a long time, however, before one could speak even superficially of a radar-equipped night fighter force. The *Lichtenstein* set that Becker had in his Do 215 was the only one in existence, and after his fourth or fifth victory – the record is not clear – on 2 October 1941 that set itself became unserviceable and could not be repaired. The *Nachtjagd* was blind again, and it was not until well into 1942 that sets began to arrive on the fighting units, and only towards the end of the year that they were widely operational. 1941 passed, therefore, without the *Nachtjagd* in general having the operational benefit of AI radar.

In proving that *Lichtenstein* had a future, however, Becker had spread the seeds of enthusiasm for the device and for the concept of hunting in the dark. He had also begun to formulate tactics for interception by night, and the tactics he developed were to prove to be so soundly conceived that they were adopted in outline by generations of night-fighter pilots after him. Firstly, in common with other German night-fighters, the aircraft that Becker flew, the Do 215, was only marginally faster than the British bombers, so that a simple tail-chase would involve a long time catching up, during which the fighter, as it closed, would come under the fire of the four-gun rear turret of the bomber. Secondly, the best position from which to attack was, from the defensive point of view, from below, so that the fighter would be hidden against the darkness of the ground beneath from the searching eyes of the rear gunner, and a further degree of safety would be guaranteed by the fact that as a rule RAF bombers did not have a defensive position below the fuselage. Becker's solution was pure common sense. When going out to meet the approaching British bombers he would climb as high as possible, aiming to be above the RAF machines. Having picked up a target on his *Lichtenstein*, which would usually be at a range of something over a mile, he would position himself astern and dive down in pursuit, gaining speed but keeping the bomber within the scan of his radar, and aim to come out flying level at about the same speed as the bomber but perhaps 500 metres below, by which time he would hope to have his target in sight, possibly silhouetted against the sky above. Hidden from the view of the British gunners, he would gradually gain height until he was just beneath his victim and then pull up his nose and open fire, letting the bomber fly through the burst of bullets and explosive shells from his forward-firing armament, which in the case of the Do 215B-5 amounted to the formidable package of four 7.9 mm MG 17 machine-guns and two 20 mm MG FF cannon. Once the fighter was in an attack position, this was an almost infallible recipe for success, as very many RAF aircrew might testify, had they lived.

But during 1941 it was still the German anti-aircraft artillery that represented the primary hazard to RAF bombers venturing over German territory. The direct hit, which often brought with it instant oblivion for the unfortunate men in the aircraft, was comparatively rare. More frequent was the damage caused by one of the countless fragments of shrapnel scattered from the exploding shells, damage that caused the bomber to die slowly and the crew to endure the mental agony of not knowing whether they would make it home or hit the ground in a violent impact from which they stood little chance of escaping alive; or whether, perhaps even worse, their machine would come down in the inhospitable North Sea where, if they managed to survive the impact and to struggle into their fragile rubber dinghy, the balance of probability was that they would perish slowly of exposure or eventual drowning. One man who survived such an ordeal in July 1941 was Pilot Officer Ivan Kayes of No. 77 Squadron, navigator of a Whitley V piloted by the nineteen-year-old Sergeant Bernard Harpur:

'We were last to take off at Topcliffe and arrived last at the target over Bremen, thus attracting the attention of all the searchlights and flak. Dropping the bombs, we turned for home only to find that the glycol jacket around one of the engines had been punctured. With glycol streaming out behind us we had to cut the engine, but found a little later that it was impossible to continue flying on only one engine. Bernard Harpur, having given instructions to prepare for ditching, successfully ditched about 100 miles off Flamborough. We opened the back door and threw out the dinghy, which floated upside down. Sgt Mayson, the wireless operator, jumped into the water to right the dinghy and it was then that we found that Flying Officer Dean and Sgt Thuell, second pilot and air gunner respectively, had been injured and were temporarily out of action. I had packed the cartridges for the flare pistol, but the pistol itself was lost in the course of ditching. This was a nuisance, but we got over the problem by holding the cartridge in a gloved hand and striking the base with the spike of my jack knife. This worked very well, and the flare soared up into the sky.

'Just before we ditched the wireless operator had sent out a Mayday call with our estimated position, and four hours later an aircraft from our Squadron was overhead dropping a bag containing water bottles but, in spite of great efforts by our intrepid swimmer, Sgt Mayson, this drifted away. A Hampden arrived later to drop a Lindholme dinghy with four containers attached, but this dinghy was only half inflated. Bernard Harpur climbed into it while we secured the containers but was unable to cause it to inflate. We thought we had tied the two dinghies together, but they were suddenly yards apart and drifting. Sgt Mayson again went into the sea to get them together, but failed, and the dinghy containing Bernard Harpur was soon out of sight. We attended to the injured men, putting them into sleeping bags and then, having had some food, we settled down to wait. We waited for two-and-a-half days, during which time we had visits from a Wellington, a Spitfire and an Me 109. We also saw what we thought was a German E-boat, which fortunately didn't see us. Two motor gun-boats of the Royal Navy then appeared, and we were taken to land in Felixstowe. Bernard Harpur was found at about the same time, but sadly he was dead, having apparently drowned in three inches of water in the faulty dinghy.'

If he had to ditch, Ivan Kayes was fortunate to do so in July, when the North Sea was possibly as warm as at any time of the year. The chances of surviving a ditching in the winter months were minimal. But Ivan's luck was short lived, and just the following month it ran out. With a new crew he was in a Whitley that set out from Topcliffe to attack Frankfurt am Main on 5/6 August, and once again a shell splinter put an engine out of action. This time the crew had to take to their parachutes, and Ivan Kayes spent the remainder of the war in a prisoner-of-war camp.

On the world scene 1941 was a year of mighty developments. It began with Britain standing virtually alone against the Berlin-Rome Axis and, by all logic, apparently destined to eventual subjugation, and it ended with two vast nations, the Soviet Union and the United States of America, ranged alongside her, but with the Japanese added to the sum of her foes. Both the Russians and the Americans had been compelled into direct participation in the fighting by the treachery and aggression of the Germans and the Japanese respectively. There was however a fundamental difference of nature between the two new alliances that Britain now enjoyed. The Americans were already committed to supporting the British cause by supplying great quantities of war materiel. Possibly of even more importance in the long term was the unequivocal American declaration of intent in what came to be known as the Atlantic Charter, signed by Winston Churchill and the American President, Franklin D. Roosevelt, on 12 August 1941, which looked forward to 'the final destruction of Nazi tyranny'. In bleak contrast, the alliance with the Soviet Union was an enforced alignment lacking any element of fundamental ideological principle, one of practical necessity rather than community of political belief. As recently as 10 January 1941, only five months before Hitler's invasion of Russia, Nazi Germany and the Soviet Union had signed a large-scale economic agreement under which the Germans would receive industrial raw materials, including oil, in return for machine tools with which the Soviets could modernise their factories. Yet despite the odd nature of the Triple Alliance, as it came to be called, in the European war zone it was now Germany rather than Great Britain to whose disadvantage the logic of the odds could be interpreted. But it was to be a long time before those odds would assert themselves.

During a year of disaster for British arms that saw, among other unhappy events, early progress in North Africa turn to retreat before Erwin Rommel's *Afrika Korps*: the Dunkirk-like evacuation of British, Commonwealth and Polish forces from Greece; heavy bombing by the *Luftwaffe* throughout Great Britain; the capture of Crete by German airborne forces and serious naval setbacks including the loss of the aircraft carrier *Ark Royal* to a U-boat off Gibraltar and the battleships *Repulse* and *Prince of Wales* to Japanese aircraft, Bomber Command represented virtually the only easily understandable and readily perceptible way of hitting back at the Third Reich, and as such it had enormous public support. Despite the seemingly unstoppable series of triumphs by the German forces, here was an area in which Britain was on the attack and the Germans were suffering. It can now be seen that the physical impact of the Bomber Command attacks at that time was not what it was made out to be by the propagandists nor, indeed, what the majority of the Air Staff believed it to be. Of the psychological impact in Great Britain, on the other hand, there can be no doubt. The RAF fighter pilots had won the Battle of Britain, and now their colleagues in the heavies were perpetuating the tradition that they had created. The British public awoke to headlines in the press telling of losses and of defeats on land and at sea, but there were also stirring headlines announcing apparent successes in the air – 'RAF BOMBERS BLAST BERLIN', 'HAMM MAR-SHALLING YARDS STRUCK AGAIN', 'GERMAN NAVAL TARGETS HIT HARD', and so on. This, they saw, they felt, was what Churchill meant when, in his broadcast to the nation following the German invasion of Russia, he said: 'We will never parley, we will never negotiate with Hitler or any of his gang. We shall fight him by land, we shall fight him by sea, we shall fight him in the air, until, with God's help, we have rid the earth of his shadow and liberated its peoples from his yoke.' The news on land was not good, the news at sea was not good, but, by God, there was something to be proud of in the air.

Nor should the physical impact of the Bomber Command attacks, exaggerated though it might have been, be dismissed as insignificant, even though the way in which the efforts of the bomber crews were directed may legitimately be criticised. As noted above, the year had begun with German oil supplies the main target; in March the emphasis was transferred to maritime targets, towns connected with U-boat construction and ports, like Brest, that harboured German capital ships such as the *Scharnhorst* and the *Gneisenau*. This phase lasted until July, when priorities were again readjusted. On the ninth of the month the Deputy Chief of the Air Staff, Air Vice-Marshal N. H. Bottomley, sent a directive to Peirse, Commander-in-Chief, Bomber Command. The missive is worth considering in some detail in an attempt to understand the way in which the forward momentum of Bomber Command developed. It began:

'1. I am directed to inform you that a comprehensive review of the enemy's present political, economic and military situation discloses that the weakest points in his armour lie in the morale of the civil population and in his inland transportation system. The wide extension of his military activities is placing an ever-increasing strain on the German transportation system, and there are many signs that our recent attacks on industrial towns are having a great effect on the morale of the civil population.

'Subject, therefore, to para. 7 below, I am to request that you will direct the main effort of the bomber force, until further instructions, towards dislocating the German transportation system and to destroying the morale of the civil population.'

The para. 7 mentioned by Bottomley simply allowed for attacks on priority targets that might emerge in the light of the current situation, and for a continuation as appropriate of raids on naval units at Brest and on submarine-building yards and bases. The directive attempted to define and identify 'transportation' targets: roads as such were ruled out 'owing to their tactical unsuitability as bombing targets': Synthetic rubber plants at Schkopau and Hüls were specified (albeit misspelt); in them, it was optimistically stated, almost the whole of the enemy rubber industry was concentrated, and their destruction would have far-reaching effects on road transportation generally and 'might have an immediate influence on operations in the Russian theatre'. The directive also listed nine rail bottlenecks, to be attacked in moonlight, and four targets adjacent to water 'suitable for concentrated and continuous area attack on moonless nights', which lay 'in congested industrial towns, where the psychological effect' would be the greatest. Inland waterways such as the Dortmund-Ems and Ems-Weser canals and the River Rhine, for use against which a new type of mine was under development, were included.

Who was fooling whom? Was this yet another case of self-delusion on the part of whoever – presumably the Ministry of Economic Warfare – had produced the 'comprehensive review of the enemy's political, economic and military situation' on which the directive purported to be based? And what were the 'many signs that our recent attacks' were 'having a great effect on the morale of the civilian population'? At this juncture Britain had been far harder hit by German bombers than Germany had been by the RAF, yet there had been no sign of a collapse of the morale of the British civil population: if anything, just the reverse. Was there any real reason to believe that the German man-in-the-street would react differently from his British counterpart? It is hard to avoid the very strong suspicion that here was an attempt to justify the decision to adopt area bombing while retaining a façade of respectability; and that the decision in question was in itself a reflection of the growing, if belated, realisation that bombing from the air with the aircraft and the navigational and bombing aids then available was a bludgeon rather than a rapier.

To some extent the directive conceded this latter point by including what was intended to be a mathematical consideration of the effect that might be expected from attacks on railway centres. But even so the suppositional and mathematical bases of the argument were so unsound that the authors of the directive were either victims of self-hypnotism or fools or knaves: fools because they were incompetent or knaves because they were concealing the real nature of what they were ordering to be done not only from the country at large but also from those who would have to do it. 'In the opinion of railway experts,' the directive said, 'the dropping of 50 to 100 bombs (say 15 tons) on any one of the railway centres listed in para. 2 is likely to lead to a complete stoppage for a period of at least one week . . . ' The centres listed were not pinpoint targets but city areas – Hamm, Osnabrück, Cologne (Kalk Nord) etc. The *Luftwaffe* had dropped about 450 tons of bombs on Coventry, itself a rail centre, the previous year with considerably more accuracy than Bomber Command could yet hope to achieve, yet there had been no 'complete stoppage for at least one week'. The next assumption was that ninety aircraft would attack the target and would achieve an average aiming error of 600 yards, with the result that 112 high-explosive and 1,874 incendiary bombs would fall in the target area (the dimensions of which were not specified) and fifty-six HE bombs would hit vulnerable points within it. How wildly inaccurate these latter figures were would be seen when, as will be described below, a formal study of Bomber Command effectiveness was conducted soon afterwards.

Let us, therefore, concede that at this juncture, indeed since the beginning of the war, the fundamental nature of the contribution that Bomber Command could make to winning had been misunderstood and misrepresented, sometimes, it might seem, wilfully. The analogy of the rapier and the bludgeon is a nice one:

the rapier is the weapon of gentlemen, the bludgeon that of the blackguard. The rapier leaves a nice, clean wound; the bludgeon leaves a bloody mess. But if you don't have a rapier, or if you are not one of the élite skilled in its use, it is the bludgeon that you will seize when your family and your life are threatened, and you will be thankful that you have one to hand. And, gentlemanly though the rapier is, few would dispute that a ruthless battering with a blunt instrument is a very satisfactory way of discouraging aggressive intent. And so it was with Bomber Command. The threat was there, and the weapon was there, and there was none other to reach for. It was not a nice weapon – but, then, what weapon is 'nice'? The machine-gun bullets that tear man apart? The bayonet that disembowels him? The high-explosive shell that reduces him to pulp or, possibly worse, leaves him a hopeless cripple, physically or mentally or both? The long-range gun that pounds an enemy's coastal towns regardless of the fact that there are women and children living there? Or perhaps the submarine or the blockade ship that prevents food reaching the women and children and commits them to slow starvation and lingering death from disease, as happened in Germany in the First World War?

There could be no better indication of the increasing impact of the bomber offensive during 1941 than the way in which the Germans built up their night-fighter force during the same period. By the end of the year it had grown to about ten *Gruppen* and an establishment of about 350 aircraft. In August 1941 a further *Nachtjagddivision* had been created and absorbed, together with the first one, into the XII. *Fliegerkorps*, which also included all the day-fighter units remaining in Germany, two searchlight divisions and three Air Signals Regiments, with Kammhuber as Commanding General.

Hamburg, after Berlin the second largest German city, was a frequent recipient of visits from the RAF in 1941 and forms a useful example of the way in which the operations of Bomber Command were affecting German cities. At the same time its experiences exemplify the random nature of area bombing as it was then practised. Large forces – the average was 128 machines – went there during the nights of 6/7 May, 8/9 May, 10/11 May and 11/12 May. Crews returning from the first attack were optimistic concerning their results, but reports from the ground belie their claims. The following three attacks, however, caused 233 deaths, injured 713 and rendered 2,195 homeless. Much damage was done to private property, but in the early morning of 9 May the *Deutsche Erdölwerke* were struck and the thirty-four oil-tanks there ignited; on 10/11 May the financial area of Hamburg was hit, and the stock exchange building was among those severely damaged.

Just after one o'clock on the morning of 28 June there was another air-raid alert that lasted one hour and forty minutes, during which, it was estimated, thirty-five bombers attacked the city. Five RAF aircraft were shot down by night fighters actually over Hamburg, four of them falling to Oberleutnant Eckhardt of II./NJG 1, who had taken off from nearby Stade. Seven people were killed, thirty-nine injured and 280 made homeless. Yet the bombers had not set out that night to attack Hamburg: the target for which they were briefed was Bremen, some 110 kilometres to the south-west.

It is a further reflection of the haphazard nature of the Bomber Command attack that during 1941 the city authorities recorded forty raids in the course of which bombs were dropped, just twice as many attacks as Bomber Command crews were briefed to carry out. In the other twenty, Hamburg was bombed in error for other targets, mainly north German ports such as Kiel and Bremen. The RAF directed a total of 2,034 sorties against the city, while the total number of aircraft that the Germans estimated as having attacked it altogether during the year was 1,240, including those nights when Hamburg was not the intended target. The figure for nights when the crews were briefed to raid Hamburg was 923. A great many aircraft were not finding their proper target. Yet the suffering to the city was not inconsiderable, an estimated 3,201 HE bombs and 29,939 incendiaries landing there, killing 626 persons, injuring 1,959 and making 7,025 homeless. There was very considerable damage to residential property, less to targets with a more clearly defined importance to the war effort, and the total cost of damage was estimated at 175 million *Reichsmark*. Of the 2,034 RAF crews sent to attack Hamburg, sixty-seven failed to return. The majority of the approximately 350 men crewing them were killed.

It would, in all fairness, be difficult to describe the bombing of Hamburg, or indeed of the rest of Germany, during the greater part of 1941 as anything other than indiscriminate, whether by intent or otherwise. Of course, the full extent of the inaccuracy was not then known, even though it was suspected in some circles. That was a realisation yet to come. And Hamburg was just one of many German cities and towns that had suffered similarly. Between the outbreak of war and early August 1941 the number of deaths in the whole of the *Reich* came to 3,853, and scarcely a night passed without air-raid warnings being sounded and bombs dropped somewhere in the Fatherland. But it must not be overlooked that during the same period Great Britain, with a death toll of almost 42,000, had suffered more than ten-fold from the attentions of the Heinkels, the Dorniers and the Junkers of the *Luftwaffe*, against whose crews the same charges of terror bombing could justifiably be levelled. Bombing was intrinsically indiscriminate, as is the bludgeon.

To Lord Trenchard, long retired from active service but as a Marshal of the Royal Air Force and a member of the House of Lords still retaining considerable influence, the practical issues were clear. He saw the bomber as first and foremost a weapon to be used against enemy morale. In a memorandum arguing for a larger bomber force that he addressed to the Chiefs of Staff in May 1941 he said, without providing a basis for his statement but with a degree of correctness unusual for the period, '. . . the percentage of bombs which hit the military target at which they are aimed is not more than one per cent.' With a staggering degree of incorrectness quite typical of the period, on the other hand, he averred that 'all the evidence of the last war and this shows that the German nation is particularly susceptible to air bombing', a statement he sought to justify with a grotesque description, which could only have originated in his own prejudice, of the German civilian under attack:

'While the ARP services are probably organised with typical German efficiency, their total disregard for the well-being of the population leads to a dislocation of ordinary life which has its inevitable reaction on civilian morale. The ordinary people are neither allowed, nor offer, to play their part in rescue or restoration work; virtually imprisoned within their shelters or within the bombed area, they remain passive and easy prey to hysteria and panic without anything to mitigate the inevitable confusion and chaos. There is no joking in the German shelters as in ours, nor the bond which unites the public with ARP and Military services here of all working together in a common cause to defeat the attacks of the enemy.

'This, then, is their weak point compared with ourselves, and it is at this weak point that we should strike and strike again.'

Sir Charles Portal, Chief of the Air Staff, agreed with Trenchard that the Germans' most vulnerable point was the morale of her civilian population under air attack, and he supported Trenchard's call for more bombers. Surprisingly he did not contest Trenchard's 'not more than one per cent' statement. It might be thought noteworthy that neither Trenchard – who, having retired in 1929, might be forgiven – nor Portal, the officer ultimately responsible for RAF policy, including that of Bomber Command, suggested that better results might be obtained by doing something to make sure that a larger proportion of bombs dropped actually hit their target.

Fortunately for the future of Bomber Command there were others who were apprised of the inaccuracy of aerial bombing and thought that something should be done about it. Among them was Professor Frederick Alexander Lindemann, soon to become Lord Cherwell. Lindemann was a close friend of, and scientific adviser to, the Prime Minister, Winston Churchill, with whom he wielded considerable influence. Like Trenchard, he was a strong advocate of the bomber and of its use as a weapon to break the morale of the Germans; in contrast to Trenchard, however, he was a scientist and not so prone to irrational and emotive justification of his opinions. As a preliminary to considering ways in which Bomber Command might be made a more effective weapon he commissioned Mr D. M. B. Butt, a member of the secretariat of the War Cabinet, to carry out an objective study on the accuracy of Bomber Command attacks.

Butt had little to go on. By far the major source of information on the accuracy of the attacks comprised the bomber aircrew themselves who, for a variety of reasons, not necessarily discreditable, were unreliable witnesses. Intelligence from Germany on the effects of RAF bombing was superficial and frequently exaggerated. Butt perceived that properly analysed photographic evidence would be his most valuable aid in reaching his findings. In 1941 the RAF had a comparatively small photographic reconnaissance capability, and such small evidence of damage created by Bomber Command that the long-range Spitfires of the Photographic Reconnaissance Unit (PRU), set up as late as November 1940, had brought back from occasional visits to targets after they had been raided was less than encouraging; the sample, however, was too small to be of real value in any objective analysis of results. There remained, as a source for Butt, cameras carried by the bombers themselves. Unhappily, these too provided only limited data. Of the many bombers flying operationally, only a very small proportion carried a camera: trials of photography by aircraft participating in the raids themselves had not begun until February 1941, and by June the same year only one in ten of Bomber Command aircraft carried an F24 camera in the fuselage. Photographs were taken by the light of comparatively long-burning magnesium flares dropped from the aircraft. Butt used about 650 selected photographs taken in this way as the basis of his study. An idea of the comparative size of the sample used in the study may be formed by considering that these 650 photographs were taken in the course of 100 raids in a two-month period, June and July 1941, and that the total number of sorties – flights by individual aircraft – in those raids was in the region of 6,000. Of the photographs taken, only about half were of the target itself, but from the remaining ones, Butt said, he was able to check accuracy of navigation.

Butt was, it might be thought, very liberal in the criteria that he set himself: for example, he defined 'target area' as 'anywhere within five miles of the aiming point', or an area of seventy-eight square miles (200 square kilometres). As a comparison, a bomb aimed at the Houses of Parliament would be counted as having landed in the target area if it impacted in Hammersmith, Holloway, Crystal Palace or Greenwich. Even with this wide latitude for inaccuracy, Butt's findings were devastating. Of all aircraft recorded as having attacked their target, only one in three actually bombed within the target area: if one considered all sorties, the proportion dropped to one in five. The results varied with the degree of moonlight and the amount of flak experienced. They also varied according to the difficulty of the target: for example, two out of three machines claiming to have attacked the French ports had landed their bombs within five miles of the aiming point, but in the case of the Ruhr, Bomber Command's prime target, the proportion was as low as one in ten. Although Butt did not state it in his conclusions, it follows that when Bomber Command's target was in the Ruhr area only one bomber in every seventeen dispatched, as opposed to those that claimed to have attacked their target, had bombed within five miles of its allocated aiming point. On the night of 3/4 July 1941, ninety bombers were sent to bomb the Krupps arms works and rail targets in Essen. Applying Butt's findings to that raid, one would expect the probability to be that only five had hit the town itself or its environs, not necessarily their specific targets, with eighty-five dropping their loads elsewhere. That extrapolation is supported by the military historian Martin Middlebrook: 'Essen reported only light housing damage with two people injured, but many bombs fell in the towns of Bochum, Dortmund, Duisburg, Hagen and Wuppertal as well as in other places.'[1]

The Butt Report was issued on 18 August 1941. At the command level it was not well received. The Commander-in-Chief of Bomber Command, Sir Richard Peirse, was sceptical of its findings, minuting, 'I don't think at this rate we could have hoped to produce the damage which is known to have been achieved.' There were other objections and criticisms, some valid, some frankly straw-clutching: into the latter category must come the assertion made by Air Vice-Marshal Saundby, Senior Air Staff Officer at Bomber Command, that squadron commanders tended to give cameras to the crews in whom they had least confidence, so that the photographs that Butt had used could not be considered representative. Lord Cherwell, however, went above the heads of the Air Staff, minuting to Churchill on 2 September 1941 to the effect that the figures, even though they might be inaccurate, were 'sufficiently striking to emphasise the supreme

[1] *The Bomber Command War Diaries*, by Martin Middlebrook and Chris Everitt, first published 1985 by the Viking Press.

importance of improving our navigational methods'. Churchill took Cherwell's point and wrote to Portal, Chief of Air Staff. 'This,' he said, 'is a very serious paper, and seems to require your most urgent attention . . . I await your proposals for action.' With just a hint of petulance – he thought Butt's figures 'might be wide of the mark' – Portal conceded that the need for an improvement in night bombing represented 'perhaps the greatest of the operational problems confronting us at the present time', and he added that operational research, improved training, developed tactics and above all science were to be brought to bear on the problem.

There was an additional suggestion. If bombing was so inaccurate, it was suggested by the Air Staff, the answer was to concentrate on area attack and ensure that a greater number of bombs hit German cities by increasing the size of the force to 4,000. Portal, passing on the Air Staff paper on 25 September, said that with that number of bombers the Command could break Germany within six months. Churchill was sceptical, particularly as the Air Staff had attempted to justify their demands on a mathematical basis, extrapolating from the weight of bombs dropped on Coventry and the effect they had had there to the impact that an increased RAF force would have on Germany. He queried the logic of the arguments. He disputed whether bombing itself would be a decisive factor in the war. He argued that the effects of bombing, both physical and moral, were greatly exaggerated. He pointed out that under German attack the British people had been 'stimulated and strengthened'. He drew attention to the inherent inaccuracy of aerial bombing and concluded, 'The most we can say is that it will be a heavy and I trust a seriously increasing annoyance.'

During the remainder of the year the debate continued: so did the bomber offensive, with results little different from those that had been achieved previously. There were heavy losses among aircraft sent to Berlin, Cologne and Mannheim on the night of 7/8 November 1941, 9.4 per cent of 392 bombers in the attacking force failing to return. Churchill, whose attention was much focused on Bomber Command by this time, suggested, first to Sir Richard Peirse and then to Portal and Sir Archibald Sinclair, the Air Minister, that Bomber Command effort should be conserved with a view to reopening the offensive in the following spring. The Cabinet endorsed this suggestion. This was a time of low morale in Bomber Command, spreading from the top downwards, and a time of intense debate in high places as to the future of the Command. From mid-November 1941 to late February 1942 only comparatively modest raids were carried out, the majority of them against coastal targets in France and Germany. There was, however, no improvement in the accuracy of the bombing or of the navigation. There had to be a change, either in strategy, in tactics, in equipment, in leadership or in a combination of some or all of these areas. New navigational aids, including those described above, Gee and Oboe, were being developed, and high hopes reposed in them. Gee was almost ready for full operational use, and a further reason for optimism was that re-equipment with four-engined bombers was going ahead.

Both the strategy and the tactics were largely dictated by the navigational and bomb-aiming capabilities of the bomber force: at the strategic level the choice was between pinpoint bombing and area bombing, and pinpoint bombing, no matter how attractive as an ideal, had been shown to be well outside the

Command's capabilities, for the time being at least. The alternatives seemed to be area bombing or no bombing at all, and, given that Bomber Command was at the time virtually the only means of carrying the war to the enemy, not to speak of the vast investment already made in the force, simply to abandon the bombing of Germany could scarcely be contemplated. A change of leadership was a matter that could, and would, be addressed.

Scientifically accurate or not, the Butt Report had focused attention very compellingly on the performance of Bomber Command, indeed calling into question the very existence of the force. Complacency was shattered, cloud-cuckoo-land revealed as the refuge for the self-deluding and incompetent that it was. More than anyone else, more than any of the Air Marshals, the comparatively lowly Mr Butt had provided the impetus that would quite rapidly turn Bomber Command from a clumsy, blundering adolescent into a vastly powerful and sophisticated fighting adult.

During 1941 *Luftwaffe* night-fighters accounted for over 400 of the 700-plus machines of Bomber Command that failed to return from a total of 27,101 operational sorties. The most successful months, from the *Nachtjagd* point of view, were June, July and August, when the better weather meant that there were more attackers flying, hence more targets for the fighters, and the shorter nights and clearer skies of summer militated in favour of the night-fighter crews. It was an ominous sign that the night-fighters had accounted for nearly fifty-six per cent of the year's successes as against the *Flak*'s forty-four per cent, whereas the previous year the percentages had been 15.5 for the *Nachtjagd* and 84.5 for the *Flak*. Bomber Command's overall losses in 1940 had been 1.95 per cent of all sorties, and they had risen to 2.6 per cent in 1941. Flying bombers over Germany was becoming steadily more dangerous, while flying night fighters against those bombers was equally steadily becoming a more rewarding occupation.

Above: Crew compartment of the He 219 "Uhu" night fighter, looking to the stern. The radio operator sat back-to-back with the pilot. *(Hinchliffe)*

Left: Oberst Lent (left) visits St Trond (Belgium) in 1943. He is seen here in conversation with *Hauptmann* Schnaufer, *Kommandeur* of IV./NJG 1. *(Greiner)*

Above: 1943, 5./NJG 3, Schleswig. From left: *Unteroffizier* Busch (flight mechanic), *Unteroffizier* Kutzner (pilot), *Unteroffizier* Klotz (radio operator). Terribly injured, Kutzner survived when his Ju 88 crashed in December 1944, but his fellow-crewmen perished. *(Kutzner)*

Above right: Oberleutnant Rudolf Szardenings, *Staffelkapitän* of 7./NJG 3. He scored twelve confirmed victories. *(Szardenings)*

Right: Flying Officer Terry Bolter DFC, who "walked back" after being shot down over Belgium during the night of 20–21 December 1943. In his tie he is wearing the golden emblem of the Caterpillar Club, exclusive to those who have saved their life by parachute. *(Bolter)*

CHAPTER FOUR

The End of the Beginning: Millennium, *Himmelbett* and PFF

January to November 1942

Oberleutnant Walter Knickmeier was a fighter controller, a *JLO*, with I./NJG 1, which, equipped with the Bf 110E, was based at Venlo. NJG 1 was destined to be by far the most successful night-fighter *Geschwader*, recording 2,209 confirmed victories by the end of hostilities out of the total of 5,833 achieved by the entire *Nachtjagd* on the Western Front. A pre-war officer in the *Luftwaffe* and a trained pilot, Knickmeier had served as a navigation instructor before joining the night-fighter force. Although not himself accommodated at Venlo, Knickmeier, like the majority of other controllers at that period, when the world of fighter controlling was more intimate than it later became, made it his practice to visit the base as frequently as he could and to discuss tactics with the aircrews, at the same time developing an intimacy with them that added greatly to the working relationship that evolved. The first 'kill' in which Knickmeier participated, that of a Handley Page Hampden, was achieved by the redoubtable Hauptmann Werner Streib on 10 March 1941, just before I./NJG 1 occupied the newly constructed airfield at Venlo. The Hampden was one of nineteen bombers briefed to attack Cologne. By the end of 1941 Knickmeier's tally stood at twenty-four, of which Streib was the pilot who had shot down six. Another six had fallen to Oberleutnant Wolfgang Thimmig, and five to Oberleutnant Reinhold Knacke. All of Knickmeier's successes had been achieved in *helle Nachtjagd* (searchlight-assisted night fighting) with the exception of one, a Wellington shot down by Oberleutnant Thimmig by the AN close-control procedure on 11 July. From March 1942 onwards, when *Lichtenstein* was beginning to reach I./NJG 1, every successful interception that Knickmeier controlled, which by July 1943 amounted to a further sixty-four, was finalised by the use of AI radar, and of them Streib was responsible for twenty-three.

Werner Streib, it will be recalled, had, as a member of Wolfgang Falck's *Gruppe* in Norway in April/May 1940, been one of the first pilots to be involved in experimental night-fighting, and on 20 July the same year, as an officer of Falck's newly formed NJG 1 flying from Gütersloh, he had achieved the first confirmed destruction of a British bomber by that unit, a Whitley of No. 78 Squadron piloted by Sergeant V. C. Monkhouse. Ironically this Whitley, the first destroyed by Kammhuber's *Nachtjagd*, was also the first of the 192 aircraft lost by 78 Squadron during the war.

Streib, like Falck, was a pre-war *Wehrmacht* officer. His first flying duties were as an observer, but then he underwent pilot's training, and by the outbreak of war he had joined Falck's Bf 110 *Staffel*. In October 1940, as a Hauptmann, he was *Kommandeur* of I./NJG 1. After his first night-time success on 20 July he had rapidly established himself as an expert at the craft of night-fighting. In the *Luftwaffe* the word *Experte* was synonymous with the word 'ace' in the RAF. His success as the leading night-fighter ace during this period, however, was due not only to his natural genius, but also to his position as *Gruppenkommandeur*, which meant that he could choose when to fly, selecting opportunities that seemed to him most likely to provide him with good targets. For this he had the rapidly improving raid warning service, the *Flugmeldedienst*, to show him when and where enemy attacks might be expected, so that he could arrange it so that he took off when the chances of action were best. It was the general practice of leading aces in the *Nachtjagd* to ensure in this way that they got the best pickings, and the practice would persist long into the war. The more opportunities the aces got to shoot down British bombers, the more their expertise grew, with the result that the officers among them were given positions of command as *Staffelkapitäne* or *Gruppenkommandeure*, which then gave them even more chances to increase their score. In terms of the overall potency of the *Nachtjagd*, this was a double-edged weapon. It contributed to the emergence of an *élite* among the pilots who ran up impressive scores, but at the same time it meant that many young crewmen got little chance to build up their own expertise. Of their ambitious seniors, determined to be at the head of the table of successes against British bombers, the lower-placed pilots said, '*Die haben Halsschmerzen!*' – 'They've got a sore throat' – a euphemism for being eager to earn the coveted Knight's Cross, a decoration worn at the throat on a ribbon round the neck.

In January 1942 and in the wake of the Butt Report the Commander-in-Chief of Bomber Command, Peirse, was appointed C-in-C of the Air Forces in India and South-East Asia. Air-Vice Marshal J. E. A. Baldwin, Air Officer Commanding No. 3 Group, was made Acting Commander-in-Chief of the bombers. It was during Baldwin's short tenure of office that, on 12 February, the German warships *Scharnhorst, Gneisenau* and *Prinz Eugen* made their break from Brest and passed through the Channel on the way to northern ports. Among the RAF aircraft that took off to attack them were 242 from Bomber Command, but bad weather meant that the majority did not even find their targets and that none of those that did bomb scored hits. Among the fighters escorting the German capital ships were Me 110s from the *Nachtjagd*. Although Bomber Command did not achieve any success against the German ships during their escape, their departure from Brest meant that there was no longer any need to divert effort there from the main task, the assault on Germany.

Peirse's permanent successor as Commander-in-Chief was Air Marshal Arthur Travers Harris, but he was absent from the UK at the time leading a mission to Washington negotiating the provision of military supplies for the RAF by the American Government. On his return from the States, Harris took over command of the bomber force in February 1942, retaining it for the remainder of the war.

Harris, born in 1892, had been an RFC pilot in the First World War, seeing service first with anti-Zeppelin flights in England and then as a fighter pilot in France. He had attained the rank of Major by the end of the war and was granted a permanent commission as a Squadron Leader in the post-war RAF. In 1921 he was appointed to the command of No. 31 Squadron in India, and the following year took over No. 45 Squadron in Mesopotamia, later to become Iraq. Exercising Trenchard's policy of air control, Harris oversaw the conversion of Vickers Vernon troop-carrying aircraft to the job of bomb-dropping, so beginning a long association with the aggressive application of air power that would eventually earn him fame, some would say notoriety, as 'Bomber' Harris. On his return to England in 1925 Harris commanded No. 58 Heavy Bomber Squadron, and then followed a number of 'career' postings, including staff and training appointments, until 1937 when, as an Air Commodore, he became AOC No. 4 Group, Bomber Command, the Yorkshire-based heavy-bomber group equipped with the Vickers Armstrong Whitley. After a purchasing-mission interlude in the USA, Harris assumed command of No. 5 Group, equipped with Hampdens, at the outbreak of war, a job he held until, now an Air Vice-Marshal, he was appointed Deputy Chief of Air Staff in November 1940. In May 1941 he returned to the United States to lead the diplomatic mission based there to deal with the supply of materials to the RAF, being promoted to Air Marshal the following month.

By experience and by personality Harris was primarily a 'bomber man'. He had a reputation for directness in his dealings with both superiors and subordinates and in his approach to problems, which he saw in terms of black and white and thus as meriting black-and-white solutions. He did not suffer gladly those whom he regarded as fools. To him fell the formidable task of establishing Bomber Command as a viable organic part of the British war effort.

The brief to which Harris began to work as Commander-in-Chief of Bomber Command had been issued to his predecessor, Air Vice-Marshal Baldwin, just a week before Harris assumed his appointment on 21 February 1942. It lifted the restrictions placed on the use of the bombers as a result of the Butt Report, and it stressed the hopes reposing in the TR 1335 (Gee) as 'an aid to target location and blind bombing'. Despite this prospect of better things to come in the field of bombing accuracy, it nevertheless stated unequivocally, '. . . it has been decided that the primary objective of your operations should now be focused on the morale of the enemy civil population, and in particular, of the industrial workers.' Envisaging only a short operational life for Gee of about six months, by which time, it was assumed, the enemy would have managed to render it ineffective by means of jamming, the directive urged Harris to concentrate on a number of selected primary targets – industrial cities such as Essen, Duisburg, Düsseldorf and Cologne and ports such as Bremen, Wilhelmshaven and Emden, all of which were within the range of Gee. Secondary targets outside Gee range, including Berlin, were also listed. The confidence that the Air Staff placed in Gee may be seen in the sentence, 'When experience in the employment of TR 1335 has proved that, under favourable conditions, effective attacks on precise targets are possible, I am to request that you will consider the practicability of attacking first the precise targets within TR 1335 range and, later, those beyond this range listed in Annex "B".'

It might have been thought that the Air Staff, shown by Butt to have been disastrously wrong in their earlier assumptions about the accuracy of the bomber, would have been a little more cautious when it came to predicting the precision that could be achieved by a device as yet not proved under operational conditions. They did not say, 'If experience should prove . . .' but, 'When experience has proved . . .' as if such proof were a foregone conclusion. Yet such was not the case, as was abundantly clear from the geometry of Gee, the targets listed being at the extreme range of the device, where the lattice lines were wide apart and intersected at a very oblique angle, dictating that precise fixing was an impossibility. Yet the directive listed eight precision targets, mainly oil refineries, within the range of Gee, plus a further four well outside such range; there was no suggestion as to how these latter four might be accurately bombed.

Only a few Bomber Command aircraft were equipped with Gee at this time. There had been one or two flights over Germany using it, beginning in August 1941, but the loss of a Wellington carrying the equipment, and the knowledge that once the Germans had the technical details it would be an easy matter for them to jam it, had led to the sensible decision not to risk it again over Germany until a substantial proportion of the force could be equipped. In February 1942, just before Harris took over, an exercise was held using a railway station in North Wales as a simulated target. Results were promising. Recognising that it would be some considerable time before more than a small proportion of bombers could be equipped with Gee, the exercise involved Gee-equipped aircraft dropping flares over the target to attract other bombers and to provide illumination for them to bomb by, a technique used by the Germans over British targets including Coventry which would later be exploited to devastating effect by Bomber Command's future Pathfinder Force.

Harris was more clear-sighted about the capabilities of his new command, even with Gee, than the Air Staff apparently were. Later, speaking of the task that confronted him, he would write:

'Far more was expected of this extremely useful device, one of the many really brilliant things that the scientists gave us, than it could in fact achieve. And, of course, far more was expected of a very small bomber force than was at all reasonable, even if the new Gee equipment should come up to the most optimistic forecasts; so I had to prove, not only what an adequate and adequately equipped force could not achieve, but also what a small and inadequately equipped force could achieve. I had to dispose of all wishful thinking, while at the same time making perfectly clear the grounds of my complete confidence in a bomber offensive if this were given a real chance.'[1]

This was at least, and at last, a down-to-earth approach to the problems of Bomber Command which, with the advent of Harris to lead it, could now move out of the realms of self-deluding optimism into those of harsh reality.

Harris's tenure of office began with a number of 'the mixture as before' raids on north German ports followed by a very significant attack on the Renault factory at Billancourt, situated in the centre of Paris to the south of the Bois de Boulogne and producing large numbers of military vehicles for the Germans. The tactics that were employed were largely dictated by the clear necessity of causing as few casualties as possible among French civilians. The target was com-

[1] *Bomber Offensive* by Sir Arthur Harris, published 1947 by Collins.

paratively easy to identify visually, being located on the north bank of a U-shaped curve in the River Seine, and the bombers in the first of the three waves dispatched were crewed by men selected for their operational experience. These crews identified the target and illuminated it with flares so that the following two waves could bomb visually from low level. Some 235 RAF bombers took part in the attack, the highest number yet deployed on a single target, and a high level of concentration in time, for the period, was planned, all 235 bombing within one hour and fifty minutes. There was no enemy opposition, and a very satisfactory degree of accuracy was achieved. About three quarters of the bombs dropped hit the factory and caused such damage that production of military vehicles was halted for a month. Sadly the hope that French civilian casualties would be light was not realised: despite the measures taken by the planners and crews to ensure that only the factory was hit, 367 civilians were killed and almost 10,000 rendered homeless, civilian casualties more numerous than any so far caused in a single attack on Germany. This was the grim reality: even so-called precision bombing could not distinguish between the guilty and the innocent.

Essen, in the heart of the Ruhr area, was at the top of the list of area-bombing targets included in the Air Staff's directive to Harris, and Bomber Command flew three attacks against the city on successive nights on 8/9, 9/10 and 10/11 March 1942 with 211, 187 and 126 aircraft respectively. Among the bombers taking part in the third attack were two Lancasters, the first of the type to be deployed against a German target. The raids were planned along the lines of that on Billancourt, except that the leading aircraft were equipped with Gee, in which such high hopes reposed. They were, in all ways, a great disappointment. Industrial haze prevented target identification by the light of the flares, and in any case Gee was shown, as might have been foreseen but was not, to lack accuracy at extreme range, so that the flares did not fall where they were intended to. From the RAF point of view these were major attacks, but to those within the target area they were light raids only. The vast Krupp armaments factory, the main *raison d'être* for attacks on Essen, was not hit, and indeed very little damage at all was caused to the city. Only twenty-five individuals were killed and about forty reported missing in Essen itself, although ironically seventy-four were killed in neighbouring towns in the course of the second raid alone. A total of sixteen bombers failed to return to their bases, most of which were probably shot down by night-fighters.

Following the three attacks on Essen, the cities of Kiel and Cologne were Harris's next targets. Sixty-eight Wellingtons carried out a comparatively successful attack on Kiel on the night of 12/13 March, with five Wellingtons – 7.36 per cent of the attacking force – being lost, one of which fell victim to Oberleutnant Reinhold Knacke of I./NJG 1 at Venlo, controlled to a *Lichtenstein* kill by Walter Knickmeier.

A future ace who was also flying with I./NJG 1 at this period was the nineteen-year-old Leutnant Wilhelm 'Wim' Johnen of the 3rd *Staffel*. He had joined the *Gruppe* in mid-1941, but so far had not opened his score against the RAF bombers despite having flown his first operation on 11 July 1941. Another attack on Essen, Harris's fifth since taking over Bomber Command, was to be the occasion of Johnen's first victory; but that victory was not the young pilot's only memorable experience that night.

With his *Bordfunker*, Berlin-born Unteroffizier Risop, Johnen took off from Venlo in his Bf 110, one of the forty night fighters available at the base that night. He was the first aircraft to be scrambled, lifting off from the runway at about 2203 hrs. His aircraft, C9-FL, was not carrying *Lichtenstein*. The early-warning system had already forecast that the bombers' target was in the Ruhr area. That night, 26/27 March 1942, Harris had committed 104 Wellingtons and eleven Stirlings.

It took Johnen about twenty minutes to reach his operating height of 5,500 metres (about 18,000 feet) above his allocated radio beacon to the west of Wesel, about fifty kilometres to the north-east of Venlo and a similar distance to the north-west of Essen, where he went into a holding circle, well located to intercept the incoming bombers on their way across Holland. It was a clear night, and from his high position of vantage Johnen had a magnificent view of the wide panorama of the Ruhr industrial region, with Essen at its centre. On the R/T he had already heard colleagues' cries of '*Sieg Heil*', the code word that announced that they had shot down a bomber. Streib had already got two.

Johnen saw the bombers' flares go down, and he saw the concentrated flak from the hundreds of guns on the ground bespatter the sky through which the Wellingtons and Stirlings had to fly. He saw bombers coned in the searchlights, 'their silver fuselages gleaming like the pale bodies of fish against the dark night sky'. He saw bombers going down in flames – 'Three, four, five Tommys catch fire in the sky and dive to earth like comets.'

Johnen's controller vectored him in the direction of Duisburg and told him to switch R/T channels to another controller, call sign *Wolfsburg*. The new *JLO* ordered him to attack any opportunity targets above 5,000 metres, leaving those below that level to the flak. As was usual, however, the anti-aircraft gunners did not observe the 'below 5,000 metres' restriction, and Johnen found his machine shaken by near misses. He saw a Wellington at about 4,800 metres, and he decided to attack despite the fact that the bomber was under flak fire. Risop transmitted the code word *Pauke Pauke* – 'I am attacking!' Johnen writes:

> 'From my position above him I put my machine into a dive and get him into my sights. My air-speed indicator moves up to 550 kph. The bomber shines larger and larger in my gun-sight. Now I can clearly see the high rudder and the rear gunner in his glazed tail-turret. My aircraft enters the field of the searchlights, and as it does so my well-directed bursts of fire rattle into his fuselage and tear his right wing open. The Tommy catches fire and tips over on his port wing. It all happens in fractions of a second. I race past the burning Englishman at enormous speed, pull up steeply into the night sky to get away from the threatening flak . . . I cast a quick glance downwards. The Tommy hits the ground and explodes.'[2]

But Johnen's baptism of fire was not yet finished. Suddenly Risop shouted, 'There's another one above us.' Seeing this as a further opportunity to shoot down a bomber, Johnen positioned his Messerschmitt close beneath the enemy

---

[2] *Duell unter den Sternen* (*Duel under the Stars*) by Wilhelm Johnen, published 1956.

machine, which to his surprise he recognised as a *Viermot*, a Stirling. Risop asked him how he proposed to attack:

'I think a moment and then say I think the best way will be a climbing attack from below so that the bomber will pass through my sights and I will be able to hit the fuselage with a long burst. The most dangerous moment will be when I come out close behind the rear turret and the wake from his engines hits my machine . . . "We'd better fire now," says Risop, "or else he'll see us . . ." Those are his last words. I throttle back, let the Englishman shoot ahead and pull the stick back. I see the huge, projecting nose in my sight. At the same moment our bursts of gunfire cross. As if from a watering can the Briton's tracers, coming from all his guns, rush towards me, dazzling me completely . . . bullets spray into my cabin, my fuselage, my fuel tanks. In a fraction of a second my aeroplane is a burning torch. Thousands of litres of petrol are ablaze. A salvo of machine-gun fire hits my left leg, exploding the belt of signal cartridges around my left calf. The cabin roof is torn off with the force of the explosion, and it flies away. In the moment of certain death I look at Risop again. He is lying lifeless, slumped over his radio set. The burst of fire has killed him. I myself see no hope of escaping from the burning machine; I am diving vertically, on fire, into the yawning depths. The indescribable heat in this sea of flames makes me half-unconscious.

'I feel no fear. I get my shattered leg out of the cabin only with desperate effort. But the centrifugal force is too great, and I am pressed back into the machine. I give up all hope of survival, and I put my hand over my eyes to protect them. After we have fallen 3,000 metres the aircraft explodes in the air and I am hurled out. I spin through the air, a burning torch, somersaulting backwards. The cool night air whips against my face and brings me back to consciousness. A thought flashes through my brain: the parachute will catch fire! The silken canopy is still protected in its pack, but the pack has already been attacked by the flames. Swiftly I beat out the flames with my both hands, then I tear off my fur boots and my gloves. Thank God, I manage it well. Now it's high time to pull the ripcord – the red fires on the ground are rapidly coming nearer. The ground comes closer and closer. A jerk, and my downward rush is halted. The parachute opens. My joy is indescribable – but short-lived. The parachute is torn and bullet-holed.'

Johnen's chute was streaming out above him, not properly opened. By manipulating the lines he managed to get it to deploy properly, and almost at the same instant he hit the ground. He landed in a flooded meadow, the mud into which he sank nearly up to his waist taking some of the shock of his over-rapid arrival. He was taken unconscious into a farmhouse and from there to hospital. So terribly was his face burnt that it was thought at first that he must have lost his eyesight; as happened many more times during the war, however, eyelids proved to have protected eyes from damage by fire. Surgeons also managed to save his badly damaged left leg, so that after two months he was able to walk again. Despite being told immediately after being shot down that he would never return to flying, by July Johnen was back with his unit and flying operationally again.

By 13 April 1942 Essen had been attacked eight times in furtherance of Harris's execution of his directive from the Air Staff. Bombing results were poor, losses of bombers slightly above four per cent. There was still a long way to go. Area bombing, even with the aid of Gee, remained of very questionable value. Air Staff optimism, this time as to the value of Gee, had again proved to be wildly misplaced. In the meantime, however, Harris had been experimenting along other lines. On the night of 28/29 March 1942 he had sent 234 bombers to attack Lübeck.

Lübeck was one of the 'Alternative Industrial Areas' that were listed in the February 1942 directive to Bomber Command as targets for non-precision attack. It was outside Gee range but was fairly easy to find in conditions such as clear moonlight, lying on the River Trave, which flows into the distinctively shaped Lübeck Bay on the Baltic. It had negligible *flak* defences. Knowing that the old town was composed virtually entirely of wooden buildings, Harris chose the Hanseatic city as the objective in an experiment 'to learn to what extent a first wave of aircraft could guide a second wave to the aiming point by starting a conflagration'. Lübeck was not a vital target, but it did contain war-related establishments, including submarine-building yards. It seemed to Harris that in carrying out his experiment it was better 'to destroy an industrial town of moderate importance than to fail to destroy a large industrial city'[3]. The experiment was a success, in that the centre of Lübeck was largely destroyed, with a death toll of over 300, and the concept of sending a fire-raising force ahead of the main force to mark the target was shown to be a valid one.

Successful though the Lübeck attack might have been, however, there was a sombre side to the profit-and-loss account. Seven Wellingtons, three Stirlings, one Hampden and one Manchester failed to return to their bases, just over five per cent of the raiding force. From the point of view of its static defences, Lübeck was looked upon as an easy target. The potential of Kammhuber's *Nachtjagd* was becoming increasingly apparent.

Following the Lübeck raid another Baltic port, Rostock, suffered a series of four similar attacks during April. Bombing was effective and RAF losses only eight machines out of the total of 520 that took part.

Feldwebel Walter von Berg and Unteroffizier Walter Heidenreich, a Sudeten German and former *Zerstörer* radio operator transferred to II./NJG 3, took off from Schleswig as the RAF bombers were approaching Lübeck on 24/25 April. They were assigned to the *Konajagebiet* centred on Kiel, code named '*Kiebitz*'. Heidenreich takes up the story:

> 'I saw something gleaming in the searchlights behind us and we turned and tried to get into a firing position, but we couldn't go slow enough. He was doing about 200 kph and we were flying at about 250. It was a Wellington. We made another approach and got to within thirty or forty metres of him. I shouted, "Open fire!" We fired and fired, but didn't seem to hit him. We pulled away, and when we were about 300 metres distant he opened fire

[3] *Bomber Offensive.*

and hit us immediately. I could hear every hit. Von Berg put the nose down and we dived to about 250 metres. I told him that one of the engines was at its maximum temperature. Then the engine stopped. The pilot yelled, "Bale out, I can't hold her!" I jumped out, but couldn't get out cleanly. I had trouble with my legs. I hit the tail unit, catching my chin and the tip of my nose. I must have jumped at about 120 metres, and I landed just a few seconds after pulling the ripcord. Von Berg's parachute didn't open. The unopened pack was found about five metres from his body. Possibly he had turned and pressed the quick-release wheel instead of pulling the ripcord.'

Six nights later five Manchesters from No. 50 Squadron took off from Skellingthorpe, Lincolnshire, to lay mines off the Danish coast. One, VN-N, serial number L7516, was destined not to come back. The trip had been quite uneventful until the aircraft turned for home, when it was discovered that one of the four mines it had been carrying had 'hung up' – that is, it had not dropped with the others when the release button had been pressed. No sooner had this discovery been made than the Manchester came under attack by a night-fighter at an altitude of about 10,000 feet. The Manchester's three gunners returned fire, but when the pilot, Flight Sergeant Tim Willett DFM, called up the rear gunner he did not get a reply. One of the two wireless operators the machine was carrying, Flight Sergeant Hector Macdonald, went to the rear of the fuselage and found the rear gunner slumped over his guns, apparently dead. He was about to operate the 'dead man's handle' to rotate the turret so that he could get at the gunner and help him if necessary when the bomber came under attack again. Cannon shells riddled the bomber, and Macdonald was flung along the fuselage. By this time both VN-N's engines were ablaze, and the pilot gave the order to abandon aircraft, presumably believing that they were over land. Immediately, however, he cancelled the order and told the crew they were over water and he would have to ditch. The aircraft hit the surface but came to an abrupt, skidding halt. It had landed, wheels-up, on a sand bank just covered by water. Macdonald had been hit in the hand during the attack, and his fingers were hanging from the rest of his hand, attached only by skin. He managed to get out of the escape hatch together with the pilot, the navigator and the mid-upper gunner. Then the second pilot's head appeared above the water; he had been badly injured in the leg. Of the Australian front gunner, Sgt Williams, there was no sign. When his body was found later it seemed that he had either fallen out or jumped out of the front escape hatch without his parachute. He had been flying on his first operation.

The survivors from the bomber were taken prisoner. The pilot of the Bf 110 that had shot it down was Oberleutnant Günter Köberich, *Staffelkapitän* of 11./NJG 3. The fire from the Manchester's gunners had had its effect, hitting Köberich's Messerschmitt and badly wounding his *Funker*, Unteroffizier Schubert, in the stomach. Despite the damage to his machine, which included two burst tyres, Köberich managed to put it down safely on the airfield on Sylt. Half an hour then passed, despite Köberich's R/T calls for assistance, before the airfield emergency services arrived on the scene. Schubert died in hospital from his wounds the following morning. Somehow the news of this happening reached Reichsmarschall Hermann Göring, who summarily replaced the airfield commandant.

Günter Köberich was now without a *Funker*, while Walter Heidenreich was without a pilot. The two had known each other for some time, having been at night-fighter school at Echterdingen simultaneously, and it was quite natural that they should decide to make up a new crew. This they did, flying together and shooting down twelve RAF bombers before, in April 1944, Köberich was killed in an air raid on Quakenbrück only a month after he and Heidenreich were posted there.

Even as Harris was bringing a new dynamism and constructive, aggressive thinking to bear on the task of converting Bomber Command into a more potent instrument of offence, so on the German side developments were in train to enhance the defensive potential of the night-fighter force. *Lichtenstein* was being produced in increasing numbers and the technique of controlling fighters into the proximity of the bomber by means of the red and blue Würzburg Giants was improving with practice. The *Würzburg* operators, however, experienced difficulty in distinguishing on their screens between the return from the fighter and the ever-increasing number of returns from hostile aircraft. To assist them an IFF (Identification Friend or Foe) device, FuG 25, code named '*Erstling*', was introduced. The fighter carried a transponder which, when it was 'interrogated' by the ground radar – that is, when it picked up signals from the radar – transmitted a reply on a slightly different frequency, which showed up on the operator's CRT as a distinctive signal. *Erstling* worked in conjunction with both *Würzburg-Riese* and *Freya* radars, but it proved, in the initial stages, to be very difficult for the radar operators, inexperienced as they were, to pick out even an *Erstling* return when there were a large number of enemy bombers in the vicinity. There were also production difficulties, so that sets reached the front-line units only very slowly.

From his predecessor Harris had inherited a comparatively small force of front-line night bombers, most of which were obsolescent. There were 469 machines in all, of which twenty were Manchesters and only sixty were Stirlings, Halifaxes and Lancasters. Of the latter type there were only four. Kammhuber's *Nachtjagd* had, in the meantime, expanded to seven *Gruppen* (twenty-one *Staffeln*) plus one extra *Staffel*, with an establishment of 367 aircraft, although the actual strength was only about 265. The Bf 110 was by far the predominant aircraft, but there were still some Do 215s and Do 217s. The Ju 88 was available only in very small numbers. There had been hopes that the planned replacement for the Bf 110 *Zerstörer*, the Me 210, would become an effective night-fighter, but the whole Me 210 project, in which great hopes had reposed, had foundered when the machine proved to be of fundamentally unsound design and production was discontinued. The abandonment of the project, however, was not decided before most of the Bf 110 production lines had been altered to accommodate the new design, so that when it was decided to revert to the 110 it took some significant time before production could be fully resumed. In addition there was a pressing demand for aircraft for the Russian front, which inevitably had its effect on the number of 110s that could be allocated to the *Nachtjagd*.

By May 1942 Kammhuber's command, expanded in August 1941 into the *XII.*

Fliegerkorps, comprised three divisions, responsible for fighter defence around the clock. *1. Jagddivision* covered Holland, Belgium and the Ruhr area and included NJG 1; *2. Jagddivision* covered north-west Germany and Berlin (NJG 3); and *3. Jagdivision* (NJG 2 and NJG 4) was responsible for the defence of south-western Germany, south Belgium and northern France. Kammhuber, as *General der Nachtjagd*, retained direct command of the night-fighter force in addition to his overall command.

With his experimental attacks on Lübeck and Rostock, Harris had demonstrated that carefully planned area attacks against selected targets, concentrated in time and with target-marking aircraft illuminating the aiming point and setting the target on fire before the mass of high-explosive bombs were dropped on it, offered a much greater prospect of success than previous operational methods, which relied largely on the ability and initiative of individual captains of aircraft. The two targets had however been comparatively easy ones to find and were not as strongly defended as the major inland industrial cities that were his priority objectives. Harris therefore looked for a major target on which to demonstrate that a bomber force properly used was a weapon well worth further investment. The Commander-in-Chief and his immediate staff were still conscious that despite the successes against the Baltic ports other raids since he had assumed command had been little, if at all, more successful than those that had been carried out before the Butt investigation. Harris was also concerned about the morale of his crews, which, although to some extent boosted by the better results shown by the attacks on Billancourt, Lübeck and Rostock, was still low. Together with, particularly, his Senior Air Staff Officer, Air Vice-Marshal Robert Saundby, Harris conceived the idea of mounting a massive raid that would, if successful, not only restore faith in Bomber Command but also fire the bomber crews with enthusiasm. The raid envisaged would also be an opportunity to establish whether an attacking force tightly concentrated in time and space could achieve better results than hitherto.

Harris set the size of the force he proposed to use at 1,000 bombers, despite the fact that he only had about half that number of front-line aircraft: his plan became 'The Thousand Plan' and later, when a code word was allocated, Operation 'Millennium'. It was an extraordinarily bold concept, because not only would the Command's full front-line strength have to be committed, but so also would all its reserves. While success would certainly establish the credibility of Bomber Command under its new leader, failure could well mean its demise. The Chief of the Air Staff, Portal, gave the scheme his blessing, and Winston Churchill was enthusiastic. Two possible targets were selected, Hamburg and Cologne. Churchill favoured the former, Harris preferred the latter. The final choice would depend on the weather conditions prevailing at the time scheduled for the attack.

The story of the first thousand-bomber raid has been told many times, and it does not need to be repeated here in detail. At first Harris had the promise of 250 machines from Coastal Command, but at almost the last moment the Admiralty, never on close working terms with Bomber Command, withdrew the support it had promised. By bringing in crews in the latter stages of their training and scratch crews made up of tour-expired aircrew working as instructors, and by using every available machine from training and other support units within his

Command, Harris managed not only to reach, but indeed to exceed, his target figure. On the night of 30/31 May 1942 a total of 1,047 bombers – 602 Wellingtons, 131 Halifaxes, eighty-eight Stirlings, seventy-nine Hampdens, seventy-three Lancasters, forty-six Manchesters and twenty-eight Whitleys – took off for Cologne, the target selected on the morning of the chosen day on the basis of the synoptic situation over Europe.

The attack, in three waves, was concentrated into ninety minutes, each crew being briefed to maintain its allocated place and height in the stream as accurately as was possible: Gee, with which about half the force was by now equipped, and with which navigators were becoming increasingly competent, proved an invaluable aid in this connection. Although unsatisfactory for blind-bombing, its precision over Britain and the approaches to Germany enabled the navigators to fix their position while within good range and so to calculate an accurate wind velocity with which to maintain track and timing closer in to the target. The aircraft in the first wave carried marker flares and a higher proportion of incendiary bombs than those following. The location of Cologne on the Rhine, with the bombers approaching from the north and following the broad river southward, made it comparatively easy for the bombs to be aimed by eye. The raid had been planned for the full-moon period, and crews in the second and third waves were able to see the burning city from many miles away and head directly towards it.

Statistics were, by standards hitherto attained, impressive. Nearly 900 of the aircraft that set off attacked the city, dropping over 460,000 incendiaries and 1,349 high-explosive bombs, mostly of 500 lb in weight. Incendiaries accounted for two-thirds of the total tonnage dropped: 13,000 homes – principally flats, because the proportion of flats to individual houses is high in Germany, particularly in large towns – were destroyed, while 30,000 suffered damage to some extent. Against these figures, the number of human casualties – about 480 killed and 5,000 injured – looks low and was no doubt to some extent influenced not only by the high proportion of incendiary to high-explosive bombs, but also by the fact that most German dwellings, and particularly the large apartment blocks, had substantial cellars that lent themselves to conversion into solid air-raid shelters.

In his planning Harris had reckoned with a possible five per cent loss rate. In fact forty-one aircraft, representing 3.9 per cent of the total force, failed to return. In human terms, Bomber Command lost well over 200 men, the majority of them killed.

In support of the attack on Cologne itself, thirty-four Blenheims of No. 2 Group, Bomber Command, plus sixteen Blenheims of Army Co-operation Command and seven Havoc night fighters of Fighter Command, were dispatched to attack enemy night-fighter bases in an attempt to hinder the German defensive effort against the bombers. Although these operations were not very effective, they were the first steps on an ever-increasing policy of intruder activity in support of Bomber Command, a policy that would eventually represent a very considerable thorn in the flesh of the *Luftwaffe*.

The Cologne raid succeeded in its immediate operational aims; in addition it was an enormous propaganda success not only at home, where the figure of one thousand understandably caught the imagination of the public and gave a powerful boost to the morale of the man in the street, but also in the United States, where planning for American participation in the air war against Germany was under way. Harris's gamble, it has frequently been said, had paid off. But to talk in terms of gambling is to underestimate the ability and achievements of Harris and his staff. At last someone saw the problems of aerial bombing clearly and was confronting them logically and without the quixotic detachment from reality that had, until his arrival on the scene, characterised those in charge. Guidelines were at last being set for the use of the blunt weapon, the bomber, and those guidelines would serve, with constant modifications and refinements, until Germany was conquered. The German people would suffer terribly, and the RAF bomber crews would demonstrate singular bravery and incur appalling losses. Let no one decry their effort, nor that of Harris in his use of the weapon given to him. But at the same time let no one decry the valour and the tenacity of the German night-fighter men who defended their homeland and their people against the terror visited upon them by British bombers.

While Harris's thousand-force was still *in situ* on its operational airfields another nominal thousand-bomber raid was mounted two nights later, this time against Essen. The city lived up to its reputation as a target of extreme difficulty: 956 bombers were sent out, but industrial haze and layered cloud made the aiming points extremely difficult for the crews to find, despite the use of a higher proportion of flares than had been used on the Cologne raid. Given the size of Harris's force, the results were petty, only eleven houses in Essen being destroyed and fifteen people being killed there. Bombs were scattered over the Ruhr area, with Oberhausen and Duisburg, among the eleven or more other towns hit, suffering more heavily than Essen itself.

In a final thousand-bomber attack at this period, 1,067 bombers set out for Bremen during the night of 25/26 June. This time, at Churchill's insistence, aircraft of Coastal Command participated. The city was badly damaged, though not as severely as Cologne had been just over three weeks previously; whereas the skies had been comparatively clear over Cologne, those over Bremen were cloud-covered, which meant that bombers in waves other than the first one had to aim through the cloud at the glow of fires started by the leading aircraft, which were *Gee*-equipped and carried a high proportion of incendiary bombs. Nevertheless, the concentration of the attack was unsatisfactory. Just as had happened even at Cologne, the German authorities at first refused to believe that anything approaching one thousand bombers had participated. Indeed, they estimated that the fifty-two bombers they claimed as destroyed represented more than half the attacking force and that the British claim that there had been a thousand bombers was a propaganda device designed to minimise the proportion lost. In fact the number missing was fifty-five, representing 4.9 per cent of the total number of aircraft operating that night, including those despatched on intruder raids in support of the main attack.

The three thousand-bomber raids had cost the RAF 127 aircraft and roughly 700 trained men. The *Nachtjagd* had accounted for more than half of the bombers destroyed. Exact figures are not available, but it seems that on the Cologne raid twenty-three of the forty-one bombers lost had fallen to the cannon and machine-guns of the *Luftwaffe* night-fighters, predominantly Bf 110s. On the Bremen raid one *Gruppe* alone, II./NJG 2, commanded by Helmut Lent and flying from Leeuwarden, shot down sixteen. It is significant that the aircraft of II./NJG 2 were by this time mostly equipped with *Lichtenstein* interception radar. The *Jägerleitoffizier* of I./NJG 1 from Venlo, Walter Knickmeier, controlled Oberleutnant Knacke in successful interceptions against a Blenheim intruder, a Stirling and a Wellington; and also under his control Oberleutnant Loos destroyed a Halifax. While in the bombers the flickering cathode-ray tubes of Gee were helping the Bomber Command navigators to find their target with some improvement in accuracy, and also to achieve greater concentration on their way to and over the target itself, those in the Messerschmitts were enabling their radar operators, the *Funker*, to direct their pilots close enough to the bombers to bring the murderous power of their forward-firing guns to bear.

Kammhuber's defensive system had been progressively designed to cope with attackers arriving singly on a broad front and over a comparatively extended period of time. Now the Bomber Command machines, thanks to Gee and Harris's new policy of concentration in space and time, were coming in on a narrower front and in more rapid sequence. This 'streaming', as it came to be called, meant that fewer night-fighter areas were being penetrated by a greater number of bombers than previously. Because only one fighter was normally deployed in each area at any one time, this in turn dictated that while the fighter controller and the fighter were busy attempting to intercept one bomber, others were able to pass through the area unchallenged. The inflexibility of the system also meant that while there were rich pickings for individual *Gruppen*, other units had to remain on the ground at stand-by, unable to be brought into action unless a bomber strayed into their dedicated control area. While the advent of *Lichtenstein* made it easier for individual fighters to destroy bombers, the way in which the system had developed rendered it impossible for his force, by this time numerically very strong, to be used to its maximum potential, a situation that caused much frustration to the aircrew themselves – except of course to those belonging to *Gruppen* conveniently located in control areas on the 'main road' to regular Bomber Command targets – and led them to criticise the system and wonder whether some form of freelance operation might be more effective. Such a system would eventually emerge, but not for a long time yet, and even then only when sophisticated changes in the tactics and technology employed by Bomber Command exposed the fundamental vulnerabilities of Kammhuber's organisation and forced changes upon him.

In the meantime, however, the installation of *Lichtenstein* in a growing number of fighters, the acceptance of it by the aircrew and their increasing proficiency in its use were having their effect on Bomber Command's losses. Twenty major night raids were mounted against Germany in the months of June and July 1942, and 307 bombers were destroyed, representing 4.9 per cent of the attacking force. Against a Bomber Command total of 370 losses from all night raids, including minor ones, the *Nachtjagd* claimed 224 kills. The overall impression that new radar generated on the leadership was enhanced by the fact that these kills were shared by a comparatively small number of night-fighter units, those whose defended areas the bombers had penetrated. The efficiency of the *Dunaja* system when a bomber entered one of the fighter control areas can be illustrated by a typical success scored by Hauptmann Streib of I./NJG 1, controlled by Oberleutnant Knickmeier, in the early hours of 3 June 1942, when he shot down a Wellington, one of the force of 197 bombers with Essen as their target.

Knickmeier picked up a target for Streib in *Raum* 5B, between Venlo and Eindhoven, at 0123 hrs on 3 June. Within fourteen minutes Streib had destroyed the bomber.

Imagine the scene. In the control post Knickmeier has in front of him a *Seeburgtisch*, a plotting table on the ground-glass surface of which, projected from below, he can see two dots of coloured light, one red to indicate the position of a hostile bomber, one green representing the fighter he is controlling. (A word of clarification is necessary: although the Würzburg Giant following the fighter was still known as the *blaue Riese*, the light projected from beneath on to the ground-glass screen of the plotting table was in fact green.) These positions are being reported by tellers directly from two separate Würzburg Giant radars, the 'Red Giant' and the 'Blue Giant' (*roter Riese* and *blauer Riese*) respectively. Plotters around the *Seeburgtisch* are using coloured wax pencils to draw in the track of both bomber and fighter as the positions change, so giving the controller a picture of the progress of the interception. Although, depending on the efficiency of the tellers and plotters, the picture that Knickmeier sees is a short time out of date, the relative positions of bomber and fighter are tolerably accurate.

There is a good working relationship between Oberleutnant Knickmeier and Hauptmann Streib. Knickmeier is acknowledged to be the most expert fighter controller of NJG 1. He already has twenty-six successful interceptions to his credit, of which Streib has been the victorious pilot on six occasions. Streib is one of the leading aces of the *Nachtjagd*: in 1941 alone he shot down twenty-two bombers. The R/T conversation between fighter controller and pilot is economical, because the pilot also has his *Funker*'s commentary to listen to, and it is conducted in code words. Knickmeier's information and instructions to Streib are clipped, Streib's replies laconic, limited mainly to a curt '*Viktor*', the equivalent of the English language '*Roger*'. Streib is circling in his Bf 110. The British bomber stream is approaching from the west. Knickmeier, having selected a target, judges that it will pass to the south of Streib, so he turns him on to a southerly heading. What follows is taken directly from the fighter controller's assistant's original log, and explanatory comment is interspersed:

0123 hrs	Knickmeier:	*Antreten 170*	Steer 170 degrees Magnetic.
		Tampen 160	Alter course to 160.
		Kirchturm 4,300	Target height 4,300 metres.
0124 hrs	Knickmeier:	*Fahren Sie Express*	Increase speed.
	Streib:	*Viktor, Viktor*	Roger, Roger.
0125 hrs	Knickmeier:	*Kirchturm 4,300*	Target height 4,300 metres.

Knickmeier, sensing that on this heading Streib will pass behind his target, tells him to turn to the left. ('*Lisa*' is the R/T code word for 'turn ten degrees to port': '*Zweimal*' means 'twice'.)

	Knickmeier:	*Zweimal Lisa*	Turn twenty degrees port.
	Streib:	*Viktor*	Roger.
0126 hrs	Knickmeier:	*Einmal Lisa*	Turn ten degrees port.
	Streib:	*Viktor*	Roger.
	Knickmeier:	*Marie 9*	Target range nine kilometres.
	Streib:	*Viktor*	Roger.

0127 hrs	Knickmeier:	*Kirchturm 4,200*	Target height 4,200 metres.
	Streib:	*Viktor*	Roger.
		Frage Marie	Query target range.
0128 hrs	Knickmeier:	*Marie 8*	Target range eight kilometres.
	Streib:	*Viktor*	Roger.
	Knickmeier:	*Einmal Lisa*	Ten degrees port.
	Streib:	*Viktor*	Roger.
	Knickmeier:	*Einmal Lisa*	Ten degrees port.
	Streib:	*Viktor*	Roger.

As the target passes ahead of the fighter, controller Knickmeier is turning Streib ten degrees at a time. These instructions come in rapid sequence, resulting in a gentle turn by the fighter aimed at bringing him out behind the bomber and heading in the same direction.

0129 hrs	Knickmeier:	*Marie 5.5*	Target range 5.5 km.
	Streib:	*Viktor*	Roger.
	Knickmeier:	*Einmal Lisa*	Ten degrees port.
	Streib:	*Viktor*	Roger.
	Knickmeier:	*Einmal Lisa*	Ten degrees port.
		Marie 4,5	Range 4.5 kilometres.
	Streib:	*Viktor*	Roger.
	Knickmeier:	*Einmal Lisa*	Ten degrees port.
		Marie 4	Range four kilometres.
	Streib:	*Viktor*	Roger.
0130 hrs	Knickmeier:	*Marie 2!*	Target range two kilometres!

At this range the radar operator in the Messerschmitt should be able to identify the blips on his minute *Lichtenstein* screens that represent the Wellington. In the RAF machine the crew members are performing their individual tasks. The pilot is steering the aircraft, maintaining the course given to him by his navigator. The wireless operator is listening out for broadcasts from England: he does not transmit over enemy territory. The navigator is possibly, like the Streib's *Funker*, also concentrating on a green radar screen, in his case that of the Gee equipment. Gee is heavily jammed, but it is just possible that he might be able to make out a good signal amongst the 'grass' on the tube. The bomb aimer is peering downward, hoping to find a visual fix to help the navigator with his calculations. The two gunners, one in the front turret and one in the rear turret, are scanning the sky for either night-fighters or other friendly bombers. But Streib's black-painted Bf 110, being below, will merge into the darkness of the ground beneath. Knickmeier senses that the fighter is passing ahead of the target, and tells Streib to slow down a little.

Knickmeier:	*Halten!*	Decrease speed!
Streib:	*Viktor*	Roger.
Knickmeier:	*Zweimal Rolf!*	Twenty degrees starboard!
Streib:	*Viktor*	Roger.
Knickmeier:	*Halten!*	Decrease speed!
Streib:	*Viktor*	Roger
Knickmeier:	*Noch mehr halten!*	Slow down still more!

It becomes clear to Knickmeier that despite slowing down Streib has overshot his target. He therefore tells him to do a complete left-hand turn, hoping that this will then bring him out behind the bomber.

0131 hrs	Knickmeier:	*Salto Lisa!*	Turn 360° port!
	Streib:	*Viktor.*	Roger.
	Knickmeier:	*Antreten 150*	Steer 150.
	Streib:	*Viktor*	Roger.
	Knickmeier:	*Marie 4*	Target range four kilometres.
	Streib	*Viktor*	Roger.
	Knickmeier:	*Marie 3*	Range three kilometres.
0132 hrs		*Zweimal Lisa!*	Twenty degrees port!
		Halten!	Slow down!
		Zweimal Lisa!	Twenty degrees port!
		Marie 2.5	Range 2.5 kilometres.
		Antreten 110	Steer 110.
0133 hrs		*Marie 2.5*	Range 2.5 kilometres.
	Streib:	*Viktor*	Roger.

Streib has not responded to some of these recent instructions. Possibly he is listening to his *Funker*. Everything is happening very fast. If the *Funker* gets a radar contact, the code word to report that would be '*Emil Emil!*', but it is not forthcoming. Possibly this is just an oversight on Streib's part, possibly the *Funker* has not found the target.

	Knickmeier:	*Kirchturm 4,100*	Target height 4,100 metres.
		Marie 2!	Range two!
0133 hrs		*Kirchturm 4,100*	Target height 4,100 metres.
0134 hrs		*Marie 1!*	Range one!
		Genau vor Ihnen!	Dead ahead of you!
		Sie sind dicht bei Kurier!	You're right on top of the bomber!
0136 hrs	Streib:	*Ich berühre!*	I have visual contact!
		Bitte warten!	Please wait!
0137 hrs		*Sieg Heil!*	Bomber destroyed!

The Wellington is now another statistic among Bomber Command losses. In all probability the six-man crew are dead or dying. Streib is one night-time victory nearer to the sixty-five that he will finally achieve before the end of the war.

The gathering success of the *Nachtjagd* with the advent of *Lichtenstein* and the improvement in close-control procedures had an unforeseen, and at first sight seemingly adverse, outcome on Kammhuber's defence against the RAF's nightly visits. In building up his vast *helle Gürtel* Kammhuber had progressively robbed German towns and cities of their searchlights, much to the displeasure of the *Gauleiter* of cities that had suffered the attentions of the RAF, and they had therefore made representations at the highest level, to Adolf Hitler himself, to have them restored. From the date of the thousand-bomber raid on Cologne there had been a gradual withdrawal of searchlights from the Kammhuber Line to strengthen the point defence of cities, and with effect from 31 July 1942 the order was given to disband the searchlight units operating in the *helle Gürtel* completely. *Henaja*, until a short time before the most successful method of night fighting, was no more. In the event, however, the arbitrary withdrawal of the searchlights was rapidly turned to the advantage of the fighters.

As the searchlight belt had been developed, permanent or semi-permanent control posts had been built in each of the twenty-seven areas that went to make up its 800-kilometre length, and in each area there were two *Würzburg-Riese* radars. Kammhuber retained these control posts and their *Riesen* and converted each *Henaja* area into a *Dunaja* area, with one of the Würzburg Giants acting as *blauer Riese* and the other as *roter Riese*, thus replacing the searchlight barrier with an even more formidable close-control barrier, and because each *Riese* covered a circular area of about sixty kilometres radius that barrier was deeper than the former searchlight barrier had been. The 'red' and 'blue' procedure, now standardised, was christened the *Himmelbettverfahren,* or, for no apparent reason, the 'four-poster bed system'. As the war progressed very many more Würzburg Giants were deployed throughout Germany, so that almost the whole of the country and the occupied territories in the west was eventually covered with overlapping *Himmelbett* areas and it was virtually impossible for a British bomber to penetrate the area without being picked up and risking having a fighter vectored on to it.

The months of June, July and August 1942 showed a very marked increase in the number of British bombers destroyed by the *Nachtjagd*. Whereas from January to May that year the average number of kills had been just over thirty-four per month, in the following three months they averaged 116. This was, of course, to some extent due to the fact that in the better weather of the summer the RAF were mounting many more attacks, but even so the growing impact of German night-fighters could not be overlooked. In 1942, up to and including May, Bomber Command had dispatched a total of 12,029 sorties, of which the *Nachtjagd* had shot down 167. Total RAF losses during the period were 396, of which the night-fighters' share represented forty-two per cent. In the following three months, up to and including August, Bomber Command sent out 11,169 sorties and the fighters claimed 349, a 65.7 per cent share of those missing.

The effect of the growing ability on the part of the German night-fighter crews to find and destroy their enemies can also be discerned from a consideration of the gradual increase in the proportion of Bomber Command aircraft failing to return from night raids against the Third Reich. In the winter period 1941/42 average losses had been 2.5 per cent; from February to May 1942 the figure had risen to 3.7 per cent. From June onwards there was a further marked increase, with the mean hovering around the five per cent mark, the maximum average over a period which, it was calculated, would ensure that supplies of aircraft and crews could maintain the strength and striking power of the Command. On an ominous number of occasions losses went far beyond the acceptable norm. An attack on Hamburg on 28/29 July resulted in 11.7 per cent of the force of 256 bombers failing to return; in the raid on Kassel on 27/28 August it was 10.1 per cent of 306; against Nuremberg the following night it was 14.5 per cent of the 159 bombers dispatched; and on 16/17 September 10.6 per cent of 369.

It is perhaps of contextual value to ponder a moment on the implication of loss percentages in terms of the individual aircrew member. A tour of operations was set at thirty, after which a man would be 'screened' – posted to a non-operational job, most frequently in an instructional capacity. If the average of losses during his tour was one per cent, he ran a thirty per cent risk of being shot down, so that the odds would be ten to three in favour of his escaping either death or imprisonment. The number who came out of a shot-down bomber alive was far lower than that of those who perished, so death was the more likely outcome. Average losses of two per cent meant that the chances of survival were less than evens – ten to six. At a loss rate of 3.3 per cent, there was mathematically no chance of survival, and those lucky enough to keep coming back were living on borrowed time. The losses in the final months of the year, which were verging on the prohibitive, did however accompany a marked improvement in target-finding and bombing accuracy.

For Bomber Command the final quarter of 1942 was a period of some easing of the growing operational pressure generated by the strategic attack on Germany. Beginning on the night of 22/23 October and continuing until 11/12 December, Harris mounted a series of fourteen night attacks against the north Italian targets of Genoa, Milan and Turin, plus one daylight attack against Turin, in support of operations in North Africa, where Montgomery's Eighth Army defeated Rommel's *Afrika Korps* in the Second Battle of El Alamein and where November saw Operation 'Torch', the landing of the Allied Expeditionary Force. In the same period there were only five major attacks by night against Germany. Because the bomber stream could fly most of the way over occupied territory rather than over the *Reich* itself, thus bypassing the Kammhuber Line, casualties on the raids against Italy were significantly lower than on those against Germany, amounting to only thirty-one aircraft out of the total of 1,752 that took part, or 1.8 per cent overall. To some small extent these operations against Italy were also an opportunity for the recently formed Pathfinder Force to practise and develop its techniques.

The way in which the Pathfinders came about and the way in which their leader was selected are not without interest, providing insight as they do into facets of Commander-in-Chief Harris's character. The need for some method of combining the efforts of individual pilots and crews in order to inflict maximum damage on the enemy had long been perceived, and while considerable hope had rested on Gee and other electronic devices that were under active development – Oboe, discussed above, and H2S – it was generally accepted that although such systems could, in ideal circumstances, increase the efficiency of individual crews, a means of ensuring visually that the correct target was hit in adequate concentration was needed. A start had been made during the trials of Gee when long-burning illuminating flares had been dropped to mark practice targets in Britain and later when, in February 1942 and under the code word 'Shaker', the technique had been extended to light up objectives such as Essen so that follow-up crews would have a clearly defined target on which to drop their missiles; first incendiaries to mark the target specifically and then high-explosive bombs to create maximum structural damage.

One of the foremost advocates of what first came to be referred to as a Target-Finding Force was the Deputy Director of Bomber Operations at the Air Ministry, Group Captain S. O. 'Sid' Bufton, an officer of considerable operational and command experience and an advocate of precision bombing. The concept also had the backing of Lord Cherwell who, of course, had the ear of

Churchill. It is sometimes claimed that the Target-Finding Force was in fact Cherwell's own brain-child, but in fact Cherwell toyed with many ideas, some good and many somewhat wild, and to attribute what was in fact a widely discussed concept to him alone would be wrong: nevertheless, he was a powerful man, and his support was invaluable. Harris, on the other hand, was initially strongly opposed to the idea. Bufton suggested that target-finding crews should be selected on the basis of their operational experience and proven efficiency and formed into a specialist force. In essence, for the argument was heated and many-sided, Harris stubbornly opposed the formation of a *corps d'élite* in the belief that it would adversely affect the morale, and thus the operational effectiveness, of the remainder of Bomber Command squadrons and crews. Nor, in general, did the concept find much support from Group Commanders, who did not much like the idea of their best crews being taken from them. Surprisingly, too, Harris seems to have been satisfied by the way in which the bomber offensive under his command was developing. He noted, he said, that the Shaker technique had led to the majority of his force's bombs landing usefully in built-up areas of the Ruhr. Even Harris was not immune to wishful thinking, and, dedicated as he was to area bombing, he tended to be dismissive, even scornful, of ideas such as that propagated by Bufton that seemed to be furthering the concept of precision bombing. This aspect of Harris's personality would come increasingly apparent as the war progressed, particularly in his intolerance with what he called 'panacea targets' – targets imposed upon him in directives and by bodies such as the Ministry of Economic Warfare with which he happened not to agree. That is not to say that in such cases Harris was wrong: on the contrary, his undoubted single-mindedness and instinct for what was possible and likely to be effective were, with hindsight, more often than not correct. But in the matter of the Target-Finding Force experience would show that his objections were ill-founded.

By June 1942 – the argument had begun in about March the same year – Harris had given ground to the extent of accepting that there might be 'raid leaders' within individual squadrons, but he was still resisting the formation of a separate force. At Air Ministry, however, Bufton's arguments and those of his supporters had attracted the support of the Air Staff, and in particular that of the chief of that body, Marshal of the Royal Air Force Sir Charles Portal. Portal wrote to Harris 'suggesting' that a separate target-finding force should be created. Even the tenacious and frequently intractable Harris could not lightly ignore a suggestion from the supreme authority on the RAF: it may, indeed, well be that he was already half-convinced of the logic of what Bufton and others were advocating but that his ingrained recalcitrance prevented him from taking a step that others might perceive as surrender. Whatever the truth of the matter, Harris accepted Portal's suggestion, and he did so gracefully: and having done so he gave the proposal his unstinted support. Nevertheless, he imposed his authority on the creation of the special force in a number of ways, some minor but one of major and decisive significance.

The official directive from the Air Staff formalising Portal's suggestion reached Harris on 11 August 1942. Among Harris's smaller initiatives was his insistence that the new force should be called the 'Pathfinder Force' rather than 'Target-Finding Force': his major one was the selection of a commander for PFF, as it came to be known.

It would have seemed natural for Harris to give the responsibility for inaugurating and operating PFF to one of his Group Commanders. Instead he selected a comparatively lowly officer, Wing Commander Donald C. T. Bennett, the commander of No. 10 Squadron, which was operating Halifaxes from Leeming in North Yorkshire. Bennett was an outstanding aviator, already a legendary figure in the world of flying. Of Australian birth, he had trained as a pilot in the RAF in the mid-nineteen-thirties. After his short-service commission had expired he had become a senior captain with Imperial Airways, later the British Overseas Airways Corporation, and had, among other things in a short but wide-ranging career, flown *Mercury*, the four-engined upper component of the Short Mayo Composite, a seaplane riding piggyback on a flying boat; also in *Mercury* he had set up a world long-distance seaplane record, and he had piloted the flying boat inaugurating the first regular Imperial Airways two-way transatlantic service. Bennett was skilled not only as a pilot, but also in navigation, signalling and aircraft engineering. He was the author of a book, *The Complete Air Navigator.* His service with British Overseas Airways had lasted until July 1940, when he had joined a body of pilots ferrying aircraft from the United States to Great Britain. He had re-entered the RAF with the acting rank of Wing Commander and the job of assistant commander of a school of air navigation.

Unhappy with a non-operational job, Bennett had made representations at Bomber Command that resulted in his taking command of No. 77 Squadron, 4 Group. No. 77 Squadron was equipped with Whitleys at the time, and Bennett lost no time in going on operations himself as often as he could, taking a different crew each night and thus checking the capabilities of individual crews and also that of his squadron. His experiences on operations had impressed him unfavourably: he saw the bomber offensive for the inaccurate, unco-ordinated effort that it was, and he had persistently represented his views to the Directorate of Bomber Operations, during which period he had been among those advocating a target-finding force. In April 1942 Bennett had taken over No. 10 Squadron, also in No. 4 Group, equipped with the four-engined Halifax. On the night of the twenty-seventh of the same month he had been shot down when flying a Halifax attacking the German battleship *Tirpitz* in Trondheim, Norway, but had managed to return to England within five weeks or so after successfully finding his way to neutral Sweden.

It has been said that Bennett was an arrogant man. The word has an unfortunate connotation, and it might be more correct to describe him as intolerant of those whose standards of professionalism did not match his own; and because his own standards were so very high, that meant the majority of his RAF peers and superiors. He was very clear-sighted, and once he had decided upon a course of action he pursued it with dedication, dynamism, even ruthlessness, the same qualities that Harris was bringing to bear on the bomber offensive as a whole. Harris's choice of Bennett as commander of the Pathfinders was nothing but inspired. It is hard to think of any other senior officer of the RAF at that time who would have done the job nearly as well as he did: nor, incidentally, is it easy to think of one who would have earned the respect and devotion of the crews that flew with PFF – or, indeed, with Bomber Command as a whole – to the extent that Bennett did, because the aircrew knew that not only was Bennett capable of doing their own jobs as well as, if not better than, they themselves could, but they also knew that, unlike many officers in senior command positions, Bennett frequently flew operationally himself, leading by example and from the front.

Harris gave Bennett the acting rank of Group Captain and, within certain limits, *carte blanche* in selecting, in consultation with Group Commanders, the squadrons and crews that would form PFF and the stations at which they would be based. Bennett was to have one squadron each of Lancasters, Halifaxes, Stirlings and Wellingtons, plus a special squadron for using Oboe, the blind-bombing device described earlier. A tour of operations for PFF crews would be twice that for the rest of Bomber Command – sixty operations – which meant that the chances of survival were very slight indeed. To mark the specialist status of PFF flyers, each man would, after a certain number of operations, be promoted by one rank and become entitled to wear a special badge, a bronze eagle, below his medal ribbons.

At the time of Bennett's appointment to the command of PFF Gee was in wide use in the Command, but the Germans were on the threshold of jamming it, while Oboe was in an advanced stage of development. Another radar aid also arriving on the scene offered the eventual prospect of improved navigation by individual crews. It was called H2S.

The concept of H2S had derived from work on AI, and at its heart was the cavity magnetron, an ahead-of-its-time device that enabled very powerful pulses of electromagnetic energy to be transmitted at a very short wavelength. H2S used a small dish aerial that rotated about once per second and was housed in a plastic blister beneath the fuselage of the aircraft. In the navigator's position inside the aircraft was a CRT, but instead of a horizontal or vertical time-base it had a rotating one, rather like the hand of a clock, that went round in synchronism with the aerial. The transmitted pulses of energy travelled outward until they hit the surface of the earth, when they were reflected. If they hit a smooth patch of earth or water, they bounced off the surface and went out into space: if they hit a rough surface – perhaps trees, hills or so on – part of the energy was reflected and came back to the H2S aerial in the bomber, causing a slight 'bright-up' on the rotating time base. Because the screen was coated internally with a substance that retained the glow for a short time, a series of such echoes in one area appeared to the navigator's eye as a bright spot or blob, 'painted' by successive rotations. An area on the ground that contained vertical surfaces – towns, villages, large factories and so on, reflected the majority of the transmitted pulses of energy, causing an even brighter echo on the CRT. This type of radar presentation is known as a Plan Position Indicator (PPI), and will nowadays be very familiar to most readers. In 1942 it was a comparatively new idea, and when used in H2S it provided the navigator with a rough map of the terrain over which he was flying. It was particularly useful in showing coastlines and areas of water such as broad rivers and large lakes. Though not intrinsically as accurate as Gee and Oboe , it had the priceless advantage over those systems of being self-contained within a single aircraft and thus independent of range from a base; furthermore, it could not be jammed by the enemy. It was not an easy gadget to use, and operators needed a certain amount of practice before they became efficient with it. Its potential as an aid to navigation, and especially to blind bombing, was exciting.

THE PRINCIPLE OF H2S

A small aerial, or "scanner" in a plastic housing beneath the fuselage rotated about once a second and transmitted very-high-frequency impulses. Depending on the nature of the terrain below, a varying amount of the radio energy was reflected and picked up by the same aerial.

Aerial-housing

The reflected impulses were then made visible on the navigator's Plan-Position Indicator (PPI) in the form of a rudimentary map of the surface beneath the aircraft, as shown below in the left-hand column. The rotating time-base seen to the right of the PPI was in synchronism with the scanner, while the fixed line shown to the left indicated the aircraft's heading. The diagrams show respectively an aircraft heading west over the sea, approaching the coast, and over the land:

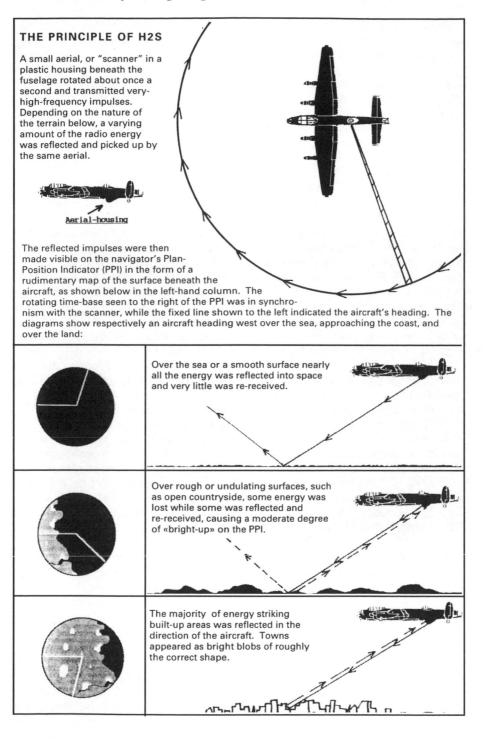

Over the sea or a smooth surface nearly all the energy was reflected into space and very little was re-received.

Over rough or undulating surfaces, such as open countryside, some energy was lost while some was reflected and re-received, causing a moderate degree of «bright-up» on the PPI.

The majority of energy striking built-up areas was reflected in the direction of the aircraft. Towns appeared as bright blobs of roughly the correct shape.

Bomber Command was taking on a new look. It had a dynamic leader with clear ideas about the way in which the force should be used, and it had an equally dynamic officer of brilliant ingenuity, expertise and powers of leadership whose task it was to create a mechanism to direct that force to its targets. Newer, more potent types of bomber were gradually replacing the obsolescent types with which Bomber Command crews had so far been going into battle, and revolutionary modern electronic aids to navigation were emerging.

When Harris instructed Bennett to form a Pathfinder Force, Bennett lost no time whatsoever in setting about the task. He spoke with Group Commanders, and with Harris's authority behind him – for as a Group Captain he was much junior to the Air Vice-Marshals commanding Groups – he persuaded them of the potential of PFF and, with no little difficulty in certain cases, to let him have some of their squadrons and crews. He selected Wyton in Cambridgeshire as his headquarters because it had a very good weather record, and Oakington, Gravely and Warboys as other bases for his bombers. PFF began with five squadrons: No. 7 Squadron (Oakington) was equipped with Stirlings; No. 35 Squadron (Gravely) with Halifaxes; No. 83 Squadron (Wyton) with Lancasters; and No. 156 Squadron (Warboys) with Wellingtons. Bennett's fifth squadron, No. 109, was the squadron he proposed to use for target-marking by means of Oboe, and it too went to Wyton. No. 109 was a specialist squadron, having been used by TRE for the development of Oboe, and when Bennett took it under his wing it was equipped with a pressurised version of the Wellington bomber capable of operating at heights of more than 30,000 feet.

While involving himself in the daunting administrative and representational work necessary to launch PFF, Bennett took part personally in advancing H2S and Oboe from the developmental stage to the operational, flying with the TRE aircraft testing H2S and with No. 109 Squadron testing Oboe.

PFF squadrons assembled at their allocated airfields on 17 August 1942, six short weeks after Bennett's appointment. Harris instructed that they should operate the same night, but weather caused the cancellation of operations so that the first attack led by PFF took place on the following night, the eighteenth. The target was the submarine base at Flensburg, located on an inlet on the Baltic coast of the Schleswig-Holstein peninsula and just south of the Danish border. PFF had no radar aids functioning, nor were they yet equipped with special target-indicator bombs, so they had to rely on standard magnesium flares suspended from parachutes. The raid was a complete failure, the perennial problems of DR navigation and unassisted target finding occurring yet again. Half the thirty-one PFF crews committed claimed to have marked the target, and seventy-eight of the eighty-seven main force crews claimed to have bombed it. In the event Flensburg escaped any damage whatsoever, while two towns in Denmark, Sönderborg and Abenra, well to the north-east and north respectively, reported being bombed; but even that bombing was scattered. Four bombers failed to return, including one from PFF.

Nor was the attack against Frankfurt six nights later an improvement, most of the bombs from the 226 aircraft falling well to the west of the target. Losses were high, amounting to sixteen aircraft, among them five PFF machines. Over a tenth of the 306 bombers sent to Kassel on 27/28 August failed to return, many of them falling to night-fighters. Losses of that magnitude could not be long sustained. On the credit side, the skies over the target were clear, and the raid was more concentrated, so that the bombers following up were able to aim by the light of PFF flares and so carry out a moderately successful attack. Another attack the following night, on Nuremberg, also achieved some success, but then, on 1/2 September, a raid was mounted that again focused attention on the continuing hit-or-miss nature of night bombing, even with a specialist force as a spearhead. A total of 231 bombers set out for Saarbrücken, located, as its name applies, in the Saarland near the border between Germany and France. The Pathfinders found and marked a town, which a total of 205 crews claimed to have bombed accurately. The town that PFF marked, however, was not Saarbrücken but a different, much smaller, town fifteen kilometres to the north-west, Saarlouis. One of the reasons for the faulty target finding was undoubtedly the fact that Gee, with which the majority of Bomber Command aircraft were by now equipped, was by now heavily jammed.

While waiting for Oboe and H2S to become operationally available, and while exerting all his efforts to ensure that they should do so, Bennett also concentrated on the way in which targets, once found, could be marked pyrotechnically to provide an aiming point for the follow-up bomber crews. Experience had shown in the clearest possible way that long-burning parachute flares were unsatisfactory. In addition, the Germans had introduced, with considerable success, dummy targets, areas of open countryside or marshland in which fires could be ignited and anti-aircraft guns sited to simulate real towns and so attract the attention of RAF bomber crews away from the real thing. What was needed was some form of bombs or flares that would provide colours, on the ground or in the air, so distinctive that Main Force crews might reasonably be expected to aim at them to the exclusion of other lights or conflagrations. Stimulated by Bennett, the Aircraft and Armament Experimental Establishment at Boscombe Down produced 'Red Blob' by filling the case of the standard 250 lb 'Bomb Incendiary' with a mixture of benzol, rubber, phosphorus and suitable dyestuffs, a long-burning mixture producing a distinctive shade of red. This was the first of the Target Indicators, or TIs, as the markers came to be known. Red Blob was first used in the comparatively successful attack on Nuremberg on 28/29 August. Also conceived at this time was a larger TI, 'Pink Pansy', a converted 4,000 lb HC bomb case that gave an instantaneous pink flash and was used to indicate the location of the target to crews, but which did not, as Red Blob did, provide an aiming point. The first Pink Pansy was dropped on Düsseldorf from an 83 Squadron Lancaster on the night of 10/11 September. This, a heavy attack, was probably the most successful PFF-led raid to date, but once more the price was high, further evidence of the growing strength and capability of the night fighters. Over seven per cent of the force of 479 bombers was lost, which represented thirty-three machines and well over 200 men.

Just less than a week before the Düsseldorf raid the port of Bremen had been hit hard by 251 bombers, 153 four-engined aircraft and ninety-eight Wellingtons. For the Bremen raid Bennett had experimentally split his PFF force into three waves: so-called 'illuminators' went in first and lit up the target area with long-burning white flares; they were followed by 'visual markers' who, as the name indicates, dropped coloured TIs on specific aiming points; and finally, 'backers-up', who dropped all-incendiary loads on to the coloured markers.

Results achieved during the remainder of the year were inevitably mixed, but there was no doubt that now, at last, Bomber Command was emerging from the shadows. The Harris/Bennett combination was proving formidable, to say the least. On 20/21 December Squadron Leader H. E. Bufton of No. 109 Squadron, the brother of the influential 'Sid' Bufton at Air Ministry, dropped the first Oboe-aimed bombs used operationally, a happening of not inconsiderable significance in the development of the strategic bomber offensive. The raid was an experimental, and not enormously successful, one and the target was a power station at Lutterade in Holland. What was possibly even more significant than the introduction of Oboe into the battle was the fact that the aircraft used was not a pressurised Wellington, with which No. 109 Squadron had been equipped when Bennett formed PFF, but a Mosquito.

Unlike the bombers that made up Harris's striking force, the Mosquito was not originally designed to an Air Ministry specification. It was the concept of Geoffrey de Havilland of the de Havilland aircraft company and a descendant of a fast civil airliner of wooden construction, the 1937 DH 91 Albatross. De Havilland envisaged a twin-seat fighter-bomber made of special plywood which, unencumbered by the weight and air resistance of heavy gun-turrets, would, in the bomber role, rely for its defence on its ability to outclimb and outpace the opposition. Following informal discussions with Geoffrey de Havilland just after the outbreak of war in 1939, the Air Ministry, although not markedly enthusiastic, endorsed an experimental programme and issued a specification based on de Havilland's plans. The prototype Mosquito flew in November 1940 and a limited number were constructed; they showed remarkable promise, but still the Air Ministry were not converted, despite the fact that the performance of the machine was far superior to that of contemporary fighters. When Bennett founded PFF he was unhappy with the idea of using the slow, clumsy pressurised Wellingtons for the task of Oboe marking, and he eagerly accepted the opinion held by members of No. 109 Squadron that the Mosquito was a better prospect. It could climb higher and more quickly than the Wellington and was more than twice as fast at operating height. Bennett flew the machine and was delighted with every aspect of its performance. He then intervened directly with Air Ministry with the result that No. 109 Squadron was able to get rid of its Wellingtons and adopt the Mosquito. The Squadron continued to fly Oboe Mosquitos until the end of the war, and the remarkable invulnerability of the unarmed 'Wooden Wonder' to enemy flak and night-fighters is illustrated by the fact that from 5,421 sorties the Squadron lost only eighteen machines. As a comparison, another Pathfinder squadron, No. 156, made 4,238 sorties from the inauguration of PFF until the end of the war and lost 121 aircraft. In percentage terms this was between nine and ten times as high.

During the remainder of the month of December 1942 PFF Mosquitos, a maximum of five in a night, made a number of attacks on targets in the Ruhr, where Bomber Command had hitherto shown very poor results. Their bombs fell with remarkable precision. Bennett carried out an experimental attack on Düsseldorf on the last night of the year. Two Mosquitos went to the city, but due to a fault in the transmitting system in the UK – a gale had blown down one of the masts – only one aircraft was able to use Oboe. The follow-up force of eight PFF Lancasters bombed on sky markers. This was another 'first'. Previously the TIs that the Pathfinders had dropped had been ground markers, of little if any use in overcast conditions. In future the bombers would be able to bomb through ten-tenths cloud.

In 1940 the *Nachtjagd* had shot down a mere forty-two British bombers in defence of the Third *Reich*; in 1941 it had been ten times as many, 421; in 1942 the total was 687, a remarkable upsurge accompanying the arrival of *Lichtenstein* and the gradual introduction of the *Himmelbett* fighter control system. In the peak months of 1942, June, July, August and September, the night fighters' tally was 435. In one night, 16/17 September, one pilot, Hauptmann Knacke – he had been promoted – had shot down five RAF bombers during the costly attack on Essen. These figures were a chilling indication of the mounting efficiency of the night-fighting capability of the *Luftwaffe*. But for the Germans the portents were even more daunting. The threat posed by Bomber Command was consolidating, increasing. The bludgeon was being wielded less randomly, its blows falling more heavily and more tellingly.

On 22 November 1942 the Prime Minister had made a speech at the Mansion House in which he had spoken of the Eighth Army's success at El Alamein. 'This is not the end,' Churchill said. 'It is not even the beginning of the end. But it is, perhaps, the end of the beginning.' His words might possibly have been spoken even more appropriately about the Royal Air Force's strategic bomber offensive.

CHAPTER FIVE

The Turning Tide: Casablanca, the Ruhr and the Wild Boars

1943: The First Half

The year just ended had seen many changes, many developments in the equipment, tactics and techniques of the nocturnal bombing war. On the British side Bomber Command had discarded its disappointing Manchesters, its lumbering Whitleys and its inferior Hampdens, all aircraft that in truth were simply not up to the task of bombing Germany effectively. The Wellington, a much better all-round machine, still survived as the only twin-engined heavy bomber taking a direct part in the main offensive: it was, in fact, the most numerous single type on 1 January, with the Lancaster a close second, but it too was in the process of being replaced by four-engined aircraft. By February the front-line striking force that Harris could use at night comprised fifty-three squadrons in six Groups with a total of just under 1,000 aircraft, of which about 650 were four-engined Stirlings, Halifaxes and Lancasters and nine were Mosquitos for target-marking duties with the Pathfinder Force, which had been elevated to the status of No. 8 Group in January. Just two Whitleys survived in No. 4 Group, but would take no further part in the offensive.

It was not only in the field of bomb carriers that telling advances had been made. Bombs, too, had been improved and enlarged. The RAF had gone to war with explosive bombs that, if anything, were even more obsolescent than their aircraft, mainly the 250 lb and 500 lb general purpose (GP) bombs, which had their origins in the First World War and which proved in action to be only about half as efficient as the equivalent weapons used by the *Luftwaffe*. As far as incendiary bombs went, however, the RAF were much better placed, having a stock of something like 5,000,000 4 lb 'stick' incendiaries, highly efficient weapons, and factories had a production capacity of 60,000 per week. These missiles would continue to be used, in slightly modified forms, until the end of the war, by which time a staggering total of about 80,000,000 had been dropped on Germany. In the early stages of the bomber offensive the proportion of incendiaries to high explosives carried was comparatively small, so that their full potential was not realised, and the proportion had only begun to increase significantly in 1942 when Harris arrived on the scene and brought his ideas to bear.

The increasing awareness of the inefficiency of the high-explosive (HE) bombs that the RAF had at their disposal, the changing appreciation of the relative effectiveness of incendiary and HE bombs, and the advent of aircraft that could carry larger missiles and heavier loads had led to the design and production of bigger and better bombs. By 1941 GP bombs weighing 1,000 lb and 1,900 lb were in use, and towards the end of the same year production of 2,000 lb and 4,000 lb

HC (high capacity) bombs had begun. The HC bombs were essentially designed to explode on the surface, rather than after penetration, and therefore to create a blast that would destroy buildings. The 4,000 lb version attracted the nickname 'Cookie', and was widely used throughout the war, in the course of which over 68,000 were dropped by Bomber Command in both instantaneous and delayed-action versions. It was first used in an attack on Emden during the night of 31 March/1 April 1942. There was also a 'Super Cookie' weighing 8,000 lb, two 4,000 lb explosive cylinders bolted together and fitted with a tail unit. Contrary to popular belief, the Super Cookie was not two Cookies in tandem; the cylinders of which it was made had a diameter of 38in against the 30in of the Cookie. Only the bomb bays of the Lancaster and the Halifax would accept this monstrous weapon, those of the Wellington and the Stirling being too small. The first one was dropped from a Halifax during the attack on Essen on 10/11 April 1942. In addition, bigger incendiary bombs had been produced, with a 30 lb phosphorus version coming into service late in 1941. There were also less successful incendiaries weighing 50 lb, 250 lb and even more, but the 4 lb bomb, carried and dropped in small 'cluster' containers that opened in the air after release, would remain by far the most used fire-raiser.

Progress was also being made with electronic navigational aids, if not as quickly as many – and in particular Bennett – would have wished. Gee, although still extremely valuable in the early stages of an operation and when returning to base, had become a much diminished asset over the Continent as soon as the Germans had discovered how to jam it. By the end of 1942 twenty-four PFF bombers, twelve Halifaxes and twelve Stirlings, had been equipped with the blind-navigation device H2S, and it was first used operationally against Hamburg during the night of 30/31 January 1943. Crews were enthusiastic, but bombing results were poor. So far Oboe was working well and without interference from the enemy.

There was increasing investment, too, in electronic and radio countermeasures. A very successful advance was the British jamming of *Freya*, which had begun on December 1942 with a device code named 'Mandrel', a fairly simple transmitter that sent out signals on the same wavelength as that of the enemy radar and so blotted out the echoes from aircraft. It appeared in two forms, a ground one and an airborne one, the airborne equipment first being carried in twin-seat, single-engined Defiants of No. 515 Squadron, Fighter Command, flying a patrol line off the Dutch coast, the first so-called 'Mandrel Screen'. High-powered ground transmitters in the south-east of England – there were eventually six of them at four sites – later added to the confusion of the enemy early-warning radars.

Also first introduced with considerable effect in the same month was a jammer known as 'Tinsel', a microphone fitted inside one of the engine nacelles of a bomber and coupled to a T1154 transmitter. Some bombers carried an extra, German-speaking crew member whose task it was to listen out for enemy fighter R/T broadcasts and then tune the Tinsel transmitter to the same frequency and so flood the fighter control communications with engine noise. Both Mandrel and Tinsel continued to operate, in various improved versions, throughout the war.

At this time the Germans were bringing a larger long-range reporting radar, the *Mammut*, into service. A development of *Freya*, it had a very large 'bedstead' aerial array ten metres tall and thirty metres wide that scanned electrically backwards and forwards over a sector of 100 degrees. In performance it outdid the *Freya* by a considerable margin. With a target at 8,000 metres (26,000 feet) it had a range of 300 kilometres (190 miles). Unfortunately for the Germans, however, both these early-warning radars operated within the same frequency band, so that jamming devices used by the RAF against *Freya* were similarly effective against *Mammut*.

The contest of radio and radar measures and counter-measures between the British and the Germans was in its early stages, but it was destined to develop with bewildering rapidity into one of the most fascinating aspects of the battle. It was at the time a science only understood by comparatively few, and that lack of understanding cost more than a few RAF lives. That any radio device that transmits can in its turn be jammed by means of signals on the same frequency is a very simple concept. Almost equally simple, although perhaps not so readily apparent, is the fact that in general, because radio energy travels in a straight line, it is possible to use any transmitter as a direction indicator or a homing aid. We saw earlier how the Germans used the *Lorenz* beam system with their *Knickebein* and *X-Gerät* bombing aids, and how Wellingtons of No. 109 Squadron flew along the beam to bomb the *X-Gerät* transmitter on the Cherbourg peninsula. Quite early on in the offensive the crews of Bomber Command had attempted their own do-it-yourself radar jamming without thinking that by doing so they might be providing the Germans with a signal they could turn to their own advantage.

Early in 1942, when the searchlights were the principal embarrassment, the idea had developed among crews that they could jam the radar controlling the lights by switching on their IFF set to transmit, and that the searchlights would no longer be able to pick them up or hold them in their beam. So widespread had this practice become that it received official approval by the fitting of a 'J' (for 'Jamming') switch on the IFF Mk II sets in the bombers. By any standards this was a nonsense. IFF normally only transmits when it is 'interrogated' by a radar signal on the correct frequency, and there was no possible scientific explanation that would support the crews' belief that in switching the IFF on they were jamming the enemy searchlight radars. By providing a switch that permitted active transmissions – signals, that is, that were not in reply to a radar interrogation – the powers-that-be were providing the German monitoring services with a gratuitous supply of radio signals to help them to plot the track of the RAF bombers, a bonus that the *Funkhorchdienst* put to good use.

Just as the RAF was expanding, so was the *Nachtjagd*. By the end of 1942 it had evolved into a huge organisation. The flying component comprised five *Geschwader* with fifteen *Gruppen*, and there were about 100 overlapping fighter control areas covering the approach routes to the Third *Reich*, each with its minimum of two Würzburg Giant radars and its associated *Freya* early-warning radar. The ground personnel of the *Luftnachrichtendienst* – the Air Signals Service – to man these control areas and their co-ordinating centres alone amounted to almost 40,000 servicemen and servicewomen. To form an idea of the full man-power requirements that were consequent upon the Bomber Command offensive one has to bear in mind also the vast number of personnel

– one estimate puts it at about 900,000 – needed to man the anti-aircraft guns and searchlight positions deployed throughout Germany. Nor must it be forgotten that a vast armada of American bombers was gathering in Britain, poised to attack Germany, and that this in its turn would dictate a huge increase in the number of men and women needed to man the defences of the *Reich*, many of whom might otherwise have been used directly or indirectly to add weight to German offensive operations elsewhere, particularly on the Russian Front.

Although growing, the *Nachtjagd* was slower than Bomber Command in getting new aircraft. The Bf 110, originally designed as a heavy day fighter, a *Zerstörer*, was still by far the most numerous German night fighter at the turn of the year. Gradually coming into wider use, however, was the Ju 88C. Like the Bf 110, the Ju 88C was originally designed as a *Zerstörer*, but one version, the C-4, was built on the production lines specifically as a fighter, evolving, with new engines, into the Ju 88C-5 and then, with extra armour-plating for the crew, into the C-6. There were some Ju 88C-6s operating with the *Nachtjagd* during 1942, but not a great many in the defence of the *Reich* itself. I./NJG 2, the intruder *Gruppe*, which was equipped with the Ju 88, had been moved to the Mediterranean area when Hitler decided that intruders were not necessary, and another *Gruppe*, II./NJG 2, was also operating from Sicily with the same machine. In 1942 only 257 Ju 88Cs had been produced, of which the great majority went to *Zerstörerstaffeln* for service on the Eastern Front. A few, however, had found their way into night-fighter units, the first of the many that would follow. Although crews that stayed with the Bf 110 were in general unstinting in its praise and remained loyally convinced that it was the best night-fighter, there can be little doubt that, with the exception of the Heinkel 219, which entered service later, the Ju 88 in its several specialist versions was the most potent night-fighting machine that RAF bombers had to face.

Whereas the crew of the 110 was originally two, that of the 88 was three, a pilot (*Flugzeugführer*), a radio/radar operator (*Funker*) and a flight mechanic (*Bordmechaniker*). The pilot flew the aircraft from the left-hand seat, and the *Mechaniker* sat alongside him on the starboard seat, while the *Funker*, as was the norm in *Luftwaffe* night-fighters, sat back-to-back with the pilot. The Ju 88, if not as manoeuvrable as its Messerschmitt counterpart, was a splendidly stable gun platform. With the assistance of its on-board radar it could creep up on its target and deliver a devastating 'punch' from its forward-firing armament which, in the C-6 version, comprised three 20 mm MG FF/M cannon and three 7.9 mm MG 17 machine-guns. The *Funker* had a single rear-facing 13 mm MG 131 machine-gun in a flexible mount designed for defensive purposes, which was also sometimes used to attack bombers. Each 20 mm MG FF/M cannon fired 540 shots a minute, while each MG 17 fired 1,180 rounds in the same time, so that a three-second burst from a Ju 88C's forward armament would launch eighty-one explosive shells and 177 heavy machine-gun bullets in the direction of its target. As the guns were synchronised to give a narrow cone of fire, the damage that an enemy aircraft incurred from a short, accurately aimed salvo, and the terrible, tearing injuries that such a burst could inflict on the members of the crew, might well be imagined.

Mention has been made above of the Heinkel 219, potentially probably the best night-fighter conceived during the Second World War, which could have been available for the *Luftwaffe* at the beginning of 1943. Had it been introduced earlier and in greater numbers than it actually was, it might just have pushed Bomber Command's losses above the level of acceptability. Unfortunately for the *Nachtjagd*, and very fortunately for those who flew in the Lancasters, Halifaxes and Wellingtons – and, indeed, in the apparently almost invulnerable Mosquitos – production of the He 219 and its introduction into service were delayed by prejudice at a high level in the *Luftwaffe* to such an extent that it made only a limited impact on RAF losses. The He 219 night-fighter's first live action, and then only an experimental one, against Bomber Command came in the early hours of 12 June 1943 when Werner Streib, who had been promoted to the rank of Major at the beginning of the year, flew in a 219 with his *Funker,* Unteroffizier Helmut Fischer, under the control of Walter Knickmeier and shot down four Halifaxes and a Lancaster in the course of one sortie. But that is a story to be told later.

A directive from the Assistant Chief of Air Staff (Operations) to the Commander-in-Chief of Bomber Command dated 14 January 1943 ensured for Germany a period of three months during which she would be given some slight respite from the full might of Harris's force. U-boats were still a major threat to Britain's maritime traffic, and large numbers of the deadly vessels were operating into the Atlantic from their heavily fortified bases in the French ports of Brest, Lorient, St Nazaire and La Pallice on the Bay of Biscay. The directive authorised area bombing of these ports, in contrast to previous attempts at precision bombing, and from 14 January until 1 March Lorient was the target for major attacks on nine occasions and Brest once. It was then accepted that the massive concrete shelters that the Germans had constructed for their underwater predators were impervious to even direct hits from RAF bombs, and Harris could again concentrate his attentions fully on the Third *Reich*. In the meanwhile, the French towns and their inhabitants had suffered grievously.

For the Germans the respite was only comparative. During approximately the same period – the beginning of January to the beginning of March – large-scale raids were mounted against Berlin and Hamburg on three occasions each; against Wilhelmshaven four times: Cologne three times: and Düsseldorf, Nuremberg and Bremen once each. Nor did Italy escape Bomber Command's attentions, both Milan and Turin receiving visits. In addition to the major raids, the Command carried out numerous lesser raids. The Mosquito was being increasingly used both in its PFF marking role and also as a nuisance raider, flying in high and fast, sometimes with the aid of Oboe and sometimes without, and dropping its 2,000 lb bomb-load, so ensuring that even when and where there were no major bombing attacks the German air raid organisation would be forced into action and the night-time rest of German workers disturbed.

Until now the markers that Oboe Mosquitos had dropped in their pathfinding role had been sky markers; markers, that is, that were suspended from a parachute. Target indicators (TIs) of this nature were, of course, indispensable when the ground was not visible because of cloud or haze, but were inherently less accurate than ground markers, drifting as they did with the wind. On the night of 27/28 January the city of Düsseldorf was ground-marked by Oboe Mosquitos, and there was a clear improvement in the accuracy of the bombs dropped by the aircraft following up. The ground markers were in fact so constructed that they exploded at a predetermined height above the surface, ejecting candles of various colours – red, green or yellow as selected for the particular raid – that fell in a cascade to the ground, where they continued to burn for several minutes. The German civilians soon nicknamed them *Christbäume* (Christmas trees).

For Harris, Berlin remained a tantalising and tempting target. After a handful of minor raids on Germany at the beginning of 1943, largely tests of Oboe which was still undergoing teething troubles, and two rather heavier attacks on Lorient, Bomber Command attacked the German capital on two successive nights in mid-January. In terms of accurate bombing neither raid was successful, Berlin being well outside the range of both Gee and Oboe. Bomber Command casualties on the first attack, 16/17 January, were slight, but the *Nachtjagd* took a heavy toll of the Lancasters and Halifaxes on the night of 17/18, accounting for twenty-two bombers, 11.8 per cent of the force. At this stage in the battle the defences seemed to be gaining the upper hand: these two attacks on Berlin had shown once again that without some such device as H2S, which was not yet operational, long-range targets could not be marked by PFF and bombed successfully, while the growing capabilities of Kammhuber's night-fighting system and the aircraft and crews that manned it were making the task of the British crews increasingly perilous. Nor was it only in the fields of organisation, machines and men that the Germans were improving their night-fighter defence. As their radio-monitoring capabilities and their understanding of Bomber Command's tactics grew they were able to forecast likely targets and deploy their fighters accordingly, moving them at short notice to airfields in the area of the assumed target and having them at readiness to take off as soon as the expected stream of bombers was detected. One aspect of Bomber Command practice that had not escaped their notice was that of bombing the same town on two or three nights in succession, and after the first Berlin raid in January 1943 they correctly deduced that the capital was to be revisited, and that correct deduction cost the RAF about 150 trained and valuable aircrew.

During the first three months of 1943 Bomber Command losses amounted to 348 machines, only 2.7 per cent of the 12,760 sorties made. The *Nachtjagd* accounted for 201 of them. This was proportionately a slight decrease in the night fighters' share of the kills in comparison to that of the *Flak*, but it must of course be realised that attacks on the French ports did not expose the bomber force to the attentions of the night fighters to anything like the extent that penetrations of the mainland did. Targets in Germany cost more dearly. An attack on Hamburg on the night of 3/4 February, for example, resulted in the loss of sixteen bombers from the 263 that had set out, mostly the victims of the Bf 110s of NJG 1.

It was not only the British that suffered. The most dangerous period of their night-fighting career for the German flyers was understandably while they were scoring their first few victories, before they had learned to kill without being killed. Losses among fledglings were persistently higher than among more experienced crews. But even experience could not guarantee survival. In February the *Nachtjagd* lost three of its leading *Experten*, Reinhold Knacke, Paul Gildner and Ludwig Becker, all of NJG 1; coincidentally, each had forty-four night victories to his credit, so that among them they had destroyed 132 RAF bombers, the equivalent of over eight full squadrons. When they died only Helmut Lent, *Kommodore* of IV./NJG 1, had more kills to his name.

Oberleutnant Knacke and his *Funker*, Unteroffizier Heu, members of 1./NJG 1 and based at Venlo, had shot down three bombers in one night during the third of Harris's thousand-bomber raids, that against Bremen on 25/26 June 1942. On 16/17 September the crew had exceeded even that performance by destroying five enemy machines in a night during the RAF's costly attack on Essen, the first time such a feat had ever been accomplished. The last kill of this series of five was attended by gruesome circumstances. Knacke was pressing home his attack from the stern when the Lancaster's rear gunner baled out from his turret. Knacke felt a heavy jolt, and his engine began to vibrate to such an extent that he had to switch it off and make a single-engine landing back at Venlo. When his ground crew inspected the aircraft they found fragments of flesh and hair attached to the twisted airscrew and scraps of RAF uniform caught on the radar aerials. Knacke, born in Strelitz on New Year's Day 1919, was *Kapitän* of the first *Staffel* of I./NJG 1. His luck ran out when he was shot down on 3 February 1943 in combat with a Halifax, which he also destroyed: both machines with their dead crews were found close to each other the following morning.

Paul Gildner, five years older than Knacke, was a Silesian by birth. He had volunteered for the *Wehrmacht* in 1934 as an infantry officer, but had transferred to the *Luftwaffe* and become a *Zerstörer* pilot, joining the *Nachtjagd* in July 1940 as one of the founder pilots of I./NJG 1. He had attained his first victory on 3 September 1940, shooting down a Whitley near Sittard, just on the German side of the border with Holland. After Falck and Streib, Gildner was the third night fighter pilot to be decorated with the *Ritterkreuz,* the Knight's Cross to the Iron Cross. When his friend Knacke died, having in the meantime moved to Gilze-Rijen to take over 3./NJG 1, Gildner became the next *Kapitän* of the *Staffel*; his command was only to last three short weeks before he, too, died in action. On the evening of 24 February 1943 a force of RAF bombers set out to attack Wilhelmshaven, and Gildner and his *Funker*, Heinz Huhn, were ordered off to the close-control area '*Hamster*' above the Schelde Estuary, but despite obtaining a *Lichtenstein* contact on a bomber they failed to complete the interception. Suffering an electrical fault and the loss of power on the port motor, they decided to return to base. Gilze-Rijen was shrouded in mist, so Gildner ordered Huhn to take to his parachute. After some difficulty, Huhn succeeded in abandoning the machine at low level and came to earth safely. Gildner, however, was unable to get out of the stricken Messerschmitt and died in its wreckage.

The third of the night-fighter aces to die in the same month was Hauptmann Ludwig Becker who, it will be remembered, had achieved the double distinction of shooting down the first British bomber by the *Dunaja* method on 2 October 1940 and making the *Nachtjagd's* first *Lichtenstein* kill on 9 August 1941. Becker came from the Ruhr area, having been born in Dortmund in August 1911. He had joined the *Luftwaffe* as a volunteer in 1934. Originally a *Stuka* pilot, he had later flown Bf 110 *Zerstörer* before, like Gildner, becoming a night-fighter pilot when Falck inaugurated NJG 1 in July 1940. When he died he was flying with IV./NJG 1 from Leeuwarden on the north-west coast of Holland. His *Funker* was Feldwebel Josef Staub. Despite being one of the foremost night-fighter pilots, he was destined to die while on a daylight mission. Since August 1942 American heavy bombers of the 8th USAAF had been bombing by day in Europe, first venturing over Germany itself to attack Wilhelmshaven on 27 January 1943. On the morning of 26 February the German early-warning service reported a concentration of bombers off Great Yarmouth, and at 1055 hrs the *Gruppe* was brought to stand-by. At about 1130 hrs twelve Bf 110s took off in three sections of four, led by the *Gruppenkommandeur*, Major Helmut Lent, to attack 8th USAAF Liberators of the 44th Bomb Group returning from an attack on Emden. The Americans lost seven bombers on this raid, of which Oberleutnant Rudolf Sigmund and Unteroffizier Georg Kraft of IV./NJG 1 claimed one each. Of the twelve fighters that took off from Leeuwarden just one, Ludwig Becker's Bf 110, G9+LZ, failed to return. The exact nature of his fate remains a mystery. The *Luftwaffe* had lost one of its great tacticians and practitioners of night-fighting, the man known to his fellow flyers as the *Nachtjagdprofessor*.

On the world stage, the first quarter of 1943 saw, in January, the Casablanca Conference at which Winston Churchill and President Franklin D. Roosevelt of the United States discussed the future high-level policy of the conduct of the war, while February saw the massive Soviet victory at Stalingrad. Stalin, invited to be present at Casablanca, pleaded pressure of military responsibilities and did not attend. Nevertheless, he urged the Western Allies to open a second front as soon as possible to relieve pressure on his armies. Stalin did not get his Second Front as promptly as he would have liked, but from the conference, attended as it was by the Combined Chiefs of Staff of Britain and the United States, emerged the controversial decision that the war would be waged until the unconditional surrender of Germany and Japan. Broad guidelines were set for the future conduct of hostilities with the aim of achieving that goal, and an attempt was made to define the combined role of Bomber Command and the Eighth USAAF in the strategic bomber offensive against Germany. For Harris, the directive agreed at the conference and passed to him on 4 February 1943 seemed to endorse his policy of mass raids on German cities, beginning as it did:

> 'Your primary object will be the progressive destruction and dislocation of the German military, industrial and economic system, and the undermining of the morale of the German people to a point where their capacity for armed resistance is fatally weakened.'

The directive, which came to be known as 'Pointblank', then went on to list priorities 'within that general concept' – submarine construction yards, the German aircraft industry, transportation, oil plants and so on – but Harris, as ever, was impatient with such niceties. His personal perception of the way ahead was clear, and that way was one from which he would not easily be diverted. Accepting that precision of bombing could not yet be expected, despite the advances in electronics and the introduction of PFF, Harris remained firm in his belief that ruthless bombing of German cities was the best contribution that Bomber Command could make towards victory, and indeed it could be, and was, argued by him and his supporters that any major German township would contain factories and other installations coming on to the list of agreed priorities. Harris wrote later:

'At long last we were ready and equipped . . . the scope of my instructions had been enlarged, as a result of the Casablanca Conference . . . I was now required to proceed with the general "disorganisation" of German industry . . . which gave me a very wide range of choice and allowed me to attack pretty well any German industrial city of 100,000 inhabitants or above. But the Ruhr remained a principal objective because it was the most important industrial area in the whole of Germany, which was why it had been originally chosen for morale-breaking attacks; the new instructions therefore made no difference.'[1]

The Ruhr area, situated as it was neatly within Oboe range and therefore easier to hit accurately, was clearly the correct choice as a target for the new-look bomber offensive, and beginning on the night of 5/6 March 1943 Harris directed the might of his force primarily against the vast complex of adjacent and overlapping towns that made up, for the bomber crews, 'Happy Valley'. It fell to Essen to be the first of a series of twenty-nine major attacks against targets in the Ruhr and Rhineland that subsequently came to be known as the 'Battle of the Ruhr' and lasted until 13/14 July. In that period Essen itself was bombed five times, as was Duisburg. Cologne was hit four times and Bochum three times, with other towns attracting the bombers once or twice each. In the same period Harris also mounted eighteen attacks on other major targets in France, Italy and Germany. Berlin was visited twice, and the bombers ranged as far as Munich, Stettin and the Skoda arms works in the Czechoslovak town of Pilsen. In Italy, Turin and La Spezia were targeted. In addition, Bomber Command carried out large mine-laying operations – a task they fulfilled throughout the war – sometimes with over 100 bombers, but it was the Ruhr that attracted the most devastating retribution.

While Oboe and the PFF tactics led to a dramatic improvement in the accuracy and concentration of the bombing, the increasing numbers of four-engined load-carriers added to Bomber Command's striking power. If the Germans had sowed the wind, they were at last reaping the whirlwind many times over. Now Pathfinders could leave the British Isles on an eastward heading with a much greater degree of confidence that they would find and mark their target, and now the crews in the main-force bombers following up knew that they had a reasonable chance of striking home hard and sure instead of, as previously, dropping their bombs more or less haphazardly over the Fatherland. There was an upsurge in confidence among the flyers whose task it was to carry the war to Germany, a confidence that stood them in good stead in face of the rising casualty rates that assailed their numbers.

Essen had always been a most difficult target to locate and to hit: the countless chimneys, coke ovens and other pollution-producing installations associated with the vast Krupp steel works and with the very many other industrial premises in the city generated a permanent haze that made precise map reading on even the clearest of moonlit nights a virtual impossibility, while the light of

[1]   *Bomber Offensive*

flares simply failed to pierce the murk but was reflected back to produce an even more impenetrable blanket. Until now Krupp, despite its huge area and its location near the centre of the town, had incurred only comparatively slight damage. In the Oboe-marked attack on 5/6 March 1943 fifty-three separate buildings within the Krupps complex were hit by bombs, according to subsequent photographic reconnaissance reports, and 160 acres of the town devastated. Further damage was caused to Krupps in each of the three ensuing raids during this period, the second bombardment on 12/13 March causing even greater devastation than the first one had. Figures for damage to private premises make sobering reading: 4,830 accommodation units – houses, flats and so on – were completely destroyed, while innumerable others suffered structurally to a greater or lesser extent. Human suffering, too, reached a new level for Germany, 1,037 dying in the assaults and approximately 3,500 being severely injured.

In addition to Oboe, H2S was also progressively, if rather slowly, being introduced into PFF operations. H2S could not be jammed, but its use carried with it other, more direct, potential dangers to the RAF crews. In common with any radar device that transmitted, it could in theory be used as a homing beacon. In the course of only the second raid on which H2S was used operationally, on 2/3 February, a Pathfinder Stirling carrying it was shot down – possibly one of the two bombers claimed by Major Streib – and it crashed close to the village of Hendrik-Ido-Ambracht near Rotterdam. The equipment, with the exception of the navigator's PPI, was relatively undamaged, and when *Telefunken* engineers inspected it they were able to recover its revolutionary component, the cavity magnetron, undamaged. By the nature of its construction the magnetron was virtually indestructible, and it had proved impossible to fit it with an explosive detonating device to destroy it should it seem likely to fall into enemy hands. The Germans called H2S the *Rotterdamgerät*, but despite further acquisitions of components in various stages of damage as other bombers were shot down – the second one was a Halifax of No. 32 Squadron that crashed near the Dutch village of Markelo during the night of 1/2 March – they were slow to reach a full understanding of the way in which the device functioned, and fortunately for the crews of the bombers it was to be some time before they produced a gadget that would enable their fighters to pick out and focus on H2S-carrying aircraft. One thing they rapidly determined, however, was that the RAF bombers were transmitting pulsed energy on a wavelength of about 10 cm, and the *Funkhorchdienst* was soon able to monitor the transmissions. It was the RAF practice to use H2S during pre-operation air tests and to ground-test the equipment before take-off and keep it switched on throughout the flight. As the number of aircraft fitted with it increased, so the monitoring of H2S transmissions proved to be a most valuable aid for the German early-warning organisation in knowing when a raid was likely and, once the bombers were airborne, from which direction they were approaching.

Düsseldorf, capital of the *Land* of Nordrhein-Westfalen and a most important industrial and commercial centre, lies on the Rhine to the south of the Ruhr area proper. Primitive bombing raids had been carried out against *Zeppelin* sheds there as early as October 1914. Now, in 1943, Düsseldorf was again to suffer, but to an infinitely greater degree. The attack on the night of 11/12 June was destined to be perhaps the worst of the very many that the city would undergo before the end of the war. But just about a fortnight earlier Düsseldorf had been the target for 759 RAF bombers led by Oboe Mosquitos and other aircraft of PFF, and the raid had been a failure. For some reason PFF had failed to mark in concentration, and Main Force had scattered bombs over a wide area. Although remarkable improvements were being made, bombing remained a haphazard weapon. According to an official report issued by the city authorities:

'The first heavy attack during the period under review took place against Düsseldorf on 26 May. The number of aircraft that entered German territory this night was considerable: the majority, however, did not reach Düsseldorf but dropped their bombs in a wide area, with villages on the west of the Rhine in the districts of Grevenbroich, Mönchengladbach and Neuss being hit particularly hard. Although relative to the size of the individual localities the damage was great, in comparison to the extraordinarily large weight of bombs used it remained within narrow limits. Individual villages received thirty heavy bombs and over 10,000 incendiaries, but the majority of the bombs fell in open countryside and missed their target.'

It was to be a different story in the early morning of 12 June. The bombing began just after 0100 hrs and left 1,236 persons dead and thirteen missing, with 2,600 injured. Official reports and statistics numb the mind, and to form an impression of what bombing was really like one has to try to translate the cold language into human terms. Think of a major IRA terrorist attack in Belfast, Enniskillen, Coleraine or London that you have seen reported on your television screen; think of the destruction, the deaths, the blood, the maiming, the widows, the orphans; and then multiply it by a thousand.

'In Düsseldorf itself the centre of gravity of the attack was in the inner town, in the main shopping area, particularly in the districts of Altstadt, Stadtmitte, Derendorf, Zoo, Flingern, Friedrichsstadt, Oberbilk and Bilk. As there are in these areas virtually no military or war-economic targets, it was clearly a terror attack on the civilian population.
'In addition to many large, medium and small fires an area of fire extending to four square kilometres was caused inside a total area of destruction measuring 5 × 5 kilometres = twenty-five square kilometres. In comparison to earlier attacks, the number of high-explosive mines dropped was especially high, so that great destruction and damage was caused to buildings and other installations. There were 180 major collapses of buildings. The explosive material tore many buildings open, shattered windows and doors and so facilitated the very rapid spread of fire throughout whole buildings, blocks of buildings and streets. Fire-storms occurred in many places . . .
'As a result of direct hits to a large number of principal and secondary water conduits the supply from the mains failed, with a few exceptions, very soon after the beginning of the attack, and it was necessary to fall back on reserve water supplies for fighting the fires. In some cases the demand on these water points was so great that the supply was rapidly exhausted . . .
'Work on digging out the dead began while the attack was still in

progress. In addition to the normal ARP units, the Air Raid Rescue Service was brought into action with thirteen large items of earth-moving machinery (baggers and bulldozers) . . .

'Very many self-help centres were destroyed or damaged, among them thirteen hospitals, twenty-eight schools and eighteen churches.

'As far as can be discovered so far 100 per cent loss of production occurred:

for 1 week	in 37 factories,
for 2 weeks	in 19 factories,
for 3 weeks	in 11 factories
for 4 weeks	in 7 factories,
until reconstruction or removal	in 46 factories.

'The attack on *Reichsbahn* [railway] land was many times heavier this time than on any previous occasion. Damage was so extensive that for the first time the main railway station and the stations at Derendorf, Bilk and Lierenfeld were completely out of action for several days. Others, such as the goods station and the station at Grafenberg, were cut off as a result of damage to the approach tracks.

'Particular difficulty was caused by unexploded bombs, which impeded repair work at various places for a considerable time. In the three-kilometre stretch between the main railway station and the station at Derendorf six delayed-action bombs were discovered and cleared by bomb disposal squads in five days.

'Damage to bridges by bombs showed that the heavy bombs, although they should certainly have been quite capable of penetrating the 70 cm-thick load-bearing foundations (roller girders sunk in concrete), always exploded on the surface without causing any damage to the foundations.

'In all twenty *Wehrmacht* buildings were lightly, moderately or heavily damaged. These are premises that are at dispersed points within the town area. At the Ludendorf Barracks moderate structural damage was caused, as a result of which an important *Wehrmacht* telephone exchange was put out of action.

'About 140,000 individuals – about twenty-five per cent of the population of the town – were rendered homeless. As had been planned they were first of all gathered together and looked after by the Party and the NSV in a Refugee Reception Centre, after which some of them were temporarily accommodated by neighbours, relatives or acquaintances. As far as was necessary the Town equipped schools as emergency accommodation, because many buildings previously earmarked for the purpose had been destroyed in the mass attack.

'The feeding of the population was a difficult and very urgent matter, all the more so because, as a result of enemy action, not only was the food distribution system greatly interrupted, but also there were no longer supplies of food in sufficient quantities.

'Local public transport in the town of Düsseldorf was extremely badly affected by the attack. Principal tram routes received fifteen direct hits. Ten direct hits were counted on secondary routes and sheds. In addition the overhead cables were severely damaged throughout the main area of heavy destruction and on some suburban routes. There were heavy losses to the stock of vehicles . . . . After the attack the whole public transport system came to a standstill.

'Of the 154 schools in the town twenty were completely destroyed, twenty-four heavily damaged and twenty-six lightly damaged.'

Three miles above the city of Düsseldorf, while scenes such as this were being created, young men were running the gauntlet of thousands upon thousands of anti-aircraft shells that burst into countless vicious fragments of shrapnel, any one of which might tear through the thin aluminium sides of their aircraft, perhaps to maim those inside it, perhaps to strike a vital component and turn the machine into a flaming comet carrying its occupants to their death. On their way into the target they had passed through Kammhuber's *Himmelbett* areas, where some of their colleagues and friends had already been blasted out of the sky, and on their way out they would run the same hazard again. Just as it is impossible to describe what it was like to be on the receiving end of a concentrated bombing attack in anything other than the most general of terms, so it is equally impossible to put into words the experience of flying in a heavy bomber over Germany. The sense of aloneness even though you knew that your machine was one of hundreds; the stomach-sinking fear, because any minute might be your last; and the fear of being seen by the other members of the crew to be afraid; the noise, the cold, the lurching and jolting and bumping of the aircraft; and the smell, indescribable, a mixture of petrol, dope, rubber, chemical-toilet fluid, possibly vomit. But no thought of what you were doing to the people on the ground, because it was just a job, after all, and there were things of more immediate importance to think about, and the most important ones were doing your job and surviving.

The night of 21/22 June saw 705 of Harris's bombers attacking nearby Krefeld and suffering heavy casualties, forty-four failing to return. One flyer who, for that night at least, was spared the stress of yet another operation over the Ruhr and, as it turned out, the trauma of being shot down, was Flying Officer Harry 'Nick' Nock, a bomb-aimer belonging to No. 51 Squadron stationed at Snaith in Yorkshire. An accidental injury meant that he was unable to fly and his skipper, Sgt Fred Heathfield, took Sgt. Allan Poulton with him as a temporary replacement. No crew liked to fly with a 'spare bod' on board: a crew was usually a comfortable unit, each member knowing just how to work with the others, and a stranger tended to upset the working rhythm. Additionally, crews carrying a replacement member seemed to suffer a higher 'chop rate' than others. This was possibly no more than superstition, but lonely-looking aircrew who had lost the remainder of their crew were a frequent sight on operational squadrons.

The flak over Krefeld was, as usual, intense, and Heathfield's Halifax II, MH-K, serial number JD 244, was hit over the target. One engine on the port side caught fire and the other was put out of action. Heathfield managed to extinguish the fire but the Halifax could not maintain altitude on two engines, so Heathfield, realising the hopelessness of the situation, ordered the crew to abandon aircraft. After they had baled out Heathfield crash-landed the aircraft near the small town of Balen-Neet, fortunately escaping with only minor injuries. The remainder of the crew also survived, in itself a very rare occurrence, and all seven were taken prisoner.

Nock was lucky on that occasion, but Luck is a fickle friend. In the early hours of 4 July Oberleutnant Ludwig Meister and his radar man, Unteroffizier Forke, a Bf 110 crew belonging to I./NJG 4 stationed at Florennes in Belgium, were scrambled against bombers attacking Cologne. At about 0215 hrs they picked up a contact between the townships of Beaumont and Chimnay. The bomber was the No. 51 Squadron Halifax MH-E, JD 262, and it was flown by a pilot who had only recently arrived at the Squadron's 4 Group base at Snaith, Sergeant John Garnham. It was Garnham's first operational flight. Flying as bomb aimer on his first mission since the trip that had ended his former pilot's operational career was Nick Nock. At about 0240 hrs, after a long chase, Meister's cannon fire destroyed the Halifax near the village of Rance. Only three of its occupants lived, the navigator, the wireless operator and Nock himself, all of whom baled out. While the other two were taken prisoner, Nock managed to evade. He eventually joined the Maquis, with whom he fought a war quite different from the one he had trained for.

The raid against Cologne during which Nock was shot down was the third of four mounted against the city during the Battle of the Ruhr. Whereas the first had not been very successful, the second, on 28/29 June, was, for the people of the Rhineland city, the worst of the four; much, much worse, even, than their ordeal at the hands of Harris's makeshift 'thousand-force' of the previous year, even though about 439 fewer bombers participated. A statistical comparison is of interest as an illustration of the way in which Bomber Command was growing in both its size and its ability to visit frightfulness on Britain's enemies.

Whereas in the May 1942 attack 755 of the force had been twin-engined machines, with 602 Wellingtons forming the bulk of the armada, in June 1943 all the force, with the exception of twelve PFF Mosquitos and eighty-five Wellingtons, were four-engined – 267 Lancasters, 169 Halifaxes and seventy-five Stirlings. It is probable that the total bomb-load dropped in 1943 was slightly below that dropped in the first thousand-bomber raid, yet the precision with which the missiles fell – despite the fact that the first raid had been carried out in conditions of good visibility while in the second attack the bomb aimers were unable to see the ground but had to aim at coloured sky-markers dropped by PFF – was incomparably greater, as may be seen from the respective casualty figures. Operation 'Millennium' had cost the Germans about 470 dead and 5,000 injured: this time the figures were 4,377 killed and about 10,000 injured. Some 230,000 citizens of Cologne were made homeless as compared to 45,000 in May 1942. This was by far the highest number of dead for any RAF attack in the war so far, but it would pale into comparative insignificance before what was yet to come. But still it was not the end, even temporarily, of Cologne's suffering. In the final two raids of the series there were more than 1,000 further deaths, while another 120,000 were made homeless.

Harris's twenty-nine attacks in the Battle of the Ruhr cost him 672 machines and approximately 4,400 men. At 4.8 per cent of the sorties dispatched, this was nudging the five per cent 'acceptable' attrition rate. When the battle began the front-line strength of Bomber Command in four-engined bombers and

Wellingtons was about 1,000, so that in just over four months the Command lost the equivalent of sixty-seven per cent of its force; and that figure did not include the many aircraft that made it back to Britain but were damaged to a degree that varied from 'repairable' to 'write-off'. During the same period PFF Mosquitos flew 302 sorties for the loss of only two, a remarkable comment on the character of the unique aeroplane. At the other end of the scale Stirlings, which had to fly lower than the other heavies and so tended to attract special attention from the flak, lost 6.4 per cent.

Although the Air Staff's general policy for Bomber Command was one of area bombing, it was realised that not all targets were suitable for such treatment, and objectives were sometimes perceived that required special attention in the form of a precision bombing. The outstanding example of such an attack carried out by night was of course the renowned Dams Raid in the early hours of 17 May, chronologically in the middle of the Battle of the Ruhr, and Sir Arthur Harris allowed it to go ahead despite an initial, presumably instinctive, adverse reaction to the idea. It has sometimes been quoted in support of the contention that Bomber Command efforts would have been better employed in precision attacks rather than in the wholesale destruction of cities. The story of the raid itself has been told many times, and it is in any case somewhat outside the scope of this chronicle, but it is worth diverting slightly from the main stream of the narrative to consider whether the Dams Raid does indeed contribute to the 'precision versus area' argument.

A saturation raid against the dams would not have been practical, because, as the many wasted attempts to destroy the U-boat pens on the Bay of Biscay had shown, ordinary bombs dropped from the vertical would not have caused any significant damage to the massive structures, even if the necessary precision of aim could have been realised. To destroy the dams required a special weapon dropped from a low level so that it would sink into place below the water before exploding and causing the 'earthquake' effect needed to start the chain reaction that would permit the enormous weight of water to break open the dams. Such a weapon had to be conceived, designed, tested and produced, and it was a weapon that would never be of more than specialised use.

To drop the weapon needed specially modified Lancasters, and to fly the Lancasters needed the best crews that could be found, and the crews and the necessary aircraft had to be withdrawn from operations for a period of intensive training until the time was ripe, which was a tricky calculation in itself, because the dams needed to be full for the necessary knock-on effect to be achieved when the bombs exploded. A completely new squadron, No. 617, was formed from highly experienced and competent flyers and put under the command of Wing Commander Guy Gibson DSO DFC, whose leadership of the raid was to earn him the Victoria Cross, and the specialised training for the crews lasted for six weeks. Three dams were attacked, the Möhne, the Sorpe and the Eder, by nineteen Lancasters. Two of the dams, the Möhne and the Eder, were breached in spectacular style, but at the cost of eight of the attacking force of Lancasters and their fifty-six crew members, of whom only three survived to become prisoners of war. The aim had been to deprive the Ruhr area of its water supplies and thus wreck its economy, but in fact one of the two dams successfully breached, the Eder, was of little significance in that context, its waters being used almost entirely for agricultural purposes. The ultimate value of the attack has been the subject of debate ever since the end of the war, when insight not previously available was gained. While the Official History describes the effects of the raids as 'not, in themselves, of fundamental importance', Albert Speer, Hitler's Armaments Minister, is not quite so dismissive:

'A torrent of water had flooded the Ruhr Valley. That had the seemingly insignificant but grave consequence that the electrical installations at the pumping stations were soaked and muddied, so that industry was brought to a standstill and the water supply of the population imperilled . . .

'We immediately summoned experts from all over Germany who had the electrical insulation dried out and also confiscated other motors of this type from other factories, regardless of the consequences. Thus the Ruhr industries could be supplied with water within a few weeks . . .

'A few days after this attack seven thousand men, whom I had ordered shifted from the Atlantic Wall to the Möhne and Eder areas, were hard at work repairing the dams. On 23 September, 1943, in the nick of time before the beginning of the rains, the breach in the Möhne Dam was closed.'[2]

In *Bomber Offensive* Harris himself states, ' . . . the destruction caused by flooding was not, and was never expected to be, as serious as the subsequent shortage of water for industrial purposes.' Yet Speer makes it clear that that shortage was of a very temporary nature. The direct damage caused by the floods was, however, extensive, and 1,300 people were drowned in their inundated homes, itself a remarkable achievement on the part of only nineteen Lancasters. But one cannot take this achievement and claim that the case for precision attack is proven. The Dams Raid was a one-off, costly and unsuited to the weapons and men available to Bomber Command's Main Force. There were other precision attacks by No. 617 Squadron, which remained in existence as a specialised unit within No. 5 Group and would add many outstanding exploits to this, its first, but not against the sort of targets that were visited night after night in the pursuance of the main strategic offensive.

Among the raids mounted by Harris against the Ruhr during the three-month period there were two that marked significant developments in the history of the *Nachtjagd*, one negative in terms of the battle against the bombers and one positive. They were the operation against Düsseldorf on 11/12 June and the one against Cologne on 3/4 July, both already mentioned.

It had been clear to General Kammhuber from the very first that the Bf 110 was at best a stop-gap solution to the long-term problem of catching and shooting down British bombers. Even in its improved form it was still only marginally faster in level flight than the *Viermots* that it was its job to intercept, and when the Mosquito began to arrive on the scene a further limitation of the

---

[2] *Inside the Third Reich*, by Albert Speer, first published 1970 by Weidenfeld and Nicolson.

Messerschmitt, that of altitude, was highlighted. The Ju 88 was not much better: both were adaptations of aircraft originally conceived for other purposes, and neither was ideal. In 1942, despite strong objections from the very influential Director General of Equipment (Air), General Erhard Milch, and from Reichsmarschall Göring himself, both of whom remained convinced that existing types such as the Bf 110 and the Ju 88 could do the job of night interception adequately, the *Technische Amt* of the Ministry of Aviation issued urgent instructions to the firms of Heinkel and Focke-Wulf to design a new aircraft specifically for night fighting. The Focke-Wulf offering, the Ta 154 ('Ta' after the firm's chief designer, Kurt Tank) may be dismissed here and now, only two or three production models ever reaching a front-line night fighter unit, Stab/NJG 3, in late 1944. Interestingly the Ta 154, like the British Mosquito, was largely of wooden construction. Focke-Wulf never produced a satisfactory adhesive to join the components, and it was largely on this consideration that the Ta 154 project foundered. In the world of the press and radio in Germany the aircraft was referred to as the *Moskito*, presumably in a vain attempt to show the population that anything Britain could do, Germany could do better.

There is no doubt that Hermann Göring's cavalier opinions as to the type of aircraft required, coupled with his immense personal power and influence with the *Führer*, played a great – and very damaging – part in the equipping of the flying units, including the *Nachtjagd*. In March 1943, for example, he was demanding that, because the *Luftwaffe* lacked a conventional four-engined bomber, the German aircraft industry should copy 'the enemy's best aircraft, the latest model Stirling . . . ' ! On the same occasion, at one of Generalfeldmarschall Milch's fortnightly conferences that he attended personally, Göring also addressed the subject of the Mosquito in these terms:

'And we haven't got a wooden aircraft, either, and that brings me straight to the point. I could go mad when I think of the Mosquito. I go green and yellow with envy. The British, who can afford more aluminium than we can, build themselves a wooden aeroplane without any trouble, one with a speed that has even just been increased again. The Mosquito that photographed Linz was flying, according to our precise calculation, not that of the British, at a speed of 530 kph – and that was a bomber, would you believe it? And that is a machine that any piano factory over there can make! Unfortunately – I could kill myself! – I didn't insist with the Generaloberst, because at that time I gave him the benefit of the doubt when it came to making decisions. When war broke out, I demanded this wooden aeroplane time and time again, because there was no harm in building wooden fighters and bombers as well. But they said that that was impossible; no pilot could imagine such a thing; the whole world would laugh at us – now the whole world can laugh at us because we haven't got it. The day before yesterday Mosquitos made another low-level attack on Paderborn. They didn't lose any, or perhaps only one. Our fighters didn't see them. The Mosquitos flew around like mad things, and they relied on their speed alone, and they were incredibly fast. Even though they were only flying at fifty metres they didn't have any guns, they relied on their speed, and they got away with it. Gentlemen, you should have a good look at this aeroplane – perhaps you might learn something. The primitiveness of this aircraft is astounding. And here too I say, "Why waste time looking?" We should be copying the Mosquito. That's the easiest thing for us to do!'

The second of the two firms approached, Heinkel, came up with the He 219, but the production of that aircraft too was bedevilled by internal differences of opinion and clashes of personality at a high level – and, it must be said, by the effects of RAF bombing – so that it never reached the front line in numbers large enough to make as significant an impact on the RAF's bomber offensive as it might otherwise have done.

To trace the irregular nature of the development of the He 219 it is necessary to go back to 1940 when, just as de Havillands had done with the Mosquito, the Heinkel firm embarked upon a private venture, in their case the design of an aircraft in the heavy multi-purpose category known as the *Kampfzerstörer* (battle destroyer). Again similarly to the Mosquito, the design, *Projekt 1060*, included revolutionary features, which in the case of the Heinkel proposal extended to cockpit pressurisation and a nose-wheel undercarriage. The concept did not find the approval of the Technical Department of the Aviation Ministry, and nothing more was done. In late 1941 Kammhuber was pressing for a purpose-built night fighter, but was not receiving the support of his superiors: he therefore made a personal *démarche* to Hitler himself, and with the support of the *Führer* he was able to discuss his requirements directly with the aircraft firms, among them Heinkel. *Projekt 1060* seemed to embody desirable characteristics, and design work on a night-fighter version of the He 219, as the aircraft was christened, began. The construction of a prototype started at the Heinkel factory at Rostock/Marienehe soon afterwards, and Kammhuber was able to inspect it on 22 January 1942. In the course of Bomber Command attacks during March and April the majority of the design documents for the machine were destroyed, although the prototype itself was not damaged. Soon afterwards design work was transferred to Vienna/Schwechat in Austria.

Milch, as *Generalluftzeugmeister*, was opposed to quantity production of the He 219. Milch entertained personal animosity towards both Kammhuber and Ernst Heinkel, and he indulged this animosity with the excuse that it was counter-productive to embark upon too many projects at the same time by putting a series of administrative obstacles in the way of the development and construction of the He 219. The first test version of the aircraft flew from Marienehe in November 1942 and the test pilot, Peters, was enthusiastic about its handling, commenting particularly favourably on the excellent taxying, take-off and landing characteristics that stemmed from the fine forward vision and the nose-wheel undercarriage. An order was placed for twelve pre-production examples, and the start of series production was promised for mid-1943. Milch hastily revised this, however, announcing at a conference the same month that the original estimate had been a year out – series production would not be possible before 1944.

In March 1943 a comparative test was conducted between one of the pre-production He 219s and the most up-to-date version of the Ju 88, the 'S', an aircraft which, it was hoped, would emulate the Mosquito by flying fast enough to outstrip enemy fighters. The Ju 88S was flown by Oberst Viktor von Lossberg, a

Head of Department (*Abteilungsleiter*) in the *Technische Amt* of the *Reichsluftfahrtministerium*; the He 219 by Major Werner Streib, *Gruppen-kommandeur* of I./NJG 1, who already had over forty kills to his credit. Von Lossberg was an experienced bomber pilot, having commanded II./KG 26. The He 219 proved itself far superior, and as a result it was decided to place a pro-duction order with Heinkel of 200 machines a month. Heinkel, however, maintained that the most they could promise in the immediate future was ten.

Streib's unit was instructed to carry out operational testing of the He 219, and the first aircraft arrived at Venlo in early June 1943. Streib himself flew the first fully operational test sortie in a machine carrying the marking G9+FB during the night of 11/12 June, when, as recounted above, 783 RAF bombers attacked Düsseldorf. Under the control of Oberleutnant Walter Knickmeier, *JLO* for *Himmelbettraum 5B*, and with Unteroffizier Helmut Fischer as his *Funker*, Streib took off from Venlo at 0038 hrs on the twelfth. At 0105 hrs he shot down a Halifax, and by 0222 hrs he had added three more Halifaxes and a Lancaster to his toll.

By any standards this was an impressive début for a new aircraft, but the over-all effect was somewhat marred when the aircraft's flaps failed on the approach to Venlo and Streib had to land at high speed, with the result that he left the run-way on touchdown and the aircraft was wrecked completely. Both pilot and *Funker* escaped without injury.

Even this remarkable achievement failed to move Milch, who commented that it was possible that Streib would have achieved the same result had he been fly-ing another type of aircraft. Nevertheless, enthusiasm for the 219 among the *Nachtjagd* was high, and Milch had no alternative but to sanction full produc-tion, at that time estimated by Heinkel at a mere twenty-four per month. The *Stabsschwarm* (Staff Flight) of I./NJG 1 continued to operate the few evaluation aircraft with some success, although often-repeated reports that they destroyed six Mosquitos in the days immediately following Major Streib's successful sor-tie are most unlikely to be true. Indeed the only recorded destruction of a Mosquito by a He 219 during the remainder of 1943 was by Hauptmann Manfred Meurer on the night of 12/13 December. By then Meurer was the incumbent of Streib's previous position as *Kommandeur* of I./NJG1. Streib had been promoted to Oberstleutnant on 1 July 1943 on his appointment as *Kommodore* of NJG 1, and he had been replaced by Hauptmann Hans-Dieter Frank who, however, had died in a collision with another night fighter over Hanover on 27 September 1943 with fifty-five kills to his account. Frank in his turn had been replaced by Meurer, but Meurer was destined to survive only until 21 January 1944, when he too was killed in a mid-air collision, this time with a Lancaster over Magdeburg. At his death, Meurer's score was sixty-five.

It was not until March 1944 that the permanent re-equipping of I./NJG 1 with the He 219, which was nicknamed the *Uhu* ('Owl'), began. Even then, *Generalluftzeugmeister* Milch continued to place endless obstacles in the way of its mass production. It was a specialised aircraft, he said, and the *Luftwaffe* wanted multi-purpose machines; it was uneconomical in production, needing 30,000 man hours per machine; and so on, and so on. By the end of the war the only *Gruppe* to operate the He 219 in any strength was I./NJG 1, and even then the aircraft, despite continued successes, was in permanently short supply.

Although, then, it first made an appearance during the Battle of the Ruhr, it was not until well into the following year, when the later Battle of Berlin had virtually run its course, that the *Luftwaffe* could begin to think seriously of using the He 219 against Harris's bombers. RAF losses during the Battle of Berlin were high, on occasion verging on the intolerable, and it is interesting to speculate what the extent of casualties might have been had the Bf 110s and the Ju 88s been strongly supported by He 219s. But that is jumping ahead of our story. It is acceptable, nevertheless, to consider at this point, ahead of the chronology as it is, what sort of a machine the He 219 was.

The *Uhu* was a twin-engined aeroplane of remarkably thin fuselage section in which the pilot and the *Funker* sat back to back. It had a high, fully glazed cockpit which, with the nose-wheel undercarriage, gave excellent forward vision not only in the air but also on take-off and landing, and which was fully pressurised for flight at high altitudes. Both pilot and radar operator were equipped with an ejector seat, making the He 219 the first operational aircraft to have the device. The definitive night-fighter version, the He 219 A-7/R1, was powered by two Daimler-Benz 603G motors which gave it a maximum speed of 416 mph (665 kph) at 23,000 feet (7,000 metres). Its ceiling was in the region of 42,000 feet (12,700 metres), which it could reach in twenty minutes, and its time to 20,000 feet, an average operating height for Bomber Command aircraft, was under twelve minutes. These figures made it the only true night-fighter in the *Luftwaffe*'s armoury that could, in theory at least, compete with the Mosquito on equal, or better than equal, terms, and the 219 became known as the *Mosquitojäger* – the 'Mosquito Hunter'. Performance figures quoted without qualification can, however, give a very wrong impression. Times to height, ceilings and altitudes are dependent, for example, on other factors such as the weight of fuel carried, the weight of ammunition and so on. The capabilities and potentials of the He 219 have often been exaggerated, but it was nevertheless a very good machine indeed. Its armament was frightening. In the wing roots it carried two 20 mm MG 151 cannon, each firing 800 rounds per minute, and in a ventral tray two 30 mm MG 103 cannon that fired 440 rounds per minute each. Its forward 'punch' per second, therefore, comprised over forty heavy shells in a tracer, armour-piercing and incendiary mixture. Equally deadly, for attacking bombers in their unprotected belly, were the two 30 mm MK 108 upward-pointing cannon (660 rounds per minute each) in a so-called *Schräge Musik* installation in the fuselage roof, of which we will speak later at greater length. For detecting its foe the He 219 was fitted with the most advanced radar then available, plus, of course, standard navigation, communications and flight safety equipment.

Streib's accomplishment in destroying five RAF bombers when flying the He 219 on its first operational sortie was followed just over three weeks later by another virtuoso performance by a different *Luftwaffe* officer, but this time the aircraft involved were not twin-engined night fighters but single-engined day-fighters, and the officer concerned was not a fighter pilot. What he achieved had a considerable effect on the way the battle between the bombers and the night-fighters evolved, and to see how that came about we must first of all take a look at the officer's career.

Hajo Herrmann was a bomber pilot. He had seen action in Spain during the

Civil War and had flown operationally in the attack on Poland, the Norwegian campaign, the invasion of France and the Low Countries, the Battle of Britain, the *Blitz* against British cities, the attacks on Malta and the Greek campaign. In the first half of 1942 he was stationed at Banak, in the north of Norway, flying against the North Cape convoys. He was twenty-nine years old and held the rank of Hauptmann. In July 1942 he was posted to a desk job in Berlin, a move that he accepted only with great reluctance. With considerable and indisputable justification he looked upon himself as first and foremost an operational pilot.

The staff job to which Herrmann was posted was in *Gruppe T* of the Command Staff of the *Luftwaffe*, located at Wildpark-Werder near Potsdam. *Gruppe T* was a small section staffed by six junior officers, and its responsibilities were specified as 'Technical/Tactical Requirements'. Each officer dealt with a separate field of operational activity, and Herrmann took over the Bomber Desk. As Fate dictated, however, and as will be described below, Herrmann found himself increasingly concerned with the defensive rather than the offensive side of *Luftwaffe* operations.

In *Gruppe T* Herrmann met a situation common to every organisation that has the task of deciding priorities and allocating resources: demand invariably outstrips supply, and everyone submitting requirements equally invariably sets a figure higher than that which he thinks he really needs, so that when that figure has been cut he will get, he hopes, his basic requirement. The demands for aircraft were great, with the Russian front a clear priority as far as bombers, fighter-bombers and fighters went, but the defence of the *Reich*, beset as it was by Bomber Command by night and facing the imminent threat of American attacks by day, was also looming large. Herrmann had at his disposal figures from German intelligence assessments, one setting the production capacity of the Americans and British alone, not to speak of the Russians, at 29,200 bombers a year, a figure that far outstripped the forecast annual German production of fighters, at that time about 10,000. As a bomber pilot himself he could imagine very clearly the progressively growing disadvantage under which the German fighter force would suffer. Among the several ideas that occurred to him was that the night-fighters should be reinforced in their operations against Bomber Command by single-engined fighters, which traditionally flew only during the hours of daylight. With proper organisation, he suggested, the Bf 109s and Fw 190s of the *Tagjagd* could perform a twenty-four hour function, being available for their traditional role by day and, with different pilots, taking off by night to join in the fight against the *Viermots*.

Herrmann's idea harked back in two respects to the original, tentative attempts at night-fighting in the very early stages of the war, when the Bf 109s of JG 2 freelanced by night and when night interceptions with the aid of searchlights seemed to offer the best prospects of success. There were elements, too, of the later *Konaja* method, but there was a fundamental difference from all these ideas. Herrmann reasoned that the best place to catch British bombers was immediately above the town or city they were attacking, and it was there that the fast, manoeuvrable, single-engined fighters could come into their own, hunting visually among the swarm of Lancasters, Halifaxes and Wellingtons, if necessary among the searchlights and flak, although, of course, it would be safer if arrangements could be made to limit the latter to a specific ceiling so

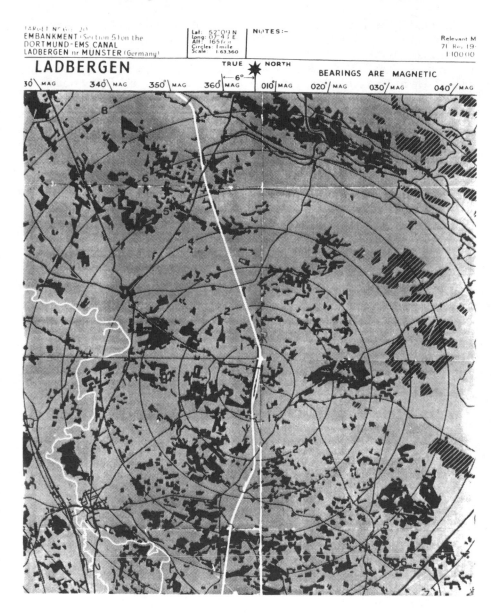

TARGET Nº 6-20
EMBANKMENT (Section 5) on the
DORTMUND-EMS CANAL
LADBERGEN nr MUNSTER (Germany)

Lat: 52°09 N
Long: 07°43 E
Alt: 165 ft
Circles: 1 mile
Scale: 1 63,360

NOTES:—

Relevant M
71 Rev 19·
1 100 00

LADBERGEN

TRUE NORTH
←—6°→
BEARINGS ARE MAGNETIC

30° MAG   340° MAG   350° MAG   360° MAG   010° MAG   020° MAG   030° MAG   040° MAG

that the fighters could operate without having to run the extra hazard of 'friendly' fire.

To test the feasibility of his concept – papers on the subject that he had sent up to a higher level in the *Luftwaffe* had not seemed to generate noticeable enthusiasm – Herrmann approached a senior officer sympathetic to his ideas, Oberst i.G. Eschenauer, and asked if he might borrow a single-engined fighter to test his theory, and Eschenauer agreed. Herrmann also obtained the co-operation of the General in command of the Berlin *Flak*, Schaller, and the services of a He 111 bomber and crew to act as target for him in practices over the city of Berlin, flying from the day-fighter base at Staaken on the western edge of the German capital. He had no difficulty in finding other pilots with night-flying qualification and experience to join him in his scheme, the first coming from among the instructors at the flying school at Brandenburg-Briest, about seventy miles to the west of Berlin, men prepared to do their normal work by day and to join Herrmann in the hazardous occupation of flying day-fighters at night over cities being attacked by hundreds of RAF bombers. Herrmann extended his experiments to participation in live operations, despite an order originating from the *Führer* himself that there should not be any restriction on the height to which the anti-aircraft guns fired.

In April 1943 he and seven other pilots took off in single-seater fighters in an attempt to intercept a Mosquito that the radar had picked up approaching Berlin from the west. Herrmann himself was at 11,000 metres when he saw the Mosquito 2,000 metres below him, and he went in to attack among the dense flak that was surrounding the British machine, but although he fired at it he did not succeed in shooting it down. Two of his volunteer pilots also opened fire unsuccessfully. Although the Mosquito had not been destroyed, Herrmann had shown that it was not the invulnerable 'miracle bird' it was reputed to be, although in some high quarters, among which Feldmarschall Milch and Kammhuber were prominent, there was reluctance to believe his story. The charismatic Generalmajor Galland, however, who was General of Fighters (*General der Jagdflieger*), was favourably impressed both by Herrmann himself and by his theories, and he made further fighters available. Throughout May and June 1943, night after night, Herrmann and his volunteers practised their night flying and their tactics, in addition to carrying out their day-time jobs, waiting for a raid on Berlin so that they could prove their worth, but none came.

What sort of a man was Herrmann? He was, as his record proved, a brilliant, courageous pilot. He was a clear-thinking man impatient of bureaucracy and of inflexibility in his superiors, a man of great powers of leadership, an officer in the best tradition of the *Wehrmacht*. A regular officer of the *Luftwaffe* with an outstanding reputation, he was well connected and more influential than his comparatively lowly rank of Major – he had been promoted in April 1943 – might suggest. An officer who knew him in Berlin when he was first calling for volunteers, and who later commanded one of Herrmann's single-seater units, was Gerd Stamp, himself a Major at the time. Like Herrmann, Stamp too was a bomber pilot, and he had achieved considerable distinction in the eastern Mediterranean, flying the Ju 88 with *Lehrgeschwader 1*:

'In April 1943 I was sent home to Berlin to work on the Staff. It was there that I met Hajo Herrmann. It was a rest period from operations for me; I already had several hundred missions to my credit. Herrmann had been in Berlin since 1942, and in his spare time he went over to Brandenburg/Briest to practise night flying. It was at a time when Bomber Command were coming increasingly frequently. People said a Messerschmitt 109 couldn't be flown at night, but he said, "We'll see!" When I heard he wanted pilots I asked him if I could join him. At that time I already had the *Ritterkreuz*, so my ability was established, but I had never flown the Bf 109 before.

'You ask me what sort of a man Herrmann was. I must say that at first I didn't like him at all. He knew who he was – self-confident, assured, aloof, cold, arrogant. As I was the same rank as he was I could speak to him on equal terms, however, and I told him he was a flying calculating machine, and he thought everyone should be able to do as well as he could. I told him that this was not so: "Not everyone is a flying genius like you are." He really was a flying genius.'

Herrmann's endeavours met with approval on the one hand, opposition on the other. Prominent among the sceptics was Generaloberst Weise, in overall charge of air defence (*Befehlshaber Mitte*), who refused categorically to issue orders limiting the *Flak* to a specific height 'for the sake of a handful of fighters'. At a meeting chaired by Weise in Berlin to discuss the subject one Oberstleutnant i.G. Boehm-Tettelbach referred to Herrmann's ideas in dismissive terms, calling them '*Wilde Sau*', which in German means crazy, bull-at-a-gate, irresponsible, a reference to the frenetic behaviour of the wild sow when cornered. It was a name that would stick. Despite Weise's opposition, however, it was arranged that Herrmann should outline his ideas personally to the Reichsmarschall, Hermann Göring, and he did so at Obersalzberg on 27 June 1943. The Chief of Staff of the *Luftwaffe*, Generaloberst Jeschonnek, was also present at what was a small meeting. Herrmann was supported by his close associate in *Gruppe T*, Major Werner Baumbach, probably the greatest bomber pilot on the German side in the Second World War. The minutes of the meeting include the following passage:

'Major Hermann [sic] outlines his plans for freelance single-engined night fighting. As grounds for this plan he points out that the current building-up of a defensive belt and the control of individual fighters in small areas closely tied to the organisation on the ground is only appropriate to incoming flights that are widely separated. When the attacks are concentrated in space and time this system can only produce a set number of shootings-down. The establishment of a true defensive concentration by this means is impossible.

'Major Hermann therefore proposes: That in addition to the night-fighting method so far used, *helle Nachtjagd* should be carried out in the light of the searchlights in *Flak* areas provided with lights, using standard single-engined fighter aircraft. This will be particularly effective in that the searchlights coupled to *Würzburg* radars can hold their targets sufficiently long even in hazy weather. During major attacks in the Ruhr area (Düsseldorf, Essen etc.) there have regularly been fifty to 140 aircraft held in the searchlights for more than three minutes. That means that the conditions for interception are similar to those by day. Indeed, finding targets is probably easier than in daylight, because the targets are identified optically by the lights, so that target-finding by eye is easy without the necessity for radar control. By this method it is possible to carry out single-engined night-fighting over the target with between eighty and a hundred single-engined fighters and so achieve a considerable increase in the number shot down.

'In addition, because the system is not dependent upon the ground organisation, it is possible to alter the defensive focus rapidly as the bombers approach, so that single-engined night-fighter *Gruppen* positioned in the *Ruhrgebiet* and promptly scrambled to height when there are enemy penetrations from the west can cover individual targets in the *Ruhrgebiet* and further, should the bombers continue onward in the direction of e.g. Berlin or Hamburg, accompany the bombers and then attack them over the target in the light of the searchlights.

'Co-operation with the *Flak*, already discussed with General Hintz, has been guaranteed. There is no question of stopping the *Flak* firing completely or by sectors, but it may be stopped by means of an optical signal indicating that a specific enemy aircraft is coming under fire from a friendly fighter attacking from astern. Recognition of friendly aircraft is guaranteed by the use of *Häuptling*.[3]

'The Reichsmarschall suggests as an extra means of optical identification, a 'cat's eye' type of reflecting system by means of a suitable paint or something similar. Recognition *vis-à-vis* friendly fighters can be ensured by means of a tail-light. It would be particularly advantageous if the fighter could remain in the darkness so that the rear gunner in the bomber would be dazzled by the searchlight and could not see the night-fighter.'

Göring liked Herrmann's ideas, and he and his volunteers became known as the *Nachtjagdversuchskommando*, or 'Night-Fighting Experimental Unit'. He was given permission to test his theories in the West, where his chances of action would be greater because the Ruhr was a more likely target than Berlin in the shorter nights of summer. Herrmann had already been in touch with the Commanding General of the *II. Flakkorps*, Hintz, responsible for the Ruhr area, who was co-operative and promised him that when an opportunity came for the *Wilde Sau* irregulars to go into action he would order the *Flak* to confine itself to 5,500 metres, or 18,000 feet.

Herrmann's chance came on 3 July 1943, when in the early evening the air raid warning system forecast a heavy raid on the Ruhr area. Herrmann rapidly contacted his pilots, obtained permission from their superiors for them to join in his live experiment – he himself had no powers of command – and took off from Berlin/Staaken for the airfield at Mönchengladbach. When he arrived there nine of his volunteer pilots who had flown on ahead of him from Berlin in their Bf 109s and Fw 190s had already taken off and were circling as planned at between 6,000 and 7,000 metres above the centre of the sprawling Ruhr complex of towns. Herrmann took off after them as soon as his machine had been refuelled. He was pleased to find that Hintz's agreement not to fire above 5,500 metres was obviously in force and that the *Flak* was was not engaging his planes, as it certainly would have done in normal circumstances.

[3] *Häuptling* was an IFF device that operated in conjunction with the *Würzburg* radar.

The approach of the bomber stream to the south of the Ruhr was clearly shown by the searchlights, the bursting flak shells and the explosions in the air and on the ground that marked the end of British bombers whose unhappy fate it had been to be intercepted by Kammhuber's conventional night-fighters, up in strength. When the leading bombers reached the Krefeld area, however, they did not turn north towards Essen, as had been expected, but south towards Düsseldorf and Cologne. Herrmann's fighters sped after them. Harris's target for that night was in fact Cologne, which had already undergone the devastating raid described earlier just five nights previously, and he had dispatched a further 653 aircraft to the hard-hit city. For Herrmann and his fellow fighters this meant an unforeseen complication: the anti-aircraft guns that defended the cathedral city did not belong to General Hintz's *II. Flakkorps* but to the *7. Flakdivision* under General Burchardt, and to fly over Cologne meant with certainty that Herrmann's pilots would come under fire from the hundreds of heavy- and medium-calibre guns defending the city.

The first of Herrmann's pilots to shoot down a British bomber in the midst of the *Flak* over Cologne was Karl Friedrich Müller, whose large nose had earned him the affectionate nickname '*Nasenmüller*', and when the ten of them who had taken part submitted their reports on landing, their claims amounted to a total of twelve bombers. That twelve bombers were indeed destroyed over Cologne was certain, but the *Flak*, who had never destroyed more than one or two in any previous night raid, also claimed them all. There followed a period of horse-trading, and it was finally decided that Burchardt's gunners and Herrmann's *Wilde Sau* pilots would be credited with six bombers each.

On completion of the operation Herrmann landed at Bonn/Hangelar airfield, although he did not know exactly where he was until he got out of his aircraft; he had put down at the first convenient field that he saw, a practice that was to become normal operating procedure for the *Wilde Sau*. Physically and emotionally exhausted by his experiences, he went to bed, and early the following morning he was woken by an orderly – Hermann Göring was on the telephone. Göring told Herrmann that he was to report to Generaloberst Hans Jeschonnek at Berchtesgaden that morning. He, Göring, wished to speak to him. The outcome of Herrmann's visit was that he was instructed to set up a night-fighter *Geschwader* of single-engined machines, JG 300, of which he was to be *Kommodore*. A first *Gruppe*, with its own aircraft, would be formed immediately at Bonn/Hangelar, and he was to select pilots both for that *Gruppe* and for two others, which would be stationed at Rheine and Oldenburg but would share aircraft with the day-fighter units there as so-called *Aufsitzgruppen*, or lodger units. His first task, apart from gathering together the necessary pilots with experience of flying at night and the qualities appropriate to the swashbuckling nature of the job they were to do, was to begin devising and practising techniques and tactics. Herrmann said that he estimated that it would be the end of September before JG 300 could engage in operations. He was mistaken.

CHAPTER SIX

Wittgenstein, Window and Gomorrah

Summer 1943

Operational techniques and electronic and weapons technology were developing apace, spawning even more new code names and jargon words in both English and German. Many of these developments occurred while the Battle of the Ruhr was being fought, but have not yet been covered.

The Pathfinder Force used three basic methods of marking targets, and Bennett named them 'Newhaven', 'Parramatta' and 'Wanganui', visual ground-marking, blind ground-marking by means of H2S, and sky-marking – in which the crews following up aimed at flares suspended from parachutes – respectively. Marking by means of Oboe was shown by prefixing the codeword with 'Musical', so that 'Musical Parramatta' meant ground-marking by Oboe, while 'Musical Wanganui' was sky-marking by the same means. Once the Germans had recognised that the British were using a highly accurate method of marking targets in the Ruhr area, and that the pathfinding Mosquito approached on a track that was an arc of a circle, they named the technique the *Bumerang-verfahren*, or 'Boomerang procedure'. German long-range early-warning radar was improving, too, with the more efficient *Wassermann* joining, and in some cases replacing, the *Freya* and the *Mammut*, particularly on the coastal approaches.

It had first been recognised in 1942 that the German night-fighters had begun to use radar to intercept the British bombers when the stations in England monitoring German fighter control R/T frequencies increasingly heard the German pilots using the words '*Emil, Emil*' to report contact with a target. On 3 December that year a Wellington bomber of No. 1474 (Wireless Investigation) Flight, flown by Pilot Officer Paulton of the Royal Canadian Air Force, carrying electronic measuring equipment and acting as a 'decoy duck' during a raid on Frankfurt, was attacked about twelve times and terribly damaged by a German night-fighter, but the special radio operator, Pilot Officer Harold Jordan, also RCAF, had already accurately measured the frequency of the fighter's *Lichtenstein* radar. Jordan, badly wounded in the jaw, one arm and one eye, drafted a message reporting his findings, and the regular radio operator, Flight Sergeant Bigoray, who was also severely wounded in both legs, transmitted it to Britain. Bigoray, unable to receive an acknowledgement to his message because his receiver had been damaged in the fighter attacks, continued to send the message until shortly before the Wellington reached the English coast. Rather than risk putting the extensively damaged Wellington down on land, Paulton decided to attempt a ditching just off the coast, but, because he did not know whether the vital message had in fact been received, he dropped the badly injured Bigoray by parachute over land first. Happily, Paulton's landing on the sea just off Kent was successful, and none of the four crew members that had been wounded succumbed to their injuries.

Possession of the precise frequency on which *Lichtenstein* operated made it possible to devise methods of jamming it, the first of which was 'Ground Grocer', which came into operational use on the night of 26/27 April 1943. Ground Grocer transmitters were situated on the ground in England and their range, in common with that of radar, was limited by the curvature of the earth, so that their jamming was not very effective as the majority of attacks on bombers were carried out at a range and altitude that put the night fighters below the transmitters' coverage. There would eventually be a development with the self-explanatory name 'Airborne Grocer', but that was for the future.

British knowledge of German airborne interception radar was greatly enhanced when, literally out of the blue, a *Lichtenstein*-equipped Ju 88R-1, D5+EV, landed at the RAF station at Dyce, Aberdeen. The pilot was Oberleutnant Heinrich Schmitt, a veteran of the Spanish Civil War and the Battle of Britain, the radar operator Oberfeldwebel Paul Rosenberger, and the flight mechanic Oberfeldwebel Erich Kantwill, and they had planned their flight to the British Isles and their defection very carefully. Members of 10./NJG 3 stationed at Grove in Denmark, they had been temporarily detached to the airfield at Kristiansund on the southern coast of Norway in response to a requirement voiced by Hitler that the nightly RAF courier flight between Stockholm and London should be intercepted and shot down. At about 1530 hrs on 9 May 1943 the Ju 88 took off, ostensibly for a routine air test, and shortly afterwards the radio operator, in accordance with their plan, transmitted an SOS message to the effect that there was an engine on fire and they were ditching in the sea. Air-sea rescue machines sent off in response to the distress call found floating rubber dinghies, but understandably no sign of the aircraft itself. Walter Heidenreich, radio operator to Günter Köberich, takes up the story:

'I knew Schmitt and Rosenberger well. They were with me at Grove with IV./NJG 3; we were in the 11th *Staffel* and they were in the 10th. I knew Oberfeldwebel Rosenberger particularly well – we were both chasing the same girl, a Luftwaffe auxiliary. In the twenties Schmitt's father had been secretary to a leading Social Democrat.

'At that period we were often moved around, and I remember once, while we were on attachment at Nordholz, near Bremen, we were in the crew room listening to a British propaganda radio station. I heard someone talking and I recognised his voice. It was Rosenberger. He was broadcasting primitive gossip about individual members of the Luftwaffe who were misbehaving themselves with women and so on. Someone called our *Staffelkapitän* on the telephone, and he came in and listened. Then Hauptmann Schmitt came on the radio, and he said similar things – for example, he was saying that Luftwaffe crews had to fly long distances over enemy territory without parachutes, and so on. No one minded us listening in to the British stations – we never took any notice of what they said, and it was all a big joke to us.'

135

To have a *Lichtenstein* set delivered into their hands was, of course, a considerable windfall for the British scientists and tacticians, but by this time work was already well advanced on a most potent device that utilised *Lichtenstein* transmissions to the advantage of the RAF, 'Serrate'.

Serrate, developed by the Telecommunications Research Establishment, was a passive homing device that detected the signals sent out by a German fighter's intercept radar. It was first fitted to Fighter Command Beaufighter Mk IVF aircraft of No. 141 Squadron based at Wittering, which began regular bomber-support operations in June 1943. The device could, in favourable conditions, detect *Lichtenstein* emissions at a range of up to eighty kilometres when the night fighter was pointing towards it, and at a much lesser distance when the fighter was transmitting in a different direction. When the navigator in the Beaufighter picked up a *Lichtenstein* signal on his CRT he would endeavour to direct the pilot towards the enemy fighter until, ideally, he picked it up on his own AI Mk IV radar and was in a position to finalise the interception.

The night of 14/15 June 1943, when Bomber Command attacked Oberhausen in the Ruhr industrial area, saw the first operational use of Serrate, five Beaufighters setting out to patrol the *Luftwaffe* airfields at Eindhoven, Deelen and Gilze-Rijen while eight Mosquitos of PFF used Oboe to mark Oberhausen for a main force of 197 Lancasters. Although the Beaufighters did not enjoy any success in the form of kills, the operation was an example of the way in which the science of electronics was continuing to change the nature of Bomber Command's methodology. All the British aircraft participating now had Gee to refine their navigation; some of the Lancasters were carrying H2S to assist them to find their target; the Mosquitos marked the target with a remarkable degree of accuracy using Oboe; and the Fighter Command Beaufighters, carried Serrate in addition to AI to assist them in the defence of the bombers against the attentions of the *Nachtjagd*. The other side of the coin, unhappily for the British flyers, was that this was the period during which the night-fighter crews were also exploiting the revolutionary capabilities of radar. Seventeen Lancasters were lost, the majority to fighters. Controlled by Walter Knickmeier, Major Günter Radusch of I./NJG 1 shot down two Lancasters within a quarter of an hour.

In an attempt to increase the defensive capability of the British bombers against German fighters, two new devices were also introduced into Bomber Command in June 1943, 'Boozer' and 'Monica'. Boozer was a passive device – that is, it did not transmit – which showed, by a system of red and yellow lights, when the aircraft was being illuminated by impulses from *Lichtenstein* or *Würzburg* radars. Monica, on the other hand, was an active system: it transmitted radio pulses that were then reflected from other aircraft in the vicinity to produce a clicking sound in the pilot's headphones. The quicker the clicking, the nearer the other machine, so that a series of clicks in ascending tempo would indicate a rapidly approaching aircraft. Neither of these devices was much liked by the aircrew, Boozer because the very large number of radars active over Germany meant that the lights were constantly flickering on and off, and Monica because when a bomber was in the stream there were so many other machines about that the sheer volume of clicking in the headsets formed a real irritant.

On the German side there was emerging a new weapon which, carried principally by the Ju 88s, would prove to be frighteningly efficient against the RAF heavy bombers. As is very often the case, it is unclear who first thought of mounting machine-guns or cannon on the top surface of a night fighter so that all the pilot had to do was to position his machine under the bomber and then open fire. The idea was not a new one: there had reportedly been experiments along the same lines as early as the First World War. In World War Two the concept seems to have developed logically from the 'Becker' method of attack in which the fighter approached his target from astern and below (*von hinten unten*) and pulled up to fire before diving away when his shells had done their work.

Although there had been even earlier suggestions along similar lines, it is generally agreed that it was the then Oberleutnant Rudolf Schoenert, *Staffelkapitän* of 4./NJG 2, who initiated the process that led to the general adoption of what came to be known as *Schräge Musik*. Unlike the majority of his contemporaries, Schoenert preferred the night-fighter version of the Do 217 to the Bf 110. The number of Bf 110s reaching the front-line units had been falling as the Messerschmitt factories were re-equipped to produce the ill-fated Me 210, and the Do 217 bomber had been brought into service as a stop-gap replacement. The first night-fighter conversion, designated the Do 217J-1, was delivered to II./NJG 1 at Gilze-Rijen in about March 1942. Schoenert was already accustomed to flying Dornier aircraft, his *Gruppe* having until then flown the Do 215 and Schoenert himself having experimented with upward-firing 7.9 mm MG 15 machine-guns in a Do 17Z-10 *Kauz II* that had been passed on to 4./NJG 2 when the *Fernnachtjäger* were disestablished in autumn 1941. He had already unsuccessfully suggested the use of upward-firing guns to Kammhuber, but other aces such as Helmut Lent and Werner Streib were opposed to the idea. In July 1942, however, he was decorated by Kammhuber with the *Ritterkreuz* and took the opportunity of this further meeting with the Generalmajor to renew his suggestion. This time Kammhuber was more receptive, and he authorised official experiments to be conducted.

At the end of 1942 Schoenert, who already had twenty-three kills to his credit, was given command of II./NJG 5, equipped with the Bf 110, but he took with him one of the Do 217s that had already been experimentally equipped with upward-firing machine-guns. The installation attracted the attention of an armaments NCO, Oberfeldwebel Mahler, who built two 20 mm Oerlikon MG FF machine-guns into the cabin roof of a Bf 110. Using this 'do-it-yourself' weaponry, Schoenert achieved the first acknowledged *Schräge Musik* kill in about May 1943. In addition to this success, which was soon followed by others, the experiments that Kammhuber had authorised had shown that the concept of guns or cannon firing upwards was a valid one, and design work on a custom-made modification for the Do 217 and the Ju 88-C, the R 22, had been completed. Installation began in June 1943.

While Schoenert was successfully promoting the concept of upward-firing armament, other pilots were also pursuing the idea separately. One was Hauptmann Wittgenstein of IV./NJG 5, operating on the Eastern Front. His *Funker* at that time, Herbert Kümmritz, recalls:

> 'This idea was attracting enthusiastic attention all over the place from the end of 1942 onward. That led to experiments being carried out. A few of the better-known crews started building a gun or guns in on a trial basis,

often against armament regulations. Wittgenstein was one of them. When I joined him at about the beginning of March 1943 the guns had just been installed – two MG FFs. I took part in the first test firings. We used them successfully against the Russians. For the main part of the *Nachtjagd*, however, it took several months before the official conversion kits were approved and installation authorised.'

Trials showed that the best results were achieved when the upward-firing guns were mounted at an angle of about 70° to the fuselage. The early experimental installations used machine-guns, but the R 22 modification comprised two Mauser 20 mm MG 151 cannon, each with 200 rounds. In the interests of maintaining the element of surprise, only non-tracer ammunition was used, and each cannon was capable of firing at a rate of 800 rounds per minute. The name *Schräge Musik* derives from the slanting (*schräg*) position of the cannon. In the contemporary vernacular '*schräg*' could also mean 'off-beat' or, when applied to music, 'hot'. Jazz music – proscribed by the Nazis – was therefore '*schräge Musik*', a combination of words that seemed nicely to fit Schoenert's invention, and *Schräge Musik* it became.

In action, *Schräge Musik* was comparatively simple to use, and in the hands of many of the *Nachtjagd* crews it was a devastating weapon, although there were pilots who never came to terms with it, preferring to use their forward-firing armament. Once either radar or visual contact with a target was established, the pilot would manoeuvre his aircraft to a position up to thirty metres – some pilots preferred to get in even closer – below the bomber, enjoying the advantage of concealment against the dark earth below and avoiding the hazard of the bomber's rear turret. His prey would loom large above him, silhouetted against the lighter sky. Using an optical sight located in the cabin roof to which the cannon were precisely synchronised, if possible to his preferred aiming distance, he would, in the case of a four-engined bomber, aim between the two engines on one wing, chosen because the main fuel tanks were situated there. The *Schräge Musik* cannon fired a lethal mixture of armour-piercing, explosive and incendiary ammunition, and a split-second burst, a single pressure of the thumb on the firing-button, was usually sufficient to set the wing ablaze and damage the Stirling, Lancaster or Halifax beyond hope of recovery. Once he had seen that his shells had struck home the pilot would attempt to avoid a collision with his victim by peeling off in the direction away from the wing at which he had aimed, knowing that the bomber would inevitably dive to its destruction in the opposite direction.

In addition to the vulnerability of the wing area, there was another powerful argument in favour of not aiming at the fuselage of the bomber. Many fighter attacks in which cannon shells struck the bomber's fuselage caused bombs still on board to explode, and an aircraft immediately below was in great danger of being damaged, in all likelihood beyond hope, by falling débris. There was also, it is often claimed, another reason for aiming at a wing. In that way, say many former *Nachtjagd* flyers, the members of the British crew would have a better chance of taking to their parachutes and escaping with their lives instead of perishing in the explosion that would surely occur in the air a few moments later or when the bomber impacted with tremendous force into the ground below.

Should one of the gunners in the bomber see the fighter in advance he would warn the pilot and initiate a so-called 'corkscrew', a sequence of violent, stomach-wrenching, diving and climbing turns to port and starboard alternately that was designed to make the task of the night-fighter difficult. Many *Luftwaffe* pilots abandoned their attack when their target began to corkscrew, preferring to find easier, more unsuspecting, game. There were, however, those who looked upon a corkscrewing bomber as a challenge, persisting until they either shot it down or lost it from visual or radar sight. But most British crews did not know they were in danger from a fighter beneath them until they heard a short series of violent explosions and realised almost simultaneously that their aircraft was on fire. The fortunate ones had time to bale out; the unfortunate ones had only a few moments to live. As will be described, *Schräge Musik* came into its own with devastating effect during the second half of 1943 and the first half of 1944.

Both in Bomber Command and in the *Nachtjagd* names were being made and becoming known both in the respective air forces and to the public. Donald Bennett had progressed from being a squadron commander to leadership of the Pathfinders. Wing Commander Guy Gibson's outstanding achievement in the extraordinary raid on the Ruhr dams had captured the public imagination; from his three tours of bomber operations he had earned the DSO and bar and the DFC and bar, and he had been awarded the Victoria Cross for his gallantry and leadership on the Dams raid. Between bomber tours he had flown as a night fighter pilot. Leonard Cheshire, with two tours of hazardous operations behind him and a solid reputation for professionalism and bravery, wore the DSO and bar and the DFC, and when he was made Group Captain in April 1943 he was, at the age of twenty-five, the youngest man ever to have held that rank. He had been awarded his first DSO for gallantry as a Pilot Officer; the DSO was only very rarely awarded to anyone of so lowly a rank. His DFC had come at the end of his first tour, an extended one of about fifty operations on Whitleys with No. 102 Squadron and Halifaxes with No. 35 Squadron. He had then been appointed to the command of No. 76 Squadron, also flying Halifaxes, and the bar to his DSO had come at the end of his tour there. There were other outstanding pilots, but by now the ranks of those who had begun flying on operations in the early days of the bomber offensive were very thin. To survive one tour was against the odds, to survive a second one a comparative rarity. By the end of June 1943 the total of Bomber Command machines that had not returned from night raids amounted to 3,448, and the tally of aircrew lost had reached a figure in the order of 20,000. *Nachtjagd* kills during the same period were about 1,600, but included in the overall total of Bomber Command losses were the figures for the earlier period, when the night fighters were non-existent or only marginally successful compared to the *Flak*. In April, May and June 1943 Kammhuber's crews claimed 551, or seventy-two per cent, of the 762 British bombers destroyed.

It was in the nature of aerial warfare that more glamour, and hence more individual fame, attached to fighter pilots than to bomber crews. Whereas in England the names of only a very few bomber men were known to the public – or, indeed, to the mass of Bomber Command crews themselves – those of a much larger number of fighter pilots had become household words. Successful accomplishments by fighter pilots tended, by their very nature, to be spectacular, those of the bomber men to be anonymous. A fighter pilot shot down twenty enemy aircraft, and he was a national hero, invariably recognised as such by the award of at least a DSO, DFC or DFM: a bomber crew flew thirty, forty or fifty operations and, if they were fortunate enough to survive, the pilot, and possibly the navigator, might be decorated. Awards for other crew members tended to come only if the individual distinguished himself by some perceived act of unusual gallantry.

So it was, too, in the *Luftwaffe*, but German fighter pilots' scores were in general much, much higher than those of their RAF counterparts. There were two main reasons for this: firstly, the Germans had far more targets than the British ones did; and secondly, as has already been mentioned, senior *Nachtjagd* pilots frequently enhanced their own opportunities to augment their scores, and therefore to win decorations, by making sure, if necessary by 'pulling rank', that they were in the right place at the right time to shoot down the bombers attacking their country. But let there be no misunderstanding here. The German aces were very brave men and highly accomplished flyers. In the night-time war of fighter against bomber in the West there were no easy pickings. Pilots' expertise grew with the number of missions they flew, as did that of their radar operators, so that individual crews came to stand out from their contemporaries.

A combination epitomising these points was that of Hauptmann Heinrich Wittgenstein and Unteroffizier Herbert Kümmritz. When he joined Wittgenstein's crew in February 1943, Kümmritz had already had six months' operational experience, although no victories, flying in the Bf 110 with II./NJG 3 from Stade, near Hamburg. Kümmritz brought another important qualification to bear as a radar operator. Before the war he had studied high-frequency technology with *Telefunken* in Berlin. At the time, Wittgenstein was *Kommandeur* of IV./NJG 5 and had about twenty-five kills to his credit: he was a man who, for a number of reasons, did not get on well with many of his fellow aircrew and who was intolerant of inefficiency, and until then he had had a series of wireless operators, rejecting each of them after a short period. Immediately after Kümmritz joined Wittgenstein, IV./NJG 5 was transferred to Döberitz, to the west of Berlin, from where crews were detached to Insterburg for night-fighting operations against the Russians in the East Prussian area. Carrying *Lichtenstein* and operating out of Insterburg, Wittgenstein shot down six or seven Russian bombers, easy targets that nevertheless provided useful experience for the Wittgenstein/Kümmritz combination and for the third man in the crew, the *Bordfunker* or flight mechanic/air gunner.

In March or April 1943 IV./NJG 5 was moved temporarily to France, to Rennes, to support Kammhuber's defence of the German U-boat bases. The so-called Battle of the Ruhr was at its height, and in May many of the best *Nachtjagd* crews were sent to the Netherlands to reinforce the night-fighter units already stationed there. Wittgenstein went to Gilze-Rijen: simultaneously came the order for the unit to convert to the Bf 110. Wittgenstein and Kümmritz flew in this machine for just one day: that same night, in late May, their Bf 110 was unserviceable, so they took off in their Ju 88C and shot down four Lancasters, after which Wittgenstein, whose seniority and status put him to some extent beyond the usual restrictions of subordination, refused to fly the Bf 110 and continued to use his 'own' Ju 88. In late June or early July Wittgenstein's unit went back to

Döberitz for Eastern Front operations, but they would return to the West after only a very short absence.

Wittgenstein was one of the most interesting personalities of the *Luftwaffe*, in some ways a paradox. Although he insisted on being known simply as Hauptmann Wittgenstein, his full style was Heinrich, Prinz zu Sayn-Wittgenstein. Of a delicate constitution, he had demonstrated in childhood a determination to succeed, setting himself high targets in, for example, physical activities, and persevering ruthlessly, despite his physical weakness, until he achieved them. His life-style was austere, and to his subordinates he was the complete German officer and a remote, not to say arrogant, aristocrat. He had volunteered to transfer from bombers to night fighters because he preferred the idea of defending Germany to that of attacking its enemies, and to his work in his chosen field he brought the same selfless application that had characterised his younger days. As in everything he did, he was determined to be the best, and he drove himself and his crew members hard, expecting from them the same high standards that he imposed upon himself. Honours inevitably came his way, and he invariably manipulated things to ensure that he was in the forefront of the action. In Wittgenstein's case, however, there was never any suggestion that his principal aim in doing so was glory: he had a bitter revulsion towards the slaughter that was being exacted by Bomber Command, and he was resolved to do everything in his power to fight against it, if needs be to the death. Herbert Kümmritz recalls:

'There was the man, and there was also the ace, a phenomenon that was, by reason of its unique nature, almost impossible to describe. Imagine if you can a nature unremitting and ready at any time, regardless of his own health, to carry out his self-imposed duty even to the death. And the whole coupled with an obsession bordering on fanaticism. Many saw this as the expression of extreme ambition. In my view, that was a superficial judgement. Agreed, ambition was part of it – indeed, there was an unusual degree of ambition – but it was also his conviction that as a member of the German aristocracy he was duty-bound to attain high achievement. He demanded that of himself, and he also believed that he could take such an inner resolve for granted on the part of other participants in the struggle. In doing so, in my assessment, he was deceiving himself: others set themselves limits on the extent of their commitment to operations. They were not prepared to die at any cost – they wanted to survive the war. That meant that they had no sympathy for Wittgenstein's unconditional operational dedication. These two very different philosophies led quite naturally to tensions, which were always present and occasionally led to explosions on the part of the Prince. He did not make things easy for either his subordinates or his superior officers. That also applied to his relationship with his crew. I was the only radar operator who stuck it out with him for a year (1943): had I not been detached for a period of study, I might have gone to my death with him. It follows that we were to a certain extent on friendly terms, while still observing military protocol. At first he did not make it easy for me. I still remember his pointless, stereotyped question, "Why can't you see anything?" when he wanted information from the radar and the radar wasn't picking anything up. At first I had great difficulty in convincing him that when the equipment was looking for a target and there wasn't one there, there just wasn't a blip on the screen.'

Herbert Kümmritz also tells how Wittgenstein 'pulled rank' to ensure that he got first crack at the incoming bombers. He would remain in the Operations Room until it was quite clear from the general situation map where the stream was heading, and only then would he take off and fly to the beacon that seemed to offer the best chance of 'trade'. If, as was usual, there was another fighter already on the beacon, Wittgenstein would peremptorily tell him on R/T, '*Hier Wittgenstein – geh' weg!*' ('Wittgenstein here – clear off!').

Following the raid on Cologne on 3/4 July when Hajo Herrmann's Wild Boars first went into action, the RAF hit the same city again the following week. Gelsenkirchen, Turin, Aachen and the French town of Montbéliard suffered major attacks. On the Turin raid an acknowledged Bomber Command hero fell victim to *Luftwaffe* cannon when Wing Commander J. D. Nettleton VC, the Commanding Officer of No. 44 (Rhodesia) Squadron, was shot down over the Channel on his way back to base, losing his life along with the other members of his crew. Like Gibson, Nettleton had won his Victoria Cross in a spectacular raid outside the routine of Bomber Command operations. On 17 April 1942 he had led a low-level daylight attack by twelve Lancasters on a diesel engine factory at Augsburg in Bavaria in the course of which seven of the attacking bombers were shot down while that flown by Nettleton himself was severely damaged. Personified by the *Nachtjagd* the Deadly Reaper respected neither rank nor reputation.

Verses twenty-four to twenty-eight of the Nineteenth Chapter of the Book of Genesis record that: '. . . the Lord rained upon Sodom and upon Gomorrah brimstone and fire from the Lord out of heaven . . . and he [Abraham] looked toward Sodom and Gomorrah, and toward all the land of the plain, and beheld, and, lo, the smoke of the country went up as the smoke of a furnace.' With a degree of prescience, one might speculate, the Commander-in-Chief of Bomber Command chose 'Gomorrah' as the code word for a short but intensive series of operations to be mounted against the great, strategically important northern port of Hamburg, Germany's second-largest city. The overall directive under which Harris was working at the time of the Battle of Hamburg, as he christened it, was the one issued to him on 10 June 1943, which confirmed that Bomber Command's primary task remained '. . . the progressive destruction and dislocation of the German military, industrial and economic system, and the undermining of the morale of the German people to a point where their capacity for armed resistance is fatally weakened.' The increasing success of the German night-fighter force, and particularly the mounting casualties that the *Luftwaffe* day-fighters were inflicting upon the American Fortresses and Liberators, had resulted in a new priority being inserted in the directive, which was issued, under the authority of the Combined Chiefs of Staff, as 'Pointblank'. This new requirement was to attack, as a matter of urgency, German fighter strength. While the Americans, with many more guns of heavier calibre in their bombers than the RAF had, were able to pursue this objective by doing battle with the fighters in the air, that option was not a realistic one for Bomber Command at that time. Their contribution would of necessity have to be confined to attacks on production facilities.

There can be no doubt that Hamburg was a 'legitimate' target within the terms of Harris's directive, although there can equally be no doubt that the Commander-in-Chief preferred to interpret his overall brief in his own way and to be somewhat impatient of specific priorities set by the Chiefs of Staff. Nevertheless, Hamburg, apart from being a good 'morale' target, contained many maritime and industrial targets that were consistent with the suggestions of the Chiefs of Staff. In addition to its position as Germany's largest port, with all the war-related implications that go with that, Hamburg housed the vast Blohm und Voss shipyards, feverishly engaged in 1943 in the production of U-boats, a function they shared with several other Hamburg yards. That alone justified the choice of Hamburg as a target for a major attack. As a further attraction, the very many industrial factories and workshops within the city included a large number producing aircraft parts.

Anticipating the end of his campaign against Ruhr towns, Harris had begun as early as May 1943 to give shape to his thoughts on the destruction of Hamburg; his aim was no less than that. In an operational instruction dated 27 May 1943 and addressed to the Commanders of Bomber Command Groups Harris had bluntly written under the formal 'Intention' heading, 'To destroy HAMBURG', predicting that:

> 'The total destruction of this city would achieve immeasurable results in reducing the industrial capacity of the enemy's war machine. This, together with the effect on German morale, which would be felt throughout the country, would play a very important part in shortening and winning the war.'

This paragraph encapsulated Harris's concept of a strategic bomber offensive. The policy that he pursued was straightforward, untrammelled by moralistic inhibitions or by niceties of target selection based on the theoretical impact that attacks on individual industrial sectors – oil, rubber, ball-bearings and so on – might have, which he contemptuously dubbed 'panacea targets'.

Hamburg was no stranger to air-raid warnings. By the beginning of July 1943 the municipal authorities had already logged 137 attacks of varying strength, with 1,387 people killed and 4,496 injured. By the end of the month these casualty figures would have receded into comparative insignificance.

There were other considerations besides its fundamental target-worthiness behind Harris's choice of Hamburg for a major assault. Although the port did not come within Oboe range, its geographical location on the broad River Elbe, leading south-east from the distinctive coastline of the *Deutsche Bucht*, made it a very good target for marking and bombing by H2S, and additional navigational accuracy could be achieved because an approach over the North Sea would enable the navigators to use Gee, already heavily jammed over the mainland, to a much greater range. Additionally, Harris now had clearance to introduce a technical innovation 'Window', aimed at jamming enemy ground and air radar, which would, he foresaw, come as a major tactical surprise. Until the introduction of Window, jamming of radars had been conducted electronically, and not very effectively, with such devices as Grocer and Mandrel, but Window was basically a physical expedient, comprising innumerable narrow strips of coarse paper, aluminium-coated on one side and cut, for optimum effect, to half the wavelength of the German gun-laying and fighter control radars, the *Würzburg*s. As the wavelength of these radars was 53.5 cm, this dictated that the length of a strip should be approximately 27 cm. Dropped by aircraft into the field of the radars, each bundle of strips became a radar reflector, sending back an echo, so that the *Flak* gunners' and fighter controllers' radar screens would be swamped by a multiplicity of spurious signals through which it was virtually impossible to detect echoes originating from enemy bombers. There was a bonus: although originally designed to jam the *Würzburg* family of radars, Window was also highly effective against the *Lichtenstein* in the German night-fighters, the wavelength of which was 61 cms, near enough to twice the length of a strip for Window to reflect *Lichtenstein* transmissions almost as efficiently as it did those from the *Würzburg*. The principle of Window had long been known to both sides, the Germans calling it *Düppel*, but each side had hesitated to use it in case they should put themselves at an overall disadvantage by stimulating the opposition to retaliate in kind and then finding their own radars rendered unseeing.

Two minutes before midnight on 24 July 1943 the first British heavy bombers penetrated German air space. Since that morning the radio-monitoring services had been reporting heavy signals activity over Britain that indicated that preparations were under way for a major attack, and the fact that the nights were short made it reasonable to expect a comparatively short-range target, possibly in north Germany or the Ruhr area. That the former possibility was the correct one was confirmed when a strong force of bombers was detected over the North Sea by the *Wassermann* and *Freya* long-range radars, heading initially for Schleswig-Holstein. At 0019 hrs on the morning of Sunday, 25 July, the first air-raid alert, the thirty-minute warning, was issued for North Germany. Five minutes later the warning was upgraded to fifteen minutes, and the public air-raid sirens in Hamburg sounded at 0033 hrs. The sirens were not, however, the first intimation that all the people of city had of their impending ordeal: throughout Germany there was a system of air situation reporting on domestic radio and the *Drahtfunk*, or cable radio, with programmes being interrupted whenever it seemed likely that a raid was in the offing, so that those listening to late-night radio were already aware that a large force of British bombers was on its way.

Long before the first of Harris's force of 347 Lancasters, 246 Halifaxes, 125 Stirlings and seventy-three Wellingtons reached Hamburg from the north-west – they had turned on to a south-easterly heading about 100 kilometres short of the island of Sylt, shortly afterwards beginning to drop their packets of Window at the prescribed one-minute intervals – the coastal anti-aircraft and fighter control radars were reporting that their equipment was not functioning correctly, and when the fighters of NJG 3, responsible for the defence of the northern area, were scrambled to meet the incoming stream of bombers the radar operators, instead of picking up the familiar returns from hostile machines, found that their screens were swamped with countless flickering signals that gave the impression that the sky was full of an incalculable number of bombers, some of which seemed to be flying at impossible speeds. As the RAF force approached their target the effect of the Window, and with it the frustration of the defences, became more and more intense, with pilots having to listen to a confusing commentary from the baffled radar operators seated behind them and equally incoherent reporting and instructions from the fighter controllers on the ground.

The aiming point chosen by the Bomber Command planners was in the centre of the city and just north of the River Elbe, near to the town hall and the Church of St Nicholas, the *Nicolaikirche*. Since the war the choice of an aiming point so near to a House of God has many times been cited by critics of the bomber offensive as evidence of the cold-bloodedness of the Bomber Command planners, Harris in particular. Such criticism in fact trivialises the anti-bombing case: any area bombing attack on a city is bound to destroy and damage buildings of religious significance, because neither the bomb aimer nor the bomb can distinguish between them and other edifices. It was not intended that the attack would centre on that point, however, because experience since the introduction of target-marking by Pathfinders had revealed a phenomenon in RAF attacks that had come to be known as 'creep-back', a pronounced tendency for backer-up markers and main force bombs to fall progressively short of the target markers themselves and so produce an elongated pattern of bombing reaching back along the bombers' run-in track. In all probability this was an outcome of an understandable inclination on the part of bomb aimers, tense in the nose of the aircraft and 'talking' the pilot in to the attack, to press the bomb-release button just marginally early and, along with the other members of the crew, to experience the indescribable, if only momentary, relief that came with the announcement 'Bombs gone!', even though there were long seconds yet to wait before the photoflash had exploded and the pilot was clear to take evasive action. In the planning of the attack it was envisaged that the creep-back would spread the carpet of destruction across the mainly residential areas of Hamburg to the north-west of the aiming point. Given the multiplicity of naval and maritime objectives within the city, most of which lay to the *south* of the river, the choice of aiming point emphasised Harris's unwavering belief in area bombing and his view that civilian morale was the target most likely to win the war. Hans Brunswig, in his detailed book *Feuersturm über Hamburg*, incorrectly puts a slightly more charitable interpretation on Harris's choice of aiming point:

> 'The strategic aim of the bombing of Hamburg was certainly primarily the elimination of the armaments factories concentrated here, in particular the U-boat yards and the mineral-oil industry, not by destroying the individual industrial installations, but more by destroying the homes of the workers. As a secondary objective Bomber Command also hoped to make a considerable impact on the population's will to resist . . .'

The tactics to be used in 'Gomorrah' were carefully planned to exploit to their utmost the technical facilities that Bomber Command now enjoyed and to optimise the chances of achieving Harris's avowed aim, the destruction of the city. The bomber stream would be concentrated in space and time, and PFF markers would be used not only to provide aiming points for the main force bomb aimers but also to mark the crossing-in and crossing-out points on the German coast. To help in track-keeping and bombing accuracy, selected crews were to calculate the wind velocity at altitude between their final Gee fix and their first accurate H2S fix and transmit the results to headquarters in England, from where, after a process of mathematical and meteorological refinement, the average would be re-broadcast for use by the other aircraft on their approach to the target and for setting on their bomb-sights. The raid was to be supported by Fighter Command, about twenty-five of whose Mosquitos were to fly intruder operations against enemy night-fighter airfields.

In brief, the Pathfinder plan for the bombing itself was that the aircraft starting the attack should be twenty so-called 'Blind Marker-Illuminators', who would light up the target by dropping yellow markers and flares, aiming by means of their H2S radar. They would also drop high-explosive bombs. Almost immediately afterwards 'Visual Markers', eight in number, would each drop five red target indicators, identifying the aiming point by eye. It was at the red markers that, ideally, the main force bombers were to aim. As the raid progressed further Pathfinder aircraft, 'Backers-up', would attempt to re-centre the raid by dropping green target indicators, which would then be the datum point for those crews following up.

The raid started punctually at 0058 hrs, but the initial marking was scattered, some of the yellows and reds falling up to eight kilometres away to the north-west. This contributed to the extent of the ensuing creep-back, which stretched even further than had been envisaged when the planning was being done. A very high degree of concentration was achieved in the heavily populated residential areas in the north-west of the city, largely made up of workers' apartment blocks, but whereas the plan had envisaged that the devastation should be confined within the city limits, the area in which bombs fell stretched much further out, as far as outlying villages fifteen kilometres or so from the aiming point, with many bomb-loads falling into open country. Indeed, post-raid calculations indicated that only thirty-nine per cent of the attackers had dropped their bombs within three miles of the aiming point. Even so, the damage caused was immense and approximately 1,500 lives were lost on the ground. Had the PFF marking and the bomb aiming been more accurate, a vastly higher casualty rate would have ensued. Even as it was, more people had lost their lives in Hamburg in that one raid than in the 137 attacks that had preceded it. It is, incidentally, worth bearing in mind that casualties of this order had been suffered in England two years previously. The difference was that what in 1941 was outside the norm was now becoming commonplace in Germany.

But statistics are cold, impersonal, inadequate to give any idea of the human suffering, on both sides, involved in raids such as this. Let one family die in a motor accident, let twenty die in a terrorist bomb attack, let two hundred die in a ferry disaster, and the sense of shock is real, the grief understandably profound. Show the wounded in a Balkan or African skirmish on television, and the sensitive viewers who ignore the announcer's warning that 'some of these scenes might cause distress' will, at least briefly, begin to realise the horror of what is going on. Write '500 people died in Coventry', or '1,436 lost their lives in London during the night of 10/11 May 1941', or 'About 1,500 were killed in Hamburg', and already the enormity of what is being reported is such that the mind is incapable of other than superficial, numerical comprehension. Try to read the figures in terms of individual pain and anguish, not only in those directly affected but also in those who grieve and mourn, and soon the mind rebels, rejects what it is trying to envisage, finds palliative explanations and excuses for what was done. And refuses to come to terms with the fact that Man is inherently barbarous, be he German or British.

The value of Window was reflected in the Bomber Command loss rate. Whereas the average rate of attrition on major targets during the Battle of the Ruhr had been approaching five per cent, twelve aircraft failed to return from this, the opening move in the Battle of Hamburg, representing only 1.5 per cent of the force dispatched. Had the average suffered over the Ruhr been maintained the figure would have been thirty-five, so the introduction of Window may be assumed to have saved twenty-three bombers at a stroke. More importantly, because machines could be comparatively easily replaced, it had saved about 150 aircrew from death, injury or imprisonment.

Walter Heidenreich had been flying with Oberleutnant Günter Köberich, *Staffelkapitän* of 11./NJG 3, since April 1942 when, as related earlier, they had formed a crew after losing their pilot and *Funker* respectively. They had by now destroyed three British bombers. In the early hours of 25 July 1943 they took off from Grove to stand by in *Nachtjagdraum 'Ameise'*:

'We were sent to "*Ameise*", and we shot a Halifax down. The attack that night was on Hamburg, and I cannot think what he was doing so far north. Perhaps he was flying on a special operation. Or it is possible that he had made a navigational error and had mistaken the coastline on his *Rotterdamgerät*. And although the RAF were dropping *Düppel* that night, he didn't drop any. The ground controller took us in very close. We picked him up on *Lichtenstein* and got very near to him, so near that I could read his squadron letters – I wrote them down somewhere – and we almost collided with him. I even saw the face of the rear gunner. When we shot him down the sun was just rising, we were so far north. He came down near Sönderborg on the Flensburg Fjord.

'After we had landed we went out to where the Halifax had crashed. They told us not to go too close because there were still bombs on board. There was an aerial mine in a crater just by the aeroplane, and sentries were guarding it. A Feldwebel from the navy, the *Kriegsmarine*, went and looked into the crater, and the mine exploded. There was a terrible bang, and they never found his body.'

The Halifax that Köberich shot down was not on a special flight but was clearly well off track: possibly Heidenreich was correct when he suggested that the navigator had made an H2S error. If the bomber had drifted well to the north of its flight-plan track it would have crossed the Danish coast in an area where the H2S returns would not be greatly different from those at the correct crossing point. In his meticulous book *The Battle of Hamburg*, Martin Middlebrook identifies the hapless bomber as one from No. 51 Squadron captained by a pilot newly arrived on the unit and flying only his second operation, Sergeant W. J. Murray. Middlebrook describes how five of the crew members were killed when the machine crashed, and the remaining two gravely injured. Local inhabitants sent heaps of flowers to the two men, who had been put into the Sönderborg hospital, but when the German authorities heard of this they ordered that the flowers be removed. The two flyers died soon afterwards.

Murray's Halifax was, according to Middlebrook, 'flying the correct heading but sixty miles from the bomber stream'. Its destruction is a graphic illustration of the vital nature of the navigator's contribution to the safety of the aircraft in which he flew. Now that the bombers were concentrated in a stream, it was the straggler or the one that was to one side of the stream that would stand out on the *Würzburg* or *Lichtenstein* operator's screen and so invite attack. Those that remained on track and kept to their flight-plan times enjoyed the anonymity of one in a crowd and were less likely to be singled out for attention. Even Window could provide little, if any, protection for an isolated bomber dropping it, because it naturally lagged behind and only provided cover for following machines, which is why Heidenreich was possibly wrong in thinking that Murray's Halifax was not 'windowing' at the time.

In strategic terms, Window had done much more than jam the German radars, the frequency of which could, in the fulness of time, be altered to minimise its effects, while other anti-jamming devices could be, and indeed were, conceived and introduced. But such measures would only trigger off the next reactive step in the electronics war, for example the use of Window of different size and the introduction of other measures to overcome the hostile anti-jamming equipment. What the silver strips had achieved was to render Kammhuber's complex, laboriously developed night-fighter organisation completely ineffective.

There had for a time been unease in some quarters, particularly among the night-fighter crews themselves, at the inflexibility of the *Himmelbett* defensive system. The overlapping areas, each covered by two Würzburg Giants, could only handle one, or at the most two, fighters at a time, and the bomber stream would only cross a small number of areas. Because of the concentration in time there could be up to fifty or so bombers in any one area simultaneously, which meant that even if both fighters made successful interceptions the majority of the raiders would cross the Kammhuber Line unchallenged. Even more tellingly, the nature of the system meant that many fighters would be scrambled to orbit beacons in areas that would not be penetrated by the incoming bomber stream, and so would have no hope of 'trade'. Some crews took it into their own hands to leave their allocated fighter control area and infiltrate the bomber stream, but the practice was frowned upon, particularly when the pilot was of junior rank and lacking in hierarchical status. But Kammhuber had invested so much in his *Himmelbett* system that he was implacably reluctant to change it for something new. By making both the *Würzburgs* on the ground and the *Lichtensteins* in the air blind, Window forced the Germans to think again.

The shock-waves reached to the very highest level of the *Luftwaffe* hierarchy. Any remaining complacency that Göring might have had about the threat that Bomber Command presented was shattered. By this time in the war the Reichsmarschall was becoming increasingly remote from the day-to-day oversight of the *Luftwaffe*, and indeed from his other state responsibilities, spending much of his time travelling through occupied territories in search of art treasures to add to his private collection. The attack on Hamburg affected Hitler, too, even more so, it seems, than the equally destructive ones on Düsseldorf and Cologne shortly before had done. During the morning following the attack, Göring rang

Hajo Herrmann from his Karinhall estate and asked him how far advanced his training programme with the newly established JG 300 was (it will be recalled that Herrmann had estimated that his *Wilde Sau* fighters would not be operational until the middle of September, and he told Göring that such was still the case). Göring ordered him to bring JG 300 to operational readiness immediately.

This is an appropriate point to outline the way in which Herrmann envisaged his single-seater Bf 109s and Fw 190s being used. Training for the pilots in blind flying and air-to-air firing were of course a *sine qua non*, but without any form of navigational equipment in their machines other than a compass the pilots needed some means of finding their way about Germany in the darkness that they could use with confidence in their cramped cockpits. They would carry a small-scale map of the country on which were marked the major cities and towns and airfields suitable for landing by night, and the map would be annotated with courses, distances and approximate flying times between airfields and towns, and ideally they would also commit the principal figures to memory so that their reaction to instructions from the ground would be automatic. Because of wind effect, however, courses and times could be extremely inaccurate, so some physical aid was necessary to ensure that the fighters would reach the target under attack and then have a reasonable chance of finding their way back to either their own or some other suitable airfield. The duration of the single-engined aircraft was limited, particularly after combat, even though supplementary drop-tanks could be carried. Herrmann was therefore in the process of arranging searchlight 'avenues' between the major cities, with individual searchlights pointing the direction to follow and with combinations of searchlights in easily recognisable arrangements – triangles, parallel beams, crossing beams and so on – to identify the towns themselves. The *Flak* would also play its part, firing combinations of coloured shells to mark individual towns. These and other measures were in the process of being implemented and practised when Göring rang Herrmann.

The night after the attack on Hamburg Harris's force returned to Essen, hoping to inflict a major blow on this most important target before the Germans could devise and implement counter-measures to Window. Oboe Mosquitos accurately marked the Krupp works, which suffered considerable damage. Six Mosquitos also paid a harassing visit to the hard-hit city of Hamburg. Ominously, 3.7 per cent of the force directed against Essen failed to return, mostly victims of night-fighters that had been scrambled towards the approaching bomber stream and who had hunted freelance. Some controller/pilot combinations, however, still managed to achieve close-control success, Major Werner Streib, newly promoted *Kommodore* of NJG 1, destroying two Lancasters, a Stirling and a Halifax between 0028 hrs and 0142 hrs under the control of Oberleutnant Walter Knickmeier. Streib's final kill that morning was the eighty-eighth that Knickmeier had to his credit, and Knickmeier's last close-controlled intercept.

Another night-fighter ace who enjoyed a close-controlled success that night despite Window was Oberleutnant Paul Zorner, who scored his tenth kill. In December 1942 Zorner had joined 2./NJG 3, stationed at Wittmundhafen, the second *Staffel* of I./NJG 3, which in March 1943 was detached to Grove, Zorner being made *Staffelkapitän*. His *Gruppenkommandeur*, like Wittgenstein of IV./NJG 5, was an officer of aristocratic line, Prinz zur Lippe-Weissenfeld, and

NIGHT-TIME VISUAL NAVIGATION AIDS

First introduced in 1943 to help Herrmann's *Wild Boar* single-seat fighters to find their way around blacked-out Germany by night, visual aids to navigation became of more and more importance to all night-fighter crews as British jamming of radio frequencies made accurate navigation by traditional means increasingly difficult. Represented on this and the next page are some of the systems in use in mid-1944

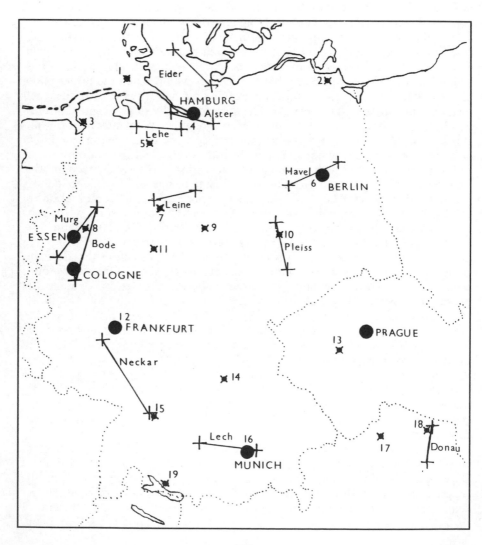

Searchlight Lanes: Lanes of vertically-shining searchlights were set up between airfields in the vicinity of important towns. They were code-named after local rivers. For example:

Eider: Between Schleswig and Lübeck.
Alster: Between Lüneburg and Stade.
Lehe: Between Oldenburg and Rotenburg.
Havel: Between Brandenburg and Werneuchen.
Murg: Between Münster/Handorf and Mönchengladbach.
Bode: Between Bonn/Hangelar and Münster/Handorf.

Leine: Between Wesendorf and Wunstorf.
Pleiss: Between Altenburg and Köthen.
Neckar: Between Mainz/Finthen and Echterdingen.
Lech: Between Leipheim and München/Riem.
Donau: Between Seyring and Wiener Neustadt.

Starshells: The *Flak* fired starshells in given combinations to mark navigationally important towns. For example:

1. Heligoland: Three, one above another.
2. Danzig: Three side by side.
3. Emden: Four side by side.
4. Hamburg: Two side by side.
5. Bremen: Two, one above another.
6. Berlin: Two, one above another.
7. Hannover: Three side by side.
8. Dortmund: Three side by side.
9. Brunswick: Three, one above another.
10. Halle: Three side by side.
11. Kassel: Two side by side.
12. Frankfurt/Main: Two, one above another.
13. Pilsen: Three, one above another.
14. Nuremberg: Three side by side.
15. Stuttgart: Three, one above another.
16. Munich: Two side by side.
17. Linz: Three, one above another.
18. Vienna: Three side by side.
19. Friedrichshafen: Two, one above another.

Searchlight Town-Codes: Important towns could be identified by groups of two to four searchlights arranged to form a distinctive pattern;

Augsburg :

Berlin Centre (6) :

Bremen (5) :

Danzig (2) :

Emden (3) :

Halle (10) :

Hamburg (4) :

Hannover (7) :

Kassel (11) :

Kiel :

Linz (17) :

Munich (16) :

Münster :

Nuremberg (14) :

Pilsen (13) :

Vienna (18) :

also like Wittgenstein he was a highly successful night-fighter. The *Gruppe* was equipped with the Bf 110, except for the second *Staffel*, which had the Do 217, an aircraft which Zorner did not like, and he refused to fly it operationally, so incurring the displeasure of the prince: Zorner, however, already had a good reputation with the Bf 110, in which he had shot down six enemy aircraft, and Weissenfeld, less uncompromising than Wittgenstein, relented. On 17 April 1943 Zorner had taken off in daylight against American bombers, and because his Bf 110 was unserviceable Weissenfeld had let him fly his. Weissenfeld was not flying that day: he already had thirty-six kills to his credit and crews with more than ten were banned from flying on daylight operations. Zorner was shot down by an American bomber, but managed to make a belly landing near a *Luftwaffe* observation bunker, where he and his radio operator were treated as heroes by the fifty or so *Luftwaffe* girls manning it, who were enormously impressed when they saw the thirty-six victories painted on his rudder.

Zorner describes his tenth victory graphically:

'In the summer of 1943 experienced crews were moved into the front line, but there was considerable confusion when it came to using them. Between 12 and 15 June, for example, I was moved to Vechta, St Trond, Leeuwarden, Gilze-Rijen, back to St Trond and then to Leeuwarden again. I was not scrambled for the first attack on Hamburg – I can't remember why not. At the time I was at St Trond in Belgium, and I see from my log book that I was sent to Wunstorf the following day, landing there at 1828 hrs. Very soon afterwards I was ordered back to Wittmundhafen, taking off at 1957 hrs. All we carried was a small bag with shaving kit and so on. I was scrambled at 2326 hrs. Bombers were approaching on an easterly heading and were approximately over the Friesian island of Nordeney. We thought it might be Hamburg again, but in the region of Borkum they turned south. Their target was Essen. I was sent to circle a beacon in the Jüst area. I had an excellent *JLO*, Oberleutnant Janssen, who had already controlled me in six of my victories. This time, however, Janssen did something that made me angry – he tried to talk me in from the north. As it was summer, the northern sky was very bright, so the bomber's crew would be able to see me in silhouette. What I didn't know was that the stream had already turned south, so Janssen had no choice.

'I decided to stay high, in any case. The bomber was at 6,000 metres, so I went up to 6,600. I positioned myself to one side and closed in to a range of two to three hundred metres and slightly below. I don't know whether the rear gunner saw me, because I didn't see any fire from the turret. After a very short burst from my guns the Halifax's starboard wing caught fire, and then I saw it hit the ground. I think it was probably a Pathfinder machine, because there were lots of coloured lights, reds and greens, in the explosion.

'Possibly I had in fact been fired at and hit, because almost immediately my starboard engine cut out and the airscrew began windmilling. The port engine couldn't cope with the air resistance. I tried to reach Wittmundhafen, but I couldn't feather the starboard propeller and it was clear I wasn't going to make it, so I ordered my *Funker* to bale out. He jettisoned the cabin roof and I thought he had gone, and I attempted to follow him. In the Bf 110 there was a so-called *Überschlagbügel*, a curved metal tube that strengthened the cabin so that in the event of landing upside-down the crew would not be crushed. My parachute caught in this, and we were going down vertically. I clambered back into the cockpit, and I realised that I had forgotten to lower the flaps, which was part of the drill when abandoning aircraft, so that it would go into a relatively flat glide. The hydraulics were out, because they were operated by the starboard engine, but I managed to lower them with the emergency compressed-air system. The aircraft came out of the dive and slowed down, and I was able to get out without difficulty. I counted slowly as I had been taught at training school – 22 pause, 23 pause, 24 – and pulled the ripcord. I hit the ground immediately afterwards. A few seconds later and I would have been killed.

'When I baled out I could see the lights of the airfield. I landed in a ditch by the side of the road. A young man came past on a motorcycle and gave me a lift back to base. I had lost one boot when I jumped. I got into the sidecar and put my parachute on the pillion. I had shot the Halifax down at 0106 hrs, and I was back at Wittmundhafen by 0130.

'I was very disturbed to hear that there was no news of my *Funker*, Heinz Wilke. I had flown with him for twenty-one months, and we were an excellent team. There was naturally a very close bond between us. Next morning he phoned in. He had landed in a waterlogged meadow, so he had inflated his dinghy and lain in it to wait for dawn. When it was light enough he went to the nearest village and phoned in. I was surprised when he told me that after jettisoning the canopy he too had been unable to get out, but had stayed in the aircraft until I had pulled it out of its dive, and then he had jumped. In my confusion I just hadn't seen him.'

It is arguable that Harris's decision to strike at Essen on 25/26 July instead of going back to Hamburg immediately was in principle tactically unsound. Public and air-raid services had been very badly hit: telephones were out, water mains ruptured and public transport in the affected area disrupted, with many streets virtually impassable. Fires were still burning, even though brigades had been brought in from surrounding towns – Bremen, Lübeck and Kiel – and, on the day following the attack, from as far away as Berlin. Work on digging out the dead and the survivors was being carried out as quickly as the hard-pressed rescue services could manage. Hans Brunswig (*Feuersturm über Hamburg*) finds Harris's decision incomprehensible: 'It was just impossible to understand why Bomber Command didn't continue with Operation 'Gomorrah' – if they had done so, it would certainly have been fatal for Hamburg!' Paradoxically, as will be recounted, it is probable that the postponement of a second major blow against the stricken city contributed enormously to Harris's self-imposed aim of destroying Hamburg completely.

The following night the sirens sounded again, but once more the only British machines that visited the city were a few Mosquitos, and minimal damage was caused. Possibly the switch of the Bomber Command attack to Essen and two nights' relative peace gave the more optimistic of the citizens to imagine that their nocturnal tribulations were over, for the time being at least. In the daylight hours of 26 and 27 July, however, formations of American heavy bombers joined in the battle; but they did not do so in strength comparable to that of the RAF, even allowing for the fact that their commander, Major-General Ira C. Eaker, only had some 350 bombers to call upon against Harris's 800-plus. The Pointblank directive for a combined bomber offensive, which in simple terms envisaged the RAF hitting a target by night and the 8th Air Force striking at the same, or a related, target by day, which would have required joint planning of a very intimate and closely co-ordinated nature, was in fact never fully realised, as was exemplified by the American contribution to Gomorrah.

Instead of concentrating all his bombers on Hamburg with the aim of furthering the destruction of the city, Brigadier-General Fred Anderson, commanding the US VIII Bomber Command, decided to carry out several attacks on various targets in northern Germany, and as part of this general effort about one hundred B-17 Fortresses attacked Hamburg on the afternoon of the twenty-fifth and about sixty on the morning of the twenty-sixth. Following the American policy of precision attack, specific targets in accordance with priorities specified in the Pointblank directive were chosen, those in Hamburg being the Blohm und Voss U-boat yard and the Klöckner aero-engine factory. Both of these objectives lay to the south of the River Elbe and in an area that had escaped major damage in the earlier Bomber Command attack. The targets, partly obscured by smoke drifting from the fires caused by the RAF, were hit, but the effect on production was comparatively insignificant, much more damage being caused by random bombs that fell outside the immediate target area. Overall, the American formations operating against Hamburg and other objectives suffered heavily at the hands of German day fighters. Night fighters were also scrambled from Leeuwarden against Fortresses returning from the northerly targets, and they achieved three successes. On 25 July Leutnant Gerhard Dittmann of 12./NJG 1 shot down a B-17 into the North Sea, his first success, but his *Staffelkapitän*, Oberleutnant Gerhard Gardiewski, was himself shot down by the Americans in the same area. He and his radio operator, Unteroffizier Fritz Abromeit, were rescued by the British Air-Sea Rescue Service and made prisoners of war. Most of the night-fighters had already flown operationally that day, in the very early hours of the morning against the RAF attack, and one of them, Oberleutnant Ernst-Georg Drünkler, had shot down an off-track Lancaster: in the afternoon he destroyed a B-17. The redoubtable Oberleutnant Martin Drewes of 11./NJG 1 claimed the third kill for the Leeuwarden *Gruppe* the following day, and Gerhard Dittmann claimed his second victory which was, however, not confirmed.

To write of what happened on the night of 27/28 July 1943 is to attempt to describe the indescribable. Harris resumed his attack on Hamburg, committing 787 bombers, approximately the same number as he had used on the same target three nights previously. In concept it was a routine raid by the standards of the day. A similar route over the North Sea was followed and the same aiming point chosen, but this time the bomber stream's final approach was from slightly north of east, heading marginally south of west so that the creep-back would take in residential areas largely unaffected by the first raid. Window would of course be used once more, as indeed it would be as a matter of routine throughout the remainder of the war, and the whole raid was to last forty-five minutes as against the fifty minutes planned for the first attack. The composition of the overall bomb tonnage was altered so that a significantly higher proportion of incendiaries was carried, but this seems not to have been specifically in order to create more fires, but rather because the longer distance to be flown to enable the bombers to approach from the east dictated a lighter bomb-load, particularly for the Stirlings and Halifaxes, and incendiaries did not weigh as much as high-explosive bombs. Fate took a hand in that night's events, and Fate was on Harris's side to an extent that even he could not have envisaged. A new word, a new concept, was born into the language of aerial bombing. The word was 'fire-storm'.

Rising air expands and so becomes cooler. In simple terms this is because the same amount of heat is spread throughout a larger volume of air. The effect is known as adiabatic cooling, and the rate at which that cooling takes place as the air rises is called the adiabatic lapse rate, and it is a constant figure. There is also a different lapse rate: as everyone knows, if you go up through still air, in an air-craft for example, or up a mountain, it gets colder. The rate at which the temperature falls off in still air is called the environmental lapse rate, and it varies according to the physical composition of the air mass. In normal circumstances the environmental lapse rate is less than the adiabatic rate, so that if air is caused to rise – by heat, for example, or at a weather front, or by the wind blowing up a hillside – that air will cool down until it becomes colder than the air surrounding it, and therefore more heavy, when it will cease to rise and begin to sink. Sometimes, however, the adiabatic lapse rate will be slightly less than the environmental lapse rate, which means that when air starts to rise it stays warmer, and therefore lighter, than the air around it, and so continues to go upwards. In the right conditions the rising air reaches almost unimaginable volumes and speeds, and commonly the result is a thunderstorm. Everyone is familiar with the increase of wind speed, sometimes to gale force, that is experienced when there is a thunderstorm. This is because air is being sucked in at the base of the storm to replace the air that is rushing upwards.

On what has come to be known as 'the night of the fire-storm' the atmospheric conditions in the Hamburg area were such that, had Bomber Command not intervened, the citizen's sleep would in any case have been disturbed by thunderstorms. It was a beautiful summer's evening, if very close, with temperatures on the ground approaching 30° centigrade. The skies were clear of cloud, but hazy. There had been no rain for some time, and buildings, trees and so on were dry. The majority of the available fire services were still working in the western suburbs of Hamburg, anticipating a further raid and attempting to douse the fires started in the earlier attack.

Dropping their target indicators by means of H2S, the first PFF machines, the blind markers, opened the attack at 0055 hrs on the morning of 28 July, the majority of markers landing in a good concentration approximately two miles to the east-south-east of the aiming point itself. The concentration of markers provided a good datum point for those following up, and in a very short time high-explosive and incendiary bombs were raining down in the Borgfelde, Hamm and Hammerbrook areas. Pathfinder backers-up performed well in limiting creep-back, but they did not move the centre of attack to the main aiming point.

By 0130 hrs the many fires that were ignited were combining into one vast con-flagration, and the enormous heat generated had triggered off upcurrents that sucked in more and more air which, in its turn, joined that already shooting upwards, always remaining warmer than the remainder of the surrounding air mass so that there was no meteorological mechanism to stop it. The fire-storm, once triggered off, was self-propagating, the oxygen in the gale-force winds it created feeding the hungry flames to unheard-of temperatures so that fires leaped from building to building in a holocaust defying comprehension or description. Countless human beings died in the flames, burnt and charred beyond recogni-tion, hundreds upon hundreds more suffocated in their shelters when the fire-storm sucked out the air. Much has been written about that terrible night, but nothing even remotely adequate to convey the reality of what happened. To this day the number who perished is not known with any accuracy, but a con-servative estimate puts it at 40,000.

To the Bomber Command aircrew taking part it was clear that this was no ordinary raid. Some spoke of a sea of flames, of smoke rising to their bombing altitude, even of smelling the smoke within their aircraft, of pity for the people caught in the inferno below them; all were impressed, many deeply shaken, by the extent and significance of what they had experienced.

Window again proved its worth, with only seventeen bombers being lost, 2.2 per cent of the force. Just as had happened on the first Window-assisted attack, the Hamburg *Flak*, usually highly efficient, had to resort to a comparatively innocuous barrage. On the night-fighter front, however, the first steps were already being taken along the path towards recovery from the shock created by Window. The command and control structure of the *Nachtjagd* was in a turmoil of indecision, which meant that local commanders had more latitude for tactical decision. Some adhered strictly to the *Himmelbett* procedure, others preferred to send the fighters up to operate freelance, even over the target itself. After the first bewilderment of finding their radar screens saturated with spurious blips, some of the more competent *Würzburg* operators were beginning to be able to differ-entiate between Window-induced returns and those originating from bombers, and in the aircraft some radio operators were making similar progress. To help the freelance fighters, ground stations were broadcasting rudimentary running commentaries on the bombers' target and the location, route and height of the attackers.

The night-fighter pilots held in the *Himmelbett* boxes could do little but watch in frustration while Hamburg burned. Leutnant Peter Spoden, then twenty-two years old, made his first operational flight in a Bf 110 of 5./NJG 5 from Parchim during the Battle of Hamburg. On the night of the fire-storm he was scrambled to a beacon in a *Himmelbett* area near Rügen on the Baltic coast. He comments:

'I was in *Raum* "*Reiher*", forty or fifty kilometres away from Hamburg, but I could see it burning, and I could make out aircraft like moths in the light from the fires. I was angry – I went crazy. I called up on my R/T asking for permission to go to Hamburg and hunt freelance, but I was told to stay where I was. And then I had to land. We young officers were crazy with frustration. It was stupidity to keep us up there in a *Raum* where there were no targets. I asked to be allowed to take off again and go there, and I was told no. I was a young man, and I had to obey my superiors, like Hauptmann Schoenert, Hauptmann Fellerer, Wim Johnen. But I should have disobeyed them on this occasion, I should have gone and flown *"Wilde Sau".'*

Major Hajo Herrmann's Wild Boars were up in such strength as they could muster. Under his command he now had three embryo *Gruppen*, I./JG 300 at Bonn/Hangelar under Major Ewald Janssen; II./JG 300 at Rheine led by Major Kettner; and III./JG 300 under Major von Buchwaldt at Oldenburg. He had his Staff Flight at Hangelar, but his headquarters were in a country house near Bonn, the *Schloss Allner*, from where he would commute to Hangelar in a Fieseler Storch when leading his *Wilde Sau* men into action. The *Gruppen* at Rheine and Oldenburg were lodger units, II./JG 300 with the day-fighter *Gruppe* II./JG 1, equipped with the Fw 109; and III./JG 300 flying the Bf 109 day-fighters of III./JG 1. The *Stab* and I./JG 300 at Hangelar had a mixture of both types of machines, including some Bf 109Ts, a version originally designed for operation from the aircraft carrier *Graf Zeppelin*, which was never completed. JG 300 had already experienced fatalities. Its first loss had been that of the twenty-three-year-old Leutnant Heinz Strauss of 4./JG 300, whose Fw 190 had crashed near Staaken, Berlin, during a searchlight practice on the night of 21 July. The *Geschwader* had suffered a heavy blow when the officer whom Herrmann had first appointed to command I./JG 300, Major Willy Gutsche, had been killed when his aircraft crashed from unknown causes the following night. Even this early the dangers of flying a single-engined machine, not equipped with blind-flying aids, by night were becoming apparent. Some *Wilde Sau* machines had operated *ad hoc* during the night of the attack on Essen that had come between the first two major attacks on Hamburg, and four machines had been lost, three pilots, Feldwebel Günther Hattendorf, Leutnant Hans-Werner Schmidt and Feldwebel Heinrich Grill, paying the ultimate price. During the same raid Feldwebel Wolfgang Knobloch, severely wounded by machine-gun fire from a British bomber, had crash-landed his damaged Fw 190 at Rheine.

By the time, then, that JG 300, or the *Geschwader Herrmann* as it had come to be colloquially known, flew its first full-scale defensive mission over Hamburg on the night of 27/28 July 1943 it had already lost six aircraft, the pilots of five of which had been killed. It had not been an auspicious beginning. But that night Herrmann's Wild Boar concept came closer to being vindicated. Twelve machines took off from Hangelar, Rheine and Oldenburg to hunt in the light of the fires from the inferno below, where they were joined by a small number of conventional night-fighters, some under orders and some, more self-assured or senior than Peter Spoden, at their own initiative. Herrmann's pilots shot down four bombers over the city out of the total of seventeen that Bomber Command lost that night. Herrmann lost just one of his machines, the Fw 190 of Leutnant Fritz Tesch of 5./JG 300, at thirty-two years of age one of the older of the Wild Boar pilots, who had to crash-land, severely injured, after his fighter had been damaged in combat with a British bomber.

Two further raids completed the Battle of Hamburg, the first comparatively successful, the second one a failure. The aiming point for the attack during the night of 29/30 July was the same as that chosen for the two previous raids, with the bombers approaching from the north. The intention was to hit undamaged areas in the northern part of the great city. A total of 777 bombers took part, with the Pathfinders marking by H2S. Again the first markers were inaccurately placed, this time between two and three miles too far to the east. A good concentration of bombing was achieved, the creep-back extending about four miles, and intense fires generated. Fortunately for the people living in the areas that were struck on this occasion, the atmospheric conditions had changed and there was no fire-storm. Nevertheless, something approaching 1,000 are believed to have perished – it proved impossible to compile an accurate figure because of the complete breakdown of the normal damage reporting and assessment mechanism after the cataclysmic events two nights previously.

The final attack in the series, which took place on 2/3 August 1943, was a clear demonstration of the inherent potential for failure that still characterised Harris's bombing methods despite the technical and tactical innovations since he had taken over Bomber Command. This time 740 RAF machines were directed to bomb an aiming point in the north of the city, coming in from the south. On the three previous occasions the bombers' initial course had taken them over the North Sea and Schleswig-Holstein, but this time they were routed to cross the north German coast between Bremerhaven and Cuxhaven. They met violent thunderstorms over Germany, and the force was scattered, many crews turning back and/or dropping their bombs at random. The Pathfinders were unable to mark the target because the city itself was cloud-covered, and such bombing as there was was widely distributed throughout the flat countryside of Lower Saxony. Some bombs fell in Hamburg, but the people in the shelters could not distinguish the noise of the explosions from that of the violent thunder that was occurring simultaneously. Casualties were light, to some extent as a result of the fact that approaching a million people had fled the city following the night of the fire-storm.

Sandwiched between these two final attacks of the series was a raid led by Oboe Mosquitos against Remscheid on the periphery of the *Ruhrgebiet*. Only a comparatively small number of bombers took part, but heavy damage and casualties were caused in the industrial town.

Already, only nine days since the introduction of Window, Bomber Command losses were beginning to rise again, as the following table shows:

Date	Target	Bombers	Lost	Percentage
24/25 July	Hamburg	791	12	1.5
25/26 July	Essen	705	26	3.7
27/28 July	Hamburg	787	17	2.2
29/30 July	Hamburg	777	28	3.6
30/31 July	Remscheid	273	15	5.5
2/3 August	Hamburg	740	30	4.1
Total		4,073	128	3.1 (average)

The rise in Bomber Command losses was certainly due to the quick reaction to the initial setback on the part of both the leadership and the operational units of the *Nachtjagd*. Herrmann's *Wilde Sau* tactics, practised above the target by both his own single-engined fighters and the conventional twin-engined machines, played a large part in the recovery, and many of the crews of the traditional night-fighter units, now freed from the restrictions of Kammhuber's *Himmelbett* system, took enthusiastically to a new, freelance role. Pilots of Hajo Herrmann's JG 300 claimed approximately twenty kills for the loss of three more machines and one more pilot, while the majority of the rest of the bombers destroyed fell to Kammhuber's men.

Even before the introduction of Window minds other than that of Hajo Herrmann had been focusing on ways in which Harris's night bombers might be combated. Bomber Command's fundamental potential to wreak havoc within German cities had increased enormously with the advent of the four-engined load-carriers, Gee and H2S had revolutionised navigational methods, and PFF techniques meant that the bombers' loads were falling nearer to their allocated aiming points. Kammhuber's *Himmelbett* defences, designed and developed in response to Bomber Command's earlier haphazard, unco-ordinated tactics, were not inflicting sufficient casualties on the enemy to prevent him striking hard or to deter him from pursuing his ruthless course of destruction.

On 21 July 1943, three days before the opening raid of the Battle of Hamburg, Generalfeldmarschall Erhard Milch, Director-General of Equipment (Air), had written to Dr Rottgardt of the electronics firm *Telefunken* outlining his thoughts on the way in which he saw the future development of night fighting. He had begun by stating that the urgent need was to destroy at least twenty to thirty per cent of the attackers, with the longer-term aim of increasing that figure to fifty per cent. In order to achieve these aims it would be necessary to introduce a system of long-range freelance night fighting to augment the efforts of the close-controlled fighters, for which purpose a wider range of AI and other radars would be necessary. *Telefunken* were already working on a range of new radar devices, and Milch urged the speedy development and production of, for example, *Lichtenstein SN-2*, which operated on a lower frequency than the commonly used *Lichtenstein BC*; the wide-angle version, *Lichtenstein C-1 Weitwinkel*; *Lichtenstein C-1* with a tunable frequency range; *Pauke A*, a blind-firing device; and *Biene W*, an IFF equipment. To some extent, then, the scene was already set for a rapid response to Window, and on 29 July, almost immediately after the second Hamburg attack, Oberst Viktor von Lossberg, now working with Milch as his adviser on night-fighting matters, was able to present proposals for a new night-fighting system to a meeting attended by twenty-eight senior *Luftwaffe* personalities presided over by Milch and including Generaloberst Weise who, as *Befehlshaber Mitte,* exercised overall command and control of the air defence of the *Reich.* Also present were night-fighter chief Kammhuber, Generalmajor Adolf Galland, General of Fighters (*General der Jagdflieger*), and Hajo Herrmann, as a mere Major one of the most lowly in rank.

The concept that von Lossberg outlined envisaged a strong reserve of night fighters being brought up from the rear and deployed in the Dutch area to supplement the *Himmelbett*-controlled machines. One aircraft from each *Staffel* would be a so-called *Fühlungshalter*, literally a 'contact-keeper', but perhaps better translated as 'lead aircraft', which would navigate by means of the 'Y' system, which will be described later. The lead aircraft would transmit a continuous signal on a spot frequency, which would allow the other machines of the *Staffel* to home on to it by means of their direction-finding (D/F) equipment. All the night-fighters should be equipped as soon as possible with *SN-2* interception radar and/or wide-angle *Lichtenstein*. As Window did not protect the foremost aircraft of the bomber stream, the lead aircraft would home on to them, followed by the rest of the *Staffel*, and they would then freelance within the stream. The lead aircraft, the remainder of the *Staffel* and the ground control organisation would operate on a common R/T frequency. To prevent friendly aircraft being shot down, until a reliable IFF system was available there should be a complete ban on firing at anything other than four-engined machines.

Von Lossberg advocated the strengthening of Herrmann's *Wilde Sau* units, the possible equipping of some of the single-engined machines with *Lichtenstein B/C*, the use of twin-engined fighters on *Wilde Sau* operations above the target, and the restriction of the anti-aircraft guns to a certain level. Thought should also be given to the use of infra-red homers in the fighters and to the dropping of parachute flares within the bomber stream to illuminate the attackers.

The committee unanimously accepted von Lossberg's proposals and forwarded them to Göring. On 31 July, after discussion with Kammhuber, Generaloberst Weise issued the following signal to all units:

> 'The present enormous difficulties in defence against the heavy night attacks caused by the jamming of radar demand extraordinary measures everywhere. All crews must understand clearly that success can only come through the most self-sacrificing operations.
>
> 'I therefore order the operation of *Geschwader Herrmann*, as previously laid down, above the target of attack. Moreover, insofar as there are no other favourable operational possibilities, all available night-fighter squadrons are to be deployed over the *Flak* area. *Flak* fire will be restricted to 4,500 metres when night fighters are over the target. The operation of *Fühlungshalter* aircraft against the approach and withdrawal flights of the enemy are to be furthered by all possible means. For the information of other arms of defence, Fighter Divisions are to notify the *Luftgau* and *Flak* commands immediately fighter units take off. *Flak* Divisions and *Luftgaue* are to inform *Jagddivisionen* at all times of the probable target, the dropping of the first bombs, the dropping of target markers etc. Night-fighter *Gruppen* are to be scrambled at times calculated to enable them to arrive over the target simultaneously with enemy units. For this purpose, the searchlight organisation and *Flak* position-finding aids are to be at their disposal. Telephone and teleprinter communications are to be set up immediately between the headquarters of *Befehlshaber Mitte* and *Fliegerkorps XII* respectively.'

The Battle of Hamburg was a significant event in the development of both the strategic bomber offensive and the German night-fighter force. For the latter it was a turning-point, forcing its commanders to abandon the rigidity and discipline of close-controlled interception in favour of a more flexible, and ultimately more effective, means of combating the bombers. Sir Arthur Harris, despite having demonstrated in a most terrifying way the power of the bomber, had failed in his declared intention of destroying Hamburg completely. The advantage furnished by Window was already showing signs of being short-lived. Nature, in the form of atmospheric conditions, had shown two sides of her character: on the second of the four night raids against Hamburg she had demonstrated how she could change what otherwise would have been a normal area-bombing attack into a catastrophe beyond description, and on the night of the final attack she had made part amends to the hard-pressed people of Hamburg by scattering the bomber force and sparing the city yet another major ordeal.

CHAPTER SEVEN

Peenemünde and Changing Defences

August 1943

Kammhuber's *Nachtjagd* was disorganised but already regrouping. By now it had grown, in the West, to four *Geschwader* of conventional night fighters, a total of sixteen *Gruppen* plus the Staff Flights with a paper strength of about 700 machines, although the actual number available for operations fell far short of that figure. To some extent the inherent inflexibility of the *Himmelbett* system had influenced the attitudes of the night-fighter crews, who in general had grown accustomed to operating in a static defensive environment, taking off from their parent airfields to nearby close-control boxes and returning to the comfort and stability of their bases after the bombers had left. The Battle of the Ruhr had forced Kammhuber to bring up reserves temporarily from the rear areas into the front line, but they too had more often than not been tied to individual airfields when going into action against the British bombers. Navigation had made no great demands on the member of the crew responsible for it, the *Funker*, because the aircraft were normally under radar surveillance for the whole of a sortie and did not, in any case, stray far from base. In very broad terms, the effect had been to stifle initiative on the part of the pilots. Now Window had deprived them of the security of their home and parental environment, so to speak, and they had to go out into the night and fend for themselves.

The first problem was that of navigation, and fortunately for them there was already a highly accurate system in existence, the *Y-Verfahren* (spoken as '*Ypsilon-Verfahren*') or 'Y' System, which had been widely used in its basic form by German bombers and by the day-fighters of the *Luftwaffe* but for which the night-fighters had so far had little use, relying more on the *Würzburg* radars. It was a comparatively simple method of position-finding that could easily be expanded. In its original form the position of a *Y*-equipped aircraft was plotted on a *Seeburg* plotting table in the same manner as a position read off from a *Würzburg* screen, but soon the *Seeburgtisch* would be abandoned in favour of a huge vertical transparent map, already in use to show the overall air situation, which will be described below.

Ypsilon was not a radar system but worked in the VHF spectrum. There was a series of *Y* sites (*Ypsilon-Stellungen*) throughout the territory of the *Reich* and the occupied countries, each with a range of between 250 and 300 kilometres. Each site had five separate stations so that up to five aircraft could be handled separately, and sites and stations operated on a number of different frequencies in order to avoid confusion with one another. There was a central plotting room at each site, into which the stations passed their readings.

The position of a fighter was calculated by bearing and range. When a controller on the ground spoke to an aircraft on R/T an extra signal was superimposed on the speech, audible as a soft whistle. This was received by a transponder in the aircraft, which replied on a slightly different frequency. By means of a so-called phase-modulation comparison at the ground station the range of the aircraft was measured, while its bearing was simultaneously assessed by a traditional D/F (direction-finding) aerial. In this way the position of a machine equipped with *Y* could be shown continuously on the general situation map, and in the aircraft radio operators or pilots in need of navigational assistance could call up and ask for their positions at any time.

The suggestion made by Oberst von Lossberg of a lead aircraft, the *Fühlungshalter*, came from a practice that was being used in day-fighter operations, in which such an aircraft would maintain visual contact with the American bomber formations and broadcast their position to the fighters. Lossberg's suggestion, it will be recalled, was that by night the lead aircraft should be controlled to the head of the bomber stream and then broadcast a homing signal so that other night-fighters could keep in contact with it by conventional radio direction-finding. This was not really a very practical idea, and was certainly a very unpopular one with the crews. To broadcast a continuous radio signal was to invite intruders – Beaufighters or, even worse, Mosquitos – to home in on it, and for that very reason the scheme was never fully adopted. *Y*-equipped aircraft, originally those of the *Staffelkapitäne* and other senior pilots, were used to call in other freelance fighters into the bomber stream by R/T, but gradually more and more night-fighters were equipped and so became able to operate independently.

While some *Himmelbett* close-control centres continued to operate with *Y* plots replacing the Blue Giant (*blauer Riese*) radar plots of the fighters, broadcast control, in which ground stations transmitted a running commentary (*Reportage*) on the position, strength, direction and altitude of the bomber stream so that the fighters could attempt to find their own way into the stream, became more and more the norm. From being a hindrance to the ground controllers, Window became a considerable advantage, because the millions of descending silver-foil strips 'painted' the track of the bomber stream on the radars. This change from close control to broadcast control was, of course, a gradual process of evolution as new ideas were conceived and new technology introduced, particularly in the field of communications. The most important prerequisite, central locations on the ground from which the battle could be directed, already existed. Huge Divisional Battle Command posts (*Divisionsgefechtsstände*) had been erected, or were in the course of completion, at Deelen in Holland (*1 Jagddivision*), which had begun limited operation in July 1942; Stade (*2 Jagddivision*); Metz (*3 Jagddivision*); Döberitz, Berlin (*4 Jagddivision*); and Schleissheim, Munich (*5 Jagddivision*), and were used both day and by night to show the overall air situation, although until the shattering attacks on Hamburg only day fighters had been directly controlled from them.

The Divisional Battle posts, or to give them their generic title *Grossgefechtsstände* ('large Battle Command posts') merited the adjective 'large' in every way. Above the ground the main building measured about sixty by forty metres by twelve metres high, with a smaller annexe sixty metres by eight by nine high. The construction extended about four metres beneath the earth. The walls,

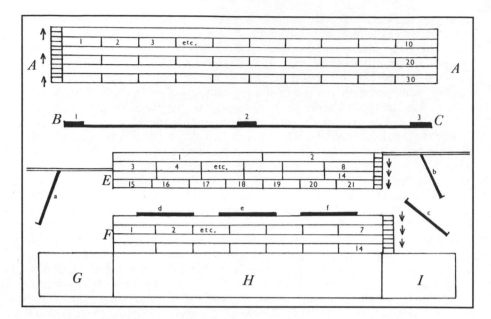

SCHEMATIC LAYOUT OF A TYPICAL *GROSSGEFECHTSSTAND*

A *Grossgefechtsstand* was a large, central battle Control Centre, roughly analogous to fighter Command Operations Room during the Battle of Britain, but much bigger. It operated by both day and night. The dominant feature (BC in the sketch) was a translucent vertical General Situation Map (GSM) about 40 feet in length and 30 feet high. Behind the map were a number of long tables

of bomb-proof ferro-concrete, were more than a metre thick. It is estimated that 33,000 cubic metres of concrete were needed for each building.

Much of the internal space was of course occupied by offices, accommodation, workshops, telephone exchanges, radio centres, generators and so, but the heart of the complex was the control centre itself, the *Gefechtsraum* ('Battle Room'), a huge hall, the dominant feature of which was a translucent matt-glass vertical screen twelve metres long by nine metres high – forty feet by thirty – that divided the hall into two unequal parts, the one in front of the screen approximately three times the area of the one behind. On the front of the screen was marked a map of the operational area covered by the *Division*. For example, that of the post at Deelen, near Arnhem, covered the whole of Holland and extended over the Ruhr area of Germany. The map was divided into grid squares, so-called *Planquadrate*, each designated by two letters. Prominent features – cities, airfields, radar sites, rivers, lakes and so on – were also shown. To the sides of the hall there were smaller-scale maps of the surrounding areas, meteorological charts and so on.

Behind the screen and across its entire breadth were three long rows of tables, staggered in height rather like the seats in a theatre auditorium, if rather more

(AA), at which sat *Luftwaffe* auxiliaries (1 to 30), usually female, each connected by telephone directly to a ground radar (*Freya, Würzburg Riese, Elefant, Wassermann, Mammut etc.*) and each equipped with a narrow-beam light projector with which they beamed a coloured dot (red for the position of a bomber, green for that of a fighter) on to the map. These tables were stacked rather like seats in a theatre. The arrows show a flight of stairs upwards.

1, 2 and 3 on BC show the position of three displays, visible from the front of the map. 1 showed the altitude of the bomber stream as given by the so-called «red» radars, 3 the altitude of fighters («blue» radar), while 2 was simply a large-faced clock.

The operational control officers, similarly «stacked», sat in front of the map. Officers of the air-reporting service (*Flugmeldedienst*) at table 1, Flak officers at 2, each with his own communications to operational units. Seats 3 to 14 inclusive were occupied by Fighter Control Officers (*Jägerleitoffiziere*), with R/T equipment with which to talk to their allocated fighters. Senior operations officers were located at tables 15 to 21 inclusive, with the officer in overall control, the *Jagdführer*, usually with the rank of *General*, at table 18

Rows of tables at F (1 to 14 inclusive) accommodated controllers using the «Y» system for locating and directing fighters. G, H and I were occupied by personnel involved in technical aspects of the battle – the monitoring service, radio- and radar-jamming etc.

In addition to the GSM there were a number of smaller displays, for example: a. raid-reporting chart; b. night-fighter availability «tote»; c. Intelligence data; d. fighters committed; e. current weather details; f. synoptic maps.

General Galland christened these vast structures «Battle Opera Houses».

steeply. These were the 'radar tables', and behind them sat female *Luftwaffe* auxiliaries, *Luftwaffenhelferinnen*, each connected via a land-line and headphones to a teller at a radar site – a *Würzburg Riese*, a *Freya*, a *Mammut*, a *Wassermann* and so on. Each of these girls had at her disposition a light projector – *Lichtspucker*, literally 'light-spitter' – either red or green, with which she showed on the vertical map the position of enemy bombers or friendly fighters, depending upon her allocated task.

In front of the vertical display, in the larger area, were up to ten or so staggered rows of tables. The central position was occupied by the General in command of the *Division* or his deputy, who was in overall control of the defensive battle and had the functional title of *Jafü (Jagdführer*, or Fighter Commander). Other positions were occupied by officers, airmen and airwomen in contact with such services as the *Flak* and smaller formations, all with their own telephone communications. Most importantly, from the tactical point of view, there were the fighter controllers whose task it was to direct the fighters by means of R/T. Behind the fighter controllers were the *Ypsilon* tables, occupied by men and women in contact with the *Y* stations, who, like the plotters connected to the radars, marked with coloured lights the position of those fighters using the *Y* navigational system. Adolf Galland christened these vast, complex centres *Gefechtsopernhäuser* – 'Battle Opera Houses'. When fully operational *Diogenes*, as the site at Deelen was code named, occupied a staff numbering approximately one thousand. There was a vast and intricate system of internal and external communications by land-line and radio.

There was inevitably a transitional period before the change could be made from the close control of night-fighters by the *Himmelbett* technique to loose control from the Divisional Battle Command posts and until improved intercept radars, less susceptible to Window, could be fitted into the fighters. It was during this period that Hajo Herrmann's Wild Boars, boosted by considerable official publicity, achieved fame and hero status among the German population. The conventional night-fighter men were more critical.

In the immediate aftermath of the Hamburg catastrophe, Göring once more demonstrated his inherent capacity for peremptory, impulsive and irrational decision-making and disregard of protocol. Herrmann attended a short series of meetings that Göring convened to discuss the performance of Kammhuber's night fighters and the way ahead, and at one of the meetings it emerged that Kammhuber, who was not himself present, had been less than sympathetic to Herrmann's original proposals for single-engined participation in the night battle against Bomber Command and that he had taken no action following the encounter between Herrmann's pilots and the RAF Mosquito over Berlin in April. Göring thereupon criticised Kammhuber severely, turned to Herrmann and told him, 'I am subordinating the *XII. Fliegerkorps* to you!' The Reichsmarschall went on to say that henceforth Herrmann would be responsible for everything that happened in the field of night-fighters, and that he, Herrmann, should issue orders to that effect to Kammhuber. It was as if the Chief of Staff of the RAF was placing a Squadron Leader in a position of authority above an Air Marshal, and it put Herrmann in an impossible position. Herrmann decided to interpret Göring's instruction in his own way: he would co-operate with Kammhuber's officers to his utmost, but not from a position of superiority. He could not blatantly disobey Göring's instruction, and he would not embarrass Kammhuber by demanding from Göring strict terms of reference and a formal statement of the extent of his powers of control and command. In effect he relied on Göring's reputation for not following through his off-the-cuff decisions, a reliance that proved to be justified. It inevitably became accepted that Herrmann was now Göring's protégé, and he was able to exercise a degree of authority far above that implicit in his comparatively lowly rank of Major. Recalling those days in 1993, Herrmann writes:

> 'You express surprise that Göring should wish to put me in a position of authority above the Commanding General; I was equally surprised at the time. But such measures on the part of Göring were not all that unprecedented. Drastic measures usually followed drastic statements. Galland, too, was a very young operational commander without command experience when he was made Inspector of Fighters. Dieter Peltz was a highly talented *Stuka* pilot and was promoted from Captain to Staff Colonel and appointed *Fliegerführer England* [Officer in Charge of Air Operations

against England]. My case was easier to explain. Göring was up to his neck. I was his last hope in a situation of extreme emergency . . . He clearly felt that he was progressively losing Hitler's confidence. And Hitler was his shining example.

'At the time I did not fully appreciate Göring's inner conflict. Of course I was aware, when he spoke to me on the telephone about Hamburg, that he was in a state of agitation. But I also felt that he was well in control of himself, and I formed the opinion that he was motivated by fear and dismay.

'So it is understandable that he should simply leave me with orders to go to the *XII. Korps* in Deelen, take over command and see that my instructions were obeyed, and then himself go home to Emmy. All I could do, flabbergasted as I was, was to look at his Adjutant, Oberst von Brauchitsch, and ask him what was going on. I told Brauchitsch that I would not act in such a way towards Kammhuber, even though I considered him a bureaucratic air commander. I said I was prepared to fly to Deelen and call together the whole of the senior command staff and give a presentation of my ideas. Brauchitsch said that I should do that for a start.'

While Herrmann was not prepared to go over Kammhuber's head, he was equally unprepared to allow his Wild Boars to be subordinated to Kammhuber and integrated into the overall air defence system. He therefore asked for, and was granted, independence of control:

'When I later reported personally to Göring he said to Loerzer, his old comrade from World War One and now his Head of Personnel, "Bruno, you'd better think what sort of a job we can find for Hajo Herrmann – *Jagdführer* [Fighter Commander] or something like that." I protested. I said that the correct status of my operational command could only be a Fighter Division directly subordinate to him, Göring, and not on any account subordinate to Kammhuber or Stumpff, in overall control of air defence. Generaloberst Stumpff had just come down from Norway, where he had led a comfortable life.'

Herrmann was destined to achieve high rank and a considerable reputation before the end of the war. Few would describe him as ordinary. But what of the mass of aircrew, British and German, the ordinary men who flew the lethal machines of war, dropped the bombs, shot down the bombers, risked their lives night after night? They came from widely differing backgrounds, but they had all been motivated by a desire to fly. For some, flying had been a peace-time ambition, while for others the coming of war gave birth to a desire to fly and also provided an unexpected opportunity to fulfil that desire. Re-armament and militaristic patriotism in Germany in the nineteen-thirties had stimulated many young men there to volunteer for the *Luftwaffe* well before the outbreak of hostilities, so that the Germans began the war with a considerable advantage over the RAF in terms of men qualified to fly and to command. The overwhelming majority of those who manned the Bomber Command machines were civilians when the war began.

By the time of Operation 'Gomorrah' the crew of a Stirling, Halifax or Lancaster was standardised as pilot, navigator, bomb aimer, signaller (more often referred to as wireless operator), flight engineer and two gunners. The basic aircrew rank on completion of training was sergeant, but some men, particularly pilots and navigators, received a commission on qualification. The majority of crew members did their flying training abroad under the self-explanatory Empire Air Training Scheme and in the United States, while a smaller number were trained from beginning to end in the British Isles. The basic crew usually came together at an Operational Training Unit by an entirely haphazard process known as 'crewing-up', in which all the recently arrived aircrew would assemble, possibly in a hangar, and the pilot would approach men who were available and who seemed congenial and ask them, in effect, 'Would you like to fly with me?' So casually were fates decided. Flying at an OTU would be on a twin-engined bomber, the Wellington being by far the most numerous, and then, if the crew was earmarked for a squadron flying four-engined machines, the next stage would be a Conversion Unit, where an engineer joined the crew and the handling of the operational aircraft was practised. This is an appropriate moment to look at a small selection of aircrew, both British and German, who were operationally active in 1943.

Terry Bolter and John Chaloner were typical members of Bomber Command at that time. What was not typical was that against the odds, they survived. They were not heroes, they would argue, but just everyday chaps who had volunteered for aircrew – all aircrew were volunteers – because they wanted to 'do their bit' to beat Hitler. Paul Zorner and Peter Spoden had both joined the *Luftwaffe* as officer-cadets with a firm belief in the rightness of German territorial claims in Europe and in Hitler as the leader of their country.

Born in Islington in December 1922, Terry Bolter was sixteen when the war began, the son of a civil servant who had served as an officer with the Royal West Kent Regiment during the First World War. When he left secondary school at the age of sixteen he followed his father into the Civil Service, but, as with the overwhelming majority of young men of his age in the heady atmosphere of those days, thoughts of joining the armed forces to continue the fight against German imperialism that had been suspended two-and-a-half decades previously following the 'war to end all wars' predominated over thoughts of a civilian career. In May 1941 he joined the Air Training Corps, which had been formed the previous year to prepare young men for service in the RAF, and he volunteered for aircrew just a month later. To his initial disappointment, a medical examination at Adastral House in Kingsway, London revealed that he was partly colour-blind, which meant that he could not become a pilot, but he was accepted for observer's duties. At that comparatively early stage in the war the separate functions of navigator and bomb aimer had not yet been fully adopted. He was called up in October 1941 and reported at Air Crew Reception Centre at St John's Wood. Initial Training Wing at Torquay and Elementary Air Observer School at Eastbourne lasted until March 1942, when he was posted to Blackpool to await embarkation:

'There we were issued with tropical kit, which seemed to point to southern Rhodesia or South Africa as our likely destination under the Empire Air

Training Scheme. We embarked on the *Highland Chieftain* from Avonmouth on 13 April, and after five weeks at sea in convoy we arrived at Durban in South Africa. We spent some weeks at Lyttleton Transit Camp, about thirty-eight miles from Johannesburg. There we participated with hundreds of South African servicemen in a march past General Jan Smuts, who took the salute in a very smart turn-out. We also relished the honour of paying our respects to General Smuts, under whose wise premiership, albeit on a majority vote, South Africa had entered the war on the British side as in the Great War of 1914–1918.

'From there I was posted to No. 45 Air School at Oudtshoorn in Cape Province. We took to the air for the first time on 4 July 1942. The fifteen-week instruction comprised the Air Observer Navigation Course followed by the Bombing Course on Avro Ansons and Airspeed Oxfords respectively. At the end of these courses we went to No. 43 Air School in Port Alfred for the Gunnery Course on Oxfords. Wings Parade took place on 10 October 1942. After an enjoyable interlude at a transit camp near Cape Town we sailed for the UK on the *Île de France* in early December, arriving, after a fast solo trip, three weeks later at Liverpool.'

As an observer, and wearing the coveted 'Winged 0' brevet, Bolter was qualified in both functions, navigation and bomb aiming. Because bomb aimers were in short supply in Bomber Command he was given the option of either flying on heavy bombers in that position or going to the Middle East on aircraft in which the navigator also dropped the bombs. He chose the former, and in February 1943 he went for his operational training to No. 20 OTU at Lossiemouth, on the Moray Firth, where he crewed up. His crew were all Londoners – it was formed largely on the basis of that common factor – except for the pilot, Sandy Sunderland, who was a Yorkshireman. The navigator was Bob Prendergrest, from Tooting; Ron Walter, a near neighbour and former school friend of Prendergrest, was the wireless operator; Biff Hagen, the gunner, was, unusually among aircrew, a married man with children, admitting to thirty-five years of age but actually being three years older. Terry Bolter takes up the story:

'The Wellington bomber had five crew members, so we now had a full crew and were posted to the satellite station at Elgin, a few miles away from Lossiemouth, to begin our operational training. The crew knitted well together in the air, and we completed OTU at the end of March and went on seven days' leave. Our posting to No. 1658 Conversion Unit at Riccall in Yorkshire, where we would convert to the Halifax four-engined bomber, came through while we were still on leave. At Riccall we chose the two new crew members to make up our complement of seven. They were both Londoners, Bunny Kearley, the engineer, and Mac Maculloch, the other gunner.

'After a forty-eight hour stand-down at the end of the first week I was back at Riccall in time for the 8.30 a.m. parade, when I was told by a bomb aimer whom I knew casually that my pilot had been killed over the weekend in a fall from his hotel room. He had landed on the concrete pavement below, where a policeman found him moaning and barely conscious just before 6.00 a.m. Sandy had died on the way to Leeds Hospital. Within a few days we were told that our new pilot, Squadron Leader Derek Duder DFC, was on his way to join us from Moreton-in-the-Marsh, where he had been Commanding Officer before volunteering for a further tour of operations. He was an experienced pilot, having been awarded his DFC in June 1941, having already completed two tours of operations in the Middle East. He was a Cambridge University graduate with a cultured and incisive voice, and was a natural leader. The general view was that we had been lucky to have such an experienced flyer to take over from Sandy.'

Terry Bolter arrived on his operational station in May 1943. Elvington lay just to the south-east of York and was the home base for No. 77 Squadron, a unit of No. 4 Group equipped at that time with Merlin-engined Halifax B Mk IIs. As a senior officer his pilot, Derek Duder, was appointed to command 'B' Flight. As it was Squadron policy that Flight Commanders should be around long enough to exert a stabilising influence, they and their crews were restricted to flying a maximum of three or four operations a month, which meant that a full tour would take longer to complete than normal, perhaps seven or eight months. Bolter's first operation was against Düsseldorf on 25 May, and he then went to such high-risk targets as Essen, Wuppertal and Krefeld in the Battle of the Ruhr, experiencing the full intensity of the 'Happy Valley' flak. Coming back from Wuppertal in the early hours of 30 May his aircraft reached England low on fuel, with poor visibility making landing hazardous: after initiating a distress call the pilot finally landed at Newmarket, breaking cloud at 500 feet. The crew considered themselves lucky to get down in one piece. Bolter visited Düsseldorf for a second time on the night of 11/12 June, the night in which Streib and his radar operator Fischer shot down five bombers in the first operational flight of the He 219 and when Bomber Command's losses for the night, including an attack on Münster, amounted to five per cent. He flew on two of the Gomorrah operations against Hamburg, but today he only remembers the searchlights waving around aimlessly on the night of 27/28 July, the extensive fires in the target area the same night, and the cloud on 2 August that made the red and green TIs difficult to distinguish.

The other RAF flyer whose career with Bomber Command we shall look at in some detail is John Chaloner. John, born in Burnley in 1921, left the local grammar school at the age of sixteen. When the war came along he realised that in all probability he would eventually be called up, and thought that he might end up in the Royal Navy. The idea of becoming something as glamorous as aircrew seemed to him to be so remote as to be impossible, until a former school friend, Stanley Owen, appeared in Burnley wearing the rank badges and wings of a Sergeant Pilot. Chaloner realised that there was a chance that he, too, could be a flyer, and he volunteered for flying duties in the RAF and, to his surprise, was accepted for pilot's training. Called up on 3 September 1941, exactly two years after the declaration of war, he did his initial training at No. 9 ITW, Stratford, and then went to start learning to fly at an Elementary Flying Training School outside Coventry. In spring 1942 he found himself on board the Canadian Pacific ship *Montcalm* bound for Canada, which sailed via Iceland to avoid the U-boat packs that haunted the direct Atlantic route further to the south:

'We reached Canada after about thirteen days, and I was posted to Americus US Air Force base in Georgia to begin flying training on Stearman biplanes. We had a strict military regime – up before dawn for PT and so on. The course was very intensive, and only about twenty-five per cent passed it. I was one who was washed out after about twenty hours' flying, and I was regraded observer. After a short period back in Canada, at Trenton near Toronto, I went to Miami, Florida to do a navigation course with PANAM. Compared to Americus, life was luxurious. We lived in the Coral Gables Hotel and did our theoretical study at Miami University and our flying at San Sebastian. Towards the end of 1942 I sailed back to the UK on board the *Queen Elizabeth*, and the trip to Greenock only took three-and-a-half days. At the end of the course at Miami we had been promoted to Leading Aircraftman and had been given the observer's brevet, but we lost our flying pay. I was not promoted to Sergeant until I had finished another course, this time at No. 3 Advanced Flying Unit at Bobbington in Staffordshire – I think the airfield was later renamed Halfpenny Green. After AFU I went on to Wellingtons at No. 14 OTU, Cottesmore, and then to Heavy Conversion Unit at Wigsley, Lincolnshire, where we flew first Manchesters and then Lancs.'

From Wigsley John Chaloner was posted to RAF Station Fiskerton, also on the flat Lincolnshire plain, in late July 1943. His Flying Log Book showed a total of 215 flying hours, slightly less than half of them by night. Fiskerton was one of the stations of No. 5 Group and was the home of No. 49 Squadron, equipped with Lancasters. The practice of doing all one's operational training with the same crew before joining a front-line squadron was designed to ensure that the seven men would work together with a degree of mutual proficiency enhanced by 'crew spirit'; as Chaloner relates, in his case this consideration was apparently deemed less important than that of in-crew status:

'I did my OTU and Conversion Unit with an Australian, Flight Sergeant N. They always gave the Australians commissions very quickly. I was a Sergeant, and he was a Flight Sergeant, but at the end of the time, as N. was going on to 467 Squadron, an Australian squadron, they gave him his commission. They thought he might as well have a commissioned navigator, and there happened to be one in another crew, so they teamed N. up with this Flying Officer somebody-or-other, and I replaced him in his crew, which had an NCO pilot. It was a straight swap. N's crew had been together all the way through to finishing school – Wellingtons, Manchesters, Lancasters – and I was looking forward to being posted to 467 Squadron, because it was nicely situated near Nottingham – you know, civilisation – and with the Australian squadrons they always seemed to get rather better conditions than the RAF squadrons. But some bright guy comes up, straight out of the blue, "Ah, you're not going with N's crew, because he's going to be commissioned," which gave me a bit of a jolt, because it meant, "*You*'re not going to be commissioned," so I went to 49 Squadron. Fortunately for me, it was a jolly good move, because the new pilot, Ernie Webb, was a Yorkshire lad, while N. was an up-and-thrusting, ambitious sort of Australian. As it turned out, he'd got feet of clay. During our training he would often talk to me: "We don't want to do just this tour, we'll do two tours, we'll go on to night-fighters," and that sort of thing. The idea was to get lots of flying time in to go back to civvy street on airlines. He took every opportunity to get flying in. Ernie Webb was a much more quiet, reserved sort of Yorkshireman.

'Shortly afterwards I heard on the grapevine that N's first trip was pretty disastrous. They did a bull's-eye[1], and they had engine trouble, and the crew baled out, and N. tried to bring the aircraft down, and he damaged himself in the process. He wasn't damaged too badly, but it damaged his morale somewhat. N. then did a couple of ops, and he had more painful experiences, and he went LMF[2]. He went back to Aussieland, and the rest of the crew was split up. They went off to different crews, as odd bodies, and they were all killed or fell by the wayside in one way or another.'

Chaloner's first operation was against Mannheim on the night of 9/10 August. Mannheim/Ludwigshafen had the reputation of being a tough target, especially for one's first trip, but in the event it was quite an easy ride for Webb's crew. In his diary Chaloner later recorded: 'Six large fires and numerous incendiaries flashing all around. Five-tenths cloud, everything illuminated like daylight with the fires from the target. A lively reception over Boulogne on our return.' His second operation, to Milan five nights later, he found 'very relaxing: sight-seeing over the Alps. We saw a few searchlights coming up, but as soon as the bombs started going down the Italians lost heart!'

Like the majority of Bomber Command aircrew at that period, Bolter and Chaloner had entered the RAF as wartime volunteers. In contrast, the greater proportion of German aircrew, particularly those flying in night fighters, had joined the service before 1939. Training, particularly for pilots and radio operators, tended to last much longer in the *Luftwaffe* than in the RAF. One of the reasons for that lay in the fact that the *Luftwaffe* was not a completely independent force but just one component of the *Wehrmacht*, so the training was much broader than that of aircrew in the RAF, covering basic military theory, history and skills as well as specialisations. The normal sequence in the *Luftwaffe* was that one entered the service with a view to a set career and did one's training as an officer or NCO before embarking on flying training.

There were, of course, variations to this pattern in time of war. In the wartime RAF one trained as aircrew and whether one was commissioned or not depended

---

1 'Bull's-eye': a training exercise under operational conditions, often including short penetration of enemy territory.
2 'LMF': abbreviation for 'Lack of Moral Fibre'. Aircrew so categorised were removed from flying duties and, frequently, reduced to the ranks in disgrace.

on several factors – the number of officer vacancies, 'officer qualities', marks in ground and air work, recommendations and so on. In 1943, it is fair to say, the majority of night-fighter crew members were professional soldiers, while those flying on Bomber Command might, by contrast, be referred to as amateurs, serving as they were 'for the duration only', the product of conveyor-belt training. One German who joined the *Luftwaffe* as an officer-trainee after the beginning of the war was Peter Spoden, whose frustration over Hamburg on the night of the fire-storm, when he made his first operational flight, has already been described:

'I was born in 1921 and I joined the *Luftwaffe* in October 1940. My father was very pro-Hitler at first, but his views changed after the take-over of Czechoslovakia. I remember the anti-synagogue actions in 1938, and I remember too that when I was seventeen or eighteen there were three Jewish boys in our class at senior school who suddenly didn't appear any more. One was Stern, who eventually became the proprietor of a successful chain of airport stores. They had been expelled by the headmaster. Nevertheless I believed in Hitler as a leader and I never asked any questions about government policies. In fact there was no government, only the *'Führerprinzip'* – the *Führer* concept. I thought we were doing the right thing in building a new Europe under German leadership, in correcting the Treaty of Versailles, where the Allies took away so much German land, such as the Sudetenland, South Tyrol, Memel, West Prussia and the German town of Danzig. I and, I think, millions of young German boys and girls were full of these ideas – crazy and extremely nationalistic, as I know today but did not understand at the time. Between 1939 and 1945 it was compulsory for all men to serve in the forces. I was always interested in flying, and I had a great admiration for bomber pilots. I was already registered before the beginning of the war at the Technical University of Hanover to study aerodynamics, and in 1939 I volunteered for an officer's career in the *Luftwaffe*. My father had told me of his terrible experiences on the Western Front between 1914 and 1918. He was badly wounded there and did not live to see old age. I was called up into the air force in October 1940. When I was on my flying course we could volunteer for different branches of the service and I selected night-fighting, although I had originally been intended to be a day-fighter pilot and had trained on the Bf 109. I chose night fighting because I came from the Ruhr area – my family lived in Essen – and since the beginning of the war it had been under heavy attack by British bombers. I joined 5./NJG 5 on 1 June 1943, and my first live operation was during the attack on Hamburg. As a new crew we were always in the second or third waves. There was Hauptmann Schoenert, then Hauptmann Fellerer, then Wim Johnen, then came Spoden. The senior ones were hogging it – it was like a sport. Many kills meant many decorations. After one's first kill one got the Iron Cross First Class, then after four the *Ehrenpokal* [cup of honour], after the tenth the German Cross in Gold, and after twenty the Knight's Cross. It was a crazy kind of sport. And a lot of them, when they had got their Knight's Cross, they weren't so keen. They didn't want to tempt Fate!'

We have also met Paul Zorner: it was he who scored his tenth victory over Hamburg, also on the night of the fire-storm, and had himself been shot down in return. A year older than Spoden, Zorner was born in a small village, Roben, in what is now Polish Upper Silesia. He passed his *Abitur* in early 1938. The *Abitur*, the rough equivalent of the then Higher School Certificate, was a pre-requisite for officer training. Zorner then completed the six months' labour service (*Arbeitsdienst*) that was compulsory under the National Socialist gov-ernment, having in the meanwhile volunteered for an officer's career in the *Luftwaffe*, hoping to fulfil a long-felt desire to fly. For him to learn to fly privately was beyond his parents' comparatively modest means, and a career in the air force offered him the chance of learning free and earning a salary at the same time. He began his service in October 1938 and went to the School of Air Warfare at Berlin/Gatow in March 1939, studying simultaneously to be an officer and to fly. By November he had qualified on single-engined aircraft, and he then went to the so-called *C-Schule*, where he learned to fly twin-engined machines. By March 1940 he was qualified on eleven types of aircraft, and was selected for training as a instructor.

Just a year later, in March 1941, there was an urgent need for pilots qualified as multi-engined pilots to fly Junkers 52 three-engined transports in support of Rommel's advance in North Africa, and Zorner was posted to the newly formed KGzbV 104, based at Wiener-Neustadt but operating in the Middle East. In September 1941 he was posted as a transport pilot to the Ukrainian front. Zorner himself takes up the story:

'I was with a Ju 52 unit in the Ukraine until October 1941. I didn't like it in Russia. The night-fighter force was being built up at that time, and there were calls for volunteers. There was also a lot of publicity being given to night-fighter pilots, and I remember reading an article in a newspaper by Wilhelm Beier, who had been awarded the *Ritterkreuz*. I was well qual-ified, with lots of flying hours, wide experience and I had my blind flying certificate, so I put my name forward. In October 1941 I was posted to the day-fighter school at Munich/Schleissheim, where we flew the He 51, the Ar 96 and the Bf 110, and in January 1941 I began the night-fighting course at Manching, near Ingolstadt. The whole training, day and night, was sup-posed to last for four months, but there was a shortage of fuel because of the demands of the Russian front, so I didn't finish until May 1942. What surprised me was that although many of the pilots had very little night-flying practice, the majority of our training was still done by day. In my case I only flew 16.5 hours at Manching by night out of a total of seventy-two hours. Nevertheless, it was a very pleasant time, and I had two four-week periods of leave.

'My first operational unit was II./NJG 2 at Gilze-Rijen, where I flew the Ju 88. We were also given theoretical instruction there by successful pilots such as Strüning and Prinz zu Sayn-Wittgenstein. From them, two things always remained in my mind. Firstly, that at night you could creep up on an enemy aircraft like a Red Indian: in other words, there were heights and directions, depending on the weather conditions, from which to approach with minimum risk of being seen. The second point was to keep your nerve and aim carefully between the fuselage and engine, in the case of a twin-engined bomber, and between the two engines on one wing with a four-engined machine, and then the enemy would catch fire after the first burst.

'From Gilze-Rijen I was posted in October to Grove in Denmark. On 2 December I was transferred to I./NJG 3 at Wittmundhafen in East Friesland, where I became Kapitän of the 2nd *Staffel*. Basically the *Staffel* was flying the Do 217, which I didn't like. It could stay up for five hours, but was not as manoeuvrable as the Bf 110, so the Gruppenkommandeur, Prinz Egmont zur Lippe-Weissenfeld, let me fly the 110 when I wanted to. If it seemed that the British were coming in over the sea I would take a Do 217, but if they were approaching over the land I would use a Messerschmitt 110. My first kill was in January 1943, and I got my tenth during the raids on Hamburg, by which time I was Staffelkapitän of 3./NJG 3 at Vechta, north of Diepholz.'

Terry Bolter, John Chaloner, Peter Spoden and Paul Zorner were just four of the thousands of young men on both sides confronting each other in the dark skies over Europe, combatants in the longest and most intensive air battle the world had ever seen, probably ever will see. Individually they would live to see either triumph or defeat, but before that time they would experience the anguish of seeing innumerable of their fellows killed or maimed, and they would know the mental and physical demands placed upon them by the need to fly in an inhospitable and perilous environment impossible to describe or, to those who have not known it, even to imagine.

In the first two weeks immediately following the Battle of Hamburg, Bomber Command flew only two attacks against German cities, Mannheim and Nuremberg, neither raid being other than routine. At about two per cent of the forces committed, losses were still encouragingly low. But Italy, hovering on the brink of capitulation, was less fortunate than her senior Axis ally, Germany. Harris carried out a series of telling attacks on Italian cities at low cost to the Command, attacks which certainly contributed to the Italian surrender the following month.

The attack on Turin on the night of 7/8 August 1943 saw an innovation in main-force bombing. Although the introduction of the Pathfinder Force's marking techniques had vastly improved target finding and bombing concentration, experience, including that over Hamburg, was showing that the success of the raid was very much dependent upon accurate placement of the target indicators by both the initial markers and the backers-up. Once an attack began to develop against a target inaccurately marked the tendency was for bombing to become progressively more scattered or, even if a degree of concentration was achieved, to achieve it in areas outside the selected objective. There was another problem, too. Smoke from explosions and fires, and sometimes from smoke-screen generators on the ground, obscured the TIs and led to further imprecision in bombing. There was also the phenomenon, mentioned earlier, of creep-back. The urgent necessity existed for some method of concentrating, and if appropriate shifting, the bombing pattern.

During the attack on the Ruhr dams in May, Wing Commander Guy Gibson had remained in the target area after dropping his own bombs and had directed the other members of his Squadron into the attack by broadcasting instructions to them on R/T. Within Bomber Command thoughts were now turning to the possible extension of this technique to main-force raids, with specially selected, experienced officers circling the target area throughout the attack and directing the bombing by means of an R/T commentary, and an experiment had been carried out during an attack on Friedrichshafen in June, but without conspicuous success. Turin, a less hazardous target than the majority of German cities, was chosen for a further trial of the proposed technique, and Group Captain John Searby DSO DFC was selected as 'Master of Ceremonies'. Searby had been a Flight Commander with Gibson on No. 106 Squadron and then Squadron Commander when Gibson left to form No. 617 Squadron in March 1943. Later, in May 1943, he became Squadron Commander of No. 83 Squadron in No. 8 Group, PFF. Although this trial, too, was in its turn not an outstanding success, the principle had been established and Master Bombers, as they later came to be known, featured increasingly from then on in Bomber Command operations. What was known to only a very few people at the time of the Turin raid, however, was that there was another reason for experimenting with the technique at that very time, and indeed for using Searby, who was himself kept in ignorance of the specific reason for having been chosen for the job.

An urgent requirement had arisen for a precision attack by night to be made by Bomber Command, in contrast to the area bombing that was its standard practice. Intelligence reports, confirmed by aerial reconnaissance photographs, had shown that rocket missiles were being developed and tested at a top-secret experimental installation at Peenemünde on the Baltic coast, and it was calculated that the Germans would be in a position to open a rocket attack on the British Isles in the near future. Harris's brief was to inflict the maximum possible damage on the several separate sites that made up the Peenemünde rocket research complex, and to do so it was clear that standard Pathfinder and area-bombing techniques would not be adequate to ensure the necessary degree of accuracy. Harris therefore decided that the attack should be made in conditions of clear visibility and full moon, usually avoided by Bomber Command because of the advantage to the night fighters, and that Searby should act as Master Bomber in an attempt to ensure as far as possible that the bombs fell on their intended targets. Because of the importance of the project unusual security precautions were taken, and no one apart from a very small circle of senior officers at Bomber Command knew the location of the target until the very last moment. The crews were not told at their pre-flight briefing the true nature of what was being developed there. They were, however, warned that if they failed in the task of destroying the Peenemünde site they would have to go back again and again until the job was properly done.

Not all main-force Group Commanders were totally convinced that Bennett's Pathfinders represented the best means of achieving good bombing results. Foremost, and most forceful, among Bennett's critics was the pertinacious Air Vice-Marshal The Hon. Sir Ralph A. Cochrane KBE CB AFC commanding No. 5 Group, to which the élite No. 617 Squadron belonged. Cochrane had a degree of influence with Harris, who agreed that as an alternative to bombing on PFF markers he could, if circumstances at the time made it appropriate, use his own preferred technique of 'time-and-distance bombing', in which individual bombers measured their ground speed with reference to fixed visible datum points on the ground on the run-in to the target, bombing blind if necessary at a moment calculated on that basis.

The attack on Peenemünde saw the introduction of an improved target marker, the 250 lb Spotfire, which after bursting at a height of 3,000 feet then burnt on the ground as a single spot of colour for up to twenty minutes. The colours in which this marker was available – red, yellow or green; red was used at Peenemünde – were very distinctive and proved difficult for the Germans to copy, something they were by now doing on an increasing scale in conjunction with decoy target sites that they were constructing in the vicinity of cities in an attempt, often successful, to divert British bombing. There was another important 'first' on the night of the attack, a carefully planned scheme intended to suggest to the German early-warning organisation that the bombers were on their way to another target and so divert the night fighters from the real one.

After the pounding of the Ruhr cities and the destruction of Hamburg, and with the longer nights approaching, it was reasonable for the Germans to expect that the RAF would launch further massive attacks against major targets deeper inside the territory of the *Reich*, and it was a natural assumption that Berlin would be at the head of the list. Harris encouraged this thought by sending small forces of Mosquitos to the capital city on three nights out of the four immediately preceding the planned attack on the Peenemünde rocket development complex, persuading the defences to expect that a major attack would follow. He sent the Mosquitos by the northern route, approaching, that is, from the Baltic, ensuring that air-raid warnings would sound in and around the Peenemünde area and so, because no bombs were dropped there, that the defences and personnel would be lulled into a false sense of security. Harris wanted to kill rocket scientists, and the chances of doing that were greater if they were caught in their beds rather than in the shelters when the bombs started to drop.

Accordingly on the night of 17/18 August just under 600 Lancasters, Halifaxes and Stirlings set out on this momentous raid, preceded by a diversion force of seven Mosquitos heading for Berlin. The heavies' route, and that of the Mosquitos, took them over the narrow Schleswig-Holstein/Denmark peninsula on a south-easterly heading, the Mosquitos turning off directly for Berlin while the heavy bombers continued on to a point to the north of their target before turning in on the approach. Window was dropped by both forces, making it difficult for the Germans to assess the strength of the Berlin force. For Terry Bolter, Peenemünde was his thirteenth operation. He writes:

'Back off leave in late July, we had successful operations over Essen and Hamburg . . . On the 17 August operation the target was Peenemünde on the Baltic, which, we were told at briefing, was a most vital target. German scientists there were working on secret equipment that could make our bombers much more vulnerable to attack from their fighters. We were not told the truth! We learned after the war that Peenemünde was a Nazi rocket research station . . .

'As we flew over Denmark the moon came up, and as we approached

Hiddensee Island, our last turning point, map reading up-moon enabled me to pinpoint our position, which Bob came forward to verify before we started to lose height on our run-in to Peenemünde. Our target was the living quarters of the scientists, and from 5,000 feet these could be clearly seen in the moonlight. The Master Bomber was already in control of the operation. "Attention Ravens, attention Ravens. Bomb the green ground markers, bomb the green ground markers." It was exciting to hear the far-back voice of the Master Bomber directing operations as I released the bombs with the green markers exactly in the centre of the illuminated cross-section of my bomb-sight, with the red light on my camera blinking away. "Bombs away" and "Photoflash" had gone. We could see the bomb-bursts on the ground as we came over the target with bomb doors closed and Derek pulled the stick right back to begin our steady climb back to 22,000 feet and turned on our westerly course, heading for home. We were lucky. Being on the first wave we saw no fighters. For the first and second waves the Mosquito decoy over Berlin had drawn off the German night-fighters. But they were there for the third wave of our bombers on that night, aided by the full moon, and it was the final wave that sustained most of the forty losses.

'When the Master Bomber left the target area it was impossible to distinguish individual buildings because of tremendous fires. Dr Thiel, chief scientific officer in charge of the development of Hitler's "V" weapons, and his chief assistant had been killed. Even more important, the drawing offices were destroyed and with them the production drawings of the V-2 rocket. They had just been completed for issue to the firms who were to manufacture the rockets, and their destruction delayed production for many months.'

The Peenemünde raid was, it is fair to say, only a qualified success. Errors of marking by the Pathfinders in the early stages of the attack compounded by slight scatter by the backers-up; German smoke-screens and the confusion of explosions, fire and smoke caused by the bombardment; indecision on the part of some of the No. 5 Group crews whether to bomb markers or use Cochrane's time-and-distance technique; a wind from the west stronger than forecast that blew the markers to the east of the aiming points: these and other factors combined to result in two of the three main targets, the Development Factory (*Entwicklungswerk*) and the Assembly Shop, known as the South Factory (*Werk Süd*), suffering less damage than they might otherwise have done. The third objective, the large accommodation area for German scientists and workers, was very hard hit, and approaching two hundred were killed there. Tragically a foreign workers' camp to the south of the main target area suffered grievously when main-force crews bombed misplaced PFF markers. The Master Bomber detected this error quite early in the attack and was able to move the bombing away from the camp, but not before between five and six hundred of the inmates had lost their lives.

The results achieved by the raid were limited only in comparison to the ideal, which would have been the complete destruction of all three objectives. By contemporary standards it was an impressive attack, a chilling demonstration of the advances being made in the deadly business of strategic bombing, and an ominous warning to the Germans of what lay ahead. The full extent of the effect it had on V-2 development and production has been the subject of controversy since the end of the war, when scientists involved in the programme and other leading German authorities became available for questioning. Estimates of the degree to which the rocket offensive against Great Britain was delayed vary from two months to six months and more, and it is generally accepted that the total production of the deadly weapons was adversely affected.

The attrition among the British and Commonwealth crews manning the Bomber Command machines was high but, in view of the nature of the target, acceptable. Forty machines failed to return, 6.7 per cent of those dispatched. The *Flak* at Peenemünde from both the local defences and a flak ship anchored off the coast was comparatively light, probably a combination of the effect of Window and the fact that the bombers were attacking from a much lower level than they normally did, between 8,000 and 10,000 feet. The night fighters, when they arrived on the scene, had a field day, a cliché that fits in nicely with the German concept of night-fighting (*Nachtjagd* – night-hunting) as well as with Herrmann's Wild Boars.

With *Himmelbett* largely ineffective and the reorganisation of the night-fighter defences only just beginning, Kammhuber resorted to the Wild Boar concept. Harris's feint towards Berlin with Mosquitos had served its purpose, and the majority of the conventional night-fighters, scrambled to holding beacons and listening out for instructions on selected R/T frequencies, were dispatched to the capital to hunt freelance. They converged on Berlin from all points of the compass – from St Trond in Belgium, for example, from the Dutch airfields, from Parchim, from Greifswald, from Schleswig. Herrmann's own fighters, the Bf 109s and the Fw 190s, operating independently but listening out on the same R/T frequencies, also sped towards Berlin from their bases at Bonn/Hangelar, Rheine and Oldenburg, attracted by target markers that were being dropped by the Mosquito deceivers. They were greeted by a heavy flak barrage. Sensibly, the majority of the Wild Boars remained on the periphery of the city, awaiting the arrival of the *Viermots* that did not come.

Even before the controllers on the ground had begun to divert the fighters towards the true target, some of the pilots, seeing markers going down, anti-aircraft fire and the glow of fires far to the north, ignored the R/T instructions and flew at full throttle towards Peenemünde, 180 kilometres to the north. One was Leutnant Peter Spoden of 5./NGJ 5, still looking for his first kill:

'I took off from Parchim for a radio beacon with instructions to listen out for the Jagddivision. It was an "Alarmstart". Everybody expected Berlin, and because it was a clear night we could see bombers going down in flames to the west of us. I waited and went higher, and I saw fires burning to the north, and I sped for them, but I went a bit to the west, because that was the direction the bombers would be likely to fly after bombing. I didn't know where it was – it could have been Stettin or Rostock. My decision to leave the beacon was a result of my experience over Hamburg, when I had seen bombers but had waited to be told to go there, but the instructions never came. I got there towards the end of the attack, and I got a Lancaster. I hadn't got *Schräge Musik* – I used my front guns from astern and below. The successful pilots in our *Gruppe* always tried to hit between the engines, and that is where I aimed, between number one and number two engines – those on the left wing – and I fired quite a long burst. The wing began to burn and I followed him down. I was so excited at my first victory that I didn't wait to see if there were any more targets, as I should have done. I saw him crash and I landed at the nearest airfield, Greifswald. I borrowed a motorcycle from the airfield Kommandant, and I drove out to the Forst Hagen, where he had crashed. It was a terrible sight, the fires and the dead crewmen, and I never went to see any of my victims again afterwards. There was one survivor, and I spoke with him. He was a young man, about my own age, and he was wearing a white sweater. He wouldn't tell me anything except his number, rank and name. He probably thought I was an interrogation officer. His name was Sergeant Sparkes, and he wrote to me after the war and told me he had baled out.'

Sergeant Bill Sparkes was the bomb aimer of a Lancaster from No. 44 (Rhodesia) Squadron, No. 5 Group, based at Dunholme Lodge, Lincolnshire, one of the aircraft experimenting with Cochrane's time-and-distance bombing technique, and as such in the final wave of the attack. The Squadron lost three of the thirteen Lancasters it sent on the raid, and the Group seventeen out of 117, losses only exceeded proportionately by No. 6 (Canadian) Group, also in the final wave, which lost twelve out of sixty-one. Those in the earlier waves, who bombed before the delayed night-fighters arrived, had a comparatively easy ride. Of the forty bombers destroyed, twenty-seven came down in the immediate vicinity of the target.

Paul Zorner, an Oberleutnant and *Staffelkapitän* of 3./NJG 3 flying from Kastrup near Copenhagen, chalked up his eleventh and his twelfth kills, two Lancasters, within the space of ten minutes. They were, he says, among the easiest of his many victories, the moonlight making conditions almost as bright as day. His Bf 110 was one of the few not sent towards Berlin. He was rather late in taking off because there were thunderstorms in the vicinity, and from Kastrup he was vectored south-south-west towards the bomber stream as it was leaving the target. Zorner has the impression that the Window was not as thick as previously, or possibly his *Funker* was learning to cope with it. In any event, they soon had a radar contact and shot down their first Lancaster at 0153 hrs, German time. Some of the crew left the aircraft by parachute, and it crashed in the sea. There was no close control, Zorner comments, and he probably found his way into the bomber stream by chance. Having destroyed his first bomber, Zorner headed towards Peenemünde, although he did not at that stage know what the target was, and almost immediately saw another four-engined bomber beneath him, silhouetted against the haze below. It was a simple matter to turn in astern of his victim and dispatch it with a burst from his forward guns. It exploded in the air. Like Spoden, Zorner landed at Greifswald.

Given the times of Zorner's two kills, it is likely that they too had formed part of the final wave of the attack, scheduled to begin at 0143 hrs and to end at 0155 hrs, although, not unusually, some bombers attacked late. It is possible that they were a No. 57 Squadron Lancaster captained by Wing Commander Haskill DFC and one from No. 426 Squadron flown by Flight Lieutenant Shuttleworth DFC of the Royal Canadian Air Force. There were no survivors.

Single-seater fighters from JG 300 had mixed success. Hajo Herrmann himself took off from Hangelar and reached Berlin. In his book *Eagle's Wings*[1] he writes, 'I felt a personal responsibility for guarding Berlin, so I tore into the sea of searchlights and anti-aircraft fire as the Mosquitos were dropping their Pathfinder markers, usually a sign for the heavy bombers to open their bomb doors. When I saw that there were no bombs bursting below and that the Mosquitos had flown swiftly through, I looked around and saw that the bell had tolled in the north. It was there that the main bomber stream was causing its havoc. For us above Berlin it was too late to engage them.'[1]

One *Wilde Sau* pilot who did enjoy success that night was Oberleutnant Friedrich Karl Müller, *Nasenmüller*, who was the Operations Officer of JG 300 and had the callsign *Wilde Sau Drei*. He had taken off from Bonn after Herrmann, and he saw the conflagrations at Peenemünde immediately he arrived to the south of Berlin. He flew directly towards them, crossing the capital city and coming under flak fire on the way, and he was one of the first to tell the ground control system that the raid appeared to be on the Baltic coast. When he arrived at Peenemünde he found plenty of targets, and he shot down two bombers. Another JG 300 pilot claimed a bomber, and the *Gruppe* lost one machine from II./JG 300 at Rheine, that of Leutnant Max Krähwinkel, who had to bale out when his Fw 190 ran out of fuel. Feldwebel Werner Hakenjoos of I./JG 300, flying a Bf 109G-6, enjoyed the distinction of destroying the one Mosquito lost from the eight that mounted the diversionary attack on Berlin, which was crewed by Flying Officer A. S. Cooke and Sergeant D. A. H. Dixon.

Despite initial scepticism in certain quarters, the principle of *Wilde Sau*, that of fighters operating freelance above the target under attack, had been emphatically vindicated, particularly so in view of the short time the few fighters that finally arrived there had spent over Peenemünde itself. This is reflected in the minutes of a meeting held on 20 August at the *Reich* Ministry of Aviation in Berlin. Von Lossberg is speaking:

'During the night of 17 to 18 August *Wilde Sau* went into action in strength for the first time, and there were 148 night-fighters and fifty-five day-fighters over Berlin. The spoof attack by the British succeeded in that the majority of the night-fighters wasted a lot of time over Berlin and so the actual target, Peenemünde, was not identified until very late. The night-fighters were then diverted. Only thirty night-fighters arrived over Peenemünde, and in a short time they shot down twenty-four bombers. In addition a further eighteen kills were made, a few in the fighter control areas and the majority freelance. It has thus been shown that twin-engined *Wilde Sau* in good weather has extraordinary chances of success.'

---

[1] Translated from the original, *Bewegtes Leben*, and published by Airlife, 1991.

The meeting went on to discuss the confusion between *Flak* and fighters over Berlin – hardly surprising, in fact, considering that the number of German aircraft there was about 200, the strength of a moderate Bomber Command raid. It ended with Feldmarschall Milch dictating a telegram to Göring:

Milch: 'Polte, take down the following telegram to the Reichsmarschall: "Night-fighter operations over Berlin on the night of the seventeenth to the eighteenth have once more clearly shown that when there are enough night fighters above the target anti-aircraft fire must be restricted more rigidly than has been the case hitherto. There were only a very few enemy harassing aircraft, yet the *Flak* shot barrage fire unrestrictedly up to 7,500 metres while there were about 200 friendly fighters present. I suggest that when there are night-fighters above a target anti-aircraft fire should be restricted to below 3,000 metres when so requested by the night-fighter authorities. At the same time I request that in the case of non-observance by the *Flak* court-martial proceedings should be initiated, with the most severe penalties for unit commanders if a verdict of guilty is reached."'

There was another side to the night-fighters' success, however. The Americans had mounted heavy deep-penetration daylight raids against ball-bearing works at Schweinfurt and the Messerschmitt plant at nearby Regensburg on the seventeenth, the day immediately before the Bomber Command assault on Peenemünde. Some night-fighter units had been flung into the battle despite the fact, already shown in earlier operations, that the staid Bf 110s and Ju 88s were likely to suffer heavily in combat with the heavily armed B-17s and their escorting fighters. The American formations had suffered grievously, but so had the night-fighters, losing about twenty-one machines, which, therefore, were not available to oppose the British raid that night. In addition, some aircraft that might otherwise have been used were damaged or not available for other reasons, representing a further diminution of the night force that could be used against the Bomber Command attack.

Fighter Command of the RAF had also played its part in the night battle. Harris had asked for the maximum possible support for his Peenemünde operation from Fighter Command, who had provided ten Beaufighters and twenty Mosquitos, the task of the majority of which was to disrupt activity by night fighters by patrolling near to their airfields and carrying out attacks on the ground and in the air as appropriate. Some Serrate-equipped Beaufighters, however, went out to entice enemy night fighters into the air and if possible to shoot them down. The Commanding Officer of No. 141 Squadron, based at Wittering, sent nine Beaufighters out in waves of four and five respectively, and he led the first wave himself. He was Wing Commander Bob Braham DSO DFC, one of the foremost British night-fighter pilots, who already had a score of fifteen kills. Braham and his three other aircraft took off just ahead of the Peenemünde force and headed towards the north of Holland. Their aim of tempting German fighters into the air was successful.

When the first reports of enemy aircraft approaching from the west were received at No. 1 *Division*, four Bf 110s of IV./NJG 1 were scrambled from Leeuwarden to intercept them, led by the outstanding night-fighter pilot

Oberleutnant Heinz-Wolfgang Schnaufer. The other three aircraft were captained by Oberfeldwebel Karl-Heinz Scherfling, Feldwebel Heinz Vinke and Unteroffizier Georg Kraft, all experienced men. The intention was to test out the procedure that had been suggested by von Lossberg immediately after the Hamburg attacks, that of using a lead aircraft, which would be that of Schnaufer, navigating by the *Y* procedure and sending out a homing signal so that the remainder of the formation could follow him into the approaching enemy stream.

For the Germans, the operation was little short of a catastrophe. Schnaufer and Scherfling both had to return to base with engine failure, while Wing Commander Braham shot down both Kraft and Vinke. There was one survivor, Vinke himself, who baled out and spent eighteen hours in his rubber dinghy off the Dutch coast before being picked up by a Do 18 air-sea rescue flying boat. He was even luckier than he realised at the time. In his book *Scramble* Braham relates his recollection of the incident:

'Above me in a tight turn was another Me 110, and at the speed at which we were travelling we looked as if we were going to ram him. I eased back on the stick, put the sights on him and fired at point-blank range of about fifty yards. There was a blinding flash as the Me exploded in my face. Our Beau rocked violently, threatening to flick over on its back. My windscreen was flecked with oil from the exploding wreckage which hurtled seawards . . . Then as we circled I saw in the light of the moon a parachute floating gently downwards. Something made my blood boil. Perhaps it was the narrow escape from the collision that angered me, or maybe it was because I was exhausted. I called Jacko on the intercom. "One of the bastards must have been blown clear, I'm going to finish him off." I had turned towards the parachute when Jacko said, "Bob, let the poor blighter alone." This brought me to my senses, and I felt ashamed of what I had intended to do. As we flew past the forlorn figure dangling on the end of the 'chute and falling towards the sea I wished I could call out to tell him that his life had been spared because of the compassion of my AI operator – a Jew like many of those the Nazis had slaughtered in the ghettos and concentration camps of Europe.'[2]

Braham was awarded a bar to his DSO for his success that night. Another IV./NJG 1 aircraft that had taken off independently was flown by a recent arrival with the *Gruppe*, the twenty-year-old Leutnant Gerhard Dittmann, whose sole confirmed kill until then had been that of an American B-17 on 25 July. Dittmann too was shot down by one of Braham's Beaufighters, and he and his radar operator, Unteroffizier Theophil Bundschuh, also aged twenty, both lost their lives. It had been a bad night for IV./NJG 1. They had scrambled five aircraft, two of which had to make an early return while the remaining three were shot down, only one man surviving. Numerically, however, the *Nachtjagd* had won a clear victory on the night of Peenemünde in accounting for forty RAF bombers and

2 Published by William Kimber, 1961.

about 280 aircrew in return for eight of their own fighters, the crews of some of which managed to escape by parachute or survived crash-landings.

Although the Commander-in-Chief of the *Luftwaffe* was nominally Hermann Göring, in practice the function of overall command was exercised by his Chief of Staff, Generaloberst Hans Jeschonnek, who had held the post since the February before the outbreak of war. To the dilettante Göring 'his' *Luftwaffe* was something which, when things were going well, reflected glory on him, its creator, but which in bad times he criticised unmercifully, holding Jeschonnek, and indeed everyone but himself, responsible. Many of his decisions and orders were impulsive, irrational and impossible to carry out. Göring still retained the ear and the backing of Hitler, himself a man often intuitive in action and scornful of expert advice, but Hitler was becoming increasingly critical of Göring, and in particular of the *Luftwaffe*. The *Luftwaffe* was indeed undergoing a bad period, and Hitler was demanding of Göring to know the reasons why and insisting on improvements. Göring's characteristic response was to rage at his *Luftwaffe* commanders, in particular his Chief of Staff, and to interfere with traditional channels of command and control by peremptorily shortcutting them, as he had done, for example, when giving Major Herrmann precedence over General Kammhuber in the matter of operational control of the night-fighter force. In the summer of 1943 Göring's promise to supply the besieged German troops at Stalingrad from the air had proved to be an empty one. Axis air power in North Africa had been effectively quashed, and American bombers were ranging far into the Fatherland by day, and by night the RAF was wielding its destructive power to a terrifying degree, as Hamburg and Peenemünde demonstrated. Peenemünde was, it seems, the straw that broke the camel's back. The following day Jeschonnek committed suicide. He left a note saying, 'I can no longer work with the Reichsmarschall. Long live the *Führer!*' He had followed the road chosen over two years previously by another leading figure who could not cope with the despotic irrationalities of Göring and Hitler, the then Director General of Supplies, Generaloberst Ernst Udet, Göring's comrade-in-arms from the First World War and like Göring the holder of the Pour le Mérite, Germany's highest award for gallantry in the days before the Third *Reich*.

Above: Pilot Otto Fries (right) and *Funker* Alfred Staffa with their machine. They achieved eighteen victories. *(Fries)*

Above left: Oberfeldwebel Helmut Fischer, *Bordfunker* to several pilots, including Streib. Fischer participated in 29 "kills", but had to bale out four times himself. *(Fischer)*

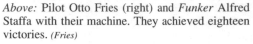

Left: Oberleutnant Fritz Krause of 1./NJGr 10 in front of his Fw 190A -5 night fighter.

Right: Pilot Officer John Chaloner, DFM, taken in February 1944. Against the odds, John completed eleven operations against Berlin during his tour. *(Chaloner)*

Below left: Rudolf Szardenings, *Staffelkapitän* of 7./NJG 3, with his crew. Szardenings had 12 confirmed victories. *(Szardenings)*

Below right: Taken in October 1943 at RAF Fiskerton. Flight Sergeant Ernie Webb and crew with a Lancaster of No.49 Squadron. Left to right: Unknown rear gunner deputising for Sgt Percy Horton (wounded during fighter attack on Mannheim operation); Flight Sergeant Webb (Pilot); Sgt John Chaloner (Navigator); Sgt Eric Lovick (Wireless Operator); Sgt Harold Olerenshaw (Bomb-Aimer). Kneeling, Sgt Fred ?, (Mid-Upper Gunner). *(Chaloner)*

CHAPTER EIGHT

The Tame Boars and the Jammers: Looking to Berlin

September to November 1943

The Battle of the Ruhr and the raids on Hamburg and Peenemünde had established a pattern of area attack by Bomber Command that was to persist, with minor variations, for the remainder of 1943 and well into the following year. *Force majeure* had compelled the *Nachtjagd* to adopt a pattern of defence against the night bombers fundamentally different from that which they had so far followed and which had brought them well over 2,000 successes. Ahead lay an all-out aerial assault on Germany. In Britain the ruthless bombing of the enemy's cities, glamorised as it was to some extent by official hand-outs and the media, enjoyed the strong support of both public opinion and the political and military establishment in Britain. In the Third *Reich*, on the other hand, Government propaganda extolling the bitter defensive action that the *Luftwaffe* was fighting, plus the condemnation of the Allies' 'unconditional surrender' policy, helped the German population to bear the ordeal served upon them by Bomber Command. Heralded in the press, with no little justification, as knights of the air defending their country against the barbarous onslaught of the British *Terrorflieger*, men such as Schnaufer, Wittgenstein, Lent, Streib and Lippe-Weissenfeld became household names. The number of kills they achieved individually, and those gained by the night-fighters collectively, made impressive reading.

The man who most attracted the imagination of the German man-in-the-street at this period, however, was without doubt Hajo Herrmann. Overnight he and his men became the focus of popular hero worship, their swashbuckling attitudes and deeds capturing the admiration of the ordinary German, rather as the Battle of Britain pilots had been acclaimed as the saviours of their country three years previously. The 'Song of the Wild Boars' became a hit on the radio. The elevation of the *Wilde Sau* pilots in the eyes of the public to the status of supermen gave rise to much cynicism, even resentment, among the crews of the conventional, twin-engined night fighters, who tended to see them as disorganised adventurers projected into a medium they did not understand and were ill-equipped to master. There can be little doubt that the fact that they were not integrated into the existing night-fighter organisation contributed considerably to the strong element of cynical rivalry and adverse criticism that developed. As time would show, such criticism was not wholly without foundation.

In a very short time the system of broadcast control and freelance operation within the bomber stream became known as *Zahme Sau*. Translated as 'Tame Boar', this was a logical progression that underlined the fundamental difference between von Lossberg's more circumspect approach and that of Herrmann. With fluctuating fortunes *Zahme Sau* operated until the end of hostilities. *Wilde Sau* became an accepted procedure for both single-engined and twin-engined fighters, and that too was practised until the end of the war. *Himmelbett* operations eventually all but petered out. By progressively concentrating his bombers in time and space Harris had presented Kammhuber with a larger, more compact, and therefore potentially more vulnerable, target, but Kammhuber had been slow to recognise and adapt to the defensive possibilities thus opened up. Now there began a fascinating, at times bewildering, duel for supremacy between the night bombers and the night-fighters, a conflict characterised by the skills and heroism of the men who took part, British, Commonwealth, Allied and German, and by the rapid cut and thrust of technical and tactical measure and counter-measure. In its basic form area bombing remained a weapon comparable to the bludgeon, but increasingly it enjoyed support that was more akin to the rapier.

With the raids on Italy and Peenemünde behind him, and greatly encouraged by the massive success against Hamburg, Harris could now turn his attention back to the rest of Germany. Inevitably Berlin was firmly in his mind as his next major objective, although the nights were not yet really long enough comfortably to accommodate the long journey the bombers would have to make. Nevertheless, after a disappointing, if low-cost, attack on the Ruhr town of Leverkusen five nights after Peenemünde, Harris tentatively sent 727 bombers to the capital of the *Reich* on the night of 23/24 August. The results were not encouraging. Poor marking by PFF and bad timing by some of the main-force machines resulted in bombs being scattered over a wide area despite the fact that a 'Master of Ceremonies', as he was still called, was present over the city throughout the attack. Even so there were comparatively heavy casualties within Berlin, at approaching 900 the highest yet experienced there. It was, indeed, hard to miss an area as large as that represented by the 'Big City', a built-up sprawl more extensive than the entire Ruhr complex. The very size of Berlin contributed greatly to the inaccuracy of the bombing. H2S operators, particularly among the blind markers, found that their screens were virtually swamped by a mass of echoes among which it was difficult to recognise specific aiming-points. Berlin was, and would remain, a poor H2S object. It lacked the nearby, readily identified coastlines of targets such as Hamburg and Peenemünde, and even the many lakes, canals and rivers within the metropolitan area did not show up as clearly as it had been hoped they would.

If the bombing results of this attack on Berlin were disappointing, that was as nothing compared to the chilling reminder served on Harris and his crews by the enemy defences that the initial optimism generated by the introduction of Window had been illusory. The Command's loss of fifty-six aircraft was the highest yet suffered in one night, and it represented 7.9 per cent of those dispatched. This was the night of the first formalised Tame Boar operation, although many more fighters, including those of Herrmann's JG 300, flew Wild Boar over Berlin, which had been recognised as the likely target long before the first markers went down. No diversionary raids were mounted, but the attacking force was supported by thirty-six Beaufighters and Mosquitos from Fighter Command flying intruder and Serrate missions.

From Bonn/Hangelar I./JG 300 took to the air, led by Hauptmann Gerd Stamp, who, after his early rebuff in Berlin, had now been accepted by Hajo

Herrmann as one of his *Gruppenkommandeure*. Herrmann himself flew from his headquarters in his Fieseler Storch to Hangelar, where he transferred to his Bf 109T, ready to take off in the company of his adjutant, Hauptmann Naroska, and his technical officer, Friedrich-Karl Müller, *Wilde Sau Zwei* and *Wilde Sau Drei* respectively, who together made up the *Stabsschwarm* or Staff Flight. They headed for the Bremen area. Then Herrmann picked up the broadcast commentary from the *Luftgau* in Münster: 'Teuto calling: leading enemy bombers approaching the Weser, heading east.' Herrmann turned on to an easterly heading, positioning himself in the air with reference to recognition signals being fired by the *Flak* over Bremen (two flares bursting one above the other), Brunswick (two flares side by side), and Kassel (three flares vertically above each other). Then came another announcement from the *Luftgau*: 'Target provisionally 1 – 3,' indicating that the bombers were expected to reach 13° east, the meridian on which Berlin lies. The broadcast commentary now placed the leading bombers to the north of Hanover, and Herrmann was to the south of the city and heading east on a parallel course. He throttled back to avoid overtaking the bombers. As he approached Berlin he heard the R/T call '*Horrido*' from *Nasenmüller, Wilde Sau Drei*, announcing that he had already made a kill. Then Müller, who had found the bomber stream and was keeping it company, contributed to the commentary: 'Enemy four-engined bombers heading east.' Now Herrmann could see the Berlin searchlights ahead of him picking up the first British bombers. There was an awe-inspiring barrage of anti-aircraft shells bespattering the sky. Herrmann was soon attacking a bomber, but lost it in the confusion of searchlights and shellfire. Then another attack, but his prey, already burning, was also being harried by a twin-engined fighter. On the R/T, Herrmann heard *Nasenmüller* reporting a second kill. Then he saw a Lancaster caught in a searchlight beam, flak shells bursting around it, and he brought his guns to bear. When the first burst of cannon fire struck home the pilot of the Lancaster began to corkscrew, but Herrmann followed him through and finally destroyed him from close range, not, however, before his own aircraft had been fatally damaged by gunfire from the Lancaster's rear turret. Herrmann had to take to his parachute, and was lucky to escape with his life when he came down in one of Berlin's many small lakes. The following day Göring personally decorated him with the Oak Leaves to the Knight's Cross.

For another German night-fighter pilot this was also a traumatic night. Peter Spoden of II./NJG 3 took off from Parchim, to the north-west of Berlin, hoping to add to his score, which he had opened over Peenemünde. Speaking in 1989 Spoden, after the war a senior *Lufthansa* pilot, recalled:

'This was to be a *Zahme Sau* mission and we were under the control of the *Division*. We were sent to a radio beacon to wait for the bombers, but it was soon clear that Berlin was the target, so I went there. Then, I suppose, it was *Wilde Sau*. I think Herrmann's idea was fantastic, very successful. But you need a pilot with better skills than I had. With a single-engined aircraft it is very hard to do instrument flying, and a night-time landing was very, very difficult. Multi-engined aeroplanes are so much more stable. I speak from experience – I still have my single-engined licence, and I still find it more difficult to make a single-engined landing at an international airport like Frankfurt than with a 747. Herrmann was a genius, an outstanding pilot, but the trouble was that he expected other pilots to be the same.

'But to revert to the Berlin attack, when we were freelancing over the city. I was flying a Bf 110. There was an incredible number of aeroplanes, bombers and fighters, over the city. I was confused by the flak and the searchlights, and I fired at a number of bombers unsuccessfully. Then I saw one ahead of me: I think it was a Lancaster. I fired at it and hit it, and it went down. Just ten minutes later I attacked another four-engined bomber, which I think was a Stirling, but the rear gunner hit me, and we both went down in flames. I ordered my crew to bale out, but got no reply. Then I tried to get out myself, which was hard because I had been hit in the leg. When I came free I hit the tailplane and the speed of the aircraft held me pinned against it for what seemed a long time while we were in a steep dive. Then somehow I managed to disengage myself and pull the ripcord. I don't remember falling – I must have lost consciousness – but I came to in the garden of a house in Berlin. I had been hit in the upper leg by a bullet and the bone was badly broken. When I came round I was being attacked by civilians, who thought I was an Englishman. But then I spoke to them in German and they stopped. My *Funker* also escaped by parachute, but my flight mechanic didn't get out and was killed.'

Spoden was taken to hospital, where he underwent surgery. Following a period of convalescence, and despite the surgeons' opinion that he would never fly again, he returned to his unit in early November, one leg shorter than the other. Later that same November he claimed his fourth victim in the course of another RAF attack on Berlin.

Other German night-fighter pilots active throughout this phase of the battle who claimed victories that night were Hauptmann Georg Hermann Greiner of IV./NJG 1, who made his tenth kill with the destruction of a Halifax, and Leutnant Günther Wolf of III./NJG 5. Wolf's two claims, for a Stirling and a Lancaster destroyed, were not confirmed because it proved impossible to match them to specific crashes, something that frequently happened when the main part of the battle was above the target itself and both the *Flak* and night-fighters claimed the same kill. There was however no doubt about what happened to Wolf himself:

'I had to bale out. The whole thing went very smoothly. I don't know who shot me down, but think it was probably our own flak. I don't think it was enemy action, because the effect is quite different. The cabin roof was shattered and flew away, and the starboard engine was on fire. Gefreiter Heinz Schmitz and I baled out – there were only two men in our Bf 110 at that time. Some were already carrying a third man, the *Bordmechaniker*, who acted as gunner and a spare pair of eyes, but we only had two in our crew. We were quite high when we jumped, and I let myself fall for a long time before I pulled the ripcord. I landed in the village of Werftpfuhl, north-east of Berlin. It was foggy on the ground, and I landed in a field with something of a bump, but I didn't break anything. I found a road, and a short time afterwards a farmer came along with a cart, and I asked him to telephone our Operations Room at Werneuchen. One of our *Staffel* came out and picked me up. Heinz Schmitz escaped without injury as well.

'One of the reasons that I had become a night-fighter pilot instead of a day fighter was that I didn't like aerobatics, which made me very airsick. On this occasion I must have been at about 6,000 metres when I jumped, and I probably opened my parachute at about 3,000. It took me about ten minutes to reach the ground. I was swinging violently, because there were big fires on the ground causing turbulence, and I was airsick all the way down. While I was coming down I was very afraid that I might land in the fires. That's what happened to Peter Spoden the same night.'

When talking of victories, one normally credits them to the pilot, but although it was the pilot whose thumb pressed the firing button the contribution to success made by the *Funker* was considerable. As navigator, radio operator, radar operator and rear gunner, the *Funker* was an extremely busy man. It was he, usually, who 'talked' the fighter into the proximity of the bomber and into a position from which a good attack could be made, and it was he, too, whose radio skills, more often than not in the face of intensive enemy jamming, saved many a badly damaged aircraft from crashing to destruction by directing it to an airfield at which it could make an emergency landing. Just as navigators, particularly, in the RAF used to call the pilot the 'driver' – the implication being that ultimately it was the navigator who ensured that the bomber went where it was supposed to go – so the German radio operators referred to their pilots as *Kutscher*, or 'coachmen'. But on both sides, RAF and *Luftwaffe*, a bad crew member more often than not meant a bad crew, while in the best crews all the members were of high quality. One *Luftwaffe* radio operator who personified this fact was Oberfeldwebel Helmut Fischer, a member of I./NJG 1 based at Venlo who had flown with Reinhold Knacke in 1942, participating in six kills between March and May. As *Funker* to Werner Streib between January and June 1943 he had had a hand in fifteen further victories, including Streib's five kills in a night in June when testing the He 219. Now he was flying again with *Oberfeldwebel* Bruno Eikmeier, a former tank commander who had volunteered for flying duties. Fischer had earlier participated in two victories in September and October 1942 with Eikmeier, and now, in the early hours of 24 August, flying Wild Boar over Berlin in Bf 110 G9+BK, he experienced his twenty-sixth victory overall but was shot down in the process. Eikmeier died.

On the British side, this was John Chaloner's third operation and his first visit to the 'Big City'. His Lancaster was carrying one 4,000 lb 'Cookie', four Standard Bomb Containers (SBCs) each loaded with 150 four-pound incendiaries, six SBCs of sixteen thirty-pound incendiaries, and one SBC with eight thirty-pound incendiaries. In his log book is entered laconically, 'Two enemy aircraft broke away.' He and his crew were fortunate that the German fighters did not press home their attacks. Unlike many Bomber Command navigators, Chaloner made a practice of leaving his 'office' on the approach to the target so that he could watch the action:

'When we were coming up into the target area I liked to be at the front, looking out. It was my own idea – no one suggested it. You see, when you'd got within range you could see the city, everything lit up, things were flying about all around you . . . I didn't give any instructions, because we were on the bombing run, under the bomb-aimer's control, so I just memorised the heading out of the target and the time and so forth, and I concentrated on looking round the aircraft. I thought that was the best contribution I could make. As soon as we'd got out of the target area, as soon as things had calmed down, I'd go back to my normal station. There was a blister in the Lancaster, just behind the engineer, and you could see directly underneath. And you could see what was going on.

'The first trip to Berlin came as a shock. I confess that I was not feeling over-confident. We had been taken off the Peenemünde battle order: the Wing Commander told us we were too inexperienced. For Berlin, it was a moonlit night. And it was a horrific night, and I was absolutely scared, petrified. The flares were going down on both sides, right into Berlin itself, and we sensed that it was going to be a bad sort of occasion. We must have been in the worst part of the raid, I suppose. The Master of Ceremonies was just going as we arrived, but he told us the green TIs had gone down and they were bang on the aiming point.'

The Master Bomber's confidence that the target indicators had landed 'bang on the aiming point' seems to have been misplaced: most of the bombs that night fell outside the city limits. Two further raids on the *Reich* capital during the following week underlined the lesson of the first one: Berlin's distance from England, its size and heavy defences made it hard to hit specific targets within the city with any real accuracy, while those same defences made bombing it a hazardous occupation for the crews taking part. The two attacks cost Bomber Command sixty-nine bombers out of the 938 sent out. At 7.4 per cent of the total, that was a daunting price to pay for the very limited bombing success achieved. Pathfinder marking on both raids was disappointingly inaccurate, while given the number of bombers involved damage to the town itself was slight and casualties were low. German fighters were up in strength for both raids, and, as was always the case with Berlin, flak was intense. On 30 August/1 September there was an ominous indication that perhaps the RAF crews, in face of the determined defences, were not pressing home the attack as resolutely as they might otherwise have done, PFF markers falling well short of the aiming point and the final creepback extending up to fifty kilometres along the approach track. Both Tame Boar and Wild Boar were in operation, and in support of the latter Herrmann introduced illuminator aircraft – *Beleuchter* – Ju 88 bombers of I.KG 7, stationed at Greifswald, whose function was to fly above the bomber stream and drop high-intensity flares into it in the vicinity of the target, so providing light by which the Wild Boars could attack their prey. The Halifaxes and Stirlings, inferior in performance to the Lancasters and operating within a lower height band, attracted the major share of the attention of the German defences during this raid, and they suffered accordingly. Twenty Halifaxes out of 176 and seventeen Stirlings out of 106 were lost, rates of 11.4 and sixteen per cent respectively. These were intolerable figures, and only Lancasters – 316 of them – were sent to Berlin on the night of 3/4 September 1943. Even so, twenty-two did not come back.

Sandwiched between the raids on Berlin in late August and early September were two operations that showed clearly the difference between the problems of accurate navigation, and in particular bomb aiming, that applied to short-range targets and those a longer distance away. On 27/28 August Nuremberg was attacked, and despite clear skies over the target and the use of a Master Bomber the majority of bombs fell in open countryside. A combined attack in similar strength the following night against the neighbouring towns of Mönchengladbach and Rheydt, just over the Dutch/German border to the west of the Ruhr and so within Oboe range, produced high-accuracy bombing.

The introduction by the Germans of running commentaries to tell their fighters where the bomber stream was and where it seemed to be heading led rapidly to a modification in the Tinsel R/T-jamming system used by the RAF. Previously, German-speaking radio operators in some bombers would scan the appropriate frequency band until they heard a fighter controller broadcasting, when they would activate a microphone mounted in one of the bomber's engines. In September the monitoring service in England began to broadcast to the bomber stream on some of the frequencies being used by the night-fighter control system. By tuning in to such a frequency the radio operators could transmit noise from their motors and so jam out the controllers' commentaries. The system, which was continued to good effect until the end of the war, was called 'Special Tinsel'. Because of the limited range of VHF broadcasts, however, Special Tinsel was confined to the HF band. In response to this further irritant the Germans began to broadcast their commentaries on an ever-increasing number of separate frequencies, VHF, short-wave and long-wave, so that the radio operators in the fighters could try to find one that was free from jamming, even momentarily, or perhaps one on which the jamming was not overwhelming. Some *Funker* became expert in deducing from ill-heard phrases and words the gist of what was being broadcast, while others never came to terms with the interference in their earphones. Morse code, the use of which had largely lapsed during the comparatively easy days of *Himmelbett*, came back into its own, but many radio operators were out of practice and found it hard to cope with, particularly as the W/T channels were also jammed by the British.

Window now became a help, rather than a hindrance, to the German controllers, providing them with a clear picture of the dimensions and approach direction of the bomber stream. The main commentary (*Reportage*) was originated at the *Korps* control centre, but *Division* centres such as *Diogenes* at Deelen initiated their own separate commentary, which they interspersed with instructions to individual fighters or groups of fighters. The running commentaries summarised the meteorological situation, with warnings being given of weather fronts, hazardous conditions over high ground, conditions of fog, airfields that were unusable and so on. They gave the latest location and dimensions of the bomber stream, its general heading and, as far as possible, its altitude. Then came the assumed target and the direction the stream was approaching it from. Once the target was confirmed by markers or bombs being dropped, this too was reported. When fighters were scrambled they were given a specific initial heading so that they could be readily identified on the defence radar screens and would not be confused with individual bombers that had strayed away from the main stream and the protection of Window.

While tactical measures such as these were being introduced post-haste into

191

the vast chess-like confrontation in the night skies, there were wide-ranging organisational and personnel changes within the *Luftwaffe*, particularly in those departments dealing with the fighter defence against the bombers. Kammhuber was among the first to experience Göring's frustration when, on 15 September 1943, he was relieved of his command of the *XII. Fliegerkorps* and replaced by Generalmajor Josef 'Beppo' Schmid. He remained *General der Nachtjagd*, but his time in that function was to be very short. At about the same time Göring approached Viktor von Lossberg and offered him Kammhuber's job, but von Lossberg declined.

The scope of Hajo Herrmann's Wild Boar command was broadened when, on 26 September, Göring ordered the setting-up of two further single-seater *Geschwader*, JG 301 and JG 302, the former to be located in Bavaria to participate in the defence of southern Germany and the latter in Brandenburg, to strengthen the defences in the Berlin area. Göring combined the three *Wilde Sau Geschwader* into the 30th Fighter Division (*30. Jagddivision*) and put them under the overall command of Herrmann, whom he had promoted to Oberstleutnant at the end of August. He also put under Herrmann's operational command a Ju 88 bomber *Gruppe*, III./KG 3, to act as illuminators. Herrmann was to exercise his command from Berlin and had his Divisional Operations Centre at Döberitz, just outside the western perimeter of the capital. As if further to emphasise Herrmann's independence from Kammhuber's command, the *30. Jagddivision* was subordinated not to him but to the General in overall command of all fighters, Adolf Galland.

Under the spotlight of criticism that was now focused on Kammhuber and his organisation other shortcomings in his static defence system became apparent. The change-over from a method based on small defensive areas to one requiring a comprehensive overview of the aerial battle in a much larger geographical context brought with it the need for a greater degree of integration not only of the night-fighter forces themselves but also in the way in which early warning and raid reporting were structured. A sweeping reorganisation was introduced in mid-October, and Kammhuber was removed from all association with the night fighters. The following month he took over as Commander of *Luftflotte 5* in Norway, a side-lining which, at that time of the war, was a clear indication that he no longer enjoyed Göring's approval. Beppo Schmid's *XII. Fliegerkorps* was renamed as the *I. Jagdkorps*, or Fighter Corps, reduced to three divisions in strength and made responsible for the air defence of the *Reich*, while the *II. Jagdkorps* was set up to defend the occupied territory of France and the *7. Jagddivision* at Munich/Schleissheim to defend against bombers approaching from the Mediterranean. The post of *General der Nachtjagd* was abolished as such and the overall responsibility for night-fighters combined under the *General der Jagdflieger* with that for day-fighters. Galland, who in principle did not support the amalgamation of both day-fighter and night-fighter arms, reluctantly accepted this extension of his responsibilities.

Meanwhile, the battle went on. On the German side urgency lent impetus to the development and introduction of electronic devices that might ease the task of the ground controllers and night-fighter crews. First on the scene was an attempt to rid the *Würzburg* control radars of the pest of Window – the Germans used the word *entlausen*, or 'delouse' – and the device introduced, with only partial success, was *Würzlaus*, which operated on the Doppler principle. Briefly, a moving target responds to a radar interrogation on a slightly different frequency from that on which a stationary target responds, so that it is possible to differentiate electronically, for example, between a moving aircraft and a cloud of Window which, after being released, descends with no forward speed except that provided by the wind. Far more promising was the thought of introducing an air-interception radar operating on a different wavelength from that of the *Lichtenstein* series in use so far. Development work was already well advanced on a lower-frequency *Lichtenstein*. A lower frequency means a longer wavelength, and series production and installation of this equipment went ahead with urgency. It was the *FuG 220*, or *Lichtenstein SN-2*, usually abbreviated simply to *SN-2*.

The *SN-2* operated on a switchable frequency of 72, 81 or 91 MHz as opposed to the fixed 54 MHz of its predecessors, and it utilised the same transmitter, receiver and switching units. The display unit comprised only two small circular screens, one for bearing and one for height, and the equipment had a range of up to six kilometres. While the longer wavelength meant that the *SN-2* was unaffected by the Window then in use, it also meant that the nose-mounted aerial dipoles had to be much longer, so that the performance of the night-fighters suffered somewhat. So big were the aerials that the array soon attracted the nickname *Hirschgeweih*, or 'stag's antlers'. The first sets were fitted in front-line aircraft in September 1943, by the end of which month some 2,000 had been produced by *Telefunken*. By early 1944 the majority of night fighters were carrying *SN-2* and improved models of the radar were being introduced, one of which, the *SN-2b*, was a combination of the basic set and a *Lichtenstein C-1* wide-angle radar. It carried the aerials for both frequencies, the smaller ones for the *Lichtenstein* mounted within those for the *SN-2*. With the lethal *Schräge Musik* upward-firing armament being fitted to an increasing number of fighters, the threat to Bomber Command aircraft was consolidating. The first He 219s, too, were coming into service with I./NJG 1 at Venlo. In July and August Hauptmann Hans-Dieter Frank, the *Geschwaderkommodore*, shot down seven RAF bombers in such a machine. But in August alone the workhorses of the *Nachtjagd*, the Bf 110s and the Ju 88s, also accounted for a total of 286.

John Chaloner's first operation had been to Mannheim, and despite the daunting reputation of Mannheim and its twin city Ludwigshafen it had not been too difficult a trip with which to start a tour. His visit on the night of 23/24 September 1943, however, redressed the balance:

'Percy was our rear gunner. He was accident-prone. There was never a trip when things went like clockwork. If we were high, he would be frozen up, or his guns would be frozen up, or his intercom, and even if you were in full communication with Percy you never got much feedback. Both the gunners – Fred was the mid-upper – were very laid-back. I remember one occasion, all was quiet, and Fred came up in his Black Country accent and without any sense of urgency, "They're firing at us!" And after another interval he said, "Get a move on in front, they're getting close to Fred's turret!" That meant that there was a number one crisis situation! And if the bloody aircraft were on fire you wouldn't get more than a murmur from Percy. He'd probably be off the intercom anyway!

'On the Mannheim trip I had the feeling it was going to be a shaky do when I saw the fighter flares dropped to illuminate us. We saw two kites shot down. I saw a parachute dropping and another combat to starboard. The searchlights were wobbling about, and then we were coned, and we stayed coned over Mannheim for about five minutes. It was a weird sensation, because we'd seen other aircraft being coned, and when you were coned it was like being on centre-stage. You were the star attraction. Every searchlight joined in, and I suppose all the other bombers were as pleased as Punch, because we were diverting the Germans' attention from everyone else. Everything was as light as day. And suddenly we got this "Bump, bump, bump", and flak explosions all around, and cordite fumes, and you knew that these were the ranging shots – you know, one short, one high, and the next one is going to be spot on. And suddenly, just after we had bombed, all the searchlights went out. What had happened was this German night-fighter was coming up behind us. He fired off the colours of the day, and the lights went out, and the guns stopped, and he came in with his attack. He came in from astern, to port and slightly below. He got in a good burst. And he hit Percy in the rear turret, and he hit down the port side of the aircraft, making twelve large holes, and he missed everybody in the front. The intercom and the hydraulics were put out of action. He only made one pass at us, and it wasn't decisive.'

Percy didn't complain about his wounds – he had been hit three times, by two bullets in the thigh and a splinter in the arm. The Lancaster had lost ten thousand feet while attempting to evade the searchlights, the flak and the Ju 88. Eventually, after eight hours in the air, 'O-Orange' landed at Fiskerton. John Chaloner continues the story:

'I went down to the back of the fuselage, and I said, "Bloody Hell, look at all these holes in the fuselage!" And Percy, lugubrious as ever, said, "Don't bother about those holes! I've got three holes in me!"'

Percy went into hospital, and from then on the rear turret was occupied by a different spare gunner for each operation.

October 1943 began with Bomber Command raids on Hagen, Munich, Kassel and Frankfurt. By now four-engined bombers were being used to mount diversionary raids in addition to the main attack, a role that had been played until then mostly by Mosquitos. On 4/5 October the main force of 406 machines went to Frankfurt while sixty-six attacked Ludwigshafen. There was an important 'first' on this night, too. A Mosquito went to Aachen to test – unsuccessfully, as it turned out on this occasion – a new navigational device, G-H, which would eventually be used to no little effect later in the war. The following week saw the introduction of a new method of jamming enemy night-fighter and control frequencies. For its time Airborne Cigar, or 'ABC' as it was perhaps more commonly known, was a very sophisticated device, and it was afforded a high security rating. Installed exclusively in Lancasters of No. 101 Squadron of No.

1 Group, ABC was operated by a specialist radio-man who flew as an extra crew member. The ABC aircraft operated as normal main-force bombers, carrying normal bomb-loads, and the regular members of the crew did not know what the 'extra bod' was doing, except that it was something very technical, highly specialised and very secret. The operator had at his disposal a cathode-ray tube which, coupled to a receiver, showed signals as blips on a horizontal base line. The receiver would automatically scan R/T frequency bands and lock on to signals. When the operator saw a blip on the CRT he would activate a switch that enabled him to hear what was being received: should it be an enemy broad-cast – the operators were German-speakers – he would tune one of his three transmitters to the appropriate frequency and broadcast a warbling tone that effectively jammed the enemy transmission. He would do this until all his three transmitters were in action. ABC could also be used to jam the signals of the German *Ypsilon* system, to which the British gave the codename 'Benito'. The introduction of this new jammer, coupled with diversionary raids by Mosquitos to Munich, Emden and Aachen and by a small Lancaster force to Friedrichs-hafen, took the *Nachtjagd* by surprise, and only 1.2 per cent of the 343 Lancasters that comprised the force against the main target, Stuttgart, were lost. The target, however, was cloud-covered and the bombing scattered.

Diversionary raids were not always successful in diverting the fighters' atten-tion from the main stream. On 22/23 October 1943, a force of 569 Lancasters and Halifaxes visited Kassel, with twenty-eight Lancasters and eight Mosquitos going to Frankfurt and a smaller force of twelve Oboe Mosquitos to the Ruhr. The German controllers correctly deduced that Kassel was the main target, with the result that forty-three bombers, representing 7.6 per cent of the force, were destroyed. One Halifax that survived the attentions of the night-fighters was that flown by Squadron Leader Derek Duder DFC, in which Terry Bolter was the bomb aimer. By this time Bolter, who had been commissioned in September, was deputy bombing leader of No. 77 Squadron:

> 'Our seventeenth operation was eventful. On the way back from bombing Kassel I heard Biff Hagen's voice through the intercom: "Rear gunner to skipper – fighter on the starboard quarter, eight hundred yards. He's clos-ing to attack. Dive to starboard – go!" Biff left his intercom on and I could hear his own guns firing and his heavy breathing. Then he called through, "It's OK. I've got him – he's going down." Mac Maculloch, the mid-upper, evidently tried to get in on the act by firing a burst, but Biff said, "It's OK Mac, leave him alone, he's finished, he's going down." Then lots of congratulations and excitement from the crew. I added my own congratu-lations with a note of warning that I could see other fighters about and to keep on the alert for other attacks.'

Fortunately no further attacks occurred, and Bolter's Halifax came home safely. The following day Hagen, who had also been commissioned a short time previously, was awarded an immediate DFC. This was Squadron Leader Derek Duder's final trip, and he received the DSO to go with the DFC he already had from a previous tour of operations. A new Flight Commander, Squadron Leader Herbert Bickerdike DFC, arrived on the station and took over the headless crew.

He brought with him his former rear gunner, Flying Officer Gordon Hills DFM. Hills replaced Maculloch in the mid-upper turret. Mac was posted to PFF.

On the German side, the Kassel attack saw Otto Fries's second kill. He and his *Funker*, Alfred Staffa, had taken off in the early evening in their Bf 110 G-4 from St Trond in Belgium flying Tame Boar under *Ypsilon* control. They had been vectored first north, then south-east, then south, but had had no contact with the enemy. It was a clear, moonless night, but ominous black clouds to the west marked the approach of a cold front. ABC was making itself felt. The German crewmen had christened its warbling note *Dudelsack*, or 'bag pipes'. On other frequencies Tinsel, noise broadcast from within bombers' engines, was also making it difficult to decipher what the fighter controller was saying. To the Germans Tinsel was *Seelenbohrer*, or 'soul-borer'. But already the German crews were learning ways of defeating British jamming. It had been discovered that if a transmitter was switched off when jamming occurred, the jamming signal too was switched off. When the transmitter was switched on again there was a short break before jamming resumed, during which alert crews could pick up a few sentences of the broadcast. In this way Fries managed to make out an instruction to turn on to a north-westerly heading, but could not hear the estimated height of the approaching bombers. He climbed to 6,000 metres, 20,000 feet, coming nearer and nearer to the bank of clouds to the west. On the aerials Fries and Staffa saw flickering lights, St Elmo's fire. The airscrews, too, showed circles of flame, and the aircraft lurched and swayed in the turbulence of the cold front they were flying into. Fries turned on to a reciprocal heading and began to lose height. Then he heard a message from the ground, another breakthrough in the jamming: '*Adler 98* from *Eisvogel*, head 300°. Bombers approaching, height 4 to 4.5 thousand metres.' Fries turned, and Staffa peered at his *Lichtenstein* screen. At first he saw nothing, not even Window returns, but very soon there was a response. 'I've got a blip! Coming in very fast. Probably *Düppel*. Climb a bit higher just in case!' At that very moment a dark shadow flashed past on a reciprocal heading and Fries flung his Messerschmitt around in a steep turn. Once on a south-easterly course he opened the throttles. His air speed indicator showed 430 kph. Staffa could see nothing on his radar until:

> ' "The bloody fool!" yelled Staffa. "It's a classic example! He's got the idea there's a night-fighter hanging around and he's trying to camouflage himself. He's chucking *Düppel* out every few seconds like a good 'un, and he's leaving us a splendid trail we just can't miss! We'll catch him! He's only two kilometres in front!" Later Staffa explained how the approach had looked on his radar screen. At first there was nothing to be seen except the circular time-base and the vertical or horizontal lines on the three CRTs, according to their individual function. Then a blip appeared from nowhere, then another, and then a third the same distance away, and then the blip from the target itself, with another blip emerging from it each time a bundle of Window was thrown out.'

They closed in on their prey. Soon Fries could see a shadow, and soon the shadow consolidated into the shape of a four-engined bomber. Fries goes on:

'The shadow grew bigger and bigger, until at last we could make out quite clearly the glowing exhausts of the four motors. We were scarcely a hundred metres away. "Open fire, before he sees us! Take it easy – just a bit closer." Then suddenly there were flashes from the rear of the bomber, and like a concentrated beam of light the bullets from the four-gun turret swept around the machine. There was a loud banging noise, and I felt a piercing pain in my left calf. I reacted instinctively, pushing the control column to the right and kicking hard right on the rudder bar. Then I pulled back gently on the control column so that the bomber's turret moved slowly across my sight. A short burst put the rear guns out of action. It was the first and only time that I fired directly at the fuselage of a bomber.'

Peeling off to port, Fries fired a second burst into the port wing root of his target. Despite the dazzling effect of his own tracer he could clearly see his cannon shells hitting home. The wing of the enemy machine broke off, and the fuselage spiralled down to earth, to crash in a great explosion. Fries saw the severed, burning port wing fluttering down until, almost a minute later, it too hit the ground. The main part of the bomber, with its bomb-load still on board, came down near Nettersheim in the Eifel region, carving out a crater twenty-five feet deep and seventy-five feet in diameter.

Fries was uninjured. A bullet from the bomber's rear turret had penetrated a joint between two armoured plates and struck a signal cartridge in a belt attached to his left flying boot. Fortunately for Fries, and no doubt for Staffa, the cartridge had not exploded.

Yet another jamming device was introduced by the RAF that same night, 'Corona'. Enemy fighter control and *Reportage* transmissions in the high-frequency band were monitored at a small station at West Kingsdown, Kent, using a captured German receiver. German-speaking operators listened in, and when they picked up a broadcast they informed one of four high-power GPO transmitters at Rugby and Leafield of the frequency, upon which the transmitter was tuned and misleading instructions were broadcast in German. Because VHF, as opposed to HF, transmissions have a limited ground range, Corona could not be used against the shorter wavelengths. Nevertheless, it proved to be a lasting irritant to the *Luftwaffe* controllers and crews, diverting fighters from their true targets, ordering them to return to base and so on. Later, when the Germans introduced females to do the *Reportage* and to broadcast control instructions to the fighters, believing that the dummy broadcasts were being made from aircraft, the RAF in their turn brought in German-speaking women to broadcast from the GPO transmitters. Many of the men and women engaging in this disruption were Jews who had fled Germany in the nineteen-thirties. It is said that on occasion the German controllers and their British tormentors, particularly the women, would abandon all pretence of broadcasting genuine and spurious instructions respectively and engage in bitter personal abuse. Another variation of the Corona technique was to broadcast a pre-recorded jumble of German voices on the fighter control frequencies, thus making the ground controllers and the *Reportage* completely incomprehensible to the *Luftwaffe* crews trying to find their targets or, often in emergency conditions, their destination airfields. Even recorded speeches by Hitler were reportedly used in this way.

Of the eighteen Lancasters among the forty-three Bomber Command aircraft destroyed during the attack on Kassel that night, Unteroffizi*er* Otto Kutzner, who had made his operational début on the night of the first Gomorrah attack and his first kill over Hanover on 9 October, claimed two. Unlike Fries and many other night-fighter pilots, he had no qualms about aiming at the rear gunner's turret. 'There was a man there, and he wanted to get home just as I did. So I always attacked from astern to eliminate him first.' Herrmann's three *Geschwader* of Wild Boars were active, too, and Hauptmann Friedrich-Karl Müller had to bale out from his Bf 109-G6 when his engine caught fire. He was slightly injured when he hit the ground. Two other pilots were less lucky. Feldwebel Horst Neumann and Feldwebel Kurt Degenkolb, both of III./JG 301, lost their lives. Since their first mission as a regular force, the Wild Boars had lost fifty-two pilots killed, forty-six of them in action, with twelve wounded or injured. This takes no account of the numerous aircraft written off in crash-landings without the pilot being hurt. A glance at the casualty lists shows that a good proportion of the losses were not directly due to enemy action but to crashing on landing, baling out on account of fuel shortage and so on. The *Wilde Sau* had had their particularly bad nights. During the Berlin raid on 31 August/1 September 1943 they had lost six, of which only one pilot survived. The twenty-seventh September, when Bomber Command hit Hanover, was even worse, with eight of Herrmann's machines being lost. Only two pilots survived, one with severe injuries.

The Kassel raid was, then, noteworthy in a number of ways. It was also, from Harris's point of view, a very successful attack. Although the blind markers, dropping their flares on H2S, overshot the aiming point, the backers-up were able to correct the error by placing their TIs correctly in the centre of the city. This was the most damaging raid since Hamburg, with a death toll among the population of about 5,600. Many industrial and military buildings were destroyed or damaged, including aircraft factories producing parts for V-1 flying bombs, which suffered so badly that it was calculated that the beginning of the flying-bomb offensive was delayed by several months.

By October 1943 aircraft of the main-force squadrons were beginning to be equipped with H2S sets. Training was 'on the job', with selected crews being the first to receive the sets and learn how to use them, after which the navigator would pass on his knowledge to the other crews as new equipments were fitted. John Chaloner became one of those selected. There was a still a shroud of secrecy around H2S. That is surprising, perhaps, because by that time so many PFF machines had been lost that it must have been beyond doubt that the Germans were well informed on the radar. Yet so secret was H2S that even in crews' flying log books the only reference was to 'Special Signals Training'. Behind the scenes, much was going on on the British side to improve the device, and on the German side to counter it.

The Mk II sets so far in use by the Pathfinders and now beginning to arrive with Main Force operated on a wavelength of ten centimetres, and, as experience over Berlin had shown, did not produce a crisp picture. Experiments had been going on for some time on an H2S working on the shorter wavelength of 3 cm and after the first disappointment of finding that a huge metropolitan area such as the German capital gave a great, largely unrecognisable blob on the screen there was much urgency to bring the improved device into service. Trials were very promising, and the new set became the Mk III. It would, however, be 13 November before the first three Lancasters equipped with it were delivered for trials to PFF, and for the time being the mass of the navigators would have to make the best of their 10 cm Mk II equipment.

There was a spin-off from H2S that did come into operation in October 1943. Reportedly the idea originated with Group Captain Dudley Saward, chief radar officer to the C-in-C of Bomber Command: if H2S would permit one to see the ground beneath the aircraft, he reasoned, could it not be used to see other aircraft in the same area? The answer was that it could, and 'Fishpond' was then a comparatively simple thing to develop. Using H2S transmissions and echoes it showed on a screen in the wireless operator's compartment small blips that represented other aircraft in the vicinity. Of course, it could only see below the bomber, because that was where the scanning aerial looked, but as most fighter attacks came from below that seemed to be a good thing. The device would show other friendly aircraft as well as hostile ones, but anything approaching on a rapidly converging course would automatically arouse alarm. From small beginnings in October, Fishpond rapidly became standard equipment on H2S aircraft.

Within three weeks of the German capture of a partly intact H2S in February 1943, as described earlier, the *Luftwaffe* had set up a commission to study means of defence against the *Rotterdamgerät*, as they called it. It was an obvious first thought on their part that if the thing transmitted it would be a simple matter to use its transmissions to their own advantage, and a detector device, code named *Naxos*, was swiftly produced and fitted experimentally to a night fighter in early September. The tests showed that it was possible to pick up and obtain a rough bearing on H2S transmissions at ranges up to about fifteen kilometres. By November that range would be increased to some 100 kilometres. *Naxos* never became a precision instrument that would permit fighters to home in on to individual H2S-carrying bombers, but it was of great defensive value, particularly in conjunction with the Tame Boar procedure, in enabling fighters to find the bomber stream, home in on it and broadcast its location so that other fighters could be brought up. Another homing device introduced into German night-fighters during this period was the FuG 227 *Flensburg* which, operating on the radio frequency used by the bombers' *Monica* tail-warning device, enabled the pilots to home directly in on to the machine. There was also the so-called *Freya Halbe* equipment, with which fighters could home in on to British airborne Mandrel transmissions that were jamming the *Freya* ground radars.

Prinz zu Sayn-Wittgenstein was back in the West from the short detachment to the Eastern Front that had kept him away from the *Reich* for the Battle of Hamburg and the attack on Peenemünde. During this short period he had added twenty-seven Soviet machines to his score. It was, says his *Funker* Herbert Kümmritz, easy: there was no jamming, the Russians didn't expect night-fighters and they didn't take evasive action. With *Schräge Musik* it was the easiest thing in the world to shoot them down, pure routine. In the West, of course, it was different. Kümmritz goes on to describe the demanding duties of the *Funker* in a German night-fighter:

'It was very crowded in the cockpit of the Ju 88 – there wasn't much room to move. At first we had a pilot, a *Funker* and a *Bordmechaniker*, but operating became so complicated that they later did without the mechanic in some machines and flew with two radio operators. Most of our navigation was by track and groundspeed, and we had a circular slide-rule to do our navigational problems on, a so-called *Kniemeyer*. We had the standard FuG 10 radio receiver with a direction-finding loop, and we would use this for "beacon-hopping", which was one of our standard forms of navigation. We could switch the D/F loop in to the automatic course-steering, and then the aircraft would head for the beacon we selected. All the beacons were of course marked on our charts, so we could use them for bearings to check our position. We could call up stations in Morse for bearings, but they were often jammed and difficult to work. We used QDMs a lot for homing. I must say that much of our navigation was "guesstimation" – we didn't keep an air plot, for instance.

'In addition to navigation and R/T and W/T communication, the *Funker* was responsible for radar. First of all we had *Lichtenstein*, then *SN-2*, sometimes a combination of both. *Naxos* came towards the end of 1943. Then we had the *Freya Halbe*, the FuG 221, for homing in on to *Freya* jamming. For R/T we had the FuG 16 or 17, and there was the transponder for the *Ypsilon* system. We had also to carry lists of operational frequencies, airfields, colours of the day and so on and be ready to answer any questions the pilot put, particularly in an emergency. Just to make things complete the *Funker* had a backward-firing gun in his cockpit, but I myself only fired it once or twice. Can I give you an example of the way in which a *Funker* might have to react in an emergency?

'We were somewhere in central Germany, and we had lost our bearings. I kept calling up ground stations on W/T for a QDM, but no one replied – Berlin, Leipzig, Dresden but no one came in. Then one of our engines failed. Then suddenly, through all the background noise, I heard a very distant signal – "AOA, AOA". But I couldn't find the letters on my list of airfields. The Prince was angry, telling me I ought to know where it was. But the signal was getting louder, so we were obviously heading in the right direction. I called up on the frequency, telling them we wanted an emergency landing because we only had one engine and were short of fuel, and they came back, "What type of aircraft are you?" I told them "Ju 88," and they told me I couldn't land there, the airfield was too small. I called up and told them to switch on the airfield lighting, we were going to attempt a landing in any case. We managed to get down – it was a small industrial airfield near Cottbus. We touched down right at the edge of the field and put full brakes on immediately, and we came to a stop just about twenty or thirty metres from the radio mast on the far boundary. The operator had already left his hut at full speed, thinking we were going to hit him!'

After the Kassel attack there were no further major raids until 3/4 November, although small numbers of Mosquitos flew nuisance raids almost every night to ensure that the population, the air-raid services and the air defence forces would not have a chance to relax. In the early evening of 3 November, John Chaloner was on board one of the 344 Lancasters which, together with 233 Halifaxes and twelve Mosquitos, paid a visit to Düsseldorf, while a smaller force flew a diversionary raid to Cologne. It was a routine night for Bomber Command. Flying *Zahme Sau*, Otto Fries shot down his third bomber, Halifax MP-X from No. 76 Squadron at Holme-on-Spalding Moor in Yorkshire. It crashed near the Dutch village of Opgrimby, near the Belgian/Dutch border to the north of Maastricht. Most unusually, all the crew managed to bale out safely before the aircraft came down. Only one crew member, Sgt Fewson, was captured immediately. The others evaded capture for various lengths of time, and the captain, Dennis Hornsey, reached Spain in the course of the following weeks with the help of the underground movement.

By the beginning of November Terry Bolter's crew had completed seventeen operations, and were now in the 'veteran' category. With Ernie Webb, John Chaloner's score stood at twelve: the Düsseldorf raid was his thirteenth, but bad luck did not strike. John recalls Düsseldorf that night because it was 'One of those shambolic occasions, when Bomber Command was scattered around coming back. We had a cookie and six cans on board. I remember that one, because it was as clear as daylight, with the loop in the river and so on. And the bombs were going down at seventy-two tons a minute! It was all concentrated in about twenty minutes. There was no question of missing the place, because it was as clear as day.'

It was during this November raid against Düsseldorf that the navigation and blind-bombing device G-H was first used operationally. With similarities to both Gee and Oboe, G-H enjoyed the advantage of greater accuracy than Gee itself, and, unlike Oboe, it could be used by a number of aircraft at the same time. In common with both its predecessors, however, its range was limited by the curvature of the earth. Whereas the active components of Oboe were on the ground, those of the G-H system were in the aircraft, a transmitter and a receiver respectively, by means of which ranges from two ground stations could be measured. The device was complicated and required a high degree of skill to operate, but its great advantage lay in its availability to a number of aircraft simultaneously.

Luck had been with Chaloner and his crew on their thirteenth operation. Now, for what would have been their fourteenth, it deserted them:

'The next one was Modane, an easy target, on 10 November. That was the one when we were going to bomb a railway tunnel in France. I think we were the first to take off. We had got sixteen 1,000-pounders on board, high explosives. And we were trundling down the runway. We'd got about half way down, and the port inner set on fire. And we went at right angles to the runway, to port, and I thought, "This is it, for sure!" – we'd got a full load of fuel and sixteen thousand pounds of bombs on board – "There's going to be one big bang any minute now!" And the wheels folded up, and we came down – well, we'd never got airborne, really. We swung off the runway. I was standing behind the pilot for take-off, and it seemed as if we were frozen, waiting for the damned explosion. We pulled down the pilot's clear-view window at the side, and Ernie went out first, and I followed head first behind him. We thought we were going to hit the inner engine, which was on fire . . . We'd come to a grinding halt, and we were expecting the explosion at any time, and we just ran like crazy towards the Air Traffic Control building. And when we'd got a couple of hundred yards away, we dropped down to the ground, but the explosion didn't come. And all the crew got out.'

The aircraft did explode, but not until some short time later, and happily there were no casualties. None of the other aircraft from Fiskerton detailed for the trip to Modane was able to take off, and the airfield was closed. Ernie Webb and his crew were not very popular with the other crews the following day, because they blamed him for spoiling their chance of an easy trip to bring the end of their tour nearer. Chaloner felt mildly aggrieved – the most 'hairy' operation that he had so far participated in didn't even count towards his own tour! Somewhat wryly he adds, 'And we had another one, later, when we were shot up over Beachy Head by a Mosquito, and that didn't count, either!'

Above left: Hans Angersbach (right) and crew. *(Angersbach)*

Above right: Fahnenjunker-Oberfeldwebel Günther Migge with mechanic in front of Fw 190. A Wild Boar pilot, Migge shot down eight bombers. *(Frau Migge)*

Left: Oberst Helmut Lent, whose score stood at 110 when he was killed in a flying accident in October 1944. *(Szardenings)*

Above left: The burial of *Major* Prinz zu Sayn-Wittgenstein, 29 January 1944. Numbered in the photograph (centre row) are 1, *Unteroffizier* Loacker; 2, *Feldwebel* Fritz Ostheimer and 4, *Oberleutnant* Erich Jung. *(Scholl)*

Above right: Hauptmann Gerhard Friedrich (NJG 6) on the airfield at Heilfingen, in conversation with *Stabsarzt* (Medical Officer) Dr Karl Buschmann. *(Buschmann)*

Below: Flight Lieutenant John Cox and crew, shot down in an attack on Nuremburg on 16 March 1944. Their aircraft was one of the eight destroyed that night by *Oberleutnant* Erich Jung. *(Cox)*

CHAPTER NINE

The Big City: Battle is Joined
November to December 1943

Now, in November 1943, the scene was to all intents and purposes set for a bloody engagement that would last until the end of the following March and would cost the lives of approaching 8,000 Bomber Command aircrew and an unrecorded, but not insignificant, number of German night-fighter men. Harris, undeterred by the experience of his earlier costly and unrewarding attacks against Berlin, once more focused on the capital city. The longer nights would provide his bombers with the cover of darkness for the entire duration of their flight to and over hostile territory, while further protection would be afforded by the increasing use of diversionary and intruder tactics and electronic and radio counter-measures. Just as had been the case with Hamburg, Harris's declared aim was nothing less than the complete destruction of Berlin. But whereas he had foreseen the annihilation of Hamburg playing 'an important part in shortening and winning the war', he now forecast, in a much-quoted minute to the Prime Minister on 3 November, that the destruction of Berlin would 'cost Germany the war'.

This was a significant document, particularly in the light it cast upon Harris's character. He claimed that the Ruhr area was as good as eliminated: the words he used were, ' . . . you will see that the Ruhr is largely "out".' Typically, he was overstating his case: whether knowingly, in order to strengthen that case, or because he genuinely believed that his bombing campaign was having a greater effect than it really was, must remain an open question. It was true that vast damage had been caused in the industrial heartland centred on Essen, but the effect on industrial capacity and output, although significant, was very far from being decisive. Harris also suggested that the Americans might join in the attack on the German capital, when he knew full well that, not having a long-range escort fighter that could meet the Messerschmitts and Focke-Wulfs on equal terms, they were not yet in a position to mount large-scale daylight raids to targets deep within the heavily defended *Reich*. On 1 August 1943 the Americans had sent 163 B-24 Liberators, flying from airfields in North Africa, to attack the Romanian oil-fields at Ploesti, and fifty-four had been shot down. Harris referred to the Ploesti raid, suggesting that the Americans should avoid 'such disastrous diversions'. But the big lesson to be learned from the Ploesti raid, as Harris must have seen, was the one that Bomber Command had learned early in the war: quite simply, unescorted heavy bombers were no match for day-fighters. There was no reason, when Harris wrote his minute, to think that similarly intolerable losses would not apply to raids mounted against Berlin by day. Later the North American P-51B, the 'Mustang' with a Rolls-Royce Merlin engine built under licence in the States by the Packard Company, would dramatically overcome this deficiency, but Berlin was not attacked by the 8th Air Force until March 1944, when the RAF offensive against the city had all but run its course.

In fact, it is not clear in just what way Harris envisaged American collaboration. Was he, possibly, hoping that they would join Bomber Command in the offensive by night? It seems more likely that he well knew that American participation in his Berlin plan was a non-starter. In addition to the specific matter of the lack of an escort fighter, there was another, more general, factor that suggested that Harris's tongue was in his cheek when he brought up the matter. By November 1943 it was clear to both sides that agreement on a common bombing policy was unlikely in the extreme. The Americans' concept of strategic bombing was at odds with Harris's: Harris unswervingly advocated the saturation bombing of cities, the Americans adamantly favoured the precision bombing of selected war-related targets, which ruled out night raids. But Harris was formally bound by the Pointblank directive, which called for a co-ordinated Anglo-American bomber offensive, and so when he suggested that the Americans should join in the Battle of Berlin, even knowing that it was a virtual impossibility, he was paying lip-service to the concept. That he did not seriously expect the Americans to accept his suggestion is strongly indicated by what he went on to say and what he went on to do. 'I await promised USAAF help in this, the greatest of air battles,' he wrote, 'but I would not propose to wait for ever, or for long if opportunity serves.' He did not wait long – his first attack in the resumed offensive on Berlin took place just fifteen days later, so the strong presumption must be that his plans for Bomber Command to go it alone were already laid.

Whatever was in Harris's mind, he was confident that bombing could 'wreck Berlin from end to end' at a cost of between four and five hundred aircraft. It is interesting, as a further indicator to Harris's character and of his, or his advisers', staff work, to speculate as to what basis was used for this estimate. Harris had sent Bomber Command to Berlin three times in August and September, losing a total of 7.5 per cent of the bombers he dispatched. This was, it should be remembered, not long after the introduction of Window, when the night-fighter force might have been expected to be at a technical disadvantage. At a similar rate of attrition, 400 losses would indicate a forecast total of about 5,300 sorties; 500 losses a total of about 6,700. No doubt Harris, nothing if not optimistic, would have hoped for a lower loss rate. But even basing calculations on predicted losses of five per cent, his forecast would mean that he envisaged that between 8,000 and 10,000 sorties by heavy bombers would be necessary to cause such damage to Berlin that the Germans would lose the war.

The official historians dubbed this period 'The Battle of Berlin', but it was not as compact as that. The first strike was against Berlin on the night of 18/19 November 1943, the last one against Nuremberg on 30/31 March 1944. During that period Bomber Command flew fourteen raids against Berlin and eighteen against other major targets in Germany. There were also mine-laying sorties, attacks on French targets and many diversionary and harassing raids to Germany.

For the front-line British crews the pattern was much as it had long been, a taxing cycle of tension and relaxation day in and day out, anticipating the demands that the coming night might make upon them and recovering from the testing experiences of their most recent operation, simultaneously trying to cope, both consciously and subconsciously, with the cumulative mental and physical strain that operational flying imposed upon them; and, joke as they might, with the persistent awareness that 'the chop' was a probability rather than a possibility. Now the frequency with which the 'Big City' and other long-range targets came up added yet another burden for young shoulders to bear. There were, it was true, regular periods of seven days' leave every six weeks or so, but to some aircrew they were a nuisance rather than a blessing because they made it necessary to readjust repeatedly to the physical and psychological demands with which they were expected to cope.

Similar tensions affected the men who flew the German night-fighters. They too knew what it was like to have to fly and fight in the small hours, to contend with the hazards of the autumn and winter weather and to face the guns of the enemy, to know that for them there might be no tomorrow. They were strongly motivated, because while flying their nightly excursions they could see their cities erupting and burning and imagine, often from personal experience, what was happening in human terms amid the explosions and the flames. For the overwhelming majority of crew members, RAF and *Luftwaffe* alike, the need to kill posed no moral dilemma: this war was a fight to the finish, and the enemy had to be defeated. That was the job to be done, and they would do it to the best of their ability and, if needs be, to the death. In that way philosophical issues of immense complexity were reduced to an over-simplification without which soldiers of all countries and all ages could arguably not do, or have done, their duty, whatever might be entailed. And so it will always be.

If life for the flyers was stressful, it was not, in some ways, unenjoyable. There was the ego-boost of knowing that they were doing their duty, fighting for their respective countries, 'doing their bit' – phrase it as you will. English or German, they subconsciously echoed the American naval officer, Stephen Decateur, in the War of Independence: 'Our country! In her intercourse with nations, may she always be in the right; but our country, right or wrong.' There was the pride of belonging to an élite force, the prestige of wearing a flying badge. And the thrill of flying, the satisfaction of mastering a specialist job, the excitement of action, the comfort of comradeship. And the tension and the fear could be offset by adapting to a life-style, with its origins in the traditions of the air forces, that had developed as the war had progressed. Each flyer was, of course, an individual. By and large aircrew were men of above-average intellect and sensitivity, and, as might be expected, there were some who retained their individuality to the extent of refusal to conform to the norm, but the majority readily fell into the pattern of working hard and playing hard. Off-duty relaxation in messes or local bars regularly took the form of hectic parties with liberal consumption of alcohol, and a lot of the participants were little more than boys and unequipped for heavy drinking. There were understandably many short-term sexual relationships, but probably not a lot more proportionately than tend to occur whenever and wherever there are soldiers and females, both serving and civilian, within reasonable proximity. In the RAF, and even more noticeably among aircrew of the Commonwealth Air Forces, there was a widespread impatience with and flouting of traditional military discipline. Superstition – or, more probably, the affectation of superstition – was endemic, taking the form of carrying mascots on operations, urinating on the tail-wheel before take-off, wearing a special item of clothing and so on. Warrant Officer James Goldie DFC DFM, an air gunner who lived through 111 operations, attributes his survival to 'Never having relaxed my vigilance from take-off to landing; removal of Perspex from rear window of rear turret; believed completely in violent evasive action when attacked – the Browning .303 was a poor match against a fighter's cannon who already had you in his sights; and always wearing a large tartan scarf (the Germans feared that colour).'

While details varied from airfield to airfield, there was a general pattern to aircrew life on a Bomber Command base in eastern England. If the return from the previous night's flying, operational or non-operational, warranted it, part of the morning might be spent in bed catching up on lost sleep. If not, crew members would usually begin the day by reporting to their respective sections for continuation training or simply to await apprehensively the appearance of the 'Battle Order', the list of those crews detailed for operations that night. Sometimes there would be training flights to be flown – cross-countries, fighter affiliation, bombing practice, air-to-sea and air-to-air firing and so on – and possibly, for the crews on the Battle Order, an air test to carry out. There was the nagging worry about the nature of the coming night's operation, the hope against hope that it would be a short-haul one, preferably to an easy target, and the stomach-sinking fear that it would be a long-penetration mission, perhaps to Berlin, the most dreaded destination of all.

Then would come the confirmation from Group that an operation was planned for that night, or alternatively that the squadron was stood down. If ops were on, a detailed telegram from Group announcing the target, the force to be deployed, routes and heights to be flown and so on would trigger off hectic activity on the base, all the complex preparations necessary to ensure that perhaps twenty heavy aircraft, fully bombed-up, fuelled and armed, would be ready to take off at times precisely calculated to ensure that the necessary concentration in space and time on the way to and above the target would be achieved. There would be great interest on the part of the crews in the bomb-load and quantity of fuel to be carried, because from those figures an idea could be gained of how long the trip was likely to be. Eventually, crew members would be called to their individual sections for pre-flight specialist briefings, but at this stage the only member of the crew who would be aware of the target itself was the navigator, who would attend a flight-planning session in the Navigation Section, plotting his routes on his charts and calculating his flight plan times and ETAs. Then would come the main briefing, at which all the crew were present.

There was an element of theatricality about main briefing, with everyone's attention focused on the covered map on the wall facing the rows of seats. Behind the covers was the outline of the planned routes out and home. When all the crews were assembled, with windows curtained and service policemen posted at the doors to ensure that unauthorised individuals did not learn details of the forthcoming operation, the station commander, squadron commander, intelligence officer, meteorological officer and section leaders would file in – the aircrew already assembled would stand and remain standing until told by the senior officer to be seated – and the proceedings would begin, usually with the squadron commander stating, 'Gentlemen, your target for tonight is . . .' Ritual cheers or groans, frequently a mixture of both depending on the nature of the target, would greet this announcement and the drawing back of the curtain in front of the map. Then would come short briefings from individual officers – intelligence, meteorological, navigation, bombing, gunnery, engineer, signals and so on – and the senior officer, either the station commander or the squadron commander, would wish the crews good fortune, and the meeting would disperse. Those who were to fly would have a period alone with their personal thoughts and fears before it was time to have a meal – usually, like the prisoner's last breakfast, of a standard higher than was customary in the days of wartime austerity – and then to gather equipment, clothing and parachute and board the vehicle that would take them to their individual aircraft, possibly to their fate.

In Germany, Belgium, Holland, France and Denmark night-fighter crews would be waiting, young men so very similar in so many ways to the Bomber Command men whom Fate had decreed they should try to shoot from the sky. They too, possibly, were tired from the previous night's flying, they too might have a hangover from the previous evening's partying, they too had their own fears and their personal thoughts, possibly of loved ones. Logically they knew they might only have hours to live, but emotionally they persuaded themselves that while Death might choose others, he would not pick them. From perhaps midday onward those detailed for operations would be at stand-by in expectation of an attack from 'the friends from the other Field Post Office Number' (*Die Freunde von der anderen Feldpostnummer*). Meanwhile their time would be spent much as that of their RAF opposite numbers was spent – training and self-briefing, checking aircraft and equipment, possibly air-testing or flying practice interceptions to the mutual benefit of aircrew and fighter controllers. In mid-to-late afternoon, depending on the time it would grow dark and bombers might be expected, the crews would go on to readiness – *Bereitschaft* – when they would assemble in the *Bereitschaftsraum*, or 'Readiness Room', and settle down in armchairs – those lucky enough to 'bag' them – or at tables. Briefing would usually be held here, although the practice varied from airfield to airfield, but it would not be as formal or as detailed as that that the RAF crews had. It would normally be given by the Gruppenkommandeur or his deputy, who might speak along these lines:

'*Meine Herren*, the weather over England is good, that over central Europe bad, which means that we must expect raids. That is confirmed by early monitoring and radar reports. Large numbers of raiders are expected, but we are well prepared. So far there is little information with which to identify the target. Diversion raids may be expected. First indications, however, are that the enemy will come in over Holland, and there must be a strong possibility that the Ruhr area is the objective. Berlin, however, cannot be excluded. We must be prepared to stay in the air a long time. We will assemble at Beacon Marie. *Hals und Beinbruch.*'

The briefing concluded, games of chess and cards – *Skat* and *Doppelkopf* were favourites – would be played, letters written, books read, jokes exchanged and thoughts thought. There was often a gramophone, and, just as in the RAF messes, there were favourite records. One was '*Kommt zurück*', the German version of the plaintive French hit '*J'attendrai*'. '*Kommt zurück*' means 'come back', but instead some crews sang 'QAC' – phonetically 'coo-ah-tsay' – the W/T Q-code signal for 'I am returning to land at base.'

At last the telephone would ring, and someone would answer it; or alternatively a loudspeaker would sound: '*Sitzbereitschaft!*' – cockpit readiness – and those detailed to fly the first defensive wave would be picked up by motor vehicle and taken to their aircraft, either at dispersal or, increasingly as RAF intruder raids became more frequent, in shelters, in clearings in woods, or in hangars. In winter the aircraft would if possible be kept in heated hangars to ensure quick starting. Once the crew was on board the engines would be started, pre-flight checks carried out, and the machines would taxi out to await the signal to take off (*Startbereitschaft*), which would be a green Very light fired into the air. The fighters' first destination would be a nearby marshalling point, most often a radio beacon but sometimes a visual beacon, where they would switch over to their allotted control, frequency and circle at their allocated height to await further instructions by R/T.

At this stage both British and German crews would be at a high peak of tension, the Bomber Command men knowing that they were entering the danger zone, very conscious that they would have to run the gauntlet of the night fighters right up to their target and back, and knowing that if they were unlucky enough to be picked out the odds were stacked against them. The men of the *Nachtjagd* would be alert for the instructions from the ground that would send them to victory or the frustration of knowing that there were bombers nearby but being unable to find one, possibly to a crash-landing, a parachute jump, even death. Both sets of flyers had lived through the loss of many of their friends and comrades, both sets knew the price they might have to pay.

So it was on the night of 18/19 November 1943, when Harris resumed his attack on Berlin by sending a force of moderate size – 440 Lancasters and seven Mosquitos – to attack the city. It was not a good raid, because the crews met thick cloud over Berlin, PFF did not mark accurately and the Main Force's bombs were scattered throughout the whole vast metropolitan area. Bomber Command also mounted an attack against Mannheim/Ludwigshafen, intended primarily to divert the Germans' attention from the Berlin raid but comprising, in fact, almost as strong a force in terms of aircraft involved – 248 Halifaxes, 114 Stirlings and twenty-three Lancasters. Just as with Berlin, the target was cloud-covered and the bombing scattered. As far as the Berlin attack was concerned, the diversionary raid seems to have achieved its purpose, only nine Lancasters being lost, most of them to flak. The bad weather over Germany also played its part in limiting RAF losses. Many night-fighter units were unable to take off because of low cloud at their bases. Nevertheless, the *Nachtjagd* did achieve not inconsiderable success against the Mannheim raid, which lost twenty-three bombers, 5.8 per cent of the force as against the two per cent lost on the Berlin raid. In addition to these two large raids, Mosquitos carried out nuisance raids on Aachen and Frankfurt, while Wellingtons laid mines off the north German coast.

Of Herrmann's Wild Boars only a few aircraft of JG 301, located in Bavaria, were able to get into the air. The *Geschwader* lost two machines, both pilots dying. One was Major Helmut Weinreich, *Geschwaderkommodore* of JG 301, a former bomber pilot who was a close friend of Hajo Herrmann, with whom he had served in KG 30. A holder of the Knight's Cross, he had flown over three hundred bomber operations before joining Herrmann's 'irregulars'. Now his Fw 190, badly damaged in combat with a British bomber, struck the ground short of the runway and exploded as Weinreich was attempting an emergency landing at the Rhein-Main airfield at Frankfurt. Weinreich had been a night-fighter pilot only two months. On the British side, John Chaloner had an uneventful nine-and-a-half-hour trip on this his third visit to Berlin and his sixteenth operation overall.

The following night a small raid against Leverkusen in the Ruhr by Halifaxes, Stirlings and Mosquitos was again dogged by bad weather in the target area, but the same bad weather prevented the majority of the night-fighters from taking off, so that only five bombers, 1.9 per cent of the attacking force of 266, were shot down. In addition to the poor weather, the unserviceability of the Oboe equipment contributed to the poor bombing results, making accurate marking of the target impossible. Almost unbelievably, only one high-explosive bomb is recorded as having fallen in the town itself. Even accepting that casualties were light, this would seem to be a poor return for the loss of five bombers and thirty-five aircrew.

One night fighter that did get airborne from St Trond despite the poor weather was a Bf 110, G9+EM, of II./NJG 1. Borrowed from the 6th *Staffel*, it was manned by Otto Fries, recently appointed Technical Officer of the *Gruppe*, and his radio operator Unteroffizier Alfred Staffa. Despite the presence of Window, the ground controller was able to close-control the Messerschmitt into contact with a target. The unfortunate bomber was a Stirling (LJ 442, JN-F) of No. 75 Squadron, which had taken off from Mepal, north of Cambridge, and it is possible that it had drifted off track and so was not within Window protection. Fries's first attack, from astern and below, was unsuccessful. The fighter had clearly been spotted, and the bomber went into a corkscrew. Fries's reaction was relaxed: 'He'll soon get fed up of that, so we'll just wait a bit!' Fries, writing in the third person, describes what happened then:

'Only a few minutes had passed since the attack when the Stirling began gradually to calm down and to fly normally once more. Obviously they thought they had shaken him off. He was positioned to the right of the bomber, about two hundred metres below, slightly astern. Slowly he eased up, very slowly. When he was to the right of the bomber, almost at the same height and about seventy metres behind it, he pushed on the rudder bar, moving his machine to the left. He gave a short burst from his guns as the starboard wing moved through his sights, another as the port wing did. Then he peeled off immediately to the left so that he would not be caught by fire from the rear turret. Like swift-moving glow-worms tracer flashed past the stern of his aircraft.

'In the port wing of the Stirling he saw a faint glow, which then exploded and expanded, enveloping the entire wing and reaching into the fuselage. A number of parts seemed to come away from the bomber and fly into space – were they members of the crew baling out? He could not tell. Within a few seconds the entire bomber was a mass of bright flame. Then it pulled up slightly, peeled off to port and fell into the depths like a stone, a trail of fire like that of a comet behind it. The ball of fire disappeared into the clouds, which were lit up a few seconds later as if by a red flash of lightning. The lightning flash went, but a red glow could be seen for a long time afterwards . . .

'The wreckage was found near the village of Horrues, three kilometres north-west of Soignies. The letters of the aircraft could still be seen – JN-F. Four members of the crew had perished: Sergeant Day, whose name was discovered on an envelope; Sgt Watkins, identified by a name-tag on his clothing; and two others who remained unidentified. Sergeant Hyde was wounded, and he was taken to the *Luftwaffe* hospital in Brussels.'

The captain of the Stirling was Flight Sergeant N. N. Parker, who managed to evade capture and reached England early the following year, as did the navigator, Sergeant Robert Griffith. A report on their debriefing on the loss of the aircraft dated 13 February 1944 describes how, after crossing the enemy coast inbound at 15,000 feet, Parker had difficulty in maintaining height, a not unusual phenomenon with the Stirling. At the estimated time of their arrival in the target area they were down at 13,500 feet and above ten-tenths cloud and coming under predicted flak fire, but there was no sign of the expected PFF markers. Parker began to orbit, but the flak intensified and the aircraft was hit by splinters, so he jettisoned his load of bombs at 12,000 feet and turned on to a southerly heading in an attempt to follow the planned route out of the target. Twenty minutes later they came under attack from a night-fighter, but the first burst of fire missed and the rear gunner, Sergeant M. I. R. Day, gave the order, 'Corkscrew port!' The report continues:

'Finally, when the pilot had begun to think that the fighter's ammunition was spent, a fourth attack was made as the Stirling was at the "top" of a corkscrew . . . The pilot heard two explosions in the starboard wing, but saw no shells go past . . . Almost directly after the last attack, the wireless operator told the pilot he could smell petrol, and the mid-upper gunner reported a fire in the starboard wing . . . He immediately ordered the crew to abandon the aircraft, height then being about 8,000 to 9,000 feet. There was no acknowledgement of this order at first. Probably the crew were putting on their parachutes and were not connected to the intercom, so the pilot repeated the order, which was then acknowledged. The rear gunner reported he was unable to open the doors of his turret. As the pilot left his seat, having put in "George", he saw the bombardier go through the front escape hatch. Looking down the aircraft the pilot saw strong flames coming up through the floor of the fuselage, suggesting that incendiaries had hung up and caught fire during one of the attacks. Taking his parachute pack, the pilot intended to go back to help the rear gunner. He put the right-hand hook on to his harness and was fumbling with the left one . . . That was the last thing he could remember doing. Seven or eight hours later he found himself on the ground, but without trace of either parachute or Mae West. The side of his face was lacerated and an eye severely bruised, a bone in his neck was broken, three ribs broken, and other lesser injuries. He heard later that the aircraft had broken up in the air and can only believe that he was thrown out and fell with his 'chute open. Presumably his 'chute and Mae West had been removed by someone who believed he was dead. The pilot found himself a little south-west of Soignies, between Mons and Brussels.'

Sgt Mike Day, identified from an envelope found on his body, was the rear gunner, Sgt 'Tuffy' Watkins the flight engineer and Sgt Jack Hyde, who was wounded, the bomb aimer. The two others killed were Flight Sergeant Bill Kell, the wireless operator, and Sergeant Jack Gilfillan, the mid-upper gunner. The pilot, commissioned on his return to England, joined the Pathfinder Force and survived the war, flying a further fifty operations, some of them as Master Bomber.

Jack Hyde, Australian by birth but a member of the Royal New Zealand Air Force, recalls the night of 19 November 1943:

'My final flight began for me under a bad omen, and I had the feeling that it would be a fateful night. Why? Well, my flying boots were stolen from my locker together with my oxygen mask, and on the same day someone pinched my cap with the RNZAF badge on it. Our encounter with the aircraft that shot us down was actually quite a good one, and we really thought we had shaken him off when he broke off his attack. Everything seemed fine for about five minutes until the petrol tank began to burn and it was time to get out pretty damn quick!

'The aircraft must have exploded just after I jumped out, because I lost consciousness and came round when I was just above the ground. I can only assume that my parachute was opened by the Good Lord. The impact on the ground was quite severe, and I was only just able to crawl. I spat out two teeth and had lost half of one of my eyelids . . . I was picked up by civilians and taken to a farmhouse, where they gave me coffee and cognac . . . I had a fractured pelvis, and after the local doctor had examined me the good people told me they would have to hand me over to the Germans so that I could be got to hospital. I was then taken by ambulance to the *Luftwaffe* hospital at St Gilles. I remained there until the end of February 1944, and I must express my gratitude for the excellent treatment I had from the Belgian and German personnel.'

Before the month of November 1943 passed there were three further major attacks on Berlin and one on Frankfurt/Main. Despite bad weather on the ground, the night fighters took their toll, but they too were experiencing mounting losses, largely due to the difficulty of landing successfully in conditions of poor visibility on the ground when returning from night operations, possibly with fuel low, possibly with damage from air combat. British jamming made navigation difficult, and there was the ever-present danger of intruder Mosquitos, which were being deployed in increasing numbers.

Particularly vulnerable to the hazards of night flying in bad weather were Hajo Herrmann's Wild Boars, single-seater, single-engined aircraft without any internal aids to navigation other than a compass. Herrmann was a hard task-master, insisting that his aircraft should take off even in conditions that grounded the better-equipped twin-engined fighters with their specialist radio operator/navigator on board. In addition, and despite the use of drop-tanks, the amount of fuel the Bf 109s and Fw 190s could carry was limited, and pursuit and combat flying at high engine power used up petrol disproportionately quickly, so reducing even further the time that the small aircraft could remain in the air. Herrmann's instructions to his pilots were uncompromising: 'Your job is to destroy enemy bombers, and the safety of your own aircraft is secondary to that. Remain in the air as long as there is a chance of shooting down a bomber. If you run out of fuel, if you get lost or cannot find an airfield, abandon your machine by parachute rather than attempt a crash-landing.' The crews of the conventional *Nachtjagd*, unconvinced, in general, that the single-engine concept was a realistic one – and possibly to some extent jealous of the glamorous reputation that they had achieved – commented wryly that most of Herrmann's pilots had more parachute jumps to their credit than kills. There is the story of the Wild Boar pilot who called up on R/T, *'Wilde Sau Sieben, Wilde Sau Sieben, ich steige aus, ich steige aus!'* ('Wild Boar 7, Wild Boar 7, I am baling out!'), only to attract the laconic comment from the pilot of a twin-engined fighter, *'Arme Sau!'*, literally translated as, 'Poor sow!' but in fact a widely used German equivalent of 'Poor bastard!' The recollections of Gerd Stamp, at the time *Gruppenkommandeur* of I./NJG 300, give some slight insight into what it was like to fly a day fighter operationally at night in the autumn and winter:

'We were in a state of air emergency whenever we took off! (*"Nach der Start waren wir immer in Luftnot!"*). Taking off in bad weather was fraught with difficulties. I was a bomber pilot, and of course I was trained in blind flying, but my conversion training on to the Bf 109 was only a few hours. And there was no automatic pilot on the 109, everything had to be done manually. Compared with what I was used to, the Messerschmitt was a very basic aircraft. There was an element of resentment among the pilots, because we were scrambled in all weathers. We had to get airborne, even if it was impossible! (*"Wir mussten, auch wenn wir das nicht konnten!"*) With a horizontal visibility of a hundred metres, no one should be expected to try to take off. Sometimes we'd be in cloud at a hundred metres (330 feet) and once, I remember, we didn't break cloud until 9,000 metres (30,000 feet). For this sort of night fighting we should have had good weather, otherwise it was quite senseless. Herrmann was the driving force, and the trouble was that he could do it himself, even if most of the others couldn't. He flew whenever he could, he set us an example. He was not in any way an armchair warrior.

'We would go on to ten-minute readiness when the British bombers were reported to be approaching, which meant that we would be in our cockpits but without the engines switched on. We couldn't afford the fuel. When we were scrambled we didn't even know, usually, what the target was. Once airborne we would switch over to the running commentary to get an idea of which city was being attacked, and then we were on our own. Then the British began jamming the commentary, and things became even more difficult. There were, however, a number of alternative frequencies for us to try to get information on.

'Normally you saw nothing of the ground once you were in the air, so you couldn't navigate visually by map reading. But there were "light roads" – strings of searchlights pointing in certain directions – and over the big cities such as Münster, Frankfurt, Cologne, Stuttgart, Hamburg, Bremen and so on – and Berlin, of course – they fired parachute flares in various colour combinations, and they put searchlights up as well, in special arrangements and combinations, so that you knew roughly where you were and which way to go. But the whole thing was a *Durcheinander* – complete confusion. If you were shot at and hit by a bomber, you simply had to get down, anywhere, anyhow. The aircraft was very light. When you got down, you slammed the brakes on – and, God, once I turned right over. I looked round, and I could hear the fuel hissing on the hot engine. Then people came, and they dragged me out.

'There was nominally co-operation between the searchlights and the *flak* over the city being attacked, but in reality the searchlights and *Flak* didn't differentiate between friend and foe. They only knew targets. Everything that appeared came under fire! It was organised that they would only fire up to a certain height, and above that level we had priority. But of course, if we saw a target, a bomber, down below that level, we'd go for it. It was no laughing matter!

'There was no standard attack procedure – it was a matter of personal preference. I used the tactics I had seen British fighters using over Alexandria when I was on bombers. I would try to come in from astern and about twenty metres below. If you come in from above you're losing height and probably going too fast. I would open fire at between fifty and a hundred metres. Further than that, you had no chance of hitting him. There was no feeling of triumph when you shot a bomber down – it was either him or you. I survived. It was the same when I was dive-bombing ships: if I hit them, I felt sorry for them. I wouldn't have liked to be in their position myself. We had no training in air-to-air firing, so I just aimed at the aircraft, not at any particular part of it.

'When it came to landing, you had to get down anywhere you could. There were a number of airfields specially allocated for night-fighters to land on if they couldn't get back to base. They usually wouldn't have their lights on, because of the Mosquitos. When you had to land you would fire the colours of the day and they would put their lights on. Then you would fire a red cartridge to show that you wanted to make an emergency landing. We didn't normally call the airfield up on R/T – there was no other help they could give us. It was a case of any port in a storm. I usually only had a vague idea of where I was, but I never knew exactly. I remember an attack on Berlin, and I should have been in the Berlin area, but I could see nothing but mountains and forests below – it was one of the rare nights when the visibility was good. So I shot off some light signals, and then I saw a searchlight pointing in a certain direction. My fuel-warning light was flickering, and I had to get down. I saw some airfield lights, and I went straight in and landed. I realised I wasn't landing on grass, which was normal, but on concrete. My engine cut out just as I was clearing the runway.

I was at Prague/Ruzyn in Czechoslovakia. Next day they discovered my compass was faulty!

'If you were above cloud and wanted to land, you just had to look for the "duty hole in the clouds" (*Loch vom Dienst*). If you couldn't find it, you baled out. It was a matter of profit and loss. It was better to shoot down an expensive British bomber with seven men on board and risk losing a comparatively cheap fighter with only one pilot.'

Major Stamp's comments on the hazardous nature of flying single-engined fighters operationally at night and in bad weather are supported by a glance at the official casualty figures for the period. The casualty lists record only those incidents in which death or injury occurred, and so are only a part of the whole truth: there were of course many occasions on which pilots crashed or abandoned their machines but were unhurt, so that their names were not listed. Between July and the end of November 1943 there are eighty-four names, sixty-four of whom died. In thirty-three cases the cause of the casualty is given in terms such as, 'Fuel shortage, emergency landing', 'Hit ground on landing', 'Hit radio mast on landing', 'Aircraft caught fire on landing', 'Ran out of fuel, baled out', 'Crashed in the sea, presumably because of bad weather', and so on. The high rate of attrition to their aircraft did nothing to increase the popularity with their hosts of those Wild Boar units who were sharing aircraft with day-fighter units, and indeed it became a frequent practice on the part of the day-fighter pilots to report their machines unserviceable so that they would not be flown at night and run the risk of being written off. 'It was surprising,' comments one source, 'how many miraculous spontaneous repairs happened between dusk and dawn.'

Whereas the figures of confirmed kills by the conventional night-fighters are by and large extremely reliable – the checking of claims was a rigidly bureaucratic procedure requiring independent witnesses and/or proof in the form of a crashed bomber at the appropriate place and time – there is no reliable record of the number of kills scored by Herrmann's pilots. As most of the kills were achieved over the target, with combats usually taking place while the anti-aircraft guns were throwing up their barrage of myriad shells of various calibres, accurate claims could usually neither be made nor checked. A Lancaster explodes over Berlin while it is under fire from *flak* and simultaneously in the sights of one or more fighters – who is to get the credit? A Halifax impacts into a block of flats in Essen during the confusion of a saturation bombing attack, and no record is made of the exact time of the crash, but a Wild Boar pilot claims that he hit an unidentified bomber somewhere in the Ruhr area while the bombs were dropping – that is not precise enough for a confirmed kill. An Fw 190 pilot fires on a Stirling over Frankfurt and damages it, but the *Viermot* doesn't hit the ground until the target is twenty minutes away – can the German pilot claim a victory, and if so will his claim be allowed?

The best available estimate of the number of kills made by JG 300, JG 301 and JG 302 during the period that they were flying *Wilde Sau* operations – from about July 1943 to about March 1944 – is 330, but many more kills were claimed. The record has it that the highest individual scorer was Oberleutnant Kurt Welter, of JG 300, with fifty-six kills, with Major Friedrich-Karl Müller ('*Nasenmüller*') in second place with thirty. Welter, however, was a controversial figure, and there are those who doubt the accuracy of his claims. For example, he is recorded as having destroyed twenty-five Mosquitos, although only officially credited with six, three when flying the Fw 190 and a further three when flying the Me 262 jet fighter later in the war. It is sad when the claims of a gallant man are doubted, but it must be said that, as described, the claims were made in conditions that made accurate checking impossible. A well-placed source who, for obvious reasons, would prefer not to be named, has this to say about Welter:

'Müller was *Wilde Sau 2*, and he was a very reliable man. You could believe him. He was a long-standing fighter pilot. Welter claimed to have shot down one after the other, and some people believed him. I was sceptical. Welter was comparatively young, and I should like you to reflect on the fact that extravagant claims by young people are not unusual. I myself know how difficult it was to shoot down bombers by night: I must have made about fifty attacks, and I only destroyed two for certain. Admittedly there were some, like Marseille for instance, who had a special gift when it came to air-to-air firing, but I do not think that Welter was one of those. What was certain was that he was a braggart, and I think that that was reflected in his claims. I also doubt Welter's claim to have shot down six Mosquitos, but presumably that can be checked against British records.'

It was in autumn 1943 that Herrmann conceived and introduced another aid to shooting down British bombers over their burning targets, a procedure to which he gave the macabre code name *Leichentuch*, or 'Shroud'. When the target was cloud-covered illuminator aircraft would fly high above it and drop flares, lighting up the bombers against the white sheet of cloud beneath them, and to enhance the effect the searchlights would be shone vertically on the cloud from below, reinforcing the light of the fires burning on the ground and creating an effect similar to that of an illuminated ground-glass screen, against which the bombers would be sharply silhouetted.

Despite Herrmann's drive and ingenuity and the gallantry of his pilots, however, it was still on the shoulders of the conventional night fighters that the heaviest responsibility for the defence of the *Reich* rested, increasingly so as the British raids intensified and RAF tactics became progressively more refined. Total *Nachtjagd* claims reached their 1943 maximum in August at 290: the highest monthly figure in 1942 had been about half that. With the onset of autumn and the deterioration of the weather the figures sank to 178 in September, 149 in October and 128 in November. These figures are, of course, only of significance when set alongside the number of sorties flown by Bomber Command. In August, September and November they are remarkably constant – 3.7 per cent, 3.2 per cent and 3.2 per cent respectively. November showed a certain respite for Bomber Command, the percentage losses to fighters being only 2.4, probably to a large extent a result of the consistently bad weather that kept the majority of the *Luftwaffe* night-fighters grounded. The scores of the *Experten* were rising steadily, with Helmut Lent, Heinrich zu Sayn-Wittgenstein, Werner Streib and Manfred Meurer leading the field with scores in the fifties and sixties. Other pilots were making a name for themselves – Heinz-Wolfgang Schnaufer, Heinz Rökker, Martin Becker and others. The *SN-2* radar and *Schräge Musik* were gradually making their presence felt, and multiple kills in one night by individual pilots were becoming more common as techniques were refined and the realisation grew that the combination of these devices was lethal if properly exploited. Gradually more and more Ju 88 night fighters were being introduced into the defence of Germany, aircraft that could stay up longer than the Bf 110 and, many would say, were more sympathetic to the demands of their pilots and represented a more formidable threat to the British bombers. The introduction of the potential match-winner, the He 219, still lagged, which was to the good fortune of the RAF aircrew.

As has already been mentioned, the unsatisfactory definition produced by 10 cm H2S, particularly over Berlin, had led to strenuous efforts to produce sets working on a 3 cm wavelength, H2S Mk III. The first sets were supplied to Bomber Command in November 1943, but not through normal channels. Impatient with the slow-grinding mills of bureaucracy, Bennett, who by this time had been promoted to the rank of Air Vice-Marshal, and Group Captain Dudley Saward, Harris's chief radar officer, had, together with Dr Philip Dee and Dr Bernard Lovell of TRE, contrived to have six sets produced ahead of schedule and installed in Lancasters. Three aircraft equipped with the device were delivered to PFF on 6 November, the remaining three on the sixteenth. It was decided that they would be used to mark Berlin as soon as feasible, and on 22 November five of them formed the vanguard of the 764 Lancasters, Halifaxes and Stirlings that took off to attack the German capital in response to a 'maximum effort' order by the Commander-in-Chief.

The meteorological forecast was, unusually, ideal for Harris's purposes. The weather in England promised fair for both take-off and landing, low cloud and poor visibility over central Germany would restrict night fighter operations, while scattered cloud in the Berlin area offered the prospect of accurate visual marking, back-up and bombing. Harris decided on a direct route to and from the target with no attempt to confuse the Germans by means of misleading routes or diversionary attacks. The bombers would cross the Dutch coast in the region of Den Helder and head for a point to the north of Hanover, making a slight turn there on to an easterly heading that would take them directly to the 'Big City'. After bombing they would, with the exception of a minor offset to the south to minimise the chance of collision, return along the reciprocal of the same route. Harris's plan laid down that the bombing should be concentrated within a period of just twenty-two minutes.

The crews of the five aircraft carrying the high-definition H2S were given clear and unequivocal orders that should the equipment fail they were to return to base, if possible bombing an alternative target, and in the event three of the sets developed faults and the Lancasters turned back. Despite a very thick and unbroken covering of cloud over Berlin – in that respect the met. forecast had been inaccurate – the two remaining PFF crews were able to mark the aiming point with encouraging precision, and there followed a highly concentrated attack, the most effective one suffered by Berlin during the course of the war. A large area of devastation was caused in the area around the Brandenburger Tor, the focus of Berlin's administrative and governmental offices. Although the success of this attack was not known to Bomber Command until much later – cloud conditions

in the target area meant that neither the crews bombing, nor the bombing photographs that they brought back, nor photographic reconnaissance in the
aftermath of the attack could provide evidence on which to base an assessment
– it was subsequently to emerge that the raid on Germany's capital city, with hails
of high-explosive and incendiary bombs falling with uncanny precision through
a covering of thick cloud reaching down to the very ground, came as an immense
shock to the Nazi leadership, including Hitler himself. Given that this was the
capital city of the *Reich*, the very heart of Germany, and despite the fact that
casualties, at about 2,000 killed, were by comparison modest, it is probable that
this raid had a greater effect, in terms of bringing the grim reality of the war home
to the leadership, than had Operation 'Gomorrah' five months before.

One member of the Government who had direct experience of the fury of the
RAF attack was the much-quoted Munitions Minister Albert Speer, whose
Ministry suffered direct hits. Speer, as was his custom, watched the raid from the
roof of a *Flak* tower. Hajo Herrmann, who had just finished a meeting with
Speer, also watched the attack from the roof of a nearby above-ground concrete
air-raid bunker, situated on which was a radar equipment manned by *Luftwaffe*
soldiers. The spectacle made a lasting impression on both of them. In his book
Inside the Third Reich, Speer writes:

> 'My nearby Ministry was one gigantic conflagration. I drove over there at
> once. A few secretaries, looking like Amazons in their steel helmets, were
> trying to save files even while isolated bombs went off in the vicinity. In
> place of my private office I found nothing but a huge bomb crater . . .
>
> 'From the *Flak* tower the air raids on Berlin were an unforgettable sight,
> and I had constantly to remind myself of the cruel reality in order not to
> be completely entranced by the scene: the illumination of smoke, the innu-
> merable probings followed by flashes of explosions which were caught by
> the clouds of searchlights, the excitement when a plane was caught and
> tried to escape the cone of light, the brief flaming torch when it was hit. No
> doubt about it, this apocalypse provided a magnificent spectacle.'[1]

Herrmann records his impressions of the spectacle in his autobiography,
Eagle's Wings:

> 'Following my talk with Speer, and while the attack was still under way, I
> went up to the roof of the tower . . . I looked around. Incendiary bombs
> were lodged high in the trees and burning on the pavements. There was a
> shrill organ concert of thousands of flak splinters whistling down and strik-
> ing sparks from the concrete as they landed, punctuated by the cracking of
> bombs and the pressure waves of aerial mines. All around me was a light
> grey to white, luminous sea of fog. In the centre of this chaos the young
> men on their exposed tower carried out their duty. I was appalled. This was
> what terror looked like in the eyes of the defenceless victim. I was not wear-
> ing a steel helmet, and I withdrew to the protection of the thick concrete
> walls.'

[1]   Published 1970 by Weidenfeld and Nicolson.

Albert Speer continues:

'As soon as the planes turned back, I drove to those districts of the city where important factories were situated. We drove over streets strewn with rubble, lined by burning houses. Bombed-out families sat or stood in front of the ruins. A few pieces of rescued furniture and other possessions lay about on the sidewalk. There was a sinister atmosphere full of biting smoke, soot, and flames. Sometimes the people displayed that curious hysterical merriment that is often observed in the midst of disasters. Above the city hung a cloud of smoke that probably reached twenty thousand feet in height. Even by day it made the macabre scene as dark as night.'

The pall of smoke of which Speer spoke was still there at eight o'clock the following evening when the first of a force of 383 bombers dropped their markers on Berlin in a follow-up raid, and the glow of fires started the previous night could be seen through the clouds. Again it was an accurate raid, but this time more night fighters were able to take off, with the consequence that the attacking force suffered losses of 5.2 per cent as compared with the 3.4 per cent sustained the previous night. Together the two raids cost Bomber Command forty-six machines.

One of the four-engined bombers lost that night fell to the cannon of the Ju 88 piloted by Oberleutnant Rudolf Szardenings, a II./NJG 3 *Staffelkapitän* flying out of Schleswig. In his log book it is recorded as a Halifax, but presumably Szardenings was mistaken in his identification and his victim was in fact a Lancaster – a common error, because the appearance of the two types was very similar, particularly at night and in the excitement of air combat. None of the ten Halifaxes engaged that night was shot down. Paul Zorner, also a *Staffelkapitän,* destroyed a Lancaster over the target itself at five minutes past eight, right within the seventeen minutes into which Harris's plan compressed the whole attack. He recalls that although he was in fact flying *Wilde Sau* that night, the *Zahme Sau* system that had evolved after Hamburg was, in his view, more efficient than the previous *Himmelbett* method. A lot depended on one's radio operator and his, Heinz Wilke, was very good indeed: he usually managed to find a channel on which the broadcast commentary could be received despite British jamming, and he had learned how to distinguish between blips from bombers and those from Window. The Lancaster was Zorner's thirteenth kill, and as yet his Bf 110 was not equipped with *Schräge Musik*, so that he had to rely on his forward-firing armament. Peter Spoden, who had been shot down and severely injured over the same target, Berlin, in August, was by this time back on operations, and he achieved his fourth victory when he shot down a Lancaster. Flying from Leeuwarden, Oberleutnant Heinz-Wolfgang Schnaufer, with his *Funker* Fritz Rumpelhardt and his gunner Wilhelm Gänsler, destroyed two PFF Lancasters as they crossed Holland only about an hour after they had taken off from their bases in East Anglia. Schnaufer was destined to end the war with 121 victories to his credit.

Warrant Officer Ernie Webb – he had had two promotions since beginning his tour as a Sergeant in August – and his crew set out from Fiskerton, heading for Berlin, in the late afternoon of 22 November, but mechanical trouble dictated that they should return to base, where they landed after two hours and fifteen minutes in the air, one of the sixty-eight crews – 8.9 per cent of the force – who aborted the mission for various reasons. Of the fifty Stirlings participating, twelve returned early and five did not come back at all, proportions of twenty-four per cent of the total and thirteen per cent of those attacking respectively. It had long been apparent that the Stirling was, for many reasons, an unsatisfactory machine, regularly suffering proportionately higher losses than the Lancasters and the Halifaxes, and morale among its crews was low. On the other hand, the crews of the Lancasters and Halifaxes always felt marginally safer when Stirlings were part of the attacking force, knowing that because the Stirling could not fly as high as they could the *flak* would tend to look for the easier prey at lower level and not concentrate on them, flying several thousand feet higher. In light of these poor figures, Harris now decided that Stirlings would no longer attack targets in Germany, which meant that ten squadrons had to be withdrawn from the battle until they had been re-equipped with more efficient machines.

With Ernie Webb, John Chaloner went to Berlin on the night of twenty-third. The direct route meant that for a target so deep inside Germany the duration of the flight, six hours and twenty minutes, was short. John's diary reads: 'Plenty of cloud. Saw three Ju 88s going in the opposite direction. Me 110 missed our starboard wing by six inches.' While 'six inches' might be something of an exaggeration, it was certainly a near thing. Remembering the incident in 1993 he says, 'I was in my usual position over the target, behind the engineer looking out, and just after we had bombed I saw this Messerschmitt 110 coming straight at us, and I had opened my mouth to give a warning, but the 110 lifted its wing over our starboard wing and banked. Otherwise we'd have had it. It was psst! – just like that. And he lifted his wing, and we could hear the sound of his engines over the sound of our own engines.' Webb and his crew had come frighteningly close to being one of the very many Bomber Command crews lost as a result of mid-air collision with another aircraft, either hostile or friendly.

Drawing breath, as it were, from the strain of two major attacks on Berlin on successive nights, Harris mounted a medium-strength, none too successful attack on Frankfurt on 25 November. Night fighters were up, and twelve bombers failed to return. Then it was back to Berlin, 443 Lancasters attacking the capital on 26/27 November, with a medium-scale – twenty-one PFF Lancasters, 157 Halifaxes – diversionary raid to Stuttgart. Both forces followed the same route across Germany as far as a position just to the north-east of Frankfurt, when the smaller one turned to the right for Stuttgart. Despite some of the night fighters being enticed away from the main attack and going for the Stuttgart force, twenty-eight of those raiding Berlin (6.2 per cent) were shot down. The diversionary contingent lost six Halifaxes. In a new tactic introduced in an attempt to diminish the high loss rate of Pathfinder machines to predicted *flak*, a small number of Mosquitos flew over Berlin just before the arrival of the Pathfinders, scattering a large amount of Window to interfere with the *Flak* radar. Although the target area was clear, the first markers were dropped by H2S. Marking was somewhat scattered, and the bombing not as concentrated as might have been wished, but all in all it was, from Harris's point of view, a moderately successful raid. The three raids on Berlin in November killed between four and five thousand people and destroyed almost 9,000 houses: but a German *Haus* is not what one envisages in English, but much more frequently a block of flats, so that the number of dwellings destroyed was in fact just under 105,000.

John Chaloner again navigated Ernie Webb to Berlin that night. All he recorded in his diary was, 'Clear, bags of searchlights, flak and fighters.' So far, five of the eighteen operations that Webb's crew had completed had been to the most feared of all targets, Berlin. They were now, by any standards, seasoned veterans, and few would argue that they were not lucky still to be alive.

The penultimate month of the year, the month that had seen the resumption of the Battle of Berlin, went out like a lamb, with nuisance raids by a small number of Mosquitos on 28/29 and 29/30 November, while on the night of 30 November/1 December, in addition to minelaying sorties and yet another minor Mosquito raid, four Wellingtons flew radio counter-measure flights. These last sorties were of great significance in the context of the overall battle, because they were the first flown by the newly formed No. 100 Group.

As explained earlier, as the Bomber Command offensive had developed and tactics had been refined, there had been a gradually increasing emphasis placed on radio counter-measures (RCM), diversionary raids and intruder operations in support of the bombing campaign. Fighter Command had provided the intruder Beaufighters and Mosquitos, while individual squadrons and aircraft of both Bomber Command and Fighter Command had carried out jamming operations of various types. Now, with the increasing complexity and importance of support work, it was decided that a new Group should be formed in Bomber Command, not only to subsume these various responsibilities and actively pursue them, but also to develop the support campaign aggressively and imaginatively. In summary, the new Group's brief was:

1. To attack German night-fighters in the air and on the ground, together with their airfields;
2. To jam enemy radar, radio and navigational aids;
3. To study enemy offensive and defensive radio and radar aids with a view to carrying out these functions; and
4. To provide information on enemy night-fighter dispositions and tactics in order to help the planning of Bomber Command attacks.

The Group was officially set up on 23 November, with its headquarters at Radlett, formerly the home of No. 80 Wing, from which came the four Wellingtons that flew the first operations mounted under the Group's auspices. The first squadron to be allocated to 100 Group was No. 141, the Fighter Command Serrate Mosquito squadron, which moved from Wittering to West Raynham. It was a quick matter to organise the Group, but it proved a longer task to make it operational. By mid-December it comprised five Special Duties (SD) squadrons and three SD flights. Its permanent headquarters were established at Bylaugh Hall. The airfields of the Group were clustered within the area of a small semi-circle between Norwich and the sweep of the Norfolk coast to the north and east, well placed both for monitoring *Luftwaffe* signals traffic in Holland and northern Germany and for sending its aircraft out operationally. Anomalously, it might be thought, No. 101 Squadron, which carried German-speaking special radio operators to monitor and jam enemy night-fighter traffic by means of Airborne Cigar (ABC), retained that function until the end of hostilities and was not taken over by No. 100 Group, although the Group did in fact carry out some independent ABC operations.

If November went out like a lamb, December came in like a lion, with two major raids, against Berlin and Leipzig, on the second/third and third/fourth respectively. The Berlin operation was ill-fated, bad weather and poor forecasting contributing to a scattered attacking force, inaccurate and widely dispersed bombing, and considerable success on the part of the German night-fighters. In England, fog in and around the Vale of York and to the north, where No. 4 Group and No. 6 Group airfields were located, meant that the overwhelming majority of the Halifaxes had to be withdrawn from the maximum effort originally planned, so that of the 442 four-engined bombers that set out 426 were Lancasters and only sixteen PFF Halifaxes took part. A high proportion of the heavies, forty-three in all, turned back for various reasons. Eighteen Mosquitos from No. 139 Squadron completed the force.

The Squadron belonged to No. 8 (Pathfinder) Group. It had come under Bennett's umbrella in June 1943, and he used it as what he called a 'supporting squadron', dropping either TIs or bombs as the occasion demanded. Bennett was a strong advocate of the Mosquito, and he had insisted, against opposition from above, that the 'wooden wonder' should form a major component of the his Pathfinder Force. By December 1943 he had four Mosquito squadrons, Nos. 109 and 105 for Oboe work, No. 139 for general support work, and No. 627, which had joined his group the previous month and which performed the same function. Bennett referred to his Mosquitos corporately as the 'Light Night Striking Force', although the name was never officially recognised by Harris, who for some reason or another did not approve of it. The adjective 'light', of course, referred to the aircraft rather than to the nights on which they operated.

The predominant feature of the weather facing the crews setting out for Berlin that night was a cold front stretching across the North Sea. Cold fronts were much disliked by Bomber Command crews. Ahead of such a front, which generally moved roughly south-west to north-east, was warm, humid air, while behind it was colder, drier air. Where the two air masses met, at the front itself, there would be a towering, inhospitable barrier of cumulo-nimbus cloud reaching up to 20,000 feet or more, with heavy precipitation in the form of snow, hail or heavy rain beneath it, frequently accompanied by electrical storms; and inside it, where the bombers had to penetrate, violent turbulence that could throw even a laden bomber about like a ship in a rough sea, and heavy icing that could load an aircraft with hundreds of pounds of ice in a matter of minutes, at the same time distorting the aerodynamic properties of the control surfaces, so that the machine might lose hundreds, even thousands, of feet in altitude before the pilot could regain control. From the navigator's point of view, a front of this nature was bad news, marking as it did a distinct change, often unpredictable, in the speed and direction of the wind. On this night the front was positioned roughly where Gee coverage ended – German jamming was having an ever-increasing effect on the equipment – so that once through the front the navigators had virtually no data on which to calculate the alteration in wind velocity and correct their onward course. The result was that the force tended to drift south of track and become widely scattered. Harris had again chosen a direct route. The

Nachtjagd, alerted in good time and correctly identifying Berlin as the target, had something approaching a field day, with forty bombers, representing about nine per cent of the four-engined aircraft that did not turn back, being lost.

Among the successful night-fighter pilots was Paul Zorner. In November Zorner's *Staffel*, 8./NJG 3, had been equipped with new Bf 110Gs equipped with the Window-proof radar *SN-2*, and the first operation that Zorner and his *Funker*, Heinz Wilke, flew in their new aircraft was against this Bomber Command attack on Berlin. They took off from Lüneburg at 1844 hrs, briefed to fly Wild Boar. Zorner recalls that on that night the commentary from the ground was unusually good, so that he was able to fly a south-westerly course directly towards the bomber stream. That he was heading in the right direction was confirmed when, at just after seven o'clock, he saw a bomber going down in flames directly ahead of him. Almost immediately, Wilke picked up a contact on his *SN-2* at a height of about 18,000 feet. Zorner turned on to an easterly heading, that of the bomber stream as given in the *Reportage*. Wilke lost the radar contact in the turn – an easy thing to do, particularly if the pilot banked steeply – but at once picked up another response, possibly from the same bomber, and very soon Zorner could make out ahead of him the silhouette of a Lancaster just above the ill-defined horizon. It was a matter of minutes to close in on the bomber from slightly below and direct a short burst from his forward guns – he had not yet got *Schräge Musik* – into the Lancaster's port wing. The British bomber hit the ground near Diepholz at 1924 hrs., Zorner's fourteenth kill.

In following his victim, Zorner had lost the bomber stream. He resumed an easterly course, and soon he could see ahead of him unmistakable signs that he was heading back in the right direction – other bombers going down in flames and the *flak*, explosions, fires and smoke that marked the target area. At 2024 hrs, in the immediate vicinity of Berlin, Zorner saw another Lancaster crossing his nose from right to left, already having dropped its bombs. He was able to turn in behind it and seal its fate with another short burst from his cannon into its left wing. It crashed just to the south-west of Berlin at 2029 hrs. As the bomber stream had been briefed to turn to the north after bombing, the southerly location of Zorner's victory suggests that the Lancaster had been well to the south of the correct aiming point. It also possibly explains why, despite then heading to the west in an attempt to infiltrate the outward-bound stream, Zorner and Wilke had no further luck. They finally landed at Stendal at 2100 hrs.

The following night Harris sent 527 four-engined bombers to Leipzig, which lies about 120 miles to the south-south-west of Berlin, where the marking and the bombing results were far better than they had been the night before, and considerable damage and many casualties ensued. Harris successfully persuaded the German raid-plotting organisation that Berlin was once more to be the target by sending his force in the direction of the capital before turning the four-engined heavies off on to a southerly heading for Leipzig, while nine Mosquitos carried on straight ahead for Berlin, where they dropped markers and bombs. The result was that the majority of the night fighters went to Berlin and few went to the correct objective. Nevertheless, the Tame Boar fighters were able to inflict not inconsiderable casualties on the bomber force both on the way to the target and on the way home. Fifteen Halifaxes out of the 220 that set out – approaching seven per cent – were lost, plus nine Lancasters out of 307, or three per cent.

Hauptmann Paul Szameitat, who had just temporarily taken over command of II./NJG 3 from Prinz zu Sayn-Wittgenstein, celebrated his appointment by shooting down five bombers.

Wittgenstein had returned from the Eastern Front in August, transferring from IV./NJG 5 to II./NJG 3 when his original *Gruppe* was taken to form the nucleus of a new unit, NJG 100. Based at Schleswig, his score was mounting rapidly, so that it now stood at about sixty-five. Only Helmut Lent, *Geschwaderkommodore* of NJG 3, with about seventy-five, had more kills to his credit. In November Herbert Kümmritz, Wittgenstein's *Funker*, was temporarily detached from flying duties to continue his study of high-frequency technology in Berlin, and his place in the crew was taken by Feldwebel Friedrich Ostheimer.

Both Terry Bolter and John Chaloner took part in the Leipzig raid, and both remember it clearly as a good attack. In Chaloner's diary is entered succinctly, '*Wizard prang!*', while Bolter is a little more explicit. It was his first operation with his new captain, a senior officer and Flight Commander at the early age of twenty-one. Bolter writes:

> 'The next and eighteenth operation was Leipzig deep into Germany. Mac Maculloch had already left for Pathfinders, so our crew was pilot and captain Squadron Leader Bickerdike DFC, navigator Bob Prendergrast, bomb aimer Terry Bolter, engineer Bunny Kearley, wireless operator Ron Walter, rear gunner Biff Hagen DFC and mid-upper gunner Flying Officer Gordon Hills DFM.
>
> 'Our route was twenty miles short of Berlin, which Pathfinder Mosquitos were attacking, and then a sharp turn due south to Leipzig. We took off around midnight and were not over the target until around 0330 in the morning. But the ruse worked. The Germans felt we were going all the way to Berlin and thought initially that the diversionary attack by Mosquitos was for real. By the time they realised we were attacking Leipzig, we were too far away for the German fighters to come after us. So we only had limited *flak* to contend with over the target and the raid was highly successful. As we neared the English coast on our return flight Ron Walker, our wireless operator, tuned in to the BBC news and we heard the BBC announcer say that a large force of RAF bombers had attacked Leipzig last night and that losses had been slight – and we were still airborne!'

'Losses were slight.' Yes, but only relatively. The total of twenty-four four-engined bombers that did not return meant that something in the region of a further 170 aircrew had either perished or been taken prisoner; some few, it is true, would escape both death and capture and eventually return to England, possibly to fly operationally again, but sadly the majority would be dead, and many families would know the ultimate grief of having lost a loved one. And on the ground a far greater number had been killed – estimates for the night's fatalities range from about seven hundred to almost twice that number – and there would be a proportionately greater incidence of grief and mourning among German families.

It had rapidly become very clear that of the three types of four-engined aircraft used in the Bomber Command main force the Lancaster was the one best suited to the task. Now Harris, who had already withdrawn the Stirling from operations against German targets, was also concerned about the capabilities of the Handley Page Halifax, with which Nos. 4 and 6 Groups, as well as a few squadrons of No. 8 and No. 100 Groups, were equipped. The Mk I version of the Halifax had first flown operationally in March 1941, and by November 1943 it had been replaced in squadron service by improved versions, the Mk II and the Mk V, both powered by Rolls-Royce Merlin in-line engines. These two versions, however, still lagged behind the Lancaster in such important performance figures as operational altitude, time to height, range and bomb-load, the last two aspects of which, of course, were inter-related. The Halifax was not as cost-effective operationally as the Lancaster, not being able to carry as many bombs as far. In addition the lower altitude at which it flew made it more vulnerable to the attentions of the German defences, both *Flak* and fighters, than the Avro machine. The comparative casualty figures in raids against German targets in which both types took part showed that Halifax losses were consistently higher than those of Lancasters, particularly on long-range operations. From the beginning of the Battle of Hamburg until the Leipzig raid on 3/4 December 1943 the overall loss rate for Lancasters was 3.2 per cent, that for Halifaxes 5.9 per cent. There had been a higher discrepancy on Berlin trips, with Halifaxes losing fifty-three of the 661 dispatched as against the Lancaster figure of thirty-eight from 1,135 – eight per cent compared with 3.3 per cent. The attack on Kassel showed a similar comparison, 6.8 per cent Halifaxes against 2.9 per cent Lancasters. Now that the Stirling was no longer there to provide easy pickings for the German night fighters, Halifax losses began to rise even further. There was however a new version of the Halifax just making its appearance in squadrons, the Halifax B Mk III. Planning for a radial-engine Halifax had been begun while the in-line-engined versions were still being developed, which was why the Mk V went into service before the Mk III.

The new Halifax was a great improvement on its predecessors, and it owed that improvement largely to its Bristol Hercules radial engines, more powerful and, some would say, less temperamental than the Merlins of the earlier marks. Its time to height and its operating altitude were markedly improved, as was its range. Alterations to the nose – the front turret was replaced by a streamlined transparent Perspex fairing – and to the tail unit, with squarish rudders replacing the earlier angular ones, not only improved the performance and handling characteristics of the aircraft, but also gave it a far more compact, workmanlike appearance. It is said that if an aeroplane looks right it is right, and the new Halifax certainly had a far more pleasing look about it than its predecessors had.

The first Halifax Mk IIIs were issued to four squadrons in November 1943, the first of them, from No. 466 Squadron (4 Group), flying operationally on a mine-laying sortie in 1 December. Over the following several months Mk IIIs gradually replaced the Merlin-engined versions, but in the meantime the Mks II and V suffered increasingly grievous losses.

Between the fourth and the fifteenth of December there were no major operations against Germany, but mine-layers and intruders were active, while up to thirty of Bennett's Mosquitos visited the Ruhr on six of the eight nights. On the night of 12/13 December Hauptmann Meurer of I./NJG 1, stationed at Venlo, shot down one of the twenty Mosquitos sent out to attack Essen. Manfred Meurer, the *Gruppenkommandeur*, was among the top scorers of the *Nachtjagd* with a tally approaching sixty, and he achieved his success in a He 219 A-0. His luck would run out the following month, when he met his death with his score standing at sixty-five kills.

On the night of 16/17 December Bomber Command returned to Berlin. Harris's force against the main target comprised fifteen Mosquitos and 483 Lancasters, but no Halifaxes, while a small force of Stirlings, Mosquitos and Lancasters, the latter from No. 617 Squadron, attacked two flying-bomb launching sites in northern France. The August attack on Peenemünde had been directed solely against the long-range rockets that the Germans were developing, but another V-weapon ('V' for *Vergeltung*, or 'Retaliation') had also been pre-occupying British Intelligence, a jet-propelled, pilotless aircraft carrying a large explosive charge designed to explode on impact with its target. Reports by agents in Belgium and France had spoken of ramp-like concrete constructions associated with these weapons, and the structures had been given, from their appearance, the generic name 'ski-sites'. The Bomber Command attack marked the beginning of a long and intensive campaign by both the RAF and the USAAF against these structures, later to be known as 'Crossbow sites', which ended only after the installations had been overrun by the advancing Allied armies following the invasion.

Many factors had to be considered by the planners at Command Headquarters at High Wycombe before the timing, the bombers' route and the tactical aspects of any raid were decided. One of these factors was the state of the moon, full-moon periods usually being avoided because of the advantage to the defending fighters. There would be a three-quarter moon on the night of 16/17 December, but not until late, so the attack was scheduled to begin at about eight o'clock in the evening and to be compressed into a period of fourteen minutes. The met. forecast spoke of a possibility of fog occurring in Germany, possibly grounding the night-fighters. Harris therefore again chose a direct approach route, from Ijmuiden on the Dutch coast to the target, a distance of about 420 miles or two hours' flying time, but he decided that after bombing the force should fly north and across the Baltic to Denmark, and then westerly over the Schleswig-Holstein peninsula, crossing out near Esbjerg on the way back to England. In this way, he hoped, his bombers would be flying over less dangerous territory when the moon rose. There was, however, the worrying possibility that the fog forecast for Germany would also affect the bombers' bases on their return. That, however, was a risk that was accepted when it came to deciding whether or not the operation should go ahead.

Alerted early by R/T and H2S transmissions and by long-range radar reports, the Germans soon determined that a major raid was approaching, but, remembering the successful feint against Berlin that Harris had made on the night of the Leipzig attack, they were very slow in confirming that Berlin was in fact the target. As forecast, there was fog in Holland, Belgium and northern Germany, but experienced crews were scrambled against the incoming bomber stream, locating it just as it crossed the Dutch coast. Illuminator aircraft were out too, and the route was soon marked by numerous fighter flares. The *Luftwaffe* fighters had to penetrate thick cloud to reach their operating altitude, and some of them met severe icing.

So bad were the conditions at the Dutch airfield of Leeuwarden that only one fighter was allowed to take off, that of Oberleutnant Heinz-Wolfgang Schnaufer, *Kapitän* of the 12th *Staffel* of NJG 1. Schnaufer already had thirty-six kills to his credit, and with him in his Bf 110, lettered G9+DZ, were his radio operator, Oberfeldwebel Fritz Rumpelhardt, and his gunner, Oberfeldwebel Wilhelm Gänsler. There was poor visibility and a cloud ceiling of less than two hundred feet, and the ground temperature was in the region of 0° Celsius, a combination in which icing was a virtual certainty. Schnaufer's machine iced up heavily as it climbed through the cloud, emerging at 5,000 metres (16,500 feet). It had taken off at 1735 hrs, and just twenty-six minutes later Schnaufer's first victim for the night fell from the sky, Lancaster JA853 (MG-L) of No. 7 (PFF) Squadron at Oakington, flown by Warrant Officer W. A. Watson. The Lancaster crashed to the north-east of the Ijsselmeer, and there were no survivors. Within minutes Schnaufer had claimed his second victim, a 101 Squadron ABC Lancaster from Ludford Magna flown by Flight Lieutenant Ronald MacFarlane DFM: once more all the crew lost their lives. Schnaufer's third Lancaster that night, a 49 Squadron (Fiskerton) machine piloted by Pilot Officer Gordon Ratcliffe, came down at 1823 hrs, and his fourth, DS831 (QO-N) of No. 432 (Leaside) Squadron, at 1841 hrs. All his victims had been shot down within a radius of fifty kilometres of his base within the space of just over an hour, further examples of the deadly potential of the *SN-2* and *Schräge Musik* combination. On being scrambled Schnaufer had come under the control of the local *Himmelbett* fighter control station *Eisbär*, callsign '*Meteor*', and it is noteworthy that all his victims came to earth well to the north of their flight plan route, suggesting the possibility that they had drifted off track and away from the protection of Window. Another No. 7 (PFF) Squadron Lancaster – the squadron lost four that night – was also shot down by NJG 1, that flown by Flying Officer Francis Rush. The successful German pilot was Leutnant Rolland, who had taken off from the airfield at Bergen and whose victim fell at 1815 hrs near Alkmaar, just after crossing the Dutch coast.

The German controller's indecision as to the bombers' target – R/T intercepts show that he directed fighters to Osnabrück, Oldenburg and Hanover respectively as the stream headed to the east – meant that fighter opposition over the target itself was comparatively slight. After a moderately successful attack, with the PFF markers, some of which were aimed by H2S Mk III, dropping well concentrated, the bombers departed to the north for a comparatively trouble-free journey back to the UK. Nevertheless, twenty-five Lancasters were lost. As had been feared, conditions back at the bomber bases were bad, even worse than had been foreseen – and a further thirty-four Lancasters crashed with, or were abandoned by, their crews when landing proved impossible due to fog. Whereas 159 aircrew had died on the operation itself, now a further 136 perished in their home country. Of the 483 bombers briefed for the raid, 6.2 per cent had aborted the operation, 5.2 per cent had been lost and six per cent had crashed on return. These were high prices to pay.

In general, the weather in Europe moves from west to east, so that it might be thought that the forecasters in Britain had a reasonably easy job, in that weather that had passed over the UK would be similar to that which would occur over the Continent in the next few days. Unhappily, however, although the general movement is easterly, many other factors of considerable complexity come into the equation: the weather moves in a series of swirls, air masses of differing characteristics interact with each other, moisture is absorbed and precipitated, surface temperatures set off physical changes in the structure of the atmosphere, gases discharged from factories not only affect visibility but also provide nuclei for the formation of raindrops, and so on. Although they frequently came up with quite precise-sounding prognoses the RAF met. men (and the *Wetterfrösche*, or 'weather frogs', in Germany) were really not in a position to give more than a very general overall picture, and even then they were frequently wrong.

In an endeavour to provide a better service to the aircrews – because an accurate knowledge of such things as wind speed and direction, temperature, cloud conditions and visibility was indispensable not only to the planning but also to the execution of a bombing raid – weather-reconnaissance aircraft flew many hours over the seas around the British Isles and deep into Continental Europe. Nevertheless, weather forecasting remained a very imprecise science, and so it was on the night of 20/21 December when Bomber Command visited Frankfurt in strength. The meteorologists had expected clear skies over the target, but the Pathfinders, intending to mark visually, arrived to find the city almost completely covered in cloud. The result was bad marking and widely scattered bombing. A diversionary attack on Mannheim failed to divert the attention of the *Nachtjagd*, and it took full advantage of a scattered force, which lost forty-one of the 647 Lancasters and Halifaxes involved. Again the Halifaxes suffered disproportionately, losing 10.5 per cent of their number while the Lancasters lost 3.6 per cent. Among the Halifaxes shot down were one by Paul Zorner at Hintermeiligen, his sixteenth kill, and one by Rudolf Szardenings of II./NJG 5. Szardenings' Halifax crashed in flames into the River Rhine. There was an incredible achievement by Hauptmann Wilhelm Herget, *Gruppenkommandeur* of I./NJG 4 who, flying from Florennes in Belgium, destroyed eight four-engined bombers to bring his total score by night into the forties. Before joining the *Nachtjagd* he had shot down twelve enemy aircraft when flying with a *Zerstörergeschwader*. As many successful German night-fighter pilots testify, *Zahme Sau*, improved radar and upward-firing guns meant that once successfully infiltrated into the bomber stream and following its course, multiple kills were a comparatively easy matter, and they could be achieved with very little risk to oneself. Still the crews of the British bombers, which had no downward-firing armament, were in fateful ignorance of the threat that lurked below.

John Chaloner's crew, who had missed the attack on Berlin three nights before, went to Frankfurt. Chaloner wrote in his diary, 'We saw four bombers go down by Liège in ten minutes.' Possibly all or some of them were among Herget's kills: possibly, even, one was a Halifax from No. 77 Squadron, the fate of which is described below. John goes on: 'Straight run to target. It was scattered but a good prang. Thirty miles north of the target fighter flares stretched in two layers for about fifty miles. We lost P/O Blackmore and Sgt Saville.'

Dame Fortune was on John's side once more, but she deserted Terry Bolter, since September a Pilot Officer and deputy bombing leader of the Squadron. This was destined to be his final operational flight. It was his second as bomb aimer to Squadron Leader Bickerdike, and it was the last flight that Bickerdike would ever make. They took off from Elvington at 2100 hrs in Halifax KN-K, heading in over Belgium with a sixty mph tail-wind, seeing to their port the searchlights over the Ruhr, where Mosquitos of Bennett's LNSF were tantalising the defences. They reached Frankfurt on ETA, and Bolter instructed Bickerdike to open the bomb doors. Then:

> 'At 2032 I snapped down the fusing switches and took the bomb tit in my right hand. Up came the red ground markers into the bomb-sight beautifully. Up to the intersection – I pressed the bomb tit. "Bombs gone! Bomb doors closed."
>
> 'Everything had gone well so far. A brief red glow from the camera indicator light confirmed that the target photograph had been taken . . . Bombs away and bomb doors closed. I felt much better. We were more manoeuvrable, less vulnerable. The aircraft rocked dangerously, a burst of *flak* just in front of the nose, the black smoke from which could be seen drifting by. I knelt right up in the nose now, behind my small Vickers machine-gun, with safety mechanism off, searching the sky intently. The sky seemed full of aircraft . . . Below me a bomber was already in trouble. I saw bursts of tracer pouring into its starboard outer engine: the bomber was weaving desperately to avoid the fire from a Messerschmitt 109, which was attacking from the starboard quarter. I watched spellbound for a moment before the bomber disappeared from my view with the damaged engine smoking.'

Ahead, Bolter saw fighter flares. He warned his skipper, and then there came a shout from the mid-upper gunner, Bill Cockburn, an Edinburgh boy on only his second operation: 'Prepare to dive port – dive port go!' As Bickerdike dived to port a fighter flashed past, apparently having failed to get in a burst of fire. Soon the fighter flares were behind them. They headed west for home.

After half an hour the Ruhr was again visible to the right, and then Bonn. K-King began to run into wispy cloud. The rear gunner saw something on the starboard, and he drew the mid-upper's attention to it. Terry Bolter reconstructs those desperate moments:

> 'Nothing more was said, and I concluded that the gunners had satisfied themselves that it was another bomber on its return flight to the UK, or otherwise an enemy aircraft which was no longer in range. I was wrong on both counts. "Dive starboard – go!" But it was too late. Bullets were thudding into the starboard wing . . . '

With the starboard wing on fire the pilot gave the order to prepare to abandon aircraft. The engineer passed the pilot his parachute, while Bolter strapped his own on. The navigator opened the emergency exit in the floor beneath his seat, and then he pressed the detonator switch on his Gee equipment to avoid it falling into German hands intact. The flames were spreading, and Bickerdike gave the order to bale out. Bolter acknowledged, and then:

'I disconnected my oxygen tube and half-turned to bale out when the air-craft bucked and stood on its nose, out of control, throwing me forward on my stomach into the Perspex nose. We dropped through the sky like a massive piece of lead. The force of gravity was so strong that it pinned me to the floor. We were screaming down, with the sound of wind and engines for harsh and throbbing accompaniment. The intercom, which had been so alive over the target, now seemed dead. There was nothing to say that mattered any more. We could not get out. With my left hand across my eyes and my right hand unconsciously still grasping the handle of my ripcord, I waited for the ground to come up. My mind was clear, and I had a fleeting picture of what this would mean to my family in England. Four words went through my mind – "This is the end, this is the end!"

'It seemed endless, that journey down. My feeling of resignation and doom gave way to one of frustration, and I had to do something. I found myself frantically dashing my left arm against the Perspex nose, when it suddenly cracked open in front of me. I fell out somehow, with no sensation of speed or falling, yet looking up I could see the aircraft burning above me.

'I pulled the ripcord, and a mass of billowy whiteness together with a tight jerk across the thighs told me that the parachute was open – to my intense relief. Bits of the aircraft fell past me as I twisted round, and K-King went by a few thousand feet away, on its last flight to earth. A burst of orange flame leapt up as it hit the ground and the stratus cloud became tinged with red as I floated down through it. Above the wind in my ears I could hear myself saying, "You were lucky to get out of that." My voice seemed lost in the vastness of the night. I had a hazy recollection of losing a flying boot before I got out, and glanced down to see that this was so. A queer way to set foot on foreign soil, one boot on, one off, but this was my smallest worry right then. I still felt pretty high up after a few moments' respite, but then as I looked down the ground seemed to come up quickly. I landed with a thud, rolling over and over to absorb the impact before coming to rest with my face embedded in the muddy bank of a small stream flowing across a field in a country region somewhere in Germany. Three miles to the west K-King burnt itself out, a solitary beacon in the enemy darkness.'

Terry Bolter and his flight engineer, Frank Shaw, were the only two survivors from the Halifax. Shaw broke his leg on landing and was made a prisoner of war, but Bolter evaded capture and was back in England before the end of June the following year.

While Frankfurt was Bolter's last operation, it was the first for Sgt Horace V. Pearce and his crew, who had joined No. 77 Squadron on 9 November. Born in April 1921, Horace Pearce was the son of a Somerset willow-grower, had won a scholarship to a Taunton grammar school and had worked in a local government office until volunteering as RAF aircrew in April 1941. He had done his basic flying training in the United States and more advanced training in Canada, passing out as a pilot in October 1942. He had returned to the UK on board the *Queen Elizabeth* and finally, after familiarisation on twin-engined aircraft in European

229

weather conditions, so different from those in America, he had been posted to No. 20 Operational Training Unit at Lossiemouth. There he flew Wellingtons and first met the other four flyers who were to form the nucleus of his operational crew:

'The first four weeks would be devoted to lectures and working in the Ground School – no flying, so we were given three weeks in which to crew up, after which it would be done for us. Frankly, I didn't have a clue how to start. In the event it seems to have come about largely by the usual RAF and British haphazard method of hit and miss.'

Horace met his navigator, George Kendal, in a pub in Lossiemouth village. Asked why he chose Horace as his pilot, George later said, 'Well, you looked a reasonable sort of chap and you looked like you could hold your beer.' He met his bomb aimer, Gordon Edwards, in a bus queue in Elgin, and George introduced him to Frank Morgan, who became his wireless operator. In turn, Frank introduced Ivor 'Taffy' Hancocks, his rear gunner. In July 1943 the crew went to Marston Moor to convert on to the four-engined Halifax at No. 1652 Heavy Conversion Unit. Before they left Lossiemouth a Canadian gunner, Sgt Roy Brooks, was allocated to the crew, and the seventh man, Flight Engineer Fred Archbold, joined them at Marston Moor.

When he arrived at Elvington, Pearce already had two operations to his credit: he had flown second-pilot trips to Mannheim and Munich with No. 102 Squadron while at Operational Training Unit. The remainder of the crew, all Sergeants, had still to experience the realities of the night battle over Germany, although they had set out for Leipzig on 3 December but had returned early with an unserviceable Gee set. They had also been on the Battle Order for an earlier attack on Berlin, but had been withdrawn at the last moment by the Squadron Commander, Wing Commander Roncoroni, who felt that they should have more experience before going to the 'Big City'. Now they took off from Elvington at 1655 hrs. Instead of their regular engineer, Fred Archbold, they were carrying a replacement, 'Tiny' Greenfield. Fred had become a casualty the previous evening, not in combat with the *Luftwaffe*, but in a fight with some Canadians in a fish-and-chip shop in York. The hazards of being a member of Bomber Command were not confined to the night sky.

Approaching the Liège area just before 1900 hrs at 18,000 feet they ran into trouble, as Horace Pearce describes:

'Indicated air speed was 158 knots and we were just east of Liège. Suddenly the mid-upper gunner shouted, "Turn port, GO!" and the clatter of machine-gun fire could be heard over the intercom. Pilot: "Christ, that was close!"

'I noticed that my compass repeater needle was swinging round like mad, and I was aware that the noise of machine-gun fire was increasing intensely as our rear gunner, Ivor Hancocks, joined in. The firing then ceased as suddenly as it had started and the mid-upper gunner called, "OK, resume course." My compass needle reverted to normal and settled down on its original course, and apart from a half-a-dozen or so words, no further conversation took place. Later we learned that our mid-upper, Roy Brooks, had spotted an unidentifiable but suspicious shape keeping station on our port beam at about 500 yards. Roy lined up his guns to cover the shape, which then banked over, giving him a plan view which he recognised as a Me 110, which turned in to attack, its tracer passing in front of our cockpit. Roy called his warning and fired at the attacking aircraft. Ivor Hancocks reported that he could see Roy's tracer registering hits on the Me 110 as he swung his own turret to join in the fight. The Me 110 closed to within 300 yards and then broke away to starboard. At the debriefing later the Me 110 was claimed as damaged.'

Wing Commander Roncoroni had wanted Horace Pearce and his crew to gain experience. The Frankfurt trip was providing it. On the way to Frankfurt Pearce's crew learned something that was well known to everyone who took part in concentrated Bomber Command attacks, that *flak* and fighters were not the only dangers:

'I was horrified to see another Halifax on a converging course to starboard, boring straight at us. It was too late for evasive action, and I realised immediately that any movements of the controls would inevitably result in a collision, so I decided to stay straight and level, hoping that the other pilot, who was probably triangulating to lose time, would also fly straight and level and that there was sufficient height difference for him to miss us. The other aircraft thundered across the top of us, a lot too close for comfort. As he passed over to port the wash from his propellers threw my aircraft all over the place.'

Wing Commander Roncoroni himself had gained a little more experience. He too was involved in a combat with a German fighter that opened fire on his machine from a range of about eight hundred yards just after he had bombed the target. Another pilot, Warrant Officer Manson, also managed to escape the attentions of a night-fighter in the area of Frankfurt. The enemy aircraft, which the gunners identified, probably erroneously, as a Me 210, came in rather closer before opening fire, and was then deterred by the Halifax's guns. It attacked again and yet again, but each time the vigilance of Manson's gunners and his violent corkscrews saved him. The enemy fighter was claimed as damaged. The combat reports by all the three crews, those of Pearce, Roncoroni and Manson, contain the words 'No warning was given by Monica.'

The eventful year of 1943 was on its way out, but there were still two more raids to Berlin before the New Year came. The force that attacked the capital on 23/24 December was, with the exception of seven Pathfinder Halifaxes, an all-Lancaster one. For this raid Harris sent small diversionary forces of Mosquitos to Leipzig, Düsseldorf and Aachen, and poor weather on the ground and confused raid-plotting by the *Zahme Sau* controllers meant that the *Nachtjagd* had difficulty finding their targets. Nevertheless, of the 379 that set out, sixteen Lancasters were lost, three falling to Paul Zorner, bringing his total to nineteen. PFF marking from a cloud-covered sky was poor, with the TIs widely scattered, so that main force bombing lacked any concentration, many of the bombs falling in wooded areas to the south-east of the city.

The problems of navigation and target-finding, particularly on long flights such as those now predominating, which took the Pathfinders well out of Oboe range and on which Gee was of no use, and with few main force machines yet equipped with H2S, continued to cause concern. Compression in space and time was necessary not only to ensure an accurate and concentrated attack – and that concentration was only rarely being achieved – but also to provide protection for the individual bombers. To the night-fighters, stragglers and those to one side or other of the main stream represented comparatively easy targets, forfeiting as they did the protection of Window. In an attempt to tighten up the stream a system first tried on the Peenemünde operation was now introduced more formally. Certain aircraft, flown by experienced crews, were designated 'Wind-Finders', and it was the navigator's task to calculate the wind velocity and have it sent back to England by the wireless operator. In England the winds would be plotted and an average strength and direction calculated: the result would then be transmitted in coded form for use by the main force navigators. The theory was that if all navigators were using the same wind velocity for their calculations they would be more likely to stay together, and it is possible, but far from certain, that some improvement in concentration was achieved. But even 'found winds' could not ensure that the stream, even if concentrated, went precisely along the correct track. One wind-finder was John Chaloner:

> 'Took off midnight – what a horrible bind. Over Berlin by 4 a.m. Route by Leipzig. Had the job of sending wind velocities back. Hit east of city.'

John also went to Berlin on the final major raid of 1943 on the night of 29/30: it was the tenth raid of the Battle of Berlin, and John had flown on eight of them. This time Halifaxes were committed, 252 of them contributing to a total force of 712. Take-off was in the early evening and time on target about eight o'clock. It was a comparatively routine trip, with only moderate and scattered damage being caused to the capital of the *Reich*, which was once again cloud-covered. Bad weather over Germany and confusion to the defences caused by Mosquito diversionary and harassing raids to Düsseldorf, Magdeburg and Leipzig, plus jamming of the fighter frequencies, meant that losses, at 2.8 per cent of the total briefed, were lighter than on earlier raids, but again the Halifaxes suffered proportionately higher losses than the Lancasters, 3.6 per cent against 2.4 per cent.

It had been a costly year for Bomber Command, with 2,225 aircraft missing on night operations and a further 5,177 damaged, 348 of them beyond repair. At a conservative estimate 14,000 aircrew had lost their lives. It is interesting to note that confirmed German night-fighter claims during the year amounted to 1,816, or eighty-one per cent of all losses. The equivalent statistics kept by Bomber Command show a marked difference in emphasis. Of the 2,225 bombers missing it was possible in only 1,537 cases to estimate the cause of the loss. 964 were attributed to fighters, 547 to *flak* and twenty-six to other causes such as aerial collision. From these figures the proportion of losses due to fighters to those due to flak comes out at rather less than two to one, but the German figures suggest something like a four-to-one ratio. There must be a strong probability that even at this advanced stage of the battle the deadly potential of the *Nachtjagd* was being underestimated at Bomber Command Headquarters.[2]

The revolution in night-fighting that had sprung from the changes in Bomber Command tactics and the introduction of Window had worked to the advantage of the night fighters, who in general found it easier and more profitable to hunt freelance in the bomber stream than to be close-controlled from the ground. With new aircraft, new weapons and modified radar, their potential was growing, but they were increasingly having to contend with the advancing sophistication and versatility of British jamming techniques, not to speak of the attentions of intruder aircraft, with the Beaufighter rapidly yielding place to the more potent Mosquito.

Seen from the point of view of the generality of night-fighter crews, there had been one welcome advantage in the change-over from *Himmelbett* to *Zahme Sau*. Whereas Kammhuber's system of close control in small, overlapping areas had favoured senior officers, who 'hogged' the boxes in order to ensure their climb up the league table of victories, the more flexible broadcast-control method meant that less experienced or less influential pilots were now able to take their chance alongside their superiors, so that new names were coming to prominence on the list of *Experten*, people like Paul Zorner. At the end of the year, however, the table was still dominated by the 'old hares', the *alte Hasen*. Lent, Wittgenstein, Streib, Meurer, Schoenert, Frank, Geiger, Lippe-Weissenfeld, all had over fifty kills to their name. Helmut Lent was in the lead with seventy-six victories, with Heinrich zu Sayn-Wittgenstein in second place, eight behind him and determined to take the lead.

[2] Based on statistics from the Official History, Part IV, Appendix 40.

Halifax Mk.III MH-L of No.51 Squadron, Snaith, Yorkshire. After an attack on marshalling yards at Lens, France, during the night of 10 May 1944, the Halifax was in mid-air collision with another Halifax, ZA-E of No.10 squadron. Note the damage to the starboard fin and wing. Miraculously, both machines landed safely. *(Terry)*

Pilot Officer Horace Pearce (No.77 Squadron, Elvington, York) with ground crew, 3 July 1944. The aircraft is Halifax Mk.III, MZ 697, KN-L. *(Pearce)*

Above: Oberleutnant Fritz Krause's Fw 190A-5 (*"Weisse Elf"* – "White Eleven") showing the aerials for the FuG 217 J2 (*Neptun*) radar. Originally designed as a tail-warning radar for heavier machines, *Neptun* was used in its J2 version as an AI radar in single-seater fighters. Krause belonged to 1./NJGr 10. In this machine he destroyed a Mosquito over Berlin on 7–8 July 1944. *(Krause)*

Below left: Oberleutnant Martin (Tino) Becker on cycle and with dog in front of his SN2-equipped Bf 110. *(Buschmann)*

Below right: MH-W *Winsome Waaf.* Wreckage at Marche-en-Famenne, after being shot down on 4 November 1944. *(Charlesworth)*

CHAPTER TEN

The Berlin Battle Continues:
The Nuremberg Disaster

January to March 1944

By the end of December 1943 Bomber Command had flown just over 4,000 sorties against the 'Big City' and had suffered 184 losses: at 4.5 per cent of those involved this was, although by no means negligible, an encouragingly low proportion. Assuming that Harris's forecast of losses had been based on some reasonable hypothesis of likely casualties, his campaign against Berlin, intended to 'cost Germany the war', was at its half-way stage. But neither in terms of civilian morale nor in terms of damage to the city was there any sign that the bombing was likely to bring the Germans to their knees. Considerable damage had been caused, since the resumption of attacks on Berlin, to the governmental and administrative area of the city centred on the Brandenburg Gate, and more than a quarter of the city's civilian accommodation had been rendered unfit for occupation. Largely as a result of persistent cloud cover over the target area, PFF marking and main force bombing had in general been very widely scattered, with damage to factories, transport and so on being only moderate, coincidental rather than a result of specific intent. Compared with some of the heavier raids against targets further west, in particular Hamburg, and considering the size of Berlin and the number of raids carried out, casualties on the ground were reasonably light, with something in the order of 5,600 having met their death.

It is hard to know how Harris assessed his Command's progress in this first half of the battle towards his stated aim of wrecking Berlin 'from end to end'. He had little to go on. Bad weather meant that only rarely was sight of the ground possible, so that crews' reports of bombing results, always optimistic, were even more unreliable than usual. The same bad weather made daylight reconnaissance flights over the target area largely fruitless. Only once, on about 20 December, were reconnaissance photographs brought back, and these showed great damage in the Tiergarten area, Berlin's equivalent of Westminster and Whitehall. The majority of this damage had resulted from the successful raids on 22/23 November and the following night, and it is possible that the photographs gave an unduly optimistic impression of the combined effect that the six attacks until then had produced. To a large extent, however, the Commander-in-Chief of Bomber Command, like his crews, was working in the dark.

The period that has come to be known as the Battle of Berlin was destined to last until the closing days of March 1944. By that time, Berlin would have been attacked a further eight times, but there would also have been thirteen major attacks on other cities deep within Germany. Additionally, with the invasion of the Continent scheduled for the middle of 1944 and with the looming threat of flying-bomb attacks on England, there was an increasing incidence of raids on France. Jamming and disruption sorties by No. 100 Group escalated rapidly, as did Mosquito diversion and intruder raids. On the German side, this was the period during which the effectiveness of the *Nachtjagd* was at its highest. Even so, thanks to the steadily increasing ability of Bomber Command to outwit those controlling the German defences and to disrupt the operations of the night fighters, its potential was never fully realised. Nevertheless the Messerschmitts, Junkers and Heinkels inflicted grievous losses on the Lancasters and Halifaxes.

Of the remaining eight raids against Berlin, six were in January and only one in February and one in March. January also saw major attacks against Stettin, Brunswick and Magdeburg. The trend that had been established in the final months of 1943 persisted: the winter that brought the long nights and allowed deep penetration also brought with it bad weather, in particular thick cloud, making navigation difficult and accurate bomb aiming virtually impossible. Despite the increased use by the Pathfinders of the more accurate three-centimetre H2S and the fact that a gradually growing number of main force bombers carried the same equipment in the ten-centimetre version, marking was on the whole inaccurate and bombing was widely dispersed, much of it falling outside the area of greater Berlin. The flak over Berlin was heavy and fighters were a constant preoccupation, with the understandable consequence that there was a strong, frequently irresistible, temptation to drop one's bombs as early as possible and 'get the hell out of it'.

But even for the most dedicated of pilots and bomb aimers, the task of placing their bombs where they were intended to strike home was impracticable: there was simply nothing to aim at. Sky markers, themselves often inaccurate and scattered, disappeared rapidly into the clouds, leaving a short-lived coloured glow that merged with those caused by innumerable fires on the ground over many square miles, so that the area covered by the bombing expanded progressively and there was no concentration. Massive damage was caused, it is true: it could hardly be otherwise when hundreds upon hundreds of four-engined bombers, each carrying up to five tons of bombs, were unloading their cargo, even without any perceivable accuracy. But this was vastly different from the terrifying success of the Hamburg attacks the previous July, the ideal upon which Harris's predictions of the effect on Germany's resolve to continue the war were largely based. Then the morale of the German citizens in the Hamburg area had been near to breaking point. The 'we can take it' phenomenon, so clearly evidenced during the German blitz on London and elsewhere during the earlier part of the war, was not an exclusively British reaction to the terror of bombing, and if anything the morale of the German citizenry, in Berlin and other afflicted places, grew stronger rather than weaker. They lived in a dictator state in which to protest or to criticise meant risking severe punishment – even, possibly, death – but that was not the only, or even the major, reason behind their resilience. Their towns were being bombed mercilessly and indiscriminately, their homes destroyed by the tens of thousands, their relatives and friends slaughtered, and any incipient thoughts that there might have been of abandoning the war faded in light of the perception that they were fighting a ruthless enemy who demanded nothing less than unconditional surrender, a demand that was much publicised and exploited by the Nazi propaganda machine.

The first two nights of the New Year saw two moderately heavy attacks on Berlin, heavy in the numbers of aircraft deployed, at least. The damage to the capital caused by the total of approximately 800 bombers was, by comparison, slight, with only about 100 houses being destroyed and about the same number of people killed. The outskirts of metropolitan Berlin contain large areas of woodland and lakes. The majority of bombs bespattered these comparatively sparsely populated areas, and in addition many fell outside the limits of the city. For this paltry return, Bomber Command paid heavily, losing fifty-five Lancasters and nearly 400 trained men.

John Chaloner went to Berlin on the night of 1/2 January, flying his last trip as navigator to Ernie Webb, now Warrant Officer Webb DFC. It was not unusual for pilots to complete their tour before the other members of their crew, because they flew one or more sorties as second pilot with an experienced crew before operating as captain of their own aircraft, and so they reached the magic number of thirty before their crew did. It was an uneventful operation, with Webb arriving to find the target cloud-covered and the Wanganui sky-markers widely dispersed, so Chaloner bombed on H2S, adding his contribution to the widespread scatter of high-explosives and incendiaries.

Of the twenty-eight Lancasters that did not come back from this raid, Major Heinrich Prinz zu Sayn-Wittgenstein claimed six. There was a change in Wittgenstein's crew. In November 1943 Herbert Kümmritz, who had flown with him as his radio/radar operator since the previous February, had been granted temporary leave of absence from flying duties in order to continue his studies in the field of high-frequency technology. With Wittgenstein, Kümmritz had participated in forty-three 'kills'. Now his place in the Prince's Ju 88 was taken by Feldwebel Friedrich Ostheimer. By the end of 1943 Wittgenstein had increased his personal tally to sixty-eight, second only to that of Helmut Lent, who had shot down seventy-six. With effect from the first day of 1944 Wittgenstein was promoted to the rank of Major and appointed *Geschwaderkommodore* of NJG 2. Friedrich Ostheimer, like Herbert Kümmritz, remembers Wittgenstein as formal, aloof, a strict disciplinarian and fanatical in his self-imposed aim of being the best night-fighter pilot ever. Speaking of the legendary man in 1990, he said:

'I was with the Prince for about three months, and during that period we shot down about sixteen bombers. Once, when we were operating from Deelen in Holland, we got a Lancaster. He was on his way home after bombing. We saw some navigation lights, and we went lower and crept up on him. I don't know why he had his lights on, and if he hadn't, we probably wouldn't have seen him. So we shot him down.

'Soon after I joined the Prince's crew we were detached from II./NJG 3 and sent to Rechlin, north of Berlin, where Wittgenstein was to set up an experimental night-fighter unit. It must have been about the beginning of December 1943. Suddenly, without any warning, we were pulled out of the friendly circle of our comrades: we knew no one at Rechlin, and most of the time Kurt Matzuleit and I just sat around feeling lonely while the Prince himself was either in conference or at the Air Ministry in Berlin. But even though he wasn't with his *Gruppe* the Prince went on flying operationally.

236

There wasn't a night-fighter unit at Rechlin, so I had to spend long periods on the telephone each day getting frequencies, callsigns and so on, all the briefing material we needed to prepare for an operation. In addition, of course, Matzuleit and I had to make sure that our aircraft and its equipment were fully serviceable and ready for take-off at any time. We lived in railway wagons with sleeping compartments.

'We were at Rechlin about three weeks, and we flew several times when Berlin was raided. I remember one flight when we lost an engine and had to make an emergency landing back at Rechlin. It was standard operating procedure in the Ju 88 to belly-land if you only had one motor, because the 88 couldn't overshoot and go round again on one. Wittgenstein, however, ignored this instruction and we made a perfect landing on one engine.

'Another time we were over Berlin – it must have been in December. It was a cloudless night, but there was a layer of haze over the city at about 1,500 metres. It looked like a matt-glass screen, what we called *Leichentuch*, and we were poised above the bombers and could see them silhouetted over the city. I had one target on my radar screen, and I was giving the pilot instructions, when we suddenly came under fire. I looked out, and ahead and to one side I saw a Lancaster, and the mid-upper gunner was firing at us, and he scored several hits. He had taken us by surprise. The Prince told me to stop working my radio and radar and to concentrate on watching the Lancaster. His night vision was not very good, and he often relied on other members of the crew if we were following an enemy aircraft visually. We flew parallel to the Lancaster and slightly below for some time, and then we moved in beneath it and shot it down with *Schräge Musik*.

'You asked me what sort of a man Wittgenstein was. He was never on close terms with us. The only time I remember him being a little more friendly was once, while we were back at Deelen – we went back there just before Christmas – when he invited Matzuleit and me to visit him in his quarters at about eight o'clock that evening. He had shot a *mouflon* – a wild sheep – in a Royal Netherlands hunting preserve near the airfield. As *Geschwaderkommodore* he had permission to hunt there. We had a *mouflon* dinner with him, and a glass of *Sekt*. That was the only time he was ever really friendly.'

The 6.7 per cent loss rate experienced by Bomber Command on New Year's Day 1944 was slightly exceeded the following night, when twenty-seven Lancasters, seven per cent of the force dispatched, failed to return. Berlin was again the target, and again the damage to the city was slight, with only thirty-seven being killed on the ground for the loss of more than 180 aircrew. Paul Zorner, flying his *SN-2*-equipped Bf 110 G, got his twentieth kill, attacking from astern with his forward-facing cannon at 19,000 feet and hitting a Lancaster in the port wing. It crashed near Luckenwalde at 0310 hrs on the morning of 3 January. Another pilot flying against Bomber Command that night, and achieving his first victory, was Leutnant Wilhelm Seuss, who to this day does not really know what moved him to fly in the night defence of Germany. Professor Dr Seuss, as he now is, is penetratingly self-critical:

'I first flew, in a glider, in 1936, and I loved flying. I volunteered for the *Luftwaffe* before the war. I was called up in April 1939. I did my basic pilot's training on single-engined machines, then I did a multi-engined course and a blind-flying course. My training took longer than expected, because there was already a shortage of fuel due to the demands of the Russian campaign. I then had to choose what sort of aircraft I would prefer to fly operationally. I volunteered for night-fighting. I didn't think I was strong enough to be a day-fighter, and for some reason or other I was averse to the idea of dropping bombs and killing people. I was interested in technical matters such as navigation, and I was attracted to long-range reconnaissance or night-fighters. What finally decided me I can no longer recall, but the fact that the RAF were bombing Germany heavily certainly played no part in my decision.

'I began my night-fighter training at Schleissheim in January 1943, and in the following July I went to my first operational unit, I./NJG 4 at Laon-Athies, in the 3rd *Staffel*. Then NJG 5 was formed, and our complete *Staffel* was transferred. That would be at the beginning of September.

'We didn't get operational for some time, because at that time the "big heroes" were hogging the *Himmelbett* areas. The aces would take off first, and we younger people would wait in vain to be scrambled. At first I flew the Do 217, but then I converted to the Messerschmitt 110. I remember my first flight on the 110 very clearly – it must have been 20 August 1943. I didn't have a *Funker* on board. There was an air-raid warning in operation. I landed, and taxied back. I saw a Ju 52 to one side of me, and as I watched I saw holes appearing in it! There were Allied fighters coming in at low level. I realised that I was going to be hit too, so I got out as quickly as I could and took cover. My machine, as well as the Ju 52, was riddled with bullets! I had been shot down on the ground! I had already had one narrow escape, about a week earlier. There had been an RAF attack on Italy, and I had been scrambled. We went a long way south, and we ran out of fuel and had to land in Luxembourg. I hit a cherry tree on the approach, and wrote the aircraft off.

'I had an enormous respect for the Bomber Command crews. In my view they were greater heroes than the German night-fighters. They were extraordinarily disciplined. I was certainly no hero. I was cowardly, I was always afraid, and I used to tremble. Once I was at the controls I was quite calm, but on the ground I was always in fear. I tried not to think about it, but I couldn't sleep at nights.'

'*Ich war feige,*' says Seuss: 'I was cowardly.' But who is the hero? Is it the man who feels no fear, or is it the man who faces up to his fear and overcomes it?

Seuss remembers a trip he made to Neuruppin, north-west of Berlin, on 15 November 1943, when night-fighter crews were summoned to meet the Commander-in-Chief of the *Luftwaffe*, Hermann Göring. It was a sad occasion, he says. All the crews were introduced to 'The Fat Man', who made a speech. It was *katastrophal*: Göring was made up, clad in a 'fantasy uniform', his nails polished. He made a very bad impression on the hardened aircrew, and any respect that he might have enjoyed vanished. One had the feeling that he still thought he was a fighter pilot in the First World War. He was nothing but *eine Tüte* – an empty bag.

Göring was not only a wind-bag, he was also fickle towards those upon whom he chose to bestow his patronage. One such man was Hajo Herrmann. Considering Herrmann's abilities as a commander too valuable for him to risk his life, the Reichsmarschall had forbidden him to fly operationally. In the early hours of 3 January, Herrmann disobeyed Göring's order. When the early-warning system had picked up a raid on the way in and had identified Berlin as the likely target, Herrmann, who had aready scrambled his experienced pilots – he did not consider the weather conditions suitable for the newer men to fly – decided that he himself would take off. There was ten-tenths cloud at below 2,000 feet, extending to 10,000, and heavy icing within the cloud was forecast. From Staaken Herrmann, flying an Fw 190, headed west towards the approaching stream of heavy bombers. Once through the cloud he climbed to about 23,000 feet: at that height he would be above the majority of the attackers. Soon he saw Lancasters in the light of flares dropped by the illuminators, and he attacked and probably destroyed one. Seven minutes later another Lancaster fell to his cannon: this time there was no doubt about the victory. But at the very same moment cannon shells struck home into his own aircraft: he had fallen victim to a British intruder. Herrmann was hit in the right leg.

Losing blood and feeling consciousness fade away, he turned his Focke-Wulf on to a westerly heading, away from the burning target. In vain he tried to establish R/T contact with the ground. Any first thoughts he had of finding somewhere to land were rapidly rejected when he descended to within a thousand feet above ground level only to find himself still in cloud. He realised that his only hope lay in his parachute, and he climbed out of cloud again, jettisoned the canopy, pulled up the aircraft's nose and thrust the control column forward, catapulting himself into space and falling to earth through snow-cloud.

In hospital next day Herrmann was visited by Oberst von Below, one of Hitler's adjutants. Von Below brought Hajo Herrmann the *Führer*'s personal congratulations on his escape. Göring, however, took a different view. He was outraged that Herrmann should have blatantly disobeyed his order not to fly operationally, and he demanded an explanation. When Hitler decorated Herrmann with the Swords to the Knight's Cross of the Iron Cross some weeks later, Göring neglected to offer even his formal congratulations.

For almost three weeks Berlin was spared further attack by heavy bombers, although Mosquitos of the Light Night Striking Force visited the city on 4/5, 5/6, 10/11 and 14/15 January. The attacks on the night of the fifth and fourteenth were diversionary raids in support of heavy main-force attacks on Stettin and Brunswick respectively, while the remainder were part of a developing pattern of nuisance raids against widely scattered targets. Flying-bomb sites, too, were attracting an increasing share of Bomber Command effort.

On the night of 5/6 January, when 358 heavies carried out a good raid on the Baltic port of Stettin, Paul Zorner claimed both Halifaxes lost out of an overall total of sixteen. Partly as a result of the Mosquito diversionary raid on Berlin, where no doubt the German fighter controllers were expecting Harris to strike yet again, losses on the Stettin raid, at 4.5 per cent, were only moderate. It was a different story on the night of 14/15 January, when the early-warning system picked up the bomber stream early on its way to Brunswick and the fighters were soon finding their prey. Of the thirty-eight Lancasters lost, eleven were Pathfinder machines: it was usually the case that the leading aircraft suffered most when the fighters were promptly on the scene, and the loss of these marker machines possibly accounted for the fact that, despite the nearly 500 bombers attacking, the city of Brunswick reported only a light raid. This was yet another case of bombs being distributed throughout a very wide area, most of them outside the target city itself. The most successful fighter pilot was Leutnant Wendelin Breukel of II./NJG 2, who shot down six. Of the others flying that night, Peter Spoden got two, while Hermann Greiner of NJG 1 and Rudolf Szardenings of NJG 3 claimed one each.

The pattern of bombing six nights later, when Berlin was again the target, was similar to that of previous raids on the capital: not inconsiderable damage within the city, but many bombs outside it. In a switch of tactics, Harris changed from the comparatively direct routes to Berlin that he had used so far to a northerly route, bringing his stream in across the North Sea and over the southern part of Schleswig-Holstein before they veered starboard to a turning point 100 kilometres to the north-west of the target, from where the city was approached on a south-easterly heading. Possibly this helped to keep the losses below five per cent of the 769 bombers dispatched, but the main factor in the moderate loss rate was the bad weather over the Continent, which kept the majority of the fighters grounded. The increasing use of broadcast control and infiltration into the bomber stream meant that multiple kills by individual pilots were becoming more frequent. This night it was the turn of Hauptmann Leopold Fellerer of II./NJG 5 to make his mark with five kills. Paul Zorner was adding steadily to his score, getting his twenty-third and twenty-fourth kills, two more Halifaxes.

On the first raid against Berlin in January 1944 Harris had sent an all-Lancaster force; on the second raid all Lancasters except nine Halifaxes from No. 35 (PFF) Squadron, already equipped with the improved B Mk III version. Now 264 Halifaxes, the majority of which were the older Mk II and Mk V versions, were among the 769 aircraft taking off during the afternoon of 20 January, briefed to bomb the German capital during the twenty minutes between 1933 and 1953 hrs. Again the Halifaxes suffered badly: thirteen Lancasters were lost, 2.6 per cent of those dispatched, but the number of Halifaxes that failed to return was twenty-two, or 8.3 per cent. No. 102 Squadron, flying from Pocklington and still equipped with the obsolescent versions of the Halifax, lost five of the sixteen machines it sent on the mission, while a further two crashed in England on return. Two other Halifax squadrons, No. 76 (4 Group) and No. 434 (6 Group), similarly equipped, lost three each.

Horace Pearce and his crew had left Elvington at 1629 hrs on 20 January in Halifax Mk II, K-King, LK 731, bound for Berlin. An error in setting course put him behind schedule, and as he crossed the North Sea problems developed with his navigator's Gee equipment and both the intercom system and the automatic pilot broke down. Rather than waste his bomb-load in the waters of the North Sea, Pearce overflew the *Flak* and searchlight positions on the island of Sylt, where he jettisoned his cargo at 1845 hrs. He then headed west, arriving back at his Yorkshire base at 2146 hrs. His Squadron, No. 77, lost just one aircraft, all but one of the crew dying, while another machine crashed on take-off, fortunately without casualties.

Major Prince Wittgenstein, only recently elevated to the command of NJG 2, increased his score of victories by three that night, dispatching two Lancasters with his *Schräge Musik. Funker* Friedrich Ostheimer takes up the story:

'We attacked a third Lancaster, and it caught fire immediately. Possibly the pilot stayed at the controls and saw us in the light of the fire, because the Lancaster went into a dive as if it was trying to follow us. Because he was heavier than we were, he was travelling faster. He came terribly near. I remember thinking to myself, "This is it!" He passed over us very close indeed – possibly as close as two metres. I was sitting there, and one of the Lancaster propellers almost hit me. Our Ju 88 went out of control. This had happened at about 7,500 to 8,000 metres, and we were down at 1,000 metres before the pilot regained control. The machine was still flyable, but only just.

'We headed south from the Berlin area, and I had to establish some sort of radio contact. But I couldn't raise any of the airfields south of Berlin. The Prince became very angry – "What sort of a Funker are you? You must be able to make contact with someone!" I tried the Air Traffic Control centre at Cologne, and they gave me a fix over Saalfeld. But Saalfeld was not marked on the map I was carrying. So I called Cologne and asked them for the callsign of Erfurt/Bindersleben, which was on the map. They gave me the callsign. These callsigns were always three letters, and you could tell the frequency from the middle letter. I called SOS, and all other aircraft on that frequency shut up. I got a bearing from Erfurt. The weather was not good, and they gave me a met. report. We headed for the airfield, and we got the signal that we were overhead, but we were still in cloud. We flew away on a set heading, and turned on to a reciprocal to make our approach.

'As soon as the Prince began to throttle back – we had our wheels and flaps down for landing – the aircraft began to stall. The Prince opened up, and we went round again, climbing to about 1,000 metres. At that height he throttled back again, and immediately the machine went into a stall. He asked whether we wanted to bale out or make a belly-landing, and we decided to stay with the aircraft and land on the grass with our wheels up. As we crossed the airfield boundary lights we jettisoned the cockpit cover. The machine hit the ground, flinging dirt up into the cabin. We had of course reported that our machine was damaged and we would have to make a belly-landing, so the fire-tender and ambulance were on the spot. Luckily we all got out safely, and we got a meal and a bed for the night in the officers' mess. We discovered that about two metres of our wing had been cut off by the Lancaster's propeller.

'As luck would have it, another aircraft from NJG 2 had also landed at Erfurt. Wittgenstein commandeered it and we flew back to our own base, while the other crew had to go back by train.'

The following night it was the turn of Magdeburg, about seventy miles to the west-south-west of Berlin, to be the target for getting on for 650 Lancasters and

Halifaxes of Bomber Command. It was not a good attack from any point of view, with cloud over the target, poor marking by the Pathfinders – Magdeburg did not show up well on H2S – and very scattered bombing by the main force, so that very few bombs fell within the target area. For the German defences, on the other hand, it was a successful night: they claimed fifty-seven bombers, 8.8 per cent of the force, with Halifaxes again taking the brunt of the retribution, losing thirty-five from the 224 that set out. The *Zahme Sau* system worked very well, and night fighters were infiltrated into the stream even before the Pathfinders crossed the north German coast.

Like No. 102 Squadron the previous evening, No. 77 Squadron lost five of its Halifaxes. Sergeant George Kendal, navigator to Horace Pearce, recalls heavy fighter activity and scattered *flak* over the target. A brush with an enemy fighter and the evasive action involved just after 'bombs gone' resulted in Kendal being unsure of his position. On the way home they ran into a heavily defended area, possibly Hamburg, which meant further violent evasive action, so that the course they steered for home over the North Sea was an approximate one only: Kendal knew he would soon pick up Gee signals and be able to make the necessary corrections. Some seventy or eighty miles short of Flamborough Head, and to the north of the flight-plan track, Horace Pearce saw an aircraft on the port quarter. It was flying slowly, had its navigation lights switched on, and it looked to be in trouble. Pearce went down to 2,000 feet, while George Kendal struggled in vain to get a Gee fix. Pearce's bomb-aimer, Gordon Edwards, saw the stricken aircraft's landing lights come on, and then disappear as the machine hit the water. Pearce flew his Halifax over the spot, flashing his navigation lights to show that he had seen the aircraft come down. After about twenty minutes Kendal was able to get an accurate fix from his Gee set and to back-plot the estimated position of the ditching, which the wireless operator attempted to transmit to England, only to be foiled by heavy static interference on his equipment. When they reached base, they told their story, and the result was, they later heard, that the crew of the ditched aircraft was rescued. 'Had we not been off track at the right time,' writes George, 'the story may have been different. The North Sea in January is a very inhospitable place to be, and survival depended on being rescued in the shortest possible time.'

If this was a bad night for Bomber Command, it was also an unhappy one for the *Nachtjagd*, with two of their foremost operational commanders being lost. The leading pilots, in terms of their score, at the end of 1943 had been Lent, Wittgenstein, Streib and Meurer with seventy-six, sixty-eight, sixty-three and sixty-two kills respectively. When they took off on the evening of 21 January 1944, Meurer, *Kommandeur* of I./NJG 1, had increased his score to sixty-five, while Wittgenstein, still in second place to Lent, had reached seventy-eight: Lent had eighty-two. Both aces, Wittgenstein and Meurer, perished that night. Wittgenstein never knew that during that sortie he had achieved his driving ambition of overtaking Lent and reaching the top of the night fighters' 'league table' of kills.

As recounted above, Wittgenstein had flown back to Deelen from Erfurt on the morning of 21 January after his collision with a Lancaster the previous night and the emergency landing that followed. *Funker* Ostheimer and *Mechaniker* Matzuleit had, understandably, hoped that they would have a short break to get over the experience, but in that they were disappointed. In the early afternoon Wittgenstein rang Ostheimer up from his control post. The early-warning system had already given notice of a Bomber Command attack that night, he said, and he would be flying in the technical officer's machine: Ostheimer and Matzuleit were to prepare the aircraft and themselves.

It was not until well into the evening that the bombers began to cross the coast and the fighters took off. As usual, Wittgenstein was among the first, his position as *Kommodore* of NJG 2 giving him complete choice as to when he scrambled, and he was soon at operational height and seeing the first bombers go down in flames. At about 2200 hrs his first victim fell from the sky, twenty minutes later the second, and then, at intervals of about ten minutes, the third and the fourth. Although he did not know it at the time, he had now reached parity with Lent as the leading scorer. All this time the battle had been moving eastwards, and Ostheimer now had a fifth target on his *SN-2* screen. Wittgenstein eased his Ju 88 below the Lancaster and shot it into flames with his *Schräge Musik*. Then Nemesis struck in the form of, probably, an intruding Mosquito. All that Ostheimer remembers is that suddenly there was a violent banging and a blinding flashing in their own aircraft, and the port wing began to burn intensely. Then the cabin hood flew off, and Wittgenstein shouted, '*Raus!*' Tearing off his helmet and oxygen mask, Ostheimer felt himself flung out of the aircraft. His next recollection is of finding himself spinning and somersaulting through space. By stretching out his arms he was able to control the motion, and beneath him he saw, like a snow-covered landscape, the top of the layer of clouds. Around him he could hear the engine noise of aircraft, and a spasm of fear passed through him – what if he were rammed by one of them? He waited some time, remembering his training, when he had been taught not to pull the ripcord at too great a height lest he suffer from oxygen failure. He deployed his parachute. He was still far above the clouds, and he felt a biting coldness in his right foot. One of his fur-lined flying boots had come off, but he was able to pull up his left leg, unzip the left boot and push his right foot into it. Soon he went into the cloud, and when he came out and could see the ground below he fired off a signal light. He had just put his Very pistol back into his overalls when he came to earth in a small plantation of young trees. When he tried to walk his right ankle caused him pain, but he limped away from the spot at which he had landed. Increasingly painfully he hobbled for about two hours, until he came across a small group of houses. He fired off another signal, and he heard voices. With memories of German flyers who had been mistaken for British ones and badly beaten by civilians, he called out, '*Deutscher Flieger – nicht schiessen!*' Ostheimer was taken into a house, and soon afterwards an ambulance arrived from the nearby airfield of Stendal and took him to hospital.

Two days later Wittgenstein's body was found near the wreckage of the Ju 88, his parachute unopened. It was thought that he had possibly hit his head against the tail unit when attempting to escape from the machine, been knocked unconscious and so been unable to pull his ripcord. He had ended his life as the *Nachtjagd*'s top scorer. Matzuleit, like Ostheimer, had been able to save his life by parachute. The day following his death Wittgenstein was awarded the Swords to the Knight's Cross of the Iron Cross, Germany's second highest decoration for gallantry.

Who was responsible for bringing an abrupt and bloody end to Wittgenstein's life and career as a fighter pilot is not known. Friedrich Ostheimer remains convinced that the Prince fell to the guns of a Mosquito, yet no claims were logged by Mosquito pilots that night. It is possible that Wittgenstein was the unlucky victim of a chance burst from a British gunner, or even of 'friendly' fire from another German fighter. Such things happened. There have been claims that the man who shot him down was probably the rear gunner of a No. 156 Squadron Lancaster that was itself shot down in combat with a night fighter near Magdeburg. The snag about that explanation is that Magdeburg is some long distance, about fifty kilometres, from the spot, Schönhausen, where Wittgenstein's Ju 88 crashed, and according to Ostheimer the machine went down almost vertically when it was so unexpectedly hit by a burst of fire from an unseen enemy. There is an alternative explanation that seems more attractive.

Mosquito action in direct support of the raid on Magdeburg on the night of 21/22 January 1944 was minor, only three aircraft taking part, two from No. 141 Squadron and one from No. 239. Squadron Leader Hitchin of No. 239 Squadron returned to his base, West Raynham, and reported that he had not made any contact with the enemy. No. 141 Squadron, also based at West Raynham, sent two Serrate aircraft to patrol in the Brandenburg area, between Magdeburg and Berlin. Of these two, only one made contact, Mosquito FII No. DZ303 piloted by Flight Sergeant D. Snape and with Flying Officer L. Fowler as radar navigator. The machine took off at 2135 hrs on the night of 21 January and landed back at base just over four hours later. The relevant entry in the Squadron Diary makes very interesting reading:

> 'Intruder to BRANDENBURG. Crossed enemy coast 2205. Target reached and patrolled. While on patrol at 2315 hours south of Brandenburg at 20,000 feet, AI contact obtained above and 20° port. Chase lasting 3/4 minutes on AI only resulting in visual about 200 yards closing in a dive about 210 ASI. Enemy aircraft burning navigation lights (? Ju 88). Combat ensued. Aircraft damaged in fuselage aft of cabin. Our aircraft fired 4/5 seconds but makes no claim pending examination of cine film. No contacts on return journey after combat. No other chase during flight. Recrossed enemy coast 0039 and landed at base 0120. Weather: thin wispy cloud at 20,000 feet – hazy over Dutch coast – 6/10ths low thin cloud below – visibility above 20,000 feet good.'

This report puts the action precisely in the area in which Wittgenstein was shot down and, which is equally important, at within a measurable distance of the correct time. If it were Snape who was responsible for the death of the Prince, it would be ironical: Wittgenstein had himself, as mentioned earlier, once shot down a Lancaster that was burning its navigation lights. Perhaps human fallibility had played a part in the death of the man who had striven so hard to be infallible.

The month went out with three more heavy attacks on Berlin, on 27/28, 28/29 and 30/31 January respectively. Considerable damage was caused to the capital, even though the bombing was still not concentrated, and something like a quarter of a million people were bombed out. The most successful raid of the three was that of 28/29 January, when there was scattered cloud and some visual marking was possible. Bomber Command losses were over six per cent each night, a total of 112 heavies failing to return from the 1,726 dispatched. Among the heavies lost, Wim Johnen got four on the twenty-seventh, and Peter Spoden two, Spoden adding another to his score on the thirtieth to bring his total to nine. The same night Otto Kutzner claimed his sixth victim. A former German night-fighter pilot who still recalls the night of 27/28 January 1944 with deep sadness is Wilhelm Seuss:

'There was a very high wind that night, about 180 kilometres an hour, and I couldn't get back to our base at Erfurt. And my radio operator, Bruno Zakrzewski, didn't have the right radio papers with him. I called SOS when we were in the Leipzig area, and I decided we would have to bale out. We had been in the air over three hours, and the petrol warning lights were on. What I didn't know was that my flight mechanic pulled his parachute while he was still in the aircraft. He didn't tell me. I jettisoned the cabin roof, stood up and sat on the top of the exit preparatory to abandoning the machine, and he called, "Herr Leutnant, Herr Leutnant, I can't get out!" We were very low, and there was nothing I could do. I pushed the stick forward and was catapulted out. My *Mechaniker* went down with the aircraft. It was a frightful experience for me. I came down near Merseburg.'

After his eventful trip to Magdeburg the previous week, Horace Pearce found himself briefed to attack Berlin on the night of 28/29 January. He would be flying Halifax Mk V, serial number LK 731, KN-K, which he had taken to Magdeburg, and he found himself hoping that it would be a lucky aircraft. Some few weeks earlier Horace, acting as aerodrome control pilot, had witnessed a collision between 'K' from his Squadron, No. 77, and 'K' from No. 102 Squadron at neighbouring Pocklington: then Squadron Leader Bickerdike, captain of Terry Bolter's crew, had been lost flying the replacement 'K'. The belief that some aircraft were jinxed was strong among aircrew. Horace Pearce need not have worried: in his log book is written, '*Peaceful trip*', although 'peaceful' is not an adjective that many would choose to describe a flight of eight-and-a-half hours, most of it over Nazi-occupied Europe, running the gauntlet of enemy fighters and the *Flak* above the most heavily defended city in Germany. And uneventful as it was for Pearce and his crew, the same cannot be said for the Squadron as a whole. No. 77 lost another four Halifaxes to add to the five it had lost on the Magdeburg raid. Within a week sixty-three young aircrew from No. 77 had been written off. Nearly eleven per cent of the Halifaxes sent on the operation failed to return.

After a week's leave and a few hours' flying as H2S instructor with new crews while waiting for a pilot with whom to complete his tour of operations, John Chaloner found himself back on the Battle Order on the night of 30 January. The target was Berlin, and he was flying with a different pilot, Warrant Officer Trevor Jupp, himself nearly tour-expired, and the two gunners from his old crew, Percy and Fred, were in the turrets, Percy now recovered from the wounds he had sustained on the Mannheim operation in September. After bombing the sky markers over the German capital, Jupp's aircraft was attacked twice by a Bf 110 night fighter, but fortunately Percy and Fred gave their pilot 'corkscrew' instructions in good time and then engaged the enemy machine with their .303 machine-guns, so that the Lancaster and its crew came through unscathed, while the Bf 110 was claimed as damaged. Flight Sergeant John Chaloner had now flown on twenty-five operations, ten of them to Berlin, and soon afterwards he learned that he had been commissioned. He could now remove the three stripes and crown from the sleeve of his battledress and replace them with a thin length of braid on his shoulder-straps. On 17 February he ordered a best uniform and raincoat, which would cost him a total of £13.10.0d., and the next day he went to Lincoln and spent a further £13.5.1d. on four shirts, four pairs of socks, a pair of braces, a pair of pyjamas, two vests and two pairs of underpants. As a Pilot Officer his pay was under a pound a day, for which splendid sum he, like thousands of other young men, put his life at stake without question as often as he was called upon to do so.

After the Berlin attack on the final night of January, Harris did not mount any major raids on Germany for fourteen days. Losses had been heavy, particularly to his Halifax squadrons, and a short pause would give him the opportunity of building his forces and considering new tactics. So the first two weeks of February 1944 passed without any major raids, although Serrate patrols, Mosquitos of the Light Night Striking Force, mine-layers and supply flights for resistance groups in occupied territory ensured that the German defences were kept on the alert and much of the civilian population in the shelters. No. 617 Squadron, the 'Dam Busters', now under the command of Wing Commander Leonard Cheshire, carried out two raids by night during this period, one on 8/9 February against the Gnôme & Rhône aircraft engine factory at Limoges and one four nights later against a railway viaduct at Anthéor in the Maritime Alps between France and Italy. Since the epic raid on the Ruhr dams the squadron had been endeavouring to find a solution to the problem of accurately marking and bombing precision targets. So far they had used Oboe-equipped Mosquitos to drop markers, but success had eluded them. Cheshire believed that the answer was to mark visually from a very low level, and now he was putting his theory to the test. The first raid, by twelve Lancasters, was an excellent example of precision marking and bombing, and severe damage was done to the factory. The defences, however, were very light. Cheshire went in low, identified the target and flew backwards and forwards over it to alert the French workers and give them a chance to vacate the buildings. Then, on his fourth run, he dropped his load of 30 lb phosphorus incendiary bombs and Red Spot fires, and ten of the other eleven Lancasters each dropped their 12,000 lb HE bomb from high level precisely on to the target. The eleventh bomb missed by a short distance. It was a perfectly executed raid, and the factory was almost completely destroyed, while casualties to civilians were minimal.

In contrast, the attack on the strategically important Anthéor viaduct was unsuccessful. The target, spanning a small, steep-sided bay on the Italian coast, was heavily defended, so that both Cheshire's aircraft and that of his deputy, Squadron Leader Harold 'Mick' Martin, were damaged by gunfire, with Martin himself being wounded and his bomb aimer killed, so that Martin had to make for Corsica and land there. Despite extreme gallantry on the part of Cheshire, who made six runs over the target under intense light anti-aircraft fire before dropping his markers, the viaduct was not hit by the nine Lancasters that were carrying the 12,000-pound 'blockbusters'. There still seemed to be no strategic alternative to the comparatively crude, high-level marking of targets either by Oboe or, at long range, by H2S-equipped PFF aircraft, followed by saturation bombing to ensure the maximum possible destruction over a broad area on the ground.

In the late afternoon of 15 February 1944 Harris sent a massive force against Berlin, 891 aircraft that included 561 Lancasters and 314 Halifaxes, the maximum offensive strength he could achieve. It was numerically the largest armada of heavy bombers since the thousand-bomber raids in mid-1942, but whereas the total weight of bombs dropped on Cologne on 30/31 May 1942 had been 1,455 tons, the 875 four-engined heavies now carried almost 2,700 tons over the much further distance to the German capital, over three tons per machine on average. In addition to the main raid Mosquitos were out attacking *Luftwaffe* night-fighter bases and flying Serrate patrols, Stirlings and Halifaxes were mine-laying in Kiel Bay, there were RCM flights by No. 100 Group, and a small force of twenty-four Lancasters carried out a diversionary raid on Frankfurt/Oder, sixty miles to the east of Berlin.

Berlin's suffering continued, but the suffering was not nearly enough to break the morale of its people; nor was the damage so far inflicted by Bomber Command sufficient to cause the German government to give serious thought to surrender. There had been extensive evacuation of civilians from the city into the countryside, and many government offices, damaged and undamaged, were also moved to less vulnerable locations. Throughout Germany, including Berlin, there had already been widespread relocation of strategically important industries, so that even the extensive damage to factories that had inevitably resulted from the bombing did not have a decisive effect on production. The raid on 15/16 February continued the routine, almost ritual, pounding of the Big City, and followed the long-established pattern: cloud cover, heavy but unconcentrated bombing, vast damage to civilian premises and some damage to industrial property, many bombs outside the city limits.

John Chaloner went to Berlin yet again. This time Warrant Officer Jupp was carrying two Australian gunners, Warrant Officer Allwood and Flight Sergeant Hobbs, and Chaloner was favourably impressed by their aggressive approach. 'This,' he comments, 'was a whole new ball game. They were as keen as mustard! You really felt secure with old Juppy's gunners!' While many air gunners, Percy and Fred among them, believed that to fire on a German fighter unless it was attacking you was to risk attracting retribution, the two Australians would 'have a go' at anything that came within range. As far as details of the trip go, John Chaloner has no strong recollections. It was a quiet trip. What he does recall, however, is that it was his last to the most dreaded target of all, Berlin. Since starting his tour the previous August he had done twenty-six operations, eleven of them to Berlin. On those eleven trips alone, 340 heavy bombers had been lost, while approaching 2,400 aircrew did not come back.

The luck that had accompanied John stayed with him on the next major attack that was mounted against a German city, Leipzig, on the night of 19/20 February.

This was one of the most costly raids of the war for Bomber Command. Harris dispatched 561 Lancasters, 255 Halifaxes and seven Mosquitos, and seventy-eight of the heavies failed to return, a daunting 9.5 per cent of the total that took part. Of the Halifaxes, thirty-four were lost, 13.3 per cent, while a further twenty-seven turned back before reaching enemy territory. The loss rate to the Lancasters, at 7.8 per cent, was also severe. Of the Halifaxes lost, the greater proportion were older Mk II and Mk V machines, and the attrition to these inferior aircraft forced Harris to issue an order banning them completely from operations against German targets from then on.

It was a successful night for the German night-fighters, although a diversionary mining raid to Kiel Bay by Stirlings and Halifaxes drew off a small number of the defenders. Again airfields in Holland were attacked by Mosquitos, but nevertheless the German controller was able to feed his first fighters into the bomber stream before it crossed the coast. The *Flak* too had a better-than-average night. The tail-wind that the bombers experienced was much stronger than had been forecast, so that many of the main force arrived over Leipzig before the Pathfinder machines, whose navigators had calculated their time-on-target with their accustomed precision. The anti-aircraft guns claimed twenty bombers, many of them while they were circling and waiting for the PFF markers to go down. Unexpected cloud over the target meant that the Pathfinders had to use sky-marking rather than the ground-marking that had been planned. The sky markers disappeared rapidly into the cloud, leaving nothing for the main force bomb aimers to aim at, and the resulting attack was very scattered. The success of the *Nachtjagd* was to a considerable extent due to a high-flying *Luft-beobachterflugzeug* – air observation aircraft – being able to ascertain and broadcast the course of the bomber stream from the moment it crossed in over the northern coast of Holland, so that the Tame Boar fighters could be infiltrated early. In addition, single-seater Wild Boars were able gather over Berlin. Victories on the part of the *Nachtjagd* included five each by Oberfeldwebel Heinz Vinke and Feldwebel Rudolph Frank. Hauptmann Paul Zorner destroyed one Lancaster and three Halifaxes within the space of thirty minutes, bringing his total score to thirty.

John Chaloner remembers the fighter flares:

> 'We were just flying along, and this Dornier 217 was dropping flares along our route, running parallel with us, and there was a rattle of machine-gun fire, and the rear gunner, Phil Allwood, had shot it down. I thought, "We don't do this! Percy doesn't do this sort of thing!" This was before the target. As I visualise it, we were somewhere over the north German plain. From about two hundred miles out we used to fly to the target along the fighter flares! And he had no hesitation – he just shot the damn thing down! This was a whole new world. I thought I could do three tours with this lot! Because when we had Percy and Fred, we just used to creep about!'

John Chaloner's tour was nearing its end. Against the odds, he was still alive, and now he was only three short of the magic number of thirty. The remaining nine nights of February saw just that number of major attacks on Germany, all of them to long-range targets – Stuttgart, Schweinfurt and Augsburg respectively

– and John flew on all of them. For John, Stuttgart was a routine flight: 'Bad weather. Snow in fields clearly visible. Quiet trip.' Indeed, it was a quiet trip for Bomber Command as a whole, costing only nine bombers. Harris was increasingly experimenting with tactics designed to mislead the enemy night-fighter defences, and for this attack, on 20/21 February, he first sent a large force of training and front-line aircraft over the North Sea as a feint to draw off the fighters, while seven Mosquitos, Windowing heavily to simulate a larger force, went to Munich. The now established pattern of Mosquito attacks on fighter airfields continued. Cloud cover again bedevilled both the Pathfinders and the main force, but considerable, if scattered, damage, was caused.

In an infrequent example of close Allied bombing co-operation, 734 Bomber Command machines set out to attack ball-bearing works at Schweinfurt in southern Germany on the night of 24 February. The previous day nearly 300 Fortresses of the US 8th Air Force had attacked the same factories as part of their 'Big Week' operations, losing eleven bombers and ten escort fighters. Spaatz had also sent lesser forces to Steyr in Austria and to Gotha, and these missions had suffered considerably, losing a total of fifty-two. At Schweinfurt, the American and British raids caused considerable damage, but the ball-bearing works had already been severely damaged by earlier US attacks, capacity there considerably reduced and production dispersed, so the strategic results of the February 1944 attacks were less than had been hoped.

For the attack on Schweinfurt Harris introduced a new tactic by sending two separate main forces to the target two hours apart, the first one of 392 aircraft, the second of 342. Bomber Command lost a total of thirty-three aircraft, of which Paul Zorner destroyed five Lancasters, all of which crashed in the Stuttgart area. Another Lancaster that was nearly shot down in an encounter with a night-fighter was that of Warrant Officer Jupp, recently decorated with the Distinguished Flying Cross. But it was not a *Luftwaffe* fighter that almost put an end to Jupp's crew, including John Chaloner, but an RAF one:

'On the twenty-fourth we were going to Schweinfurt, and that's when we were shot up over Brighton and landed at Wittering. We were shot up by a Mosquito on the way out! "Friendly fire", that was! We were routed out by Beachy Head, and the bomb aimer was saying, "There's searchlights on us," and I thought that that was no problem – they could recognise a Lanc – and the next minute there were explosions in the cockpit, and it transpired that a Mosquito had come up on us. The gunners could see the Mosquito on our tail, but they didn't do anything about it. It hit underneath our aircraft, because it cut the oxygen pipe and demolished the P10 compass. Pressing on was out of the question, so we had to turn back. We had a problem, because London was being attacked by the Germans at the same time. We didn't have much option, so we turned back right across London, went to the Wash, and dropped our bombs there. There were searchlights and a bit of flak over London, but nothing like Germany. We made for Wittering, which was an American base at the time; I think they had Lightnings there. I don't think they had a runway at the time, either. And I remember when we went out the next day to pick our aeroplane up there was a Fortress parked up alongside us, and the nose of the aircraft had been blown away

– it was when the German day-fighters were doing head-on attacks – and they'd hit the bomb aimer, and there was all blood and brains and things smeared about.'

On the night of 25/26 February 1944 Harris attacked the historic Bavarian city of Augsburg. Augsburg had never suffered a major attack before, although there had been an abortive strike against the MAN diesel engine works there in April 1942, when the officer leading the attack, Squadron Leader J. D. Nettleton, had earned the Victoria Cross. Although controversial, because Augsburg seemed to have only slight attraction as a strategic target, the raid in 1944, Chaloner's last, was, by contemporary standards, a great success. Harris again sent two waves of bombers with diversionary, harassing and intruder support, so that only twenty-one of the 594 aircraft participating were lost. In exchange, the centre of Augsburg was devastated. It was a clear night, and the Pathfinders were able to mark visually and accurately, while the comparatively light anti-aircraft defences meant that the bomb aimers in the main force aircraft completed their bombing run more conscientiously than they sometimes did when the flak was more daunting. This was, in German eyes, terror bombing pure and simple. To John Chaloner it was a high note on which to end his tour. According to his diary, 'Marvellous trip, no navigation aids – looking for Lake Constance. Three minutes early. Went in with PFF. Newhaven visual markers. Town clearly visible, even hamlets at crossroads. Hit south-east edge of city.' In his log book he noted, 'Bombed river junction in town visually,' and today he recollects:

> 'We could see Augsburg on fire. We were on the second attack: there were about 400 aircraft on the target about midnight and another 400 on the target at four o'clock in the morning. Something like that. And they dropped about 2,000 tons. I was on the second wave, and by the time we got down to Lake Constance we could see Augsburg on fire. And we came up to Augsburg, and it was as clear as daylight on the ground, and we just bombed visually at our own convenience. It was just a piece of cake, really.'

The following day the officer's 'best blue' that John had ordered was delivered, and in April he was able to have the purple and silver ribbon of the Distinguished Flying Medal sewn above the left breast pocket.

Harris's tactical changes – in addition to splitting his force more than previously he was discontinuing the use of route markers, which attracted fighters, and using more southerly routes whenever possible, because the fighter opposition seemed to be much stronger in the north – appeared to be having some effect on his casualties, which showed signs of diminishing. Whereas the average losses against major German targets in January had been 6.5 per cent, and those for the first two similar raids in February seven per cent, the average for the final three in February – Stuttgart, Schweinfurt and Augsburg – was only 3.3 per cent. Harris was encouraged: in *Bomber Offensive* he writes, 'The effect of these new tactics was almost immediate,' but once more he seems to have been a victim of his own optimism. Three raids with a reduced casualty ratio would not qualify statistically as even a trend, as the following month would show with chilling clarity.

The black month of March began with a further encouraging attack on Stuttgart, with only four aircraft being lost from a force of 557. Bad weather conditions on the ground meant that the Messerschmitts and Junkers of the night-fighter force failed to locate the stream. Despite cloud over the target considerable damage was done to the town, with major industrial installations sharing in the suffering. Then it was the moon period, and attacks on long-range targets were suspended until the 15th/16th of the month, when Stuttgart was again bombed. This time the fighters found the stream, if rather late, and thirty-seven heavies failed to return.

Targets in France, with the invasion in the offing, were attracting a greater proportion of Bomber Command's efforts, and, as might be expected, these trips were comparatively risk-free for the crews. The bulk of the night-fighter force was deployed to defend the *Reich*, there was less time for the reporting organisation to locate the bomber stream and there were fewer and less powerful anti-aircraft guns to protect likely targets in France. From 1,085 sorties against important French targets in France between 2 and 14 March, only one Lancaster and one Halifax were lost. Operations in direct support of the coming invasion began on the night of 6/7 March, when a highly accurate and effective raid was mounted without loss on the strategically important railway marshalling yards at Trappes, and a further successful strike was made the following night against railway yards at Le Mans, also without the loss of a single machine from the 304 taking part. In addition to attacking main targets, aircraft of Bomber Command were also out every night except one during this period laying mines, carrying out nuisance raids, ECM sorties, supply flights for the Resistance and so on. Berlin was a regular destination for Mosquitos, which hit the capital and other German cities without loss to themselves. But the diminution in losses, if encouraging to the crews and to the senior command, was illusory. There was still much blood to be spilled before April came.

Extensive damage was caused to the city of Frankfurt in the course of two raids by Bomber Command on 18/19 and 22/23 March, each time involving more than 800 heavy bombers plus a small number of Mosquitos. Of the total of 1,662 four-engined bombers deployed, fifty-five failed to return, at an average of 3.3 per cent still on the low side for a major German target. In the course of the second visit to Frankfurt Hauptmann Martin Becker of I./NJG 6 and his radio man, Karl-Ludwig Johanssen, flying from Mainz-Finthen, accounted for six bombers. Of the six, Johanssen destroyed three with his puny rearward-firing machine-gun. Like his fallen namesake, Ludwig, 'Tino' Becker was proving himself to be a redoubtable enemy; now he was spoken of in night-fighting circles as the rising star of the *Nachtjagd*. Paul Zorner, by now well established as an ace, achieved two further kills, his thirty-sixth and thirty-seventh.

Zorner's thirty-eighth victim fell to his guns two nights later, at 2253 hrs on 24 March, but the unfortunate Lancaster proved a tenacious opponent: it took Zorner five attacks, three from below with *Schräge Musik* and two from a hundred metres astern, before it finally succumbed. The target that night was Berlin once more, with Harris sending 811 bombers in his final effort against the capital in what was later called the Battle of Berlin. Whether Harris intended that that would be the case, or whether the decision was forced upon him by the cumulative losses he incurred in his attacks, is unclear. Whatever the truth, the hammering that the Bomber Command force suffered on that night cannot have failed to have its effect on even the seemingly unshakeable Commander-in-Chief: 8.9 per cent of the force, forty-four Lancasters and twenty-eight Halifaxes, were lost, together with the lives of about a further 600 young aircrew. From the point of view of the effect of the raid, it was much the same story as before, with great damage being done to property in a diffuse attack and many of the bombs missing the metropolitan area completely, some falling in small settlements outside Berlin and many in open countryside. High winds from the north scattered the bomber stream at all stages of the route, showing once more that the position-finding aids available to the navigators were incapable of coping with unpredictable meteorological conditions. Unusually, this night the majority of Bomber Command losses seems to have fallen to the *Flak* rather than to the fighters, a result of off-course bombers straying over heavily defended areas, including the Ruhr.

Oboe Mosquitos marked Essen for 683 heavies on the night of 26/27 March, with only nine failing to return. The marking was accurate, and in a successful attack considerable damage was done to property, a high proportion of which was industrial in nature. A further force of seventy Halifaxes and thirty-two Stirlings, plus seven Pathfinder Mosquitos, went without loss to the short-range target of Courtrai in Belgium, briefed to bomb railway installations there. Surprisingly, the attack was less accurate than that on Essen, considerable damage being done to civilian property, and 252 people being killed. Some damage was caused to the targets themselves, but the railway line was open again within three days. There was another surprising, if daunting for the *Luftwaffe,* aspect to this night's operations. While the night-fighter force could claim only eight victories, they themselves lost twenty machines. Presumably the majority of these were victims of RAF air gunners, and possibly some due to German *flak*, because the Serrate aircraft of No. 100 Group made no claims except for one Ju 88 damaged in the vicinity of Essen. Of the eight kills made by the *Nachtjagd*, Paul Zorner claimed three Lancasters and one was claimed by Wilhelm Seuss of IV./NJG 5. It was Seuss's second kill, his first with *Schräge Musik*. It was, he says, so simple. He was flying a borrowed aircraft – his own machine had not yet been fitted with the upward-firing cannon – and all he had to do was to slide beneath his victim and aim between the two port engines. He does not know why the port side was preferred, but says that it was something that had been firmly implanted in his mind by other successful pilots.

After the heavy losses on the Berlin raid two nights previously, the modest 1.3 per cent toll against Essen was a relief. Perhaps Harris's tactical manoeuvres were indeed paying off, and the attrition on 24/25 March had been an aberration. On 30 March, Harris launched a maximum-effort raid by just under 800 bombers to attack the Bavarian city of Nuremberg, a prime target for both its industrial and, by reason of its close association with Nazism, its political significance. Six squadrons from No. 8 (Pathfinder) Group and forty-one main force squadrons participated. Twenty Mosquitos of No. 100 Group flew Serrate missions, while a further thirty-five Mosquitos from No. 2 Group went on intruder operations, attacking enemy airfields and carrying out spoof attacks on towns in the Ruhr area. Fifty-plus heavy bombers laid mines south of Heligoland, their approach coinciding with that of the main force in the hope that night-fighter attention might be diverted.

Much has been written about this raid, which developed into a disaster for Bomber Command. Suffice it to say that unusually the raid was mounted in conditions of moonlight and that the route chosen took the attacking bombers on long, easily plotted legs across areas readily accessible to the night-fighters. Particularly open to question was a two-hundred-mile straight leg from about thirty miles south of Brussels to another point slightly further to the north of the target, where the force was to turn south. In fairness to the planners, however, it is hard to think of an alternative route that would have seemed to be less fraught with danger. By reason of its geographical position Nuremberg was a very hazardous target to reach, because any more or less direct approach would of necessity have to take the bombers either right across the night-fighter concentrations in Holland and north Germany or through the gap between the heavy *flak* defences of the Ruhr and the Frankfurt area. Harris also wished to conceal the identity of his target from the German defences, in the hope that the night fighter force would be sent off in the wrong direction. The possibility must exist that until then British Air Intelligence had not fully understood the way in which the German night-fighter system had developed, with *Zahme Sau*, the infiltration of the bomber stream, having assumed the major role and *Wilde Sau*, the concentration of fighters over the target, falling into disfavour.

The weather too played its part. It seems that early meteorological forecasts had predicted high cloud that would dim the effect of the almost-full moon, and the attack had been planned on that basis; it was not, however, cancelled when a weather-reconnaissance flight reported that the expected high cloud would not in fact develop and that the target, which had originally been confidently expected to be free of cloud, would in fact be covered. With the change in cloud conditions came a change from the forecast wind, which eventually resulted in a scattering of the bomber stream.

By monitoring RAF radio, R/T and H2S activity in the course of air and ground testing by bomber squadrons during the morning and afternoon of the thirtieth, the Germans predicted quite early that a major attack was scheduled for that night. This came as something of a surprise, given the moon conditions, and it was expected that the attack would be a short-range one, possibly against the Ruhr. German night-fighters were brought up to readiness in the early evening, and shortly before eleven o'clock the forward radars picked up the leading aircraft. The original direction of the bombers, south-east from the Schelde Estuary, seemed to confirm early expectations that the Ruhr would again be the target, and fighters were scrambled with that possibility in mind. At that stage, unhappily for the RAF and Commonwealth crews of Bomber Command, whether the target was in the Ruhr area or further east mattered little. The German controller's task was to get his fighters into the stream, and he did that with success. The heavy concentration of Window being dropped by the attackers to jam the enemy radars on the ground, while still to a large extent hiding individual aircraft, painted a clear picture of the bombers' track. By this period, too, more fighters were carrying *SN-2* interception radar, still impervious to Window, and more and more were armed with the deadly *Schräge Musik*, the existence of which was still unsuspected by the crews in the heavy bombers – even, it seems, by the intelligence officers of Bomber Command.

The first interceptions took place soon after the bombers had turned east-wards on to the long leg to Bavaria. In the many analyses, not to say blame-casting exercises, of the Nuremberg operation, much has been made of the fact that the planned route took the bombers very close to a night-fighter beacon, '*Ida*', at Bonn-Hangelar. In fact, there were two beacons of that name, the visual one usually quoted and a radio one south-east of Aachen: but the significance of the route's proximity to beacons has been much overdone, in that it would have been impossible to plot any route across Germany that did not pass very near to one type or other. It was however tactically correct for the German controller, as he did, to direct his night-fighter *Gruppen* in the first place to *Ida* and to *Otto*, near to Frankfurt and also very close to the attackers' track. As the embattled force moved on, with more and more fighters converging on it, another meteorological quirk came into play. Some of the bombers, flying in clear air, developed condensation trails, which clearly marked the direction in which the stream was heading.

By the time those bombers that reached the target area had released their bombs, about eighty Lancasters and Halifaxes had been shot down, the over-whelming majority by fighters. So scattered had the bomber force become – largely as a result of the inaccurate wind forecasting but also partly because some crews, witnessing the carnage around them, intentionally diverted from the planned track – that the bombing, which took place through cloud that defeated the efforts of both PFF and Main Force to aim precisely, was lamentably widely scattered, so much so that the Germans failed fully to identify Nuremberg as the main target. Many crews, for example, bombed in the Schweinfurt area, sixty miles to the north. Additionally, the 'creep-back' effect was very marked. The damage to the main target, Nuremberg, was minimal.

The confusion among the Germans as to the precise objective of the Bomber Command attack had one effect beneficial to the RAF crews. The single-engined Wild Boar fighters of JG 300, JG 301 and JG 302, whose practice it was to con-verge on the target and pick off the bombers there, were largely ineffectual that night. Had the attack been more concentrated, and had the *Wilde Sau* machines been able to join in the hunt more effectively, Bomber Command losses might have been even higher. Some single-engined fighters did, nevertheless, find their way into the stream, and they were responsible for the shooting down of two bombers. Against that, three Wild Boar pilots were killed, Oberfeldwebel Willy Rose of III./JG 301, and Oberfeldwebel Friedrich Hill and Unteroffizier Erwin Völkel of III./JG 302. III./JG 302 had been scrambled early from Oldenburg when it had been thought by the raid plotters that the target was likely to be the Ruhr, III./JG 301 later from Zerbst, near Magdeburg, when it was clear that the attackers were penetrating deep into Germany.

The fighters took a further toll of the much-scattered bomber force on its homeward route, so that the final official figure failing to return was only five short of a hundred. A further nine machines crashed in England, including one flown by Pilot Officer Cyril Barton of No. 578 Squadron, whose Halifax came down near Ryhope in County Durham and who was posthumously awarded the Victoria Cross. Many bombers came back damaged, some with gravely wounded crew members on board. There were few squadrons flying that night that suffered neither loss nor damage, while some experienced dauntingly heavy casualties. No. 101 Squadron lost six Lancasters, No. 51 Squadron five Halifaxes, while Nos. 514 and 158 Squadrons each lost four aircraft.

There had been rich pickings for the *Nachtjagd* as a whole, and several pilots achieved multiple kills. Prominent among them was Oberleutnant Martin Becker of I./NJG 6. Piloting a Bf 110 without *Schräge Musik*, Tino Becker was early in the stream and within thirty minutes he had shot down three Lancasters and three Halifaxes, equalling his score during the attack on Frankfurt the previous week. But he still had one victory to come; after his first batch of successes he landed at Mainz/Finthen, refuelled and took off again. This time he was controlled by one of the largely out-of-fashion *Himmelbett* controllers into contact with a homeward-bound Halifax, which he dispatched with his cannon, bringing his score for the night to seven. His final victim of the series was Halifax LK800 of No. 429 (Bison) Squadron, No. 6 (Canadian) Group, that had taken off from Leeming, Yorkshire, flown by Pilot Officer K. H. Bowly. All the crew were able to bale out before their machine crashed south of Luxembourg, five being taken prisoner and two evading successfully and returning to Britain. Soon afterwards Martin Becker received the coveted Knight's Cross to the Iron Cross from the hands of Adolf Hitler.

Leutnant Wilhelm Seuss, the self-avowed 'coward' mentioned earlier, made four kills. He recalls the night:

'I was in the 11th *Staffel* of NJG 5, and we were at Erfurt. I was due to go on leave the following day, and I was anxious to get away. I calculated that if there hadn't been an alert by eleven they wouldn't be coming, and I would be able to go off early next morning. In any case, I was pretty confident there wouldn't be a raid, because of the moon, even though a Mosquito had flown over towards Leipzig in the afternoon. When we were ordered to readiness I was astounded, I wondered what was going on. *"Ich habe meinen Koffer nach Mond gepackt."* – "I had packed my suitcase according to the moon".

'My log book shows that I took off at 2317 hours, which means that the alert must have come through about eleven, and we were sent to a radio beacon near to Offenbach – I believe it was *"Otto"*. As soon as I arrived I could see the first Pathfinder flares, and then I could see the first bombers going down, one after the other. I flew along, following the crashes on the ground, and I saw a Lancaster in a searchlight, and I shot it down. I could have picked up bombers on my *SN-2*, but it wasn't necessary. The stream was tightly concentrated, and I shot down two more very quickly. Then I saw another, and I got under him, but my *Schräge Musik* was out of ammunition, and my *Funker* had to change the drum. It took three or four minutes, and I stayed under the *Viermot*, and he didn't see me. Then, just as I fired, he dived to one side and flew through my burst of cannon fire, and he began to burn immediately.

'I could have stayed in the stream and shot down even more, but I had simply had enough. My nerves were completely gone, and I thought that if I carried on I would be endangering my crew. So I went back and landed at Erfurt. And after I had landed a Mosquito came and attacked the airfield, and my 110 got a hole through the airscrew.'

Another German flyer who has a clear memory of the night of the Nuremberg attack is Walter Heidenreich who, as described earlier, had been radio operator to Oberleutnant Günther Köberich since April 1942. By now Köberich's score had risen to twelve, including an American Liberator he had shot down by day on 18 November 1943. On 15 March 1944 the Köberich/Heidenreich combination had destroyed three Lancasters during the attack on Stuttgart. Now they were serving with II./NJG 2 and flying a Ju 88-R2, equipped with *SN-2* and *Schräge Musik*, from Quakenbrück, north of Münster. Köberich was enthusiastic about the upward-firing cannon. Heading south from Quakenbrück, Köberich had reached the Cologne area when Heidenreich got a signal on his *SN-2* and instructed his pilot to follow it. They overtook only slowly, and as the signal strengthened Heidenreich saw that there was something unusual about it. The shape was all wrong. The first pick-up had been at a range of about five kilometres, and when they eventually closed to below one kilometre they got a visual sighting and realised why the radar blip had been strange: there were two Lancasters flying very close to each other, side by side. Köberich brought the Junkers in from astern and below, taking advantage of the dark ground beneath to hide his machine from the view of the Lancasters' gunners. Soon he had one of the bombers in the *Revi* sight in the roof of the cabin, and he gave a short burst. For some inexplicable reason tracer ammunition had been loaded into the *Schräge Musik* cannon, and Heidenreich was momentarily blinded. *Schräge Musik* usually fired non-tracer ammunition to avoid dazzling the crew and to prevent the fighter being seen by the target aircraft. Every shot went home, and the Lancaster caught fire. Köberich pulled away to one side in case the bomber should explode and slid in beneath the second *Viermot*. A further short burst, and that too caught fire. 'For quite a time,' says Heidenreich, 'the two of them went straight ahead, both on fire. Then one went off to the left and crashed on the right-hand bank of the Rhine, and the other crashed on the other bank. When they hit they seemed to burst in all directions, with all sorts of colours, reds and greens and yellows. I think they were Pathfinder machines. We landed somewhere else, and so we didn't get confirmation. I don't know whether they were found, and I don't know whether any of the crews managed to get out, but I think they probably had time to.'

There was in fact only one survivor, the wireless operator of one of the machines, who managed to bale out. As Heidenreich assumed, they were Pathfinder aircraft, both from No. 156 Squadron at Upwood, two of the four Lancasters that that Squadron lost that night. One was piloted by an Australian Warrant Officer, Jack Murphy, the other by a Captain in the Norwegian Air Force, Finn Johnsen. Both were experienced bomber pilots, with Murphy being on his fiftieth operation.

Few would maintain that, taken in isolation, the Nuremberg raid did not represent a clear defeat for Bomber Command. But what of the so-called Battle of Berlin, of which the Nuremberg operation was Harris's last attack? Views differ. The official historians, Sir Charles Webster and Dr Noble Frankland DFC, himself a navigator with Bomber Command during the war, are in no doubt: ' . . . in the operational sense, the Battle of Berlin was more than a failure. It was a defeat.'[1] Group Captain Dudley Saward OBE, chief radar officer at Bomber Command from 1942 onward, takes the opposite view in his biography of his former Commander-in-Chief: 'The suggestion that the Berlin campaign was a failure is not supported by the facts. An examination of the results reveals not failure but success . . .'[2]

A great deal has been written for and against both points of view, and the more that is written the more dogmatically sides are taken in the argument, the more attempts are made to simplify an enormously complex equation, the less clear the issue becomes. Vast damage was done to Berlin and other centres of industry and population, and the cost to Bomber Command in men and machines was heavy. Harris was the victim of his own tendency to make sweeping statements to support his unswerving faith in the bombing of cities, and much has been made of the fact that although the first part of the Commander-in-Chief's prognosis was correct, with 466 heavy bombers failing to return from attacks on Berlin alone between November 1943 and March 1944, the second part was, in the short term, demonstrably wrong. Harris said that the attacks on Berlin would win the war, goes the argument, and they didn't; that proves that the Battle of Berlin was a defeat. In fact, it proves nothing of the sort. What it proves is quite simply that Harris made a rash forecast, and that forecast was shown to be wrong.

The other side of the argument, as expounded by, *inter alia*, Dudley Saward, gathers together the statistics for damage done to industrial and other war-related premises in Berlin, adds up the unquantifiable effect of the bombing on German morale, sets that against the losses suffered by Bomber Command, and comes down in favour of a victory by Harris. There is no simple answer. There must be elements of truth in both contentions. It would be just over another year before Germany surrendered, but who can say with any certainty how much longer the war might have lasted had not Bomber Command carried out Harris's area-bombing policy, uncompromisingly ruthless as it was? And what, it is fair to ask, if only rhetorically, was the alternative? As the Battle of Berlin, not to speak of the totality of experience of night bombing over the past four-and-a-half years, had clearly demonstrated, Bomber Command was simply not yet in a position, despite Gee, Oboe, H2S and the Pathfinder Force, to find and hit anything but close-range targets with any degree of accuracy. But does that mean that Harris should simply have given up carrying the war to the enemy?

---

[1]   The Official History, Part II , Chapter 5, page 193.
[2]   *'Bomber' Harris* by Dudley Saward, first published 1984 by Cassell Ltd and Buchan & Enright Ltd, Chapter 19.

Above left: Göring meets Nachtjäger at Neuruppin. *(Szardenings)*

Above right: Anne-Marie Masson-Potier in dress made from the silk of Sergeant Charlesworth's parachute. *(Charlesworth)*

Below: Flight Lieutenant Oliver Brooks of No.XV Squadron is decorated with the DFC by King George VI. Queen Elizabeth (now the Queen Mother) and Princess Elizabeth (now Queen Elizabeth II) may be seen in the group to the left. *(Brooks)*

Below: Krupps Steel Works, Essen, from the air at the end of the War, a testimony to the hitting-power of Bomber Command. *(Smith)*

CHAPTER ELEVEN

The Run-up to Overlord

April to June 1944

In December 1943, when the final decision had been taken to invade the Continent of Europe within the measurable future, General Dwight David Eisenhower had been nominated as Supreme Allied Commander, taking up his appointment the following month. Air Chief Marshal Sir Arthur Tedder became his deputy shortly afterwards. With effect from 14 April 1944, in preparation for the invasion, Operation 'Overlord', the Combined British and American Bomber Forces were put under Eisenhower's control. This did not, however, mean that there was an abrupt change in bombing policy. Already, with the invasion clearly not a long distance in the future and the V-weapon threat increasing, a shift from targets in Germany to targets in France had begun. Included in these latter targets were those falling within the so-called 'transportation plan', aimed at disrupting enemy supply lines, and Bomber Command, with the assistance of Mosquitos carrying the remarkable short-range electronic aid Oboe, and with the more recently introduced device, Gee-H, had demonstrated that, given the right conditions, the Lancasters and Halifaxes were capable of a surprisingly high degree of precision by night against targets within range of these new radars. So it was that the transition from Harris's all-out attack on German cities to the use of Bomber Command in direct support of the preparations for invasion was a comparatively gradual one.

Throughout 1943 the *Luftwaffe* High Command had more and more been shifting fighter units from base to base at very short notice, sometimes even daily, in an attempt tactically to counter the mounting threat presented by both the United States Air Force and Bomber Command; now, with the increasing incidence of raids on targets in occupied France and the realisation that invasion could not be long delayed, the trend was to bring units forward into France and Belgium. This frequently meant, for example, moving *Gruppen* geographically from *Luftflotte Reich*, responsible for the defence of the Fatherland, to *Luftflotte 3*, covering France. It also often meant that units came under the tactical control of divisions other than those to which they were organisationally subordinate, so that the redeployment resulted in no little confusion in the fields of administration and, in particular, communications. Nevertheless, and despite the increasing priority being given to the production of day-fighters, the night-fighter force remained a formidable threat to Bomber Command, even if it was operating under increasing difficulties, as one night-fighter pilot describes.

Leutnant Otto Heinrich Fries was the technical officer of II./NJG 1. In the RAF a technical officer was not a member of aircrew but a specialist officer from the Technical Branch, whereas in the *Luftwaffe* the job was a secondary appointment held, usually, by an operational pilot. Fries had already made several kills flying the Bf 110. In the early months of 1944 his *Gruppe* was one of those moved into France. Their new base was at St Dizier, south-west of Verdun. Fries did not like the airfield. Although the runway was of adequate length, the field itself was very narrow and was bounded by water on all four sides – on three sides by canals, on the fourth by the River Marne. The large hangar used for repairs and servicing was off the airfield itself, so that to reach it the aircraft had to be taxied or towed over a very hump-backed wooden bridge. When Fries was taking an aircraft across he always had the disturbing feeling on reaching the crest of the bridge that his machine was going to stand on its nose. To prevent this possibility he would approach the bridge at fairly high speed, and when he came to the highest point he would give a further burst of throttle and hold the control column well back into his stomach so that the slipstream would keep the tail firmly down. Fries continues his description of St Dizier:

'The hut in which we used to wait every night when we were at stand-by was also on the other side of the Marne, and to reach it we had to cross a rickety wooden bridge. The hut was located several hundred metres distant from the river and in a thick beech wood. When it grew warmer the ground in the wood was covered within a day by thousands of yellow daffodils. The rooms in the stand-by barrack gave off a penetrating stink of floor-polish and tobacco smoke, even though we had the windows and doors wide open all day. When the night-time temperature allowed it we used to set up our deck chairs outside, where we would enjoy the song of the nightingales. There must have been several dozen of them, and they sang a chorus every night. I couldn't remember ever having heard so many nightingales singing at one time – it was a feast for the ears.

'Nevertheless, I felt that in some way the woods were threatening. I had no logical explanation – it was simply a feeling, but then my feeling was confirmed. When the three of us were going back to our billets in the town on a motorcycle and sidecar one night when stand-by was over, someone shot at us from out of the trees. The bullets, which by the sound of them must have come from a pistol, whistled past our ears. We already knew that Maquis activists were increasing in number from week to week, but this was the first proof that they had established themselves in the forest so near to our airfield. After this incident we stopped using the hut in the woods. The wooden bridge was broken down and a room in the operations block was made available for crews on standby.'

Fries goes on the describe how the officers' accommodation in town was broken into by thieves who took German uniforms but ignored a considerable quantity of cash that was there. But the French *Résistance* were not the only irritation that the *Luftwaffe* had to contend with:

'This was the period when the Allies were making their preparations for the invasion. Every day the "Duty Recce Aircraft" came in very high to take its pictures. Soon afterwards the sky would be full of Thunderbolts, Mustangs and Lightnings, shooting at everything on wheels. Trains bringing up supplies could only move by night; during the day they were put into sidings. The same game was played out every day: in the evening the fighter-bombers came and shot up any railway yards that the reconnaissance photographs had shown were worth attacking. The railway yards were sealed off at both sides by bombs dropped on the rails, so that the trains couldn't move. Then, during the night, dozens of RAF bombers would come and destroy the yards and the supply trains which, if the repair gangs hadn't been able to clear at least one line in the short time between dusk and the attack, had been unable to get out.

'We took off almost every night against the *Bahnhofsbomber*, as we christened them – the "railway station bombers". But every night the British "Duty Intruder" was there attempting to disrupt the air traffic at the aerodrome, and not infrequently succeeding. He always carried a few bombs with him, but fortunately he missed more often than not. Nevertheless it was a strain on our nerves. We used a few tricks to try to minimalise his chances of success.

'Our first subterfuge was to persuade him to aim at the emergency landing strip instead of the concrete runway we used for take-off. It was no easy task to take off on the grass, because the surface was very bumpy. There were even a number of rabbit holes! When we heard the droning of a Mosquito over the airfield, we knew that we would be scrambled within the next half-hour. We would let the "friend from the other Field Post Office" make one or two circuits, and then we would switch on the lights of the emergency strip on the grass for about thirty seconds. After a minute the whole thing would be repeated, with the lights being switched on and off again and again. In this way we gave the impression that a series of take-offs was taking place, and then, sooner or later, the bombs would start falling on what they thought was the runway. When the real scramble took place we had, admittedly, to reckon with the possibility of cannon attack, but no longer with bombs, which were far more unpleasant.

'Another thing we used to try was to use extreme caution when we took off. The radio operator would make R/T contact with the controller immediately the pilot started taxying, but he would only ask for the airfield lights to be switched on when he was in take-off position. The moment the runway lights went on he would push his throttles forward for full power so that he would get airborne in the shortest possible time. The moment he lifted off, the lights would be extinguished. Those who took off first had the best chance of getting away unscathed, so there was always keen competition to be first into the air.

'After the hard winter, with its heavy losses, the *Gruppe* seldom had more than eight aircraft operational; usually it was less, often only two or three. Thus it only took a relatively short time to get the whole *Gruppe* airborne – seen in the context of the activities of the British intruders, this was of course a very good thing.

'The camouflaged shelters in which our aircraft were kept were situated a good distance apart around the airfield. They had protective walls to guard against bomb splinters and were joined by means of short strips to the taxi-track that went right round the airfield. The nearest shelter to the end of the runway for a take-off towards the west, the one we used most frequently, was the *Kommandeur*'s. Mine was the next closest, because I was the technical officer, and then came the shelters for the 4th *Staffel*. On the other side of the take-off point were the shelters for the aircraft of the 5th and 6th *Staffeln*. As far as crews were concerned, at this period the *Gruppe* scarcely had the strength of a normal *Staffel*. We had had to take very heavy losses in the months of late autumn and winter just past.'

On the night of 6/7 April, Fries's *Gruppe* was called up to immediate readiness about an hour before midnight. There was no Bomber Command operation by heavy bombers that night, but Mosquitos were visiting Germany and the occupied countries in their several diversion, harassing, deception and intruder roles. It was a cold night, and the German crews sat and shivered in the machines, waiting for the Very signal that would order them into the air. Eventually it came, and Fries started up and began to taxi out at speed. He had to brake sharply to avoid colliding with the Bf 110 of the *Kommandeur,* Major Eckart-Wilhelm von Bonin, as it too swung out of its shelter. The runway lighting flashed on in response to an R/T call from the *Kommandeur*'s radio operator, and, without pausing to line up, von Bonin turned on to the runway, opening his throttles for take-off as he did so. As soon as his wheels cleared the runway the airfield lights went out, and Fries in his turn positioned to scramble, so close behind von Bonin that he had to wait for the air turbulence caused by the *Kommandeur*'s airscrews to subside before calling for the lights to come on again. Then Staffa, his radio operator, made the call, the lights came on and Fries's Bf 110 began to roll. At that moment a mushroom of flames erupted close to the left-hand side of his machine and he felt something strike his head. For a split-second he seemed to lose consciousness, but he instinctively pulled back the throttle and, treading on the brakes, swung off the runway. He taxied back to his splinter shelter, where the crew were able to inspect the damage that the Mosquito's bomb had caused. A splinter had passed through the side window of the cockpit between the radio operator and the gunner, missing both of them. What had hit Fries on the head was a medium-sized piece of concrete, presumably blown from the runway by the explosion of the bomb, which had penetrated the Perspex in the access door. The radar aerials were bent, and there were numerous dents and holes of varying size in the fuselage, wings and tail unit. Repairs to the machine took a full week.

The autumn of 1943 and the following winter had seen a falling off in the effectiveness of Hajo Herrmann's single-seater Wild Boars, which had progressively been unable to cope with the combination of bad weather, inadequately trained pilots replacing the original blind-flying experts as they fell by the wayside, and the uncompromising operating standards set by their commander. Further, the increasing effectiveness both of the *Zahme Sau* method of interception and of the twin-engined fighters in the *Wilde Sau* role, coupled with the fact that a disproportionate number of single-seater fighters urgently needed by day were being written off and damaged in the course of operations by night, mostly in flying accidents, resulted in the dissolution, on 16 March 1944, of Herrmann's 30th Fighter Division. Some of the smaller single-engined units, *Staffeln* and *Gruppen*, were retained in purely night-fighting and experimental roles. A new night-fighting *Gruppe*, NJGr 10, had been set up at the beginning of the year to work on the development of night-fighting equipment and tactics, for example, and members of JG 300 formed into 1./NJGr 10 under the command of Hauptmann Friedrich-Karl Müller, *'Nasenmüller'*, the most successful of Herrmann's original freebooters. The role of the three *Geschwader* of *30. Jagddivision*, JG 300, JG 301 and JG 302, was changed from that of night-fighter to that of all-weather fighter, and Herrmann was appointed *Kommandeur* of *1. Jagddivision* in Döberitz, which embraced both day-fighter and night-fighter units and was responsible for the defence of the area centred on Berlin.

At this time, the beginning of the month of April 1944, Bomber Command's average daily availability of four-engined bombers was in the region of 1,000, and was increasing steadily. Only a small number of the unsatisfactory Halifaxes Mk II and Mk V remained in squadron service. Ranged against Harris's force, General Schmid disposed of approaching eighty units, mostly *Gruppen*, on bases in Germany, Holland, France, Belgium and Denmark. On paper, the overall establishment strength of these units matched Bomber Command's availability figure almost one-to-one, but their actual strength, as Fries's account so clearly illustrates, fell far below the establishment figure. When it came to aircraft serviceable, the figure fell even lower, with only something in the region of 400 aircraft and crews, on average, being available to fight the bombers on any one night.

Following the staggering losses on the Nuremberg raid, it was not until the night of 11/12 April that another German city was attacked by Bomber Command heavies, and that was a comparatively short-range one, Aachen. In the meanwhile, however, Mosquitos visited the Fatherland, while targets in France were hit by the heavy squadrons at minimal cost in terms of bombers destroyed. The short penetration by the forces striking at French targets gave little time for the German night-fighters to find their prey. The night of their greatest success was 10/11 April, when they accounted for the majority of the ten Halifaxes lost against railway targets at Tergnier, to the south of St Quentin.

That night Horace Pearce was flying Halifax V, serial number LL126, KN-W. He bombed the target successfully and was in the vicinity of Amiens on the way back home when his machine came under fighter attack:

> 'The enemy aircraft came in from the port quarter and the rear gunner started his monologue: "Enemy range four hundred yards and closing, nose light out, prepare to go." I immediately heard the clatter of machine-gun fire from the rear turret over the intercom. The enemy aircraft had also fired at us but missed. I was not to know this immediately and was still waiting for Ivor's order to corkscrew, which did not come. I was aware, however, that Ivor had stopped firing and wondered if he had been hit. The flight engineer, Fred Archbold, was also worried about this, and he began to make his way to the rear to see what the score was, when Ivor came up on the intercom: "Resume course, he won't bother us any more!" I asked him, "What's going on back there, Taffy? Do I corkscrew?" Instead of replying to this Ivor reported that the enemy fighter had closed to three hundred yards, at which point he, Ivor, had opened fire and hit the enemy fighter, which had then exploded. The whole of the attack had

lasted only a few seconds and had been witnessed by the mid-upper gunner, Ray Brooks, who had been prevented from joining in due to the fin and rudder of the Halifax being in his line of fire. Ivor had done well, for, as the enemy fire was passing just over the top of his turret, had he called for a corkscrew the tail of the aircraft and his turret would have risen into the line of fire. He bided his time and, as the range closed to three hundred yards, he let him have it. Gordon Edwards saw the flaming wreckage falling, and I banked the aircraft so that I could see it burning on the ground. For this exploit and others when Ivor had been instrumental in ensuring the safety of his aircraft and crew, he was awarded an immediate DFM.'

That night No. 77 Squadron was fortunate, not losing a single machine. Crews from the Squadron did, however, witness the loss of aircraft from other squadrons, albeit unwittingly. The Operations Record Book for the squadron contains this extract: 'Amiens to French coast – only light flak. Up to twenty searchlights operating in target area. About ten new "scarecrow" flares reported on route home over France.'

In the latter months there had been an increasing number of reports of these 'scarecrows' from bomber crews, a new phenomenon – violent, flaming explosions in the vicinity of the bomber stream. These were, it was firmly believed, special shells fired by the Germans that were intended to simulate aircraft exploding and so to deter the bomber crews. The irony is that the Germans had no such devices; what the RAF aircrew were seeing were actual bombers exploding, in all probability victims of night-fighter attacks from below with the so far unsuspected *Schräge Musik*.

At this period Harris was increasingly diversifying his attacks, sending strong forces in the same night to separate targets in Germany and France, and smaller forces on diversion and mine-laying trips. Mosquitos went out every night, taking advantage of their comparative invulnerability to harass targets across the whole of the Third Reich. Very occasionally however one would fall to the guns of a night-fighter, as did the Serrate Mosquito that crashed to the south-east of Antwerp on the night of 20/21 April, shot down by Paul Zorner.

Mosquitos were active the following night too, when the main attack was against Aachen. It was gratifyingly successful in terms of the concentration of the bombing. Nine Lancasters failed to return from the 341 sent out, and all nine fell to the guns of just two night-fighter pilots. Hauptmann Helmut Bergmann of III./NJG 4 destroyed seven and Heinz-Wolfgang Schnaufer, *Gruppenkommandeur* of IV./NJG 1, the other two.

Paul Zorner's next success came on the night of 22/23 April, one of the twenty-nine four-engined bombers that the German defences, principally the *Nachtjagd*, claimed from the 577 that went to Düsseldorf. The attack against Düsseldorf was concentrated and effective, underlining the increasing vulnerability of towns that were situated closer to the bombers' base and so within range of Oboe and Gee-H.

Among the Lancasters that attacked Düsseldorf on 22/23 April 1944 was one flown by Pilot Officer Oliver Brooks. His experiences that night illustrate once more the risks that ordinary young men were called upon to run in the night skies of Europe. They also illustrate the way in which those 'ordinary' young men met the challenge.

Statistically, the Bomber Command aircrew called upon to fly an operational tour during the period from autumn 1943 to spring 1944 ran an even higher risk of death, injury or captivity than those operating at other times during the war. There had always been short periods and, of course, individual raids when the loss ratio was high, but over a tour of thirty trips these were usually offset by operations on which the casualties were comparatively light. The emphasis here is on the word 'comparatively': flying in bombers over Germany was by its very nature a high-risk occupation, but even so it was more hazardous at some times than at others. Those who manned the bombers were indisputably brave men, constantly reminded, by the absence of familiar faces from their own squadron and by the published figures of aircraft missing, of their own limited chances of survival. Yet, with few exceptions, they flew until they finished their tour or, more probably, themselves featured among the casualties. For the majority of those who perished, death came quickly, a few last moments of fear in a flaming machine screaming earthwards, and then oblivion. For others the agony was a drawn-out one, an unavailing struggle against the odds to bring a crippled machine and wounded colleagues back to safety, ending in a grave, often unmarked and even unrecorded, on land or at sea. And over and above the implicit level of bravery there were countless acts of heroism, coupled with outstanding flying skill, many of which were never recognised because those involved did not survive to tell the tale. But some did.

Oliver Brooks had joined No. XV Squadron at Mildenhall, Suffolk, as a Sergeant Pilot and flown his first operation, a mining sortie, in a Stirling in October 1943. His initiation to city bombing had been on the night of 22/23 November, when Berlin was bombed, the last raid against mainland German targets in which Stirlings took part. In December No. XV Squadron converted to Lancasters, and in January 1944, on the night of the twentieth, Oliver – now a Pilot Officer – flew his first Lancaster operation. Berlin was again the target. By the time he took part in the ill-starred Nuremberg raid on 30/31 March, Oliver Brooks had flown a total of sixteen operations. He and his crew survived an attack by a Ju 88 on the approach to the target and brought their damaged Lancaster safely back to Mildenhall. The next operation but two for which they were briefed was the one against Düsseldorf on the night of 22/23 April. The long-suffering Rhineland city was badly hit again. Heavy concentration of bombs in the central areas of Derendorf, Altstadt and Oberbilk brought the number of homeless families in the city to over 10,000, a total of 29,300 persons. On the night in question well in excess of 1,000 people were killed despite the many substantial shelters that were available. In the air, the *Nachtjagd* was in action, and twenty-nine four-engined bombers were lost from a force of 596. Among the successful fighter pilots were Paul Zorner, who shot down a four-engined bomber near Aachen, and Georg-Hermann Greiner, whose victim crashed in the target area. Zorner now had forty-three kills to his name, Greiner twenty. As usual, *flak* over Düsseldorf was heavy. Some of Hajo Herrmann's *Wilde Sau* single-seaters, now no longer used exclusively for night operations but reclassified as all-weather fighters, were among the defenders.

Oliver Brooks was flying a Packard-Merlin-engined Lancaster Mk III, LS-W, manufacturer's no. ND763. In addition to the normal crew there was an eighth man on board, Flight Lieutenant John Fabian DFC, the Squadron navigation leader, who was flying to get first-hand experience of H2S. Brooks' aircraft was one of the first on the Squadron to carry the device. All went smoothly until the bombs were released from 22,000 feet, aimed at the red markers that PFF had dropped accurately in the centre of Düsseldorf. Then an Fw 190 Wild Boar attacked from astern, setting the port engine on fire and damaging the aircraft's hydraulics so that both gun turrets were put out of action. Almost simultaneously a heavy anti-aircraft shell exploded close below the Lancaster's fuselage, causing further extensive damage and so badly injuring the bomb aimer, Allen Gerrard, that he died within minutes. Shrapnel hit the wireless operator, Flight Sergeant L. Barnes, in the leg, almost severing it. Both the mid-upper gunner, Sergeant Ron Wilson, and the navigator, Flight Sergeant Ken Pincott, suffered minor splinter wounds, Wilson on the ear and Pincott in one finger. Either the Fw 190 attack or the anti-aircraft shell had caused a short-circuit to the aircraft's electrics, which in its turn had started a fire in the fuselage. The Lancaster, Brooks struggling with the controls, was losing height at a frightening rate, and when he did regain control the altimeter read 14,000 feet. Ron Wilson managed to extinguish the fuselage fire, but the flames had damaged three of the crew's parachutes. Baling out was impossible. Ron Wilson and the extra navigator, John Fabian, attempted to stem the blood pouring from Barnes' leg, but their efforts were in vain, and Barnes died.

Heading north-west for England, Brooks' crippled aircraft, only just hanging in the sky and covering the ground at less than a hundred miles an hour, crossed the Dutch coast at 3,000 feet. Ditching was out of the question: the dinghy, stowed in the wing, had been destroyed by the *flak* burst that killed two of the crew. Brooks decided to try to reach Woodbridge, one of the three special 'crash dromes' situated on the east coast of England so that damaged aircraft could land in emergency; vast, broad, concrete runways equipped with all the necessary emergency equipment – FIDO, fire-fighting trucks, ambulances, medical facilities, heavy salvage gear and so on. John Fabian took over the navigation, while the regular navigator, Ken Pincott, occupied the seat of the dead wireless operator and transmitted SOS after SOS. Only later did he learn that the aircraft had been at too low an altitude for the calls to be received. With its port outer engine stopped and the starboard outer not giving full power, and with everything that could be spared, including the guns and ammunition, having been jettisoned, the stricken Lancaster crossed the English coast at just 500 feet. All the emergency runways, Woodbridge included, were oriented east-west, so that damaged aircraft could make a straight-in approach; it was just as well, for Brooks had neither time nor height for the normal niceties of landing. Elevator and rudder trims were unserviceable, the wheels could not be lowered, and the bomb doors were locked in the open position. Fuel was low, but that was not necessarily a bad thing, because there was less to burn if things went wrong. Oliver Brooks put the Lancaster down smoothly on its belly, and soon he and the other surviving members of the crew were in Sick Quarters for a check-up and treatment as appropriate. Meanwhile, the aircraft had been hauled from the runway by a crash party.

One might reasonably think that after such an experience a short period of leave, or at least a short time without operational flying, might have been on the cards. One would be wrong. The next night but one Oliver Brooks and his crew, with replacements for the dead Barnes and Gerrard, bombed Karlsruhe. Twice Brooks' machine was coned by searchlights, again it was attacked by a night fighter, but each time Oliver managed to manoeuvre it out of danger. Of that trip, Brooks writes, 'Our Commanding Officer, Wing Commander Watkins, was an observer, and he usually flew as bomb aimer whilst on XV. I think it was his third tour. He had the DFC and DFM, and he finished with a DSO. He was a great CO. After our Düsseldorf trip, when we were all a bit shattered, he came along with us on our next operation to Karlsruhe. That is the sort of chap he was.'

On 21 June 1944 Flight Lieutenant Brooks DFC – he had been promoted and awarded an immediate decoration in May following the Düsseldorf trip – flew his final operation. John Fabian and Ken Pincott had also been awarded decorations, Fabian a bar to his DFC, Pincott the DFM. On 5 July King George VI visited Mildenhall and held an investiture there, personally pinning on Brooks' and Pincott's medals for valour. Few decorations can have been more merited. Today, some fifty years on, Brooks tends to be dismissive of his DFC:

> 'There is just one thing I want to point out. Whether or not one survived, got a decoration etc., all was a lottery. I have just read again Brickhill's book *The Dambusters.* How people like Micky Martin, Dave Shannon, Gibson, Cheshire survived what they went through – brilliant pilots they were, but they must have had incredible luck. I feel very humble in comparison. Even so, I think I was bloody lucky, and I only did thirty trips, while some of these people did over a hundred. They were also flying back and forth over the target, usually at low level, placing their markers, often for quite long periods, while people like me were in and out like Flynn!'

In addition to Woodbridge in Suffolk, where Oliver landed, there were two other emergency landing runways on the east coast of England, one at Manston in Kent and the other at Carnaby in Yorkshire, airfields expressly designed, constructed, equipped and staffed to deal with aircraft returning to base in distress or in need as a result of enemy action, weather or a combination of misfortunes. They were impressive places.

The overwhelming majority of aircraft landing on the Emergency Landing Grounds (ELGs) were, of course, machines from Bomber Command and the USAAF returning from Germany, and for that reason the ELGs were located close to the coast with the runway running due east-west. The first one to be brought into service, Woodbridge, had its first 'customer', an American B-17, on 18 July 1943. The composite runway measured 4,500 yards – two-and-a-half miles – long and 250 yards wide. As a normal runway was about half as long and only fifty yards wide, it will be seen that the area of these emergency runways was ten times that of a runway at an ordinary bomber station. Being on the coast, the locations were less susceptible to fog than airfields inland. A pilot approaching in daylight saw a vast slab of concrete ahead of him, with very few peripheral buildings, intentionally planned that way so that there were few obstacles for an uncontrollable aircraft to crash into. There were eight parking areas, capable of accommodating fifty aircraft in all.

The landing area was in fact marked out into three adjacent and parallel runways, each with different coloured lighting for use at night – green for the southern strip, white for the centre strip and amber for the northern one. Approaching aircraft were usually told to use the strip most suitable for their condition: diverted, undamaged aircraft, or those low on petrol, were directed on to the north strip; moderately damaged machines to the centre strip, while badly damaged ones that were crash-landing aimed for the south strip. If necessary, and if there was time, a carpet of foam would be laid at the end of the southern strip to ease the landing of a badly damaged bomber. For operating in foggy weather, the ELGs were equipped, but not until June 1944, with FIDO. As with H2S, there are conflicting explanations of the acronym – 'Fog Investigation Dispersal Operation' for instance, and 'Fog, Intensive Dispersal Of'. Pipelines were laid at either side of the runway and petrol pumped along them to fuel a series of burners along their length. The intense heat generated by these burners caused air convection, which lifted the fog and so increased horizontal visibility. To someone coming in to land on an airfield when FIDO was operating – other fields besides the ELGs were subsequently fitted with it – the mass of flames and black smoke generated presented an awesome, albeit welcome, sight. It was literally like flying into a Victorian concept of hellfire; there was an unsettling lurch as the aircraft, low above the ground and throttled back for landing, passed into the field of convection; and then, when the wheels touched down, the line of flames rushing past on either side were a visible hazard that concentrated the pilot's mind on the necessity not to swerve off the centre-line of the runway. But there was always the knowledge that but for FIDO one might have run out of fuel and crashed or have had to abandon the aircraft, as happened not infrequently in foggy conditions.

The ELGs were fully equipped with mechanical and medical equipment to cope with almost any emergency, including bulldozers, cranes, crash tenders, fire engines, remotely controlled fire-fighting gear, ambulances and so on. Crashed aircraft, such as Oliver Brooks' Lancaster, were simply shoved or lifted off to keep the landing area clear for further arrivals.

Marshalling yards at Laon, near Reims, were another target hit on the night of the big raid on Düsseldorf. A *Luftwaffe* pilot who destroyed a British bomber that night was Otto Fries. His aircraft, Bf 110 C9+GC, had newly been fitted with *Schräge Musik*, and this was his first operational flight with the upward-firing weapons. After waiting for some long time, he received instructions from the ground to head towards the bomber stream, and soon *Funker* Staffa had a response on his *SN-2*. Slowly Fries was able to manoeuvre his Messerschmitt beneath the unsuspecting bomber, which he identified as a Stirling. He found that he had to adopt an uncomfortable attitude, head back, to look through the reflex sight in the roof of the cockpit to aim at the bomber, and he found it difficult to control the aircraft at the same time. At last he was in a good position, and he opened fire, but his upward-firing cannon did not respond; instead, those in the nose of his Bf 110 did. He had pressed the wrong button. For the unpractised, he says, it was an easy mistake to make. There were two triggers, *Löffel* and *Knopf* respectively. The *Knopf* (button) was on the control column and, pressed with the right thumb, fired the *Schräge Musik*. In normal flight it was protected against accidental firing by the so-called *Löffel* (spoon), a spoon-shaped device that could be pivoted down to make the button available. To make things more difficult, however, the '*Löffel*' was itself the trigger for the forward-firing cannon and machine-guns, and it was this that Fries had pressed instead of moving it out of the way and pressing the *Schräge Musik* button. Fortunately for Fries, unfortunately for the crew of the Stirling, the RAF crew had not seen Fries's fire, and next time he made no mistake. He saw the shells from his cannon strike between the two engines on the port wing. Fries counted as seven parachutes came from the bomber, and then it tipped over and hurtled to the ground, where it exploded in a ball of flame.

On the night of the major attack on Karlsruhe, 24/25 April, there was a smaller raid, by sixteen Mosquitos and 244 Lancasters, on Munich. All the aircraft, with the exception of ten Lancasters, were from squadrons of No. 5 Group, whose commander, Sir Ralph Cochrane, held views on target-marking and precision attacks that differed from those of Donald Bennett, in command of Pathfinder Force. Cochrane enjoyed the patronage of Harris to the extent that he was permitted to operate using methods different from those imposed on the remainder of Bomber Command. Munich's range from England, and its location deep within southern Germany, made it a difficult target. Cochrane had been advocating the marking of targets by low-flying Mosquitos – the original idea was that of the Commanding Officer of No. 617 Squadron, Wing Commander Leonard Cheshire – and for this operation four Mosquitos, flown by No. 617 Squadron pilots and led by Cheshire himself, marked aiming points in the city from roof top level, braving concentrated light *flak* and criss-crossing the target repeatedly until they were sure that they were dropping their target indicators in precisely the correct positions. Once the markers were down, Cheshire acted as Master Bomber, broadcasting instructions to the remainder of the force above as they dropped their high explosives and incendiaries. The result was a highly accurate attack, and soon afterwards Cheshire was awarded the Victoria Cross for this and the many other raids he had taken part in.

A raid on Schweinfurt two nights later, planned along similar lines, was a failure. This time the Mosquitos marking the target were from No. 627 Squadron, recently transferred to No. 5 Group from Bennett's Light Night Striking Force, and their marking was inaccurate. Higher winds than forecast impaired the Lancasters' time-keeping, so that by the time the majority of them arrived the markers were burning out. Possibly anticipating another attack in the south of Germany following the one on Munich, the night fighters found their way into the stream of heavies, and twenty-one Lancasters were destroyed, 9.1 per cent of the force. A larger force of approaching 400 bombers, of which only seven were lost, inflicted severe damage on Essen, while a successful attack on railway installations at Villeneuve-St-Georges by 217 machines cost only one.

Despite the daunting losses in the operation against Nuremberg four weeks previously, Harris now sent another major force to a long-range German target in conditions of moonlight, this time to Friedrichshafen on the northern shore of Lake Constance, an important objective by reason of the factories there that manufactured, *inter alia*, gearboxes for tanks. The southerly location of Friedrichshafen meant that the bombers could be directed so as not to have to penetrate the main concentration of night-fighter defences, as had been the case with the Nuremberg raid. A total of 150 OTU aircraft were sent out over the North Sea to simulate a force approaching northern Germany, while twenty-four Mosquitos of the LNSF attacked Stuttgart, and there were two heavy attacks, by 223 and 144 aircraft respectively, on railway centres in France. The tragedy of Nuremberg was not repeated, but even so the *Nachtjagd*, arriving late on the scene, enjoyed some success, and eighteen bombers failed to return. One of the raids to France, that against Montzen, attracted the French-based night fighters, and fifteen bombers were lost to them, at 10.4 per cent a higher proportion than was lost on the major raid.

Paul Zorner added three bombers to his score, and Otto Kutzner shot down his eleventh. Now, after such a long time has passed since the events described, it is frequently difficult for flyers to distinguish between one night and another. For one fighter pilot, however, the night of the RAF attack on Friedrichshafen was one that he would never forget.

As had happened on the occasion of the Nuremberg raid, the almost full moon and a thin layer of low cloud, against which bombers would be silhouetted, meant that an attack was thought to be unlikely. The pilots of the newly formed III./NJG 6, stationed at Hagenau, south of Strasbourg and just over the French border, had provisionally arranged a party for that night, but their hopes of a pleasant drinking session were doomed to disappointment when they were brought up to operational readiness. Oberleutnant Wim Johnen, *Kapitän* of the 5th *Staffel*, took off at 0048 hrs on the morning of 28 April 1944. He was flying a brand-new Bf 110 G-4, identification number C9+ES, that he had only recently collected from the workshops in Parchim. It was equipped with the latest inter-cept radar, *SN-2*, with *Naxos* anti-H2S radar and with *Schräge Musik*. Johnen's regular *Mechaniker*, Oberfeldwebel Mahle, the man who had first fitted a 'do-it-yourself' *Schräge Musik* installation in a night-fighter, was flying with him, but his regular *Funker*, Feldwebel Grasshoff, was on leave, and the signals officer of the *Gruppe*, Leutnant 'Brinos' Kamprath, was flying in his place. Kamprath, inexperienced in operational flying and therefore undecorated, had a burning ambition to wear the Iron Cross, a medal usually awarded for participation in a shooting down, and had been told that to fly with Johnen was a sure way of achieving his ambition. What Johnen did not know was that Mahle had told the somewhat naive Kamprath that it was customary to take a bottle of cognac up to drink a toast when an enemy bomber was shot down. Also unknown to Johnen, Kamprath had recently received the radio cipher material for the month of May and, in a flagrant breach of standing instructions, was carrying the documents with him.

It was not long before Kamprath picked up the first returns on his *SN-2*. All Kamprath needed to do was to point Johnen in the right direction, so that almost immediately he saw an aircraft ahead which, as he approached it, proved to be a Lancaster. But the clear visibility and the white carpet of cloud below was a mixed blessing, because just as Johnen could see the Lancaster, so could the rear gunner of the Lancaster see Johnen's Bf 110. As Johnen approached, the RAF pilot flung his heavy machine into a diving turn to port, the beginning of a corkscrew. Johnen manoeuvred beneath the bomber and, just as he opened fire with his *Schräge Musik*, saw tracer coming from the Lancaster's rear turret and apparently hitting his own port wing. He pulled to one side and saw the Lancaster begin to burn. He counted eight parachutes as the crew baled out, and then the bomber exploded and the remains curved to earth in a burning torch.

In the near distance Johnen saw another bomber on fire and going down, and he called Kamprath for instructions, but got no reply. He called up Mahle, but he, too, failed to answer. Then he heard a glugging noise over the microphone – Mahle and Kamprath were drinking the 'customary' toast to success! Johnen brought his crew back to reality by flinging the aircraft into a violent manoeuvre. The cognac bottle flew loose and shattered, and two very humbled crew members came back on to the intercom.

Over Friedrichshafen itself Johnen claimed his second bomber, and soon afterwards, over Lake Constance, he was positioning himself to attack his third, but the rear gunner's fire hit the Messerschmitt, holing the fuel tanks and setting the port engine aflame. Disorientated, Johnen managed to extinguish the fire, but had to switch off the engine and feather the airscrew. Almost immediately he found himself coned in up to twenty searchlights, and he fired off a recognition signal. The searchlights extinguished, but green signals were fired from the ground and a nearby airfield lit up – unmistakable instructions to land. Johnen realised that they were over Switzerland. Had he had two good engines, he says, he would have approached the runway as if to land and then, at the last moment, overshot and made his escape at low level; as it was, he had no alternative but to do as instructed. Where there were searchlights there were also anti-aircraft guns, and to attempt to escape back to Germany would have been to court disaster. He went in to land on his one good engine.

Johnen landed at the Swiss airfield at Dübendorf, near Zürich. His first impression on landing was of numerous American B-17s and B-24s lined up on the hard-standings, bombers that had force-landed in neutral Switzerland. Wim Johnen describes what happened then:

> 'When we had landed the Americans came out of the officers' mess and we all went there – it was, of course, during the night, about 0200 or 0300 hrs, and for the Americans the war was over, because they weren't exchanged. And of course they had heard the noise, the firing and so on, and they lifted us up on their shoulders and took us into the mess. What a party that was! German flyers, American flyers, Swiss flyers – we went on until about seven o'clock in the morning. And there was no ill will. I must say, too, that the Swiss were very friendly. They didn't question us in any depth – they were very correct.
>
> 'We already knew in 1944, although we didn't dare to say it, that the war was lost. The signs were already there – the German Army was in retreat in Russia, the German towns were being destroyed by the air superiority of the British and the Americans. But the high-ups were always talking of new rockets, new miracle weapons, the V-1 and the V-2. But even the higher command must have known that the war was hopeless. I can never understand why they didn't simply tell the German population that the war was

over and lay down their arms. It would have saved hundreds of thousands of lives.'

The Swiss treated the Germans very well, and the German air attaché at the Embassy in Berne sent a telegram to Berlin, the main sentence of which was '*Johnen und Besatzung in Dübendorf gelandet*' – 'Johnen and his crew have landed at Dübendorf'. It would have been more correct for the attaché to have used the verb '*notgelandet*' ('have made an emergency landing'), because the telegram was interpreted by the authorities in the German capital to mean that Johnen and his crew had defected. In Germany the *Gestapo* were immediately brought into action, and the families of Johnen, Kamprath and Mahle were arrested and put into prison, although, of course, the flyers were unaware of this until they were repatriated at the end of May after what amounted to a pleasant holiday in a neutral country. What mainly concerned the authorities was that the Messerschmitt was the latest model, equipped with *SN-2*, *Naxos* and *Schräge Musik*, none of which, they believed, was known to the the Allies. In Switzerland, they thought, it would be a simple matter for the British and the Americans to gain access to the aircraft, with a possibly disastrous effect on the operational efficiency of the *Nachtjagd*. It is not known whether Berlin knew that Kamprath was carrying the signals plans for April and May: in the event, the Swiss did not search the crew, so the signals information was not compromised.

Berlin's first plan, conceived by *Gestapo* chief Heinrich Himmler, was to send a sabotage team illegally into Switzerland to blow up the Messerschmitt on the airfield. There were several variants of the provisional plan, from a fully clandestine infiltration to a direct, overt attack on Dübendorf by paratroops. The man appointed to lead the mission was *SS-Standartenführer* Otto Skorzeny, who had led the successful commando operation into Italy in September 1943 to free Mussolini. Wiser councils, however, prevailed. Swiss 'neutrality' favoured the Third *Reich* much more than it did the Allies, and Hitler did not wish that valuable balance to be disturbed, as it undoubtedly would have been had any form of aggressive action been initiated. The German *Abwehr* enjoyed a close working relationship with the Swiss Military Intelligence Service, and through this channel the Germans were able to buy Swiss co-operation in preventing access by Allied Intelligence to Johnen's Messerschmitt. The Swiss refused to allow the machine to return to Germany, but in return for permission to buy twelve Bf 109 G-6 single-engined fighters from the Germans at a favourable price, the Swiss undertook to blow it up themselves. On 18 May 1944, in the presence of a technical team from Germany, Bf-110 G-4, identification letters C9+ES, went up in flames, and the next day the Bf 109s were delivered. What the Swiss did not know at the time was that the machines were fitted with worn-out engines. Interestingly, this was the subject of a court case in 1951 that resulted in Messerschmitt and Daimler Benz, the manufacturers of the engines, having to pay compensation to the Swiss.

Reaction within the *Luftwaffe* itself to the arbitrary action on the part of the *Gestapo* in arresting, imprisoning and interrogating members of the families of Johnen, Kamprath and Mahle was one of extreme indignation, reaching as high as Göring himself. When it had been established that Johnen and his crew had not landed in Switzerland with the intention of defecting, but as a result of battle damage, the relatives were released under an obligation not to discuss the matter with anyone else. Moving ahead of events, in November 1944, after further aerial victories, Johnen was awarded the Knight's Cross, and General Beppo Schmid wrote a letter to Johnen's father, Dietrich:

Dear Herr Johnen,

I am taking advantage of the occasion of the award of the Knight's Cross to our Oberleutnant Johnen to extend my congratulations to you and your wife as well. To all of us, your son is not only an exemplary officer and out-standing night-fighter pilot, but also a dear comrade. While sharing with him his pleasure at the award of this high and well-earned decoration, at the same time I cannot let the opportunity pass to thank you, his parents, for giving to us and to the whole German people so fine a son.

It was with consternation and with sincere sympathy that I learned that when your son made his emergency landing in Switzerland you were arrested, detained for a considerable period and made to suffer much unpleasantness. We regret this greatly. I ask you, my dear Herr Johnen, to take note of this: I and all your son's superior officers and comrades were fully convinced at all times of your son's loyalty and his honourable con-victions. Not for a moment did we doubt that nothing but a chain of adverse circumstances could have been the reason for Johnen not return-ing to base after a most difficult night action.

I trust that by now you and your relatives have been able to put this dif-ficult period behind you. If, however, you still feel even the slightest affront, please believe us that we recognise to the full the honour and good name of your family.

I greet you with my best wishes for a happy future in a victorious Germany,

(Signed) SCHMID

After Friedrichshafen, it was almost a month before another major attack was mounted against a German target, but there was scarcely a single night that Bomber Command aircraft were not out in force. On the two nights following the Friedrichshafen raid, small forces of Mosquitos and Lancasters from Cochrane's No. 5 Group continued to demonstrate their ability to strike accu-rately at small targets, an explosives factory near Bordeaux, an aircraft factory near Oslo, another explosives factory and the Michelin tyre factory at Clermont-Ferrand, all without loss.

Any complacency that might have been generated by the encouragingly low incidence of losses against French targets was shattered on the night of 3/4 May, when Harris sent out a large force of Lancasters to Mailly-le-Camp, to the east of Paris and about fifty miles south of Reims. Here, according to intelligence sources, was located a large military camp in use as a *Panzer* depot and train-ing centre, accommodating up to 10,000 *Wehrmacht* troops. Accurate bombing was necessary so that French casualties might be minimised, and Harris planned a very short and concentrated attack. There were two main reasons for this: firstly, Harris wanted to give the German night-fighters as short a time as possible to find and penetrate the bomber stream; and, more importantly, he wished to kill and incapacitate as many German troops as he could, so that they could not be used against the imminent invasion. A short, sharp attack would not give them, he hoped, time to get into the shelters. Time-on-target was set for midnight, so that as many troops as possible would be in the camp, and the attack was planned to last twenty-nine minutes. Because precision was essential, Wing Commander Leonard Cheshire himself, designated 'Marker Leader', was to lead four Mosquitos of No. 5 Group in marking the first of three precise aiming points that had been chosen to ensure a good distribution of bombing throughout the large area of the camp, and Lancasters from No. 5 Group were to begin the assault proper. Once Cheshire, flying low over the target, was happy that the markers were accurately placed, he was to call up on R/T and authorise the main force controller, Wing Commander Deane, to take over as Master Bomber.

The whole attack on Mailly-le-Camp was carefully planned. Cheshire, for example, flew a mock attack on a German fighter airfield before beginning his marking duties in order to give the impression that he was an intruder and not associated with the main force, which was so routed as to seem to be heading for Germany. Instead, however, the heavy bombers, which had approached at a high altitude in order to look as if they were making a deep penetration, were to descend to a low level, in the region of 5,000 feet, to bomb.

Visibility conditions were good, the Mosquitos marked accurately and Cheshire called up Wing Commander Deane to begin bringing in the main force bombers, who were orbiting at a holding position to the north. At this point the planning began to fall apart. The main cause of the breakdown was that Deane's transmitter had been incorrectly tuned, and in addition an American forces broadcast all but jammed out his R/T messages.

Cheshire and his other Mosquito pilots did valiant work in attempting to restructure the attack, and finally Squadron Leader Sparks, Deane's deputy as Master Bomber, was able to communicate with the main force and direct it in what developed into a very accurate attack. In the meantime, however, the delays incurred had given the night-fighters time to arrive on the scene. It was, for those German pilots fortunate enough to take part, possibly the easiest and most profitable night's work they were called upon to do. The holding point, around which large numbers of bombers were circling and waiting to be called up to bomb, was marked by a bright yellow flare on the ground, for which the *Nachtjagd* pilots, in both twin- and single-engined fighters, headed. There they did massive destruction among the unfortunate Lancasters. When the bombers moved on to the target, and after they had bombed it, the fighters went with them, so that by the end of the attack forty-two Lancasters had been shot down. The most successful German crew was that of Hauptmann Helmut Bergmann of II./NJG 4, operating from Juvincourt, to the north-west of Reims, who shot down six. Martin Drewes of III./NJG 1, flying from nearby Athies-Laon, scored five. Hauptmann Werner Hoffmann, Acting *Gruppenkommandeur* of I./NJG 5, with his radio operator Oberfeldwebel Köhler and his flight mechanic Unteroffizier

Modl, brought his personal score up to thirty by destroying two Lancasters over the target.

Despite the early setbacks and the delay, the bombing, thanks to the outstanding work of Cheshire and Sparks, was accurate. Enemy casualties, it was later discovered, fell well below expectations, only just over two hundred Germans dying in the attack. Happily, there were no casualties among the French population. On the debit side, however, approximately three hundred British and Commonwealth aircrew were lost, the majority of them killed. One aircraft that failed to return was that of the deputy main force controller, Squadron Leader Sparks. The whole crew did, however, survive, and Sparks managed to evade and succeeded in returning to England a short time later. Severe damage was done to accommodation and workshops, and a large number of vehicles, including thirty-seven tanks, was destroyed. As is so often the case, it is impossible to turn these figures into an estimate of the value of the raid in terms of the effect it might have had on the invasion battles destined to begin the following month. What the raid on Mailly-le-Camp did suggest was that, despite earlier experiences such as the raids on the Ruhr dams, forecasts of the possible results of individual raids, even precision ones, still tended to err on the side of over-optimism.

May 1944 was a month of much activity and encouragingly low losses, many sorties being 'milk-run' visits to pre-invasion targets in France. There were occasional shocks, however, when, as at Mailly-le-Camp, things went wrong in one way or another, but on the whole the lowering of the rate of attrition, together with the knowledge that they were contributing to the coming invasion, resulted in a much-needed improvement in the morale of the bomber crews. During May Bomber Command flew 9,261 sorties against specific targets, losing 243 machines, in addition to support, diversion and mine-laying operations. The totals for all operations were 11,353 sorties with 274 aircraft lost. Leaving aside the Mailly-le-Camp attack previously described, which was a one-off, there were only four nights during the month when more than twenty machines failed to return, and all of those nights saw major attacks against targets within Germany itself. If one removes the figures for raids against Germany from the statistics, the loss rate, for raids on targets in France, goes down to 1.7 per cent. The figures for attacks on the comparatively short-range German targets themselves, however – ninety-seven aircraft from 1,758 dispatched, or just over 5.5 per cent – were an uncomfortable reminder that German airspace could still not be penetrated with immunity. Fritz Habicht, in May 1944 a radio/radar operator with 3./NJG 1, gives a graphic description of operational flying at that period:

'From spring 1944 onwards the British long-range Mosquito intruders were increasingly trying to inhibit our successful operations with the He 219 (Uhu). Depending on the meteorological situation we often had a good idea in the late afternoon of what would be waiting for us in the evening and night. For example, the following is a description of one of the many operations we flew at that time, with a short description of the aerial combat itself and the take-off and landing being described in rather more detail.

'The night of 10/11 May promised to be a "night of the long knives" – only very little moonlight and a ceiling of ten/tenths cloud would ensure that the conditions would be favourable for an attack by the four-engined "Tommies".

'After operational briefing we aircrew go to the readiness hut on the airfield, where we play cards or try to get forty winks as an insurance against what will probably be a long, sleepless night. Soft music comes from the loud-speakers of the aerodrome broadcast system, but it is suddenly interrupted by the voice of the duty operations officer: "*Achtung*, all crews! Strong radio activity over England. A heavy attack is expected!" Then there is music again. It is the old merry-go-round. We wait. Then once again a crackling voice from the Tannoy: "*Achtung*: Mosquitos approaching Venlo. Bombs expected soon, probably in about fifteen minutes." With our relatively heavy night-fighters there is little that we can do against these fast aircraft, which approach at about 30,000 feet, and all we can do is to wait.

'Then the control tower comes on the Tannoy again: "*Achtung*! The first heavy bomber formations are over the Channel, heading towards northwest Germany. *Achtung*! First, Second and Third *Staffeln* to cockpit readiness. *Achtung*! Immediate cockpit readiness!"

'We run or drive to our aircraft and climb on board. Once we have buckled on our parachutes we check everything – the pilot checks the controls and engines, while I, as *Funker* and navigator, check all the radio and radio-navigation equipment and the *SN-2* intercept radar. Then I switch over to "Receive" just at the right moment to hear from the tower: "*Achtung*, to all *Adler*![1] Eight Mosquitos approaching on *Bumerang*[2] control beam. Altitude 9.5, heading this way. Bombs expected within three minutes!"[3] Then more sentimental music. Individual *Flak* guns open fire at the approaching high-speed bombers, but it is almost impossible to hit them. Then another message from the tower: "*Achtung*, bombs expected in the next few seconds!"

'Then – explosions on the airfield, one after another. We sit in our machines, which are still in their shelters. We duck our head and cower down, instinctively but pointlessly. Fingers crossed and be a brave boy! Silence, no music now, only a hissing in the earphones. Then there's yet another f . . . ing explosion, and then comes the order, "*Achtung* all *Adlers*. Scramble, sequence 11 to 39. Taxi to the lamp and look out for bomb craters and unexploded bombs on the taxi-track. *Achtung*! Scramble immediately for radio beacon *Biber*. *Hals- und Beinbruch*."[3] A short silence, then the soft music comes on again. "*Komm' zurück*".

'We taxi in the dark, switching the headlight in our nose only now and then. Dimmed lights lead us to the runway. Then the tower again: "*Achtung*

---

[1] *Adler* (eagle) was the *Gruppe* call sign.
[2] *Bumerang* – the German code word for Oboe.
[3] *Hals- und Beinbruch*: literally, 'Break your neck, break your leg'; figuratively, 'Good luck!'

Adler! Take great care. *Indianer* on the circuit. Take off at short intervals and head for *Biber* at full speed." *Indianer* are Mosquitos, which try to clobber us with their bombs and their cannon when we are taking off. Bomb craters and delayed-action bombs on the airfield, and above us, lying in wait, Mosquitos! Cheers! It's nice to be young and carefree!

'But all goes well, and we are soon in position for take-off. "*Adler* 31 ready to scramble!" "Roger, *Adler* 31, scramble. All the best!" My pilot, Oberleutnant Nabrich, captain of the Third *Staffel*, races our G9+AL along the runway towards the faint horizon of lamps. I peer astern to protect us from surprise. We're off, we're clear of the airfield. Hurray! No *Indianers* behind us? Not so far! We keep right down at a dangerously low level until we're away from the neighbourhood of the airfield. Behind us I see flames as an aircraft hits the ground – friend or foe? But we have to keep on, heading for *Biber*, a radio beacon to the north of the Schelde Estuary. We climb into the cloud and prepare to do battle.

'As we climb up through the cloud we meet a new enemy – icing. But this time luck is on our side, and the danger layer is only a few hundred metres thick, so we are quickly through it. Above the cloud we are greeted by the stars, and we are cleared for freelance operation above Holland. Now the control centre at Arnhem begins to give us continuous information on the position and heading of the heavy bombers. My *SN-2* radar is working well, but its efficiency unfortunately depends on the height we're flying at. There, ahead of us, a burst of fire, a bright spot grows bigger, a bomber goes down in flames, descending in a flat spin. We are in the bomber stream.

'Now I have the first contact on my radar screen, but the blips are still rather insubstantial. Suddenly our kite lurches, shakes. The slipstream of another aircraft ahead of us! One of ours or one of theirs? Now one blip on my radar is getting stronger. I take over control, directing my "driver" towards the target with short, sharp commands: "Two thousand metres ahead! Higher! Slightly right! Ahead! Left a bit, left! Ahead now! Still one thousand metres! Just below! Just to the left! *Achtung* – five hundred metres dead ahead! Just below! You must be able to see him! Up just a bit!" A cry from Jupp, "There he is!" Now I can see the four-engined crate as well, about three hundred metres ahead and a little higher in the starlit sky. It is clearly a Lancaster, making its way towards the Ruhr area, making gentle defensive alterations of course. The watching air gunners have not seen us yet, that's for sure. While this is going on I rotate my loop aerial on to the permanent D/F station and keep a good look-out astern. Despite the bomber's unsteady course my pilot brings us gradually closer to the four-engined machine, and a trifle lower. When we are a hundred metres away my pilot pulls up rapidly, and the game's on! Our six two-centimetre cannon hammer out their cruel rhythm. Our shells hit home true, and the port engines and wing of the Lancaster burst into flames. Desperately the enemy air gunners return our fire, but it is in vain. We dive away to port, while the burning bomber begins to lose height. Parachutes open one after the other, and now the burning machine is spinning down steeply. Jupp and I shout out our victory call into the ether: "*Adler* 31, one kill! *Adler* 31, one kill!" The ground station replies with congratulations, and we pass through a message with the position at which the bomber crashed to the ground in a ball of fire. In order to get a claim recognised this position must be correct to within five kilometres and be confirmed by witnesses either in the air or on the ground, together with the exact time.

'In the meantime the bomber stream has reached the Ruhr. Its track to the target from the Schelde Estuary and straight across Holland is marked by a series of fires on the ground, positive evidence of where bombers have been shot down. But ahead of us the sky is lit up with the indescribable, satanic firework display of a major air raid. The tension that goes with action mingles in our mind with pictures of the tortured human beings down there, people shivering in their shelters or dying in their houses.

'Now we attack another bomber, and we see our shells striking home; but we come under heavy defensive fire ourselves. Suddenly our port engine begins to run unevenly, possibly the result of a bullet hit. Now it is over-heating, so we have to make for Venlo as rapidly as possible. I take a bearing on the base transmitter and tell my pilot the course to fly. Letting down gradually we steer to the radio beacon at Venlo. When we break cloud we have to be alert again in case a British intruder is behind us. These "friends from the other side" have a habit of hanging around the flashing beacon about ten kilometres from the airfield that our own crews head for if their radio is out of action.

'We report to the tower that we have had to return from a successful sortie due to motor damage, and we begin a circuit at a safe distance from the airfield, which is still in darkness. More and more aircraft from our own and other night-fighter units check in. The majority of them, still hepped up, call out the victories when they check in for landing permission.

'At last we are called up: "*Adler* 31, come in to land. Look out for *Indianer*! Call in when on approach!"

'We know that on the ground everything is now being done to ensure that we land safely. The runway lights, the horizon lamps and the obstacle lamps are ready to be switched on at a moment's notice. The *flak* gunners are alert for enemy fighters that might come in behind us, because our own airborne warning radar doesn't work at low level.

'Now we begin our landing. We are at three hundred metres on a direct approach and still several kilometres from touchdown. Now the pilot has to work hard. Lose height gradually, keep on heading, flaps down, maintain correct speed, then let the undercarriage down. I watch my altimeter and the landing blip on my radar simultaneously. Just as we come to the final radio beacon I call up the tower, "*Christbaum* for *Adler* 31!" Almost simultaneously the airfield lights, the minimum necessary, go on. Two light *flak* searchlights flash on, covering our tail, and we speed towards the runway. We touch down – one, two gentle bumps, and Mother Earth has us again. As soon as the aircraft has slowed down we swing off the runway and head for the dispersal area, where our chief mechanic directs us in by means of light signals. Everybody wants to know how we got on, and we give them the important details in a few words, and then they set about checking the machine.

'A car takes us up to the Operations Room so that we can make our reports. Then *Sekt*, cigarettes and excited conversation with comrades bring home to us that we have got away with it once more. Although preliminary reports indicate that several dozen heavy bombers have been shot down, nearly all our comrades have come home safely. After our heavy losses during the past winter, today's operation makes us think that perhaps Luck is on our side again.

'Meanwhile it is growing light outside. We drive to our billets and collapse, dead tired, into our beds. Once again I relive the dangerous moments and situations, and I think of the few hours off duty I might now be able to enjoy.'

While hundreds of heavies and Mosquitos were now ranging wide and hitting relatively small targets in occupied territories with commendable accuracy, at the same time scarcely a night passed without the air-raid sirens sounding in the Fatherland, disturbing the slumbers of the population and sending them to their shelters as Mosquitos of the Light Night Striking Force sped in at high altitude, dropped their bombs and flew out again, penetrating as far as Berlin. The task of the night-fighter organisation was made much more difficult by this spread of effort on the part of Harris: it was harder to find the many smaller streams of bombers now coming from across the Channel than it had been to penetrate the much bigger and longer streams of the preceding winter. In addition, the jamming and disruptive broadcasts transmitted by No. 100 Group aircraft were steadily increasing. But despite all this the *Nachtjagd* claimed 243 kills during May from the total of 274 lost on all operations. It is of interest to note that Bomber Command's own estimates for that month attribute 137 of the losses to fighters and fifty to *flak*, with the remainder being due to causes unknown, a proportion of 2.75 to one. The German figures, on the other hand, are 243 to night fighters and only thirty-one to *flak*, a proportion in favour of the fighters of almost eight to one. The German figures are not exact, admittedly, because fighter claims tended to be exaggerated. Nevertheless, the *Luftwaffe* were scrupulous in checking fighter pilots' claims before confirming them, and any exaggeration must be only marginal. The comparative figures are a clear indication that even at this late stage of the battle, Bomber Command was still underestimating the potency of the German night-fighter arm.

In general, night operations against targets in France were less costly than those against targets in Germany. There were, however, other hazards besides *flak* and night-fighters. With the increasing concentration of bombers over individual targets, the risk of collision with a friendly machine was ever-present. In May 1944 Flight Sergeant Thomas Terry, an air gunner, was on his second tour. His pilot was Squadron Leader Robertson, and on the night of 10/11 May they raided railway installations at Lens, between Arras and Lille, flying in Halifax III MH-L of No. 51 Squadron. Tom Terry describes what happened:

'Lens was a transportation target selected in preparation for D-Day. In comparison to the German raids we considered this an easy one. We reached the target area and the flak was moderate, no sign of enemy air-craft activity. Duly bombed aiming point, left the area and set course for home. Approximately ten minutes later there was a tremendous bang. The aircraft seemed to be rammed down. Robbie succeeded in regaining control after losing a lot of height. The mid-upper gunner reported that a Halifax had collided with us. He reported severe damage to the starboard wing and that the top half of the starboard rudder had been shorn level with the tailplane and the elevator damaged. Fortunately, no engines affected. Though the aircraft had no starboard control surfaces Robbie decided to make for England. We crossed the coast north of the Thames. A Mayday call brought no reply, but an airfield showing Sandra lights came into view. Robbie ordered the crew to bale out over the airfield, but the bomb aimer stayed to help in the attempted landing. Somehow Robbie made a good landing. The airfield was Stansted, 8th USAF Fortress and Marauder base.'

The aircraft with which Terry's aircraft had collided was another No. 4 Group Halifax from No. 10 Squadron. Miraculously, it too survived the mid-air collision.

The shooting-down of Mosquitos continued to represent an almost insoluble problem. Nevertheless, the *Nachtjagd* did claim four during May, none of which was destroyed by the standard night-fighters, the Bf 110s and the Ju 88s. On the night of 6/7 May Oberleutnant Baake of 3./NJG 1, flying a He 219 A2, claimed a Mosquito during a raid on Leverkusen in the Ruhr area, while Hauptmann Friedrich-Karl Müller of 1./NJG 10, flying a Fw 190 A-6, claimed one on the night of 24/25. Another pilot who achieved success in the splendid, if under-pro-duced, He 219 was Feldwebel Rauer of 1./NJG 1, flying from Venlo, who shot down two of the three Mosquitos lost that night. This was the only occasion during the war when an individual German fighter pilot claimed more than one Mosquito in a night. From over 1,000 sorties flown by Mosquitos during May, only twelve failed to return.

The increasing strength of the Mosquito force, together with its remarkable versatility, was a factor of growing importance in the battle between Bomber Command and the German defences. By May 1944 there were fourteen full Mosquito squadrons operational in Bomber Command, seven with No. 100 (Special Duties) Group, six with No. 8 (Pathfinder) Group and one (No. 627) with No. 5 Group. In addition No. 617 Squadron, also in No. 5 Group, had a number of Mosquitos on its establishment with its Lancasters. A breakdown of Mosquito operations on a typical night in May 1944 will give an idea of the many-sided nature of the work carried out by this, probably the best all-round aircraft that ever flew operationally.

On the night of 19/20 May No. 8 (Pathfinder) Group sent out a total of twenty-two Mosquitos, mostly using Oboe, to mark railway targets for forces of Lancasters and Halifaxes at Boulogne, Orléans, Amiens and Le Mans. With the exception of that on Amiens, which was cloud-covered, all the bombing was very accurate. In an exclusively 5 Group operation, four Mosquitos marked railway installations in the town of Tours for a force of 113 Lancasters. Six Mosquitos marked each of two coastal gun positions, at Le Clipon and Merville respectively, for about sixty heavies each, and a further five Mosquitos went to Mont Couple and dropped their markers on a radar station for a following force of thirty-nine Lancasters. In support operations, Harris sent twenty-nine Mosquitos of the Light Night Striking Force to drop their bombs on Cologne, while eight flew Serrate patrols and a further twenty-three went out on intruder sorties against *Luftwaffe* night-fighter bases.

Oboe had now been in operational service for well over a year, and the Germans had initially been rather slow to appreciate that a new electronic target-marking device was being used and, once they had realised that such was the case, to divine its nature and plan counter-measures. By May 1944, however, they knew precisely how Oboe operated. They had dubbed Oboe the *Bumerangverfahren* or 'boomerang system', after the curved track that the marker aircraft used to approach their target, and they had constructed mobile jamming transmitters, *ABG23* and *ABG24*, *ABG* being short for *Anti-Bumerang Gerät*, or 'Anti-*Bumerang* equipment'. An Oboe-tracking equipment, '*Naxburg*', had also been developed, a modification of the *Würzburg* fighter-control radar and of the airborne H2S-tracker, *Naxos*, in combination. The problem that the Germans were never able fully to solve, however, was how to catch and destroy the high-flying, swift Mosquitos that carried Oboe and which the night-fighters found virtually impossible to intercept by traditional methods.

On 24 May 1944 the general officer in charge of the training of the anti-aircraft forces of the *Luftwaffe*, Generalleutnant von Axthelm, issued a paper entitled 'Combating "Boomerang" aircraft'. It drew attention to the seriousness of the threat and the precision achieved by this form of attack, and outlined in detail the way the system worked, correctly identifying the Mosquito squadrons used. 'Our own *Mosquitojäger* (Mosquito hunters) have not had any worthwhile success in shooting down aircraft prior to the release of the bombs or the beginning of Pathfinder activity,' it stated, and reached the conclusion that for the foreseeable future the only defence against Oboe aircraft rested with the *Flak*. On the fighter side, Hauptmann Friedrich-Karl Müller was persisting with the development and training of a single-engined anti-Mosquito *Gruppe*, 1./NJG 10, and, as already mentioned, during the night immediately following the issue of von Axthelm's paper he himself succeeded in destroying a Mosquito in the vicinity of the Dutch town of Roermond. The *Nachtjagd*'s record against Mosquitos, however, bore out von Axthelm's statement. Including Müller's claim, they had only shot down a further seven since Major Lent's first success in April the previous year. Four had fallen to the Bf 110, two to the He 219, one to a Bf 109, and now one to an Fw 190.

On 24/25 May an attack on railway yards at Aachen, a focal point for traffic moving from the Ruhr to France, cost Bomber Command eighteen Halifaxes and seven Lancasters. Once again the distribution of the losses is of interest – 2.7 per cent of the Lancasters taking part, eleven per cent of the Halifaxes. Oberleutnant Schnaufer of IV./NJG 1, operating from St Trond in Belgium, claimed five, four Halifaxes and one unidentified four-engined machine, achieving all his successes within the space of fourteen minutes. His victims crashed in the Tilburg/Eindhoven area. There were two principal aiming points, the Aachen-West and the Rothe Erde marshalling yards, and while the results against Aachen-West were acceptable, the Rothe Erde yards escaped serious damage, so Harris sent another force, this time of eight Mosquitos and 162 Lancasters, to attack them again three nights later. This time results were better, but achieved at a cost of twelve Lancasters. This was the final major raid against a target in Germany before the invasion.

CHAPTER TWELVE

Overlord, Normandy and Oil

June to August 1944

The invaluable contribution of Bomber Command to the invasion itself, after the weeks of preliminary softening up, particularly against transport targets, needs little more than a mention here. On the night of the landings, 5/6 June 1944, the Command flew a total of 1,211 sorties for the loss of only eight aircraft. Almost a thousand Lancasters and Halifaxes hammered coastal gun batteries in Normandy, while other machines carried out diversion, support and jamming operations. Specially trained crews from Nos. 617 and 218 Squadrons, navigating with a high degree of precision, dropped massive amounts of Window in such a way as to create the impression on the enemy radar screens of large naval forces advancing slowly but steadily over the Channel towards Boulogne and Le Havre, well to the north of the actual landing area. Other bombers dropped dummy parachutists and equipment away from the main objective as a further diversionary tactic. In response to the thousand-plus armada dispatched by Bomber Command, the *Luftwaffe* deployed only fifty-nine night fighters, and only one, a He 219 flown from Venlo by Hauptmann Heinz Strüning of 3./NJG 1, succeeded in shooting down a bomber. Ironically, greater success was achieved by a pilot from a bomber unit, KG 51, flying an Me 410. The Me 410 had been developed principally as a *Zerstörer* and fast bomber. Only a small number flew, experimentally but by and large unsuccessfully, with night-fighter units. In the latter part of 1943 two *Gruppen* of KG 51 had been set up to carry out bombing and intruder operations against the British Isles. Some aircraft from KG 51 were scrambled in the very early hours of 6 June, and one pilot, Hauptmann Helmut Eberspächer, succeeded in destroying three bombers.

By now Horace Pearce was flying the much-improved Halifax Mk III, No. 77 Squadron having converted to the type in May simultaneously with a move from their base at Elvington to Full Sutton, only a comparatively short distance away. Two Free French squadrons, Nos. 346 and 347, took over the Elvington airfield. Horace remembers D-Day:

> 'It was just seconds before start-up on the night of 5 June that a staff car containing "top brass" came round to each dispersal in turn to tell us that the destruction of our target would be so vital and essential to the incoming D-Day boats and troops. Up to then we thought it was just yet another coastal battery to be bombed.
> 'We were flying a Halifax III, MZ 697 "L", and were to carry nine 1,000 lb and four 500 lb high-explosive bombs for a coastal battery at Maisy. We had in fact suspected that this was to be something of a special operation

because at the main briefing great emphasis had been placed on the instructions that routes, turning points and altitudes had to be rigidly adhered to.

'Take-off was marred by NA 511 "C" failing to get airborne as it reached the end of the runway on its take-off run. The aircraft went straight on across fields, and fortunately the crew, although injured, were able to scramble clear of the wreck.

'The rest of us were kept waiting and fully expected a change of runway; but no, we were eventually sent off on the same runway to fly over the burning wreck, with the fear of bombs exploding beneath our aircraft. They did not, however, and we all got off safely.

'The target was bombed from 10,500 feet, the aiming point being the centre of a cluster of red and green target indicators, and the attack lasted just ten minutes from start to end. On the return flight we were unable to identify any seaborne forces, but we did see some of the aircraft carrying airborne troops below on their way to Normandy.'

For the *Nachtjagd* the Battle of Normandy, which began with the invasion, represented a hectic, frequently bewildering, period. In response to the Allied landings and the advances that followed, large numbers of fighter units, both day and night, were brought forward from the *Reich* itself to do combat. In the hours of darkness the battle between Bomber Command and the *Nachtjagd* became a game of chess on a vast scale, with the German commanders trying to forecast the next moves of Bomber Command and redeploying their forces, in both the *Reich* and the occupied territories, accordingly. Night-fighter *Gruppen* were shifted here and there from day to day, with considerable organisational confusion and, understandably, morale-sapping inconvenience to the flyers and ground personnel. In addition the period of the Normandy campaign saw a considerable intensification of the electronic war, with radio and radar counter-measures causing untold confusion to the German reporting and control organisations and the night-fighter crews.

During this time the night-fighters, in addition to their function as interceptors, were used in a tactical ground-attack role, hitting from low level at the Anglo-American invaders. The crews were untrained for this sort of warfare, and it cost them a grievous toll. From a high-point of efficacy on the night of the Nuremberg raid in March, the *Nachtjagd* was beginning a descent towards comparative impotence, a descent marked nevertheless by occasional nights on which they were able to inflict heavy losses. The trend was one of steady progress towards air superiority on the part of Bomber Command by night, which would ultimately match that already enjoyed by the Allies by day.

Although the main effort of the heavy bombers was directed against targets in France during the first few weeks after the invasion, Germany had little if any respite from the attentions of the Mosquitos of No. 100 Group and Bennett's Light Night Striking Force, which were operating almost every night in increasing numbers. Moving slightly ahead of the chronology of the story, and harking back to earlier remarks on the invulnerability of the Mosquito and the qualities of the He 219, this seems a convenient point to include a further piece written by the 3./NJG 1 *Funker* Fritz Habicht on two encounters between these machines:

'After many requests my pilot, Oberleutnant Joseph Nabrich, *Kapitän* of the Third *Staffel*, got a cleaned-up He 219 with the armour plating and four of the cannon removed, especially for hunting Mosquitos. We must already have flown about twenty trips from Venlo in spring 1944 in addition to our normal interception operations, and all we had got for our trouble was "friendly" *flak*, altitude sickness and one long but inconclusive chase of a Mosquito intruder. But things were about to change.

'We were circling on wait over the Zuider Zee at 9,800 metres at about ten o'clock on the night of 10 June 1944 when our ground station suddenly announced that a group of light bombers was approaching. We were quickly controlled by radio into the gaggle of Mosquitos, which was flying rather lower than we were, and we felt the first turbulence from slipstreams. In a few minutes I had a clear response at a range of six kilometres on my *SN-2*. The enemy machine was flying so fast that despite using our height advantage to gain speed it wasn't until we were in the Osnabrück area that we obtained visual contact. We positioned ourselves about thirty metres beneath him and identified him positively as a Mosquito. Now it was a matter of stalking this rare bird carefully and scoring a direct hit. As I was checking our position my pilot attacked, aiming at the left engine and wing in order to give the two Englishmen in the aircraft a chance to escape. At first the engine burned strongly, then more weakly. Burning gently, the Mosquito began to fly in circles, losing height gradually. After a few minutes, when we were just about to make a second attack from above, the enemy machine, together with its aerial mine, exploded. We were thrown to one side by the pressure wave, but our pilot regained control of the He 219 at 4,000 metres, just above the cloud. We made an orbit over the spot where the Mosquito hit the ground, then we made our way back to our base at Venlo without any trouble, where our combat report was received by our friends in the Operations Room with surprise and with congratulations.

'The following morning only widely scattered fragments of the Mosquito could be found where they had been flung by the explosion. And the two British flyers? They were taken prisoner almost unharmed, and a few days later told us personally how lucky they had been. Immediately after our attack they had switched on the automatic pilot and baled out, both landing uninjured. They had thought at first that they had been the victim of a new anti-aircraft weapon, because they didn't expect to meet a night-fighter at that height.

'Scarcely twenty-four hours later we were chasing another Mosquito in the direction of Berlin. This time it took us even longer to reach the fast bomber, flying as it was at 9,700 metres, because we didn't have a height advantage. At last, to the west of Salzwedel, I was able to hand over the Mosquito to my pilot for him to approach visually. We tracked him in the normal manner, but we had difficulty in getting into a firing position because the enemy aircraft was making energetic evasive manoeuvres. Finally two bursts of fire, which we saw strike home, caused the Tommy to dive vertically downwards. After a few tense seconds of waiting I saw the flash of a gigantic explosion as the aircraft hit the ground below the clouds. Even as I was reporting our kill to ground control our starboard engine began to falter. It had apparently been overstrained by the long period of running at full revolutions. It was imperative for us to get down at any available airfield in the vicinity. My Mayday call was acknowledged immediately by Perleberg, and we landed there a few minutes later. To our astonishment we were greeted on the airfield by the duty officer and a number of girls with bunches of flowers – they had heard by radio of our rare success.'

During the six nights immediately following D-Day, Harris sent 3,279 sorties to tactical targets in support of the Allied troops still battling to consolidate their foothold on the French coast. The attacks cost him seventy-nine bombers. While still not negligible, the diminished loss rate, together with the feeling that they were now making a direct, easily perceived contribution towards winning the war, was a great boost to the morale of the bomber crews. By day US heavies and countless lighter Allied aircraft carried out bombing and low-level ground-attack sorties with devastating effect. The world had never seen so massive, powerful and effective a display of air power, air power which ensured that the bloody static battles of 1914/1918 would not be repeated and that the cost in human life to the soldiers at the front would be much, much less grievous.

And in addition to the tactical contribution of the bombers, a new role for them was emerging. In the course of the Allied planning for 'Overlord' there had inevitably been much discussion, and many differences of opinion, on target priority. Harris, while accepting the orders of Eisenhower in the tactical field, still adhered unswervingly to the view that the best contribution that Bomber Command could make strategically lay in the bombing of German industrial cities and towns. At a pre-invasion meeting in London on 25 March 1944 chaired by Marshal of the RAF Sir Charles Portal, Chief of the Air Staff, and attended, *inter alia*, by General Eisenhower and the senior strategic air commanders of the RAF and the USAAF, Harris had let it be known that he was unconvinced that the transport plan, adopted at the meeting, would be effective. He doubted, he said, whether even with Oboe his force could destroy the transportation targets allocated to his Command in the time available. Major-General Kennedy, from the War Office, had advocated that the heavy bombers should be used even more widely against small tactical targets, and the minutes of the meeting record that Harris 'urged strongly against the type of plan suggested by General Kennedy which would presumably require a larger number of attacks on precise targets and present him with a task which was quite beyond the capacity of his Command. By continuing his attacks on German cities he would of course have some effect on the enemy's transportation system. He agreed that he would guide his attacks as far as possible over transportation targets but he warned General Eisenhower that the effect would be largely fortuitous. They might or might not be effective. He was of course anxious to continue attacking cities in eastern Germany for as long as the hours of darkness made this possible.'

It is difficult to know whether Harris was genuinely doubtful whether Bomber Command could achieve the precision needed to hit pin-point targets in France, or whether his belief in the ultimate value of area bombing was so firm – some would say obsessive – that he was prepared to use any arguments in support of it. As things turned out, Bomber Command had demonstrated during the pre-invasion phase that it was able, in favourable circumstances, to attain a degree of precision during the hours of darkness fully on a par with that achieved by the American heavies in daylight.

In the meantime, support was growing among Allied commanders, scientists and economists for a concentration of oil-related targets once the Allied armies were firmly established on the Continent and the need for tactical support was not as urgent. The attraction of oil and its derivatives was clear. Without them nothing mechanical could move: cut off all the enemy's supplies of the vital fluid, and you would bring his war effort to a complete standstill. This was self-evident, but earlier attempts on the part of both the RAF and the USAAF to inhibit oil supplies, particularly at long range, had failed. Much water had flowed under many bridges since the Vice-Chief of the Air Staff's rose-tinted statement in January 1941, 'On the assumption that our present scale of attack on the enemy's oil plants is maintained, the enemy's oil position may be causing them grave anxiety by the spring of 1941.' Firstly, there had been the difficulty of landing the bombs precisely where they needed to hit to do the necessary damage, while enemy fighter strength had made such operations intolerably expensive in terms of aircraft and crews. But the tide had begun to turn. The American Fortresses and Liberators, thanks to losses that had already been inflicted on the *Luftwaffe* day-fighter force and the protection that they now enjoyed from the formidable long-range Mustang, could penetrate deep into Germany. Shorter-range oil targets too could be accurately hit by Bomber Command with the aid of Oboe and Gee-H, and it was clear that as and when the front line moved further into German territory, so it would be possible to mark targets deeper within the *Reich*. Strangely, there had been no mention of oil as a target in the 'Overlord' directive issued by Eisenhower on 17 April 1944. Ball-bearings and aircraft and their components had earlier been officially categorised as the priority targets, but Lieutenant-General Carl Spaatz, now designated Commander of the United States Strategic Air Forces in Europe (USSTAF), had long been of the opinion that oil represented the best target – another 'panacea' as Harris, who was not of the same mind, would have said. Spaatz and Harris shared a common characteristic, that of stubborn independence, and each interpreted the directives he received from his masters in the way that most nearly fitted his own philosophy of bombing. In this way, Spaatz had already, as early as May, started to attack oil-related targets, and he was clearly achieving notable success.

The Fifteenth US Air Force, flying from Italy, had begun attacking oil targets in April 1944 with missions against the vast Romanian oil-fields at Ploesti, and in May Spaatz had mounted attacks from England against German oil targets, including the important works at Leuna, near Leipzig. Enigma-based intelligence reports had indicated that these attacks had been highly successful and that the Germans, who were consuming vast quantities of fuel on the Eastern Front as well as in the west, were becoming increasingly concerned about the availability of sufficient oil to pursue the war. Air Chief Marshal Arthur Tedder, Deputy Supreme Commander, had become convinced that it was in an attack on oil that the best hopes lay of bringing the German war machine to a halt, and from that time on he used his influence with Harris to promote the oil offensive. The first result of this was an attack by 303 Lancasters and Mosquitos on the Nordstern synthetic oil plant in the Ruhr town of Gelsenkirchen on the night of 12/13 June, a night that also saw 671 aircraft from Bomber Command striking at communications targets in France, plus the now routine RCM, intruder, diversion and harassment sorties. The raids to France cost twenty-three aircraft, or 3.4 per cent of those taking part, while seventeen (6.1 per cent) did not come back from the attack on the more dangerous target of Gelsenkirchen. Good Oboe marking by PFF Mosquitos and follow-up bombing by the aircraft of the main force made this a highly successful attack. Although invasion-related tactical targets remained the Command's preoccupation, Harris continued the attack on oil on two further nights during June.

On 16/17 June a synthetic oil works at Sterkrade, also in the Ruhr, attracted 321 aircraft, of which thirty-one, almost a tenth of the total, were shot down, the majority by night-fighters. A larger force bombed flying-bomb launch sites in France without loss. For the aircrew, whether you were sent to France or Germany could mean the difference between life and death. Twenty-five Halifaxes of No. 77 Squadron at Full Sutton were among those detailed to go to Sterkrade. Horace Pearce writes:

'Using MZ697 "L" with a load of fifteen 500 lb explosive bombs we took off at 2300 hrs. On arrival over Holland we found ten-tenths cloud cover with tops at 7–8,000 feet, and over the target this increased to 16,000 feet and solid. It was at first difficult to find the aiming point as only glows from the target indicators could be seen deep in the cloud. However, on the bombing run green target indicators exploding at a higher level were identified with the glow in the clouds, and an attack was made at 0126 hours from 20,000 feet.

'Heavy *flak* above and below was intense, but at our height there was slightly less action. Base was reached without incident and we landed at 0335 hrs to later find that casualties had been heavy, the main force losing thirty-one out of the 300-plus aircraft engaged, a loss rate of 9.7 per cent. No. 4 Group came off worse, losing twelve of the ninety-three aircraft sent, a loss rate of twelve per cent. At debriefing we learned that seven of the aircraft from 77 Squadron's twenty-five detailed had not returned.'

The experiences of crews from Full Sutton that night illustrate very clearly not only the everyday – or, in this case, everynight – vicissitudes of operational flying, but also the haphazard nature of the bombing of even precision targets when the weather was adverse. Twenty-five crews were briefed for the operation, of which two failed to take off because of mechanical trouble. Then there were twenty-three. One pilot experienced excessive vibration in an engine and turned back after jettisoning his bombs in the North Sea. He landed at the ELG at Carnaby, leaving twenty-two aircraft still heading for Sterkrade. The seven that failed to return, therefore, represent almost one in three of those that actually went for the target. Hauptmann Martin Drewes, taking off at 0035 hrs from Leeuwarden, claimed two Lancasters, but it seems likely that one of his victims was the 77 Squadron Halifax NA 508 'A', which crashed in Holland on its way back home with the loss of all on board. Of the fifteen bombers that returned safely to England, three reported combats with night fighters and two others reported sightings. Three Halifaxes made emergency landings away from base, and one of those missing ditched in the North Sea after suffering severe damage in combat with a Ju 88, which the gunners claimed as destroyed. Happily, all the crew of the Halifax were picked up by a motor torpedo boat and survived.

The bombing at Sterkrade, carried out through thick cloud, was scattered, and very little damage was done to the refinery. All the returning crews spoke of PFF markers sinking into the clouds and only being visible as a coloured glow. Some of the Full Sutton crews claimed to have bombed the markers, but ten said that they had bombed on ETA. But estimated times and positions could well be many minutes and miles respectively in error, so 'bombing on ETA' was little more than a euphemism for dropping the bombs and hoping to hit something or other.

The bomb aimer of one of the No. 77 Squadron Halifaxes shot down, Flying Officer Jack Stewart Nott, evaded capture and was taken under the wing of the Dutch underground. Unhappily, however, the *Gestapo* had managed to penetrate the resistance cell handling his attempted escape, and on 8 July he was shot and killed together with two other RAF flyers when a group of plain-clothes *Gestapo* workers burst into the house in Tilburg in which he was hidden, and opened fire.

An example, one might say, of German bestiality. But there had been an incident the night before the Sterkrade raid that showed another side of a German's character, and it is convenient to relate it here, even though it is slightly out of sequence. Radio operator Feldwebel Walter Heidenreich, mentioned on a number of occasions already, was flying with a new crew. His previous pilot, Oberleutnant Günter Köberich, had been killed in April in the course of an American daylight attack on the airfield at Quakenbrück. Heidenreich had participated in twelve kills while flying with Köberich. Now his pilot was Leutnant Erich Jung, and the third man in the Ju 88 crew was Oberfeldwebel Hans Reinnagel, the flight mechanic. Their unit, II./NJG 2, had been moved to the airfield at Coulommiers, about thirty miles east of Paris, to take part in the battle of Normandy. That night they were briefed to circumnavigate Paris to the south after take-off, head for the Channel coast and patrol as far as Dieppe, engaging opportunity targets on the ground. This is Erich Jung's account of that mission:

'This flight was the nineteenth night operation we had done together, and the ninth in the invasion area. On these operations we had frequently observed that in the part of France occupied by the Germans lights, apparently signals, could be seen on the ground as we approached, but that they disappeared when we were overhead. The general assumption was that these lights were signals by the *Résistance* to guide supply flights from England. On this, our eighth anti-invasion sortie, we saw these lights again.

'After we had completed our operational mission, probably between 0200 and 0230 hrs, we climbed to 4–5,000 metres in the Dieppe area and headed south-east on our return flight to Coulommiers. We usually went up high on our return flight so that we could switch our *SN-2* on and pick up any other aircraft in the vicinity. After about thirty minutes Heidenreich vectored me on to a target to the west of us on a reciprocal heading. Our curve of pursuit brought us out directly beneath a four-engined bomber, and we quickly adjusted our speed to match his. The bomber continued on its course, heading for England, without any deviation. We could see the machine-guns in its nose and tail simply hanging down, giving the impression that they were not even manned. In any event, the crew seemed to think they were safe. It would have been very simple to shoot him down with our *Schräge Musik* exactly as we had been taught.

'I had to tell Reinnagel several times to switch the guns on before he did so, but even then he told me not to open fire immediately. This was a unique opportunity, he said, for him to show me in practice everything about the attack, where one should aim for the best effect, what was the defensive coverage of the bomber's guns and so on.

'Heinz Reinnagel had already flown more than three hundred night operations and had participated in the shooting down of fifty-three bombers. Walter Heidenreich had flown about seventy missions and had taken part in twenty-two kills. I was on my thirty-eighth operational flight and had only shot three bombers down, of which two were with Reinnagel and Heidenreich. I imagine that to them, because of my youth and relative inexperience, I must have seemed rather stupid. A little instruction, therefore, was not out of place.

'And so the lesson continued. We agreed on the job the aircraft was doing, and the only question in our minds was whether he had landed and taken off in southern France. We began to talk about the crew – how many were there in the bomber? What were their respective jobs? Where did they come from? Were they all English? Married? Children? Perhaps members of their families would be waiting for them at their base in England. Heinz said that his four-year-old daughter would be waiting for him. It was that which made me suddenly break off on to a reciprocal course and head for Coulommiers. Hans switched off the guns and each of us occupied himself with his own thoughts. None of us spoke again until after we had landed.'

The Bomber Command War Diaries (Middlebrook and Everitt) does not mention any aircraft carrying out Resistance operations that night, but several targets in France were attacked. It is possible that the four-engined bomber that Jung spared was a Lancaster of No. 5 Group returning from an attack on a fuel dump at Châtelleraut, between Poitiers and Tours.

On the night of the Sterkrade raid aircraft of No. 199 Squadron, No. 100 (Special Duties) Group, mounted the first so-called 'Mandrel screen' operation. As explained earlier, Mandrel was an airborne jammer operating on the frequencies of the German early-warning radars. The 'screen' comprised a number of aircraft, each carrying up to eight specially powerful jamming sets capable of covering a wide spectrum of frequencies. These aircraft flew a fixed, compact, static 'race-course' pattern, usually over the sea, covering the track of the bomber force. It became a standard tactic for the bombers to emerge from the Mandrel screen, so depriving the German air-defence organisation of much of their accustomed advance notice of the size, location and heading of the raid.

On the thirteenth of June the long-expected V-1 attack had begun when, of ten of the pilotless aircraft fired from launching sites in the Pas-de-Calais area, four had hit London and six civilians had been killed in Bethnal Green. The campaign soon intensified, with seventy-four of the revolutionary missiles hitting London on the sixteenth. From now on, Bomber Command was called upon more and more to attack the launching sites. For the crews, these missions were generally 'a piece of cake', with very low losses. So, for example, over 400 bombers attacked four sites on the night of the Sterkrade raid already described, bombing accurately on markers dropped by Oboe Mosquitos, and they did so without loss. Then, on 21/22 June, it was back to Germany, with raids on synthetic oil plants at Wesseling, south of Cologne, and Scholven/Buer in the Ruhr area. Despite the use of Oboe at Buer and H2S at Wesseling, a covering of low cloud that swallowed up the markers meant that the bombing by the total of 256 bombers deployed was inaccurate. Against the plant at Buer, near Duisburg, eight Lancasters were lost, but a far higher toll was exacted by the *Nachtjagd* against the force attacking Wesseling, all except five of which were from No. 5 Group. Three Lancaster squadrons, Nos. 44, 49 and 619, each lost six machines from the total of thirty-seven missing. In percentage terms this, at 27.8, was one of the gravest loss rates of the war. Between them two *Gruppen* alone, I. and II./NJG 1, destroyed twenty machines, five of which were claimed by Hauptmann Modrow.

Wesseling and Scholven/Buer were the targets again the next time a major force went to Germany, which was not until a month later. This time both raids were successful and only five out of 364 bombers were lost. In the meantime, Bomber Command was hitting, usually with comparative impunity, at targets in France, mainly V-weapon sites and railways. Only occasionally did the German night-fighters manage to engage the force, as for example on the night of 7/8 July, when 208 Lancasters and thirteen Mosquitos, mainly from No. 5 Group, went to strike at an underground V-1 storage depot at St Leu d'Esserent. This time it was single-engined all-weather fighters from I./JG 301 that did the major damage, shooting down twenty of the twenty-nine Lancasters that did not come back.

Erich Jung, Walter Heidenreich and Hans Reinnagel were crewing a Ju 88-R2, registration number 4R+AP, when Bomber Command attacked St Leu d'Esserant, and they destroyed two four-engined bombers. They had taken off from Coulommiers but intended to land at Villaroche, about forty kilometres south-east of Paris. When they arrived on the circuit at Villaroche they were given a landing number and told that it would be about twenty minutes before they were called in. They decided to return to their home base of Coulommiers instead of waiting, and they headed north-east at an altitude of about 150 metres, weaving from side to side, the standard procedure against possible attack by intruders. They soon saw their base ahead, and Heidenreich was about to call up and ask for landing permission. Erich Jung takes up the story:

'What we did not know at the time was that after we had checked out of the circuit at Villaroche the ground controller there had immediately telephoned Coulommiers and told them he thought we had an enemy intruder behind us. He had seen it as we were flying away, but had been too late to tell us.

'When I saw our airfield I stopped weaving for a moment. Our pursuer used this short period of straight and level flight to get in his first burst of fire. His aim was good. He hit us in the port wing between the cockpit and the engine. Long flames shot out. I saw the metal sheeting roll back from the wing like a sardine tin opening.

'Hans Reinnagel reacted immediately, releasing the escape hatch in the floor with his left foot, unstrapping the radio operator, lifting the seat and jettisoning it through the open hatch. Then he unstrapped me, grabbed me by my chest and side and pulled me backwards from my seat, so that we both left the burning aircraft almost simultaneously. While I was falling, before I had pulled my ripcord, the Mosquito swept over me and fired a second burst at our aircraft. Our landing places – Heidenreich 200 metres, Reinnagel 100 metres, Jung 500 metres from the blazing Ju 88. It was Reinnagel's seventh parachute jump.'

That same night a single-seater pilot enjoyed a rare success when he destroyed a Mosquito. Oberleutnant Fritz Krause of 1./NJGr 10, the experimental *Gruppe* under Hauptmann Karl-Friedrich Müller, took off at 0040 hrs on 8 July from the research station at Werneuchen, just to the north-east of Berlin. He was flying a Fw 190 A-5 experimentally equipped with a *Neptun J-2* (FuG 217) AI radar. The early-warning service had reported Mosquitos approaching Berlin, and Krause climbed over the capital to an altitude of 8,500 metres. At 0148 hrs he saw a twin-engined aircraft caught in searchlights and slightly below. He headed for the Mosquito at full throttle and opened fire at a range of about 200 metres, scoring hits in the starboard engine. The Berlin *Flak* was firing, so Krause fired off a recognition signal as he closed in again on the RAF machine, which was now trailing vapour from its damaged motor. He made two more attacks, again seeing his cannon shells hit, but he lost sight of his prey at an altitude of about 2,000 metres. When he landed at Werneuchen it was to find that his own aircraft was covered in oil from the Mosquito, and soon afterwards reports came in of a burning British aircraft crashing at 0155 hrs near the spot at which Krause had estimated that his victim would come down. There was one survivor from the Mosquito, Flight Lieutenant E. V. Saunders DFC.

With the V-1 attack on London becoming an increasingly important preoccupation of the government – 2,000 of the pilotless weapons had been fired against the British capital during June alone, causing just under 2,000 deaths among the civilian population, and at the beginning of July 120 a day were being fired – much of Bomber Command's efforts were now being directed against launching sites in the Pas-de-Calais area. By day the Allied air forces had achieved such supremacy in the air that German fighters did not trouble the lumbering heavies, which were intrinsically easy targets for interceptors. The lack of effective opposition by the German day-fighter force was to no small extent a direct result of the Spaatz-initiated oil offensive by both the USAAF and Bomber Command, which was already causing the Germans a major headache. In July a total of only twelve four-engined bombers were lost in attacks on the so-called 'ski sites' used for launching the flying bombs, six by day and six by night. What is interesting about these latter figures is that while approximately 3,400 sorties were flown in the daylight, only 1,400 or so were flown in the hours of darkness, for the same cost in machines lost. Only short months before it would have been unthinkable for Halifaxes and Lancasters to venture over the French coast in daylight; had they done so they would have been simply blasted out of the sky by the Bf 109s and the Fw 190s.

With Bomber Command operating comparatively unscathed over France, hammering tactical targets in support of the Allied armies advancing from the Normandy bridgeheads as well as bombing flying-bomb sites, Harris was unable for the moment to pursue his preferred offensive against German cities to the extent that he would have wished. Despite the generally low losses against French targets there were occasional reminders that although the *Nachtjagd*'s capabilities were diminished it still remained a force to be reckoned with. On the night of 18/19 July rail installations at Aulnoye and Revigny were bombed by a total of 242 Lancasters. Both raids, but particularly the one against Revigny, involved deeper penetration of the mainland than those against V-bomb sites did, and the German night-fighters found the No. 5 Group Lancasters going for Revigny, shooting down twenty-four, almost a quarter of them. No. 619 Squadron sent thirteen Lancasters to Revigny, and only eight came back. On the *Luftwaffe* side, *Fahnenjunker* (officer-cadet) Oberfeldwebel Herbert Altner of III./NJG 3, stationed at Laon-Athies, claimed five Lancasters.

In furtherance of the oil target, refineries at Wesseling, Buer, Bottrop, Homberg and Wanne-Eikel, all in or near the Ruhr area and so within Oboe range, also received the attention of the heavies during July. The Ruhr was still a dangerous area for the bombers to venture into, and the attack on Homberg on 20/21 July cost twenty bombers from the 158 in the force, two the victims of Hermann Greiner, his thirty-fifth and thirty-sixth kills.

While V-1 launching sites, oil and support for the Allied troops advancing in Normandy still remained the priority, Harris nevertheless managed to mount four major attacks against German cities before July was out. The first, against Kiel on 23/24 July, was on a scale not seen since May, with 629 bombers dispatched. The change of tactics took the Germans by surprise, and that and the large and complex RCM, deception and support operations also mounted resulted in only four heavy bombers being lost. But large though the attack on Kiel was, it was only one facet of the total effort for the night, which amounted to 1,118 sorties and cost only five aircraft. The reduced losses over the previous two or three months meant that at last the production of heavy bombers was exceeding losses by a large margin. The far-sighted aircrew-training programme, too, was paying dividends, and there was no shortage of trained flyers to man the weapons of destruction. Kiel, by any standards an important target, suffered severe damage, particularly in the port area and U-boat yards.

The following night Harris embarked upon a three-raid offensive against the Bavarian industrial city of Stuttgart, sending 614 bombers on 24/25 July, 550 on 25/26 and 496 on 28/29. With the large number of bombers at his disposal he was able to commit these forces without neglecting the other priorities set for him. The three raids cost seventy-two Lancasters and Halifaxes, 4.3 per cent of those taking part. The attack on which the most bombers were lost – thirty-nine – was the final one. Hauptmann Walter Knickmeier, formerly the successful fighter controller at Deelen and by now operations officer of NJG I, recalls the occasion and draws attention to the shortcomings of the methods of fighter control that the Germans were using:

'In the first attacks on Stuttgart the night fighters were not very successful. I had a phone call from Oberst Wittmer, Chief of Staff of *Luftflotte Reich*. At the time I am speaking of, the First *Gruppe* was at Venlo, the Second at Eindhoven, the Third at Leeuwarden and the Fourth at St Trond in Belgium. *Geschwader* Staff was still at Deelen. I was ordered to fly to Stuttgart/Echterdingen. Wittmer told me a third heavy attack was expected on Stuttgart and that we couldn't afford another bad result. Göring had been complaining about the poor successes. Twenty kilometres west of Stuttgart an Operations Centre (*Gefechtsstand*) had been set up, and it was equipped with a *Jagdschloss* radar. This was one of the new generation of radars, very familiar nowadays but quite revolutionary in those days, which had a rotating time-base and showed an all-round picture of the air situation. There were three of them in service at that time, one near Stuttgart, one defending Berlin and one on the Lower Elbe covering Hamburg. The *Jagdschloss* had a frequency in the centimetre range, which meant that the responses were very small points, and it could see at least 120 kilometres. It was fantastic. It was technically the most advanced control device that there was at that time, but the trouble was that the technical officers at the stations were inexperienced and had no experience as controllers. It was hard for me to understand why there wasn't an expert there so that he could infiltrate the enemy bomber stream. When I began to look at it I found out that there wasn't even reliable direct communication with the Channel coast to permit early warning. It is difficult to describe the extent of the fundamental errors that were made and the unintelligent way in which the device was being used.

'The first thing I did was to find out the location of the various fighter units I could call on to defend Stuttgart and the likely direction of approach of the bombers. Then I established that there were radio beacons within 120 kilometres of Stuttgart where I could assemble my fighters. It was, of course, important that I found beacons within the range of the *Jagdschloss*.

'It was quite late in the night when the bomber stream came in. I remember we had a perfect picture of it approaching. I seem to remember the stream coming in over France and then dividing into three. However, I was able to control the fighters, which were from NJG 1 and therefore very experienced, into the stream, and kill followed kill. I think most of the victories were on the approach to the target.

'Later that night I had a telephone call from the Commanding General, Beppo Schmid. He asked how such a result was possible. I explained how easy it had been. All I had to say was, "Here are the bombers, here are the fighters, what course do they have to fly to get into the bomber stream?" There was no jamming on the equipment. It was, I told him, unforgivable that the performance capability of the equipment was not being exploited. I had carried out the control directly from the radar screen with an R/T microphone. The next day I had to fly to Jüterbog to report in detail. General Huth, the Divisional Commander, was there, and he played hell with his senior officers, and he said, "I am sending Hauptmann Knickmeier to your units, and everyone from the Signals Branch (*Nachrichtentruppen*) and the *Geschwader*, including the *Staffelkapitäne*, must listen to his views on night fighting."

'If I remember correctly, the RAF were shocked by this defeat, which was very costly in crews, and there wasn't another major attack on Germany for the next two weeks.'

It was indeed a costly night for the RAF, because in addition to the thirty-nine bombers lost against Stuttgart a further twenty-two were destroyed out of 307 that went to hard-hit Hamburg – 154 aircrew lost as against 265 individuals killed on the ground – resulting in an overall loss rate of 7.6 per cent. Again Halifaxes came off worst. None went to Stuttgart, but of those attacking Hamburg eighteen out of 187, almost ten per cent, did not come back. The unit that suffered worst was No. 431 (Iroquois) Squadron, a unit of No. 6 (Canadian) Group, which lost five machines of the seventeen that took off; almost as badly hit was another Canadian squadron, No. 408 (Goose).

Walter Knickmeier was correct in his recollection that there was not another major attack on Germany for some weeks following the raids on Stuttgart and Hamburg, but not when he thinks that the pause was due to the Bomber Command losses on that night. Harris could now call on aircraft and crews in abundance. Targets in France absorbed the majority of his effort. There was a massive break-out by Allied troops from the Normandy beach-heads in the final week of July, and much bombing effort was needed to support the rapid advances into France that followed.

In daylight on 30 July, for example, Bomber Command sent 662 heavies and thirty Mosquitos to bomb German positions in the way of the American advance. On 1 August 777 bombers went out to hit at flying-bomb sites, a total exceeded two days later when 1,114 were sent out to attack the same type of target. During the night of 7/8 August over a thousand Lancasters, Halifaxes and Mosquitos made devastatingly accurate attacks on German concentrations ahead of Allied troops, demonstrating the extreme precision which, given the right conditions, could now be achieved using Oboe, a Master Bomber and well-trained and well-briefed main force crews.

Although there were still pockets of stubborn resistance, the collapse of the Germans in France meant that now Harris could turn his sights back on the Fatherland. On 15 August, with a view to the forthcoming resumption of his strategic offensive, he sent 1,004 bombers in daylight to attack nine night-fighter airfields in Holland and Belgium. All the raids were accurate, and only three Lancasters were lost. That same day Operation 'Anvil' began when Allied troops landed in the south of France to embark upon their rapid advance northwards. In the east the Soviet armies were poised on the borders of East Prussia and well into Poland, while the Baltic states, Czechoslovakia, Hungary and Romania were under siege. The Germans were fighting a bitter defensive battle against Allied advances in Italy. Hitler still talked of 'miracle weapons' that would turn defeat into victory, but already his V-1 campaign against England was faltering. By the beginning of September all the V-1 launching sites in France had been overrun. There were still sites in Belgium and Holland, and the Germans had begun launching flying bombs against Britain from specially adapted He 111 bombers, but the threat was perceptibly diminishing. In addition to the loss of sites to the Germans, anti-aircraft guns and fighters, including the new jet fighter, the Meteor, were preventing a very large proportion of the V-1s reaching their target. There was still the V-2, the long-range rocket, to reckon with, but the occupation of France by Allied troops had already reduced the nature of that threat considerably by eliminating the many V-2 firing sites that had been constructed there in anticipation of the opening of the attack on London.

Germany, battered and bleeding, was on the ropes, and such reply as she could make to the mighty air power of the Allies was to little effect. Yet it would still take long months of punishment before the knockout came.

Above left: Oberleutnant Erich Jung (centre) with his crew, *Feldwebel* Walter Heidenreich (radio operator, left) and Hans Reinnagel (flight mechanic, right). This crew shot down eight Lancasters within thirty minutes during the RAF attack on Nuremberg on 16 March 1945. This picture was taken on 28 April 1944. The previous night Jung and his crew had destroyed a Lancaster during the RAF attack on Friedrichshafen, but on landing at St Dizier their aircraft ran into a bomb crater on the runway and burst into flames. The crew got out without injury. Photo taken at the railway station at Kassel on the way back to their base. *(Jung)*

Above right: Freddy Fairweather with air- and groundcrew, No.51 Squadron, RAF Snaith, c. March 1945.

Below: Hauptmann Paul Szameitat and crew, 5./NJG 3, at Schleswig, 1943. Szameitat was killed on 2 January 1944 with 29 kills to his credit. *(Kutzner)*

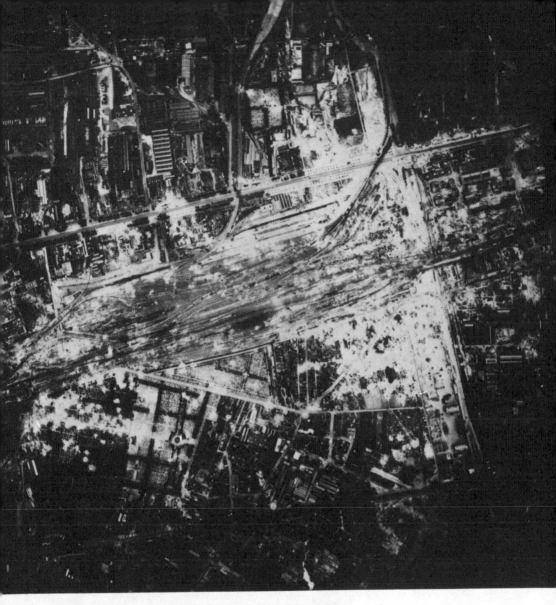

Above: A marshalling yard in France visited at night by Bomber Command during the pre-invasion period. This photograph testifies to the high degree of accuracy attained by the RAF in the latter stages of the war. *(Osborne)*

Left: SN-2 set in He 219. This example is in the possession of the Air and Space Museum, Washington DC. *(Hinchliffe)*

CHAPTER THIRTEEN

The Reich Again

August to December 1944

By having to provide direct support to the invasion and the Battle of Normandy, Harris had been obliged to make considerable changes in the part that his Command was playing in the war against Germany. Until the spring of 1944 the role of his force had been almost entirely independent, but experience during the French campaign had shown that heavy bombers could, if the circumstances were right, be used to considerable effect against targets smaller and more precise than urban areas; in other words, that by operating in co-ordination with the forces on the ground the Lancasters and Halifaxes could serve an important tactical purpose.

Alongside the heavy bombers of the USAAF and the vast Allied tactical air fleets that struck clinically and ruthlessly at transport targets, enemy troop dispositions, bases, airfields, V-weapon sites and supply depots, Bomber Command had taken advantage by daylight of the overwhelming air superiority that the Allies enjoyed over France. From June to August 1944 inclusive the Command dropped almost six times as many bombs by weight on targets in the occupied countries as it did on Germany itself, many of them by day. During the same period oil had clearly emerged as a most worthwhile target. Nevertheless, Harris's belief that the primary role of his heavies lay in the destruction of German cities had not been weakened by considerations such as these. To some extent his views were shared by Carl Spaatz, in that Spaatz, despite being *de facto* the initiator of the renewed oil offensive, was also anxious to exercise a freer hand in the choice of targets for his Fortresses and Liberators and so to exploit the gathering weakness of the German day-fighter force, a weakness that his Command had brought about by their policy of the destruction of aircraft production facilities on the ground and the fighters themselves in battles in the air. Spaatz did not, however, share Harris's belief in the power of bombing to destroy the morale of the German population in industrial cities to a degree that would have a decisive effect on the outcome of the war. By mid-August, with the Battle of Normandy won and Allied troops advancing rapidly across France, both heavy bomber forces were able to begin devoting a greater proportion of their efforts to the Third *Reich* itself.

Making good use of the increased force now at his disposal, Harris sent out almost 1,200 aircraft on the night 16/17 August, including 461 Lancasters against the Baltic port of Stettin and 348 Lancasters and Halifaxes against Kiel, also on the Baltic. One thousand-plus sorties in a night were now the norm for Bomber Command, a far cry from Harris's show piece 'Thousand Plan' against Cologne in May 1942, and the aircraft he was using, Lancasters, Halifax IIIs and Mosquitos, could carry more, bigger and better bombs and drop them more accurately than hitherto. Bombing was also less costly. Whereas an attack on Stettin in April 1943 by a similar force had cost twenty-one bombers, this time only five were lost. The Kiel attack, too, was accomplished comparatively cheaply, costing only a further five heavies.

Against this, from having attained the pinnacle of its success in late March 1944, the *Nachtjagd* now found itself in rapid decline. As the bomber campaign had grown since its early beginnings, so the night-fighter force had developed reactively into an organisation of considerable complexity. Despite the impressive results that it had achieved in total numbers of bombers destroyed, however, it had failed to attain the efficiency necessary in the long term to prevent the destruction of Germany's cities.

There were a number of fundamental reasons for the unpredictably rapid collapse of Schmid's *Nachtjagd*. Much of its earlier success had rested on the controllers' ability to get the fighters into the air in good time to intercept the bomber stream, but now much of that ability had suddenly been lost with the capture by the invading Allies of advanced long-range early-warning radars and operational airfields. The escalating shortage of petrol was making itself felt, so that not only operational flying, but even more so training flights, had to be restricted. Losses of crews, particularly experienced ones, had been severe, both in the air battle by night and in the vain attacks on ground targets following the invasion, so that now the majority of men to fly the Junkers, Messerschmitts and Heinkels were young and inexperienced, and the death toll among new initiates to the craft of night fighting was severe. Then there were the Mosquitos, an ever-present and dreaded hazard to the fighters in the air and on the ground. Harris's tactics, developed in operations in support of the invasion, of splitting his force and flying deception raids on an increasing scale, had further impeded the ability of the German controllers to bring their aircraft into action. Since July, when a Ju 88 equipped with *SN-2* and flown by an inexperienced crew had landed at Woodbridge in error, Bomber Command had been effectively jamming the night-fighters' AI radar with Window cut to correct dimensions for this longer-wavelength radar. And, over and above these many disadvantages, not only the enemy radars but also the night-fighter force's extremely complex communications system were being attacked with progressively mounting efficiency by No. 100 Group and other airborne jamming aircraft.

Both ground-to-air communications and various visual and other ways in which the fighters might find the streams of bombers had developed pragmatically since the collapse of Kammhuber's inflexible *Himmelbett* system in summer 1943. *Himmelbett* still existed on a limited scale and in certain areas as one option for interception control, but in general variations of the Wild Boar and Tame Boar freelance methods formed the basis of the aerial defence of the *Reich* by night. There had been a long battle of action by No. 100 Group and reaction by the *Nachtjagd*, making the task of the radio/radar operators in the night-fighters more and more complicated and confusing, to such an extent that some night-fighters, particularly Ju 88s, now carried an extra operator to handle the radar, leaving the established *Funker* to deal with navigation and communications.

For the night-fighter crews there was a bewildering choice of aids, both electronic and visual, to locate the bombers. There were the airborne radars for use once they were in the vicinity of the bomber stream. There was *SN-2* plus a short-range modification, the *Naxos* H2S homer and, in some aircraft, a *Neptun* rear-warning device. Some fighters carried a *Flensburg* set that picked up signals from the bombers' Monica fighter-warning radar, while there were two forms of IFF (Identification Friend or Foe) equipment, *Erstling* and *Neuling*, both of which were enthusiastically homed in on by No. 100 Group, so that night-fighter crews used them only reluctantly, which in turn caused confusion to the fighter controllers and anti-aircraft gunners.

The radio operator in a night-fighter had a vast range of frequencies at his disposal on which he might find information that would help him to locate and penetrate the bomber stream. There were the *Geschwaderbefehlswelle* (*Geschwader* command broadcast) and the *Gruppenbefehlswelle* (*Gruppe* command broadcast), both transmitted on alternative frequencies; there were the *Reportagen*, or running commentaries, on *Korps*, *Division* and *Gau* frequencies, plus the so-called *Herrmann-Welle*, the broadcast originally intended specifically for the single-seat *Wilde Sau* aircraft, which the conventional fighters also found useful. All these, plus discrete fighter-control channels, were on several R/T wavelengths, and were duplicated and supplemented in Morse code on *Luftflotte* high-powered beacons and the so-called *Korpsführungswellen* (*Korps* control broadcasts), which were also on several frequencies. Over and above this selection of broadcast and control channels there were the W/T beacons, used for holding and homing, plus airfield beacons. Civilian radio stations were also used for bearings and for the air-raid warning commentaries that they carried, so that in case of necessity the night-fighter crews could listen in and discover from the broadcasts what city was that night's target. As a further aid to finding the bombers, the forces' broadcast station 'Anne-Marie' broadcast programmes of music, so that if the fighter crews failed to find one of the more specific channels unjammed they could tell the general area that the bombers were heading for: dance music, for example, would indicate the Berlin area, sea shanties the Hamburg region, waltzes Vienna, and so on. Some night-fighter *Gruppen* used so-called *Fühlungshalter* aircraft, usually captained by experienced pilots, who would try to locate the stream and fly with it, broadcasting its location, height and heading to the other fighters. Yet so all-encompassing was the RAF jamming, from transmitters on the ground and in the air, that the night-fighters often had to fall back on visual signals to aid them in their quest for the elusive bombers.

Alternatively, the *Flak* fired star-shells in set patterns from numerous locations within the *Reich*: two star-shells, one above the other, showed Berlin; three star-shells side by side showed Nuremberg; four star-shells side by side indicated Emden, and so on. Searchlights were beamed in specific combinations and configurations: Memel, for example, was shown by two crossed beams; Hamburg by four beams showing as two letters 'V'; Vienna as a letter 'X'. Then there were searchlight lanes for use as aids to navigation, lights shining vertically at intervals of about thirty kilometres and forming a path between airfields, so that fighters in need could find somewhere to land. Over and above all this, the track, turning points and targets of the bomber stream were illuminated by the *Beleuchtergruppen*, usually comprised of Ju 88s, who flew high above the stream and the towns under attack, dropping their flares. Additionally, on an *ad hoc* basis, some night-fighter units deployed *Führerflugzeuge* (leader aircraft) which, like the *Fühlungshalter*, would find the stream and mark it for the other aircraft of their unit with distinctively coloured flares.

These enormously complicated arrangements, however, and particularly those that were radar- and radio-based, were very vulnerable to counteraction. No. 100 Group had gained enormously in knowledge, know-how and operational capacity during the months leading up to the invasion and in the Battle of Normandy, so that by late August the *Nachtjagd*'s communications were virtually swamped. The *Funker* was still, from the point of view of seeking out the enemy and navigating the fighter into contact, the most important man in the crew, but even the best of them found it virtually impossible to penetrate the obfuscation of British jamming, while the new and inexperienced operators, who were in a large majority, tended metaphorically to throw up their hands in defeat. From now on, such successes as the night-fighters achieved were more a result of chance than of organised control, and the total of bomber losses by night fell steadily.

With the cumulative losses of experienced aircrew, men from various other branches, particularly bombers, had been drafted into the *Nachtjagd* and found themselves on operations with only the minimum of conversion training. One such man was Hans Angersbach. Angersbach had been a servant in the officers' mess at the headquarters of NJG I at the country house in Zeitz, Holland, and he had volunteered for aircrew training in early 1943. In September that year he had been posted as a flight mechanic (*Bordmechaniker*) to KG 30, which was then equipped with the Ju 88, and had carried out his first bomber operation, against London, on 14 March 1943. By June, Angersbach had flown on four more operations against England, one to London, two to Plymouth and one to Portsmouth. Then III./KG 30 was disbanded, and Angersbach's crew was transferred to night-fighters. After a rushed period of training, they joined I./NJG 2 at Kassel/Rothwesten, equipped with the Ju 88, on 28 August 1944. Two nights later, when Bomber Command attacked Stettin, the very much undertrained crew took off on their first mission. They had climbed to 10,000 feet when an engine caught fire, and the three crew members, pilot Helmut Calgeer, radio operator Gerd Lutz and Hans Angersbach himself, had to take to their parachutes. All three were injured to varying degrees on landing and had to be admitted to hospital. Their first operational flight with the *Nachtjagd* had hardly been auspicious.

29/30 August was a bad night for Bomber Command, with 5.7 per cent of the all-Lancaster force of 402 that returned to Stettin, and 7.9 per cent of the 189 Lancasters from No. 5 Group that visited Königsberg, being lost, mostly to night fighters. There was still no room for complacency, particularly when raids involved penetration deep into enemy territory.

Much of Bomber Command's effort in early September was by day. Enemy positions in and around the beleaguered port of Le Havre, for example, were attacked on six separate occasions from 5 to 10 September by large forces of four-engined bombers.

Night-fighters operating from Dutch territory were still an irritant, and on 3 September a major force of Lancasters and Halifaxes, 663 in number and supported by eight Mosquitos, was dispatched to attack their six bases in Holland,

Volkel, Gilze-Rijen, Soesterberg, Eindhoven, Deelen and Venlo. In clear weather, the bombing was devastatingly accurate, and only one Halifax failed to return. A young navigator doing his first operation in Halifax III MH-Y of No. 51 Squadron was Sergeant Peter Charlesworth[1], who writes:

'We were a very young crew: the skipper, Flight Sergeant Len Berry, was twenty-three years old and he had a moustache, so we would sometimes call him "Dad". I had had my twentieth birthday the previous week, and I was not the youngest: I think that one of our gunners and the engineer were either eighteen or nineteen, so that our average age was about twenty. We were little more than schoolboys. We all got along together very well, and I remember clearly that a tremendous "crew spirit" had already developed. Despite the understandable apprehension that we felt when we went out on bombing raids, there was a strong element of fun in what we were doing. Venlo was a nice trip to start on. We had been told that short-range "daylights" were a piece of cake, but of course I was very nervous, venturing into the unknown for the first time. The weather was not too good, and take-off was postponed for over three hours, but we finally got airborne at 1545 hrs. We were not far out when our Distant-Reading Compass developed a fault, so we turned back towards England. Then we changed our minds – the idea of aborting our first operation was unthinkable – and turned round again and headed east. We climbed and broke cloud to the impressive spectacle of hundreds of four-engined bombers all heading in the same direction, so we felt more confident. The target was clear and we bombed accurately, as was later confirmed when the photographs were developed. Flak over Venlo was moderately heavy and accurate – I looked out of the nose as we began our bombing run and had a spasm of fear as I saw the sky ahead bespattered with small black cloudlets left behind by exploding shells. Over the target itself, just before we bombed, a *flak* shell burst very near to our port wing-tip, and we later found out that we had sixteen holes in the wing and outer engine. The rest of the trip was uneventful, but the weather was very bad over Yorkshire and we had to land away at Carnaby. From almost seven hundred aircraft bombing airfields in Holland that afternoon, only one was lost.'

This raid was one of many during the period against German fighter airfields. So badly was the Venlo base damaged that it was evacuated two days later after the craters in one of the runways had been filled in to make it possible for the aircraft to take off. It is difficult, even impossible, to imagine the feelings of German troops at that period of the war, with defeat and all the uncertainties it would bring with it clearly approaching. The diary of a night-fighter *Funker* of I./NJG 1 stationed at Venlo, however, gives some insight:

'31 August: I can no longer believe in victory. The best one can hope for is

---

[1] This is a pseudonym. For personal reasons the navigator does not want his real name to be used.

an armistice and a capitulation treaty on favourable terms, given that the *Wehrmacht* is to a large extent still intact. God only knows what the alternative is! In any event, we are carrying on with the usual doggedness. As long as the *Reich* continues, its soldiers can't have second thoughts. All we can do is to wait and see what happens. Somehow or other we'll come through.

1 September: Yesterday evening the fact that we don't take off after Mosquitos any more depressed me more than I can say. There was an attack on Cologne and Leverkusen, and all the bombers flew right overhead of us. It was a clear night with a full moon, and the searchlights kept on picking up bombers. The conditions were perfect for night-fighters. This morning we were woken up again by an air-raid alarm. Three fighter-bombers carried out low-level attacks on the airfield and dropped a few bombs. There seems to be ammunition on fire somewhere nearby.

2 September: A lot of new crews have arrived, mostly from bomber units that have been disbanded. But what's the point of having a lot of aircrew when we haven't got any fuel or enough aircraft? Yesterday Hauptmann Modrow got his Knight's Cross from the Divisional Commander, and Schneider got the German Cross in Gold and his promotion to Feldwebel. It's only a few months since he arrived with us as a new *Funker*. He was only a Gefreiter then, and he looked rather unsure of himself. Now he's a Feldwebel with the German Cross in Gold and thirty kills to his credit. Quite a record. Perhaps I might be forgiven for not being able to suppress a certain feeling of stupid envy. Today lorries drove through loaded with lots of wild-looking soldiers from the Western Front. That means a retreat somewhere or other. They spoke of abandoning their positions in panic, of the evacuation of Belgium and so on. Quite understandably many of us here sympathised with what they were saying.

4 September: Yesterday was Sunday, and the Tommies were here again, firstly with fighter-bombers and then with about seventy four-engined heavies. They came in one at a time at about ten thousand feet in the clearest of skies. dropping their bombs. You could see the bombs leaving the bomb bays perfectly clearly. I didn't see any shot down by *flak*. But the airfield flak claimed three. But there wasn't a fighter to be seen, and yet the bombers didn't have fighter protection. It was worse than shameful! We should have been able to do something with our 219s. The British dropped heavy bombs, and the runways weren't clear by night-time. It's obvious that such work as is being done now is getting ready for giving up the airfield. Everything is being packed up. Now Finland has deserted us. How long can we go on?

10 September: We are back in the *Reich*. The curtain has fallen on the drama of Venlo. The last things were packed during the night of the fifth, and the last machine took off from Venlo at 0900 hrs on the sixth. The move itself (to Münster/Handorf) was carried out quite smoothly according to schedule, but the evacuation of the airfield was more of a panic flight than an orderly clearance. The food store at Venlo was blown up, and thousands of kilos of urgently needed food destroyed – and only a few kilometres away German civilians were standing at the airfield gates and watching. The

Dutch plundered thousands of mattresses, beds, officers' armchairs and so on. All things that were in desperately short supply in Germany. The supplies of food in the officers' mess were destroyed too. Rabbits, hens, pigs were set free and were running around all over the place. There were requisitioned bicycles lying about at the side of the road and in the town. Innumerable radio sets provided by benevolent funds were destroyed because no one knew what to do with them in the confusion of the evacuation of the airfield.

'In the midst of all this turmoil there were columns of *Wehrmacht* soldiers retreating from the west. Every one of them thought he was going to meet the first British tank round the next corner. Using his own initiative, one senior NCO who had just got back from leave managed to rescue a Ju 88 that should already have been blown up, and he managed to take off in it before the runway was finally destroyed. And now, a week later, the British are still a long way off. Small parties are still going to the airfield to see what they can save. The camp has been occupied by the army, and the Dutch have been driven out with small-arms fire. Hitler Youth were brought in from Germany to dig trenches. The day after the attack large numbers of Dutch from the town were rounded up and taken to the airfield to fill in the craters on the runway. They say that anyone who objected was shot. In the afternoon a Ju 52 loaded with arms arrived, but it crashed on landing when it ran into a crater. The weapons – machine-guns, machine-pistols, rifles, ammunition and so on – were sold to the Dutch for cigarettes.'

Münster/Handorf in Westphalia, to which I./NJG 1 moved when it left Venlo so precipitately, had been one of the largest and best equipped military airfields in Germany, with extensive servicing and repair facilities for many types of aircraft. But in common with almost all *Luftwaffe* bases it too had suffered from the attentions of the Allied bomber fleets:

'10 September: We sit from ten until late afternoon in the street outside a ruined house in Handorf and wait to find out what is going to happen to us. The airfield looks to be in a terrible mess. There is scarcely a building in one piece; everything is terribly damaged, bombed and burnt out. Repair hangars collapsed with aircraft still in them, accommodation blocks without windows or roofs, roads and squares with vast craters and a landing and take-off area covered in bomb holes – that is Münster/Handorf. And in the ruins life goes on as well as it can. At last, as night is falling, we are taken to an accommodation area outside the aerodrome itself, where we are given somewhere very makeshift to sleep . . . '

While raids on short-range targets by daylight, virtually unopposed as they were by day fighters, were proving an effective and economical way of carrying the war into the Fatherland, Harris was not diverted from his fundamental aim of hitting major cities. During the night of 11/12 September, for instance, he sent 226 Lancasters and fourteen Mosquitos, all from No. 5 Group, to the small city of Darmstadt, so far comparatively untouched. It was a devastating attack, giving much support to the claims of the Group Commander, Cochrane, that his marking and bombing methods were more efficient than those of Bennett's Pathfinder Force. Accurate bombing in excellent weather conditions created a firestorm of Hamburg dimensions, and between ten and fifteen thousand perished and up to 70,000 out of a population of 120,000 were bombed out of their homes. But Darmstadt lay deep enough into Germany for the night fighters to be alerted and scrambled in time to find the bomber stream, and twelve Lancasters were shot down. Peter Spoden of NJG 6 claimed two of them.

That the *Nachtjagd* was not yet a completely spent force was demonstrated once more on 12/13 September when seventeen Lancasters were destroyed out of a force of 387 that attacked Frankfurt and four were lost from 217 that bombed Stuttgart. What was changing, however, was the accuracy of Bomber Command's navigation and target finding, a direct result of the fact that navigational aids such as Gee were now available far into Germany. Bombing on both targets was concentrated and accurate, and many were killed. But it was not always so. Crews of the 483 heavy bombers that attacked Kiel three nights later, a Friday, reported that the attack was 'highly concentrated', and Sunday's *News of the World*, under the headline KIEL SET ON FIRE ONCE MORE said, 'By the end of the attack fierce fires had broken out in the port, and crews could still see the glow when they were 120 miles on their way home.' The truth was that many of the bombs that were dropped fell outside the city, although some moderate damage was done in the port area and the old town. Only two Lancasters and four Halifaxes were shot down, probably by *flak*. It was a frustrating night for the *Nachtjagd*, misled as they were by a force of forty-four Mosquitos that went to Berlin and other targets, 164 heavies making a diversionary sweep over the North Sea, and mine-laying forays off Norway and Denmark. As was by now routine, No. 100 Group was out in force. These support sorties cost Bomber Command a further five aircraft, a higher proportion than the main attack, including, unusually, four Mosquitos, but still the overall losses came to no more than 1.3 per cent.

Kiel was Peter Charlesworth's sixth operation, and his first by night:

'I ambled into the Navigation Section, and someone had scrawled on the blackboard, "Ops Tonight". This rather shook me: I was looking forward to doing a tour on daylights, but I had to resign myself to this new development . . .

'At main briefing Wing Commander Ling referred to "Bomber Command's monthly visit to Kiel". Our load was one 2,000 lb bomb, the rest incendiaries. We were told to expect enemy fighter opposition. It was with rather mixed feelings that we went out to Victor, our aircraft for that night. For me this was more like my first op as I had imagined it would be. Ever since starting navigation training I had, as it were, been brought up to expect night flying as the rule rather than the exception. It had been quite a pleasant surprise to find that Halifaxes were undertaking much of the RAF's daylight bomber offensive.

'It was still light when we took off. We flew out to seven degrees east at 2,000 feet to pass beneath a cold front and to achieve tactical surprise, and then climbed to our bombing altitude of 20,000 feet. We crossed over

Schleswig-Holstein with the *flak* already bursting around us, and search-lights, like a blind man's groping fingers, feeling the sky.

'I find it impossible to describe the illusion of infinite slowness as we approached the target. The last five minutes, I thought, would never pass. At last, however, our bombs were gone and we were turning away from the target, weaving to avoid the intense flak and searchlight concentration. Then suddenly Smiler's voice came over the intercom: "Corkscrew port, Skip, for Christ's sake!" I found myself off my seat, with my chart on top of me, as Len put his stick hard over. He said afterwards that he was sure we went past the vertical. A Focke-Wulf 190 had been on our tail, but we lost him, thank God. Johnny also saw a twin-engined aircraft, probably an Me 401, on our beam, but either he didn't see us or he was interested in someone else. Bas saw it too.

'We were followed right to the coast by *flak* and searchlights, but were never once in trouble. Down again to 2,000 feet, and so to base, interrogation and bed. And next day – leave!'

The operational pattern continued throughout September, with raids by day to France, mostly to the Calais area, alternating with night raids to Germany. The Allied airborne landings at Arnhem took place on the seventeenth, and Bomber Command mounted operations in support. Hermann Greiner of IV./NJG 1, promoted to Hauptmann three months previously and now with thirty-seven victories to his credit, was flying that night from Dortmund, to which base his *Gruppe* had been withdrawn from the airfield of Leeuwarden in Holland. He had not been long in the air when, without warning, his Bf 110 was raked with cannon fire from a marauding Mosquito. With one engine on fire, Greiner managed to maintain control of the aircraft and to evade a second attack by the British intruder. He called up his *Funker*, Oberfeldwebel Kissing, and ordered him to bale out. He received no reply, and realised that Kissing had been wounded in the attack. Rather than abandon his radio operator to his fate, Greiner decided to stay with him and attempt to land the Messerschmitt. Fortunately he was close enough to Dortmund to find the airfield and make a crash-landing there, one engine still ablaze. Kissing, however, had been hit in the head by a bullet, and he was already dead.

On the night of 19/20 September almost 300 bombers went to Mönchen-gladbach and Rheydt, twin towns between Düsseldorf and the Dutch border. Four Lancasters and one Mosquito were lost, and that Mosquito was piloted by Wing Commander Guy Gibson, the Master Bomber for the attack. His valiant career, which had earned him the Victoria Cross, the Distinguished Service Order and bar and the Distinguished Flying Cross and bar, ended when his aircraft crashed in flames in Holland on the homeward flight. His navigator, Squadron Leader J. B. Warwick, died with him.

Just how Gibson's Mosquito came to grief is not known with any certainty. Gibson had remained over the target throughout the attack, broadcasting instructions to the heavy bombers, and there had been no sign that he was in trouble. His was the only Mosquito that was lost that night, and only one German fighter pilot claimed to have shot a Mosquito down. Oberleutnant Kurt Welter of 10./JG 300, one of Hajo Herrmann's most successful Wild Boars, was flying an Fw 190 A-8. With the same aircraft, he had already claimed his first Mosquito the night before, presumably the one that was lost during an attack on Bremerhaven. Kurt Welter would claim his third Mosquito on the night of 27/28 September, when the RAF's target was Kaiserslautern, although British records show all the Mosquitos operating that night as returning safely to base. Welter was destined to end the war with the reputation of being the most successful '*Mosquito-Jäger*, with at least six of the 'wooden wonders' to his credit out of a total score of sixty-one victories. Some sources claim that he destroyed up to twenty-five Mosquitos, but estimates such as this seem wild in the extreme. Part of the problem lies in the fact that Welter was a very controversial figure, with a name in some quarters for making questionable claims. It was not as easy to check out claims made by Wild Sow pilots in single-seater aircraft as it was to confirm those made by the conventional night-fighter crews. Firstly, the twin-engined fighters carried a radio operator who could usually specify fairly accurately where their victims came to the ground; secondly, the single-engined fighters scored the majority of the victories over the target itself, so that it was difficult to differentiate between bombers destroyed by *flak* and those shot down by fighters.

Hermann Greiner, too, had a successful night when Mönchengladbach and Rheydt were attacked. Flying with a new *Funker* in place of Oberfeldwebel Kissing, Greiner shot down two of the four Lancasters that Bomber Command lost.

From its small beginnings in November 1943 the Light Night Striking Force of No. 8 Group had grown to five squadrons by the end of September 1944, and was now in a position to send out sixty or more Mosquitos in any one night to mislead, harass and divert the German defences. September saw the LNSF operate on twenty-two nights against targets in Germany, deploying an average of just under fifty machines per night. Berlin was a frequent target, but Bennett kept the enemy guessing by spreading his attentions widely throughout the Third Reich, ensuring that the air-raid sirens sounded and that workers had to leave their work places to go to the shelters, those already in bed had their sleep disturbed, fighters and anti-aircraft guns were brought up to alert and the defences were misled as to the main target, if indeed one was to be attacked. The Mosquitos were formidable weapons, not only by reason of their invulnerability – of the one thousand-plus that visited Germany during September only seven failed to return – but also because of the not insignificant damage that they were capable of creating. On the final night of the month of September, sixty-three Mosquitos of the LNSF went to Germany, forty-six to Hamburg, six to Aschaffenburg, six to Heilbronn and five to Sterkrade, and none was lost. In his book *Feuersturm über Hamburg* Hans Brunswig speaks of the raid on the city, where he was a senior officer of the fire brigade. The air-raid alarm was sounded there, for the 169th time in the war, at 2107 hrs and the first bombs fell only a minute later, an indication of the speed at which the Mosquitos approached. The alarm lasted for forty-five minutes, and an estimated 107 HE bombs and 180 incendiaries were dropped, killing 103 persons and injuring 259. Later, after the bombers had gone, a further 215 were dug out from ruined buildings, ninety-five of them dead. Some 1,560 were bombed out. Official statistics categorise attacks such of this as 'minor operations', when in fact casualties and damage were greater than those caused by many previous mass attacks by heavy bombers.

In order to bring Germany to her knees by bombing alone, Harris had once stated that Bomber Command would need a force of 4,000 heavy bombers. Other calls on the war budget and production capacity, other priorities dictated by overall strategic considerations, competing claims on resources by the Army and the Navy, meant that he never came near to achieving this target. Nor, despite his single-minded individuality and determination, was he ever allowed by the Air Staff to devote those bombers that he did have exclusively to the task of eliminating German cities: as he points out in *Bomber Offensive*, during the war less than fifty per cent of the Command's efforts were devoted to area bombing. Given that the *average* availability of bombers during the period that Harris had command of the force was well below 1,000, he calculates that he did, in fact, only deploy about one-eighth of strength that he would have required to achieve his aim of bringing Germany down without the need for an invasion in the west. Be that as it may, Harris now had at his disposal an operational force of well over 1,000 and, what is more, his targets were relatively defenceless.

The Americans had a heavy-bomber force which was numerically, if not in terms of bomb-carrying capability, even stronger, and in addition both the British and the Americans had vast tactical air forces. The Air Staff, in agreement with the Deputy Supreme Allied Commander and the Commanding General of the United States Strategic Air Forces in Europe, had decided in mid-October to use their massive forces of aircraft, both strategic and tactical, in addition to striking at their primary targets – oil, transport and vehicle production – to persuade the Germans, by a mighty show of force, of the futility of continued resistance; they had, in fact, conceded, to some extent at least, that Harris's theory of victory through overwhelming bombing power had some validity. In previous directives lip-service had always been paid to the morale effect of bombing, but this was rather different, a specific endorsement of Harris's concept. Under the operational codeword 'Hurricane' the directive instructed the Commander-in-Chief to concentrate first of all on targets in the Ruhr area and to 'demonstrate to the enemy in Germany generally the overwhelming superiority of the Allied Air Forces' in the theatre in order to 'bring home to the enemy a realisation of this overwhelming superiority and the futility of continued resistance'. So it was that in the daylight hours of 14 October over 1,000 RAF heavies attacked Duisburg while 1,250 American Fortresses and Liberators hit Cologne and other targets, both forces taking with them substantial fighter escorts. Bomber Command lost fourteen aircraft, the Americans six. That night Bomber Command was out in force again, once more sending over a thousand bombers to Duisburg, this time for the loss of only seven. And that was not all: in addition to the one thousand-plus that bombed Duisburg during the hours of darkness, 240 bombers from No. 5 Group carried out a successful attack on Brunswick. Including support operations, Bomber Command alone had dispatched a total of 2,500 sorties within twenty-four hours.

And so October 1944 passed, another month closer to the end of the war and the inevitable Allied victory. In the west, virtually the whole of France and Belgium was in Allied hands, while it was clearly only a matter of time before

Holland fell. The German border town of Aachen had fallen to the Americans. In the east, October had seen the Red Army occupy Bulgaria, Romania – including the vast oilfields there – and most of Hungary. Yet still the Germans, beleaguered on all sides, did not surrender, still the relentless, merciless hammering of their country continued by day and night. With the collapse of the German day-fighter force, a reinvigorated Bomber Command had dispatched a total of 6,724 heavy-bomber sorties by day during the month, losing only fifty. Night-time figures were if anything even more impressive, with only fifty-four aircraft lost from the 8,072 that went out. In the whole of the month of October Bomber Command had only lost nine more machines than it had lost on the single failed attack on Nuremberg at the end of the previous March. For the Germans, the pendulum had swung the other way. Their night fighters claimed fifty-eight kills in October: the preceding January they had claimed over three hundred. With average losses of well below one per cent, morale among the crews of the Lancasters and Halifaxes was high. For the *Nachtjagd* crews the outlook was bleak. Their successes were few, their losses severe, and in their hearts they knew that defeat could no longer be avoided. On the increasingly rare occasions that their fuel supplies permitted them to fly at all against the huge numbers of bombers spreading destruction across their land, the hopelessness of their position was manifested in the ever-worsening conflagrations in the cities below them, and yet they fought doggedly, stubbornly.

October went out, and November came in, with heavy RAF attacks on Cologne by night. Then, on the night of 2/3 November, it was the turn of Düsseldorf to suffer yet again. Out of 961 four-engined bombers, the German night fighters managed to shoot down the majority of the nineteen that did not return.

The attack on Düsseldorf was highly concentrated, causing vast damage in the city and heavy casualties among the population. Until then the heaviest attack that Düsseldorf had suffered had been that on 23 April 1944, but the official report by the city authorities contains the paragraph, 'The terror raid on 23 April had exceeded all previous major attacks in terms of its intensity and effect, but this latest attack was carried out in strength such as the Civil Defence Area of Düsseldorf had never previously experienced.' The most successful fighter pilot that night was Oberfeldwebel Willi Morlock of I./NJG 1, who was flying a He 219, one of the ten fighters circling Düsseldorf when the bombers arrived. He had taken off from Münster/Handorf, and he shot down six. He was destined to die just two nights later. It was a good night for II./NJG 2, stationed at Cologne/Butzweilerhof, only a short distance away from the bombers' target. The most successful pilot from that *Gruppe* was their Commanding Officer, Major Paul Semrau, who achieved his first kill on that sortie at 1917 hrs and his fourth twenty-three minutes later. Oberleutnant Erich Jung claimed three victories and Feldwebel Peter Oberheid and Feldwebel Erich Kubetz one each. For Erich Kubetz, this was his first aerial victory.

Two nights later the *Nachtjagd* enjoyed further success against the 749 bombers that visited the industrial town of Bochum in the centre of the Ruhr complex and the 176 Lancasters and Mosquitos that bombed the Dortmund-Ems canal north of Münster. Altogether twenty-three Halifaxes and eight Lancasters were lost, and the night-fighters claimed all but one of them. Of the pilots who had been successful two nights previously over Düsseldorf, Paul Semrau destroyed his forty-third victim, Erich Jung and Walter Heidenreich their sixteenth and seventeenth, Peter Oberheid his fourth and Erich Kubetz his second. Other successful pilots included Hauptmann Heinz Rökker of I./NJG 2 (Kassel) with four kills; Hauptmann Hans-Heinz Augenstein of IV./NJG 1 (Dortmund) with three; and Hauptmann Hermann Greiner, also of IV./NJG 1 with two. Feldwebel Neumann of III./NJG 1 (Fritzlar) scored his first two victories.

Oberleutnant Fritz Krause, now flying with I./NJG 11, into which *Gruppe* the specialist anti-Oboe single-seater unit I./NJG 10 had just been subsumed, took off from Bonn/Hangelar at 1912 hrs. Krause was the officer who, as related earlier, had shot down a Mosquito over Berlin on 8 July. Three nights after that, again over Berlin, he had had to abandon his Fw 190 after being hit by 'friendly' *flak* at about 27,000 feet; he had had to take to his parachute once more on 8 September when flying a Bf 109 specially modified for high-altitude combat, the Bf 109H, the 'H' standing for *Höhenjäger* ('altitude fighter'). On this latter occasion the high-performance compressor on the Daimler-Benz 605 engine had exploded at 30,000 feet and his aircraft had become enveloped in flames; it was later suspected that the engine had been sabotaged. Krause speaks of his experiences during the attack on Bochum on 4 November as follows:

'I was again in a Bf 109H, and it was my 213th operational flight. I much preferred the Fw 190 to the Messerschmitt. Both landing and take-off at night in the 109 were very difficult – one might almost say that it was criminal to make pilots take off in it. It had a very narrow undercarriage and a tendency to swing and overturn. Many pilots were killed that way, particularly inexperienced ones. Landing was also extremely hazardous. On the other hand, once you were in the air it was very stable, very easy to fly on instruments. For a fighter pilot, one might say that it was almost too stable, because when you put it into a violent manoeuvre it always wanted to go back to its normal flying position, like a flying model.

'Flying a single-seater as a night fighter was intrinsically difficult. You must remember that at night there is rarely a good horizon, so that you had to concentrate very hard on your instruments. It's particularly hard when there are searchlights, because they are reflected in the cockpit canopy and dazzle you, and when you bank the aircraft there are the stars in the sky and the various lights on the ground, all of which tend to confuse you. Then we had a radar set. To search the sky for enemy bombers with all these preoccupations was a thankless task. You were trying to do what three men in a conventional night-fighter did. The idea was fine, but it was asking too much.

'Nevertheless, I managed to shoot down a Lancaster quite soon after take-off when Bochum was attacked. In fact I hadn't nearly reached my operational height, because I was supposed to be going higher to attack the Mosquitos. I was at about 12,000 feet, as far as I can remember. When I saw the Lancaster, I went for him. It's quite an experience to attack a four-engined bomber in a light aircraft like the Bf 109. You hit turbulence, and the whole machine shakes and jolts. The ideal is to remain a short distance behind and pull up the nose to fire. I was in a very good position, and I had fired two or three times, and flames and white smoke were coming from his starboard inner engine. I was concentrating so hard on my victim that I hadn't seen another Lancaster flying on my right and alongside me. He opened fire, and there was no way in which I could evade. My aircraft received a large number of hits, and all I can remember is that the instrument panel was in my lap, and there was nothing for it except to jettison the cockpit cover, pull the nose up and eject myself as was standard procedure.

'I came to the ground near a small town called Radevormwald, just to the east of Remscheid. I had baled out at above 10,000 feet, and I drifted quite a way. I was very fortunate, because I landed in a cattle field. But only about thirty or forty metres away there was a large concrete basin surrounded by heavy barbed-wire entanglements – I shudder to think what would have happened to me if I had landed in them! I was, of course, very shaken. Two dark figures came up to me, and they were speaking Russian, which didn't do much to make me feel better. But in fact they were workers at the farm, and they had been very well treated by the farmer, so they weren't in the least aggressive. That was my third parachute jump within a few months, and I had suffered only minor injuries – scratches, scrapes and bruises, but nothing serious.'

Halifaxes of No. 4 and No. 6 (Canadian) Groups made up the majority of the Bomber Command machines lost that night. Most severely hit was the Free French No. 346 (*Groupe Guyenne*) Squadron, based at Elvington in Yorkshire, which lost five of the sixteen Halifaxes it sent to Bochum. It seems likely that Krause's victim was not a Lancaster but one of the French Halifaxes – both types of bomber looked very similar at night, and identification mistakes were regularly made. Twenty Halifaxes of No. 51 Squadron, also of No. 4 Group, went to Bochum, and three failed to return. One crew that did not come back was that of Len Berry, who still wore the crown and stripes of a Flight Sergeant, not knowing that his commission in the rank of Pilot Officer had been promulgated that very day. Berry's navigator, Peter Charlesworth, writes:

'We were in MH-W, the "Winsome Waaf": it was our seventh operation in that aircraft, and our fifteenth overall. We were carrying a spare mid-upper gunner, a Canadian named Buzz Burrows, because Bob Heseltine had a cold and couldn't fly. There were no problems on the outward journey, nor over the target, which was clearly getting something of a pasting and where the *flak* was quite heavy. We descended to about 7,000 feet after the target, and we had just passed our next turning-point in the vicinity of Aachen. Without any warning there was a series of sharp explosions, and I was aware that we had been hit. It is impossible to recall with any confidence just what happened then, because everything occurred so swiftly. We were going down almost vertically. Len Berry yelled, "Bale out!" I acknowledged as one was supposed to do, and he screamed, "For Christ's sake, bale out." I always used to wear my parachute pack clipped on when over enemy territory, and happily I hadn't yet taken it off, so it was matter of seconds only to stand up, open the escape hatch beneath my seat and leave the aircraft.

'I found that my parachute pack was no longer at my chest, but was somewhere above my head. The straps on the harness had somehow come loose before the parachute opened. I was able to haul it down and pull the ripcord. I can recall no sensation of fear. As the parachute opened I saw the Winsome Waaf impact with the ground beneath me, and then, almost simultaneously, I too came to earth. I cannot remember floating down, and think I must have been very low indeed when the parachute stopped my free fall.

'I was dazed and confused, and it was very dark. My parachute was clearly caught in something, because I was swinging gently to and fro. Without thinking, I turned the mechanism that released the harness, and I fell to the ground. Presumably I was automatically braced for a long drop, but in fact must only have fallen a few inches, so that I received a jarring shock. In retrospect, I should have waited longer before releasing myself, because I could have been in a tree or snagged on a building of some sort, and I might have had much further to fall. Instead my body had apparently passed right through overhead electric or telephone cables, but my parachute hadn't.

'I heard a voice – "*Allemand?*" I hastened to announce that I was not German – "*Non, je suis anglais!*" I was approached by a man carrying a long and dangerous-looking rifle, which he was pointing at me. He took me into a nearby house, where my nationality was established and where I was made very welcome. Some time later Johnny Davies, my wireless operator, was brought in. We were in Marche-en-Famenne in Belgium, only a very short distance behind Allied lines. Johnny and I were the only survivors: there had been no time for the others to get out. That the Winsome Waaf, Johnny and I all came to earth within a few hundred yards of each other testified to the fact that we had baled out at minimum altitude and were extremely lucky to be alive.'

The remainder of November 1944 saw a continuing diversification of Bomber Command targets and methods, with the number of aircraft going to individual targets seldom exceeding 300. After the 961 heavies that went to Düsseldorf on the second and the 720 that went to Bochum on the fourth, the largest number was 551, against Duisburg on the final night of the month. By day and by night, but mainly by day, oil-related targets were still a predominant feature of Harris's attack on Germany. Results varied from the very good to the moderately accurate. Another characteristic of the development of the offensive was the increasing use that the Commander-in-Chief made of No. 5 and No. 3 Groups in specialised attacks. No. 5 Group carried out its own marking, largely by H2S, and No. 3 Group experimented with Gee-H marking and bombing. Losses by night, although proportionately heavier than in October, continued to be light. From the nine thousand or so sorties against Germany made during the month, the number of aircraft failing to return was only ninety-eight, a loss rate of only just over one per cent. Of those losses, the major attacks on Düsseldorf and

Bochum accounted for forty-seven. The Mosquito continued to demonstrate its remarkable versatility and its invulnerability, only ten being lost out of approaching 1,700 dispatched. German night-fighters made a total of eighty-seven kills during the month. By day, with no fighter opposition at all, only forty-three out of almost 4,500 heavies were lost, while all the 171 Pathfinder Mosquitos that went out came back home safely.

Bordmechaniker Hans Angersbach, whose first night-fighter operation on 29/30 August, it will be remembered, had ended in near disaster for him and the other members of his crew, had, after a short stay in hospital, returned to his unit. For their next operation he and pilot Calgeer had taken a spare radio operator in place of Gerd Lutz, whose injuries had taken rather longer to heal. Angersbach's second operation, although less traumatic than his first, had also been inauspicious. The spare radio operator, himself a 'new boy', had been unable to fix their position above thick cloud and Calgeer had been on the point of ordering the aircraft to be abandoned when a kindly Fate had intervened and a break in the cloud had enabled them to map-read their way back to base. Gerd Lutz had then rejoined the crew, and their third operation had been on 4 November, against the force attacking Bochum. Angersbach remembers arriving over the target, which he describes as 'a sea of flame', too late to intercept the bombers. Then on 11 November, Calgeer and his crew took off in their Ju 88 on their fourth operational flight. Over Dortmund their aircraft was hit by a burst of anti-aircraft fire, and they had to bale out again. Calgeer, injured rather more severely this time, went back into hospital. It was the crew's fourth and final night-fighter operation. They had achieved no kills and had baled out twice. Lady Luck, while decreeing that their night-fighter career would not be crowned with glory, had increased their chances of surviving the war. For any member of aircrew in wartime it was important to have the fickle lady on one's side, indiscriminate as she was with her favours. While experience and flying skill could increase the odds in favour of survival, they could not, in the final analysis, deny her whim. On the night of 17 November 1944 she smiled on a certain Frank Faulkner and his crew, even if it was a flirtatious, teasing smile.

Frank had completed his tour of thirty operations as an air gunner with No. 12 Squadron. His tour had included the usual number of encounters with fighters, *flak* damage and other close calls. His thirtieth operation, which would normally have been his last, was a daylight raid on Essen on 25 October, when the Lancaster he was flying in was hit by flak in the undercarriage and wing but returned safely to base. Three days afterwards he was commissioned as Pilot Officer. As the Squadron was waiting for a new gunnery leader to be posted in from the Central Gunnery School at Mamby, Frank was asked if he would take on the job on an acting basis. Liking Wickenby, he agreed, and only then was he told that to be acting gunnery leader he would have to be operational, and so he agreed to volunteer for a further five trips. As the rest of his crew were posted away, this meant that he had to fly as a spare gunner.

Freiburg im Breisgau, a university town nestling in the south-west corner of Germany, with France to the west and Switzerland to the south, was an easy target for the ten Mosquitos and 341 Lancasters sent there that night. As a target it was intrinsically of only minor importance. There was virtually no industry there, and it had not suffered attack previously. Like almost any town it was a railway junction, and so it could be put into the general category of 'transportation target'. A further justification for bombing it was that it was believed that there were a large number of German troops in the town, located to oppose the American advance across southern France, which had reached a point only about fifty kilometres to the west. The attack was based on Oboe marking from mobile sites that had been set up in liberated France. *Flak* defences were negligible, and the attack was very concentrated. The railway junction was not hit, and casualty figures of approaching three thousand dead and four thousand injured were high. Only seventy-five of the dead were military personnel. Just one Lancaster was lost on the raid, but Frank Faulkner's crew were lucky that their aircraft survived. Frank writes:

'I was never completely at ease as a spare bod, and in the case of the Freiburg raid I knew none of the crew previously. We took off at 1605 hrs, the skipper being Flying Officer Jock Murison. We had a second dickie, a Canadian by the name of Pilot Officer Kerluk. The only other detail I recall about the crew was that the bomb aimer was also Canadian. The objects of our attention were the railway and troop emplacements.

'The trip to the target was uneventful, but on the bombing run I heard, in a pronounced Canadian accent, "Bombs gone! Starboard inner gone!" My immediate reaction was to think that it was an inopportune time for an engine to pack up. It very soon transpired that the bomb aimer's comment was a literal one. The starboard inner had indeed gone, having been shot off. The mid-upper turret was damaged also, probably by bits of flying Merlin. Obviously, even the poor old Lanc was barely airworthy after that treatment, but we struggled back to England. Lincolnshire was out of the question. The skipper, not surprisingly, opted for Manston, because we needed all the help we could get.

'What happened then shows how one can get one's priorities wrong when under stress. As we were approaching Manston over the North Sea we were instructed to take up crash positions, so I duly left my turret. Now, I had been incarcerated for six hours, and I had a notoriously weak bladder. The temptation as I climbed over the Elsan en route for the main spar was too great. I had become obsessed with the thought that in the crash about to ensue I would do the unthinkable and wet myself. I therefore paused at the Elsan, removed my parachute harness (at about one hundred feet, I deemed I could spare it), my Mae West (which, in retrospect, I might have needed), and unzipped several layers of flying clothing. The next part of the operation was the most difficult, because I was very cold – with the inevitable consequences. However, I recollect the greatest relief I have ever experienced, then or since. Unfortunately, in my haste I had forgotten to plug in my intercom and my skipper, already with his hands full, could get no response from his rear gunner that he was safely in his crash position, that is, until I arrived there and plugged in, seconds before we hit the deck.'

December passed pretty much as the preceding two months had. Raids against transport targets, oil targets and cities, industrial and otherwise, predominated, but there were also a great number of minor and support operations – mine-laying, RCM flights, Light Night Striking Force raids and intruder operations by Mosquitos, and the occasional flight to supply Resistance workers in those parts of Europe not yet liberated. About twice as many attacks were mounted by night as by day, the total figure amounting to something in the region of 12,500 sorties by heavy bombers and 2,000 by Mosquitos. Losses, if not negligible, remained low, thirty Lancasters and Halifaxes by day and 104 by night, an over-all average in the region of one per cent. Only nine Mosquitos failed to return from operations.

The *Nachtjagd* claimed eighty-one heavies and four Mosquitos. This was the nadir of the *Luftwaffe* night-fighter force. There was no shortage of aircraft, because despite Allied bombing the organisational genius of the Germans, mobilised and directed by Albert Speer, had ensured that the production of fighter planes would not only be maintained, but actually increased. The avail-able strength of the night-fighter force stood at 980 in December 1944, yet shortage of fuel and the persistent harrying of the night-fighter bases by Mosquitos by night and by fighter-bombers by day meant that only a total of 1,070 Messerschmitts, Junkers and Heinkels were scrambled during the entire month against the almost 12,000 bombers that assailed the Fatherland. Against the night-fighters in the air, the British intruders continued their physical and deterrent work, so that 114 German night fighters were either shot down or crashed as a result of battle damage, bad weather or crew error, with an unknown number destroyed on the ground. New and inexperienced crews formed the majority of those who did not survive at that period. Faces appeared on the *Gruppen*, were around for a few weeks or even only days, and were not seen again; it had been the same on Bomber Command squadrons during 1943 and early 1944. But experienced crews too continued to die. In December the *Nachtjagd* lost seven aces, who among them had shot down 172 Allied machines, the vast majority British, the equivalent of more than seven complete squadrons. There was Hauptmann Heinz Strüning of NJG 2, who died on Christmas Eve with his score at fifty-six; Hauptmann Hans-Heinz Augenstein of NJG 1 (forty-six kills); Hauptmann Hans-Karl Kamp of NJG 4 (twenty-three kills), who lost his life on the last night of the year; Hauptmann Hermann Leube (NJG 3, twenty-two kills); Leutnant Heinz Roland (NJG 1, fifteen kills); and Oberleutnant Wolfgang Tonn, also of NJG 1, whose score when he died stood at about ten bombers destroyed. The might to which Bomber Command had grown may be seen in Harris's ability now to commit over 1,300 aircraft operationally in a single night, as he did on 17/18 December, when Duisburg and Ulm were the main targets.

On 16 December, the major German ground offensive in the Ardennes began, and once the prevailing bad weather had cleared the Allied Air Forces came into action in devastating fashion, predominantly in the form of ground-attack fighter-bombers operating by day. The confused conditions on the ground made action by heavy bombers in general inappropriate, but Bomber Command did contribute, hitting St Vith on Boxing Day and Koblenz, a bottleneck for German supplies to the front, on the nineteenth.

In mid-December, Peter Charlesworth and Johnny Davies, who had survived the shooting down of Halifax MH-W on 4 November, joined another crew. An abundance of available aircrew in these less demanding days meant that they had not been called upon to fly as 'spare bods'. Flying Officer Freddy Fairweather had lost his navigator, wireless operator and flight engineer during an attack on Osnabrück, so Charlesworth and Davies and Warrant Officer Taffy Isaacs filled the vacancies. After a few familiarisation flights they did their first operation with Freddy Fairweather on the night of 30/31 December, when the Kalk railway marshalling yards in Cologne were the target. It was a successful attack, and only two heavies were lost. Peter Charlesworth recalls:

'I was afraid, although I hope I did not show it. So was Johnny, as he later told me. Freddy was a competent pilot, and the rest of the crew were good blokes. But with the death of Len Berry and the others from our first crew I had lost young comrades who were simply the best friends I had ever had. I had also lost my confidence and the belief that I would survive the war. Johnny and I were destined, in fact, to do more operations with Freddy than we had done with Len, but nowadays when I think back about operational flying it is always my first crew that comes vividly to mind. My recollections of the second part of my tour are grey, and amid that greyness the only strong memory is one of dread each time I saw that we were on the Battle Order, and the certain knowledge, as it seemed to me then, that I would not survive that day or night. I know now, of course, that operational flying at that period of the war was comparatively risk-free, and presumably I was aware then, logically, that the chances of being shot down were slight. Happily, to the best of my knowledge the others in my crew never suspected that I was afraid – probably, I suppose, they were afraid as well, after their experience above Osnabrück. Possibly all members of bomber crews were afraid to some degree, and I have no way of comparing the fear I felt with their fear. Two things I know. Firstly, I did not continue the diary I had begun when flying with Len and the boys: I simply didn't have the heart. The fun had gone. Secondly, I never looked out of the aircraft again when over a target, because I was sure each time that we were going to be hit, and I could simply not face seeing the *flak* bursting. It was quite illogical – if I were going to be hit I would be hit whether I saw it or not. I used to concentrate on my Gee-box, my H2S, my charts – anything to take my mind off what was going on outside.'

The following night saw the end of 1944 and the beginning of 1945. During the early morning of 1 January the Germans mounted Operation *Bodenplatte*: in a final, despairing effort to regain at least some of their lost air superiority and to support the German offensive in the Ardennes, the *Luftwaffe* sent out over one thousand fighters and fighter-bombers, many flown by inexperienced pilots, to attack Allied airfields in Belgium, northern France and south Holland. The *Nachtjagd* provided several *Staffeln* of aircraft to act as Pathfinders. For the Germans the operation was a disaster. They succeeded in destroying or badly damaging about 200 Allied machines, mostly on the ground, but they themselves lost about 300, the majority of them with the crews. The strike also cost the

Germans a huge amount of aviation fuel, which could sorely be spared. *Bodenplatte* marked the virtual end of the German day-fighter force, while at the same time it still further reduced the already diminished effectiveness of the *Nachtjagd*.

Above: Street scenes in Hamburg, possibly Germany's most bombed city, at the end of the War. *(Johnson)*

Below: German civilians inspect a Lancaster shot down about 15 kilometres south of Paderborn during the night of 19–20 February 1944, when the target was Leipzig. This was one of seventy-eight bombers that failed to return that night. It is almost certainly PM-T of No.103 Squadron. *(Henning)*

Ladbergen, to the north of Münster, was a vulnerable point on the Dortmund-Ems Canal. Not only was it a passing point, but it lay rather above the surrounding countryside, so that a breach in the banks would drain the canal. The PR photograph above covers roughly the same area as the centre range ring on the target map to the right. Taken on Christmas Day 1944, it is testimony to the accuracy ultimately achieved by Bomber Command.

CHAPTER FOURTEEN

The Final Months

January to May 1945

The Air Staff directive to which the Commander-in-Chief of Bomber Command was working at the beginning of 1945 dated from 1 November 1944. It was itself based on a directive from the Allied Chiefs of Staff, which set two general priorities: 'the German petroleum industry, with special emphasis on petrol (gasoline)', and 'the German lines of communication'. In a rider to the second category the Chiefs of Staff had added: ' . . . with particular emphasis on the Ruhr'. It went on, 'When weather or tactical conditions are unsuitable for operations against the systems of objectives mentioned above, attacks are to be delivered on important industrial areas with blind-bombing technique as necessary. As far as operational and other conditions allow, these are to be directed so as to contribute to the maximum destruction of the petroleum industry and the dislocation of the target systems indicated above.'

Impatient with such instructions on how he should use his bomber force, Harris had scribbled at the top of his copy, 'Here we go round the mulberry bush', but despite this somewhat petty show of resistance to superior authority the directive in fact gave him considerable latitude when it came to choice of specific targets. The Ruhr Valley in its entirety was fair game, not only because it contained many oil installations but also because it formed one vast communications network; and, of course, it was one huge 'important industrial area'. Further, Harris had his own list of German cities that he was determined to eliminate one by one, and nowhere in the directive was there a definition of the term 'important industrial area', which meant that he could, if he so wished, mount an attack against any of his own favoured targets without being seen blatantly to disobey his orders. An interesting aspect of the directive from the Chiefs of Staff, addressed as it was not only to Bomber Command but to the USAAF as well, was that blind bombing was now formally recognised as an acceptable method of attack, despite the Americans' avowed adherence until then to the principle of precision bombing by visual means.

As things turned out, and despite the popular myth that has developed over the many years since the end of the war, Harris adhered very closely to the November directive, attacking many oil-related and communications targets and making very few raids that could be defined as 'city bombing' pure and simple. Accuracy, although still far from guaranteed, had increased considerably as technical devices such as Oboe and Gee-H had become more available, bombing techniques had improved and, very importantly, enemy resistance had grown weaker.

The year began with Germany under siege on every side and with the day-fighter force of the *Luftwaffe* able to offer only a token resistance. By the end of

January the Germans' last-hope offensive in the Ardennes had failed miserably, despite the gallantry of her troops on the ground. But still Goebbels' propaganda machine spoke of ultimate victory and of Hitler's wonder weapons that would help to achieve it.

There were indeed two new weapons – or, rather, one new weapon and one comparatively recently introduced ancillary device – that did give some faint hope of at least a postponement of the end. The German jet fighter, the Messerschmitt 262, was now flying operationally in sufficient numbers to cause concern among Allied commanders that it might affect their air supremacy in the west, while U-boats equipped with the *Schnorchel*, a breathing device that enabled the boats to travel submerged for long periods without having to surface to recharge their batteries, still operated with a worrying degree of success. These two thorns in the flesh of the Allied commanders led, in mid-January 1945, to their bombing directives being revised to include aircraft-manufacturing and submarine-related targets. But these were precautionary measures, and neither threat developed to any really significant extent.

As the weeks passed and the Western Allies and the Soviets relentlessly squeezed Germany from all sides, the distinction between tactical and strategic targets became more and more blurred, and as German fighter resistance became weaker and weaker, so Allied bomber strength grew. The Liberators and Fortresses by day and the Lancasters, Halifaxes and Mosquitos by both night and day were able to range wide throughout the Fatherland, striking mercilessly almost at will. Only persistent bad weather, particularly in January and February, restricted their freedom of action. And then, in addition to the heavy bombers, there were the countless tactical and ground-attack aeroplanes that swept at low level across the German countryside, hitting with frightening fire power at specifically allocated targets and marauding freelance, firing un-opposed at almost anything that moved or looked as if it might remotely have a military purpose – road vehicles, trains, buildings, troops, farm vehicles, air-fields, barracks, radars, barges on the canals, all were grist to the avengers' mill. The world had never seen so systematic a laying waste of a civilised land. Germany's industry and her economy were ruthlessly destroyed, the devastation of her cities and towns pursued to an extent that is even now hard to envisage. Yet still the German High Command, hypnotised and utterly dominated by Adolf Hitler, did not surrender.

Morale among the civilians, particularly in the bombed cities, had long been broken. But what does that really mean? There remained no will to fight, but nor was there, for the ordinary men and women of Germany, any alternative but dumb acceptance of what Fate might bring. Four-and-a-half years previously Britain had faced what looked like certain defeat, yet had not surrendered. But this was different. There could be no 'Dunkirk spirit' here. In 1940 Britain's cities had not been razed to the ground, there were twenty-one miles of water between her and the German armies, there was a new and charismatic leader who promised blood, toil, tears and sweat. There was hope. For the German man in the street there was no hope, nothing he could do but await the arrival, if he were lucky, of the American or British troops or, if luck were not on his side, of the feared Red Army. In some quarters, particularly in the *Luftwaffe*, there were vain hopes that a military confrontation would develop between the Western Allies and the Soviets, and that in it the *Wehrmacht* would fight on the side of the Americans and British, so that Germany would retain some shred of independent action and self-respect. But in extreme situations people frequently avoid facing up to the unpalatable truth by entertaining the most extreme of hopes, and almost invariably they are doomed to disappointment.

And so it was in what was left of the Third *Reich*. January saw the capture of Warsaw by the Russians and surrender by Hungary; March the capture of Cologne, the crossing of the Rhine and the arrival of the last V-2 rocket to hit England; April the fall of Vienna, the beginning of the Soviet offensive on Berlin, the capture of the Ruhr industrial area and the linking up of American and Soviet troops on the River Elbe near Torgau; and then Hitler's suicide removed the final obstacle to unconditional surrender, which took place a week later. And while all this was happening Bomber Command continued its round-the-clock campaign of attrition, while by night the *Nachtjagd* fought its desperate, hopeless defensive battle.

During January the main Bomber Command effort was by night. Daytime sorties by comparatively small forces of up to 150 bombers struck mostly at the Ruhr area and suffered average losses of about one per cent. Losses by night were proportionately almost twice as heavy, with 134 heavies failing to return from about 7,300 that set out. Official German night-fighter claims amounted to 117. In the hours of darkness, understandably, Harris was able to hit at more distant targets. Nuremberg, Munich, Leuna and Magdeburg were among those attacked. The heaviest losses occurred during the raid on Hanover on 5/6 January, which cost twenty-three Halifaxes and eight Lancasters. At 4.8 per cent of the force committed, this was much above the average loss rate for the period. The most successful German pilot was Hauptmann Georg-Hermann Greiner, who had succeeded Heinz-Wolfgang Schnaufer as *Gruppenkommandeur* of IV./NJG 1 in the previous November when the latter was appointed *Kommodore* of NJG 4. Between 1912 and 1922 hrs Greiner destroyed four bombers, claimed as three Lancasters and one Halifax, over Hanover itself – four heavy bombers and twenty-eight aircrew dispatched within ten minutes. That same night Oberleutnant Kurt Welter claimed a Mosquito destroyed. Four of the high-flying two-seater machines failed to return to base out of the 138 that were active over Germany. Welter was flying one of the 'miracle birds' in which so much hope reposed, the jet-propelled Me 262, and it was his second claim using that aircraft, his first having been two nights previously.

Following his many successes, first as one of Herrmann's *Wilde Sau* pilots and later with the specialist anti-Mosquito *Staffel* 10./JG 300, Welter had been posted in late 1944 to Rechlin to command a small unit, set up under the auspices of Herrmann, to experiment with the use of the Me 262 as a night-fighter, the *Kommando Welter*. Herrmann had first flown the Me 262 himself in mid-1943, and so impressed had he been with its handling qualities, manoeuvrability, rate of climb and speed that he had suggested to Göring that it would make an excellent night-fighter. Göring had scoffed at the idea. Much later, however, and indeed too late for the jet to have a significant impact on the night battle, Herrmann's views had been given some credence. The first few machines put at Welter's disposal were converted two-seater trainers equipped with *Lichtenstein*

SN-2 interception radar and *Naxos* for homing on to H2S. Then the *SN-2* was replaced by the FuG 216 *Neptun V. Neptun* had originally been designed as a tail-warning radar, but was then developed as an AI set, primarily for single-seater fighters, being easier for a pilot to use because it only had one indicator tube to monitor. Welter's *Kommando* was later renamed 10./NJG 11. Welter himself shot down a total of three Mosquitos with the Me 262, the only successes achieved by the few aircraft allocated to the unit. As in the day fighter field, the German jet had come into action too late to be a decisive factor in the air war, and no little blame for that must rest on the shoulders of Hitler himself who, on first hearing of the well-nigh incredible performance of the aircraft, had decreed that it must be developed as a bomber rather than as a fighter.

Herbert Kümmritz, who had flown as *Funker* with Prinz zu Sayn-Wittgenstein, flew with the *Kommando Welter:*

'I joined Welter's unit in January 1945. Welter had converted to the Me 262, and had had no trouble mastering it. Then *Geheimkommando Welter* [Secret Command Welter] was set up. At first the aircraft were single-seaters, but it soon became apparent that just as with the earlier night fighters two men were needed, and also radar. There were casualties, with pilots either crashing or having to bale out, just as there had been with Herrmann's *Wilde Sau.* Then the order came to re-equip the *Kommando* with two-seater machines with *Lichtenstein* and so on. When I was there the unit had four or five of them. Then there was training with the *Funker* on board. We did not have much success, and there were crashes. But the prospects seemed good, insofar as with good crews something should have been achievable. But five or six aircraft were not enough.

'And of course jets need a big airfield, a long runway up to 2,000 metres – what we called *Silberplätze*, or "silver fields". And as the Allies advanced there were fewer and fewer of them. And there was constant bombing. We were bombed out, for example, in Magdeburg. From there we went to Lübeck. There we were bombed out again. Then we operated from the Hamburg/Lübeck *autobahn.* That was in April 1945, and then we went to Schleswig, and the war came to an end. There were five or six machines left intact to hand over to the British. I don't know how many kills the *Staffel* achieved – I personally didn't participate in any. Towards the end I had the impression that Welter had had enough – he didn't want to carry on. He wanted to stay alive. He didn't fly a great deal, and he seemed to busy himself with organisation and so on.'

In terms of numbers of bombers destroyed, January, with 117, saw a partial resurgence of success on the part of the *Nachtjagd* when compared with the lean months of September to December 1944 inclusive. The reason lay in the fact that with the occupation by the Allies of France, nearly every raid penetrated the air-space of the *Reich.* Whereas previously many of the Bomber Command forces attacking short-range targets in France and just over the German border had been in and out before the fighters could find the stream, now most major attacks meant that the stream had a long way to travel over the Germans' home ground, so that it was easier for the night-fighters to locate and penetrate it. All the operations on which ten or more bombers were lost – Hanover (thirty-one), Munich (fifteen), Leuna (ten), Magdeburg (seventeen) and Zeitz (ten) – were deep penetrations. The night fighters paid for their successes with the loss of forty-seven of their own machines.

The statistics for February show Bomber Command dispatching approximately 2,700 sorties against Germany by day. By night the figure was over 13,000, of which more than 10,500 were by four-engined bombers. If one assumes conservatively that each heavy carried on average between three and four tons of bombs, it does not take much imagination to picture the huge amount of high-explosive and incendiary material rained down upon an almost defenceless Germany within the space of twenty-eight days. The night-fighters claimed 185 kills for a further forty-seven of their own machines, but that is somewhat suspect, because in fact Bomber Command lost only 164 aircraft operationally from all causes during February. What is worth noticing, however, is that in February there were more multiple kills by individual *Nachtjagd* aces than during any other month of the war. For example, Günther Bahr and Heinz-Wolfgang Schnaufer claimed seven each in a night, while Gerhard Rath, Johannes Hager and Heinz Rökker each claimed six. There was another macabre record too, macabre from the point of view of Bomber Command aircrew lost. Four of these claims – those of Bahr, Schnaufer, Hager and Rökker, totalling twenty-six in all – occurred in one night, 21/22 February, when losses in attacks against Duisburg, Worms and the Mittelland canal amounted to thirty-four heavies, so that about 240 RAF, Commonwealth and Allied flyers had fallen to the guns of only four German pilots. On the same night Hermann Greiner chalked up his forty-seventh and forty-eighth kills, Peter Spoden his twentieth.

By far the most significant Bomber Command attack of 1945, possibly of the entire war, took place in February. In the annals of aerial warfare the word 'Dresden' has become synonymous with terror bombing; sadly, by association, the reputation of Arthur Harris and of the crews who flew for him has also suffered. This is not the place to debate the rights and wrongs of the attack, nor would it serve any useful purpose to do so, but a short explanation would seem to be appropriate, if only in an attempt to put what happened into context.

To weaken, and if possible to break, the morale of the Germans had always been accepted by the majority, if not all, of the political and Air Force leaders in Britain as the primary function of Bomber Command, and the rightness of the nightly attacks on German cities was overwhelmingly endorsed by the media and the population. Harris was put in charge of Bomber Command because he was seen at the time of his appointment to be the senior officer most likely to carry out the policy efficiently and ruthlessly. It goes without saying that he was himself a strong advocate of the policy, but it is important to understand quite clearly that he did not initiate it; he implemented it.

In 1944 the Western Allies set foot on the Continental mainland and, with the Russians advancing relentlessly in the east, the end of the war seemed to be in sight at last. But the Germans were formidable opponents, and there was always the lurking feeling that they might still produce some last-minute surprise that would change the situation. New-technology fighters were appearing, the submarines were a continuing threat, two V-weapons had been identified and there were intelligence reports and rumours of others to come. In addition there was the real worry, to which only a handful of top people were privy, that the Germans might produce an atomic weapon. All this argued for doing everything possible to hasten the end of hostilities; and in any case the British nation was tired of war and wanted a speedy but victorious end to it. One way was to increase the bombing and force Germany into submission. In August 1944 the Chief of the Air Staff, Sir Charles Portal, put up a plan which came to be known as 'Thunderclap'. 'Thunderclap' envisaged the bombing of a number of selected cities in Germany as and when, in light of other developments, it was calculated that such a blow might stimulate revolt on the part of the German people. The plan was not enthusiastically received, but it was decided to keep it on file for reconsideration as and when circumstances seemed more likely to promise success.

In early 1945 'Thunderclap' was re-examined. By this time a new factor had emerged in favour of a major co-ordinated bombing initiative. The Russians were advancing into the Third *Reich*, and there were strong political and practical arguments for the British and Americans to do anything they could to help the Soviets. It seemed that the time might now be ripe to put Portal's outline plan into operation. Now, however, the primary aim was not to break the Germans' morale, but to give support to the Russian advance. The Joint Intelligence Committee saw advantage in a series of attacks within a short period of time on Berlin, Leipzig, Dresden and Chemnitz, all of which were important centres of communication. Not only was it envisaged that the destruction of the rail and road facilities within the cities would prevent German reinforcements and supplies being brought up to the front, but it was also calculated that the blocking-off of these focal points would cause great confusion to German military transport in the area by hindering the exodus of the very many vehicles, troops and refugees moving westwards. In this way, it was foreseen, the roads leading to the front eastwards of the targets would be blocked.

Portal, who had first suggested 'Thunderclap', was not enthusiastic about the plan in its modified form, but by late January the Prime Minister himself had become involved. He asked the Secretary of State for Air for his advice on the subject, and was impatient when Sir Archibald Sinclair sent a lukewarm reply. 'I did not ask you last night,' Churchill wrote to Sinclair, 'about harrying the German retreat from Breslau. On the contrary, I asked whether Berlin, and no doubt other large cities in East Germany, should not now be considered especially attractive targets.' In response to so unequivocal a demand from the man in supreme charge of the British conduct of the war, Sinclair minuted to Churchill of 27 January 1945, 'The Air Staff have now arranged that . . . available effort should be directed against Berlin, Dresden, Chemnitz and Leipzig or against any other cities where severe bombing would not only destroy communications vital to the evacuation from the east but would also hamper the movement of troops from the west . . . The use of the night bomber force offers the best prospect of destroying these industrial cities . . . ' Churchill took note of this minute but made no comment. This was justifiably taken as tacit approval.

All this had happened during the run-up to the Yalta Conference, which began on 4 February. In discussion of how the West could best help them, the Russians themselves suggested the bombing of communications behind the front and that in particular the Allied bombers should 'paralyse the centres, Berlin and Leipzig'.

The fact that this request came from the Russians so soon after the formulation of plans to implement 'Thunderclap' in its modified form made it inevitable that the operation would go ahead. In the meantime American participation in the plan had been agreed, and the fate of Dresden was sealed.

Operation 'Thunderclap' began during the night of 13/14 February when Bomber Command sent a total of eight hundred bombers in two separate forces three hours apart to attack Dresden, while a further large force bombed a synthetic oil plant at Böhlen near Leipzig. There was nothing special, for that period, about either the planning of the Dresden raids or the way in which they were carried out. The first wave of about 250 bombers, all from No. 5 Group, which in January had come under the command of Air Vice-Marshal H. A. Constantine, attacked just after ten o'clock in the evening using their own preferred methods of marking and bombing. Because of cloud in the target area the results were only moderately successful; the same cloud, incidentally, had resulted in scattered bombing at Böhlen just before the attack on Dresden. A larger force of about 550 Lancasters hit the unfortunate city again after midnight, by which time the cloud had cleared. The bombing, carried out this time in traditional form on markers laid by PFF, was very accurate and concentrated. As had happened at Hamburg in July 1943, the meteorological conditions were such that once fires had started – a large percentage of incendiary bombs were carried by the Lancasters – a fire-storm developed. The number of people killed will never be known. Various estimates put it at between 30,000 and 100,000. It seems probable that the true figure was in the region of 50,000, about the same number as had perished in Hamburg. The following day the Americans bombed Dresden by daylight, and they did so again on 15 February, but it was undoubtedly the second Bomber Command attack that caused the great majority of the damage and casualties.

There was virtually no defensive action by the Germans against Bomber Command. The city had never been heavily defended against air attack, and most of the small number of anti-aircraft guns that had been positioned there had been taken away for use at the Front. Confusion, in part caused by No. 100 Group's jamming of communications and in part a result of the general disorganisation prevailing within the fighter control system, reigned to such an extent that very few night-fighters were scrambled and those that did get airborne were directed from beacon to beacon and made no contact with the bomber forces. The total cost to Bomber Command was only eight Lancasters, two of which crashed in France.

The following night Harris made a second 'Thunderclap' attack, this time on Chemnitz, about forty miles south-west of Dresden. Again the attack was divided into two waves of heavy bombers arriving over the target three hours apart. There was a secondary raid against an oil refinery at Rositz, near Leipzig. The Chemnitz force comprised over 700 Lancasters and Halifaxes, while 225 Lancasters went to Rositz. In addition Bomber Command sent a total of 367 aircraft, including 197 Mosquitos and twenty-one jamming aircraft, on various support, deception, diversion and disruption operations. Again great confusion was caused to the German fighter controllers, but the *Nachtjagd* had rather more success than they had had against the Dresden bombers. In all that night twenty-three RAF aircraft were shot down. The attack was not a great success: the old enemy, cloud over the target, meant that PFF had to drop sky markers so that, as was almost invariably the case, the bombing by the main force was scattered. For Peter Charlesworth, Chemnitz was his twenty-third operation:

'At eight hours airborne, Chemnitz was the longest operation I did during my tour. Most of our trips were between five and six hours. I have no clear recollection of that night – for the navigator, all operations were much of a muchness. Some were longer than others, and you set out on some in better spirits than on others. A longer-range target naturally caused more trepidation than a shorter-range one did. But once you were airborne your main preoccupations were track-keeping and time-keeping, so your mind had other things to occupy itself with besides the danger. Because Chemnitz was a long way away, I imagine I was even more scared than usual before we took off, but I can't honestly remember. One quaint item, however, does remain in my memory. At briefing we were solemnly issued with postcard-sized cardboard Union Jacks with string attached. If we were badly damaged over the target we were advised to head east and bale out over Russian-occupied territory. The front line was only a short distance away. On the cards, in addition to the Union Jack, were the words, in Cyrillic characters, '*Ya Anglichanin*' – 'I am English'. The idea was that we should hang the cards around our neck to show the Russians that we were friends, not enemies. I have often envisaged some heavily armed, trigger-happy, possibly illiterate Soviet soldier from the depths of Uzbekistan seeing me coming down on the end of a parachute with my little flag around my neck. I wonder what he would have made of it! Fortunately, the necessity didn't arise, and the trip was uneventful. The end of the war was clearly in sight and, which was more important to me, so was the end of my tour. Perhaps I might survive, after all!'

Ten days later it was the fate of another German town to suffer as Dresden had. Like Dresden, Pforzheim in Baden-Württemberg in the south-west of Germany had come through the war so far relatively unscathed. On the night of 23/24 February that was to change. In good bombing conditions a force of approaching 400 bombers dropped over 1,500 tons of incendiary and high-explosive bombs on Pforzheim. A fire-storm developed in the closely built-up inner town, destroying it completely and killing between 17,000 and 18,000 people. After Hamburg and Dresden, this was the highest loss of life in any single attack in the war. The operation cost Bomber Command twelve Lancasters, one of which was shot down by Oberleutnant Peter Spoden:

'When the USA entered the war my father told me we could never win. He remembered 1916. I did not believe him, and it took me years to realise that he was right. On 20 July 1944, when the assassination attempt against Hitler took place, that was the end for us officers, but when the British continued to come, burning our towns night after night, we went up into the air and tried to shoot them down.

'I remember that I visited Pforzheim after a night attack by several hundred Lancasters. Within twenty minutes, from a population of 80,000,

18,000 were burned to death, mostly women and children. I cannot describe what I saw in this burning, stinking town. I was so helpless when I heard the survivors crying out in the cellars. After the war I realised that in London and Warsaw were the same pictures, the same innocent people.'

In February 1944 there had been far more raids against Germany by night than there had been by day. With improving weather and continuing lack of counter-action by the German day-fighter force, March saw a reversal of that situation: there were just over 9,000 sorties by heavy bombers by day, just under 8,000 by night. In terms of tonnage of bombs dropped, March was the leading month of the whole war. Oil-related targets predominated, but there were area attacks on cities in the Ruhr and Rhineland. Such raids were in fact largely tactical rather than strategic in nature, because the targets now lay just behind the front line. Four days after a heavy daytime attack on Cologne on 2 March, for instance, the city fell to the Americans.

As late as this in the war the danger of being attacked by enemy fighters over England did not represent a great worry to Bomber Command crews. Following Hitler's edict in 1941 that the place to shoot bombers down was over Germany, not over England, there had been a hiatus in intruder activity. In late 1944 however German thoughts again turned to the idea of using long-range fighters on the other side of the Channel, and an operation, *Gisela* by name, was planned. As in the case of the Ardennes offensive, Operation *Bodenplatte* and other similar schemes, however, it is hard to think that those who conceived and executed it could have had any confidence that it would affect the outcome of the war.

On the evening of 3 March 1945 moderately heavy Bomber Command forces set out to attack Kamen, on the eastern edge of the Ruhr area, and a viaduct on the Dortmund-Ems canal at Ladbergen. There were also, of course, the normal support, diversion and ECM operations. Losses over Germany on the Kamen raid were nil, but night-fighters penetrated the other stream and seven Lancasters were shot down. While the British bombers were attacking their targets Operation *Gisela* was launched and the first of approximately 200 *Luftwaffe* night fighters, all Ju 88s, took off and headed for England, where they shot down twenty RAF aircraft and damaged several others. About forty of the Ju 88s were either lost or damaged, mostly in crashes on the way back to Germany due to adverse weather conditions and faulty navigation at low level.

One of the pilots who took part in *Gisela* and survived was Leutnant Günther Wolf. Wolf came from the small village of Wurgwitz, just about eight kilometres from Dresden, and he had been at home during the night of the RAF attacks. 'Dresden was terrible,' he says, ' even from that distance. But for us night-fighters it was a picture we were familiar with. Everything we had seen in other cities from above, I now saw from the ground, but from a distance, thank God! It was a very strange feeling to be on the ground with everything coming down at you, when there is nothing you can do to protect yourself. Far, far worse than being in the air. The feeling is completely different.' On the night of *Gisela*, Wolf shot down a Lancaster, probably one from No. 44 (Rhodesia) Squadron, which crashed in flames near Grannington, Lincolnshire, with the loss of all on board. He gives a graphic account of the night's happenings:

'We were positioned at Lüneburg for the operation. For us night-fighters, accustomed as we were to flying over friendly territory, this was something quite new. It was the first time in our lives we had had to cross the North Sea, and they had to fit a supplementary fuel tank in our Ju 88 for the trip.

'We were briefed on the anti-aircraft defences and the barrage balloons in the vicinity of the Humber estuary, and then, at 1715 hrs on 3 March, we flew to Wittmundhafen and landed there. At 2321 hrs we took off, and we landed back there at 0256 hrs the following morning.

'Everyone flew separately, and we went out at a height of thirty metres above the water to keep below radar coverage. The weather was good, and we could see the surface of the sea. I crossed in somewhere between the Wash and the Humber. As we approached the coast I opened up and climbed higher, and we found ourselves among the returning bombers. We could see them on our radar. The unpleasant aspect of the affair was there were lots of searchlights on the coast. Just after we had crossed the coast I looked down obliquely and I saw a row of searchlights sweeping the sky, and then we saw a number of searchlights standing still and pointing directly upwards, possibly an approach lane to an airfield. I flew through them, and I came to an airfield. There was a Lancaster on the circuit, and the airfield lighting was on. I let down my wheels and flaps to slow myself down to his speed, and I shot him down.

'On the way back we passed near to Hull, and we were surprised to see the lights burning on the quays. There didn't seem to be a black-out. We fired at the lights, and they went out. We flew out very low over the Humber estuary, because we reckoned that if there were barrage balloons and we were flying over the river we wouldn't run into a cable, because they would be moored to the ground. Then I flew right into a convoy. I had seen the same convoy as I was approaching England on the way in, but then it was rather further south. I hadn't given it any further thought. They gave us a very hot reception, believe me, and we only got away by going down so low that if they had fired at us they would have hit each other. It took two minutes at the very most, but they seemed endless to me. I was more frightened during those two minutes than during the whole of the rest of the war!

'The next problem for us was that the weather forecast we had been given was very inaccurate. The wind had freshened and changed direction considerably, so we were blown off course. We had calculated that we would cross back in near to Borkum. We were unable to make radio contact with Wittmundhafen, but we were lucky enough to catch a glimpse of a visual beacon through a hole in the cloud. We read the Morse letters, and we looked for it on our maps in the area of Wittmundhafen, but we couldn't find it. Then the *Funker* said it was Leeuwarden. We couldn't believe we were so far away. Fortunately we still had some fuel, so we set course for Wittmundhafen, and we landed there a short time later.

'A lot of my comrades were killed that night. A lot had to make emergency landings or bale out because they ran out of petrol. One crashed on the dunes on the north coast of Holland because he was flying too low. The losses we had on *Gisela* were mainly due to bad weather and petrol shortage, and there were scarcely any from enemy action. We were all ready to have another go the following night. We got the firm impression that the British simply didn't know there was a war on. We put that point of view forward the following day, but the high-ups weren't interested.'

Günther Wolf claimed another Lancaster as a probable kill just a few nights later, but this time over Germany. The encounter with a Lancaster took place in the early hours of 7 March, and in his log book is written 'Hamburg'. In fact there was no Bomber Command attack on Hamburg that night, and in all probability Wolf's opponent was one of the 197 No. 5 Group Lancasters that were sent out to attack the small port of Saßnitz on the Baltic island of Rügen, some considerable distance to the east. Another pilot who has reason to remember 7 March 1945 is Otto Kutzner, who took off that evening and shot down a Halifax. But whereas Wolf returned safely to base after the combat, this was destined to be Kutzner's last operational flight.

Kutzner was a moderately successful pilot, a Feldwebel flying the Ju 88 with NJG 3. He had his share of good fortune and misfortune and had survived several crash-landings, albeit with severe injuries, and two parachute jumps, the most recent one on Christmas Eve 1944:

'At last, on 7 March 1945, I flew again operationally. We took off at about 2100 hrs in Ju 88 D5+BZ. Our radio was not working, but despite that we had been ordered off to fly freelance to the north of Lüneburg. First the *flak* showed us which way to fly, then we saw bombs dropping. By the time we got there the raid was almost over. But we decided to hang around and see what would happen, and we were lucky. A straggler, a Halifax, appeared directly in front of us and we shot it into flames, but to follow it to see where it crashed would have taken us into the Kiel *flak* zone, and I had had earlier experience of the *flak* there, so I didn't bother with the burning Halifax any more but turned my mind to the question of finding our way back on to the ground. Today, when things are calm and one isn't in any danger, one might think otherwise, but at that time Germany had become a very narrow place, from the Oder to the Rhine, so the best thing we could do seemed to be to fly south and look for somewhere to land. And that is what we did. I can't remember any longer what the weather was like, but I think there was broken cloud so we couldn't see everything below us. Eventually we did see a landing ground, but we didn't know where it was – it might even have been in enemy hands. We overflew it, and by the length of the runway lights it seemed to be very small, much too small for a Ju 88. So we flew off further south, but without any success. We flew back to the airfield timing ourselves with a stopwatch to see whether we could put the aircraft down there after all. We saw a green light from the ground, which meant that we were clear to land, although at that time I still hadn't fired off a red emergency signal, because we still had just enough fuel left to climb up and bale out. But since I had been given a green I decided to attempt a landing, and I turned in on the approach.

'What happened then I only know from what people have told me. The airfield was at Göttingen, and in practical terms it was too small for a

326

night landing. There were two goods trains standing on the line of approach. As I have said, I only know what happened from what I have been told, because I woke up in a white bed in a cellar, covered from head to foot in bandages and with both legs in traction and in splints. My head was bandaged, and the moment I recovered consciousness I was given an injection in the arm to sedate me. It appears that I had missed the first train but hit the second one, possibly with my undercarriage. The aircraft somersaulted and crashed, and I was thrown clear. The other members of my crew died in the machine, which burst into flames. Ammunition was exploding, and the emergency services couldn't get near it to rescue them. Apparently I kept on asking about my crew and trying to pull my bandages off so that I could go to them, so they had to keep on giving me injections to calm me down. Everyone was forbidden to tell me that my crew were dead, because I kept on saying that if they were dead I didn't want to live either.

'After a week I developed gangrene in my left leg, and it had to be amputated. It was also touch and go with my right foot, but at the last moment they decided to try to save it. They said they could always take it off later if they weren't successful. Many people have told me I was lucky to have crashed at Göttingen, where I could be treated in the University clinic.

'In addition to my leg injuries I had severe head injuries, severe arm injuries, badly damaged eyes, possibly as a result of hitting the gun-sight. I was in hospital in Göttingen and Bad Lauterberg from March 1945 until May 1947, when I rejoined the human race. I went back to my parents' home in Magdeburg, but left East Germany for the West in 1953. I have a one hundred per cent invalidity pension, and with one leg off and a crippled left foot which almost amounts to the same thing, any dreams of carrying on flying were out of the question. It was hard for me in the beginning, but what could I do? I have had to resign myself to going without so many of the beautiful things that life has to offer.'

The Bomber Command operations that suffered the heaviest losses during March 1945 were all night raids. In the second half of the month there were only three operations from which ten or more heavy bombers failed to return, against Lützenkendorf oil refinery on 14/15, Hagen on 15/16 and Nuremberg on 16/17. Losses were eighteen, ten and twenty-four respectively. These were the last double-figure losses from any one operation in the war. The same three raids saw the final three claims by individual *Nachtjagd* pilots of five or more kills in a night. Against the force going to Lützenkendorf Hauptmann Martin Becker of I./NJG 6 shot down nine, precisely half of the total lost. This was the highest score by a German night-fighter crew in any one night, and there was another record, too: Tino Becker's *Funker*, Leutnant Karl-Ludwig Johanssen, shot down three of the nine with his twin rearward-facing machine-guns. Johanssen was awarded the *Ritterkreuz* two days later, so becoming one of the few radio operators entitled to wear the much sought-after decoration. Coincidentally, one pilot was also responsible for half the losses on the raid on Hagen the following night, when Hauptmann Gerhard Rath of I./NJG 2 claimed five.

The last five-or-more multiple-kill claim was by Oberleutnant Erich Jung when he and his *Funker*, Walter Heidenreich, shot down eight from the 277 Lancasters, 231 of them from No. 1 Group, that attacked Nuremberg. Heidenreich destroyed one with his rear guns. Night-fighters penetrated the bomber stream in some force before it reached the target. The first Lancaster to crash was PB785 of No. 576 Squadron, Fiskerton. It collided at 2100 hrs with a Ju 88 that had taken off from Böblingen thirty minutes before, and all the seven RAF men and four Germans in the two machines died. At the controls of the Ju 88 was Major Gerhard Friedrich, *Gruppenkommandeur* of I./NJG 6, who had thirty confirmed kills to his credit. Two other senior commanders among Ju 88 and Bf 110 crews who took off scored successes, Major Hoffmann, *Kommandeur* of I./NJG 5, with three kills and Major Herbert Lütje, *Kommodore* of NJG 6, with one. Among the NCO pilots flying, Oberfeldwebel Schmidt scored his twelfth, thirteenth and fourteenth kills. Tino Becker and Wim Johnen, with one Lancaster each, were also among the successful pilots.

For this raid on Nuremberg, thirty-two Lancaster crews were briefed from the two squadrons based at RAF Wickenby, Lincolnshire, Nos. 12 and 626. Although Nuremberg was a long way to go, and despite the terrible losses on the raid against the city a year previously, there was no special reason, at this late stage of the war and with casualties generally at a low level, to feel unduly worried. Yet six of the Lancasters from No. 12 Squadron and one from No. 626 Squadron were destined not to come back, and for twenty-five of the aircrew it would be the last flight they would ever make. Six of the aircraft that did return safely to base reported combats with night-fighters, while several others reported seeing aircraft going down in flames.

Lancaster PD393, UM-N2 of No. 626 Squadron, was flown that night by Flight Lieutenant John Cox. His account of the mission gives a vivid impression of what it was like to be a member of a bomber crew at that late stage of the war:

'My own crew had completed two-thirds of their tour, and were therefore reasonably experienced. We had been to Nuremberg on 2 January 1945, during which we had moments of excitement, but we were not unduly concerned about making a second trip. My regular rear gunner had a motor cycle accident the day before and he was replaced by a Belgian whom we had not previously met but who was well recommended. The notes I made of the briefing show that we were to bomb in three waves, commencing at 2130 hrs, each wave taking three minutes to clear the target. Our aircraft was scheduled to fly in the second wave from 2133 hrs to 2136 hrs at 20,000 feet, dropping our bombs on a heading of 084°. Mosquito Pathfinders would drop illuminating flares at 2126 hrs and would follow up with red flares cascading green. If the target was visual, red target indicators would be dropped, backed up with green TIs. Aircraft would be staggered between 18,000 and 20,000 feet. The bomb-load was 1 × 4,000 lb bomb and 6,480 incendiaries.

'We had witnessed considerable night-fighter activity, particularly from the time we were south of Stuttgart, and we had seen some casualties going down. There was some heavy *flak*, but we were more concerned with night fighters, and we successfully took evasive action when the rear gunner reported a Ju 88 on our tail but out of range. Searchlights were plentiful as we approached Nuremberg, but not too troublesome, except to the extent that they made our silhouettes more easily seen. At 2124 hrs we were just short of the target and contemplating our bombing run, although our bomb bays were not yet open.

'Without any warning we were attacked from underneath and set on fire in the centre section. Flames and choking smoke funnelled forward to the cockpit. I had no intercom response from the crew. Almost immediately the Lanc went out of control and into a steep dive, and I am convinced some part of it must have fallen off or a control linkage severed.

'Having regard to the nature of our bomb-load I still cannot understand why we did not explode as it appeared to me that the incendiaries were on fire. Immediately I gave instructions to bale out, not knowing if my order would be received. The bomb aimer, engineer, navigator and rear gunner went, but the mid-upper gunner and wireless operator were presumably either injured or prevented by the fire from escaping.

'The bomb aimer and rear gunner were captured on landing about thirty miles from the crash site. The flight engineer did not survive, and I can only assume that after he jumped he was caught up by some part of the aircraft, which was in a very steep dive. The parachute of the navigator failed to open, and he was buried in the neighbouring village of Burgoberbach. For my part, I must have been no more than a few hundred feet up when I baled out. I saw the Lanc explode on the ground just below me, and within seconds I landed about three hundred yards from the burning aircraft.

'A compound fracture of the right leg resulted in a series of bone graft operations in various RAF hospitals over the next three years, and I was eventually invalided out of the RAF at the end of 1948.

'The exceptionally large losses that night, I think, could be attributed to the fact that the German night-fighters were able to penetrate the bomber stream at an early stage and on a clear night. From Stuttgart onwards we were very vulnerable. Nuremberg had always been a "hot" target. Perhaps those plotting the route should have learned from previous experience.'

John Cox and his crew had fallen victim to Oberleutnant Erich Jung. Lancaster UM-N2 was Jung's twenty-third victim and the third that night. It is interesting to read extracts from a German report of the night's happenings, based on an interview with Erich Jung, alongside that of John Cox:

'The crew of Jung, Heidenreich and Reinnagel came up to immediate readiness at Langendiebach on 16 March 1945 in their Ju 88G-6, factory number 620 045 and unit number 4R+AN. Langendiebach was not a beautiful airfield, but it had been a functional one. Now it was not even that since American four-engined bombers had accurately carpet-bombed the runway, hitting as they did so a number of barracks and hangars. All that remained was a grass strip about 800 metres in length, from which the aircraft could take off directly from the hangars. With the best will in the world, a night landing on this "pocket handkerchief" was not possible, so the airfields at Babenhausen and Rhein/Main had been earmarked as overnight accommodation.'[1]

The report goes on to describe how Jung's Ju 88 took off at 2014 hrs when a bomber stream was reported heading inbound over France. Jung made for radio beacon *Otto*, where he orbited awaiting 'trade'. Heidenreich tuned in to the commentary originating from station *Dachs* near Darmstadt, which confirmed that the bombers were still heading east. 4R+AN turned on to a heading that would bring them into the stream. The account continues:

'The *Funker* could afford not to look too often at his radar screen, given the fine weather, the clear atmosphere and the good visibility of the ground below, which led him to assume that he would be able to pick up individual bombers in the stream with his naked eye.

'And so it was. After they had been airborne for about twenty minutes they saw the first *Kuriere* passing ahead of them from left to right. Visibility could not have been better. The Ju 88 was in *Planquadrat BS*, between Strassburg and Stuttgart, right in the middle of the stream. There might have been between twenty and thirty of them, flying in loose formation. The Tommies must have taken the Ju 88 for one of their own machines, because not a single one of them took evasive action.'

The account goes on to describe how Jung and Heidenreich destroyed seven Lancasters within less than twenty minutes. Jung shot down some of them with his *Schräge Musik*, some with his forward-firing guns. After the seventh success, Jung checked his fuel and ammunition: the indicator showed that his guns were almost empty, so he decided it was time to make for a landing field, keeping what little was left of his ammunition to guard against emergencies:

'They were heading west-north-west on course for the Rhein/Main area and were about twenty kilometres from Würzburg when Reinnagel made out a moving light above them. Even on such a clear, starlit night such a rapid reaction required unusually good eyesight. Reinnagel directed his "driver" towards the light, and there it was – a Lancaster with its navigation lights burning. Jung let 4R+AN drop back a little so that he could begin his attack from astern, at the same time pulling the control column gently backwards. As he opened fire there was a burst of tracer from the rear turret – the first defensive fire he had met that night. Jung, Heidenreich and Reinnagel heard bullets striking home in the port wing. Ahead the bomber began to burn, with an ever-growing banner of flame behind it until it hit the ground.

'Now it was a matter of finding somewhere to land – the revolutions counter for the port engine made that unmistakable. No contact with Kitzingen and Wertheim, so Jung decided to go to Zellhausen, an airfield

[1] From *Achtmal Pauke Pauke in einer Nacht,* published in *Jägerblatt*, August/September 1982.

he was familiar with. After about twenty minutes they saw below the clear ribbon of the River Main, and just beyond a narrow landing strip. It was Zellhausen. When he was already on the final stages of his approach Jung realised that he had come in too close: a large number of runway lamps had flashed past to the side before the undercarriage set down with a bump. His brakes had little effect, and red hazard lights came closer and closer. Later, by daylight, they saw that the red lights were marking deep bomb craters. The Ju 88 ended up with its port undercarriage leg in a shallow ditch.'

Walter Heidenreich also remembers his personal success that night:

'The one I shot down was number two or number three. There were bombers above and below. We had often been infiltrated into the bomber stream before, and we had seen one or two, or even single ones, but this time there were bombers all over the place. It was fantastic. I had fired at *Viermots* myself on several occasions, but each time my guns had jammed after three or four rounds. He came into sight, and I said to my pilot, "There's one there in a fantastic position. Let me have a go. Throttle back." I had a stoppage on that occasion too, but only after I had got off ninety-four rounds in one long burst. Then the port wing began to blaze. I can see it to this day.

'That night he was the only one who fired at us. He went down like a blazing torch. It was my only personal kill during the whole of my operational flying.

'That night we were unable to call up our comrades and bring them into the stream. That hadn't been organised. If only we had had Very lights or something like that we could have done so, but we were quite alone. It would have been so easy to bring other fighters into the stream, and many more bombers would have been shot down. We just couldn't miss.'

Jung's eight victories in one night put him in third place on the final list of multiple-kill aces, behind Martin Becker and Wilhelm Herget. That night he had made his twenty-eighth and last kill of the war. His aircraft, 4R+AN, never flew again. It was blown up by German troops when American gliders landed on the airfield at Zellhausen nine days later.

With its defence of Nuremberg, the *Nachtjagd* had to all intents and purposes shot its bolt. Bomber Command was riding on a euphoric crest of success coupled with comparative invulnerability. From now on the heaviest loss against any one target by night, nine Lancasters, would be from a highly accurate No. 5 Group attack on the synthetic oil plant at Böhlen, near Leipzig, five nights later. In April oil plants figured large on the list of targets attacked, while there were low-cost but accurate area raids on ports such as Hamburg and Kiel in northern Germany, where penetration by troops on the ground was less advanced than further south. Like a boxer who has his opponent groggy and on the ropes and is determined to finish off the fight, Harris was hitting Germany without quarter and almost at will, determined that there would be no last-minute recovery. By day Germany was hammered by both the Americans and the RAF, which alone dispatched over 4,000 sorties as against the 5,500 or so that it sent out by night. Overall, heavy-bomber losses averaged out at less than 0.6 per cent. On the night of 3/4 May 1945, the day before the Germans surrendered, a force of Mosquitos attacked Kiel, where it was thought that troops were being put on board ships to be sent to Norway, and eighty-nine aircraft from No. 100 Group flew RCM support. Two Halifaxes and one Mosquito failed to return. Both the four-engined machines were from No. 199 Squadron, and they were lost not from enemy action but as a result of colliding with each other to the south of Kiel. All sixteen men on board died in the ensuing crashes, the last of nearly 50,000 Bomber Command aircrew who did not survive the many risks that went with operational flying.

The British, Commonwealth and Allied aircrew could now pause and reflect. With indisputable justification, as it then seemed, and with the plaudits of the nation in their ears, they could look back with sadness at the loss of so many of their comrades and friends but with deep satisfaction at terrible dangers bravely faced and a job done to the best of their human ability. It would not be until years later that critics, some honestly concerned, many lacking in understanding, many unthinking, some driven by very debatable personal, political and pacifist motivation, would begin to cast doubt on what the bomber crews had done, and by extension on the men themselves. But besides looking back, the aircrew also had to look forward to another war, this time in the Pacific theatre, to further operations and to renewed casualties. It was a duty they would certainly have faced with the same philosophical acceptance and bravery that they had demonstrated in the skies above the Third *Reich*. That they did not in the event have to meet that challenge was ironically the direct result of the atomic bomb, which in two devastating raids vindicated the theory of area bombing, city bombing, terror bombing – call it what you will – as a war-winner and a powerful instrument in the preservation of global peace.

For the German flyers, caught up in the confusion and chaos of impending defeat, the final weeks of the war represented a period characterised by a complex and often anomalous mixture of sense of duty, impotence, involuntary acceptance of what fate might bring, and the instinct of self-preservation. Then came the prisoner-of-war camp, and then some sort of resettlement in a homeland indescribably devastated. There were as many different stories as there were men, but a few of their experiences might serve to give at least a small idea of how it was for the German flyers in the cataclysmic last days of the war and the early days of peace.

Oberleutnant Rudolf Szardenings ended the war as *Staffelkapitän* of 7./NJG 3. He had flown on Operation *Gisela* on 3 March, and had come under fire from a convoy in the North Sea, possibly the same one that had so frightened Günther Wolf, and he was stationed at Uetersen, just north of Hamburg:

'My last contact with the enemy was very shortly before the end, over Hamburg on 8 April, when Bruno Rupp from my *Staffel* shot one down. My last flight was on 3 May from Uetersen to Husum. We took off at 0454 hrs. The British had reached the Elbe and the previous day they had attacked Uetersen, and I myself was on a *flak* gun trying to ward them off. And so we set off for Husum in the early hours of the morning. And that evening we were having a party in the mess to celebrate the end of the war, and an advance contingent of British came, and they gave us cigarettes and so on, and we gave them some of ours. The following day we had to set our aircraft out in lines, and the fins and rudders were removed, and we were taken from the airfield to a provisional camp and then, after a few weeks, to an internment camp at Eiderstede.

'When I had been stationed at Schleswig during the war we had got to know some farmers, and after the war I went back there. My home was in the Russian zone. At Schleswig one of the farmers picked me up with a horse and cart, and I worked there for two years as a farm labourer, carting manure, milking cows, ploughing and so on. In the meanwhile my parents had contrived to make their way from East Prussia to Saxony, and I managed to go there by rail and visit them. I travelled in a goods train by night and so on. And when I got back the British had been to the farm and carried out a house search, and they had stolen for souvenirs all the things I had managed to salvage – items of uniform, my medals and so on. But there was nothing I could do. All my worldly possessions were in a small suitcase.'

Major Paul Zorner, who finished the war with fifty-nine confirmed aerial victories to his credit, had been appointed *Gruppenkommandeur* of II./NJG 100 in October 1944 and stationed in the Vienna area:

'In February 1945 we were moved to a grass airfield at Linz. American troops were only ten or twelve kilometres away, but there was thick fog, with visibility sometimes down to fifty metres, and their advance had ground to a halt. Then, on 4 May 1945, we were ordered to go to Prague/Ruzyn. Conditions were chaotic, and I remember that we had had a signal from headquarters to the effect that Göring had "deserted to the enemy" or something like that. When I got the instruction to move to Prague the weather conditions were so terrible that I couldn't bring myself to order my pilots to take off, so I said that each one must decide for himself. We marked out a runway by sticking small branches into the ground every fifteen metres or so, and when we positioned for take-off we couldn't see the fourth one, which meant that visibility was only about forty-five metres. Eleven crews, including mine, thought they could make it. One was shot down on the way to Prague/Ruzyn.

'On 6 May there was an uprising in Czechoslovakia, and when it broke out I was on my way to *Korps* Headquarters with a motorcycle and sidecar. We were forty kilometres north of Prague, and I decided to turn back. About fifteen kilometres short of the airfield we were stopped by a large group of men, who all had their hands behind their backs. They wanted to know where we were going, and I told them the airfield at Prague/Ruzyn. They said we couldn't go on and that we would have to turn back. They were Czechs. We turned round. I was in the sidecar and one of my *Staffelkapitäne* was driving. As we were just driving away I saw one of them aiming a gun at me. I had already drawn my pistol under the waterproof cover of the sidecar, and I fired it. I don't know whether I hit him.

'We hid somewhere in the woods until it got dark and then we got through to Ruzyn in the darkness. We could see the aircraft taking off one after the other. There was a communications aircraft still there, an Arado 69, and the *Staffelkapitän* and I flew it off the next morning to Saaz, near Marienbad. When we got there we found that the other members of my crew had got hold of a car and two *Panzerfäuste* and made their way there by road. Then the Vlassov army attacked, and the capitulation took place on 8 May. We had no fuel, so we were unable to do what we most wanted to, to take off and get through to the American lines, so we commandeered a car and drove west. In this way we managed to reach the Americans, but they wouldn't let us officers through and they wouldn't issue passes for the other ranks, so I went back to my men and we lived out in the open for seven days. Then the Russians took over and we were taken prisoner. I was finally repatriated to Germany in January 1950, nearly five years later.'

Unlucky as he was to fall into Soviet hands, even so Paul Zorner was more fortunate than Hajo Herrmann, who was also taken prisoner by the Russians. Although his rank was by then Oberst, the equivalent of Colonel, he was a Divisional Commander, a post usually held by a Major-General. In Russian eyes, therefore, he was a General and so automatically a war criminal. He spent ten years in Russian captivity before his return to Germany.

But Herrmann and Zorner were senior officers, and perhaps it is not unfitting that the final personal account of the way in which his war ended should come from one of the lowly men of the *Nachtjagd*, Feldwebel Hans Angersbach. Angersbach's last operational flight, it will be recalled, had been in November 1944, when he had once again returned to earth by parachute. Angersbach, now a farmer, takes up the story:

'The official *Wehrmacht* bulletins were reporting fighting north-west of Hersfeld, which was my home area. Then I was posted to Stade, near Hamburg, and there we experienced another bombing raid, with PFF markers bursting right overhead. Dirt was flying in all directions. Then we went to Wismar, and then to Rerik, where some general or other made a high-sounding speech: the Fatherland was in great danger, he said, and we must defend it on the Elbe. He was laughed down.

'Nevertheless, we were taken by rail to the Elbe. The train was attacked by low-flying aircraft at dawn. The dead and wounded were taken off, and the train continued on its way. On the Elbe itself we were put into defensive positions and a bridgehead was formed on the eastern side of the river near Neu Darchau. There were reportedly 100 enemy tanks in front of us, but they didn't tell us what kind. Probably they thought we were going to find that out ourselves anyway. We were just spooning a very inadequate meal into ourselves when the alarm went and there was wild firing. The tanks were there, American ones. Apparently they had some wounded, because they were showing a Red Cross flag, so there was a temporary cease-fire. At dusk the tanks entered the village without further opposition, and then there was a great squealing of pigs. I imagine the Americans were stocking up with meat.

'The majority of the German soldiers had moved off sideways into the undergrowth, and I was about to do the same when suddenly an officer-cadet appeared out of the darkness. He wanted to carry on fighting, but I had had enough. We crossed the river to the other side in landing craft, and we each had to organise ourselves a dugout for the next few days. Behind me, with only a narrow path separating us, there was a big farmhouse with a thatched roof. There was a stork's nest on the roof, and the storks were back from their travels. The Americans were shelling the area indiscriminately, and one morning tank shells whistled over my head and the thatched roof with the storks' nest went up in flames. The cries of the storks still ring in my ears to this day.

'Another experience is still with me. I had to relieve a sentry in a fox-hole in front of me. He left his dugout, and I went into one about twenty metres away. This unplanned action probably saved my life. Two hours later a shell landed exactly in the hole I would otherwise have been occupying. There are things in life that one simply can't explain.

'An American patrol came over the river in a rubber boat during the night, but they were taken prisoner. Then, in the morning, heavy artillery fire began and there were three spotter planes circling above us. We were ordered to retreat from the bank of the Elbe, and as we did so we had plenty of opportunity to experience the excellent co-operation between the spotter aircraft and the artillery. Our platoon had to cross a small stretch of open field, when suddenly three shells exploded to the left of us, and then three to the right. By that time, luckily, we had taken cover in the woods.

'We passed that night only a small distance from the Americans, and we could hear our first English words. At dawn it was the same story – "Forward men, we must retreat!" The following night we spent in a stall in a stable near a farm. Next morning the leading American tanks overtook us. We went back along the path we had used the previous evening. An American jeep coming towards us did a rapid about-turn and circled round us in a wide curve. I was taken prisoner at Vehlan on 3 May 1945.

'After that I was moved to Himbergen, Vennebeck, Hesselheide, Lollar, Ziegenhain and Bebra, but by 30 May I was home, back on our farm.

'There is a lot more I could write about. One keeps remembering new things. But outside it is spring, and so there is little time for writing.'

The tumult and the shouting had died, the captains and the kings departed. History decreed that some departed to glory, acclaim and high office, some to death, some to rejection and comparative oblivion. And the flyers from both Bomber Command and the *Nachtjagd* who fought so bitterly against each other, those who had survived, departed to begin a new life, each in his own separate way. As they grow older, perhaps wiser, possibly more compassionate, they all ask the same question. Why? And there is no answer.

Glossary of German Words
and Phrases

I feel sure that some readers will consider that I have used too much German in this book. Perhaps I might be allowed a few words of explanation. I have read a good number of books on flying and related matters in which the writer or translator has tried, frequently with quite lamentable results, to anglicise German specialist words, phrases, ranks and so on, and more often than not I have felt irritated, because the practice detracts not only from the accuracy of the narrative but also from the reader's understanding and, very importantly, from the atmosphere. The fact is that there is very often no exact equivalent in English. How should *Gruppe*, for example, be translated? 'Group', although it is the literal equivalent, will not do. In the *Luftwaffe* a *Gruppe* was a formation somewhere between a Squadron and a Wing in strength, larger than the former, smaller than the latter, and very much smaller than a Group in the RAF. Although there were often variations, fundamentally nine aircraft made a *Staffel*, three *Staffeln* a *Gruppe* and three *Gruppen* a *Geschwader*. The *Staffel* was the basic fighting unit and was frequently stationed at a different airfield from the other *Staffeln* of the same *Gruppe*. And the word *Nachtjagd* – how is that to be put into English? Literally it means 'night hunt', and in its general connotation we would probably say 'night fighting' or 'night interception'. But the German night-fighting service was known specifically as *die Nachtjagd*, and I use that title quite widely because, like the *Luftwaffe*, it was an entity that had a quite distinctive individual character. And in the *Luftwaffe* a *Kapitän* was not a Captain – that was a *Hauptmann* – and so on, and so on. I hope, therefore, that readers who think that I use too much German will at least understand my reasons for preferring the original to an inadequate translation.

As an aid to understanding, should that be necessary, I am giving below a list of English equivalents (not necessarily literal translations). Again, a little explanation might be in order.

The Germans tend to join a number of words together to make a long word – sometimes a very long one – where in English we would use separate or hyphenated words. (It is also correct to hyphenate in German, but more frequent just to attach the smaller words to each other.) A good example is *Luftfahrtministerium*, which means 'Aviation Ministry'. It is made up of *Luft* (Air), *Fahrt* (Travel) and *Ministerium* (Ministry), and it could be written *Luftfahrt-Ministerium*. All German nouns, incidentally, begin with a capital letter. German plurals are rather more complicated than English ones, so where it seems necessary I will include the plural of individual words in brackets.

I hope that in practice the majority of German words will be readily understandable from the context, so that the reader will not need to refer too frequently to this glossary.

Abitur	Roughly the equivalent of Higher School Certificate or A Levels; the qualifying examination for University entrance.
Abteilung	Department; Section (military) etc. (*Abteilungen*).
Abteilungsleiter	Head of Department.
Achtung!	'Beware!' 'Look out!' 'Stand by!' (for instructions, for a broadcast etc.)
Adler	Eagle (but also, like many names of birds, animals etc., used as a code word).
Adlergeschwader	The Eagle *Geschwader* (KG 30).
Alarmstart	Immediate take-off. Scramble!
alt, alte, alter etc.	Old (adjective). As a noun (*der Alte*): the old man, the boss.
Altstadt	The Old Town (district of a city etc.)
Ameise	Ant. Codename for e.g. one fighter-control area.
Amt	An official office.
Anlage	Installation, plant (mechanical), system (technical) etc.
Antreten!	Literally, 'Fall in!' Code word for, 'Head in such-and-such a direction.' e.g. '*Antreten 270!*' = 'Steer 270 degrees!'; 'Vector 270!' etc.
Arbeitsdienst	Labour Service. In National Socialist Germany youths had to perform a period of compulsory service before going on to further education.
Armeekorps	Army Corps.
Aufsitzgruppe	Lodger unit. A *Gruppe* using the aircraft of another unit.
auswerten	To evaluate, assess etc.
Auswertetisch	A map table showing the local air situation so that controllers could make the necessary defensive assessments.
Bake	A beacon (visual or radio).
Batterie	Battery (*Batterien*).
Befehlshaber	Officer in Command.
bei	By, near etc.
Beleuchter	Illuminator (aircraft).
Beleuchtergruppe	Illuminator *Gruppe*.
Beobachter	Observer, navigator.
Bereitschaft	Readiness.
Bereitschaftsraum	Operational Readiness Room.
berühre	Literally 'touch'. '*Ich berühre!*' = 'I have visual contact with my target!'
Besatzung	Crew.
Biber	Beaver.
bitte	Please.
blau, blaue, blauer etc.	Blue.
Bodenplatte	Floor tile, paving stone, flagstone etc.

Bord-	(In compounds) indicates member of aircrew *or* airborne equipment. *Bordfunker, Bordradar* etc.
Bordfunker	Radio/radar operator.
Bordmechaniker	Air mechanic, analogous in function to flight engineer. Also acted as gunner as necessary.
Bordradar	Airborne radar equipment.
Bordschütze(r)	Air gunner.
Bucht	Bay.
Bumerang	Boomerang. Codeword for Oboe bombing system.
Bumerangverfahren	Oboe system.
Christbaum	Christmas tree. Vernacular for Pathfinder target indicators. (*Christbäume*).
dicht	Near, close.
Divisionär	Divisional Commander.
Divisionsgefechtsstand	Divisional Operations Room, Command Post etc.
Doppelkopf	Literally 'double head': a popular card game.
Drahtfunk	Cable radio.
Dudelsack	Bagpipes. German vernacular word for R/T jamming.
Dunaja	Abbr. of *Dunkelnachtjagd* (q.v.) Also used in compounds such as *Dunajagebiet, Dunajaraum* etc.
dunkel	Dark.
Dunkelnachtjagd (or *dunkle Nachtjagd*):	Night interception without the use of searchlights; radar-controlled interception. Also in compounds with '*Gebiet*' (zone), '*Raum*' (area) etc.; e.g. *Dunkelnachtjagdraum* = radar-control area, as used in *Himmelbett* procedure (q.v.).
Düppel	Window. Aluminised paper strips used for jamming radar.
Ehrenpokal	Goblet of honour.
einmal	Once.
Einsatz	Operation, (in compounds) operational; e.g. *Einsatzhafen* = operational airfield, etc.
Eisbär	Polar bear.
Eisvogel	Kingfisher.
Emil:	Proper noun. Used in codeword '*Emil-Emil*' = *Lichtenstein* airborne radar.
entlausen	Literally 'delouse': to take anti-jamming measures.
Entwicklung	Development. In compounds such as *Entwicklungswerk* = development factory.
Erdöl	Crude oil, petroleum. Also used in compounds such as *Erdölwerke* = refineries.
Erprobung	Test. *Erprobungsstelle* = test centre, testing station etc.
Erstling	Literally 'first child'. German IFF equipment.
Experte	Expert. In fighter units, ace (five or more confirmed victories). (*Experten*).
Fahnenjunker	Officer cadet.

fahren	To drive, to ride, to go etc. In R/T code, e.g. *'Fahren Sie Express!'* = 'Increase speed!'
Falk	Falcon, hawk.
Fallschirm	Parachute. *Fallschirmjäger* = paratroop(s).
Fasan	Pheasant.
feig, feige	Cowardly.
Feldmarschall	Field Marshal.
Feldwebel	NCO rank, equivalent of Sergeant.
fern	Far, distant, by extension 'long-range'. Used in compounds; see following.
Fernnachtjagd	Long-range night fighting. Intruders. Also used in compounds *Fernnachtjagdgruppe, Fernnachtjagdgeschwader* etc.
Fernnachtjäger	Intruder(s), aircraft or pilots.
Feuersturm	Fire-storm.
Flak	(Abbreviation of *Fliegerabwehrkanonen*) – anti-aircraft guns. Also used to mean the anti-aircraft service – *'die Flak'*. Subsumed into English as 'flak'. Used in compounds, see following.
Flakabteilung	Flak Section.
Flakdivision	Flak Division.
Flakkorps	Flak Corps.
Flakscheinwerfer	Flak searchlights. (The *Flak* and searchlights belonged to the *Luftwaffe*).
Flieger	Flyer, member of aircrew. Also used in compounds; see following.
Fliegerdivision	Air Division.
Fliegerführer	An appointment: Officer in Command of Air Operations. e.g. *Fliegerführer England*.
Fliegerkorps	Air Corps.
Flugmeldedienst	Air (Traffic) Reporting Centre.
Flugzeug	Aircraft.
Flugzeugbau	Aircraft construction.
Flugzeugführer	Pilot.
Flugzeugwerke	Aircraft works, aircraft factory.
Forst	Forest.
Frage	Question. In R/T code – 'Query?'; e.g. 'Frage Viktor?' = 'Do you receive?'
frei	Free, clear etc.
freie Jagd	Freelance interception.
Freiherr	Baron.
Freya	Character from Wagner. German search radar.
Fühlungshalter	Literally 'contact-keeper'. An aircraft that tried to maintain contact with the bomber stream in order to call in other fighters.
Führer	Leader – not only of the Third Reich.
Führerflugzeug	Lead aircraft; aircraft of the officer in tactical command.

Funker	Radio operator, wireless operator (air or ground). See *Bordfunker*.
Funkhorchdienst	Radio Monitoring Service.
Funkmess	Radar.
Funkmesstechnik	Radar technology, radar techniques.
Gau	A geographical administrative area of the Third Reich.
Gauleiter	Party appointment. The individual in command of a *Gau*.
Gebiet	A geographical area, e.g. *Ruhrgebiet*. Sometimes, as in '*Flakgebiet*', possibly better translated as 'Zone'.
Gefecht	Battle. See compounds below.
Gefechtsopernhaus	Vernacular, literally 'battle opera house'. One of the Divisional Control Centres used for fighter control.
Gefechtsstand	Control room, battle room etc.
Gefreiter	Junior rank equivalent to Private, LAC.
geheim	Secret, e.g. *Geheimkommando* = secret command.
genau	Exact(ly).
Generalfeldmarschall	Senior rank. General Field Marshal.
Generalleutnant	Lieutenant-General.
Generalluftzeugmeister	Senior appointment. General Officer in Charge of Equipment and Supplies (Air).
Generalmajor	Major-General.
Generaloberst	Senior rank. Colonel-General.
Gerät	Equipment, set, e.g. *Radargerät* = radar set, radar equipment.
Geschwader	Operational unit comprising three *Gruppen*.
Geschwaderbefehlshaber	Officer commanding a *Geschwader*.
Geschwaderkommodore	(Appointment) – Commanding Officer of a *Geschwader*.
Gotha	Town in East Germany. Generic name given to heavy bombers that attacked England in WWI.
Gross	Large, big. Often used in compounds.
Grossdeutschland	Greater Germany.
Grossgefechtsstand	Large control centre. See '*Gefechtsopernhaus*'.
Grossraum	Large area. Term used in connection with air defence areas. (*Grossräume*).
grün, grüne, grüner etc.	Green.
Gruppe	Operational formation comprising three *Staffeln*. See compounds.
Gruppenbefehlswelle	*Gruppe* command frequency *or* broadcast.
Gruppengefechtsstand	*Gruppe* battle room, control centre etc.
Gruppenkommandeur	Commander of a *Gruppe* (appointment).
Gürtel	Belt, as in *Scheinwerfergürtel* = searchlight belt.
Habicht	Hawk.
halb	Half.

Halsschmerzen	Sore throat. Applied jokingly to those who were ambitious to be awarded the *Ritterkreuz*, a neck decoration.
halten	To stop, to halt. In R/T code – 'Reduce speed!'
Häuptling	Chieftain, head man. Code word of a German radar.
Hauptmann	Rank equivalent to Captain (Army), Flight Lieutenant (RAF).
Haus	House, but also a block of flats etc.
Heer	The German Army, a branch of the *Wehrmacht*.
Heeresleitung	Army Command.
hell, helle, heller etc.	Bright. Used in e.g. *helle Nachtjagd*
helle Nachtjagd	Literally 'bright night fighting'. Night interception with the use of searchlights. Abbreviated *Henaja*.
Henaja	See above.
Hilfswerk	Auxiliary works, factory, plant etc.
Himmelbett	Literally 'four-poster bed'. Codeword for night-fighter control system introduced by Kammhuber.
Himmelbettraum	*Himmelbett* control area.
Himmelbettverfahren	*Himmelbett* procedure, system, method etc.
hinten	Behind, aft, astern.
Hirschgeweih	Stag's antlers. Vernacular for radar aerials for airborne intercept radar.
Höhenjäger	High-altitude interceptor.
Horrido	Code word for 'I have destroyed my target.' Used from about 1944 onwards, previously *'Sieg Heil!'*
Indianer	Red Indian. Codeword for enemy fighters.
Jafü	Abbreviation of *Jagdführer* (q.v.).
Jagd	Literally 'hunting' or 'the hunt'. General term for interceptor fighters. Used in compounds.
Jagddivision	Fighter Division.
Jagdflieger	Fighter aircrew, fighter pilot.
Jagdführer	Literally 'fighter leader', but not necessarily in the sense of the lead aircraft in a formation. Can be a ground command appointment. Abbr. *Jafü*.
Jagdgeschwader	Fighter *Geschwader*.
Jagdgruppe	Fighter *Gruppe*.
Jagdkorps	Fighter Corps.
Jagdschloss	Literally 'hunting lodge'. Codename of a German search radar.
Jäger	Literally 'hunter'. Fighter(s), interceptor(s). Can refer to either aircraft or pilot.
Jägerleitoffizier	Fighter Control Officer. Abbr. *JLO*.
JLO	See immediately above. Used as a word in its own right, pronounced 'ee-low'.
Kampf	Battle, struggle. fight etc. In compounds, Bomber', e.g., *Kampfgeschwader* (Abbr. *KG)* = Bomber *Geschwader*.

Kampfzerstörer	Ground-attack fighter-bomber.
Kapitän	Captain (Navy). In *Luftwaffe*, the appointment to command of a *Staffel*. Hence *Staffelkapitän*.
kaputt	Broken, unserviceable etc.
Kasino	Officers' Mess.
Kauz	Screech-owl. Codename for the Do 17Z night-fighter.
Kiebitz	Peewit etc.
Kirchturm	Literally 'church tower'. R/T codeword for, 'My altitude is . . . '
Knickebein	Literally 'advocaat' or 'crooked leg'. Code word for German blind-bombing device.
Knopf	Button.
kombiniert	Combined.
Kombinierte Nachtjagd	Combined Night Interception. Searchlights, flak and fighters in combination. See *Konaja*.
Kommandeur	The appointment to command of a *Gruppe*. Hence *Gruppenkommandeur*.
Kommando	A small, usually independent, fighting command or unit.
Kommodore	The appointment to command of a *Geschwader*.
Konaja	*Kombinierte Nachtjagd* (q.v.).
Konajagebiet	Combined Night-fighting Zone.
Korps	Corps.
Korpsführungswelle	Corps control wavelength or broadcast.
Kriegsmarine	The Germany Navy.
Kurier	Codeword for heavy bomber. (*Kuriere*).
Kutscher	Coachman, driver. In the vernacular, pilot.
Lagekarte	General situation map.
Lehrgeschwader	A *Geschwader* used to test operational equipment, techniques etc.
Leichentuch	Literally 'shroud'. Code word for the illumination of cloud layers from below to silhouette enemy bombers. Introduced in 1943 by the then Major Hajo Herrmann.
Leutnant	Commissioned rank. Second Lieutenant, Pilot Officer equivalent.
Lichtenstein	Air-intercept radar used in German night-fighters.
Lichtspuker	Literally 'light spitter'. A light projector used by *Luftwaffe* auxiliary to show the position of aircraft on a plotting table or GSM.
Lisa	R/T codeword for, 'Turn ten degrees to port!'
Löffel	Literally 'spoon'. Safety cover for firing button.
Lorenz	Blind-approach system.
Luft	Air. Used in many compounds.
Luftflotte	Air Fleet.
Luftgau	Air District (administrative).

Luftkreis	Air Region.
Luftnachrichtendienst	Air Signals Service.
Luftübung	Air manoeuvres, practice etc.
Luftwaffe	The German Air Arm. Was one component of the *Wehrmacht* (q.v).
Luftwaffenführung	Air Force leadership.
Luftwaffenhelferin	Air Force Auxiliary (female). Equivalent of WAAF. (*Luftenwaffenhelferinnen*).
Mammut	Mammoth. Codename for German long-range search radar.
Mechaniker	Mechanic. See *Bordmechaniker*.
mehr	More.
mein	My.
mit	With.
Mitte	Middle, centre. As in *Stadtmitte* = town centre.
Mosquitojäger	Literally 'Mosquito-hunter'. Name given to German fighter aircraft designed or modified to counter the high-flying, fast RAF Mosquitos, e.g. He 219.
Musik	Music. See *Schräge Musik*.
Nachrichtentruppen	Signals troops, the Signals and Communications Service in general.
Nacht	Night
Nachtjagd	Literally 'night hunt'. Night fighting, night interception. Also, as *die Nachtjagd*, the German night-fighter force. See numerous compounds below.
Nachtjagddivision	Night-fighter division.
Nachtjagdgebiet	Night-fighter zone.
Nachtjagdgeschwader	Night-fighter *Geschwader*.
Nachtjagdgruppe	Night-fighter *Gruppe*.
Nachtjagdraum	Night-fighter area. (*Nachtjagdräume*).
Nachtjagdversuchsstelle	Night-fighter experimental unit.
Nachtjäger	Night-fighter. Refers to either aircrew or aircraft. (*Nachtjäger*).
Naxos	A Greek island. Codeword for an H2S homing device.
Neptun	Neptune. A German AI radar.
Neuling	Literally 'newcomer'. German IFF device.
nicht	Not.
noch	Again, 'more', as in e.g. *'noch einmal'* = once more, once again.
Nord	North.
Oberfeldwebel	NCO rank roughly equivalent to e.g. Flight Sergeant.
Obergefreiter	Junior rank roughly equivalent to Lance Corporal (Army), Leading Aircraftman (RAF).

Oberleutnant	Commissioned rank equivalent to Lieutenant (Army), Flying Officer (RAF). Abbr. *Oblt.*
Oberst	Equivalent rank to Colonel (Army), Group Captain (RAF).
Oberstleutnant	Lieutenant-Colonel, Wing Commander equivalent. Abbr. *Olt.*
Offizier	Officer.
Panzer	Tank, armour, armoured fighting vehicle.
Panzerdivision	Armoured Division.
Panzertruppe(n)	Tank unit(s), armoured troops.
Parasit	Parasite.
Parasitanlage	IFF equipment used with German control radars.
Pauke	Literally 'kettledrum'. Night-fighter R/T code *'Pauke Pauke!'* = 'I am attacking!'
Peilung	Bearing (usually by radio).
Planquadrat	Geographical grid square. German system used two-letter designations, e.g *Planquadrat DS* = Bremen area, *Planquadrat JQ* = Münster area, etc.
Platz	Place. Can also be used for 'airfield', 'seat' etc.
Prinz	Prince.
Projekt	Project, plan etc.
Raum	Literally 'space', 'room' etc. In e.g. *Nachtjagraum:* area, box etc. (*Räume*).
Reichsbahn	State Railway.
Reichsmark	Unit of currency.
Reichsmarschall	Marshal of the Third Reich. A unique rank created by Hitler for Hermann Göring.
Reichswehr	German armed forces 1921-35. *Wehrmacht.*
Reise	Literally 'journey'. R/T code word as in *'Machen Sie Reise-Reise!'* = 'Break off engagement, return to base!' Not to be confused with *Riese* (q.v.).
Reportage	Fighter-control running commentary used in *Zahme Sau* system.
Revi:	Abbr. for *Reflexionsvisier* or *Reflexvisier* = reflector sight (for cannon, machine-guns etc.)
Rhein	Rhine.
Riese	Giant, as e.g. in *Würzburg Riese* = Würzburg Giant (radar).
Ritterkreuz	The Knight's Cross to the Iron Cross. See *Halsschmerzen.*
Rolf	Proper noun. As R/T codeword = 'Ten degrees right', e.g. *'Zweimal Rolf!'* = 'Turn twenty degrees starboard!'
rot, rote, roter etc.	Red.
Rotterdamgerät	German name given to H2S, the first example of which was recovered from a bomber shot down near Rotterdam.
Ruhrgebiet	The Ruhr Valley industrial area.

344

Salto	Literally 'somersault'. R/T codeword for, 'Make a 360° turn!', e.g. *'Salto Rolf!'* = 'Turn starboard!'
Sau	Literally 'sow'. But see *Wilde Sau, Zahme Sau*.
Scheinwerfer	Searchlight.
Scheinwerferregiment	Searchlight Regiment.
schiessen	To shoot, to fire.
Schnorchel	Snorkel. Device to feed diesel engines of U-boats with oxygen and so allow battery-charging while submerged.
schräg	Slanting, oblique, as in *Schräge Musik* (q.v.).
Schräge Musik	Upward-firing machine-guns or cannon in the fuselage of German night-fighters.
Schule	School.
Seeburgtisch	Horizontal screen (table) used in *Himmelbett* fighter control.
Seelenbohrer	Literally 'soul-borer'. Vernacular for some types of RAF R/T jamming.
Seelöwe	Sealion. Code word for e.g. planned invasion of Britain 1940.
Seetakt	Code name for early German naval radar.
sehr	Very.
Sicherheitsdienst	Nazi Security Service = *Gestapo*.
Sie	You.
Sieg Heil!	Night-fighter R/T code word, 'I have destroyed my target.'
sind	Are.
Sitzbereitschaft	Cockpit readiness.
Skat	A popular card game.
Spanner	Several meanings, including 'Peeping Tom'. An infra-red device for the location of enemy aircraft.
Spanneranlage	*Spanner* equipment.
Stab	Staff. In, e.g., *Stab I./NJG 1*: Staff of I./NJG 1.
Stabsschwarm	Staff Flight.
Stadtmitte	Town centre.
Staffel	The basic operational unit. Usually comprised nine aircraft. (*Staffeln*).
Staffelkapitän	The officer in command of a *Staffel*.
Startbereitschaft	Literally 'take-off readiness'. Crew in aircraft and taxying out to take-off position.
Station	Station.
Stellung	Position, site, e.g. *Funkmess-Stellung* = radar site.
Stuka	General term for 'dive bomber'. More specifically applied to the Ju 87.
süd	South.
Tagjagd	Day interception, day fighting, day-fighter organisation.
tampen	R/T code word: 'Fly in such-and-such a direction', e.g. *'Tampen Sie eins-acht-null!'* = 'Head 180°!'

technisch	Technical, e.g. *Technischer Offizier (TO)* = Technical Officer. This was an appointment, usually held by an operational pilot. Not the equivalent of an officer of the Technical Branch in the RAF.
Terrorflieger	Terror flyers.
Tisch	Table.
Tüte	Literally 'paper bag'. A windbag etc.
Über	Over, above.
Übung	Practice.
Übungsflug	Practice flight, training flight.
Uhu	Owl. Codename for, e.g., He 219 night-fighter.
Unteroffizier	NCO rank, equivalent to Corporal.
Verfahren	Procedure, method, system etc, e.g. *Bumerangverfahren* = Oboe system.
Vergeltung	Retaliation, as in e.g. *Vergeltungswaffen* = V-weapons, retaliation weapons.
Viermot	A four-engined aircraft. Abbr. of *viermotorig* = four-engined.
Viktor	Phonetic alphabet for letter 'V'. In R/T code, equivalent of 'Roger' – 'I have received and under-stood your message.'
warten	To wait. R/T code for 'Stand by!' Also seen in e.g. *Warteraum* = holding area.
Wassermann	Aquarius. Code-name for German long-range search radar.
Wehrmacht	German armed forces until end of war. Three components: *Heer* (Army), *Marine* (Navy), *Luftwaffe*.
Weitwinkel	Wide angle (radar).
Welle	Wave, wavelength, broadcast.
Werk	Works, factory.
Wetterfrosch	Literally 'weather frog'. Vernacular for meteoro-logical officer, forecaster.
wild	Wild, savage.
Wilde Sau	Freelance night-fighting, originally by single-seater aircraft. Anglicised as 'wild boar'.
Würzburg	Short-range radar used for e.g. searchlight and flak control. Also used in early stages of *Dunaja* (q.v.).
Würzburg Riese	Würzburg Giant. Radar used for close control of fighters in *Himmelbett* procedure.
Würzlaus	Anti-jamming device used with *Würzburg* radar.
Ypsilon	Letter 'Y'. *Y-Verfahren, Ypsilonverfahren*: ground-controlled navigation by means of VHF.
zahm	Tame.
Zahme Sau	'Tame boar'. Fighter control by means of broad-cast 'running commentary' (*Reportage*).

Zerstörer   Destroyer. Heavy, usually twin-engined, fighter-bomber/ ground-attack aircraft, e.g. Bf 110. In compounds such as *Zerstörergeschwader, Zerstörerstaffel* etc.

zweimal   Twice.

Selected Bibliography

ADERS, Gebhard, *Die Geschichte der Deutschen Nachtjagd* (Motorbuch Verlag, 1978).
BENNETT, D.C.T, *Pathfinder* (Frederick Muller, 1958).
BOYLE, Andrew, *Trenchard* (Boyle, 1962).
BRUNSWIG, Hans, *Feuersturm über Hamburg* (Motorbuch Verlag, 1987).
DONNELLY, Larry, *The Whitley Boys* (Air Research Publications, 1991).
GREEN, William, *Warplanes of the Third Reich* (Macdonald, 1970).
HARRIS, Sir Arthur, *Bomber Offensive* (Collins, 1947).
HASTINGS, Max, *Bomber Command* (The Dial Press, 1979).
HECKS, Karl, *Bombing 1939–45* (Robert Hale, 1990).
HERRMANN, Hajo, *Bewegtes Leben* (Motorbuch Verlag, 1986).
JANSEN, A, *Wespennest Leeuwarden* (Hollandia B.V., 1976).
JOHNEN, Wilhelm, *Duell unter den Sternen* (Richard Bärenfeld-Verlag, 1956).
LOVELL, Sir Bernard, *Echoes of War* (Adam Hilger, 1991).
MERRICK, Ken, *By Day and Night* (Ian Allan, 1989).
MacBEAN, John A., and HOGBEN, Arthur S, *Bombs Gone* (Patrick Stephens, 1990).
MIDDLEBROOK, Martin, *The Battle of Hamburg* (Scribner, 1981)
MIDDLEBROOK, Martin, *The Peenemünde Raid* (Allen Lane, 1982).
MIDDLEBROOK, Martin, and EVERITT, Chris, *The Bomber Command War Diaries* (Viking, 1985).
MIDDLEBROOK, Martin, *The Berlin Raids* (Viking, 1988).
PRICE, Alfred, *The Last Year of the Luftwaffe* (Arms and Armour, 1991).
PRICE, Alfred, *The Bomber in World War II* (Macdonald, 1976).
PRITCHARD, David, *The Radar War* (William Kimber, 1989).
SAWARD, Dudley, *'Bomber' Harris* (Cassell, 1984).
SAWARD, Dudley, *Victory Denied* (Buchan and Enright, 1985).
SPEER, Albert, *Inside the Third Reich* (Weidenfeld and Nicolson, 1970).
WEBSTER, Sir Charles, and FRANKLAND, Noble, *The Strategic Air Offensive against Germany 1939–1945* (HMSO, 1961).

Index of Personalities, Aircraft and Selected Codewords